THE BOOK OF HUMAN INSECTS

OSAMU TEZUKA

VERTICAL.

Translation — Mari Morimoto
Production — Hiroko Mizuno
Glen Isip
Tomoe Tsutsumi

Published by Vertical, an imprint of Kodansha USA Publishing, LLC.

Originally serialized in Japanese as *Ningen Konchuuki* in *Play Comic*, Akita Shoten, 1970-71.

ISBN: 978-1-935654-77-3

Printed in the United States of America

First Paperback Edition

Seventh Printing

This is a work of fiction.
The artwork of the original has been produced as a mirror-image
in order to conform with the English language.

Kodansha USA Publishing, LLC
451 Park Avenue South, 7th Floor
New York, NY 10016
www.kodansha.us

TABLE OF CONTENTS

SPRING CICADA.................................5

LEAFHOPPER................................. 69

LONGHORN BEETLE.................. 165

KATYDID................................. 289

SPRING CICADA

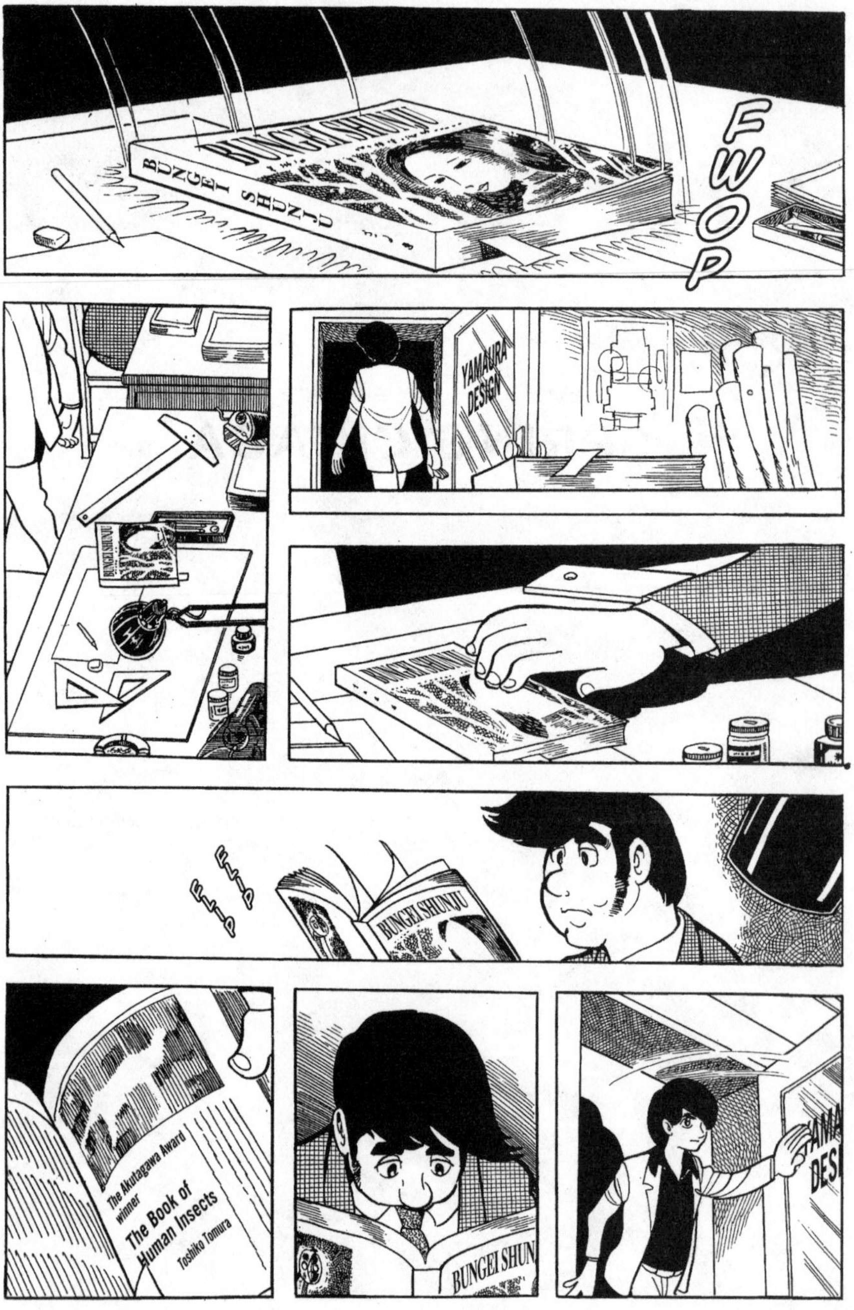
BUNGEI SHUNJU
FWOP
YAMAURA DESIGN
BUNGEI SHUNJU
FLIP FLIP
The Akutagawa Award winner
The Book of Human Insects
Toshiko Tomura
BUNGEI SHUN
DESI

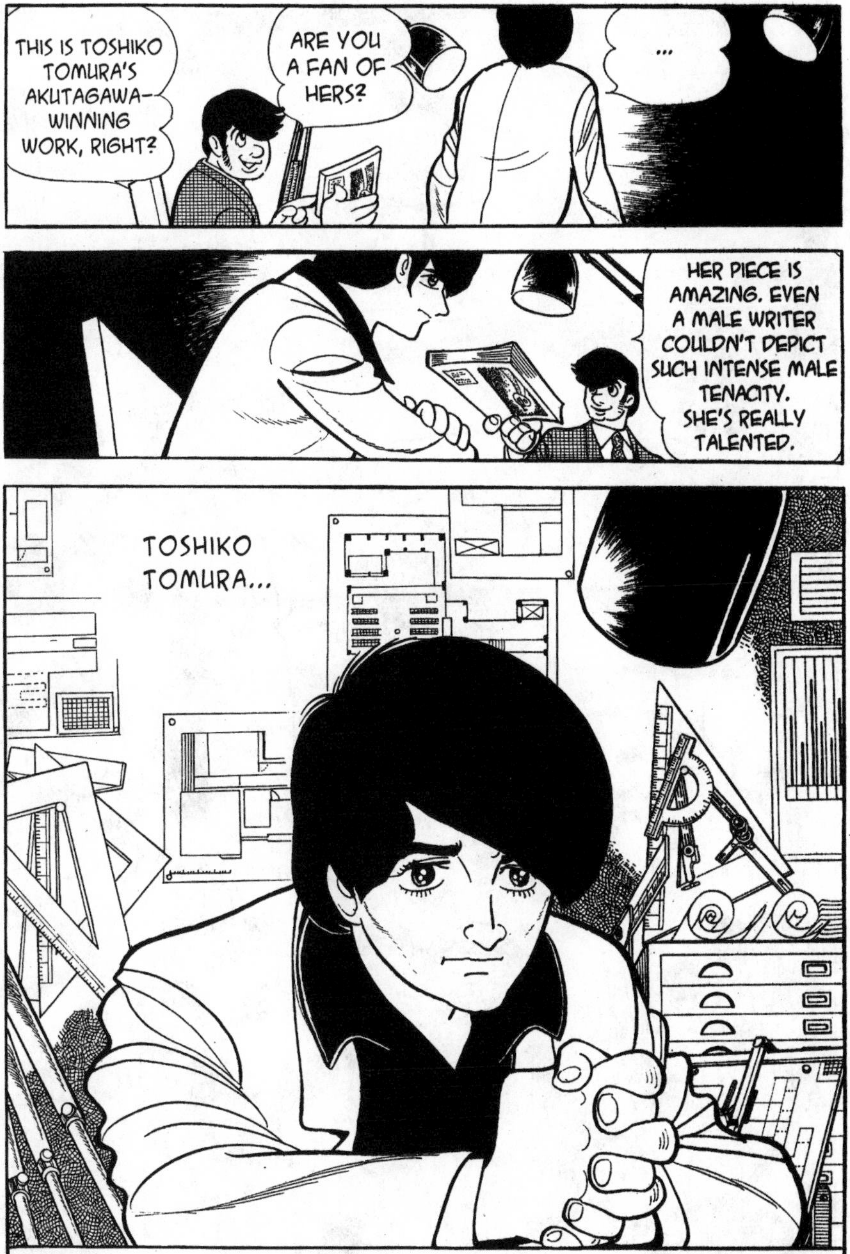
THIS IS TOSHIKO TOMURA'S AKUTAGAWA-WINNING WORK, RIGHT?
ARE YOU A FAN OF HERS?
...
HER PIECE IS AMAZING. EVEN A MALE WRITER COULDN'T DEPICT SUCH INTENSE MALE TENACITY. SHE'S REALLY TALENTED.
TOSHIKO TOMURA...

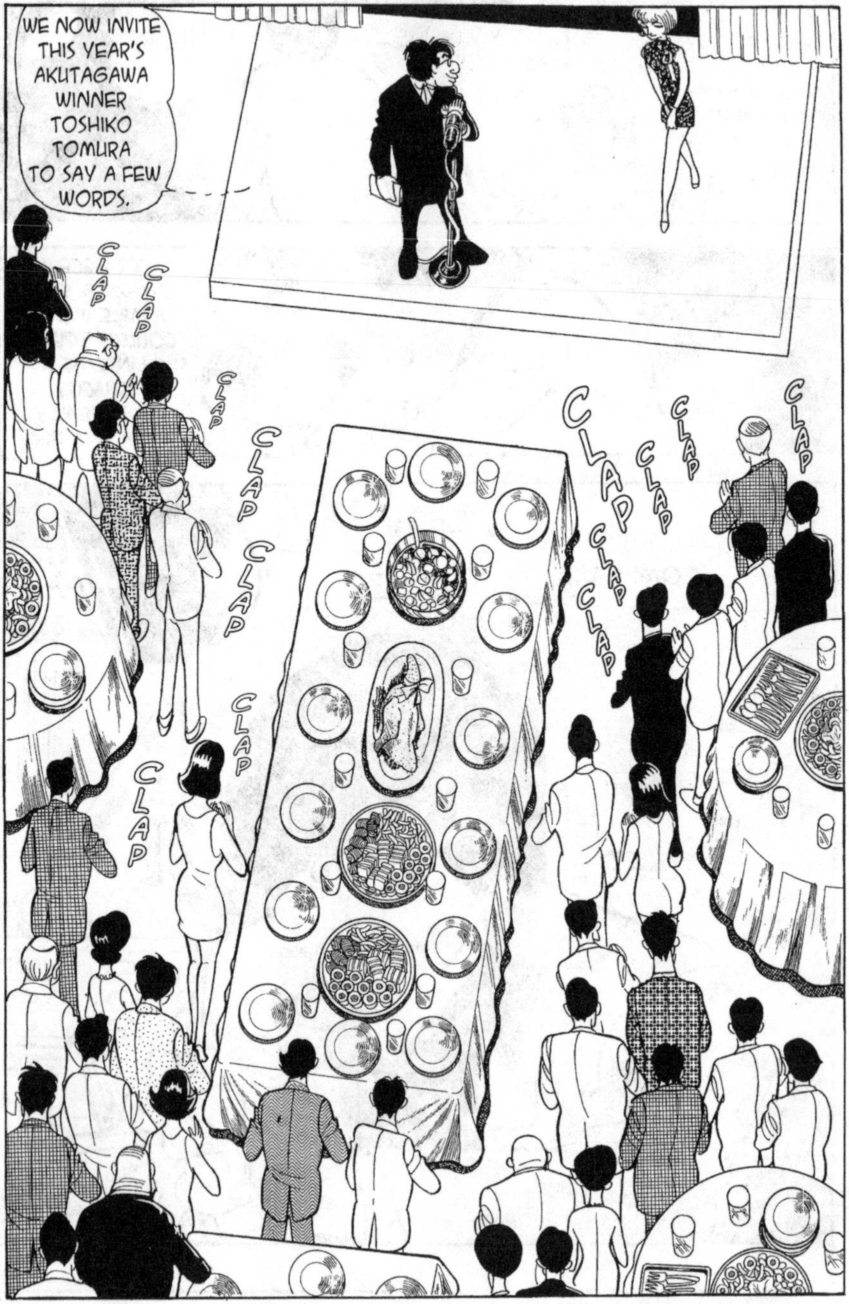
WE NOW INVITE THIS YEAR'S AKUTAGAWA WINNER TOSHIKO TOMURA TO SAY A FEW WORDS.
CLAP CLAP
CLAP
CLAP CLAP
CLAP
CLAP
CLAP CLAP
CLAP CLAP
CLAP
CLAP

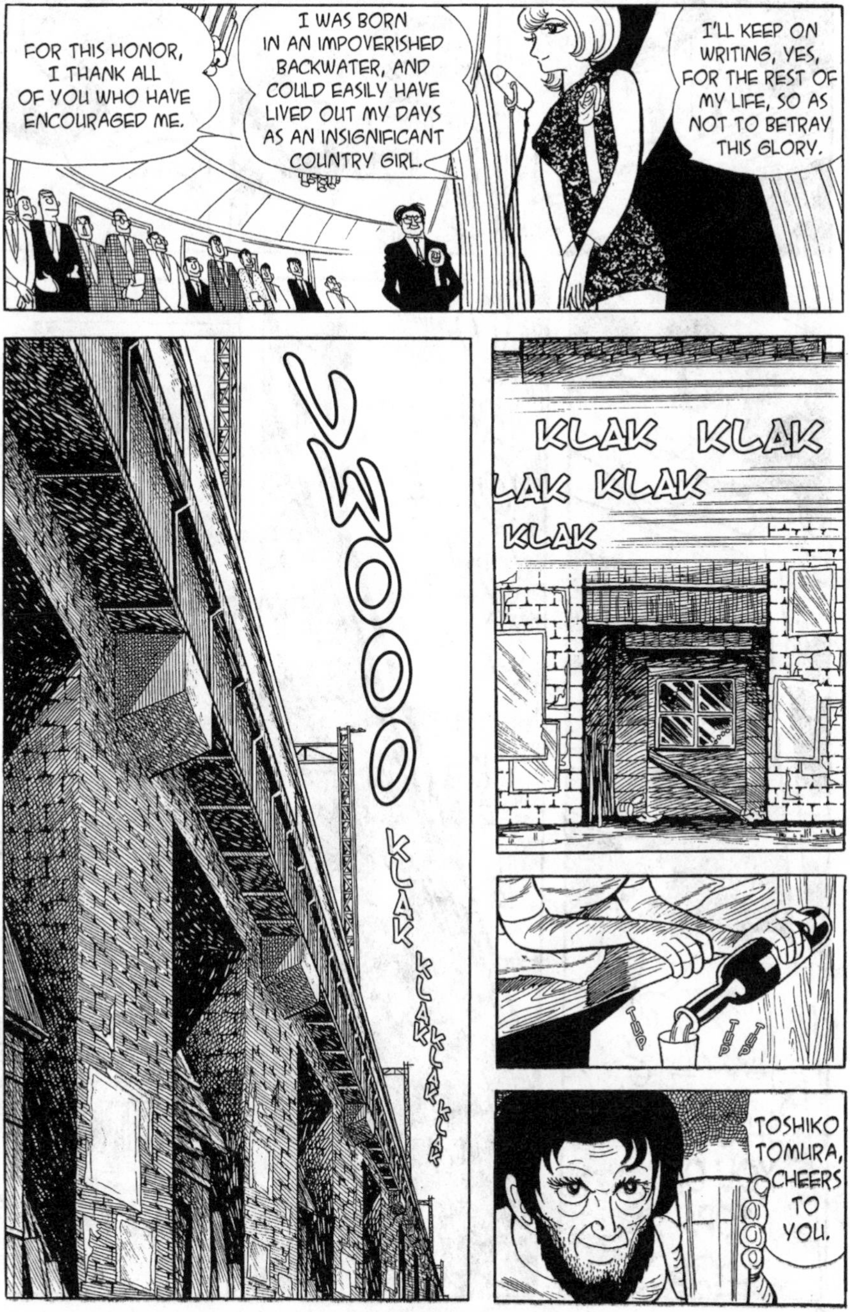
FOR THIS HONOR, I THANK ALL OF YOU WHO HAVE ENCOURAGED ME.
I WAS BORN IN AN IMPOVERISHED BACKWATER, AND COULD EASILY HAVE LIVED OUT MY DAYS AS AN INSIGNIFICANT COUNTRY GIRL.
I'LL KEEP ON WRITING, YES, FOR THE REST OF MY LIFE, SO AS NOT TO BETRAY THIS GLORY.
VWOOO
KLAK
KLAK
KLAKKLAK
KLAK KLAK
LAK KLAK
KLAK
TUP
TUP
TUP
TOSHIKO TOMURA, CHEERS TO YOU.

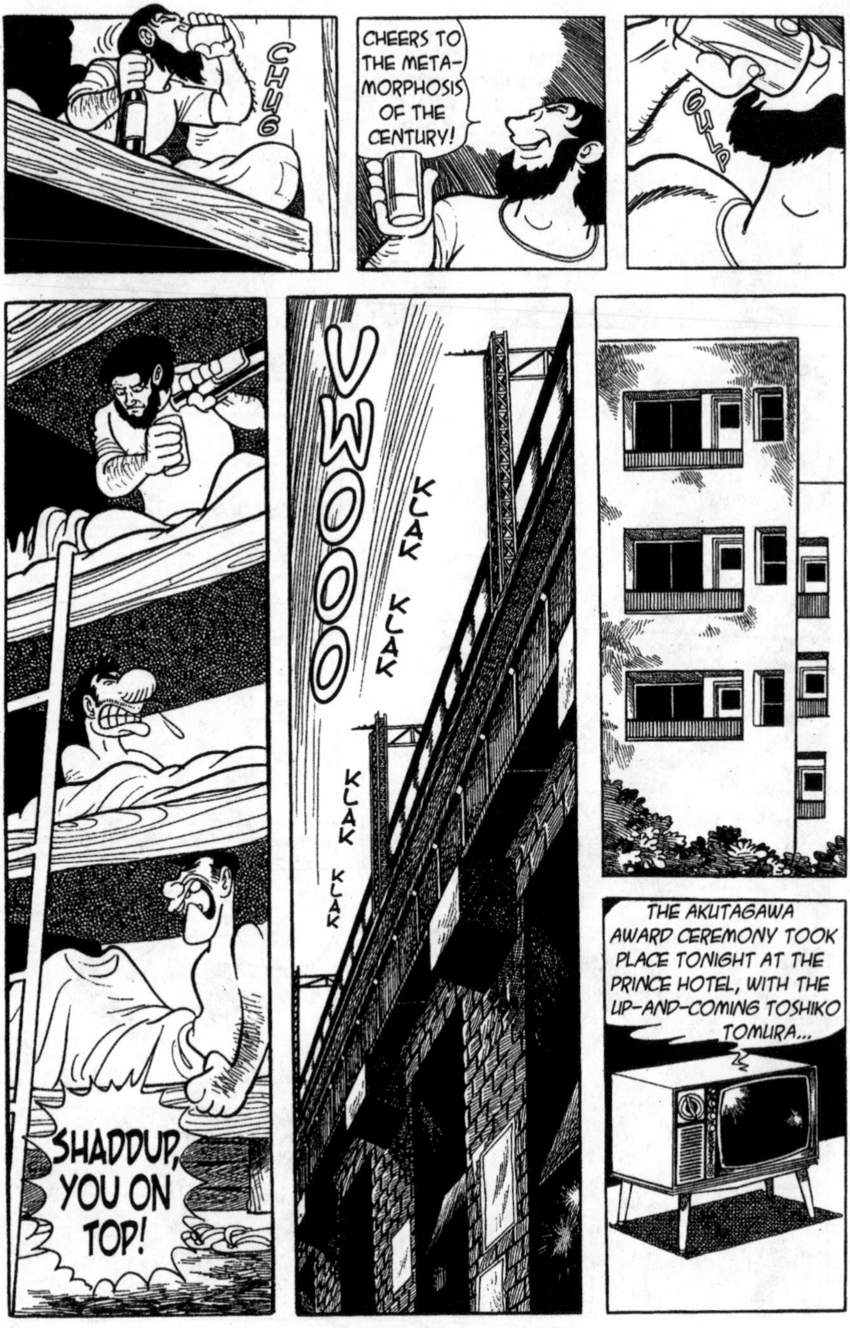
CHUG
CHEERS TO THE META-MORPHOSIS OF THE CENTURY!
GULP
SHADDUP, YOU ON TOP!
VWOOOO
KLAK KLAK KLAK KLAK KLAK
THE AKUTAGAWA AWARD CEREMONY TOOK PLACE TONIGHT AT THE PRINCE HOTEL, WITH THE UP-AND-COMING TOSHIKO TOMURA...

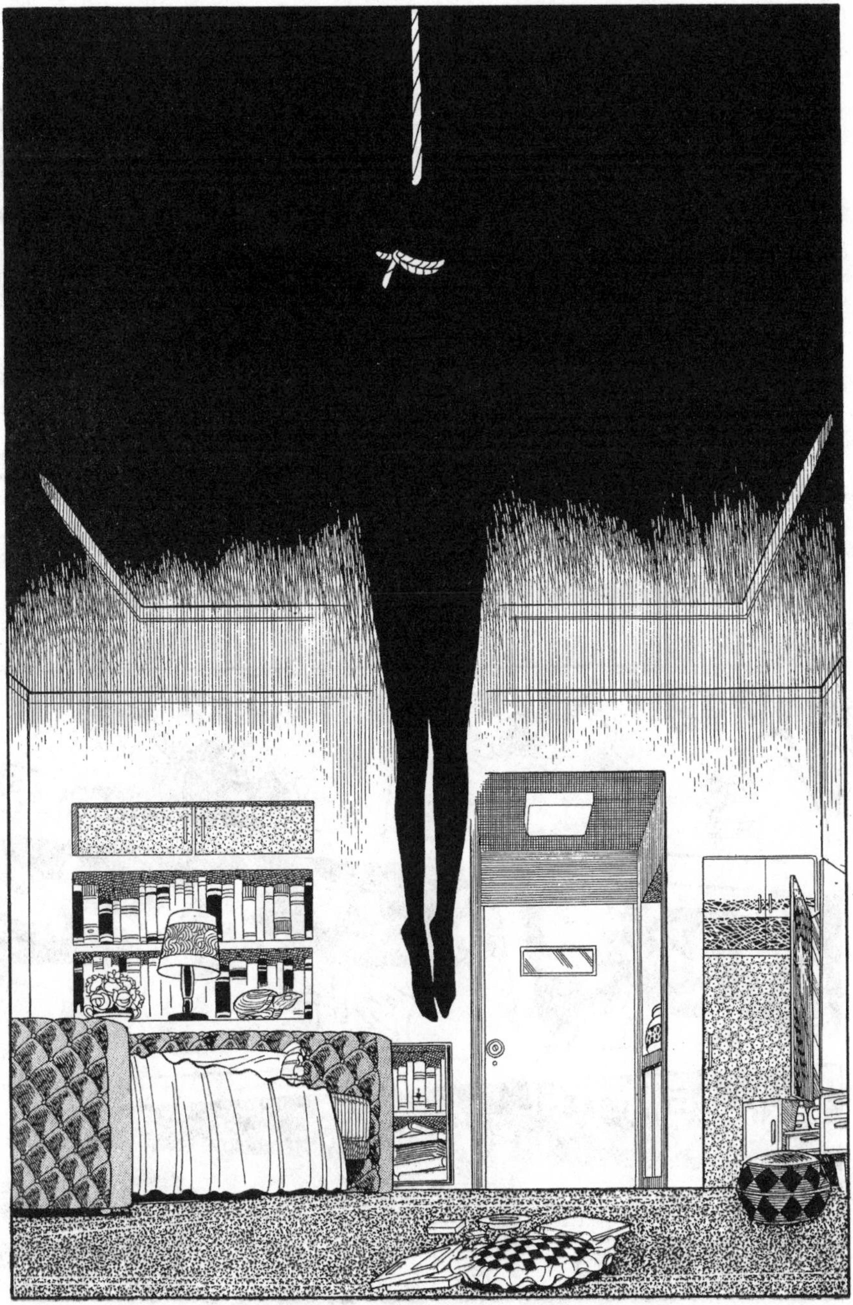

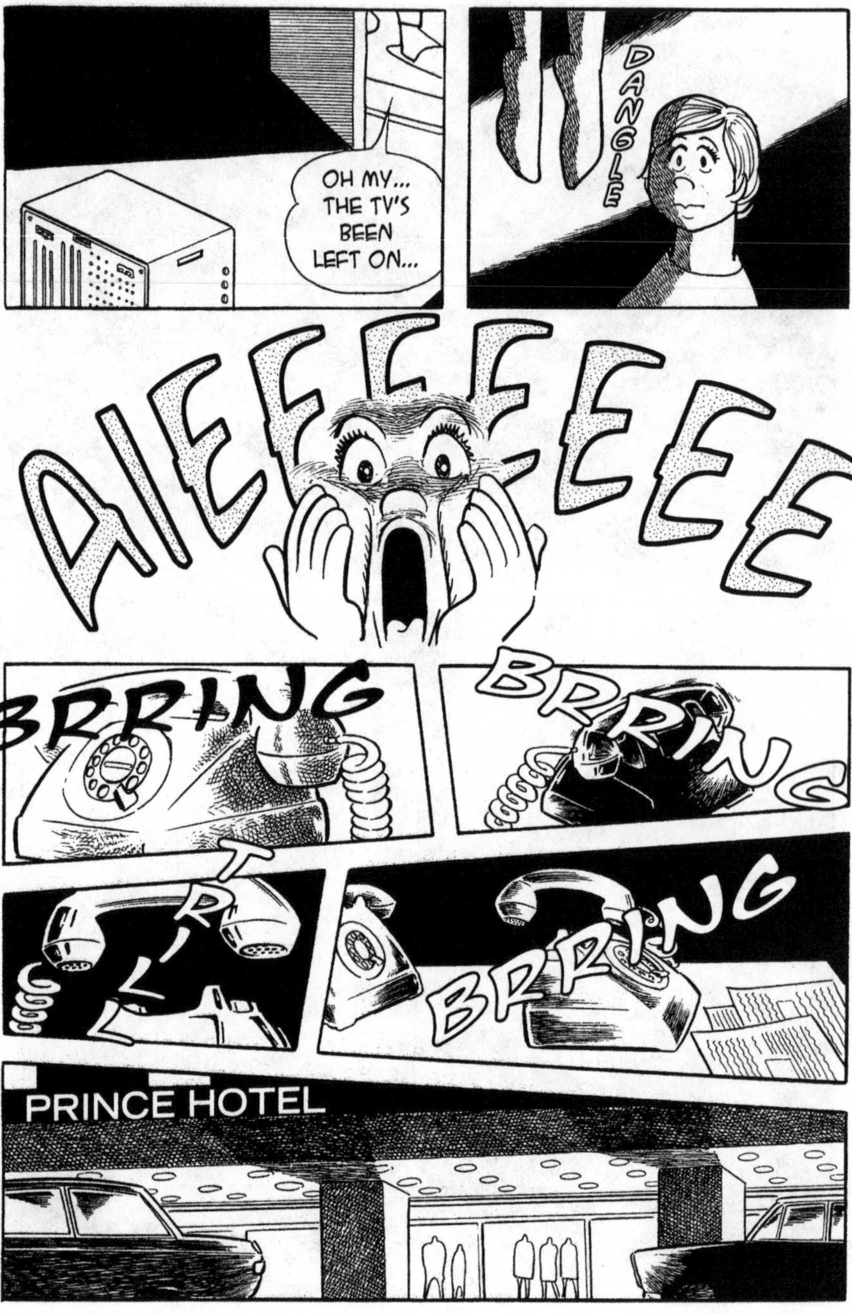
OH MY... THE TV'S BEEN LEFT ON...
DANGLE
AIEEEEEE
BRRING
BRRING
TRILL
BRRING
PRINCE HOTEL

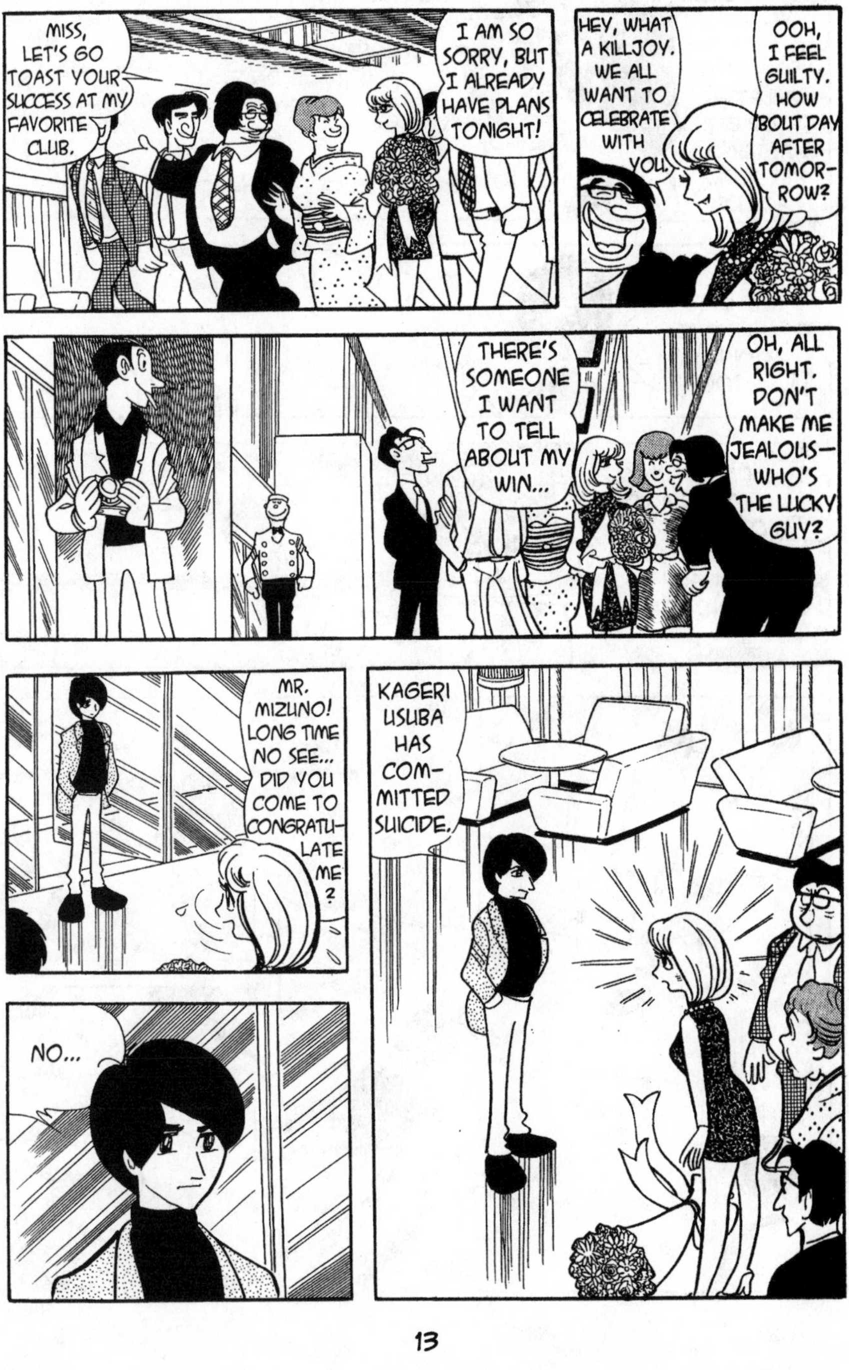
MISS, LET'S GO TOAST YOUR SUCCESS AT MY FAVORITE CLUB.
I AM SO SORRY, BUT I ALREADY HAVE PLANS TONIGHT!
HEY, WHAT A KILLJOY. WE ALL WANT TO CELEBRATE WITH YOU.
OOH, I FEEL GUILTY. HOW BOUT DAY AFTER TOMOR-ROW?
THERE'S SOMEONE I WANT TO TELL ABOUT MY WIN...
OH, ALL RIGHT. DON'T MAKE ME JEALOUS—WHO'S THE LUCKY GUY?
MR. MIZUNO! LONG TIME NO SEE... DID YOU COME TO CONGRATU-LATE ME?
NO...
KAGERI USUBA HAS COM-MITTED SUICIDE.

YOU'VE OBTAINED FAME AND STATUS, WHILE THE OTHER GIRL HAS HUNG HERSELF... THAT'S LIFE.

SHE TOOK TO THE NOOSE WHEN SHE SAW YOUR FACE ON TV. HER DOWNSTAIRS SUPER FOUND HER!

EVERYONE'S GATHERED AT HER PLACE. WANNA COME TOO?

NO...

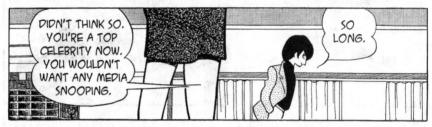

DIDN'T THINK SO. YOU'RE A TOP CELEBRITY NOW. YOU WOULDN'T WANT ANY MEDIA SNOOPING.

SO LONG.

MR. MIZU-NO!!

CAN WE MEET UP LATER?

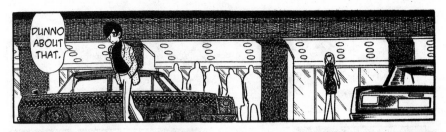

DUNNO ABOUT THAT.

FWOM

WH-WHO ARE YOU?

NAME'S AOKUSA, FROM WEEKLY TALK... NICE TO MEET YOU.

YOU'RE AN ACQUAINTANCE OF MISS TOMURA'S? I BELIEVE YOU MENTIONED A MISS USUBA JUST NOW?

...

ISN'T MISS TOMURA'S REAL NAME ALSO USUBA?

BINGO, YES? I'M PRETTY SURE IT'S KAGERI USUBA.

SOMEONE WITH THE SAME NAME COMMITTED SUICIDE?

THAT'S NONE OF THE MEDIA'S BUSINESS.

15

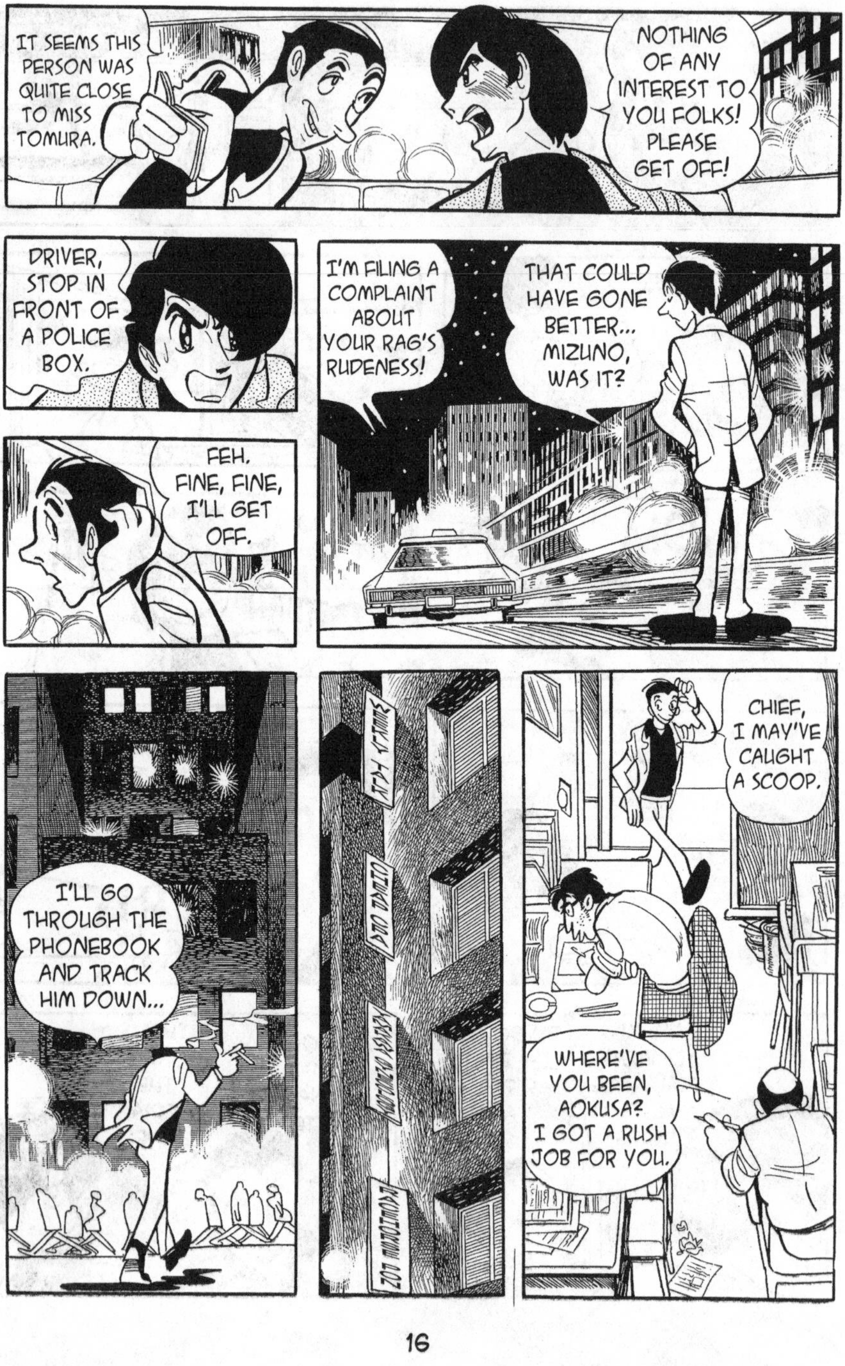
IT SEEMS THIS PERSON WAS QUITE CLOSE TO MISS TOMURA.
NOTHING OF ANY INTEREST TO YOU FOLKS! PLEASE GET OFF!
DRIVER, STOP IN FRONT OF A POLICE BOX.
FEH. FINE, FINE, I'LL GET OFF.
I'M FILING A COMPLAINT ABOUT YOUR RAG'S RUDENESS!
THAT COULD HAVE GONE BETTER... MIZUNO, WAS IT?
I'LL GO THROUGH THE PHONEBOOK AND TRACK HIM DOWN...
CHIEF, I MAY'VE CAUGHT A SCOOP.
WHERE'VE YOU BEEN, AOKUSA? I GOT A RUSH JOB FOR YOU.

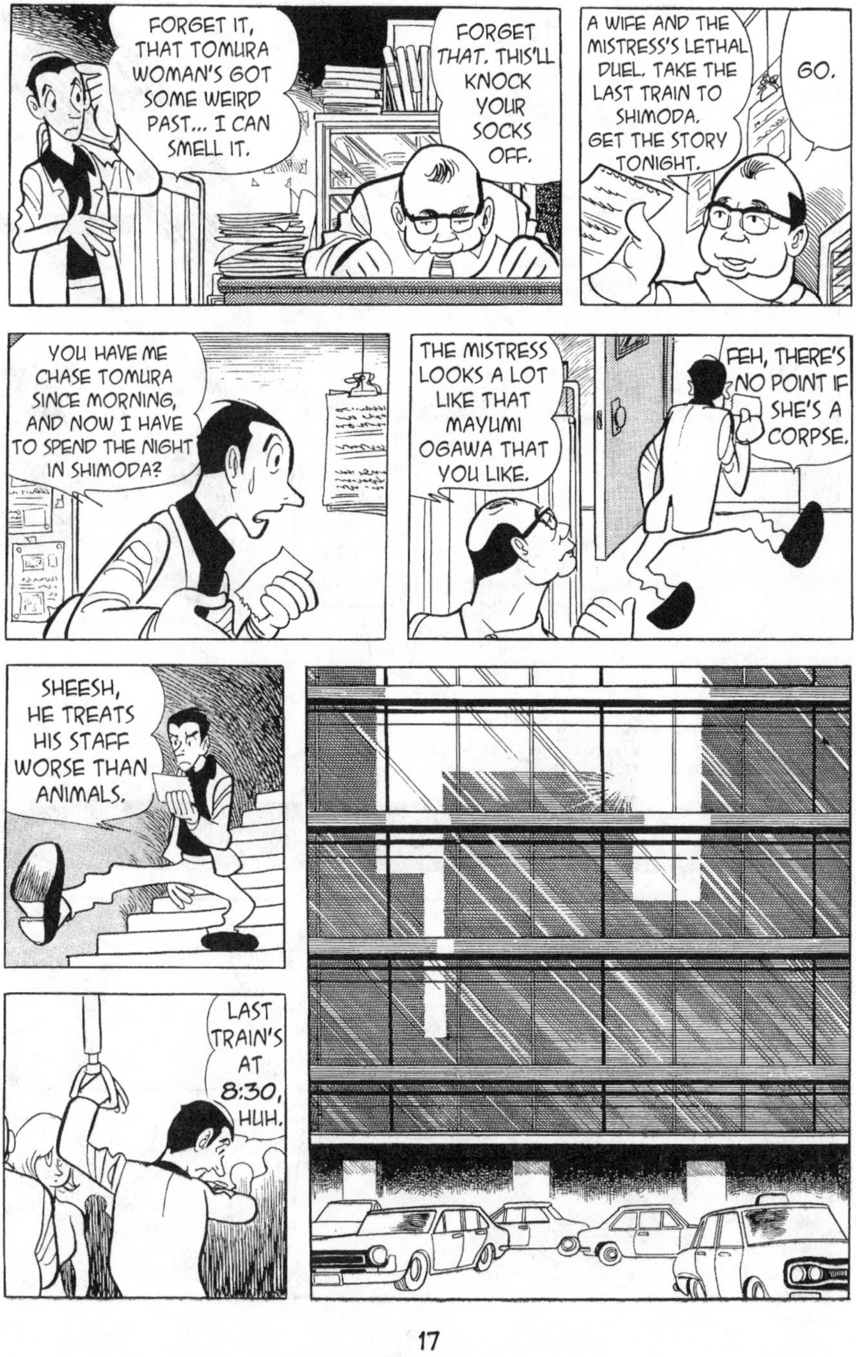
FORGET IT, THAT TOMURA WOMAN'S GOT SOME WEIRD PAST... I CAN SMELL IT.
FORGET THAT. THIS'LL KNOCK YOUR SOCKS OFF.
A WIFE AND THE MISTRESS'S LETHAL DUEL. TAKE THE LAST TRAIN TO SHIMODA. GET THE STORY TONIGHT.
GO.
YOU HAVE ME CHASE TOMURA SINCE MORNING, AND NOW I HAVE TO SPEND THE NIGHT IN SHIMODA?
THE MISTRESS LOOKS A LOT LIKE THAT MAYUMI OGAWA THAT YOU LIKE.
FEH, THERE'S NO POINT IF SHE'S A CORPSE.
SHEESH, HE TREATS HIS STAFF WORSE THAN ANIMALS.
LAST TRAIN'S AT 8:30, HUH.

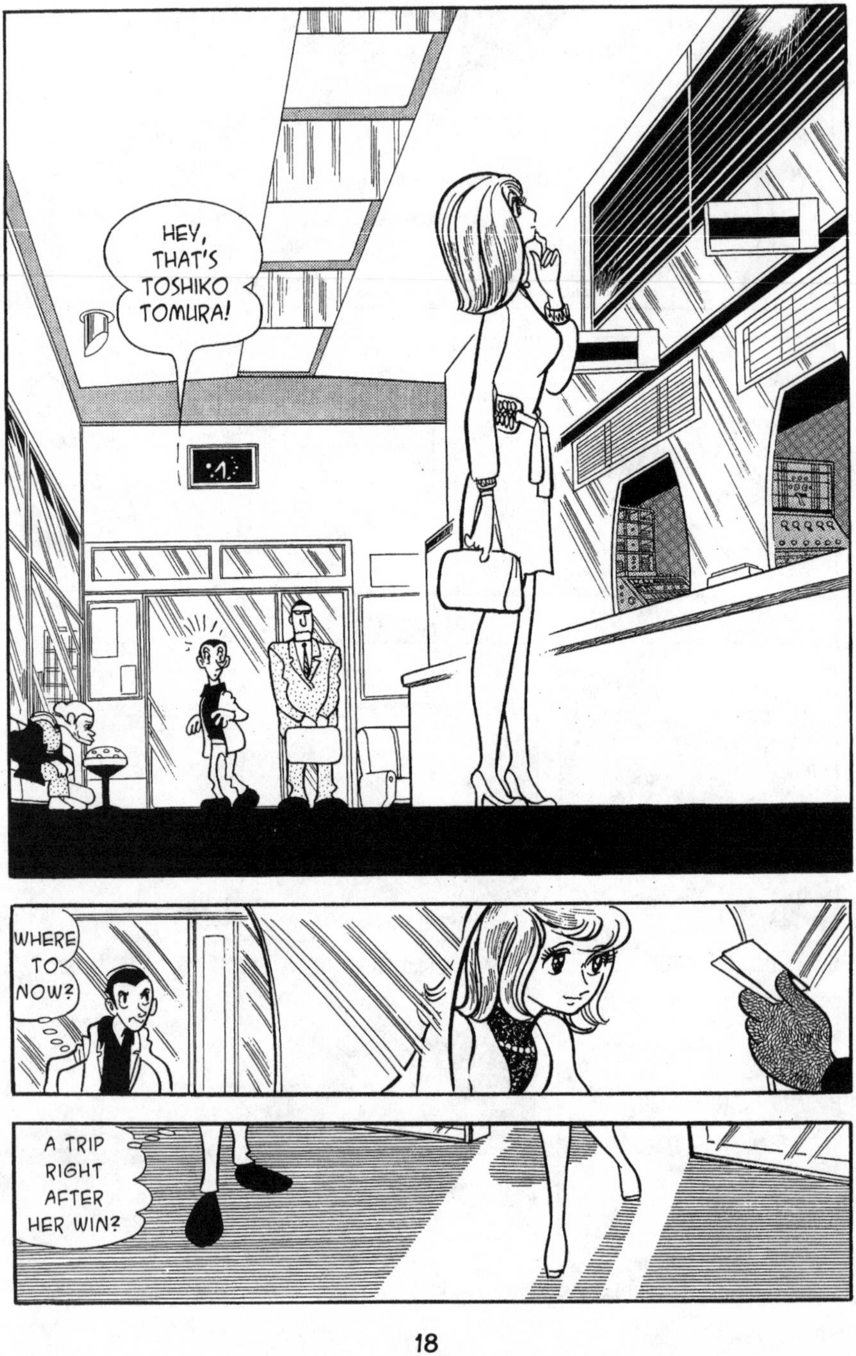
HEY, THAT'S TOSHIKO TOMURA!
WHERE TO NOW?
A TRIP RIGHT AFTER HER WIN?

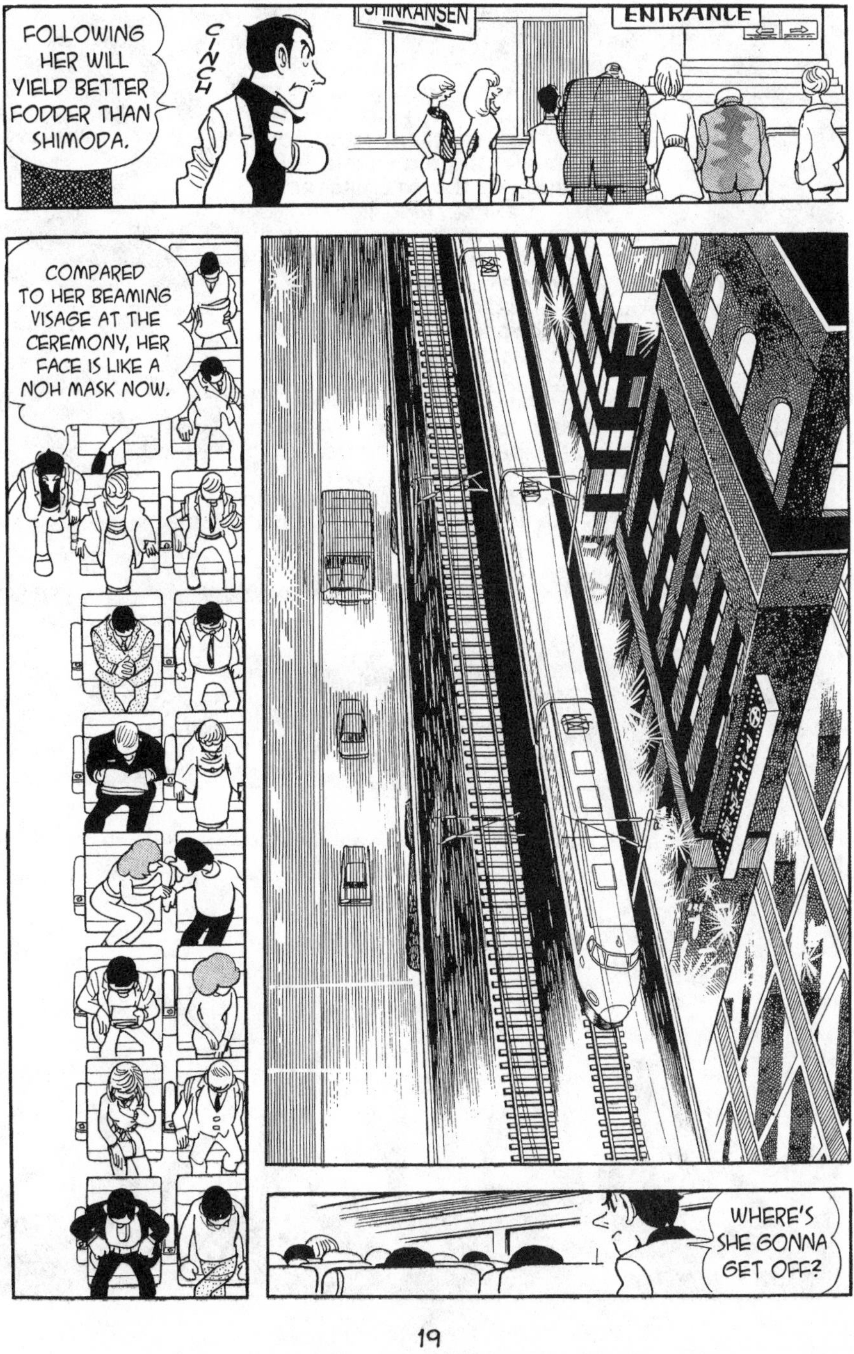
FOLLOWING HER WILL YIELD BETTER FODDER THAN SHIMODA.
CINCH
SHINKANSEN
ENTRANCE
COMPARED TO HER BEAMING VISAGE AT THE CEREMONY, HER FACE IS LIKE A NOH MASK NOW.
WHERE'S SHE GONNA GET OFF?

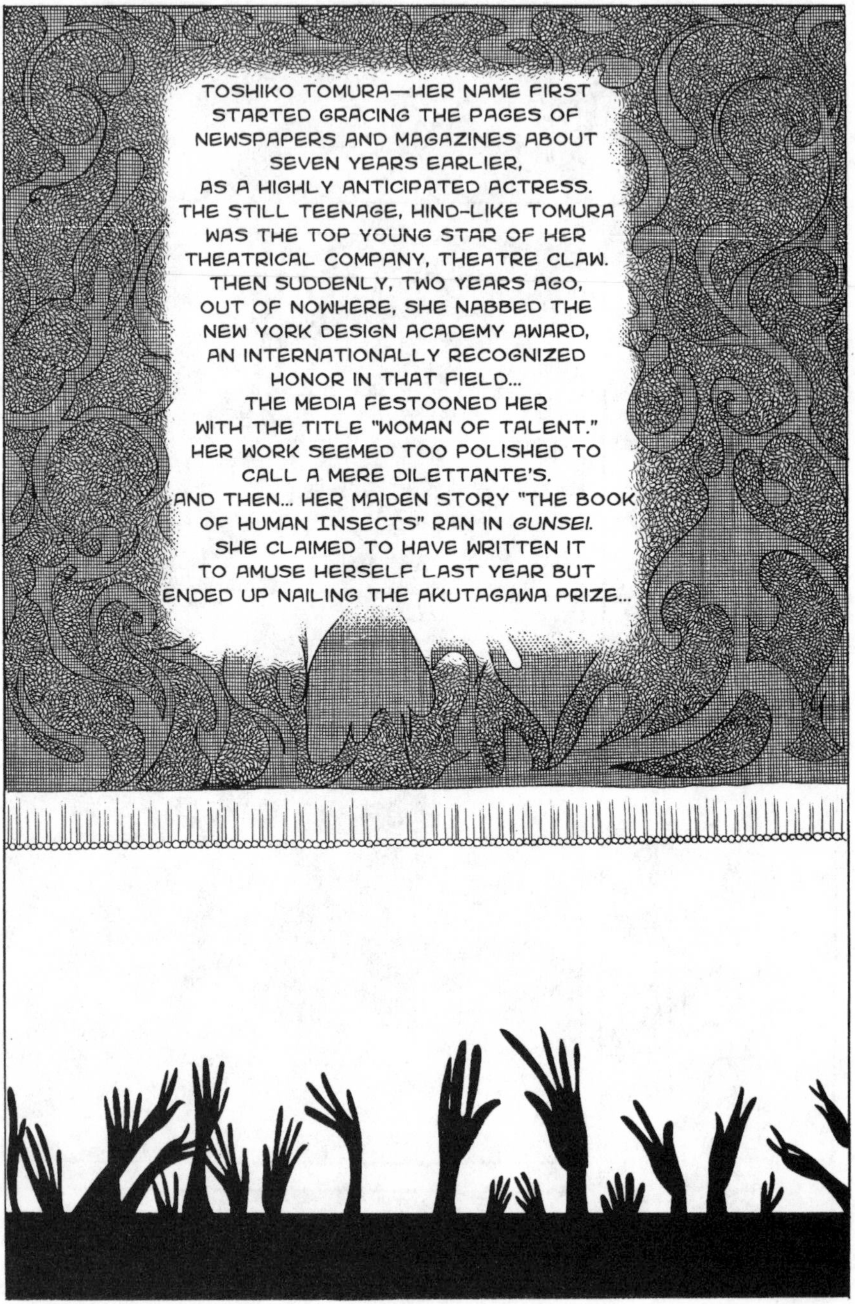
TOSHIKO TOMURA—HER NAME FIRST STARTED GRACING THE PAGES OF NEWSPAPERS AND MAGAZINES ABOUT SEVEN YEARS EARLIER, AS A HIGHLY ANTICIPATED ACTRESS. THE STILL TEENAGE, HIND-LIKE TOMURA WAS THE TOP YOUNG STAR OF HER THEATRICAL COMPANY, THEATRE CLAW. THEN SUDDENLY, TWO YEARS AGO, OUT OF NOWHERE, SHE NABBED THE NEW YORK DESIGN ACADEMY AWARD, AN INTERNATIONALLY RECOGNIZED HONOR IN THAT FIELD... THE MEDIA FESTOONED HER WITH THE TITLE "WOMAN OF TALENT." HER WORK SEEMED TOO POLISHED TO CALL A MERE DILETTANTE'S. AND THEN... HER MAIDEN STORY "THE BOOK OF HUMAN INSECTS" RAN IN *GUNSEI*. SHE CLAIMED TO HAVE WRITTEN IT TO AMUSE HERSELF LAST YEAR BUT ENDED UP NAILING THE AKUTAGAWA PRIZE...

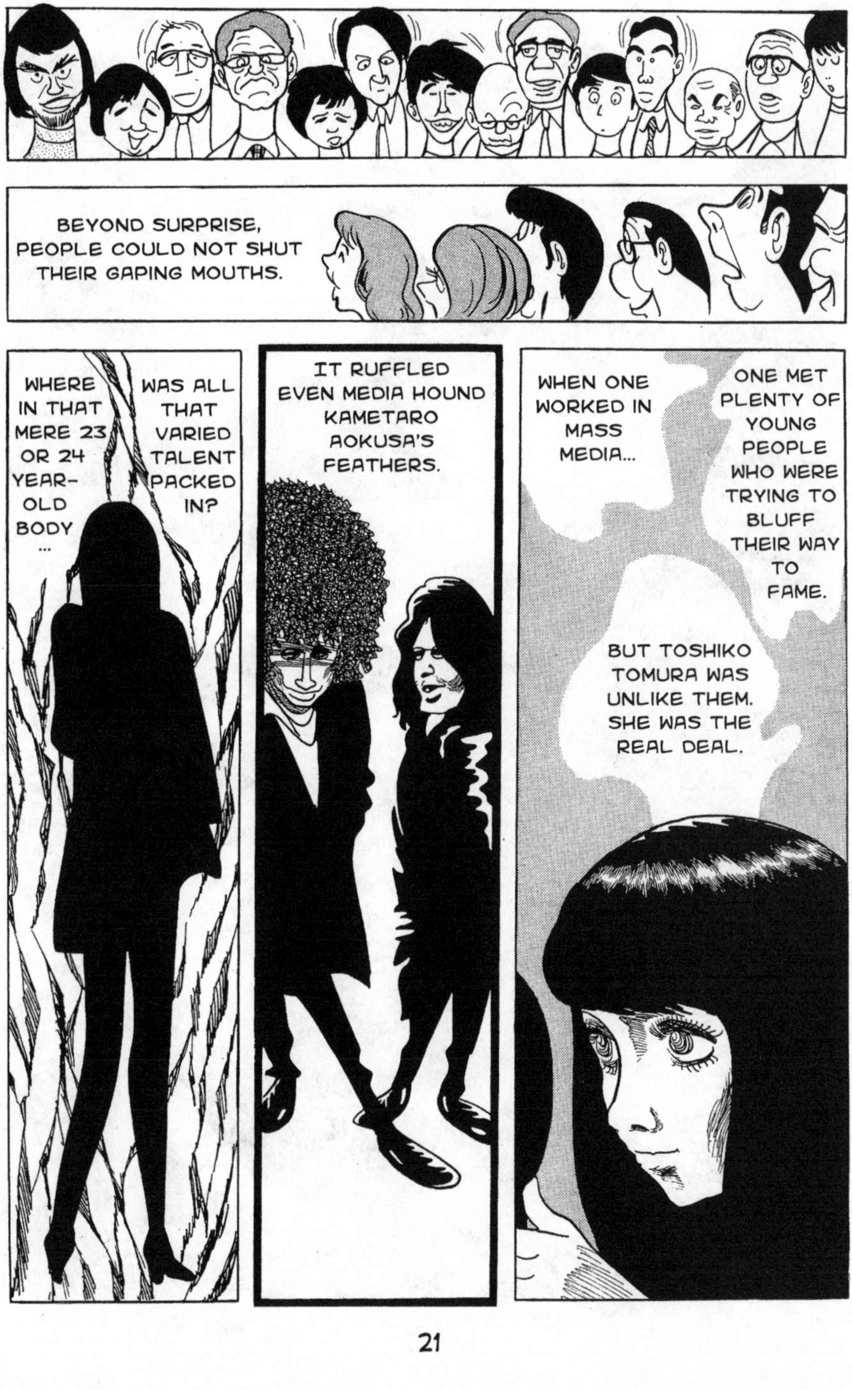
BEYOND SURPRISE, PEOPLE COULD NOT SHUT THEIR GAPING MOUTHS.
WHERE IN THAT MERE 23 OR 24 YEAR-OLD BODY ...
WAS ALL THAT VARIED TALENT PACKED IN?
IT RUFFLED EVEN MEDIA HOUND KAMETARO AOKUSA'S FEATHERS.
WHEN ONE WORKED IN MASS MEDIA...
ONE MET PLENTY OF YOUNG PEOPLE WHO WERE TRYING TO BLUFF THEIR WAY TO FAME.
BUT TOSHIKO TOMURA WAS UNLIKE THEM. SHE WAS THE REAL DEAL.

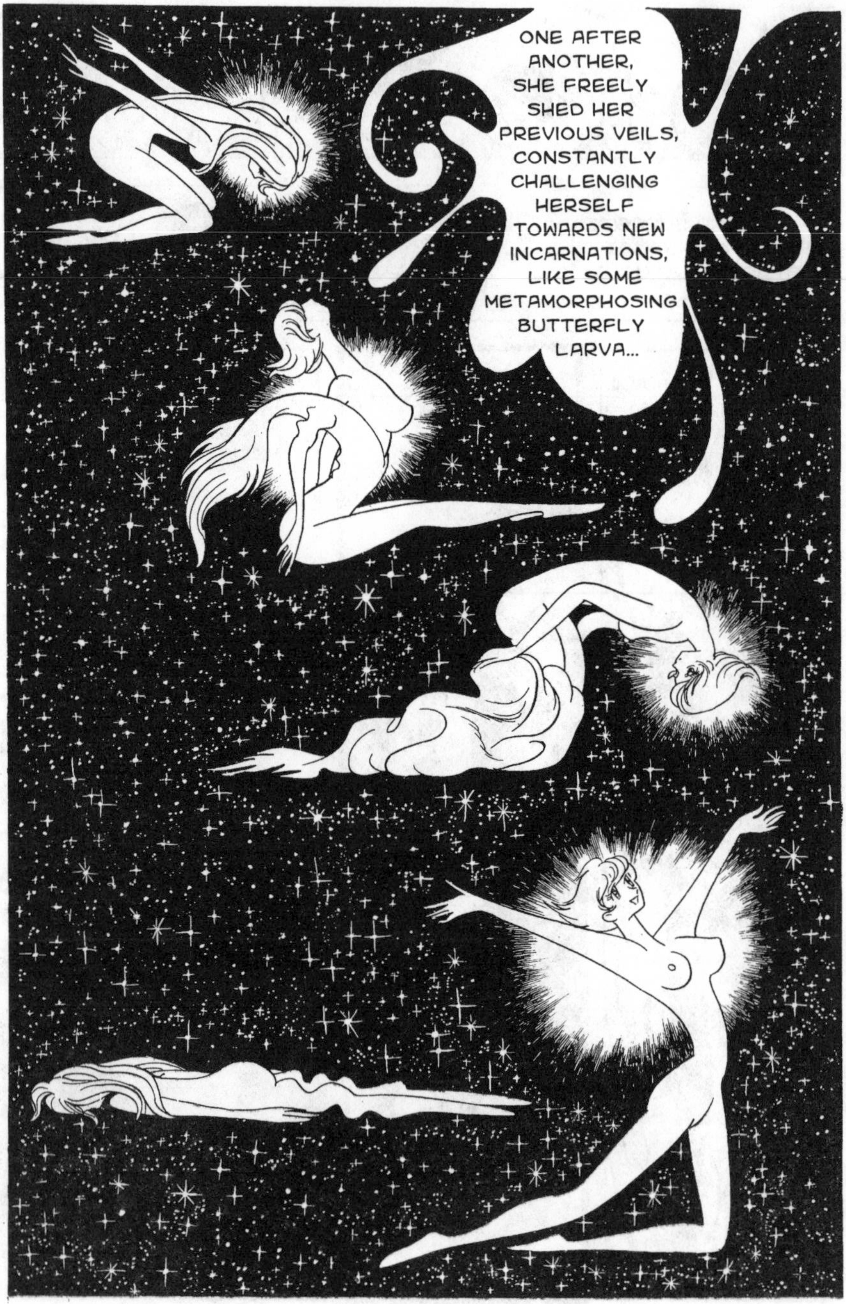
ONE AFTER ANOTHER, SHE FREELY SHED HER PREVIOUS VEILS, CONSTANTLY CHALLENGING HERSELF TOWARDS NEW INCARNATIONS, LIKE SOME METAMORPHOSING BUTTERFLY LARVA...

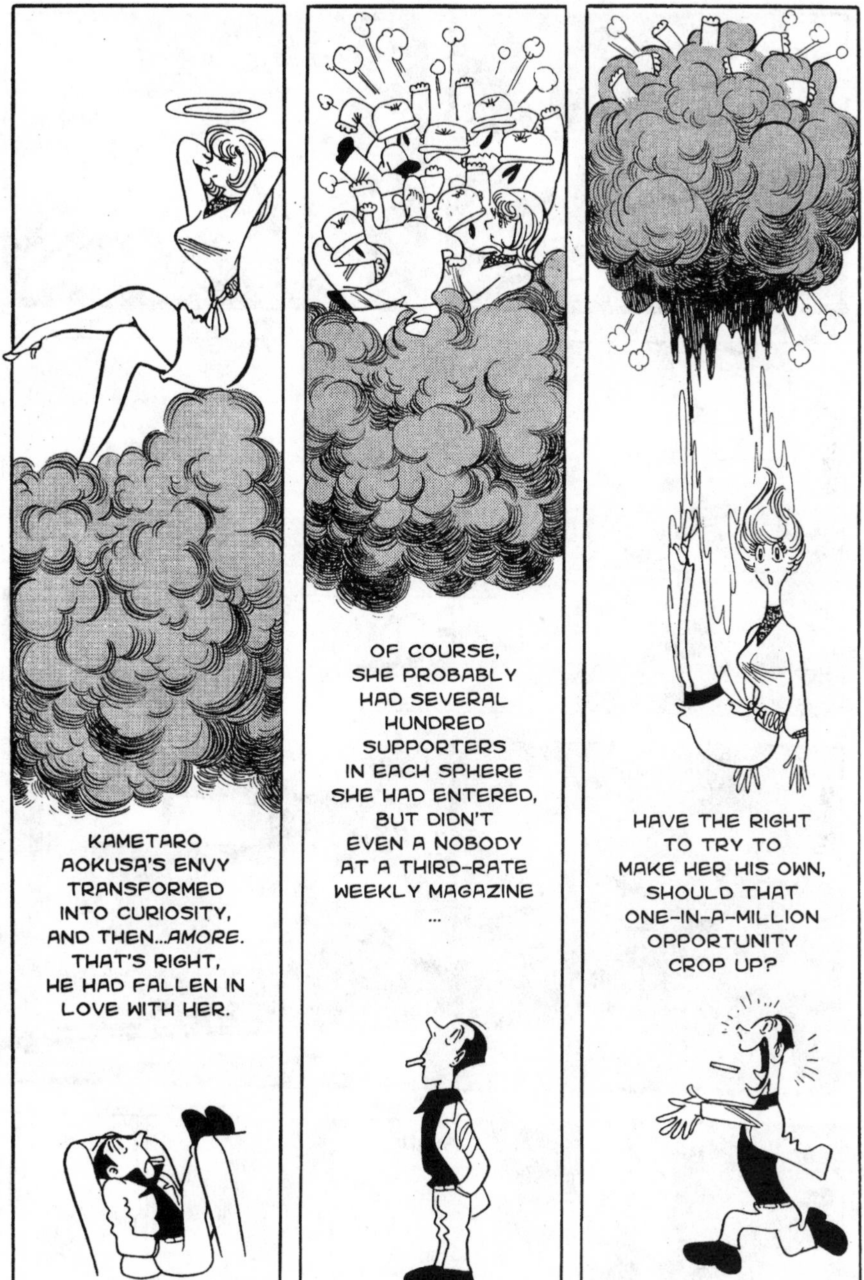
KAMETARO AOKUSA'S ENVY TRANSFORMED INTO CURIOSITY, AND THEN...*AMORE*. THAT'S RIGHT, HE HAD FALLEN IN LOVE WITH HER.
OF COURSE, SHE PROBABLY HAD SEVERAL HUNDRED SUPPORTERS IN EACH SPHERE SHE HAD ENTERED, BUT DIDN'T EVEN A NOBODY AT A THIRD-RATE WEEKLY MAGAZINE ...
HAVE THE RIGHT TO TRY TO MAKE HER HIS OWN, SHOULD THAT ONE-IN-A-MILLION OPPORTUNITY CROP UP?

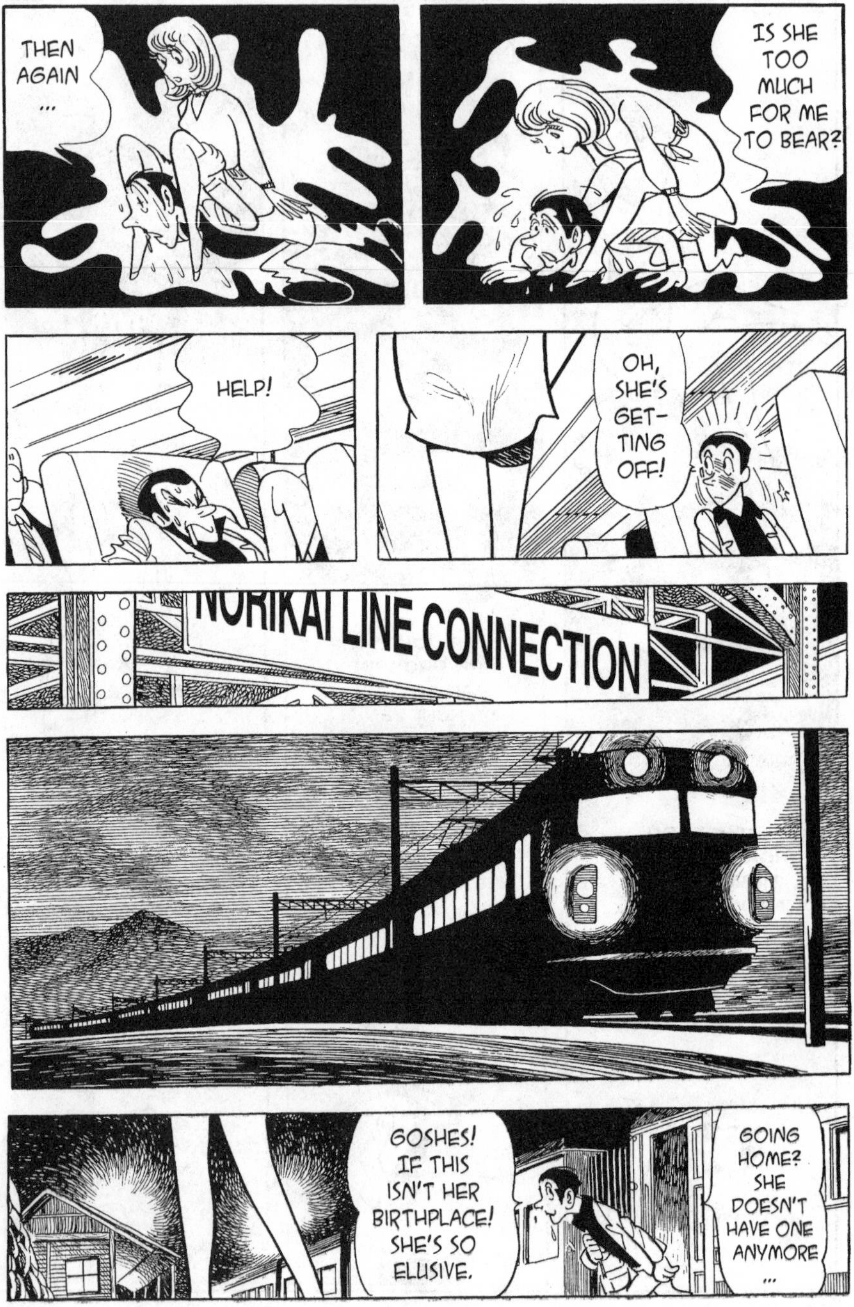
THEN AGAIN ...
IS SHE TOO MUCH FOR ME TO BEAR?
HELP!
OH, SHE'S GETTING OFF!
NORIKAI LINE CONNECTION
GOSHES! IF THIS ISN'T HER BIRTHPLACE! SHE'S SO ELUSIVE.
GOING HOME? SHE DOESN'T HAVE ONE ANYMORE ...

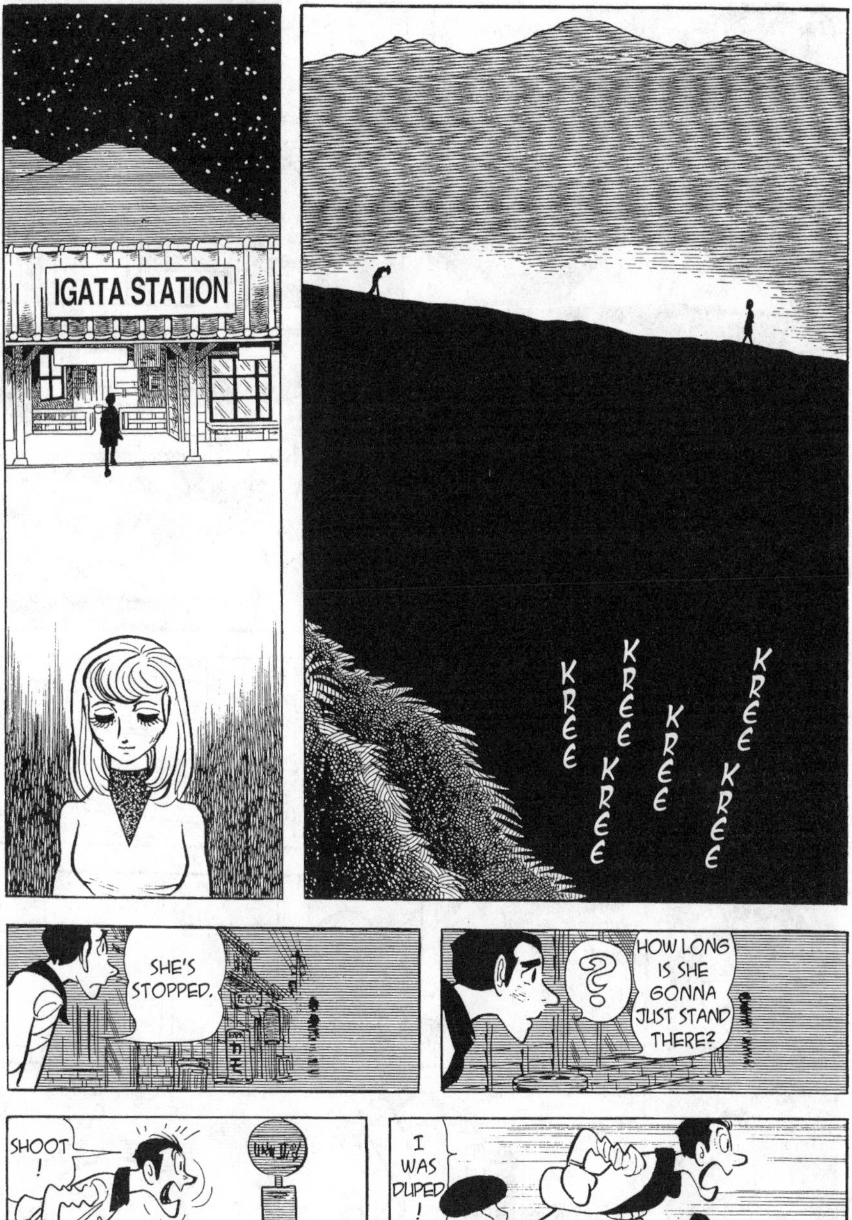
IGATA STATION
KREE
KREE
KREE
KREE
KREE
KREE
SHE'S STOPPED.
?
HOW LONG IS SHE GONNA JUST STAND THERE?
SHOOT!
I WAS DUPED!

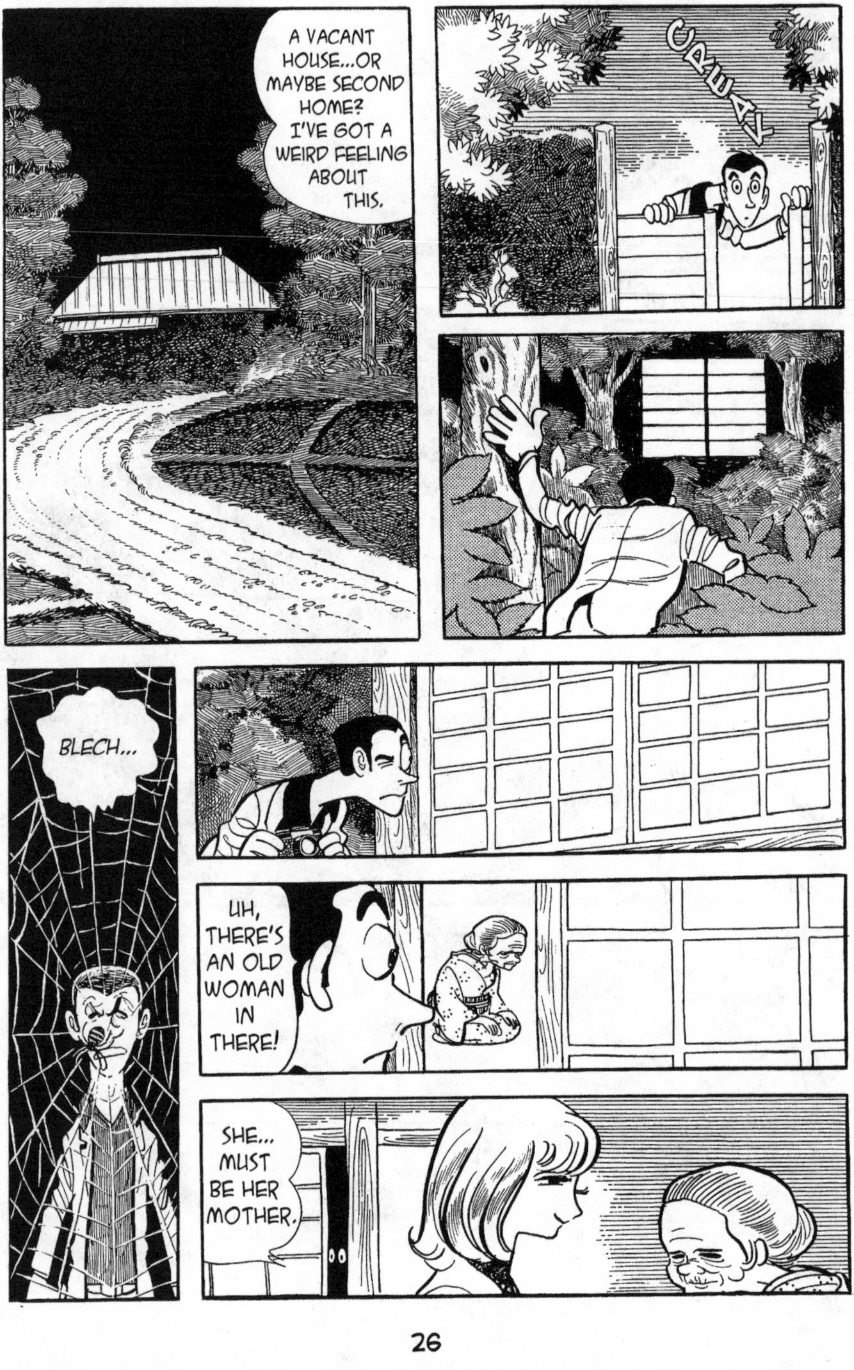
A VACANT HOUSE...OR MAYBE SECOND HOME? I'VE GOT A WEIRD FEELING ABOUT THIS.
CREAK
BLECH...
UH, THERE'S AN OLD WOMAN IN THERE!
SHE... MUST BE HER MOTHER.

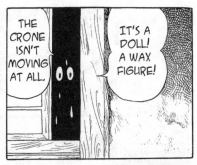

THE CRONE ISN'T MOVING AT ALL.

IT'S A DOLL! A WAX FIGURE!

IT WAS AN UNEXPECTED SIGHT.

FAR FROM A BOLD AND STATELY PRODIGY WHO HAD WON THE AKUTAGAWA PRIZE, SHE ACTED LIKE A NEWLY WEANED CHILD.

SHE'S SUCKING ON THE WAX FIGURE'S TEATS !

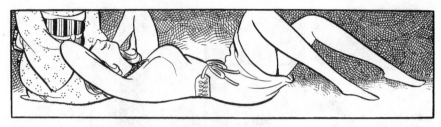

SWISH

PHEW...

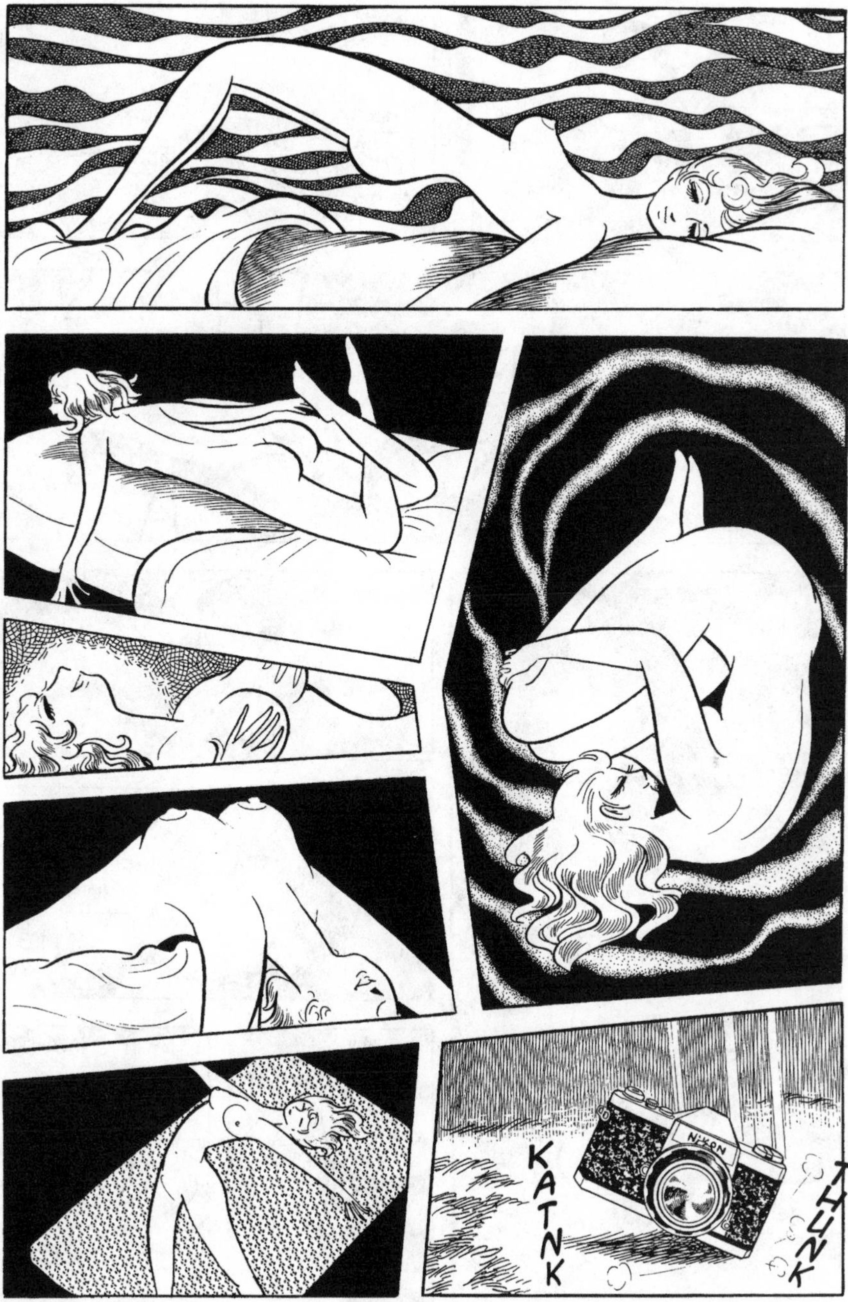
NiKON
KATNK
THUNK

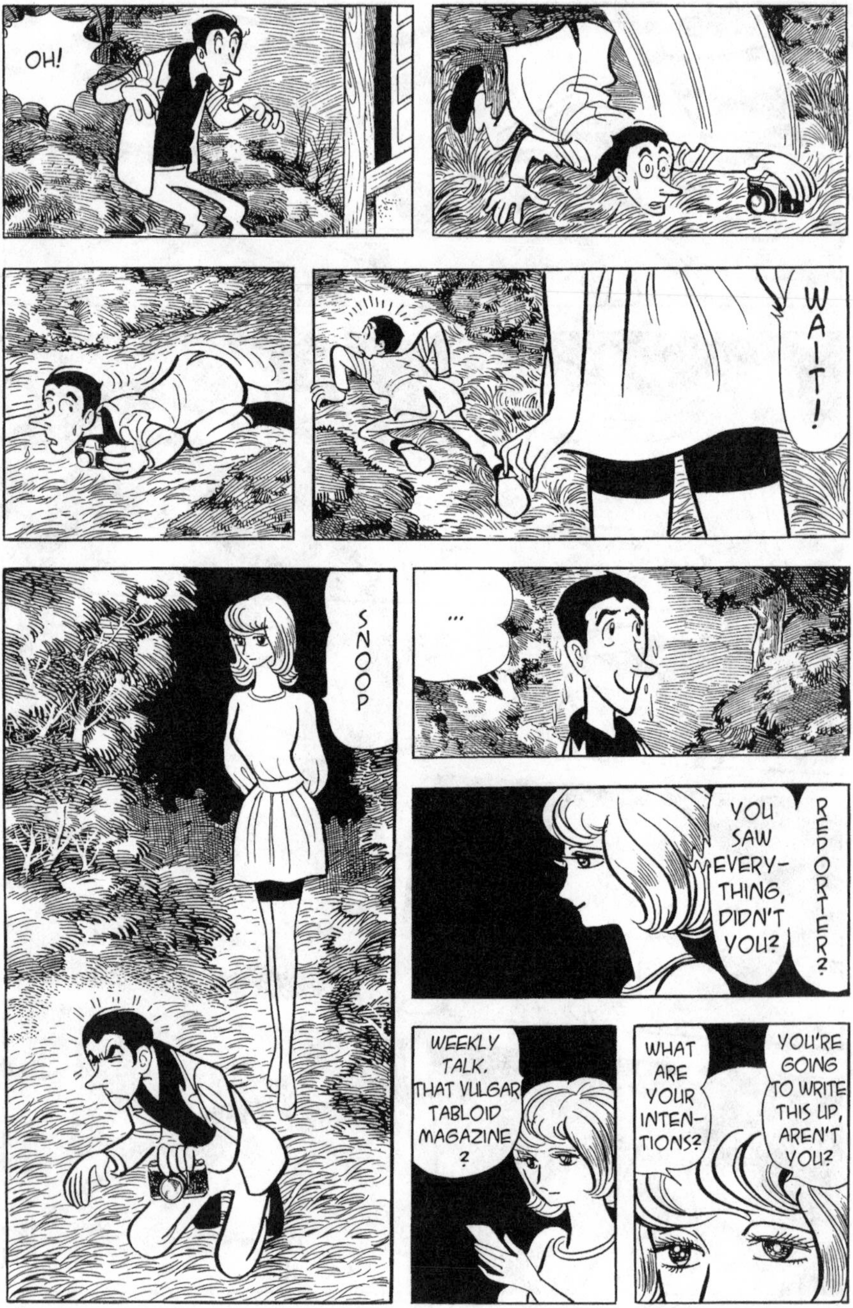
OH!
WAIT!
SNOOP
...
REPORTER?
YOU SAW EVERYTHING, DIDN'T YOU?
WEEKLY TALK. THAT VULGAR TABLOID MAGAZINE?
WHAT ARE YOUR INTENTIONS?
YOU'RE GOING TO WRITE THIS UP, AREN'T YOU?

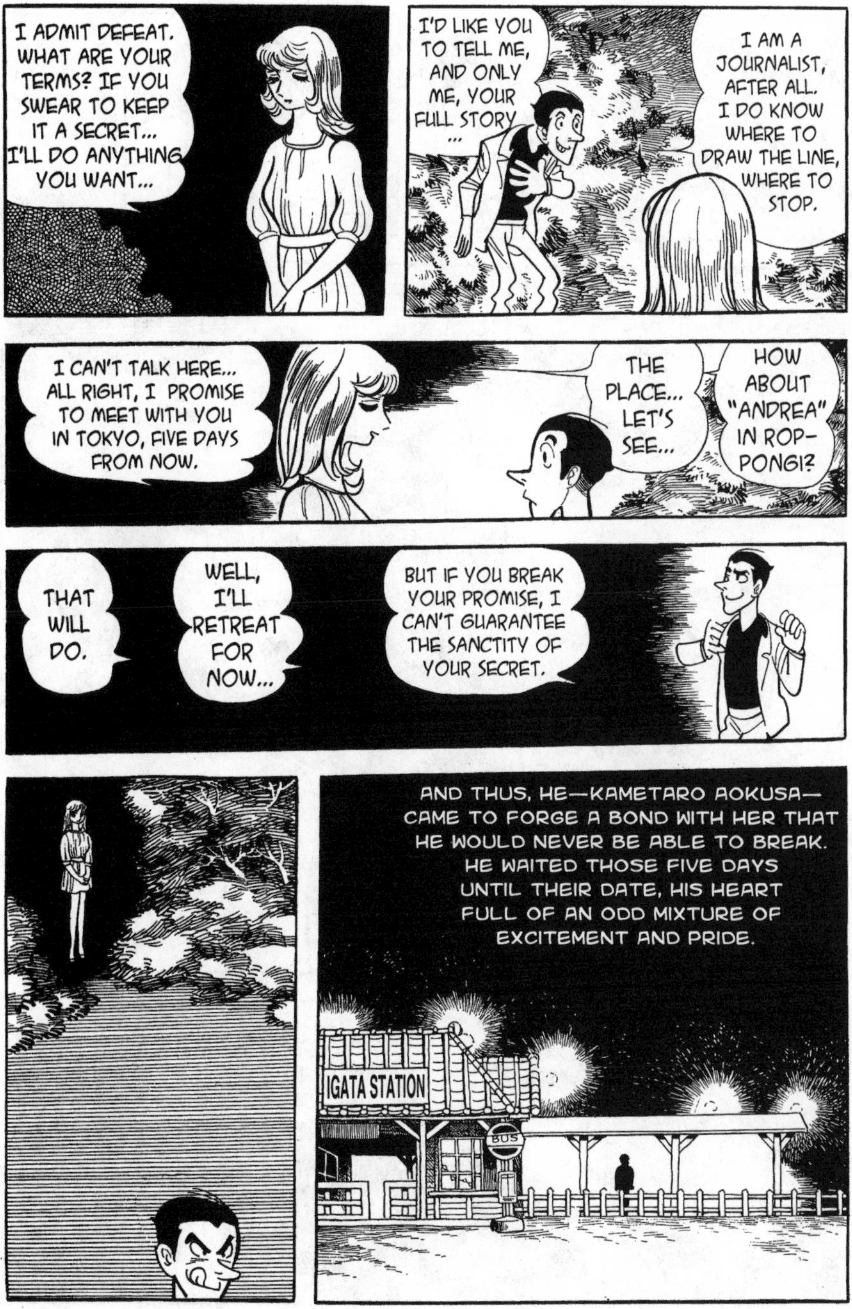
I ADMIT DEFEAT. WHAT ARE YOUR TERMS? IF YOU SWEAR TO KEEP IT A SECRET... I'LL DO ANYTHING YOU WANT...
I'D LIKE YOU TO TELL ME, AND ONLY ME, YOUR FULL STORY ...
I AM A JOURNALIST, AFTER ALL. I DO KNOW WHERE TO DRAW THE LINE, WHERE TO STOP.
I CAN'T TALK HERE... ALL RIGHT, I PROMISE TO MEET WITH YOU IN TOKYO, FIVE DAYS FROM NOW.
THE PLACE... LET'S SEE...
HOW ABOUT "ANDREA" IN ROP-PONGI?
THAT WILL DO.
WELL, I'LL RETREAT FOR NOW...
BUT IF YOU BREAK YOUR PROMISE, I CAN'T GUARANTEE THE SANCTITY OF YOUR SECRET.
AND THUS, HE—KAMETARO AOKUSA—CAME TO FORGE A BOND WITH HER THAT HE WOULD NEVER BE ABLE TO BREAK. HE WAITED THOSE FIVE DAYS UNTIL THEIR DATE, HIS HEART FULL OF AN ODD MIXTURE OF EXCITEMENT AND PRIDE.
IGATA STATION
BUS

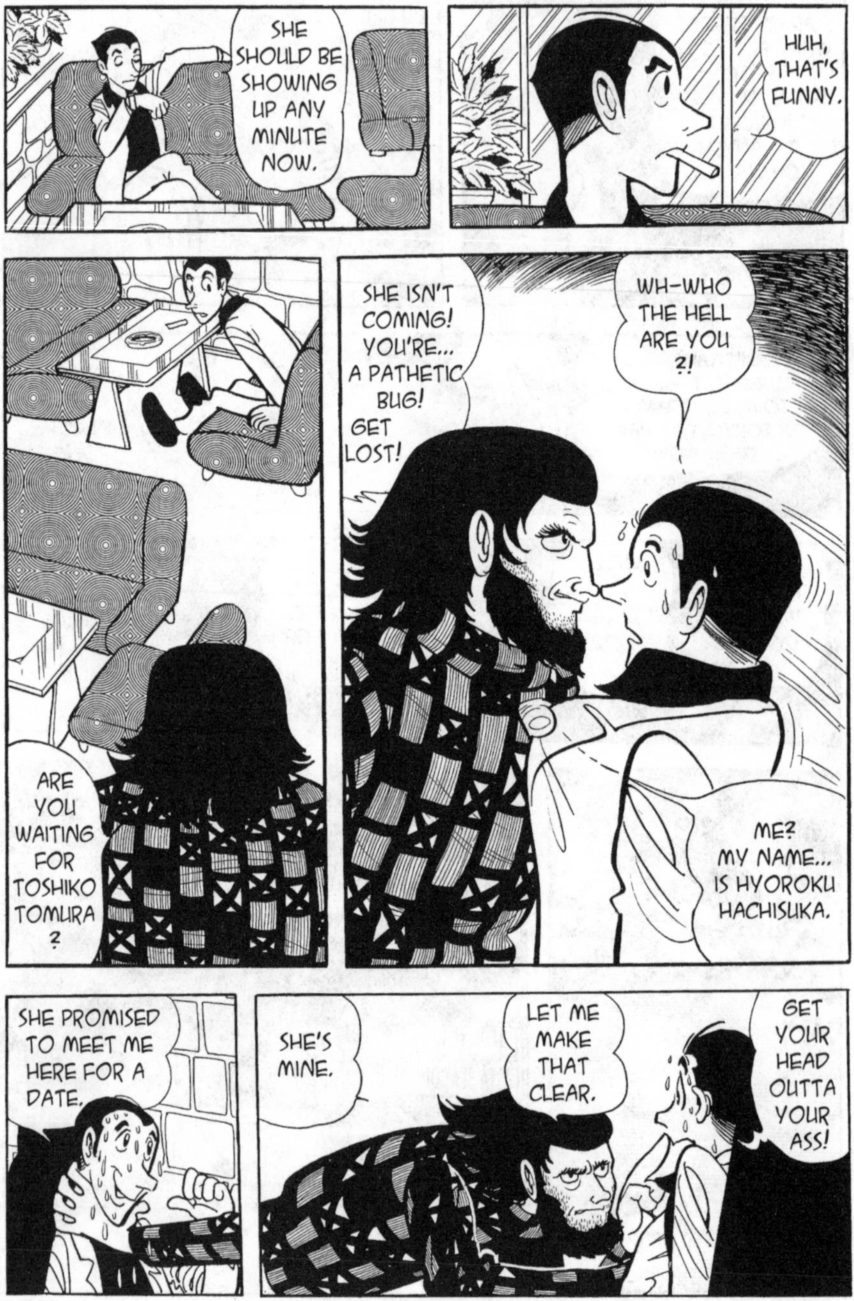

SHE SHOULD BE SHOWING UP ANY MINUTE NOW.
HUH, THAT'S FUNNY.
ARE YOU WAITING FOR TOSHIKO TOMURA?
SHE ISN'T COMING! YOU'RE... A PATHETIC BUG! GET LOST!
WH-WHO THE HELL ARE YOU?!
ME? MY NAME... IS HYOROKU HACHISUKA.
SHE PROMISED TO MEET ME HERE FOR A DATE.
SHE'S MINE.
LET ME MAKE THAT CLEAR.
GET YOUR HEAD OUTTA YOUR ASS!

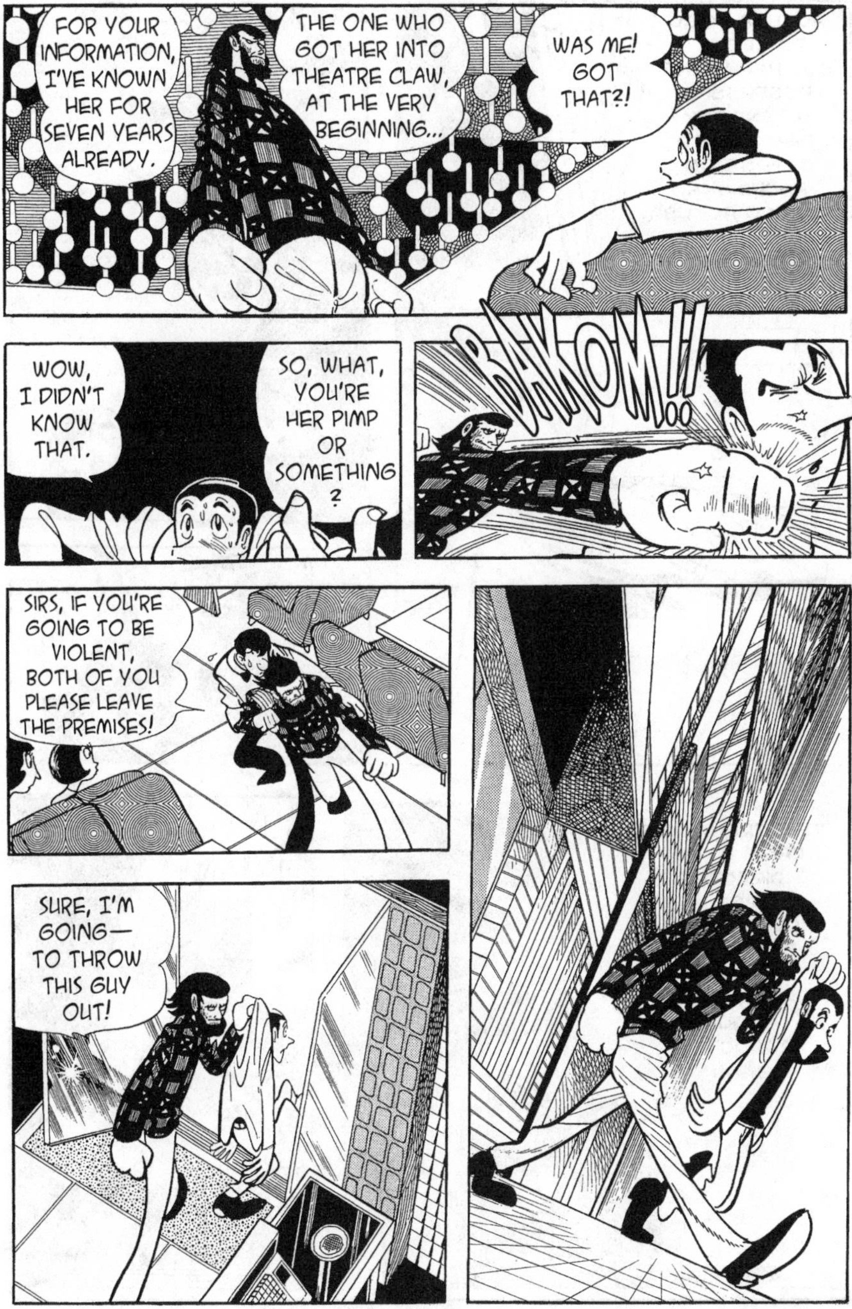
FOR YOUR INFORMATION, I'VE KNOWN HER FOR SEVEN YEARS ALREADY.
THE ONE WHO GOT HER INTO THEATRE CLAW, AT THE VERY BEGINNING...
WAS ME! GOT THAT?!
WOW, I DIDN'T KNOW THAT.
SO, WHAT, YOU'RE HER PIMP OR SOMETHING?
BAKOOM!!
SIRS, IF YOU'RE GOING TO BE VIOLENT, BOTH OF YOU PLEASE LEAVE THE PREMISES!
SURE, I'M GOING— TO THROW THIS GUY OUT!

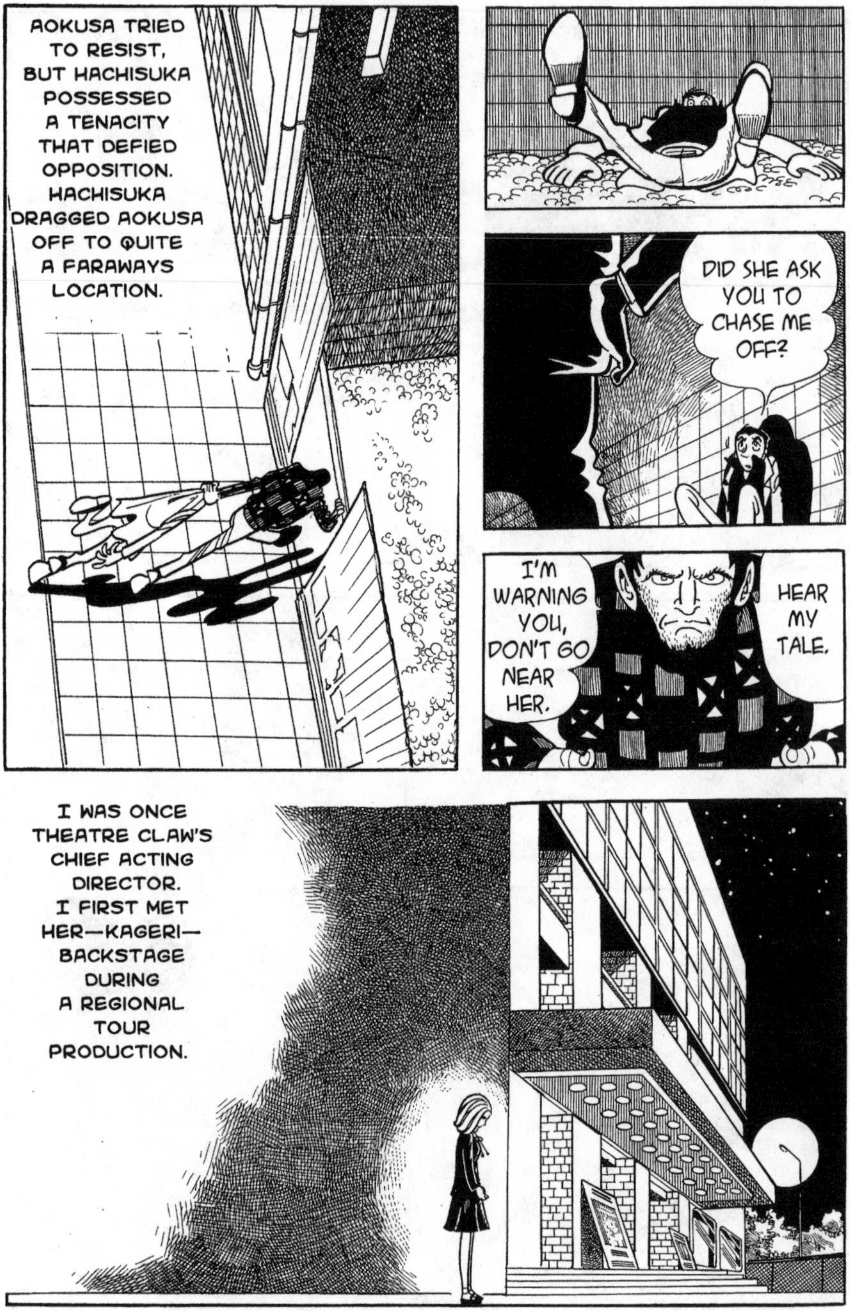
AOKUSA TRIED TO RESIST, BUT HACHISUKA POSSESSED A TENACITY THAT DEFIED OPPOSITION. HACHISUKA DRAGGED AOKUSA OFF TO QUITE A FARAWAYS LOCATION.
DID SHE ASK YOU TO CHASE ME OFF?
I'M WARNING YOU, DON'T GO NEAR HER.
HEAR MY TALE.
I WAS ONCE THEATRE CLAW'S CHIEF ACTING DIRECTOR. I FIRST MET HER—KAGERI—BACKSTAGE DURING A REGIONAL TOUR PRODUCTION.

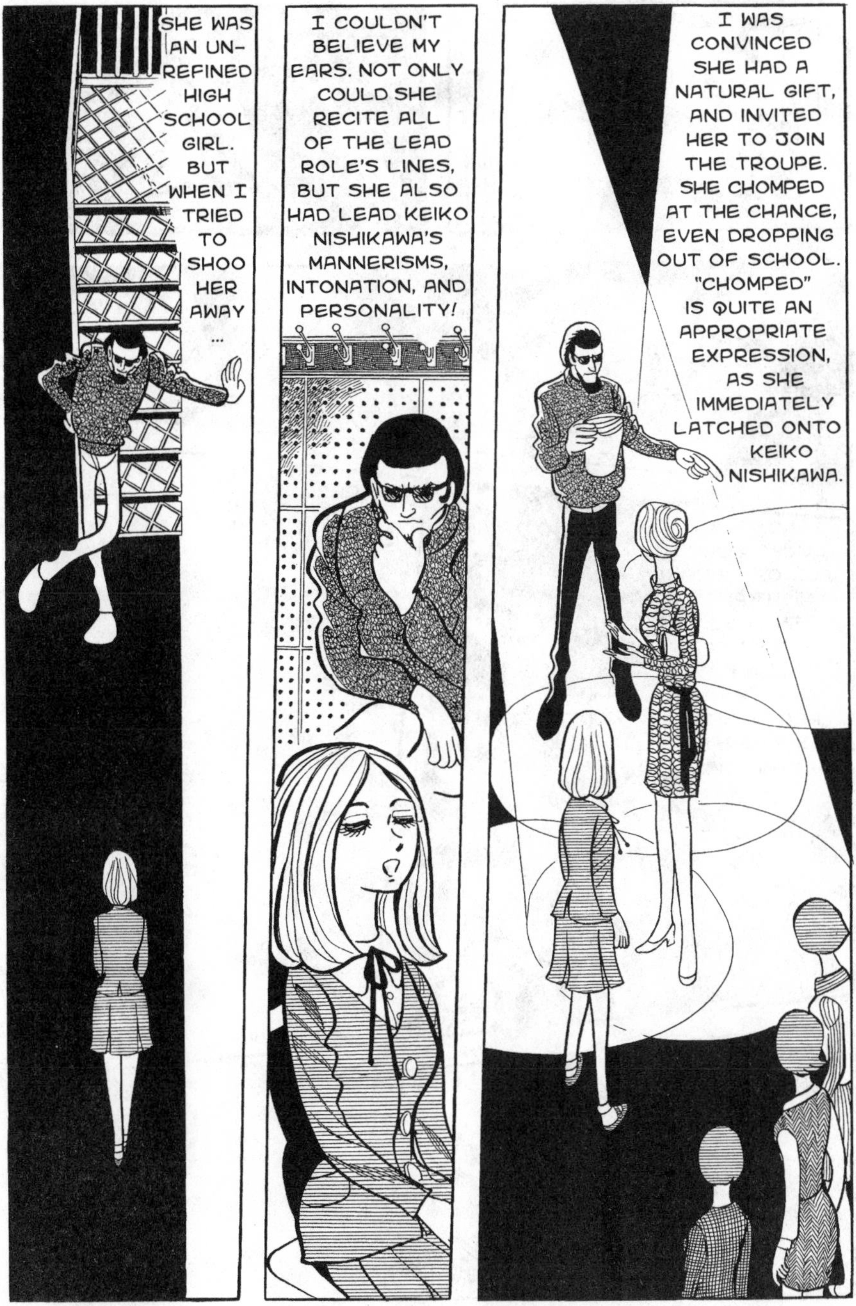
SHE WAS AN UN-REFINED HIGH SCHOOL GIRL. BUT WHEN I TRIED TO SHOO HER AWAY ...
I COULDN'T BELIEVE MY EARS. NOT ONLY COULD SHE RECITE ALL OF THE LEAD ROLE'S LINES, BUT SHE ALSO HAD LEAD KEIKO NISHIKAWA'S MANNERISMS, INTONATION, AND PERSONALITY!
I WAS CONVINCED SHE HAD A NATURAL GIFT, AND INVITED HER TO JOIN THE TROUPE. SHE CHOMPED AT THE CHANCE, EVEN DROPPING OUT OF SCHOOL. "CHOMPED" IS QUITE AN APPROPRIATE EXPRESSION, AS SHE IMMEDIATELY LATCHED ONTO KEIKO NISHIKAWA.

A Streetcar Named Des

10 ~ 10

Tennessee Williams
Theatre Claw

AND... SHE SUCKED OUT ALL OF KEIKO NISHIKAWA. IN LESS THAN A YEAR, KAGERI WAS THE LEAD. HER ACTING WAS A PERFECT NISHIKAWA.

THE REAL KEIKO NISHIKAWA, DRAINED, QUIT THE TROUPE. NO ONE KNOWS WHERE SHE WENT.

KAGERI WAS A GENIUS AT MIMICRY!

36

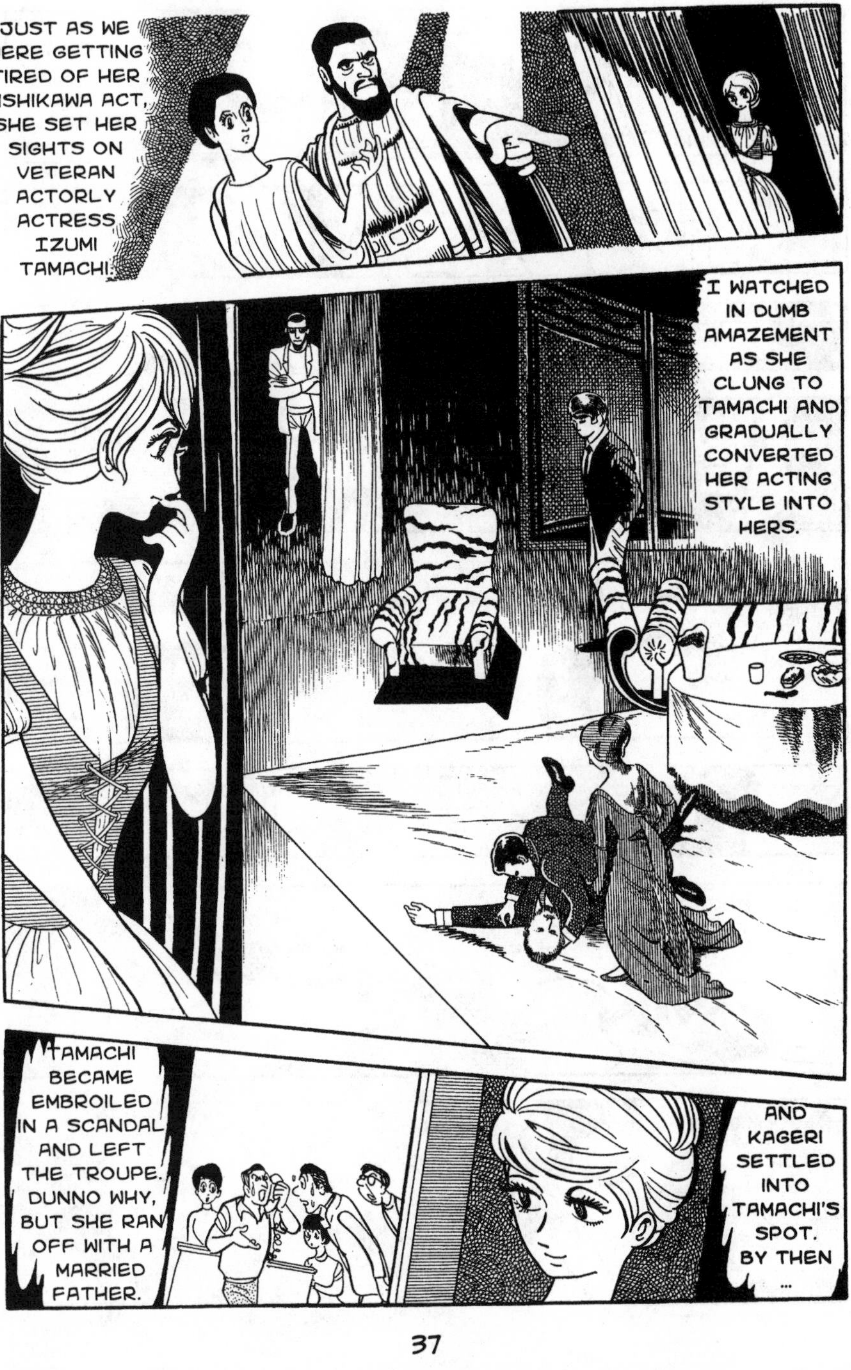
JUST AS WE WERE GETTING TIRED OF HER NISHIKAWA ACT, SHE SET HER SIGHTS ON VETERAN ACTORLY ACTRESS IZUMI TAMACHI.
I WATCHED IN DUMB AMAZEMENT AS SHE CLUNG TO TAMACHI AND GRADUALLY CONVERTED HER ACTING STYLE INTO HERS.
TAMACHI BECAME EMBROILED IN A SCANDAL AND LEFT THE TROUPE. DUNNO WHY, BUT SHE RAN OFF WITH A MARRIED FATHER.
AND KAGERI SETTLED INTO TAMACHI'S SPOT. BY THEN ...

SHE HAD TURNED INTO TAMACHI. A COMPLETE METAMORPHOSIS. LIKE A LARVA TRANSFORMING...

KAGERI CONTINUED DEVOURING TROUPE MEMBERS ONE BY ONE.

TEACH ME?

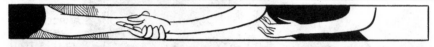

NOT ONE BIT OF IT

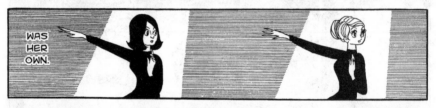

WAS HER OWN.

ALL OF IT

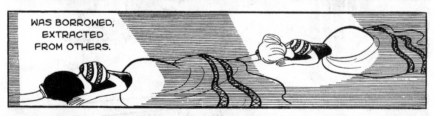

WAS BORROWED, EXTRACTED FROM OTHERS.

YET, IN HER OWN WAY, SHE WAS FLAWLESS.

38

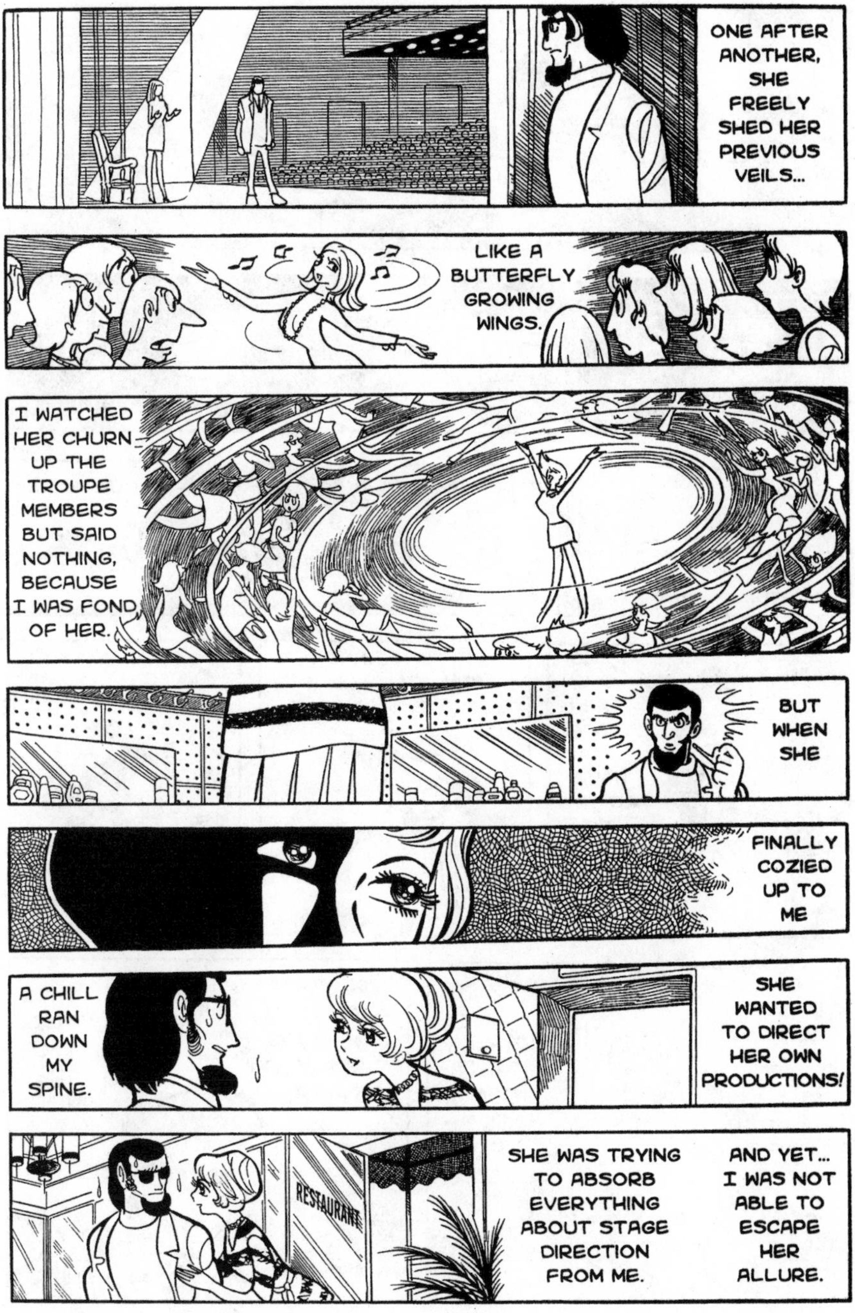
ONE AFTER ANOTHER, SHE FREELY SHED HER PREVIOUS VEILS...
LIKE A BUTTERFLY GROWING WINGS.
I WATCHED HER CHURN UP THE TROUPE MEMBERS BUT SAID NOTHING, BECAUSE I WAS FOND OF HER.
BUT WHEN SHE
FINALLY COZIED UP TO ME
A CHILL RAN DOWN MY SPINE.
SHE WANTED TO DIRECT HER OWN PRODUCTIONS!
RESTAURANT
SHE WAS TRYING TO ABSORB EVERYTHING ABOUT STAGE DIRECTION FROM ME.
AND YET... I WAS NOT ABLE TO ESCAPE HER ALLURE.

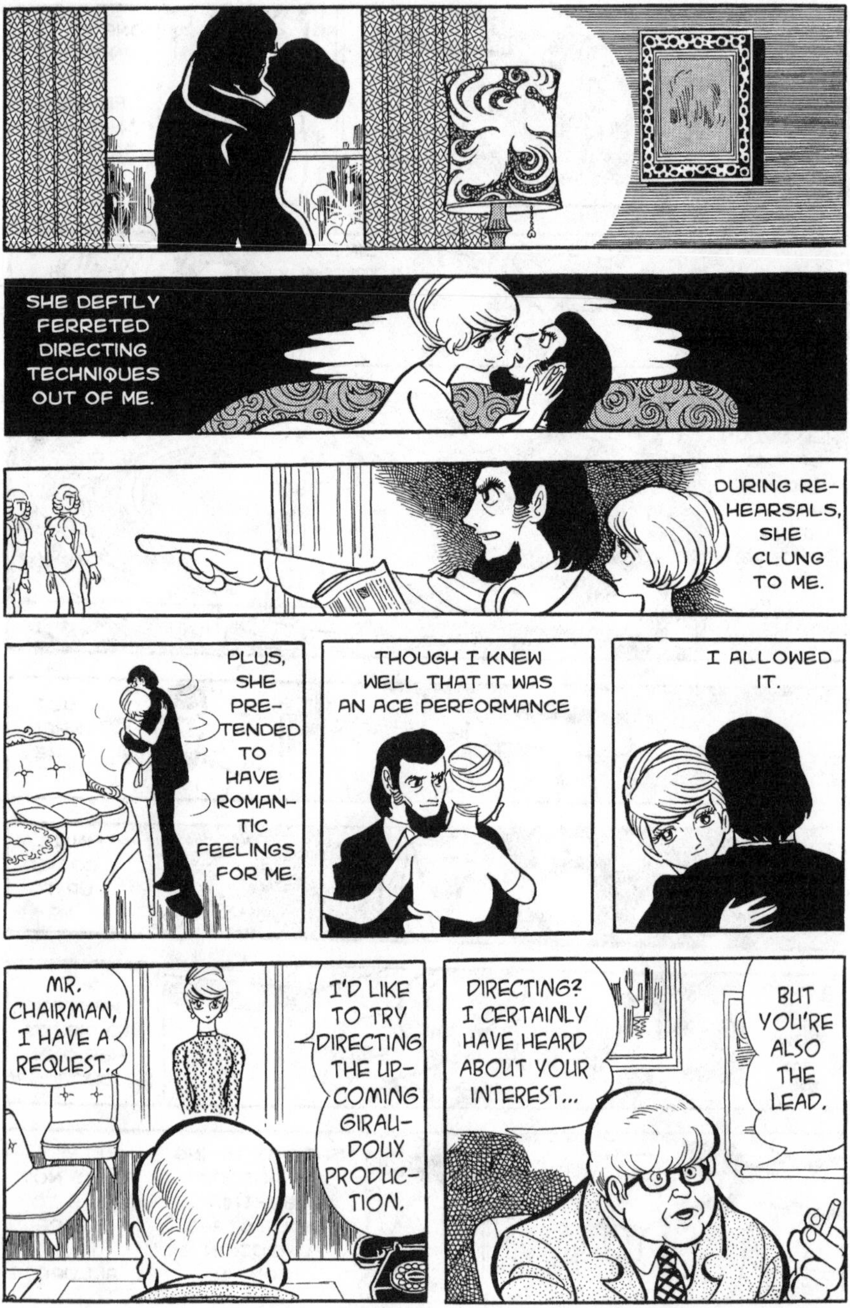
SHE DEFTLY FERRETED DIRECTING TECHNIQUES OUT OF ME.
DURING RE-HEARSALS, SHE CLUNG TO ME.
PLUS, SHE PRE-TENDED TO HAVE ROMAN-TIC FEELINGS FOR ME.
THOUGH I KNEW WELL THAT IT WAS AN ACE PERFORMANCE
I ALLOWED IT.
MR. CHAIRMAN, I HAVE A REQUEST.
I'D LIKE TO TRY DIRECTING THE UP-COMING GIRAU-DOUX PRODUC-TION.
DIRECTING? I CERTAINLY HAVE HEARD ABOUT YOUR INTEREST...
BUT YOU'RE ALSO THE LEAD.

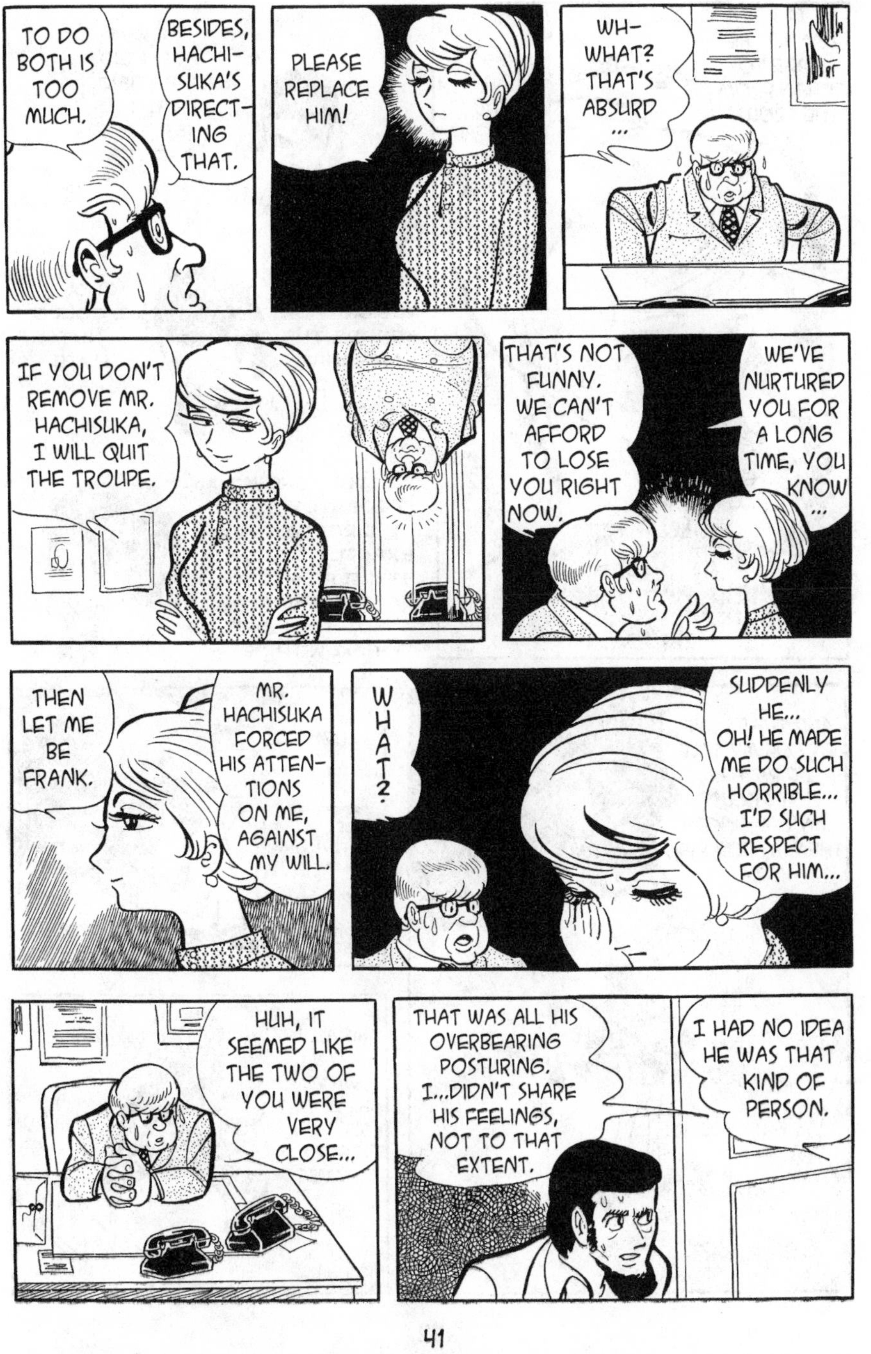
TO DO BOTH IS TOO MUCH.
BESIDES, HACHISUKA'S DIRECTING THAT.
PLEASE REPLACE HIM!
WH-WHAT? THAT'S ABSURD ...
IF YOU DON'T REMOVE MR. HACHISUKA, I WILL QUIT THE TROUPE.
THAT'S NOT FUNNY. WE CAN'T AFFORD TO LOSE YOU RIGHT NOW.
WE'VE NURTURED YOU FOR A LONG TIME, YOU KNOW ...
THEN LET ME BE FRANK.
MR. HACHISUKA FORCED HIS ATTENTIONS ON ME, AGAINST MY WILL.
WHAT?
SUDDENLY HE... OH! HE MADE ME DO SUCH HORRIBLE... I'D SUCH RESPECT FOR HIM...
HUH, IT SEEMED LIKE THE TWO OF YOU WERE VERY CLOSE...
THAT WAS ALL HIS OVERBEARING POSTURING. I...DIDN'T SHARE HIS FEELINGS, NOT TO THAT EXTENT.
I HAD NO IDEA HE WAS THAT KIND OF PERSON.

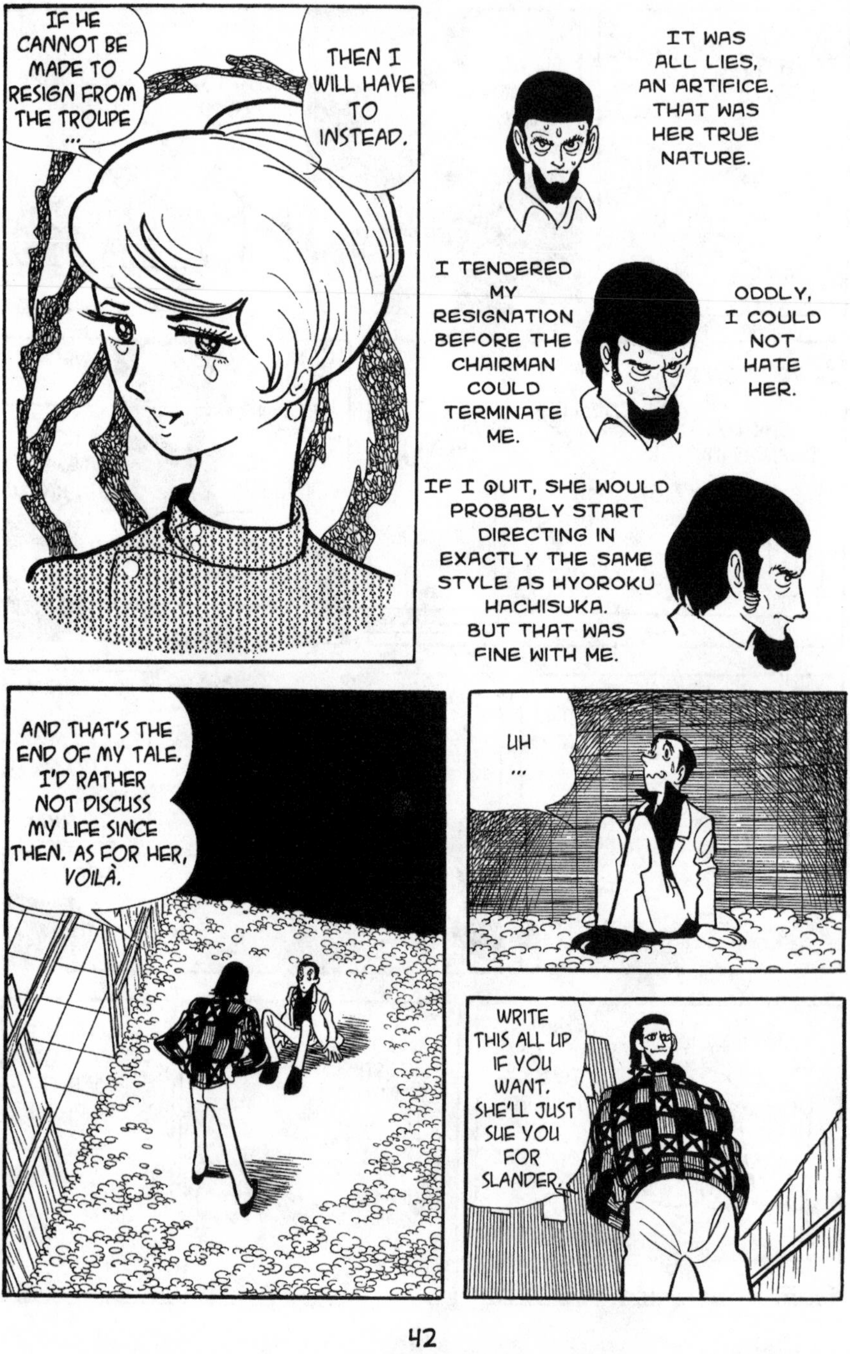
IF HE CANNOT BE MADE TO RESIGN FROM THE TROUPE ...
THEN I WILL HAVE TO INSTEAD.
IT WAS ALL LIES, AN ARTIFICE. THAT WAS HER TRUE NATURE.
I TENDERED MY RESIGNATION BEFORE THE CHAIRMAN COULD TERMINATE ME.
ODDLY, I COULD NOT HATE HER.
IF I QUIT, SHE WOULD PROBABLY START DIRECTING IN EXACTLY THE SAME STYLE AS HYOROKU HACHISUKA. BUT THAT WAS FINE WITH ME.
AND THAT'S THE END OF MY TALE. I'D RATHER NOT DISCUSS MY LIFE SINCE THEN. AS FOR HER, VOILÀ.
UH ...
WRITE THIS ALL UP IF YOU WANT. SHE'LL JUST SUE YOU FOR SLANDER.

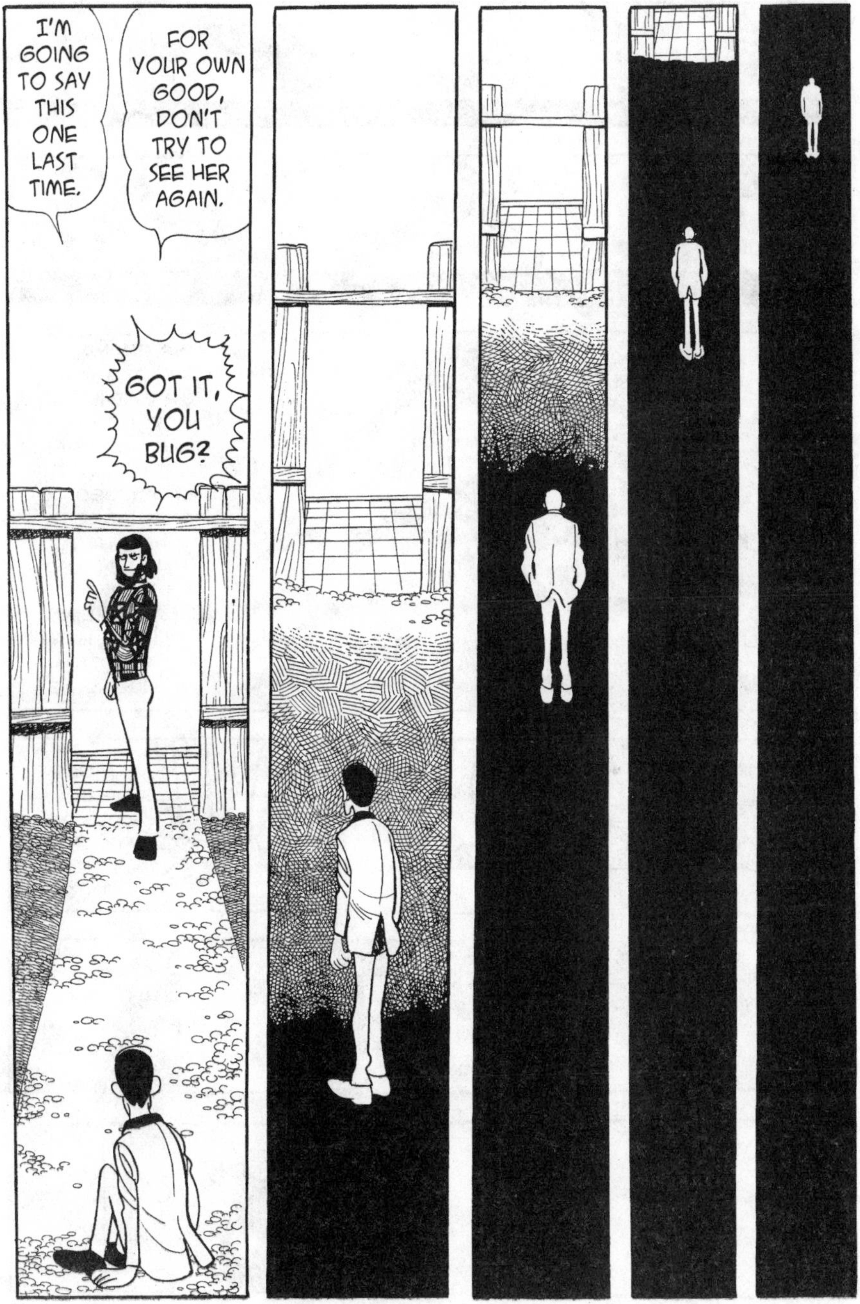
I'M GOING TO SAY THIS ONE LAST TIME.
FOR YOUR OWN GOOD, DON'T TRY TO SEE HER AGAIN.
GOT IT, YOU BUG?

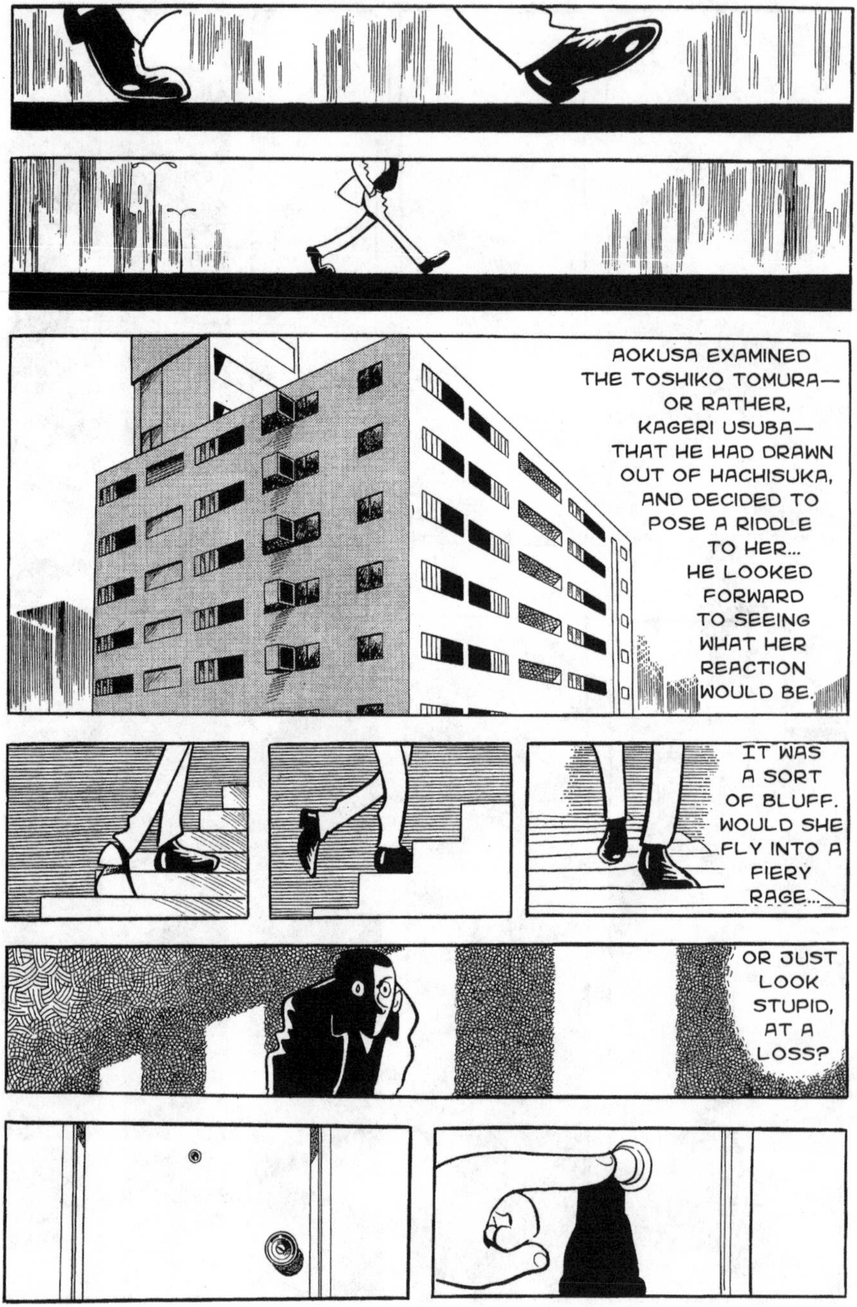
AOKUSA EXAMINED THE TOSHIKO TOMURA— OR RATHER, KAGERI USUBA— THAT HE HAD DRAWN OUT OF HACHISUKA, AND DECIDED TO POSE A RIDDLE TO HER... HE LOOKED FORWARD TO SEEING WHAT HER REACTION WOULD BE.
IT WAS A SORT OF BLUFF. WOULD SHE FLY INTO A FIERY RAGE...
OR JUST LOOK STUPID, AT A LOSS?

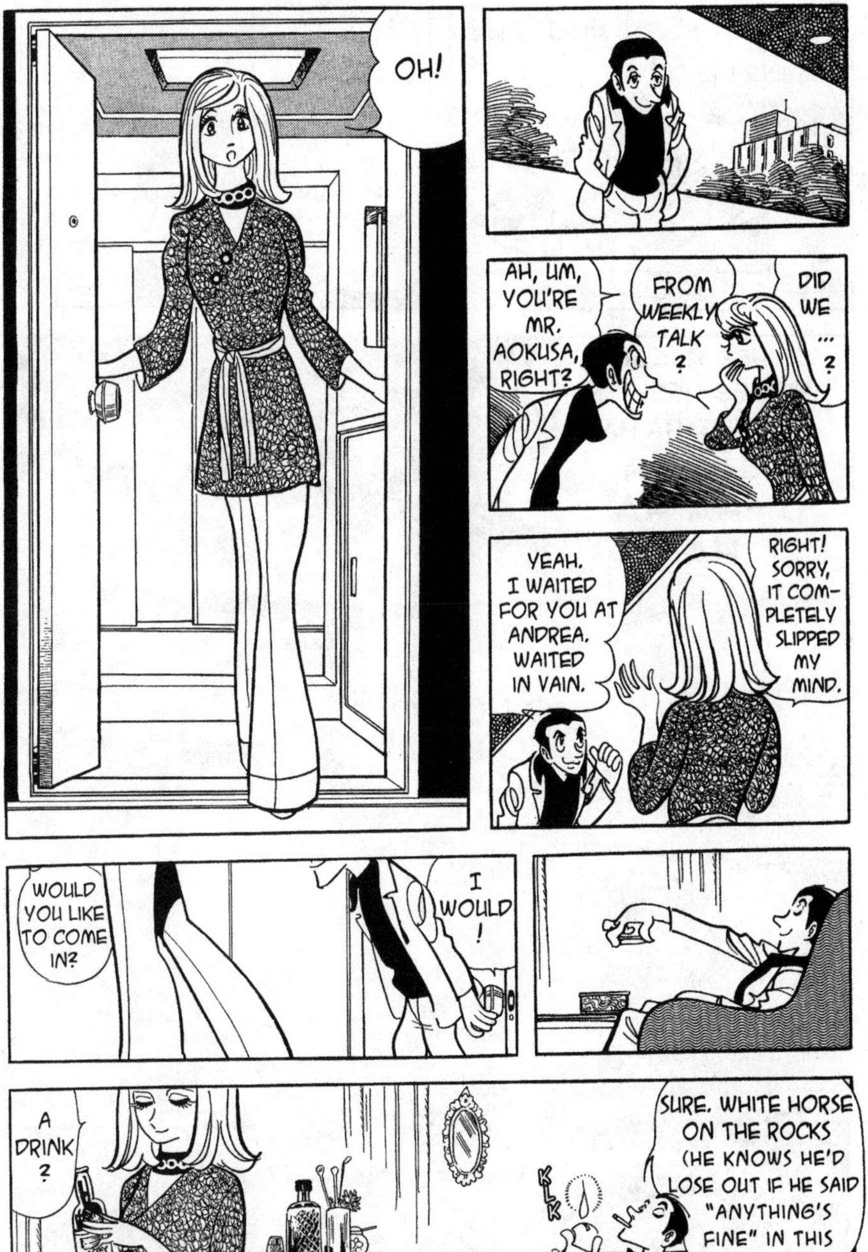

OH!
AH, UM, YOU'RE MR. AOKUSA, RIGHT?
FROM WEEKLY TALK?
DID WE ...?
YEAH. I WAITED FOR YOU AT ANDREA. WAITED IN VAIN.
RIGHT! SORRY, IT COMPLETELY SLIPPED MY MIND.
WOULD YOU LIKE TO COME IN?
I WOULD!
A DRINK?
KLIK
SURE. WHITE HORSE ON THE ROCKS (HE KNOWS HE'D LOSE OUT IF HE SAID "ANYTHING'S FINE" IN THIS SITUATION).

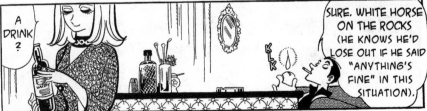

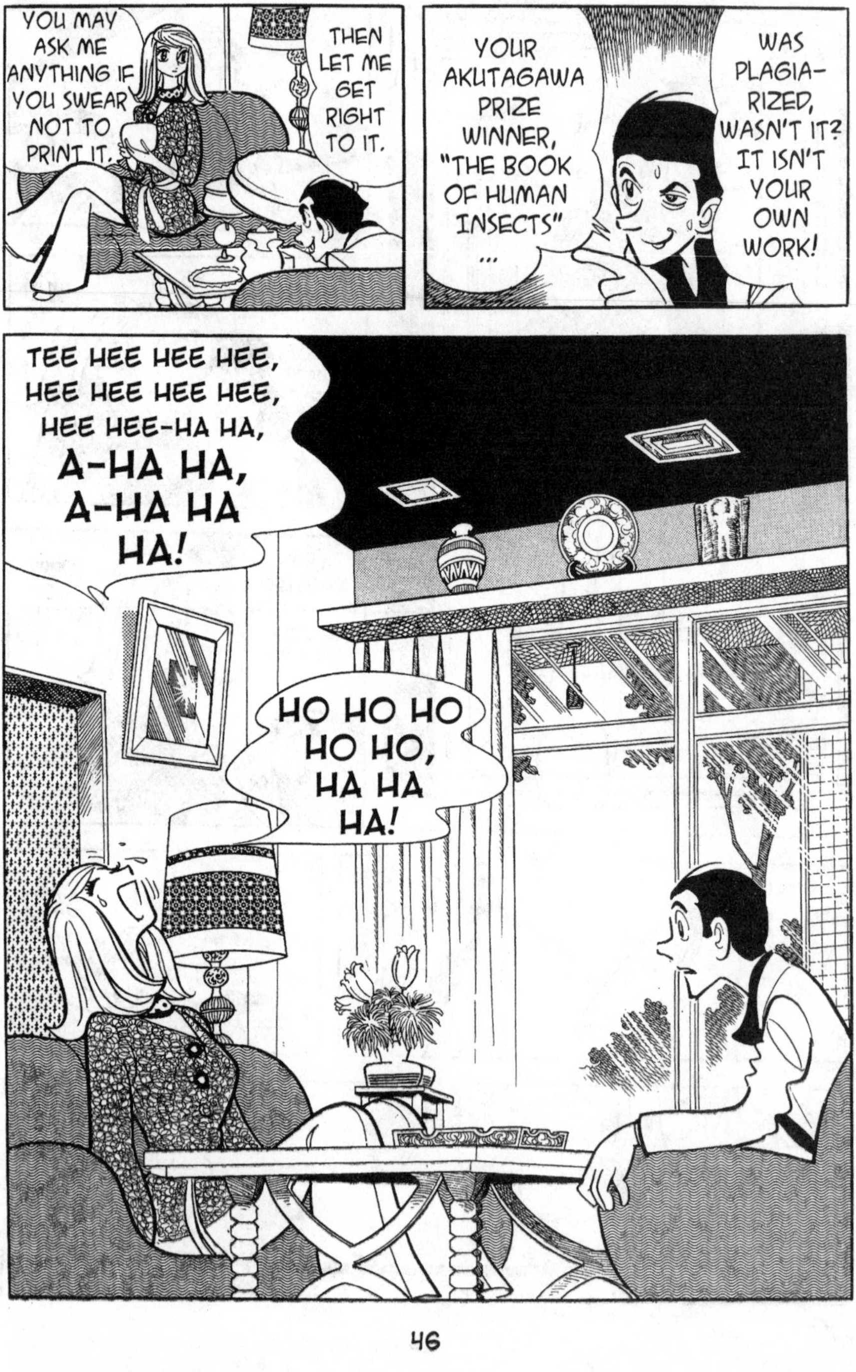
YOU MAY ASK ME ANYTHING IF YOU SWEAR NOT TO PRINT IT.
THEN LET ME GET RIGHT TO IT.
YOUR AKUTAGAWA PRIZE WINNER, "THE BOOK OF HUMAN INSECTS" ...
WAS PLAGIA-RIZED, WASN'T IT? IT ISN'T YOUR OWN WORK!
TEE HEE HEE HEE, HEE HEE HEE HEE, HEE HEE-HA HA, A-HA HA, A-HA HA HA!
HO HO HO HO HO, HA HA HA!

WA HEE HOO WA HEE HOO

GUFFAW HEAVE HEAVE

GWA-HA HA HA HA

MY AWARD-WINNER, NOT MY OWN?

OH, THAT'S HILARIOUS. WHO IN THE WORLD CAME UP WITH SUCH A...

CACKLE CACKLE CACKLE

I DID. A BOLD SURMISE, NO?

AND WHO, PRAY, AM I TO HAVE STOLEN IT FROM?

THAT, YOU OUGHT TO KNOW FAR BETTER THAN I.

DO TELL.

THE OTHER KAGERI USUBA.

SHE KILLED HERSELF THE NIGHT OF THE AWARD PARTY.

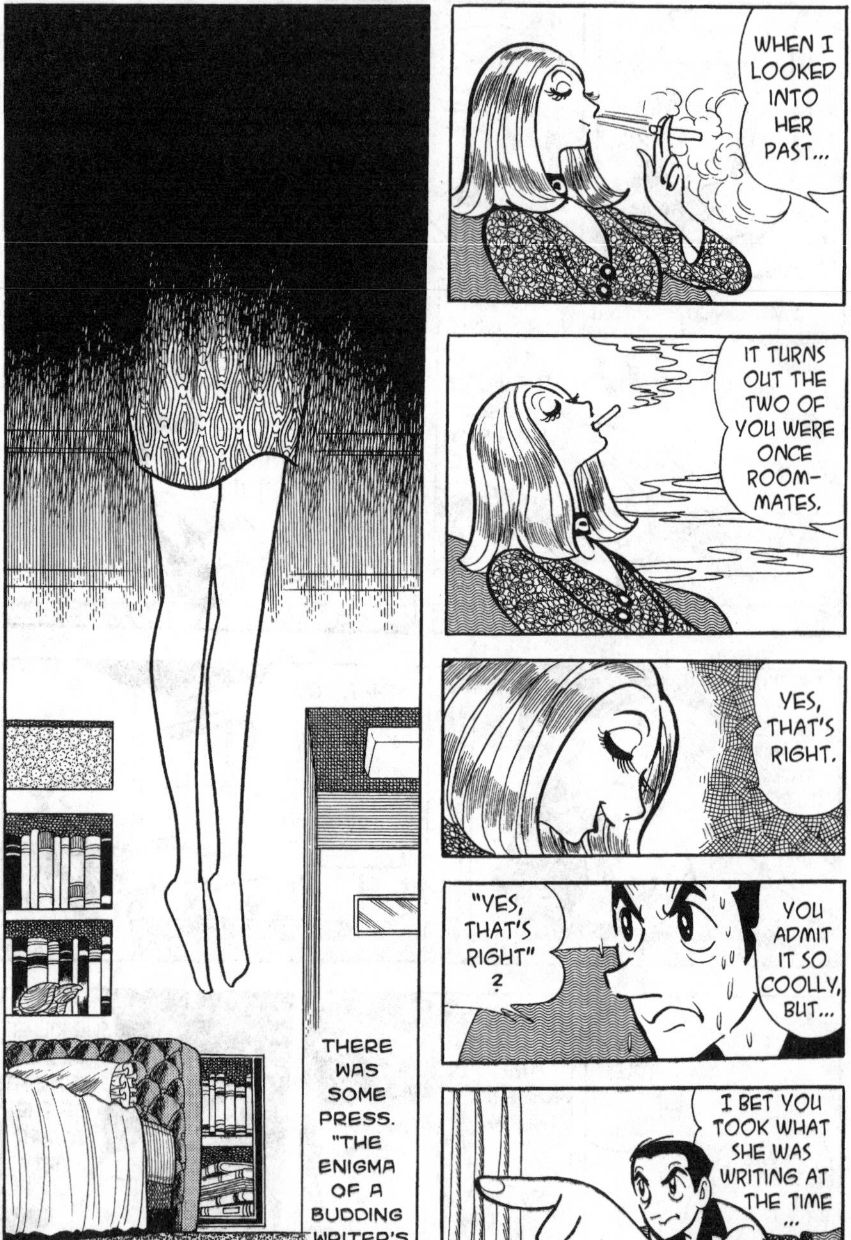
THERE WAS SOME PRESS. "THE ENIGMA OF A BUDDING WRITER'S SUICIDE."
WHEN I LOOKED INTO HER PAST...
IT TURNS OUT THE TWO OF YOU WERE ONCE ROOM-MATES.
YES, THAT'S RIGHT.
"YES, THAT'S RIGHT" ?
YOU ADMIT IT SO COOLLY, BUT...
I BET YOU TOOK WHAT SHE WAS WRITING AT THE TIME ...

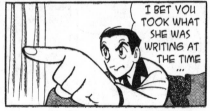

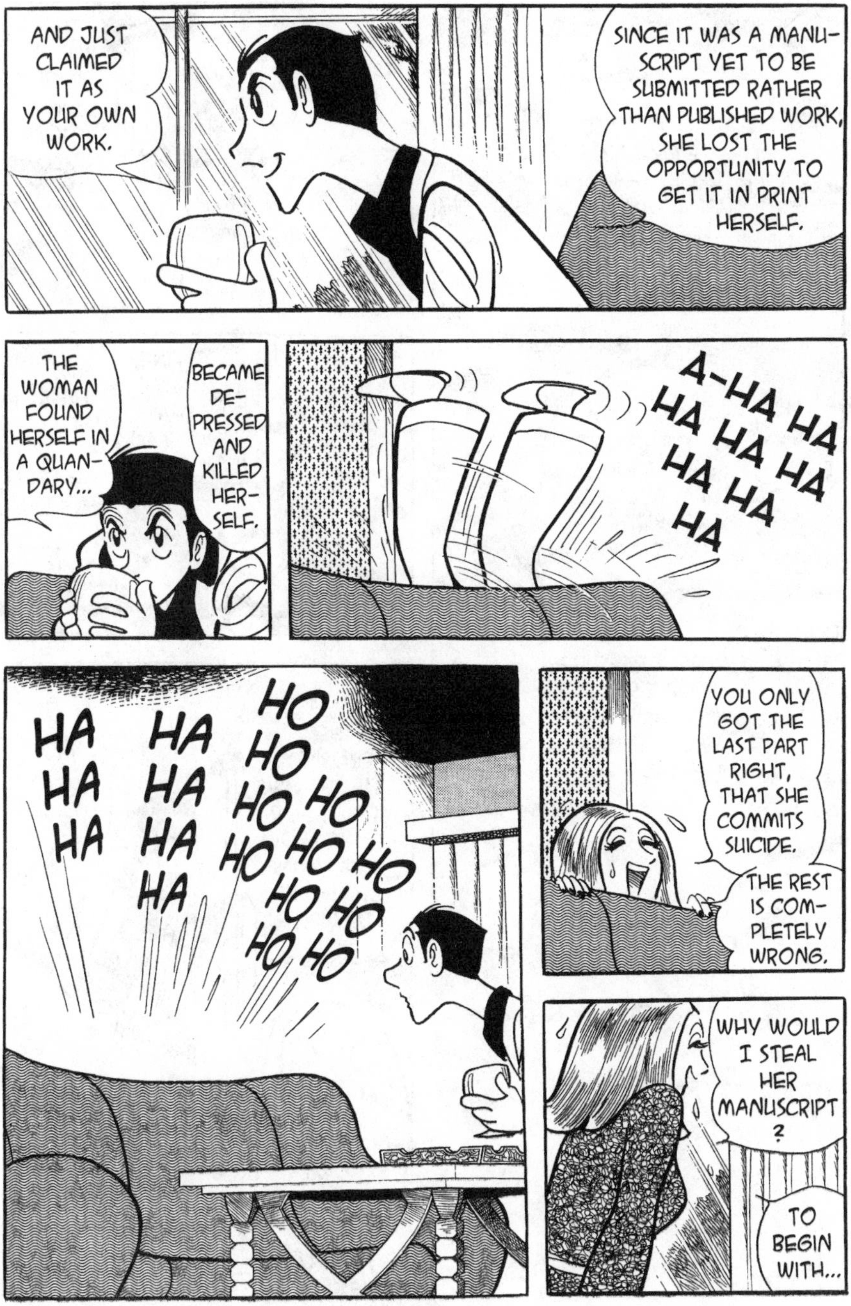
AND JUST CLAIMED IT AS YOUR OWN WORK.
SINCE IT WAS A MANU-SCRIPT YET TO BE SUBMITTED RATHER THAN PUBLISHED WORK, SHE LOST THE OPPORTUNITY TO GET IT IN PRINT HERSELF.
THE WOMAN FOUND HERSELF IN A QUAN-DARY...
BECAME DE-PRESSED AND KILLED HER-SELF.
A-HA HA HA HA HA HA HA HA HA
HA HA HA
HA HA HA HA
HO HO HO HO HO HO HO HO HO HO HO HO HO
YOU ONLY GOT THE LAST PART RIGHT, THAT SHE COMMITS SUICIDE.
THE REST IS COM-PLETELY WRONG.
WHY WOULD I STEAL HER MANUSCRIPT ?
TO BEGIN WITH...

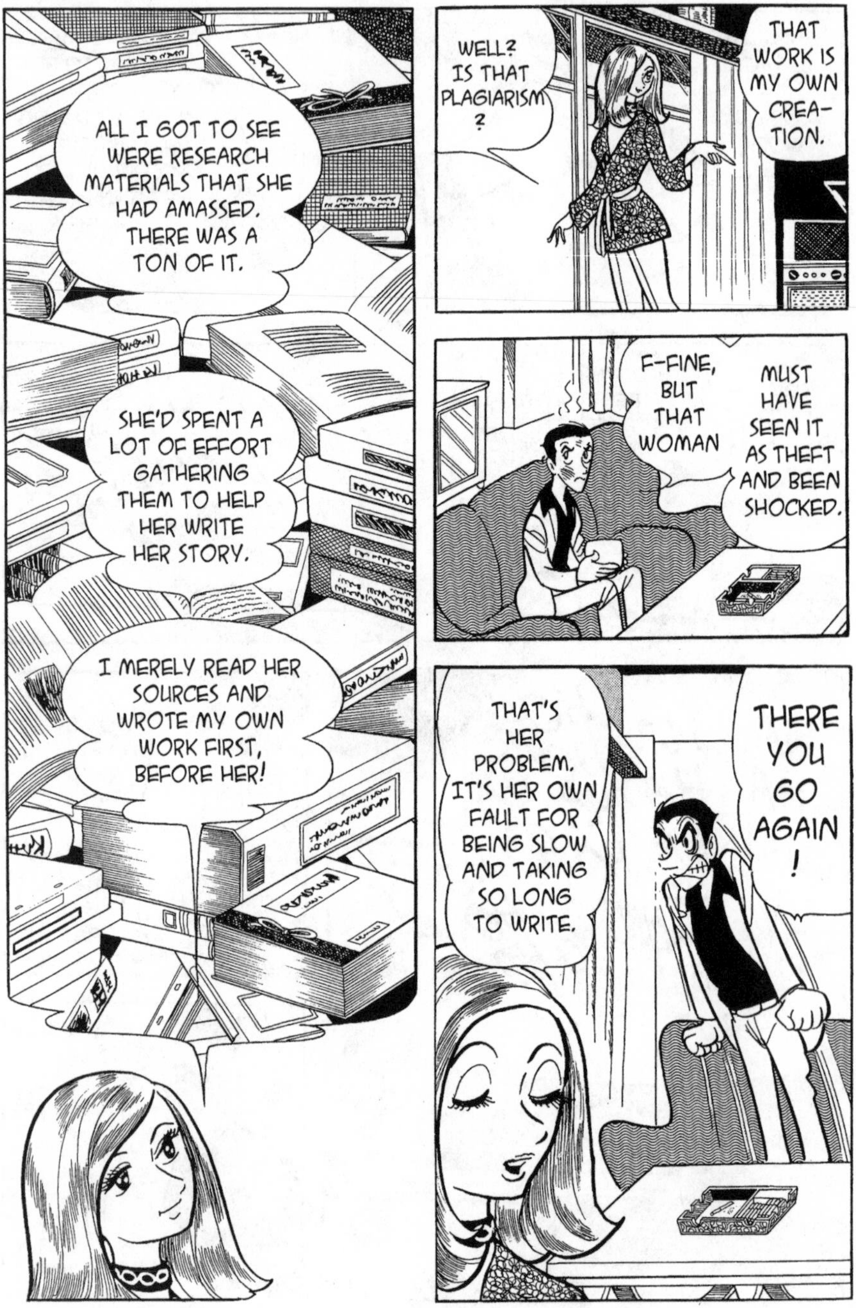
ALL I GOT TO SEE WERE RESEARCH MATERIALS THAT SHE HAD AMASSED. THERE WAS A TON OF IT.
SHE'D SPENT A LOT OF EFFORT GATHERING THEM TO HELP HER WRITE HER STORY.
I MERELY READ HER SOURCES AND WROTE MY OWN WORK FIRST, BEFORE HER!
WELL? IS THAT PLAGIARISM?
THAT WORK IS MY OWN CREA-TION.
F-FINE, BUT THAT WOMAN
MUST HAVE SEEN IT AS THEFT AND BEEN SHOCKED.
THAT'S HER PROBLEM. IT'S HER OWN FAULT FOR BEING SLOW AND TAKING SO LONG TO WRITE.
THERE YOU GO AGAIN!

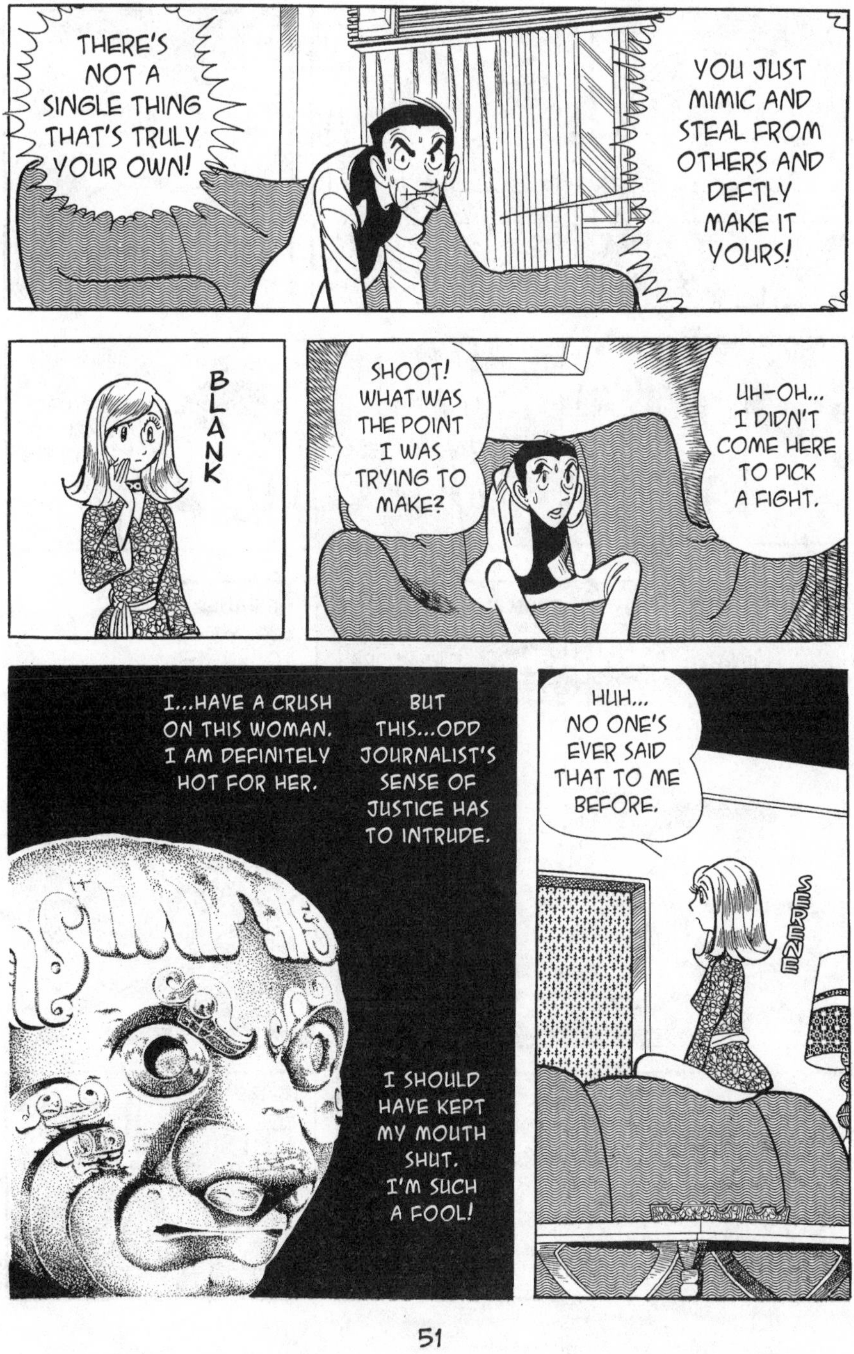
THERE'S NOT A SINGLE THING THAT'S TRULY YOUR OWN!
YOU JUST MIMIC AND STEAL FROM OTHERS AND DEFTLY MAKE IT YOURS!
BLANK
SHOOT! WHAT WAS THE POINT I WAS TRYING TO MAKE?
UH-OH... I DIDN'T COME HERE TO PICK A FIGHT.
I...HAVE A CRUSH ON THIS WOMAN. I AM DEFINITELY HOT FOR HER.
BUT THIS...ODD JOURNALIST'S SENSE OF JUSTICE HAS TO INTRUDE.
I SHOULD HAVE KEPT MY MOUTH SHUT. I'M SUCH A FOOL!
HUH... NO ONE'S EVER SAID THAT TO ME BEFORE.
SERENE

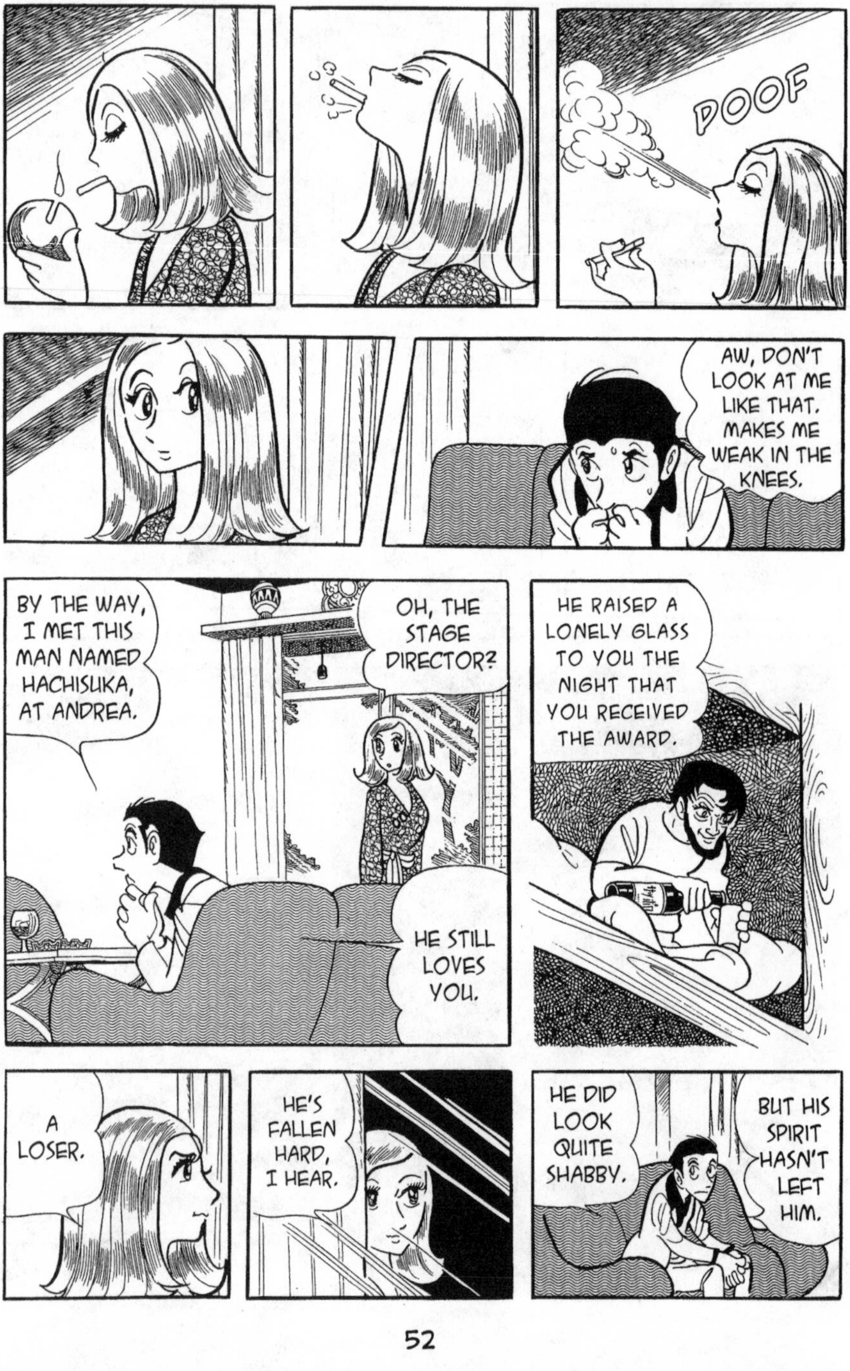

POOF
AW, DON'T LOOK AT ME LIKE THAT. MAKES ME WEAK IN THE KNEES.
BY THE WAY, I MET THIS MAN NAMED HACHISUKA, AT ANDREA.
OH, THE STAGE DIRECTOR?
HE STILL LOVES YOU.
HE RAISED A LONELY GLASS TO YOU THE NIGHT THAT YOU RECEIVED THE AWARD.
A LOSER.
HE'S FALLEN HARD, I HEAR.
HE DID LOOK QUITE SHABBY.
BUT HIS SPIRIT HASN'T LEFT HIM.

HE WAS JUST AN AVERAGE MAN.

JUST A MAN, EH...

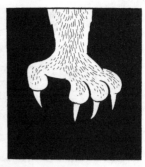

I'M A MAN, TOO, MISSY.

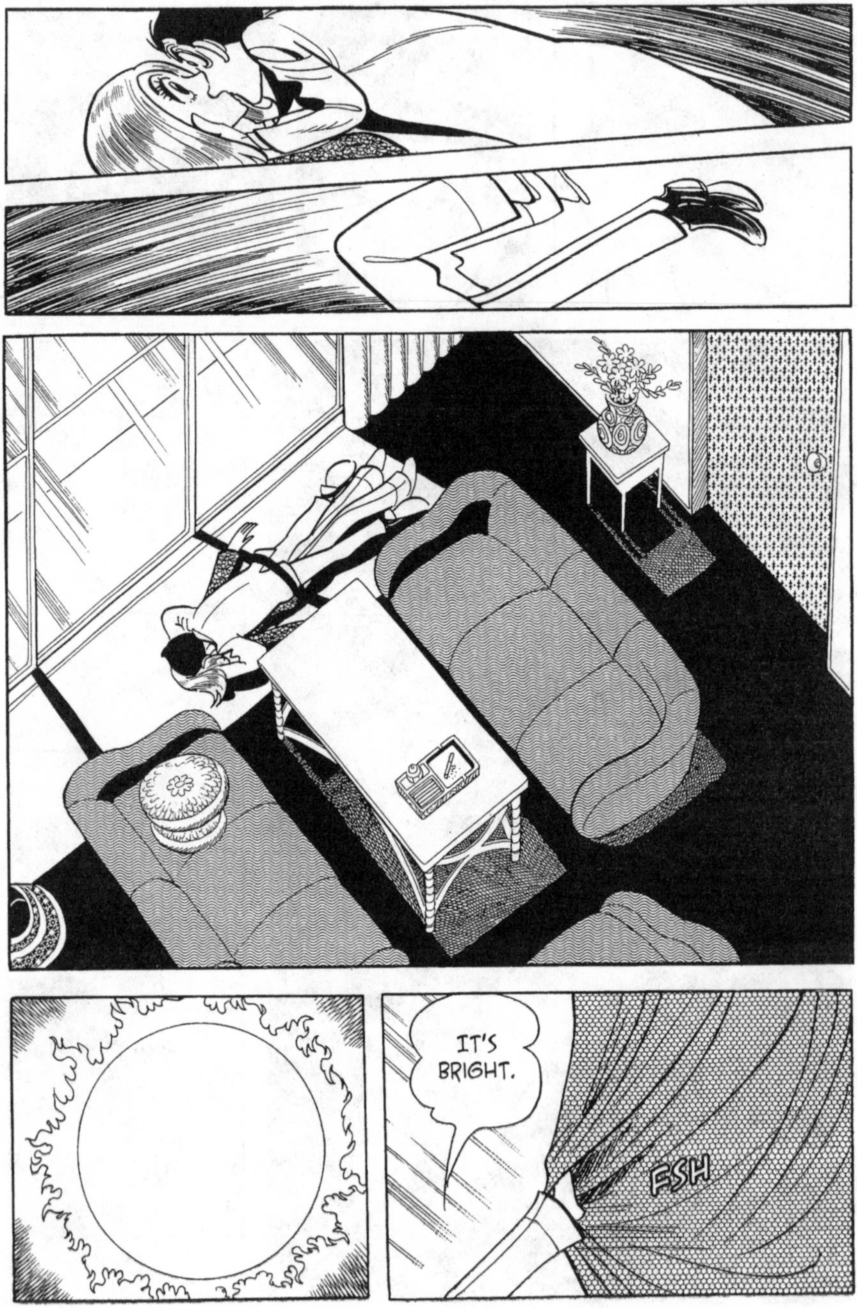
IT'S BRIGHT.
FSH

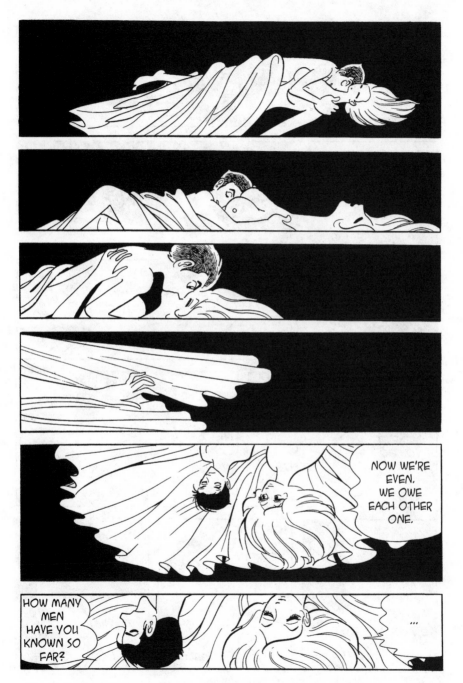

NOW WE'RE EVEN. WE OWE EACH OTHER ONE.

HOW MANY MEN HAVE YOU KNOWN SO FAR?

...

INSATIABLE... THE WAY YOU WERE GOING, YOU COULD TAKE A HUNDRED MEN IN TURN.

YOU'RE NOT HALF BAD YOURSELF, FOR A SHORTY.

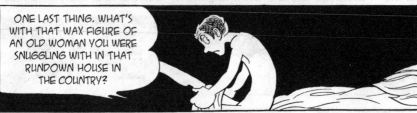

ONE LAST THING. WHAT'S WITH THAT WAX FIGURE OF AN OLD WOMAN YOU WERE SNUGGLING WITH IN THAT RUNDOWN HOUSE IN THE COUNTRY?

THAT'S MY MOTHER.

SHE DIED FIVE YEARS AGO.

YOU ACT LIKE A BABY WITH THAT DOLL WHENEVER YOU GO HOME?

EVERYONE HAS THEIR PLACE OF REPOSE.

I CAN'T ENJOY MY PRIVACY EVEN INSIDE THIS APART- MENT.

BUT WITH MOTHER, I CAN FORGET EVERYTHING AND BE A BABY AGAIN.

SO YOU'VE GOT A HORRIBLY CHILDISH SIDE, TOO.

...

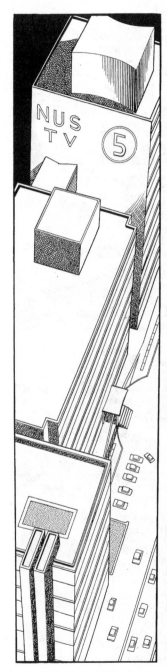

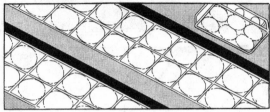

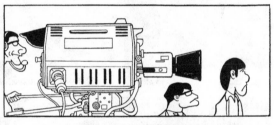

WHAT DO YOU THINK OF BEING CALLED A "WOMAN OF TALENT"?

WHAT DO I THINK? WELL...

THE MEDIA JUST DUBBED ME AS SUCH, ALL ON YOUR OWN.

NOW, YOU HAPPEN TO BE INTERNATIONALLY RENOWNED AS A GRAPHIC DESIGNER AS WELL...

WE ACTUALLY HAVE SOMEONE HERE, WAITING TO MEET YOU.

OH ?

OF COURSE, NEITHER YOU, NOR THAT PERSON, KNOWS WHO THE OTHER IS...

BUT IT IS SOMEONE YOU'RE WELL ACQUAINTED WITH.

HE'LL BE APPEARING ANY MINUTE NOW.

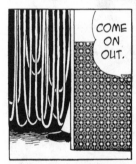

COME ON OUT.

YOU!

MR. MIZUNO...

58

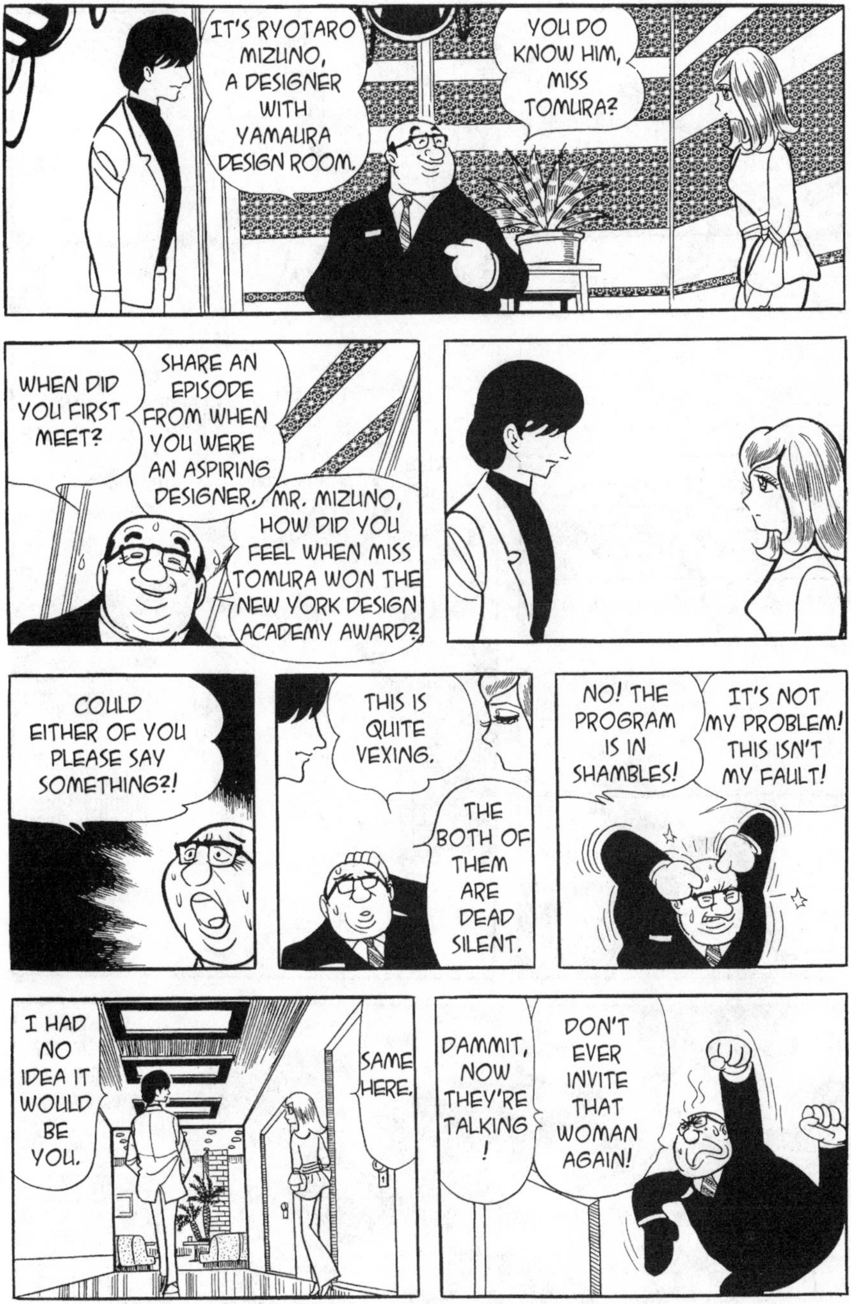
IT'S RYOTARO MIZUNO, A DESIGNER WITH YAMAURA DESIGN ROOM.
YOU DO KNOW HIM, MISS TOMURA?
WHEN DID YOU FIRST MEET?
SHARE AN EPISODE FROM WHEN YOU WERE AN ASPIRING DESIGNER.
MR. MIZUNO, HOW DID YOU FEEL WHEN MISS TOMURA WON THE NEW YORK DESIGN ACADEMY AWARD?
COULD EITHER OF YOU PLEASE SAY SOMETHING?!
THIS IS QUITE VEXING.
THE BOTH OF THEM ARE DEAD SILENT.
NO! THE PROGRAM IS IN SHAMBLES!
IT'S NOT MY PROBLEM! THIS ISN'T MY FAULT!
I HAD NO IDEA IT WOULD BE YOU.
SAME HERE.
DAMMIT, NOW THEY'RE TALKING!
DON'T EVER INVITE THAT WOMAN AGAIN!

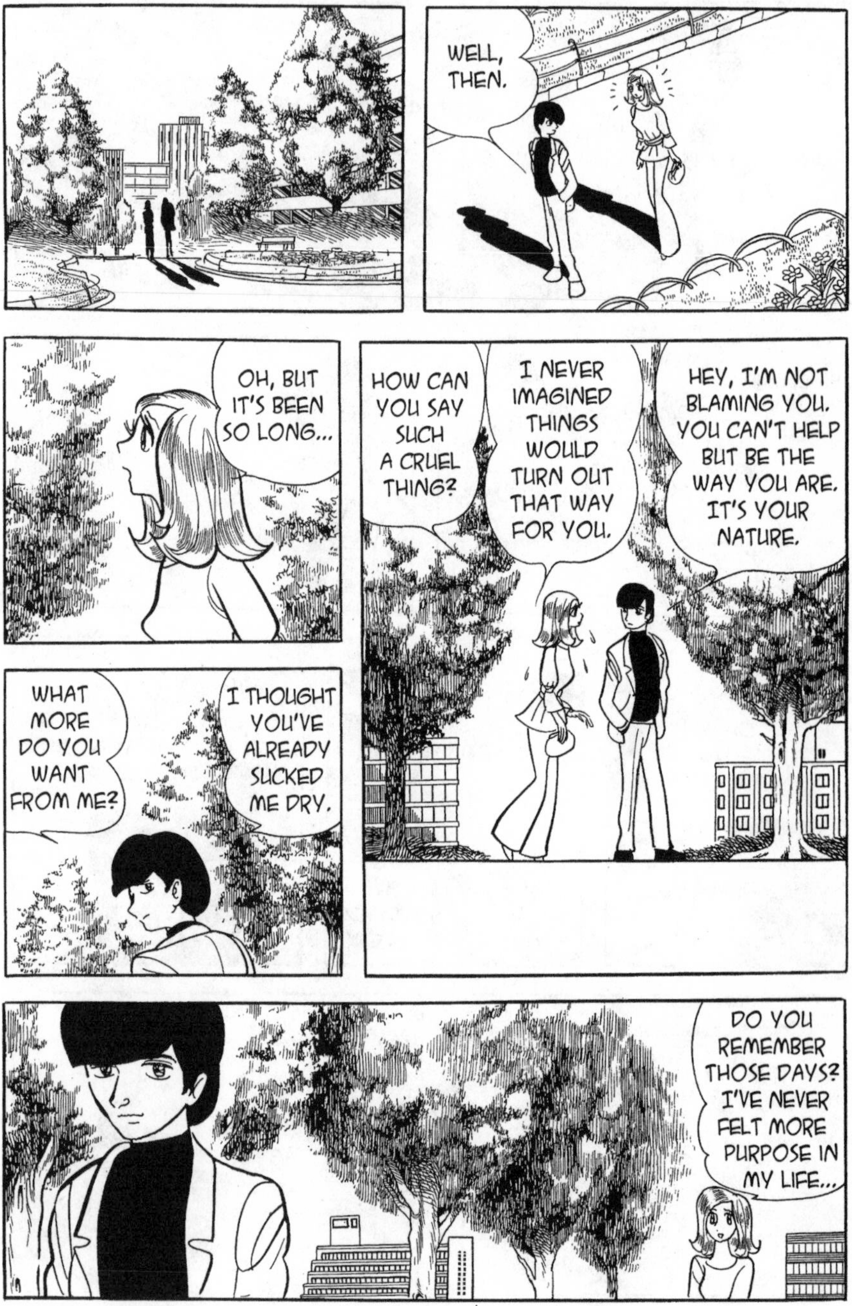
WELL, THEN.
OH, BUT IT'S BEEN SO LONG...
HOW CAN YOU SAY SUCH A CRUEL THING?
I NEVER IMAGINED THINGS WOULD TURN OUT THAT WAY FOR YOU.
HEY, I'M NOT BLAMING YOU. YOU CAN'T HELP BUT BE THE WAY YOU ARE. IT'S YOUR NATURE.
WHAT MORE DO YOU WANT FROM ME?
I THOUGHT YOU'VE ALREADY SUCKED ME DRY.
DO YOU REMEMBER THOSE DAYS? I'VE NEVER FELT MORE PURPOSE IN MY LIFE...

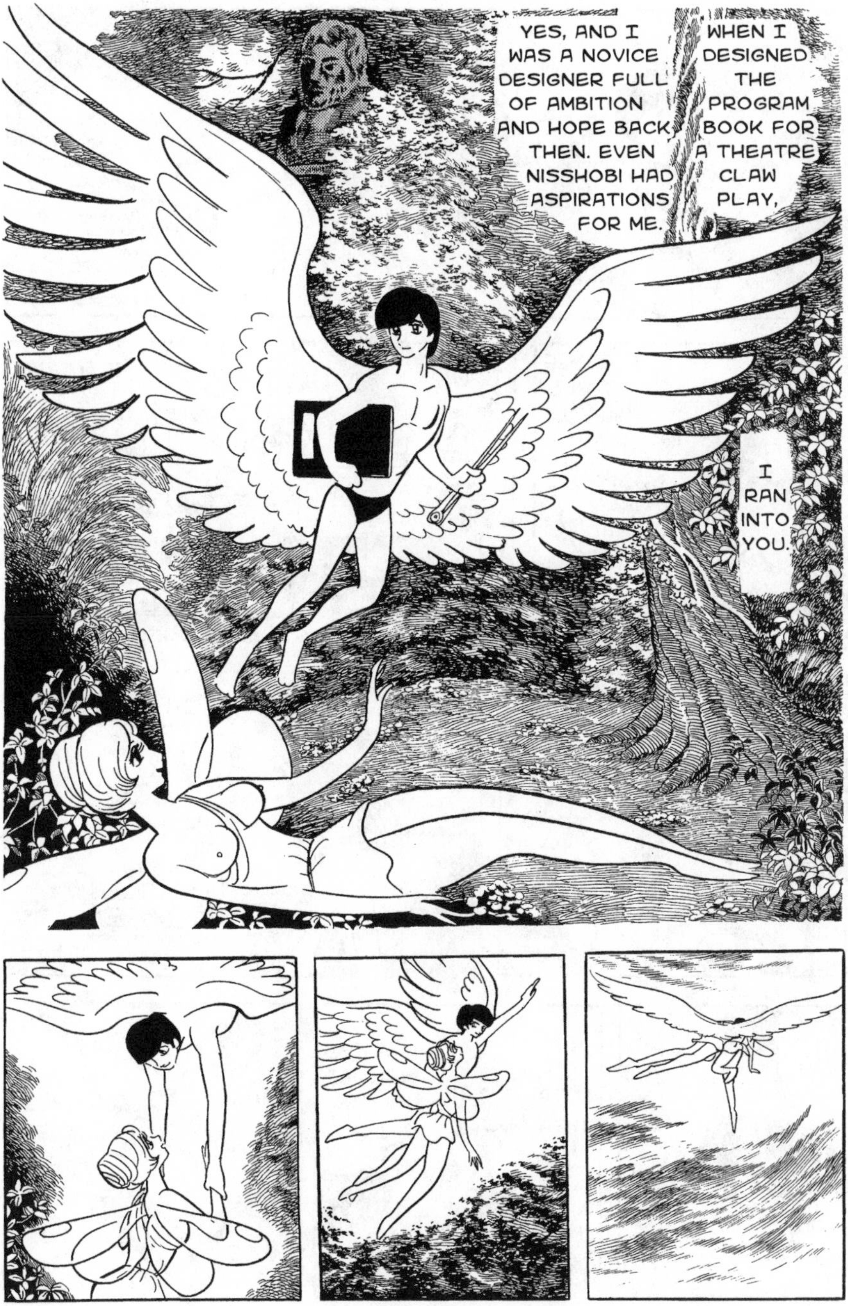
YES, AND I WAS A NOVICE DESIGNER FULL OF AMBITION AND HOPE BACK THEN. EVEN NISSHOBI HAD ASPIRATIONS FOR ME.
WHEN I DESIGNED THE PROGRAM BOOK FOR A THEATRE CLAW PLAY,
I RAN INTO YOU.

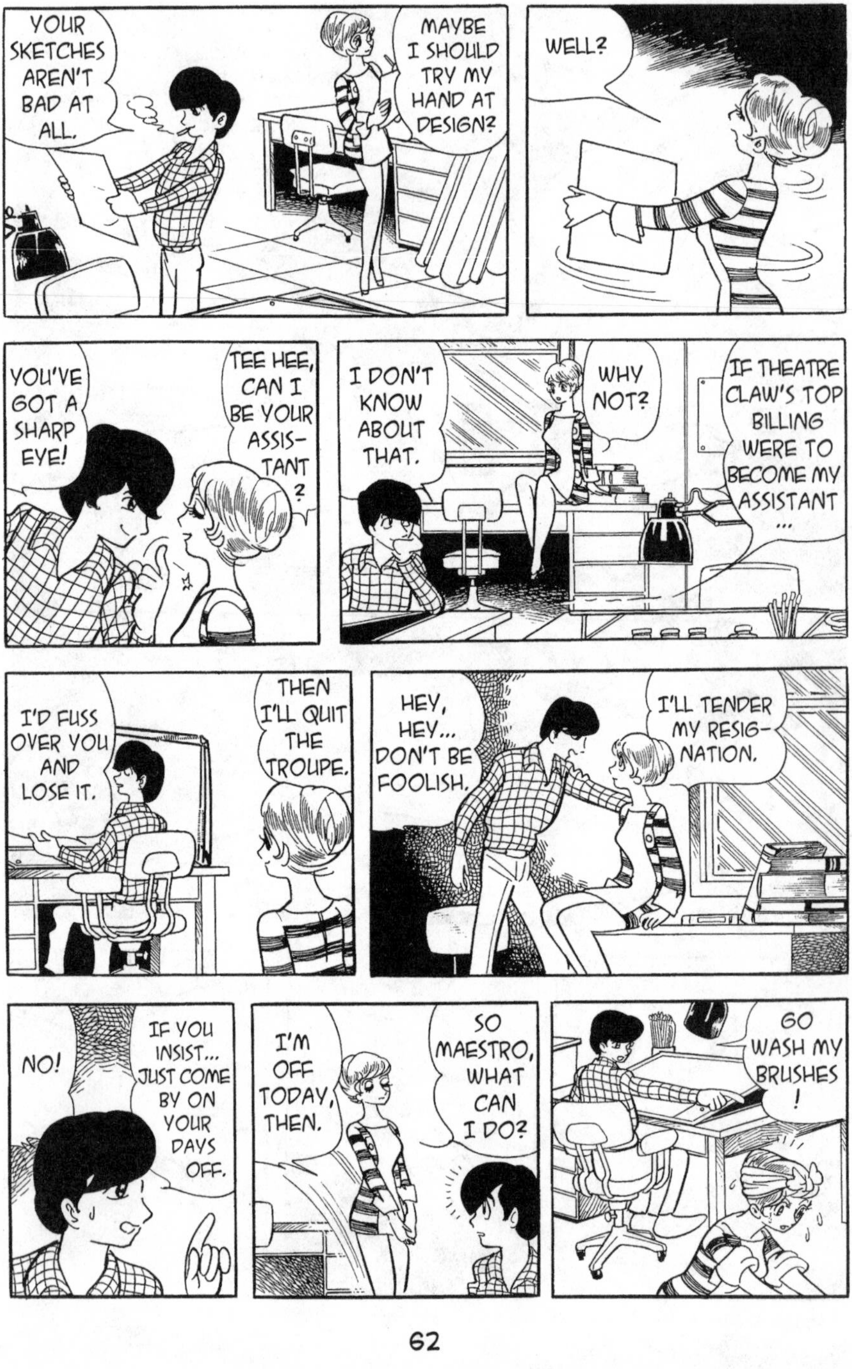
YOUR SKETCHES AREN'T BAD AT ALL.
MAYBE I SHOULD TRY MY HAND AT DESIGN?
WELL?
YOU'VE GOT A SHARP EYE!
TEE HEE, CAN I BE YOUR ASSIS-TANT?
I DON'T KNOW ABOUT THAT.
WHY NOT?
IF THEATRE CLAW'S TOP BILLING WERE TO BECOME MY ASSISTANT ...
I'D FUSS OVER YOU AND LOSE IT.
THEN I'LL QUIT THE TROUPE.
HEY, HEY... DON'T BE FOOLISH.
I'LL TENDER MY RESIG-NATION.
NO!
IF YOU INSIST... JUST COME BY ON YOUR DAYS OFF.
I'M OFF TODAY, THEN.
SO MAESTRO, WHAT CAN I DO?
GO WASH MY BRUSHES!

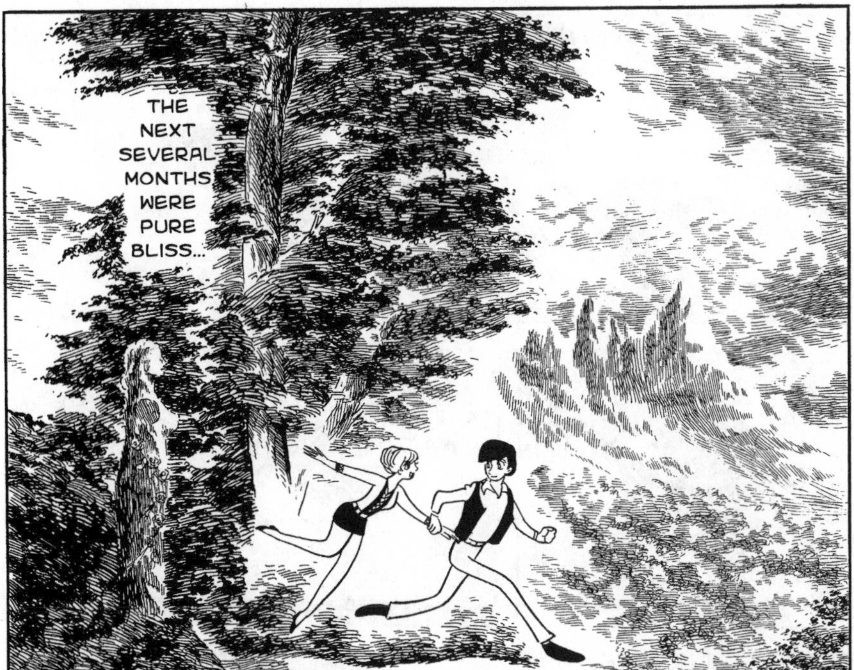
THE NEXT SEVERAL MONTHS WERE PURE BLISS...

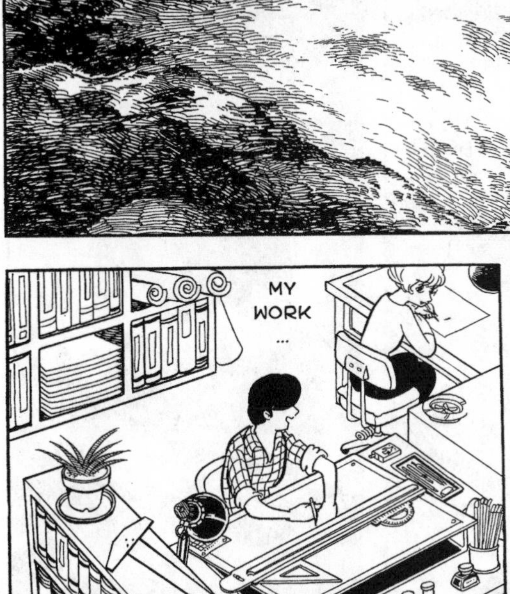
MY WORK ...

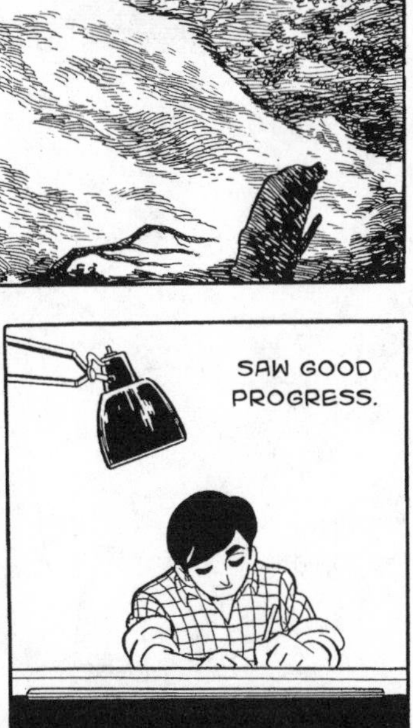
SAW GOOD PROGRESS.

I RECEIVED NISSHOBI'S ENDORSEMENT TO ENTER THE NEW YORK DESIGN ACADEMY'S CONTEST!

OH MY!

IF I MAKE THE CUT, I'LL BECOME INTERNATIONALLY KNOWN!

CONGRATS... MAESTRO.

IT'S TOO EARLY FOR THAT. I STILL HAVE TO PASS.

I'M GONNA WORK HARD!!

BUT... IF I DO MAKE IT...

KAGERI... WILL YOU MARRY ME?

MARRY?

REALLY?

A DESIGNER COUPLE! THAT'S HOW WE'LL REGISTER AT HOTELS ABROAD.

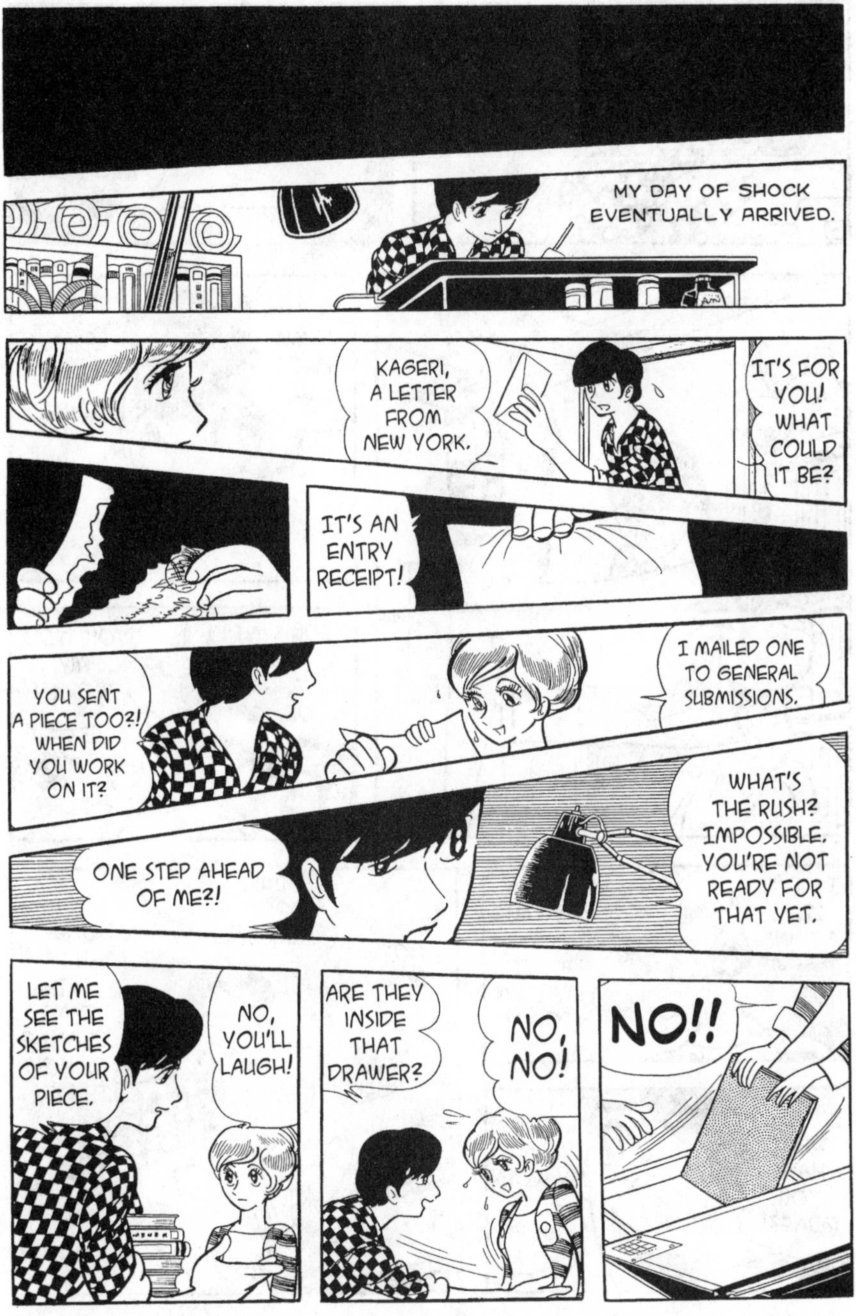
MY DAY OF SHOCK EVENTUALLY ARRIVED.
KAGERI, A LETTER FROM NEW YORK.
IT'S FOR YOU! WHAT COULD IT BE?
IT'S AN ENTRY RECEIPT!
YOU SENT A PIECE TOO?! WHEN DID YOU WORK ON IT?
I MAILED ONE TO GENERAL SUBMISSIONS.
ONE STEP AHEAD OF ME?!
WHAT'S THE RUSH? IMPOSSIBLE. YOU'RE NOT READY FOR THAT YET.
LET ME SEE THE SKETCHES OF YOUR PIECE.
NO, YOU'LL LAUGH!
ARE THEY INSIDE THAT DRAWER?
NO, NO!
NO!!

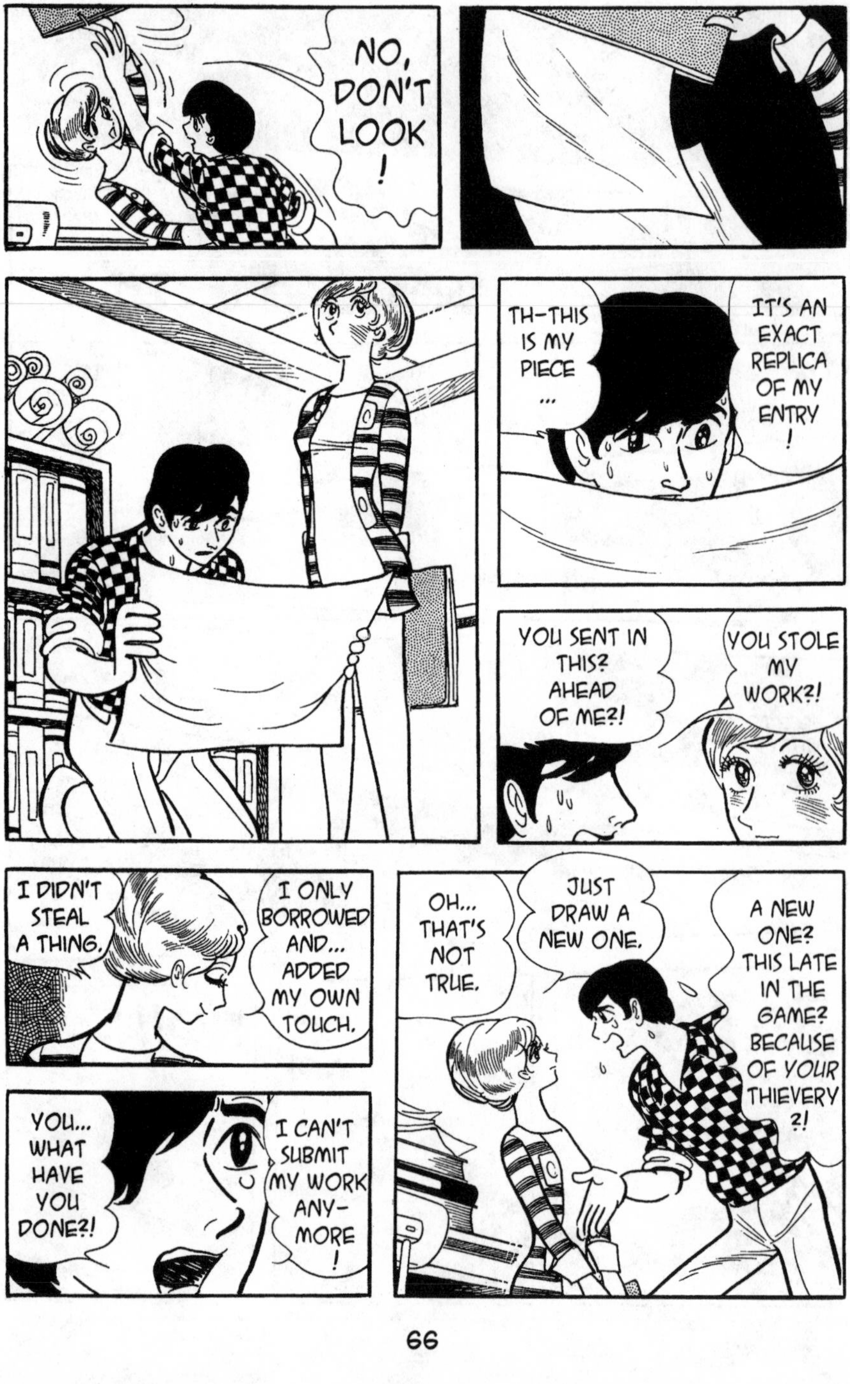
NO, DON'T LOOK !
TH-THIS IS MY PIECE ...
IT'S AN EXACT REPLICA OF MY ENTRY !
YOU SENT IN THIS? AHEAD OF ME?!
YOU STOLE MY WORK?!
I DIDN'T STEAL A THING.
I ONLY BORROWED AND... ADDED MY OWN TOUCH.
YOU... WHAT HAVE YOU DONE?!
I CAN'T SUBMIT MY WORK ANY-MORE !
OH... THAT'S NOT TRUE.
JUST DRAW A NEW ONE.
A NEW ONE? THIS LATE IN THE GAME? BECAUSE OF YOUR THIEVERY ?!

IT'S YOUR FAULT, MAESTRO. YOU'RE TOO SLOW.
SLAP
GET OUT !!
AND... DON'T EVER COME BACK! EVER...
SLAM

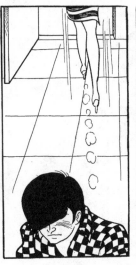

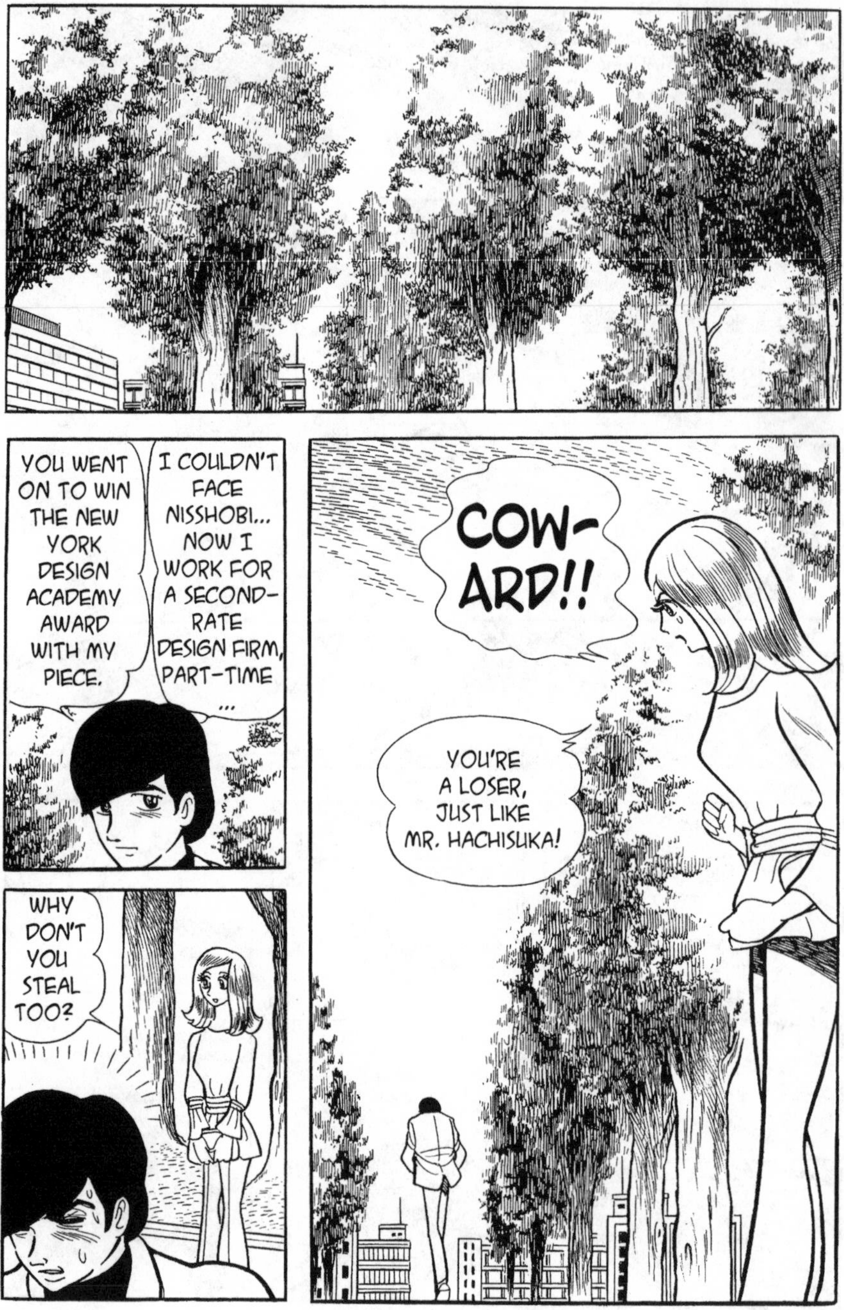

YOU WENT ON TO WIN THE NEW YORK DESIGN ACADEMY AWARD WITH MY PIECE.
I COULDN'T FACE NISSHOBI... NOW I WORK FOR A SECOND-RATE DESIGN FIRM, PART-TIME ...
WHY DON'T YOU STEAL TOO?
COW-ARD!!
YOU'RE A LOSER, JUST LIKE MR. HACHISUKA!

LEAFHOPPER

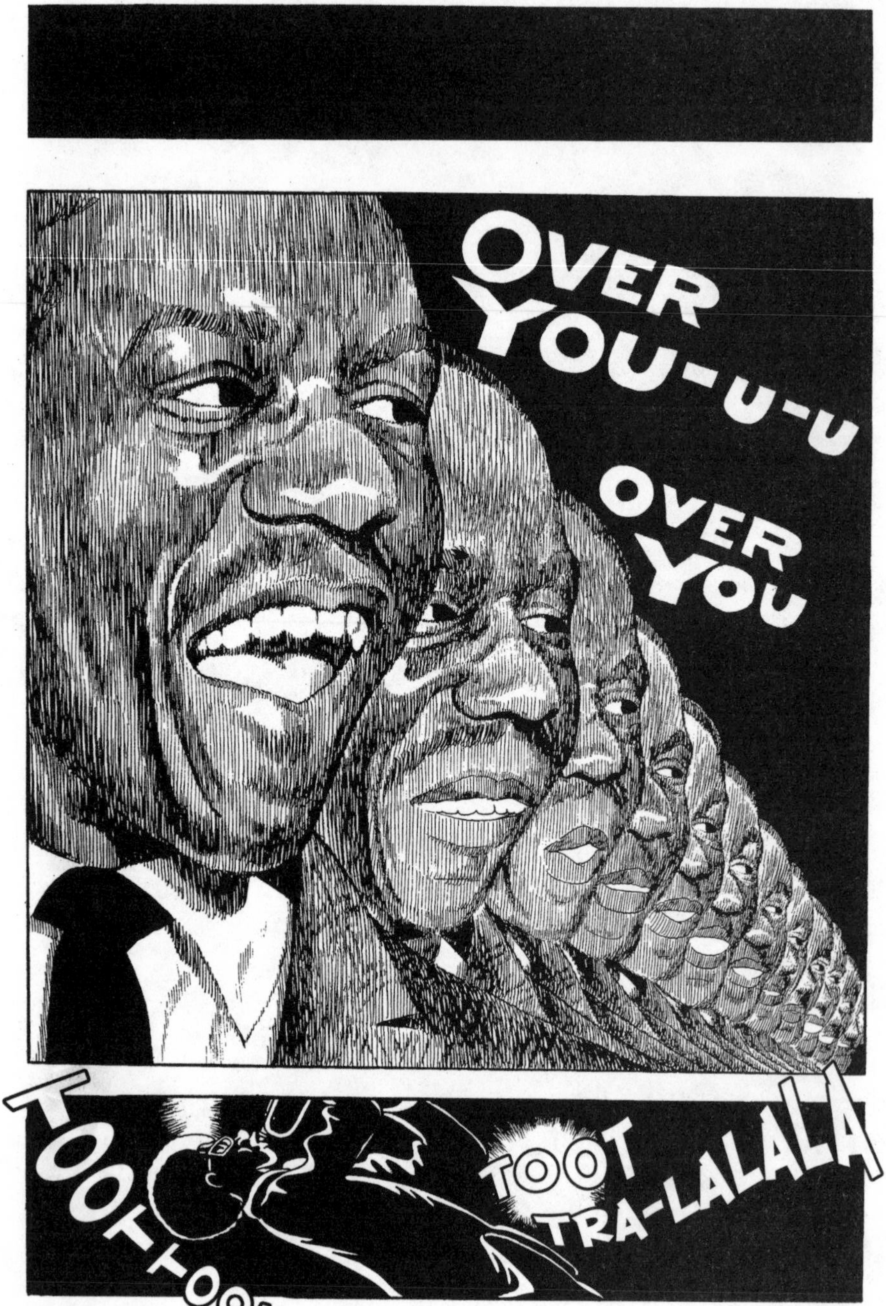
OVER
YOU-u-u
OVER
YOU
TOOT-TOOT
TOOT
TRA-LALALA

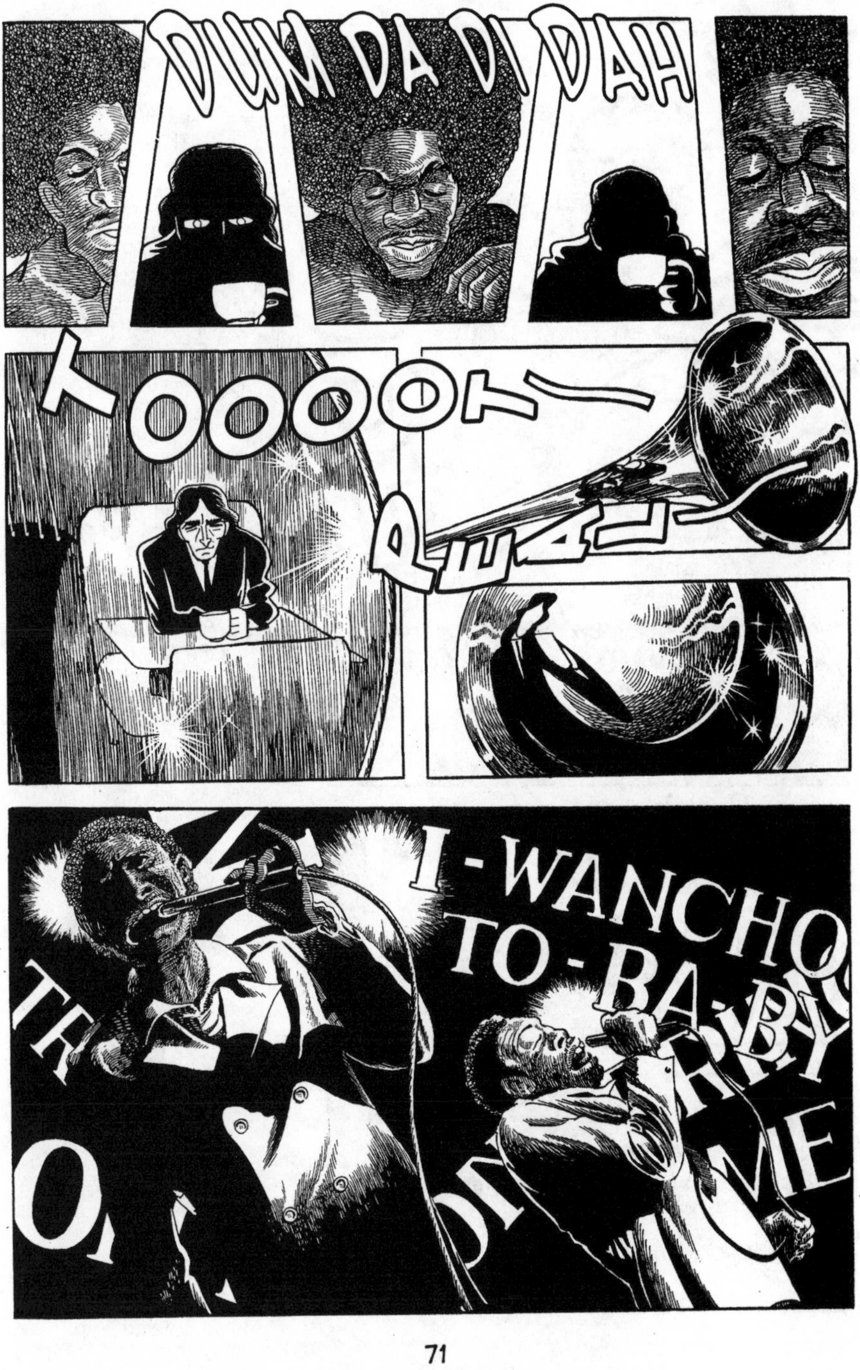
DUM DA DI DAH
TOOOOT—
PEAL
I-WANCHO
TO-BA-BY

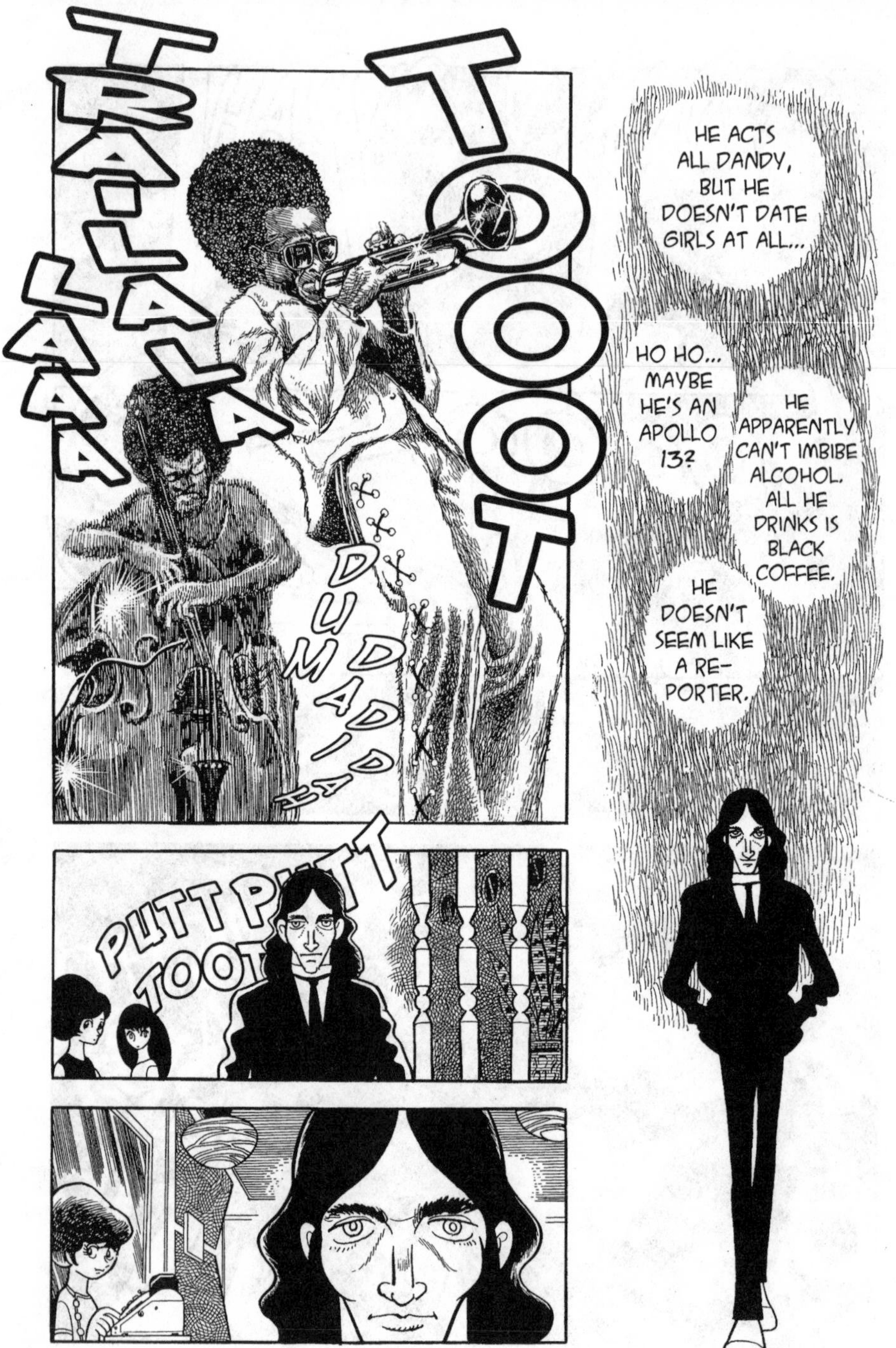
TRA-LA-LA-LAAA
TOOOT
DUDMADIDAE
PUTT PUTT TOOT
HE ACTS ALL DANDY, BUT HE DOESN'T DATE GIRLS AT ALL...
HO HO... MAYBE HE'S AN APOLLO 13?
HE APPARENTLY CAN'T IMBIBE ALCOHOL. ALL HE DRINKS IS BLACK COFFEE.
HE DOESN'T SEEM LIKE A RE-PORTER.

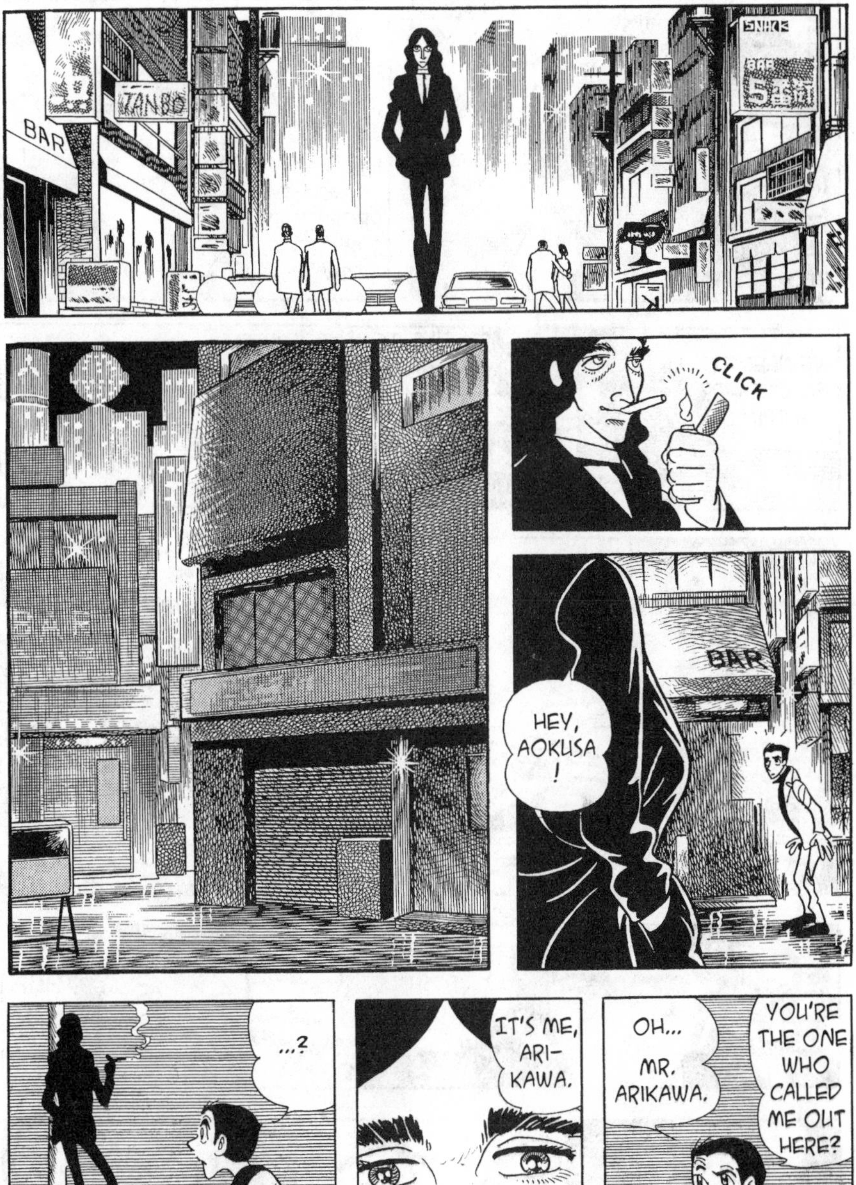
BAR
JANBO
SNACK
BAR
BAR
CLICK
HEY, AOKUSA!
BAR
...?
IT'S ME, ARI-KAWA.
OH... MR. ARIKAWA.
YOU'RE THE ONE WHO CALLED ME OUT HERE?

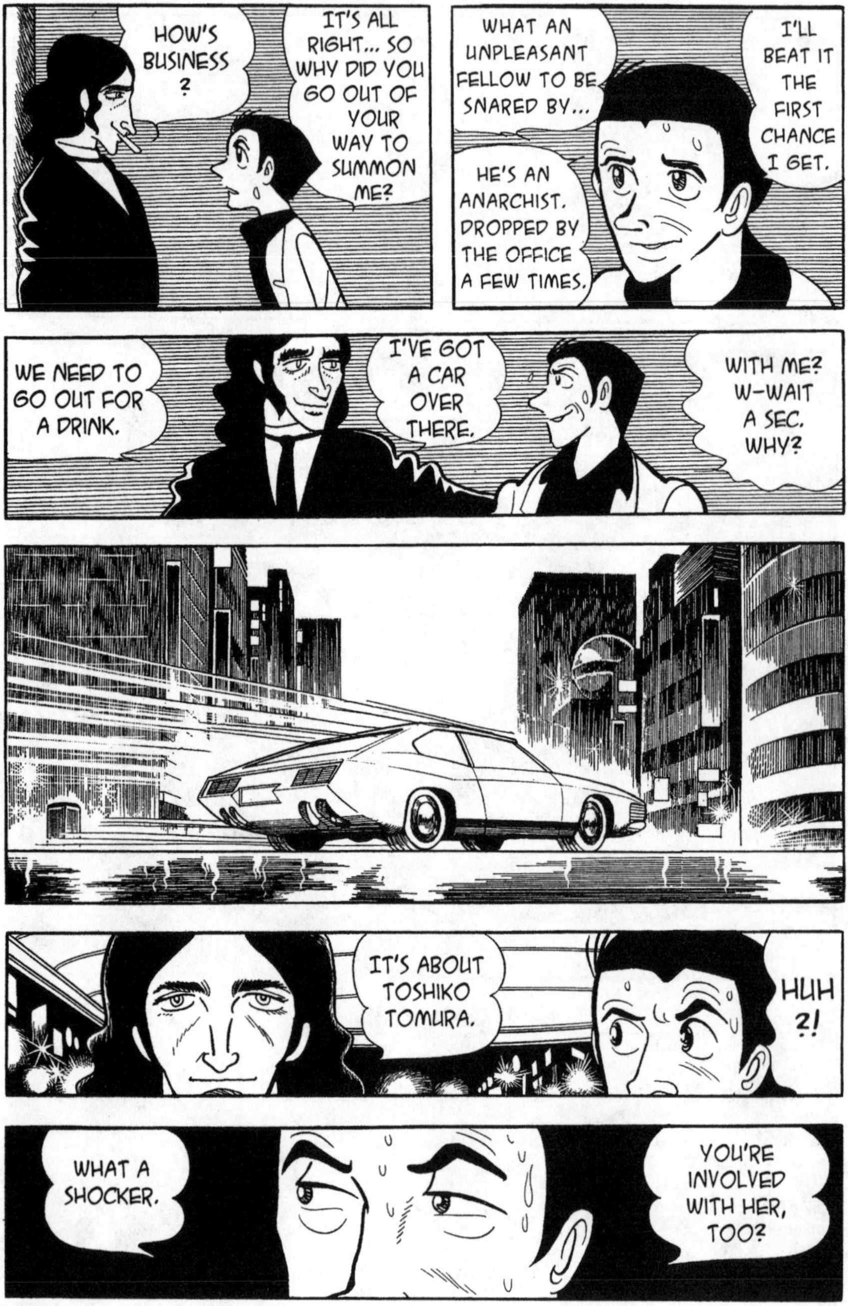
HOW'S BUSINESS ?
IT'S ALL RIGHT... SO WHY DID YOU GO OUT OF YOUR WAY TO SUMMON ME?
WHAT AN UNPLEASANT FELLOW TO BE SNARED BY...
HE'S AN ANARCHIST. DROPPED BY THE OFFICE A FEW TIMES.
I'LL BEAT IT THE FIRST CHANCE I GET.
WE NEED TO GO OUT FOR A DRINK.
I'VE GOT A CAR OVER THERE.
WITH ME? W-WAIT A SEC. WHY?
IT'S ABOUT TOSHIKO TOMURA.
HUH ?!
WHAT A SHOCKER.
YOU'RE INVOLVED WITH HER, TOO?

HA HA... I HAVE NO INTEREST IN SUCH WOMEN.

PHEW

THEN WHY DID YOU BRING HER UP?

 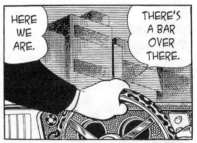

HERE WE ARE.

THERE'S A BAR OVER THERE.

THIS IS A PRETTY DESOLATE AREA.

IT'LL GET NOISY SOON ENOUGH. THEY'RE DOING BUILDING CONSTRUCTION BEHIND THIS STREET.

I THINK...

I'D LIKE TO GO HOME.

I'VE AN EARLY START TOMORROW.

YOU DON'T WANT A SCOOP?

75

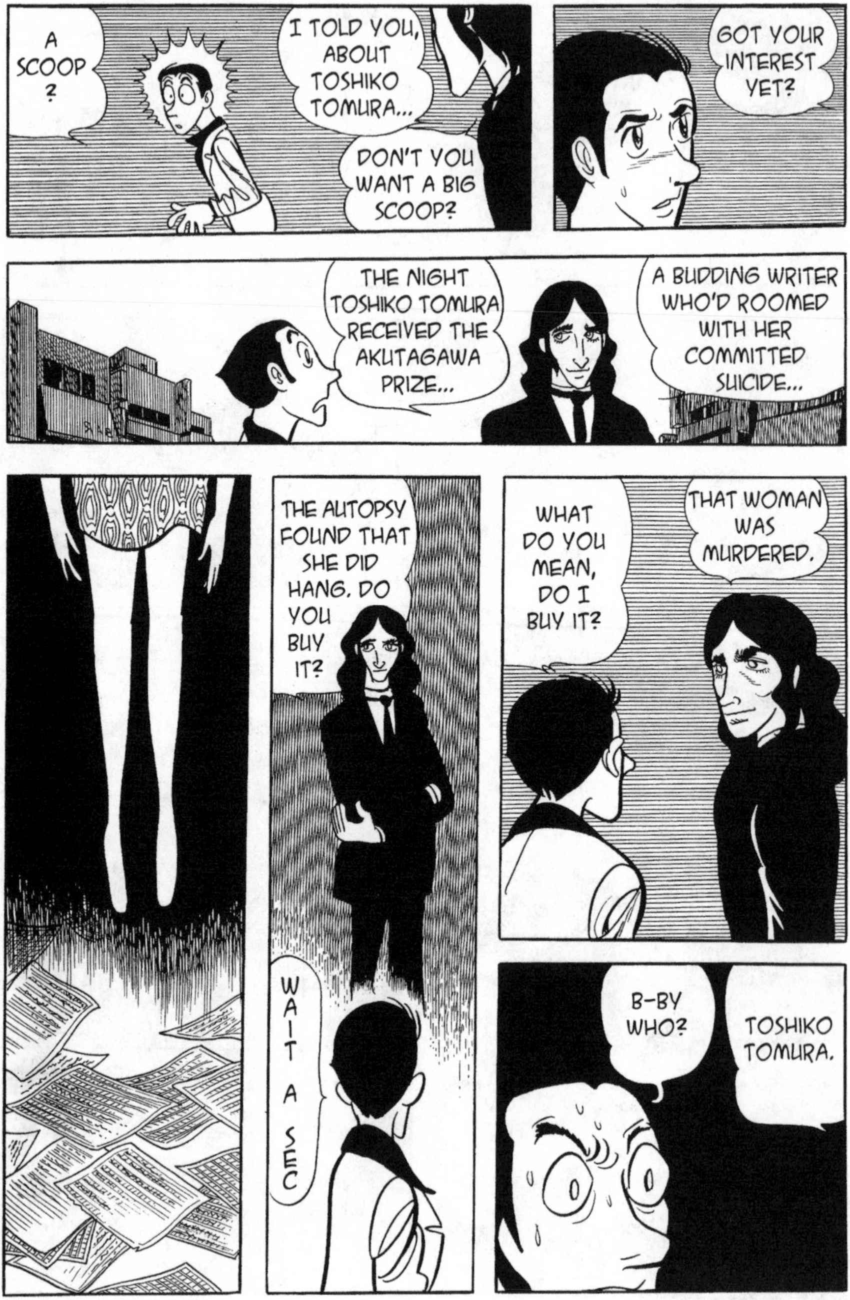
A SCOOP ?
I TOLD YOU, ABOUT TOSHIKO TOMURA...
DON'T YOU WANT A BIG SCOOP?
GOT YOUR INTEREST YET?
THE NIGHT TOSHIKO TOMURA RECEIVED THE AKUTAGAWA PRIZE...
A BUDDING WRITER WHO'D ROOMED WITH HER COMMITTED SUICIDE...
THE AUTOPSY FOUND THAT SHE DID HANG. DO YOU BUY IT?
WAIT A SEC
WHAT DO YOU MEAN, DO I BUY IT?
THAT WOMAN WAS MURDERED.
B-BY WHO?
TOSHIKO TOMURA.

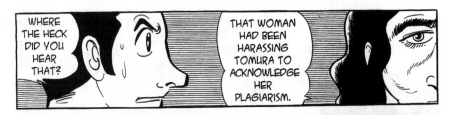

WHERE THE HECK DID YOU HEAR THAT?

THAT WOMAN HAD BEEN HARASSING TOMURA TO ACKNOWLEDGE HER PLAGIARISM.

"THE BOOK OF HUMAN INSECTS" WAS THAT WOMAN'S WORK. SHE'D COMPLETED A DRAFT.

TOSHIKO TOMURA READ AND USED IT, EVEN GOT NOMINATED FOR THE AKUTAGAWA PRIZE...

THAT WOMAN KEPT REBUKING TOMURA FOR IT.

SO... THAT'S WHY SHE KILLED HER?

YOU WANT TO HEAR MORE?

YEAH!

THEN LET'S GO TALK INSIDE THE BAR.

WHAT A DINGY BAR.

BOOM

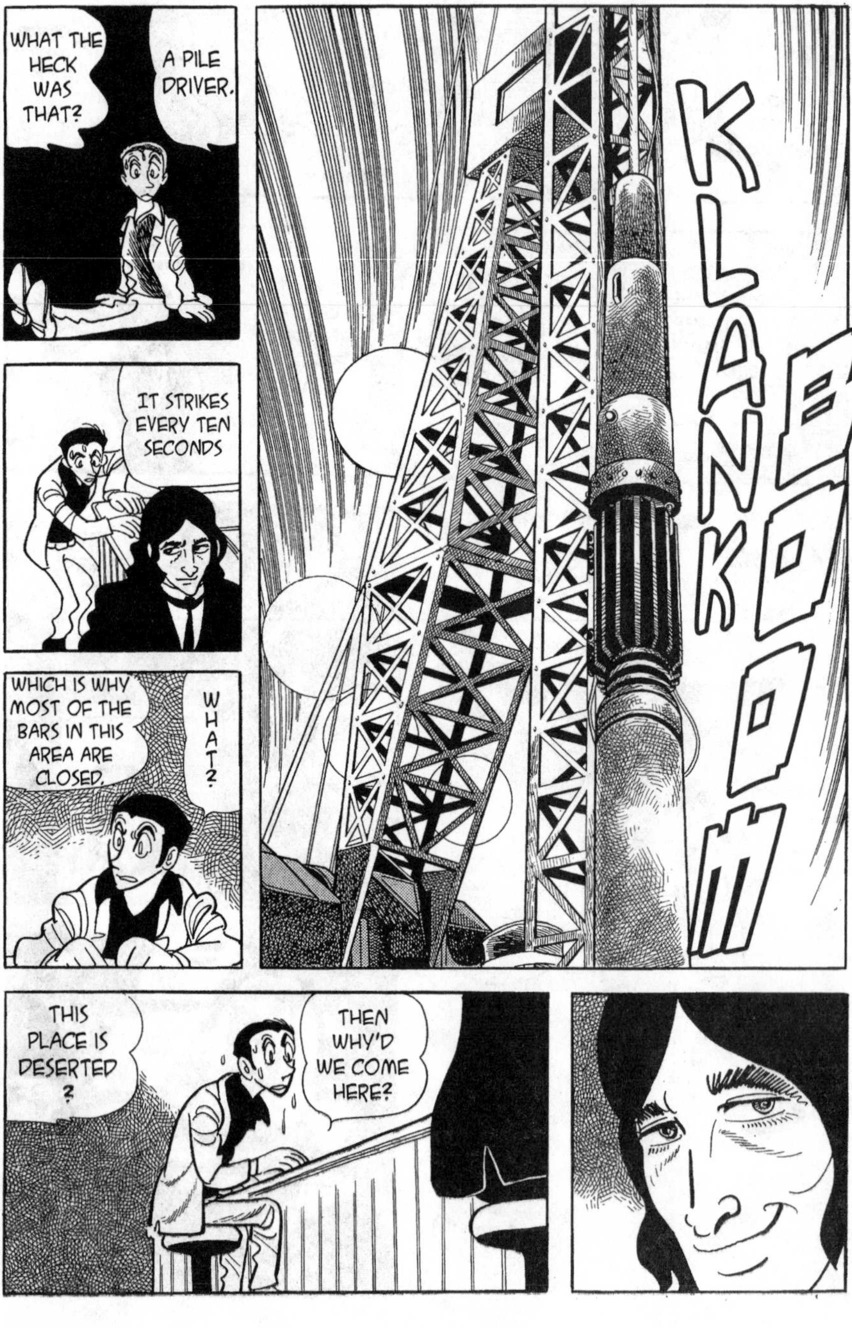

WHAT THE HECK WAS THAT?
A PILE DRIVER.
IT STRIKES EVERY TEN SECONDS
WHICH IS WHY MOST OF THE BARS IN THIS AREA ARE CLOSED.
WHAT?
KLANK
BOOM
THIS PLACE IS DESERTED?
THEN WHY'D WE COME HERE?

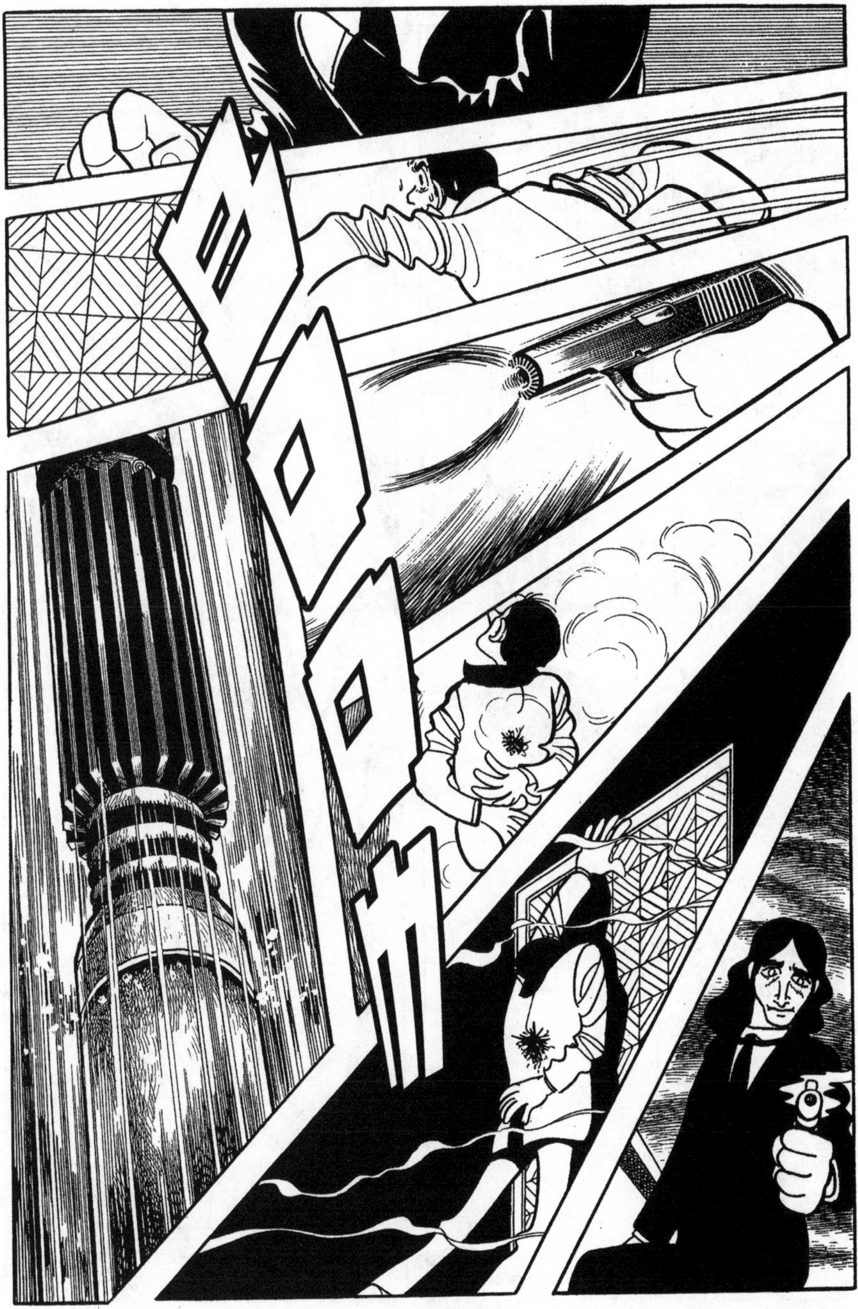

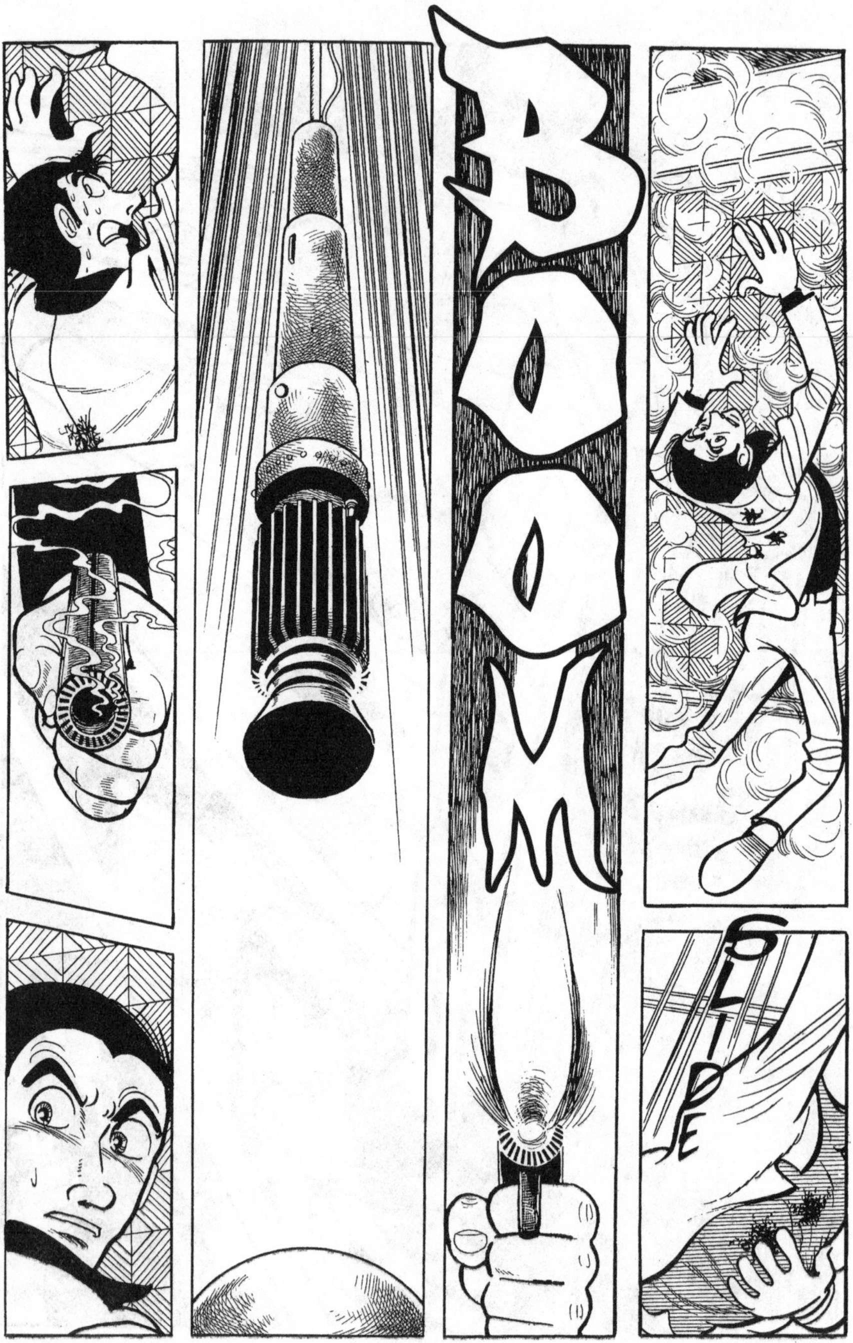
BOOM
SLIDE

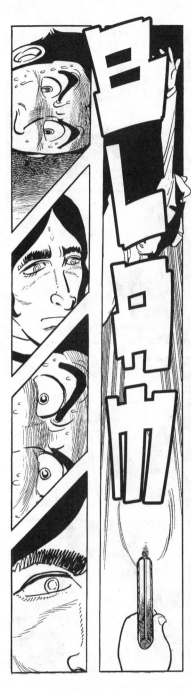

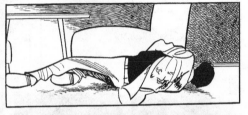

81

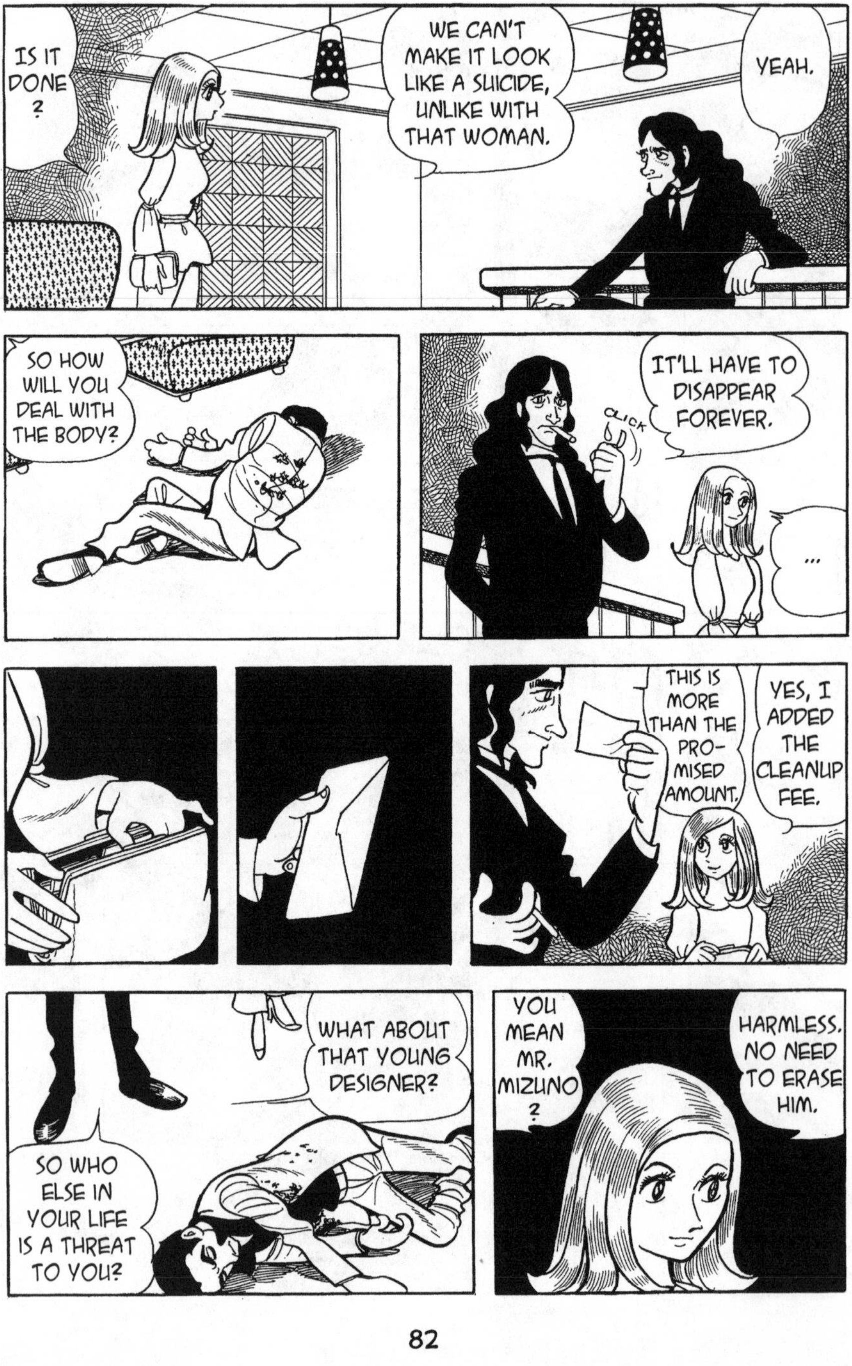
IS IT DONE?
WE CAN'T MAKE IT LOOK LIKE A SUICIDE, UNLIKE WITH THAT WOMAN.
YEAH.
SO HOW WILL YOU DEAL WITH THE BODY?
IT'LL HAVE TO DISAPPEAR FOREVER.
CLICK
...
THIS IS MORE THAN THE PRO-MISED AMOUNT.
YES, I ADDED THE CLEANUP FEE.
WHAT ABOUT THAT YOUNG DESIGNER?
SO WHO ELSE IN YOUR LIFE IS A THREAT TO YOU?
YOU MEAN MR. MIZUNO?
HARMLESS. NO NEED TO ERASE HIM.

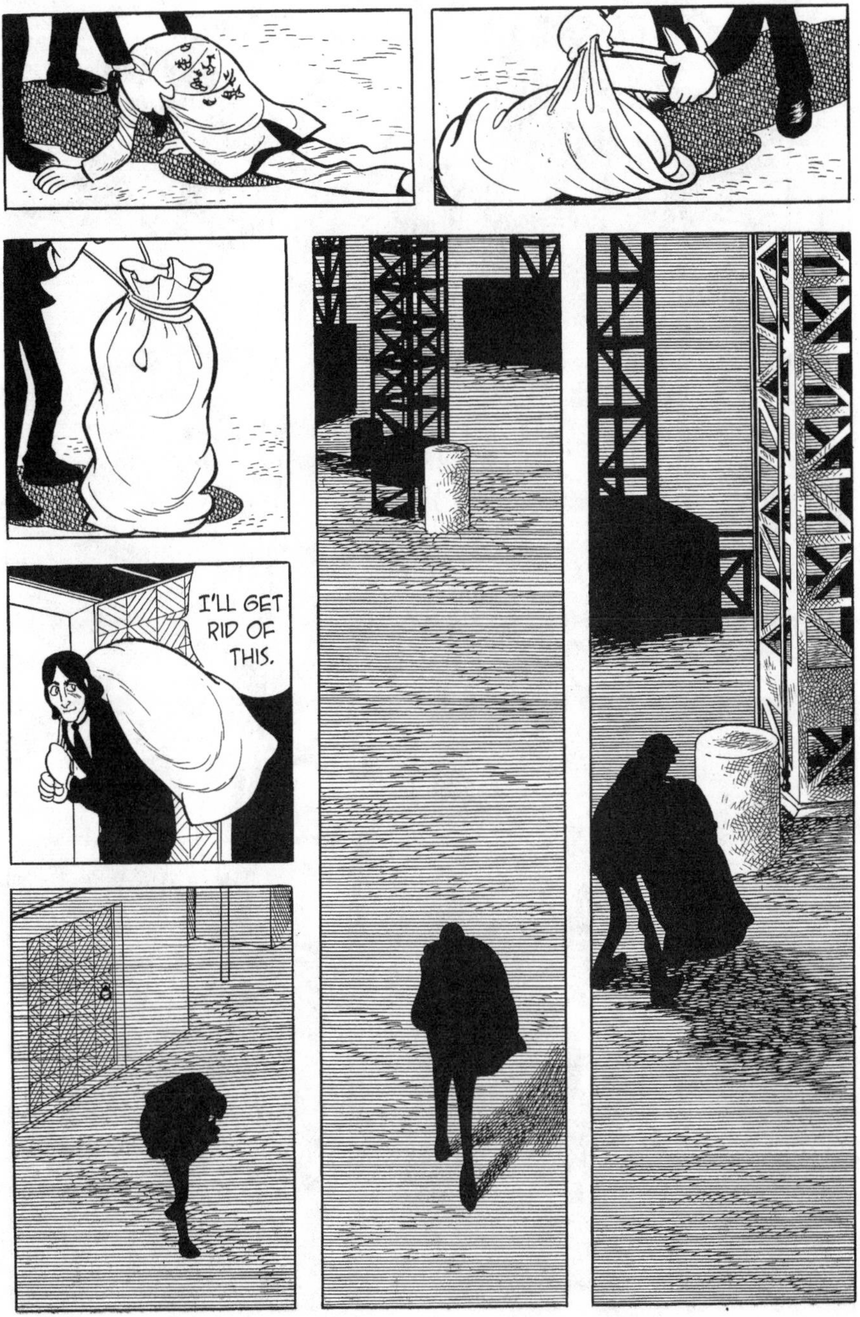
I'LL GET RID OF THIS.

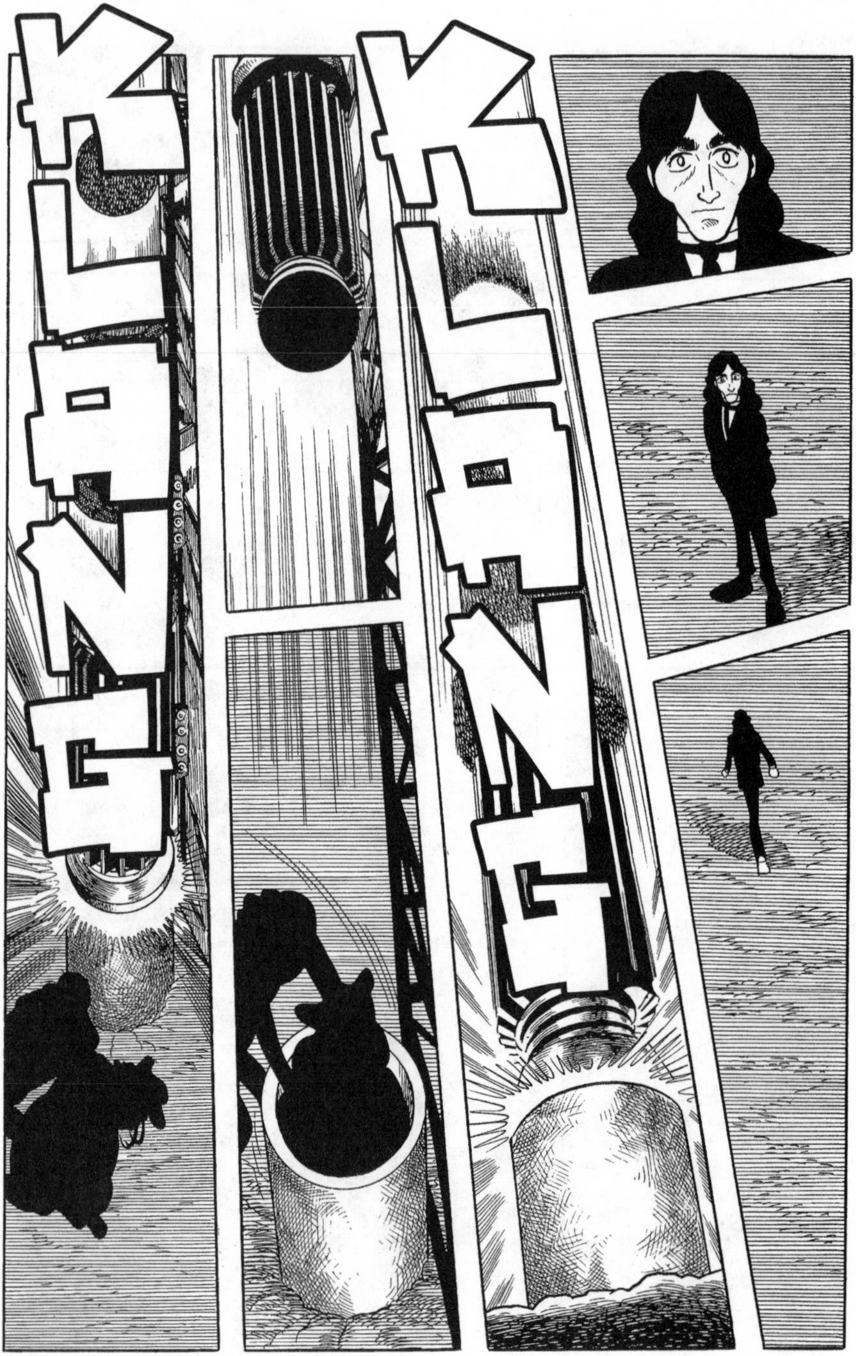
KLANG
KLANG

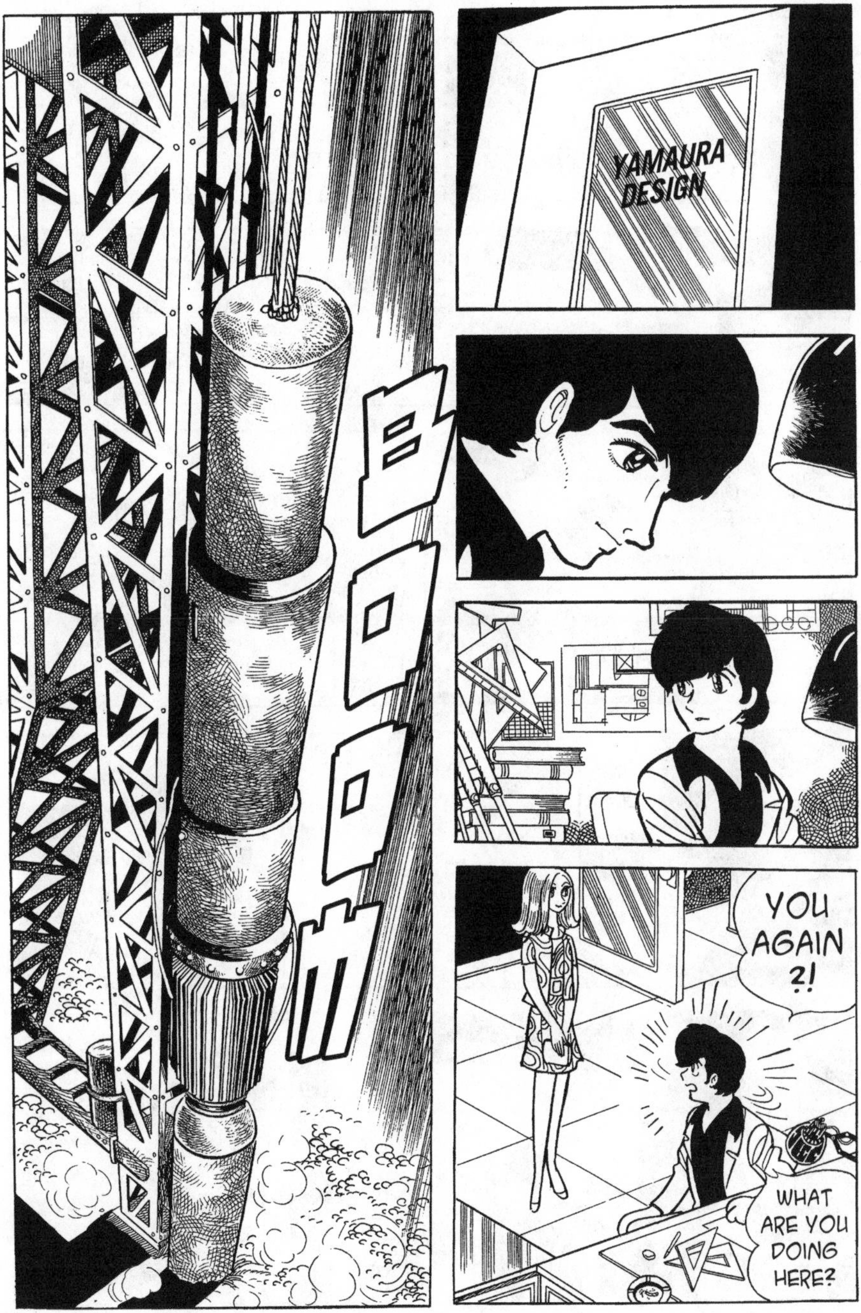
YAMAURA DESIGN
YOU AGAIN ?!
WHAT ARE YOU DOING HERE?

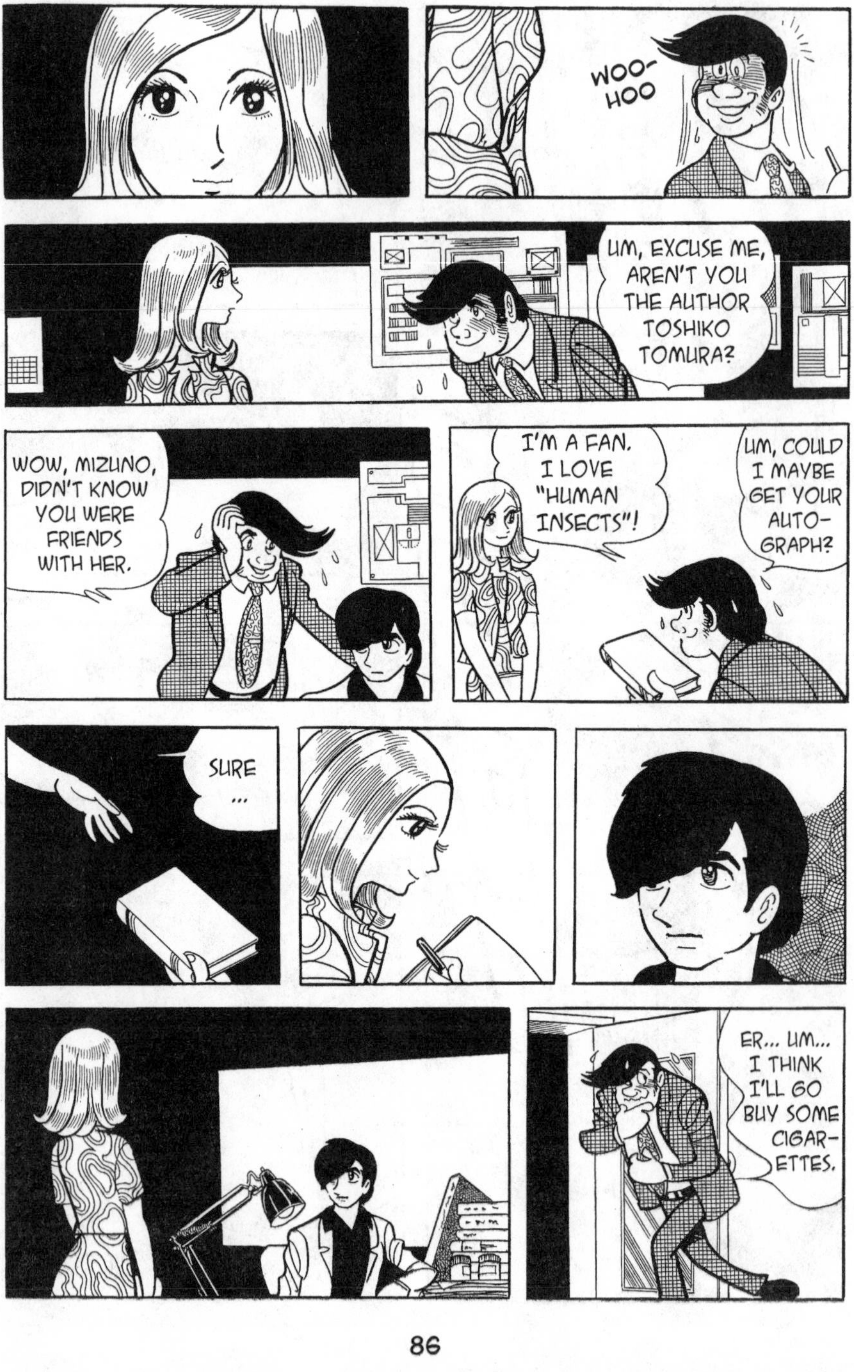
WOO-HOO
UM, EXCUSE ME, AREN'T YOU THE AUTHOR TOSHIKO TOMURA?
WOW, MIZUNO, DIDN'T KNOW YOU WERE FRIENDS WITH HER.
I'M A FAN. I LOVE "HUMAN INSECTS"!
UM, COULD I MAYBE GET YOUR AUTO-GRAPH?
SURE ...
ER... UM... I THINK I'LL GO BUY SOME CIGAR-ETTES.

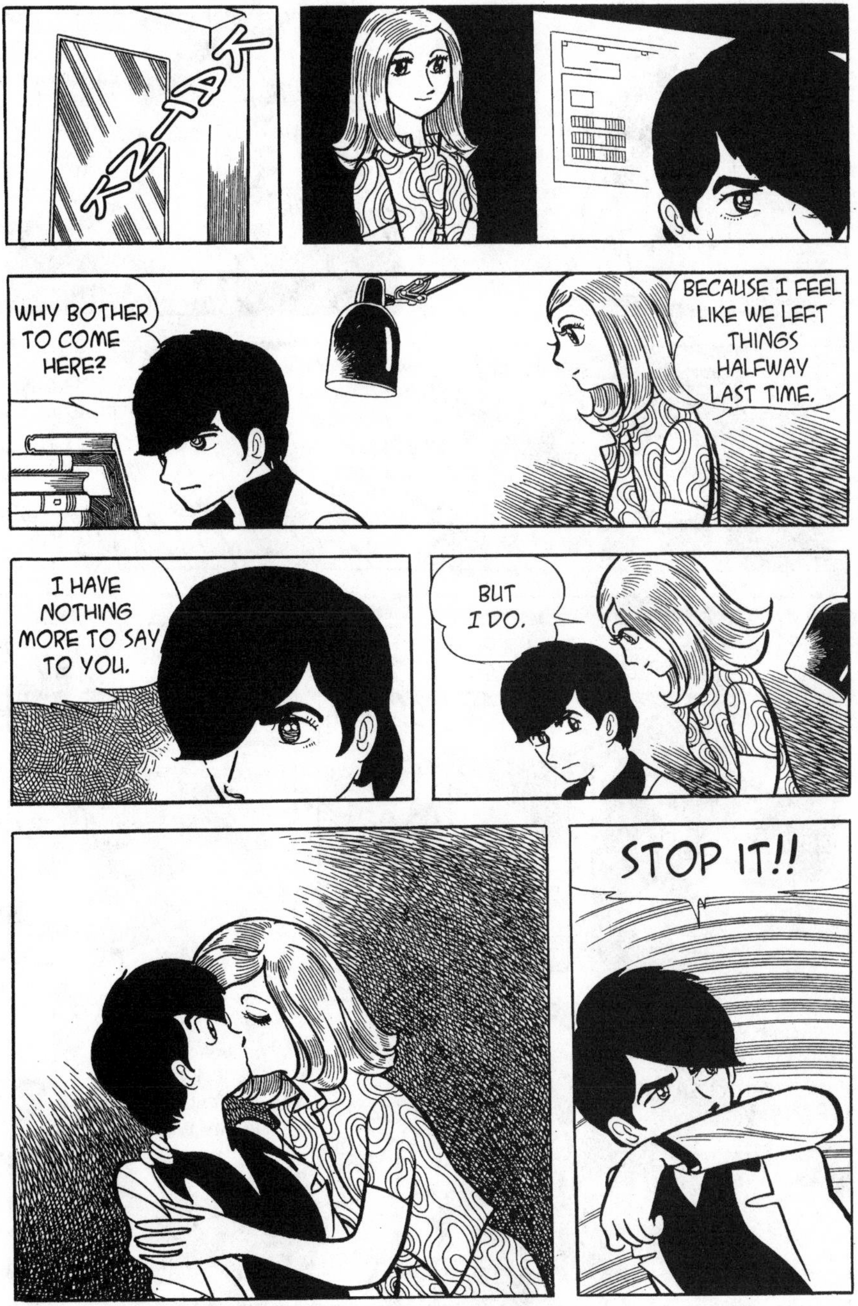
KN-TAK
WHY BOTHER TO COME HERE?
BECAUSE I FEEL LIKE WE LEFT THINGS HALFWAY LAST TIME.
I HAVE NOTHING MORE TO SAY TO YOU.
BUT I DO.
STOP IT!!

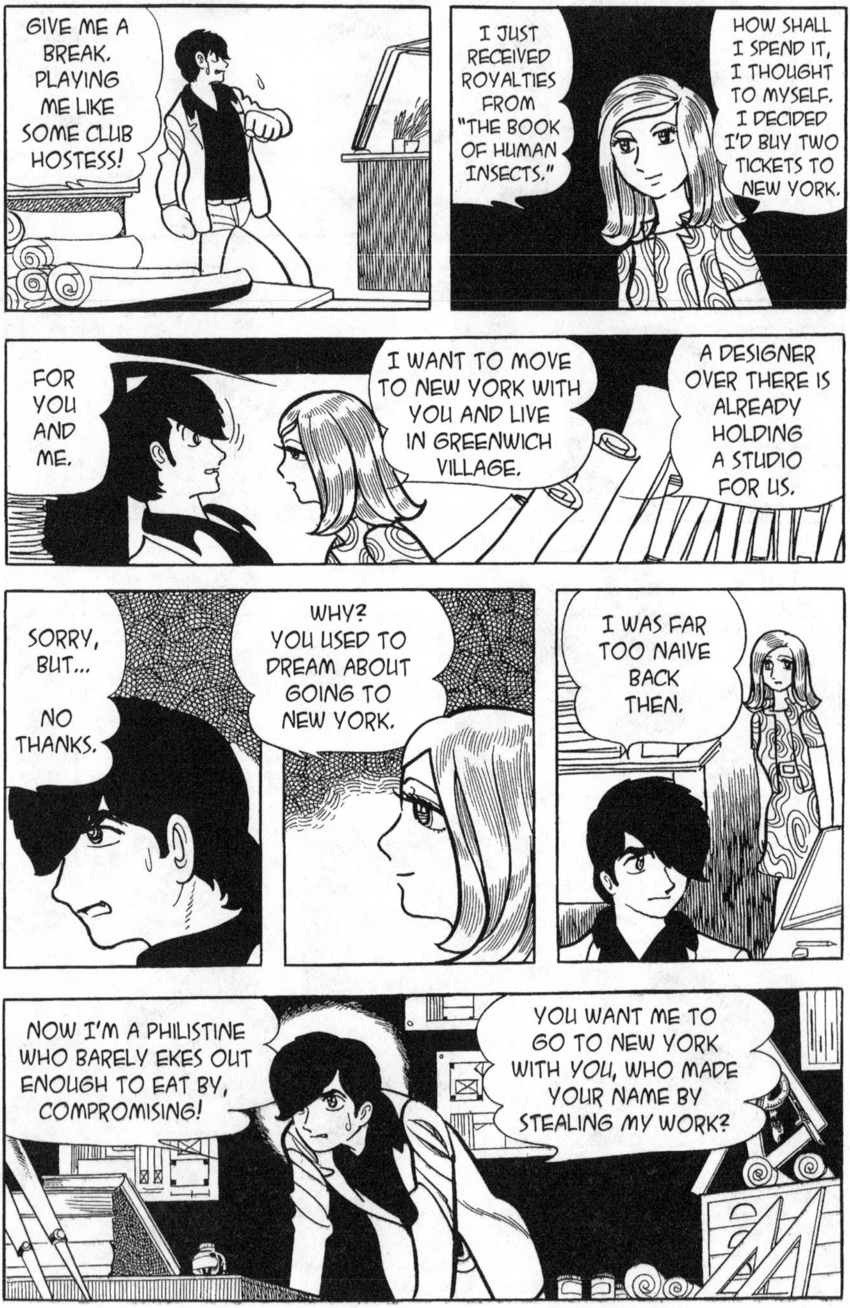
GIVE ME A BREAK. PLAYING ME LIKE SOME CLUB HOSTESS!
I JUST RECEIVED ROYALTIES FROM "THE BOOK OF HUMAN INSECTS."
HOW SHALL I SPEND IT, I THOUGHT TO MYSELF. I DECIDED I'D BUY TWO TICKETS TO NEW YORK.
FOR YOU AND ME.
I WANT TO MOVE TO NEW YORK WITH YOU AND LIVE IN GREENWICH VILLAGE.
A DESIGNER OVER THERE IS ALREADY HOLDING A STUDIO FOR US.
SORRY, BUT...
NO THANKS.
WHY? YOU USED TO DREAM ABOUT GOING TO NEW YORK.
I WAS FAR TOO NAIVE BACK THEN.
NOW I'M A PHILISTINE WHO BARELY EKES OUT ENOUGH TO EAT BY, COMPROMISING!
YOU WANT ME TO GO TO NEW YORK WITH YOU, WHO MADE YOUR NAME BY STEALING MY WORK?

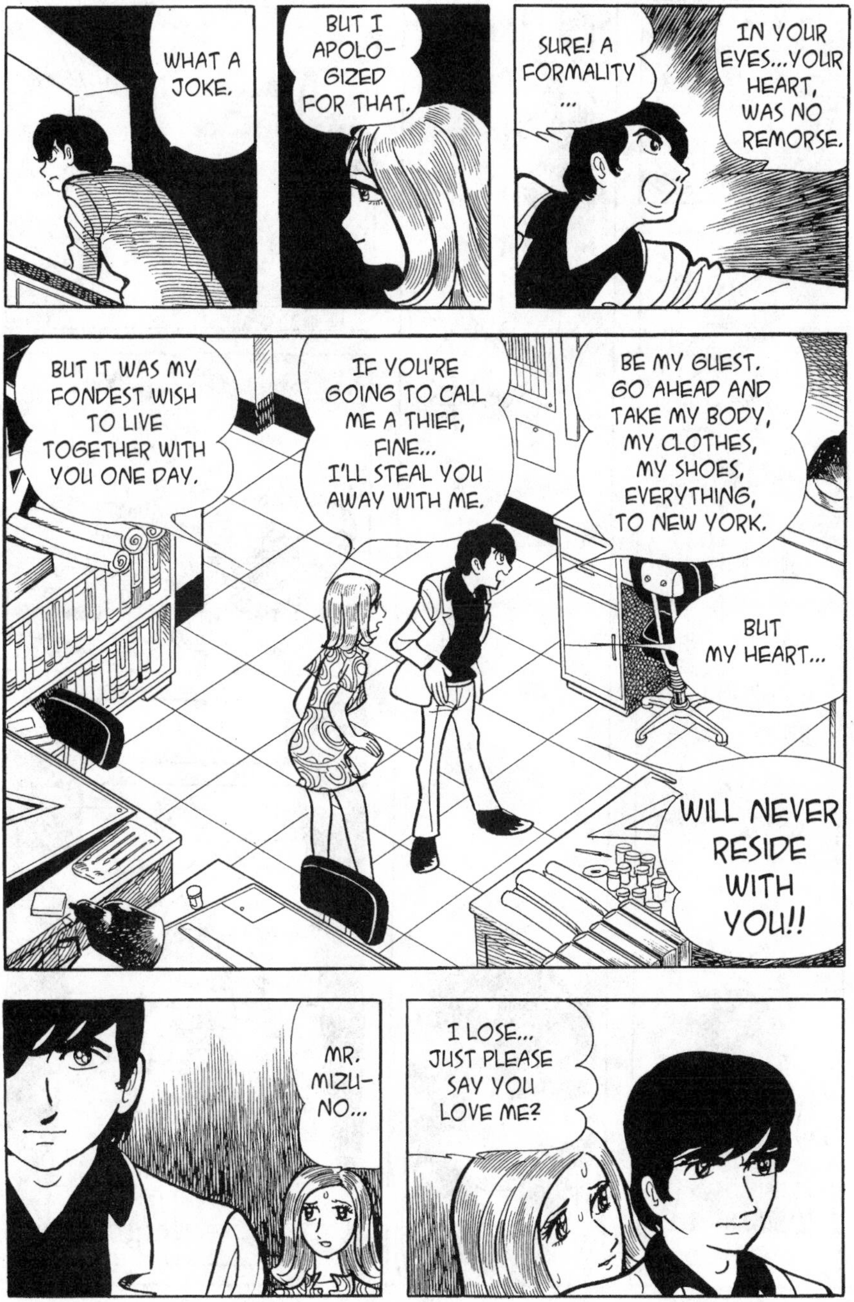
WHAT A JOKE.
BUT I APOLOGIZED FOR THAT.
SURE! A FORMALITY...
IN YOUR EYES...YOUR HEART, WAS NO REMORSE.
BUT IT WAS MY FONDEST WISH TO LIVE TOGETHER WITH YOU ONE DAY.
IF YOU'RE GOING TO CALL ME A THIEF, FINE... I'LL STEAL YOU AWAY WITH ME.
BE MY GUEST. GO AHEAD AND TAKE MY BODY, MY CLOTHES, MY SHOES, EVERYTHING, TO NEW YORK.
BUT MY HEART...
WILL NEVER RESIDE WITH YOU!!
MR. MIZUNO...
I LOSE... JUST PLEASE SAY YOU LOVE ME?

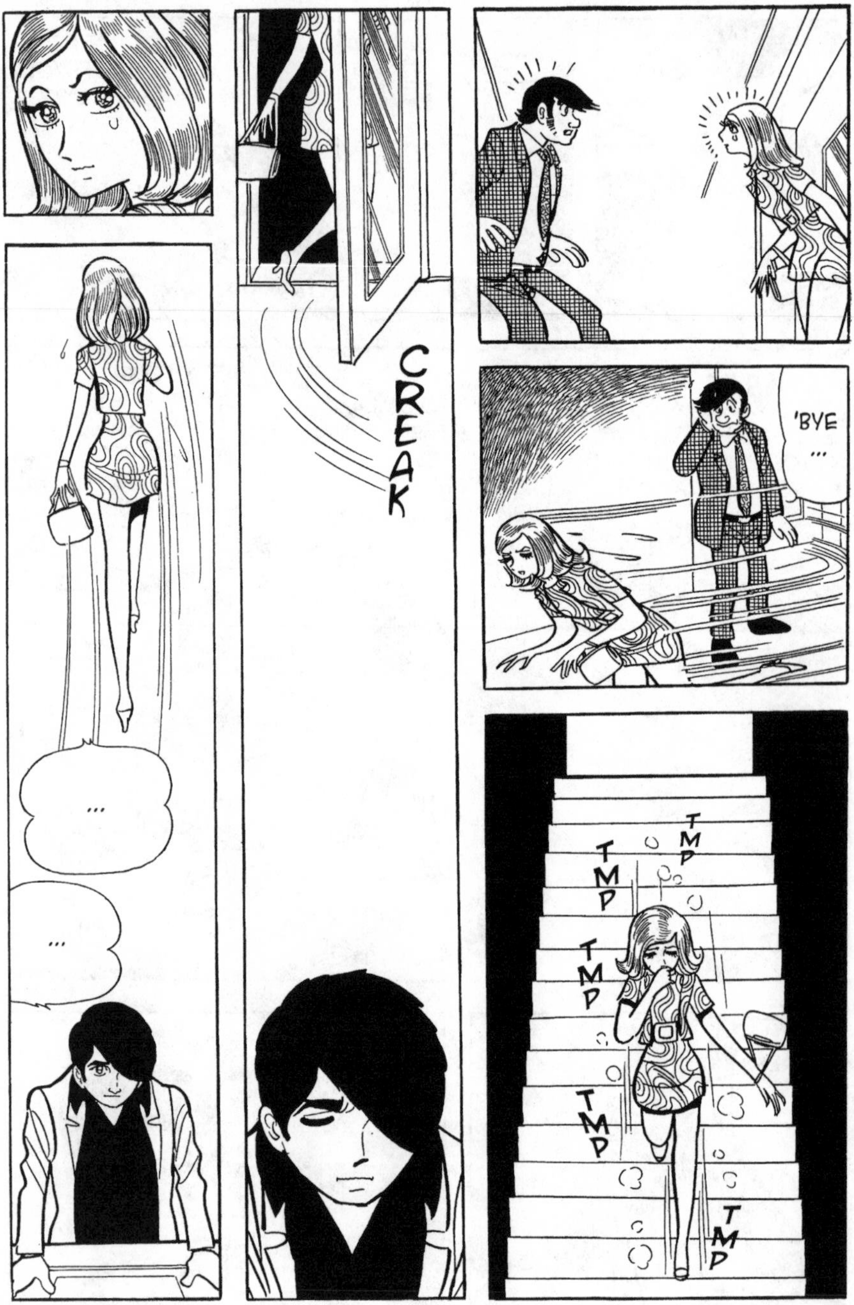
CREAK
'BYE ...
...
...
TMP TMP TMP TMP TMP

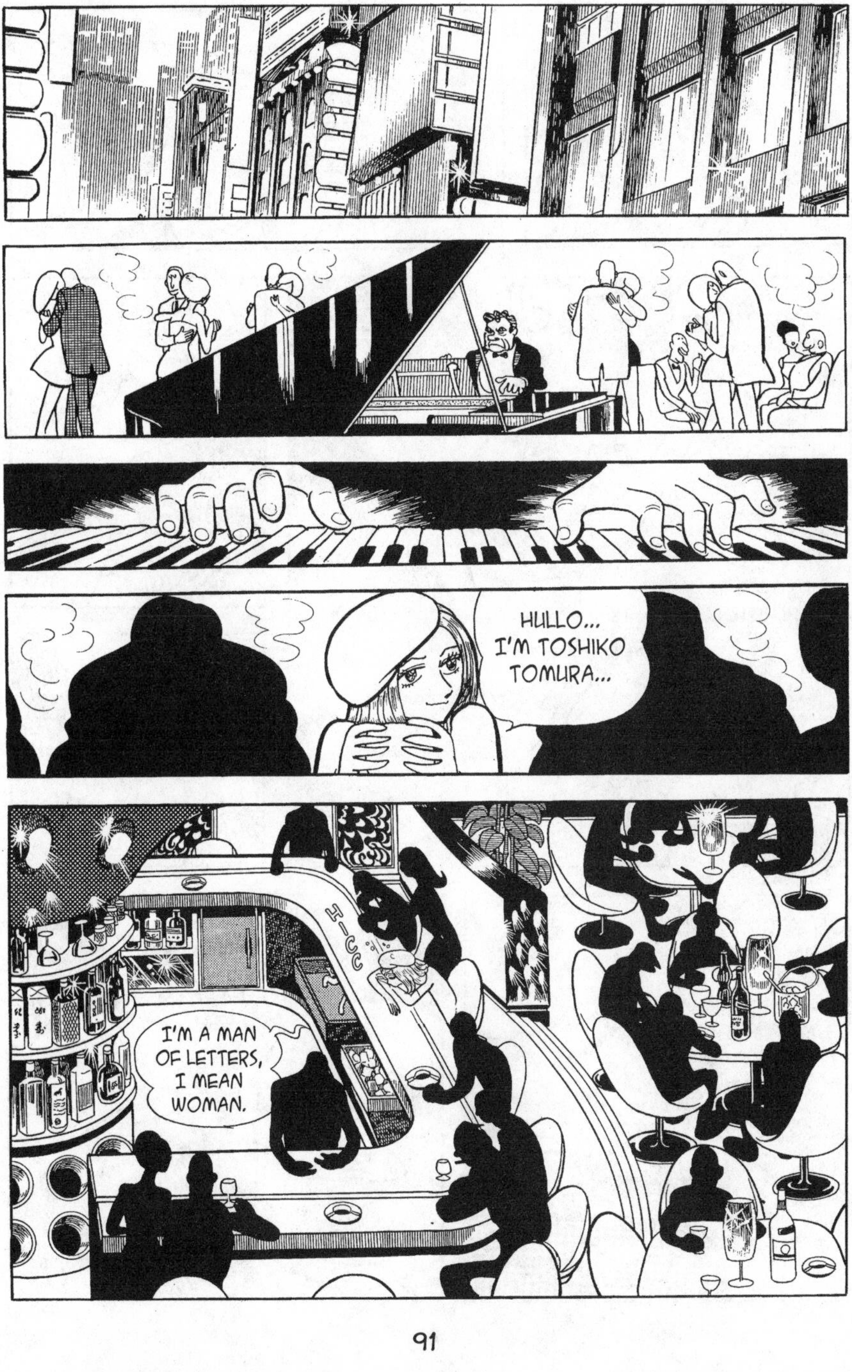
HULLO... I'M TOSHIKO TOMURA...
HICC
I'M A MAN OF LETTERS, I MEAN WOMAN.

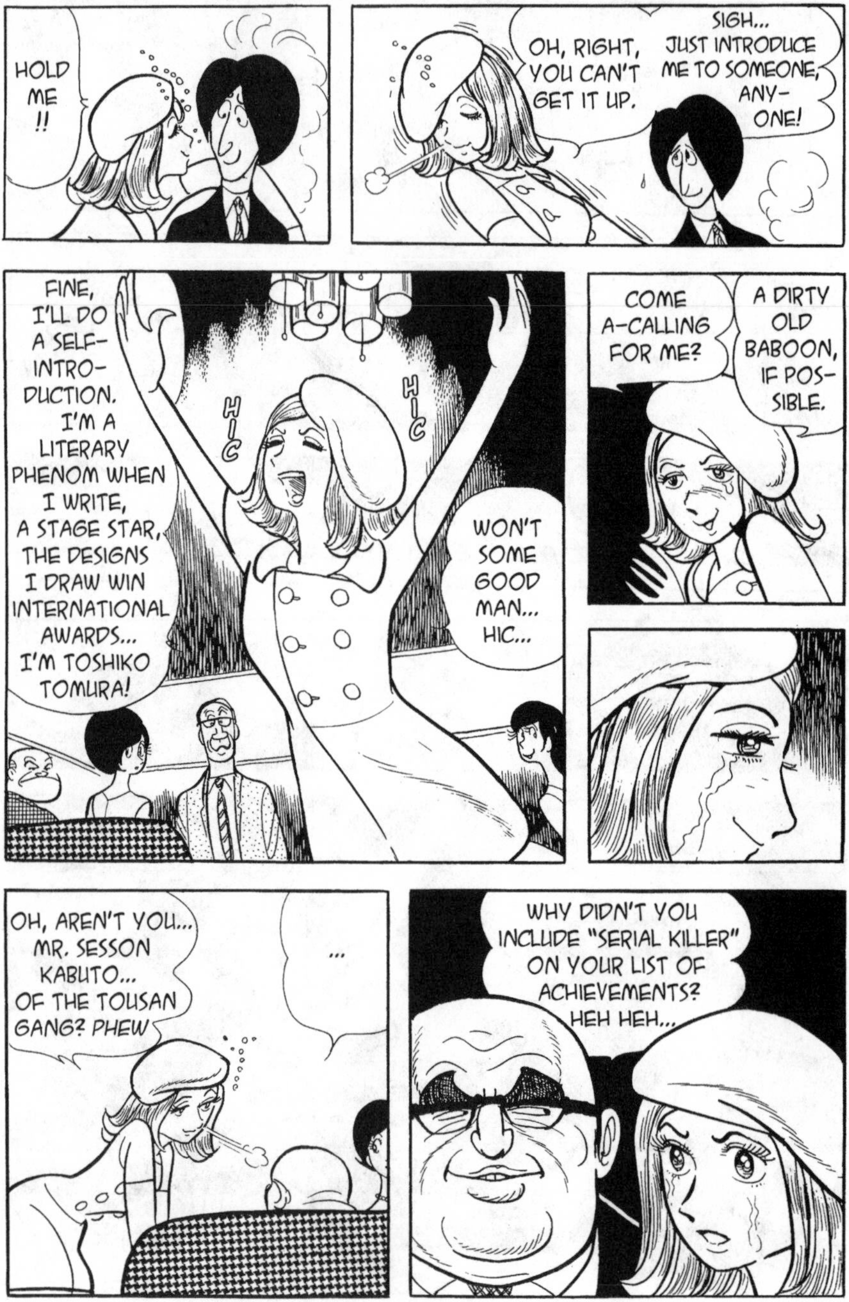
HOLD ME !!
OH, RIGHT, YOU CAN'T GET IT UP.
SIGH... JUST INTRODUCE ME TO SOMEONE, ANY-ONE!
FINE, I'LL DO A SELF-INTRO-DUCTION. I'M A LITERARY PHENOM WHEN I WRITE, A STAGE STAR, THE DESIGNS I DRAW WIN INTERNATIONAL AWARDS... I'M TOSHIKO TOMURA!
HIC
HIC
WON'T SOME GOOD MAN... HIC...
COME A-CALLING FOR ME?
A DIRTY OLD BABOON, IF POS-SIBLE.
OH, AREN'T YOU... MR. SESSON KABUTO... OF THE TOUSAN GANG? PHEW
...
WHY DIDN'T YOU INCLUDE "SERIAL KILLER" ON YOUR LIST OF ACHIEVEMENTS? HEH HEH...

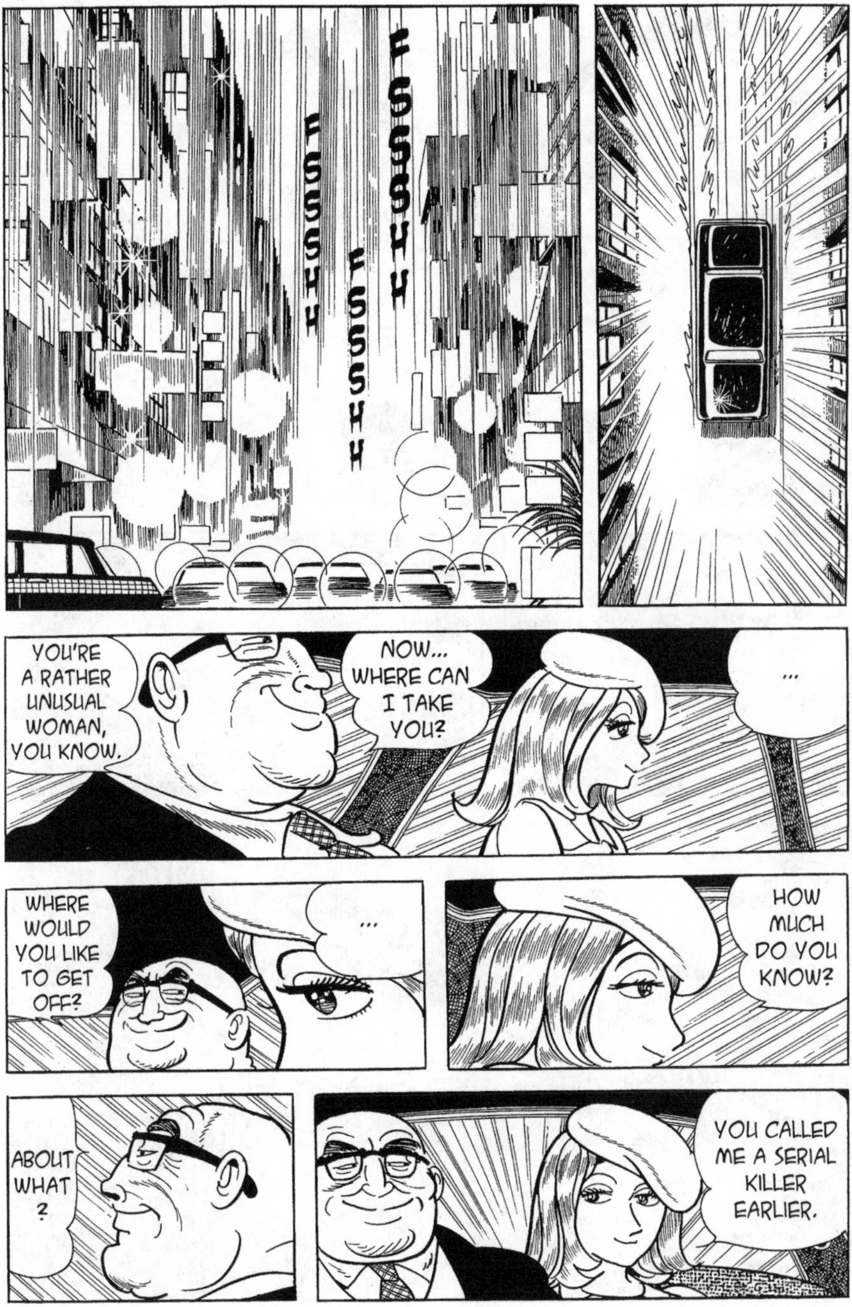
FSSSHH
FSSSHH
FSSSHH
YOU'RE A RATHER UNUSUAL WOMAN, YOU KNOW.
NOW... WHERE CAN I TAKE YOU?
...
WHERE WOULD YOU LIKE TO GET OFF?
...
HOW MUCH DO YOU KNOW?
ABOUT WHAT ?
YOU CALLED ME A SERIAL KILLER EARLIER.

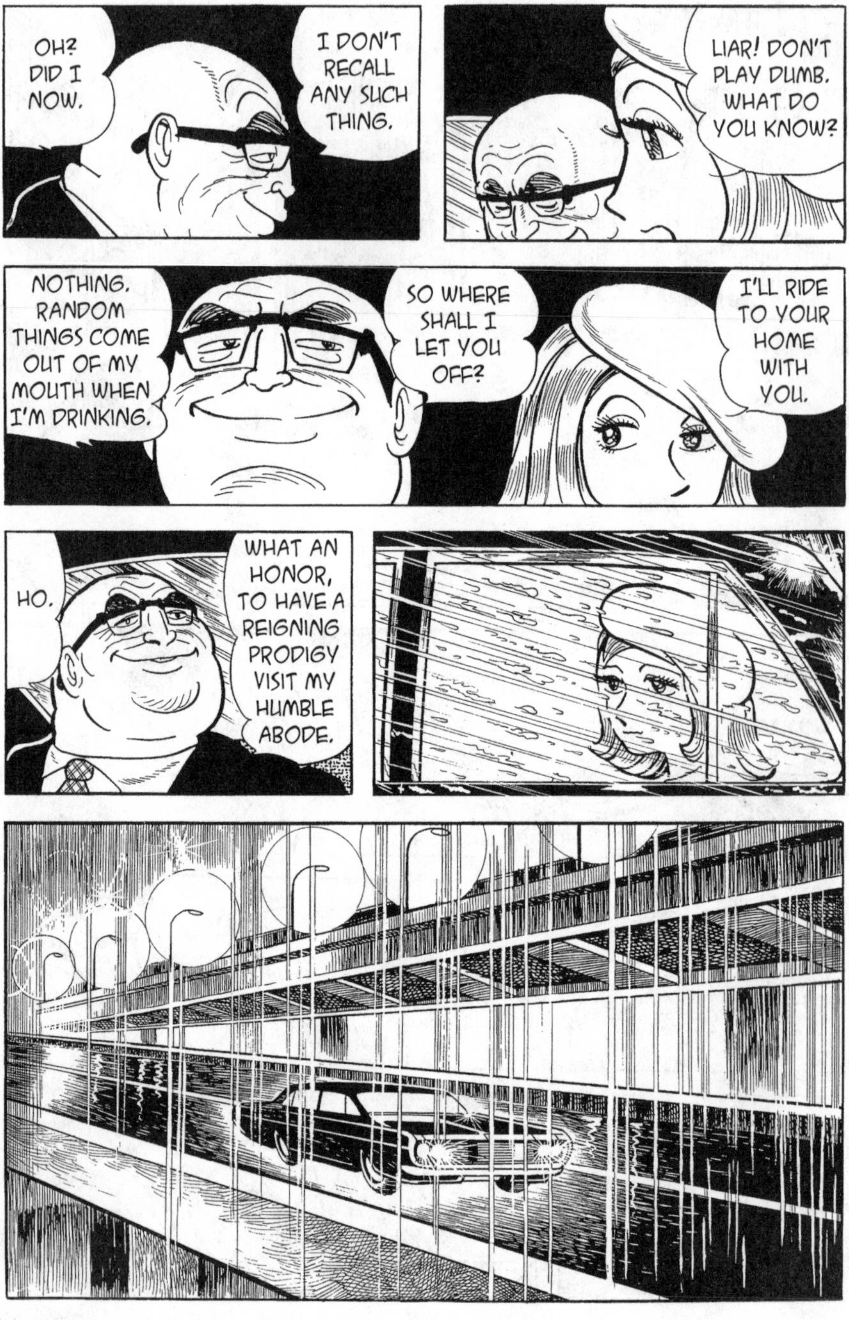
OH? DID I NOW.
I DON'T RECALL ANY SUCH THING.
LIAR! DON'T PLAY DUMB. WHAT DO YOU KNOW?
NOTHING. RANDOM THINGS COME OUT OF MY MOUTH WHEN I'M DRINKING.
SO WHERE SHALL I LET YOU OFF?
I'LL RIDE TO YOUR HOME WITH YOU.
HO.
WHAT AN HONOR, TO HAVE A REIGNING PRODIGY VISIT MY HUMBLE ABODE.

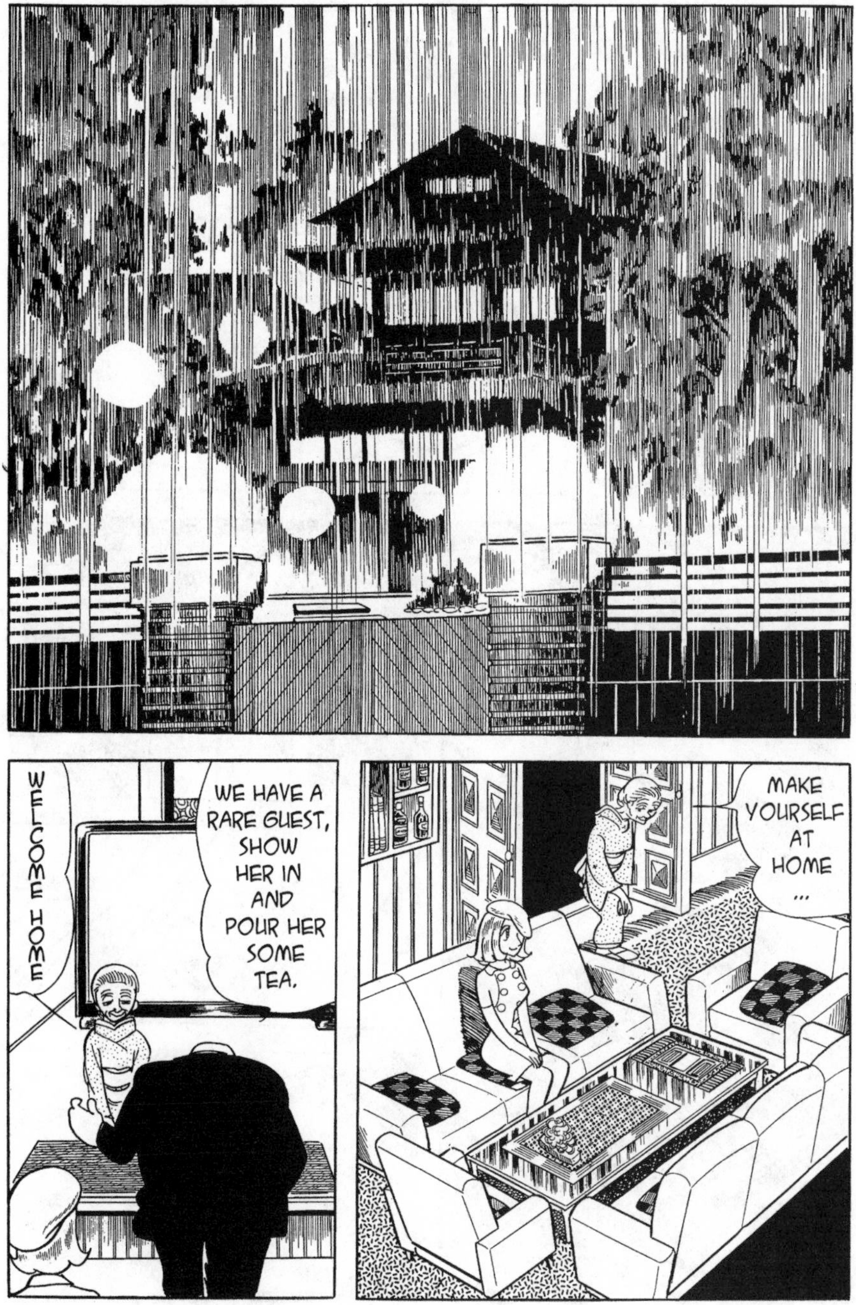
WELCOME HOME
WE HAVE A RARE GUEST, SHOW HER IN AND POUR HER SOME TEA.
MAKE YOURSELF AT HOME ...

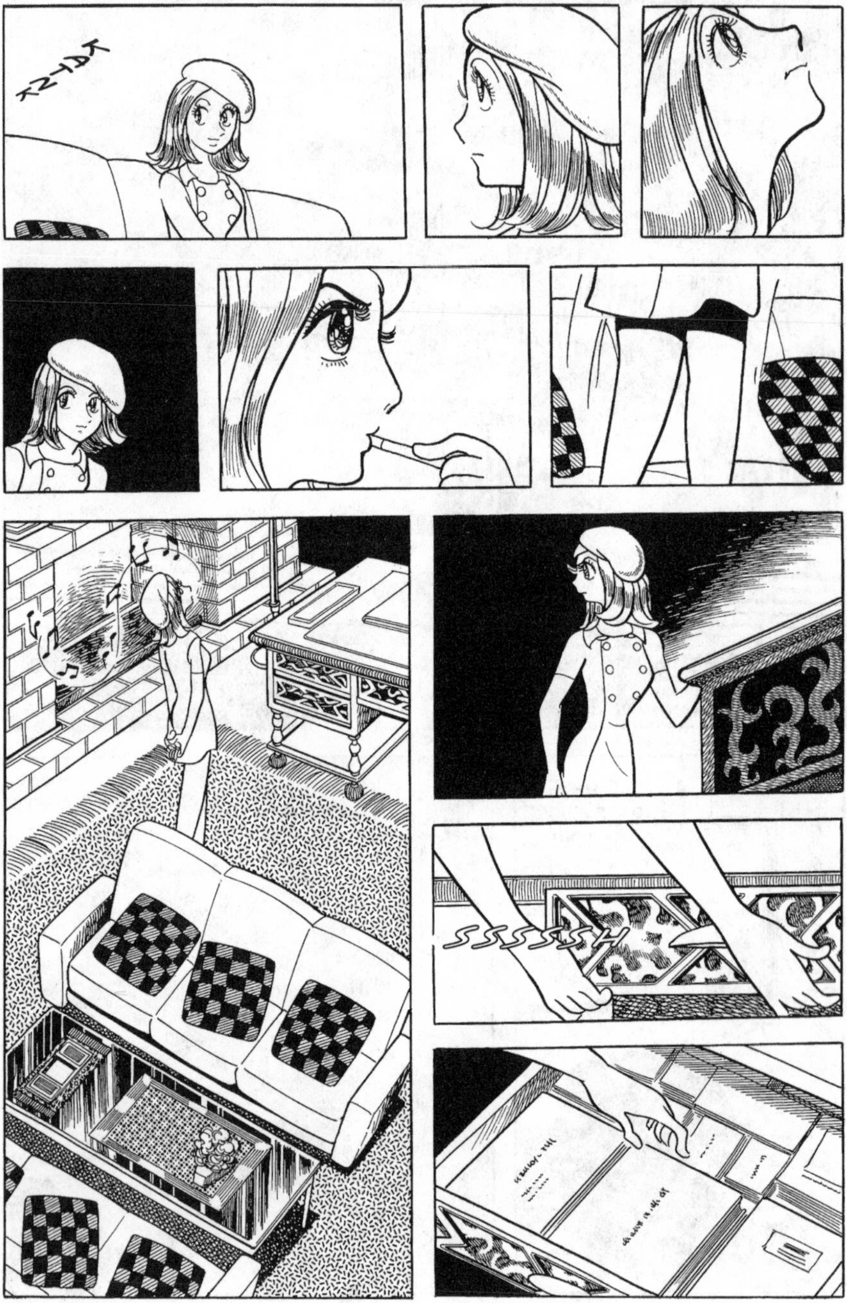

KATNK
SSSSSH

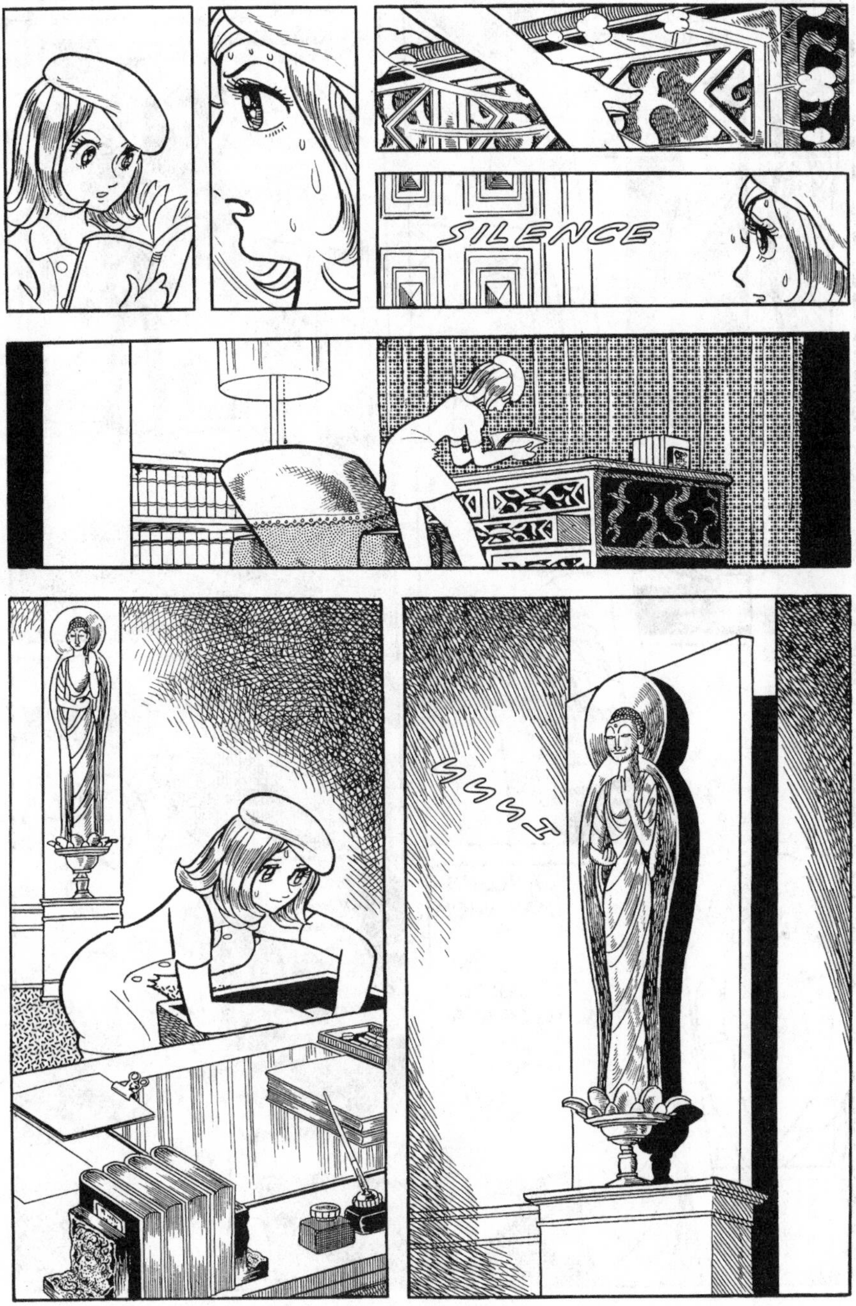
SILENCE

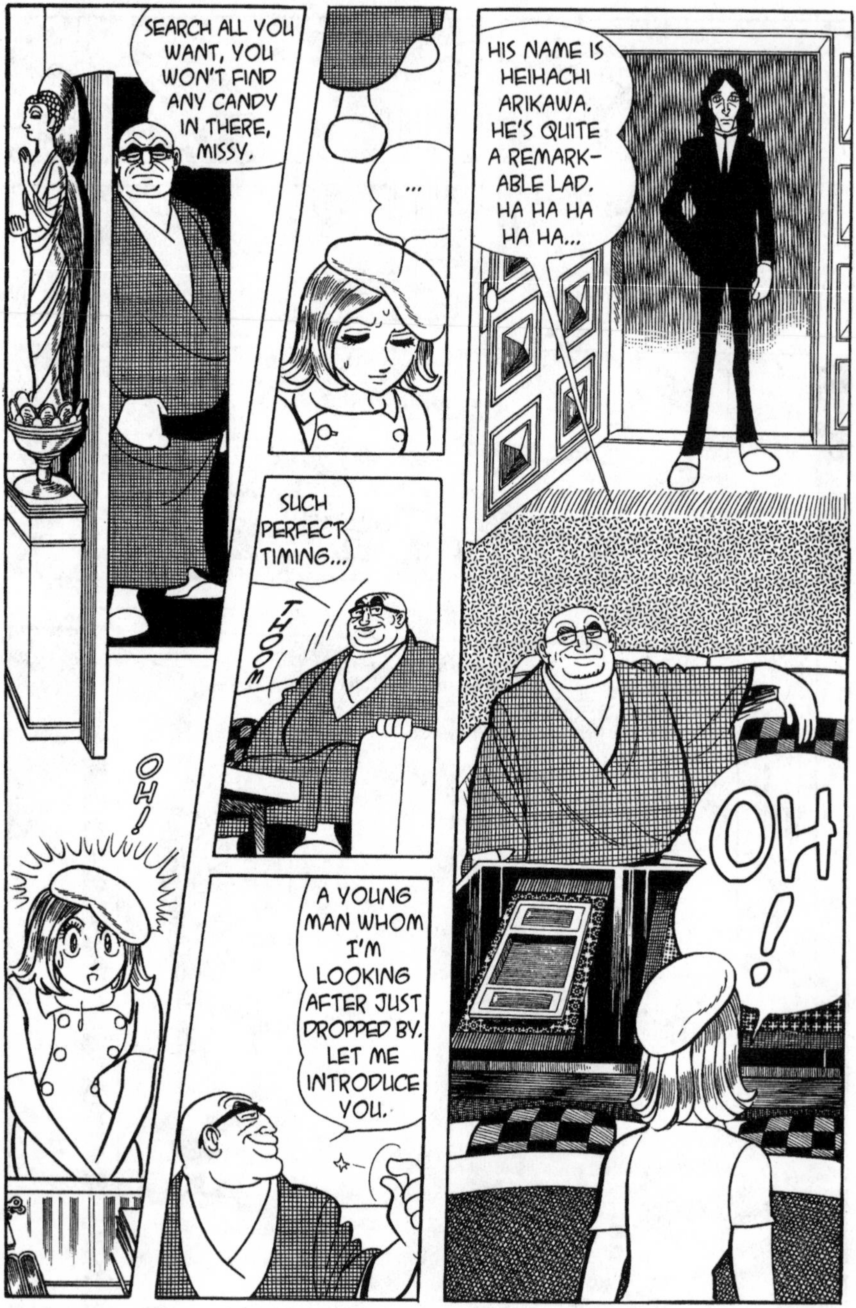
SEARCH ALL YOU WANT, YOU WON'T FIND ANY CANDY IN THERE, MISSY.
OH!
...
SUCH PERFECT TIMING...
THOOOM
A YOUNG MAN WHOM I'M LOOKING AFTER JUST DROPPED BY. LET ME INTRODUCE YOU.
HIS NAME IS HEIHACHI ARIKAWA. HE'S QUITE A REMARKABLE LAD. HA HA HA HA HA...
OH!

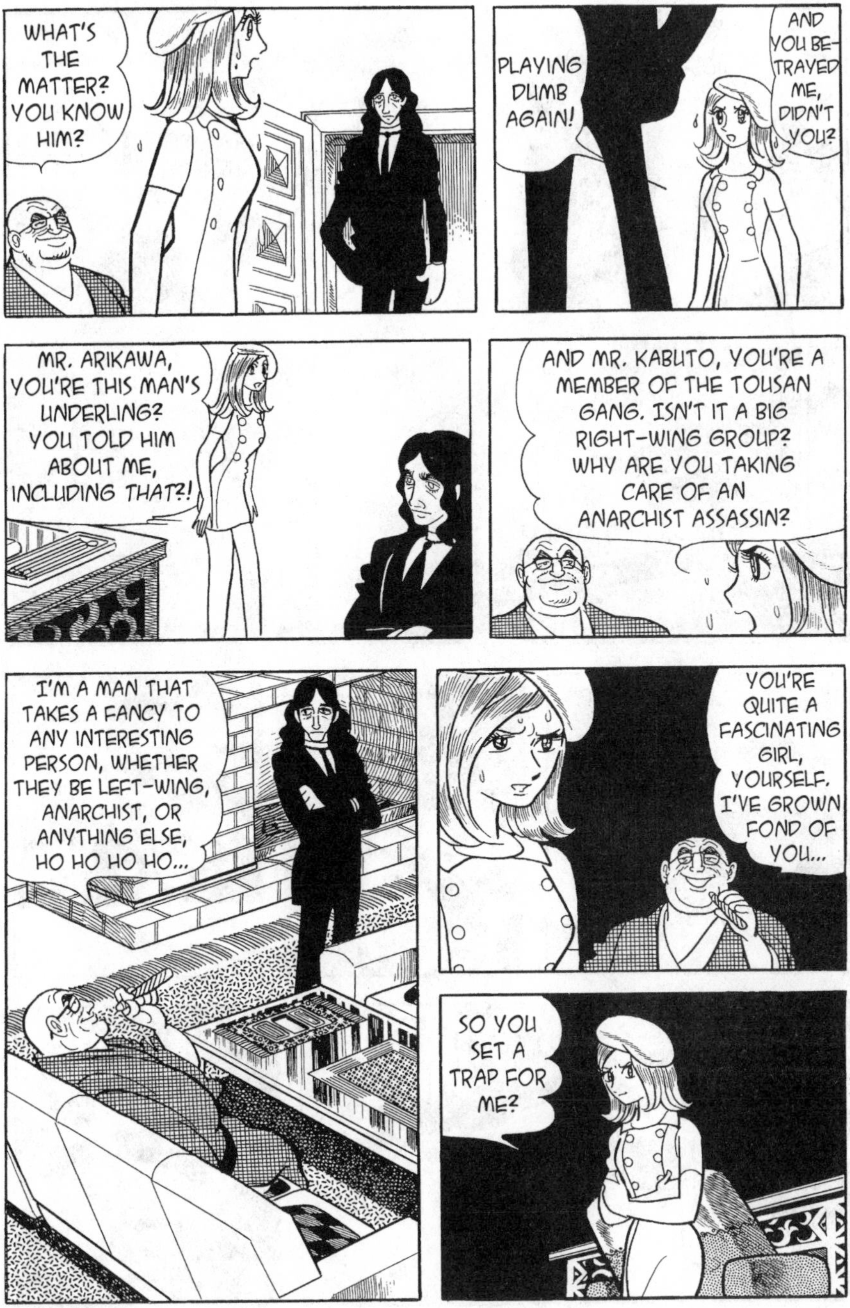

WHAT'S THE MATTER? YOU KNOW HIM?
PLAYING DUMB AGAIN!
AND YOU BE-TRAYED ME, DIDN'T YOU?
MR. ARIKAWA, YOU'RE THIS MAN'S UNDERLING? YOU TOLD HIM ABOUT ME, INCLUDING THAT?!
AND MR. KABUTO, YOU'RE A MEMBER OF THE TOUSAN GANG. ISN'T IT A BIG RIGHT-WING GROUP? WHY ARE YOU TAKING CARE OF AN ANARCHIST ASSASSIN?
I'M A MAN THAT TAKES A FANCY TO ANY INTERESTING PERSON, WHETHER THEY BE LEFT-WING, ANARCHIST, OR ANYTHING ELSE, HO HO HO HO...
YOU'RE QUITE A FASCINATING GIRL, YOURSELF. I'VE GROWN FOND OF YOU...
SO YOU SET A TRAP FOR ME?

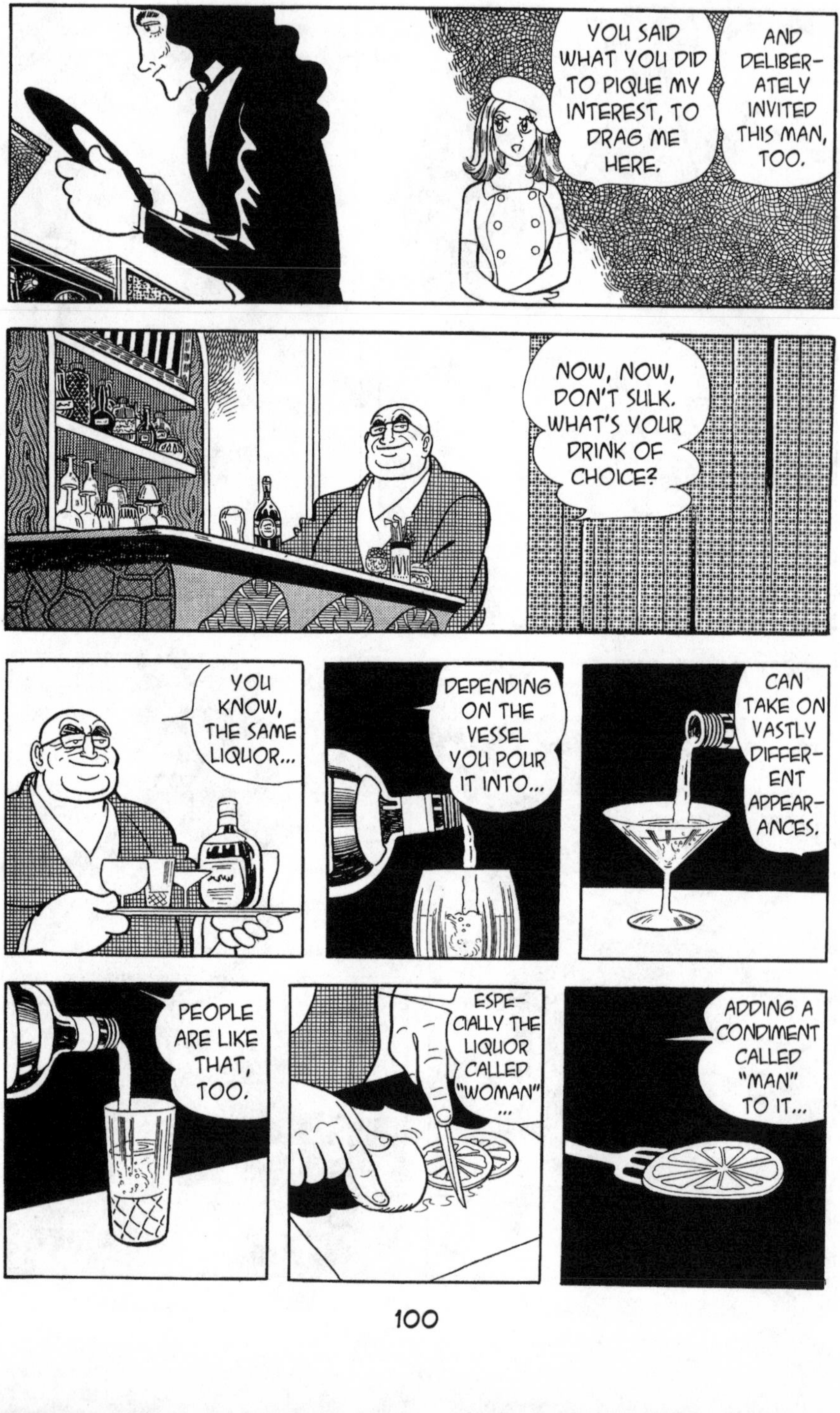
YOU SAID WHAT YOU DID TO PIQUE MY INTEREST, TO DRAG ME HERE.
AND DELIBER-ATELY INVITED THIS MAN, TOO.
NOW, NOW, DON'T SULK. WHAT'S YOUR DRINK OF CHOICE?
YOU KNOW, THE SAME LIQUOR...
DEPENDING ON THE VESSEL YOU POUR IT INTO...
CAN TAKE ON VASTLY DIFFER-ENT APPEAR-ANCES.
PEOPLE ARE LIKE THAT, TOO.
ESPE-CIALLY THE LIQUOR CALLED "WOMAN"...
ADDING A CONDIMENT CALLED "MAN" TO IT...

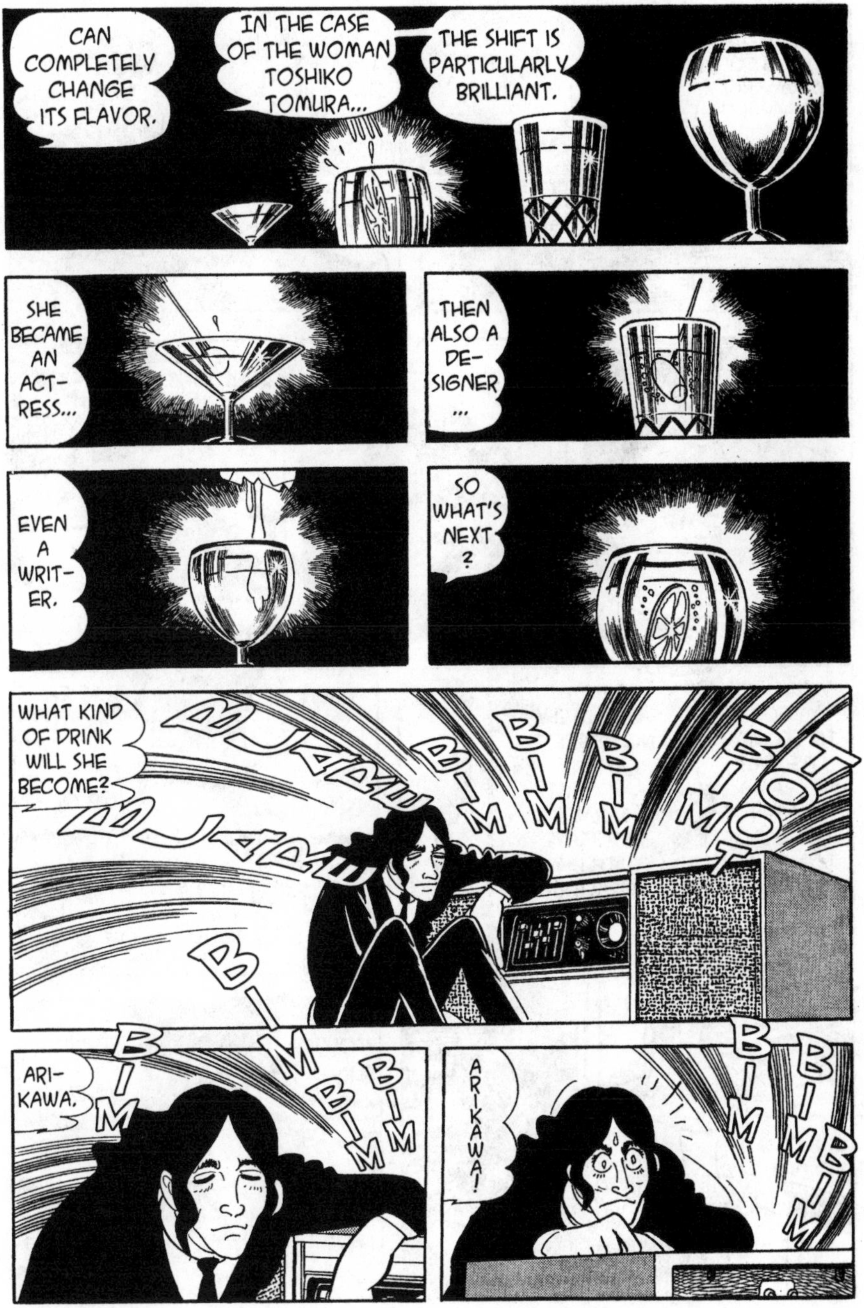
CAN COMPLETELY CHANGE ITS FLAVOR.
IN THE CASE OF THE WOMAN TOSHIKO TOMURA...
THE SHIFT IS PARTICULARLY BRILLIANT.
SHE BECAME AN ACT-RESS...
THEN ALSO A DE-SIGNER ...
EVEN A WRIT-ER.
SO WHAT'S NEXT?
WHAT KIND OF DRINK WILL SHE BECOME?
BIM
BIM
BIM
BIM
TOOT
BIM
ARI-KAWA.
BIM
BIM
BIM
ARIKAWA!
BIM
BIM

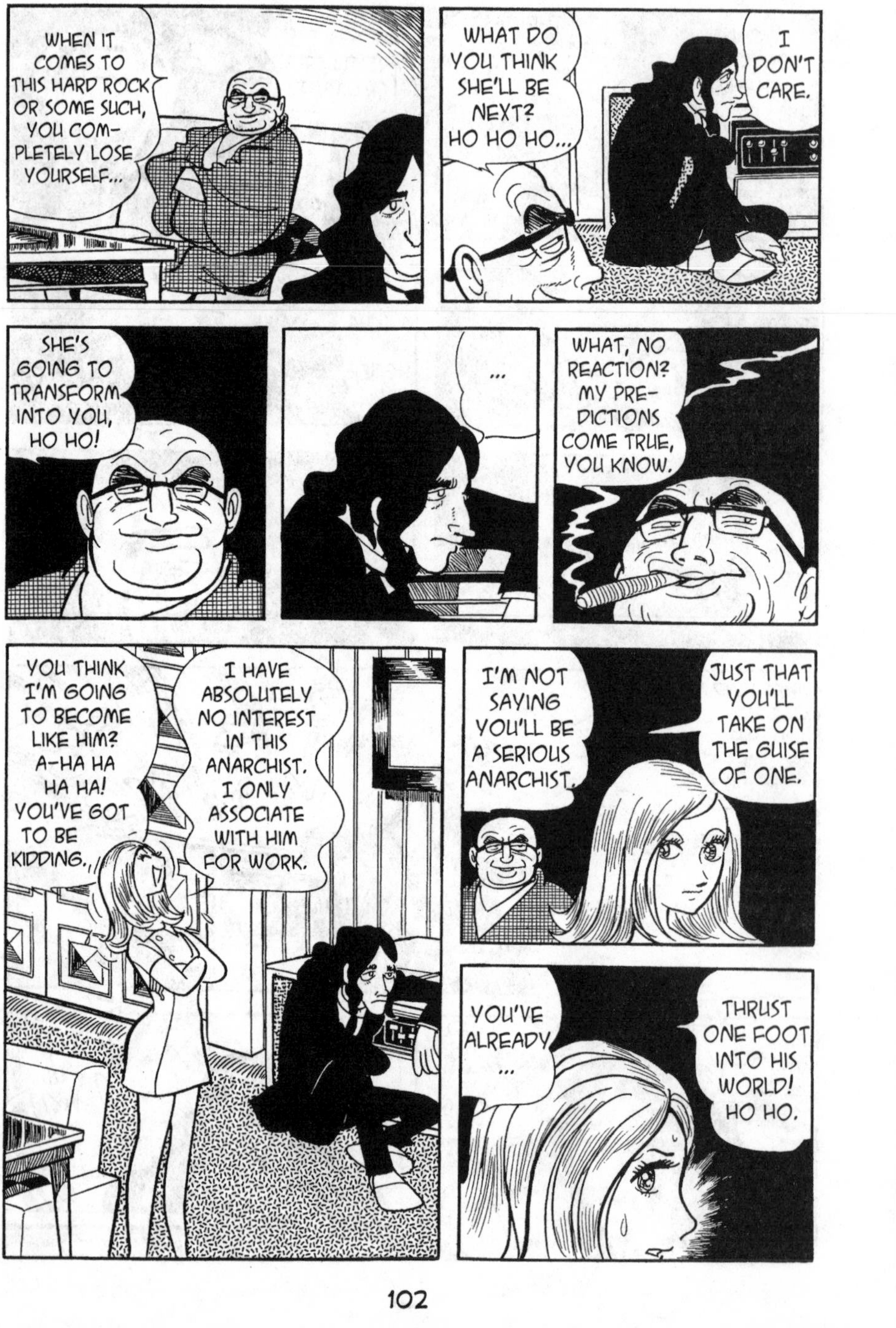

WHEN IT COMES TO THIS HARD ROCK OR SOME SUCH, YOU COMPLETELY LOSE YOURSELF...
WHAT DO YOU THINK SHE'LL BE NEXT? HO HO HO...
I DON'T CARE.
SHE'S GOING TO TRANSFORM INTO YOU, HO HO!
...
WHAT, NO REACTION? MY PREDICTIONS COME TRUE, YOU KNOW.
YOU THINK I'M GOING TO BECOME LIKE HIM? A-HA HA HA HA! YOU'VE GOT TO BE KIDDING...
I HAVE ABSOLUTELY NO INTEREST IN THIS ANARCHIST. I ONLY ASSOCIATE WITH HIM FOR WORK.
I'M NOT SAYING YOU'LL BE A SERIOUS ANARCHIST.
JUST THAT YOU'LL TAKE ON THE GUISE OF ONE.
YOU'VE ALREADY...
THRUST ONE FOOT INTO HIS WORLD! HO HO.

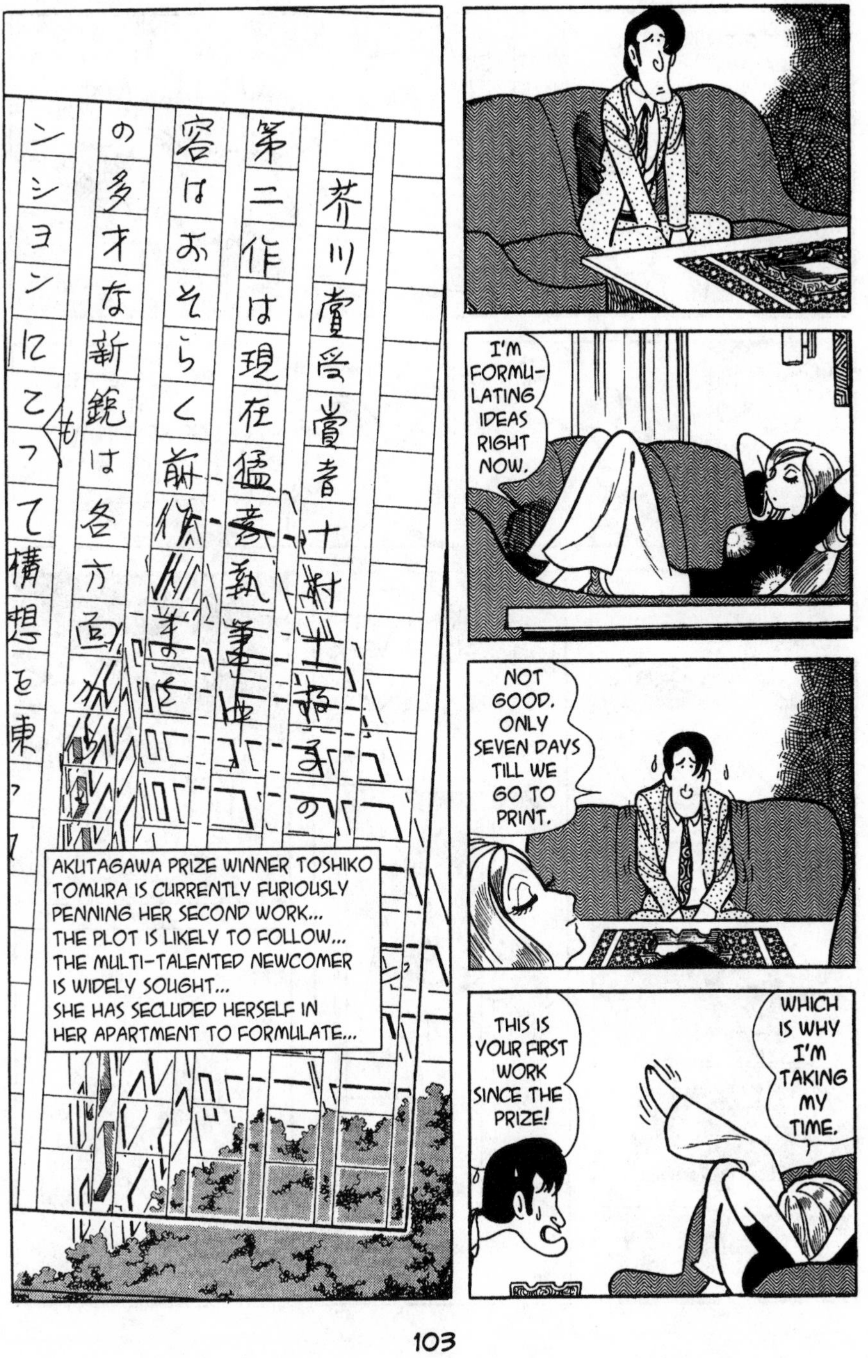
AKUTAGAWA PRIZE WINNER TOSHIKO TOMURA IS CURRENTLY FURIOUSLY PENNING HER SECOND WORK... THE PLOT IS LIKELY TO FOLLOW... THE MULTI-TALENTED NEWCOMER IS WIDELY SOUGHT... SHE HAS SECLUDED HERSELF IN HER APARTMENT TO FORMULATE...
I'M FORMULATING IDEAS RIGHT NOW.
NOT GOOD. ONLY SEVEN DAYS TILL WE GO TO PRINT.
THIS IS YOUR FIRST WORK SINCE THE PRIZE!
WHICH IS WHY I'M TAKING MY TIME.

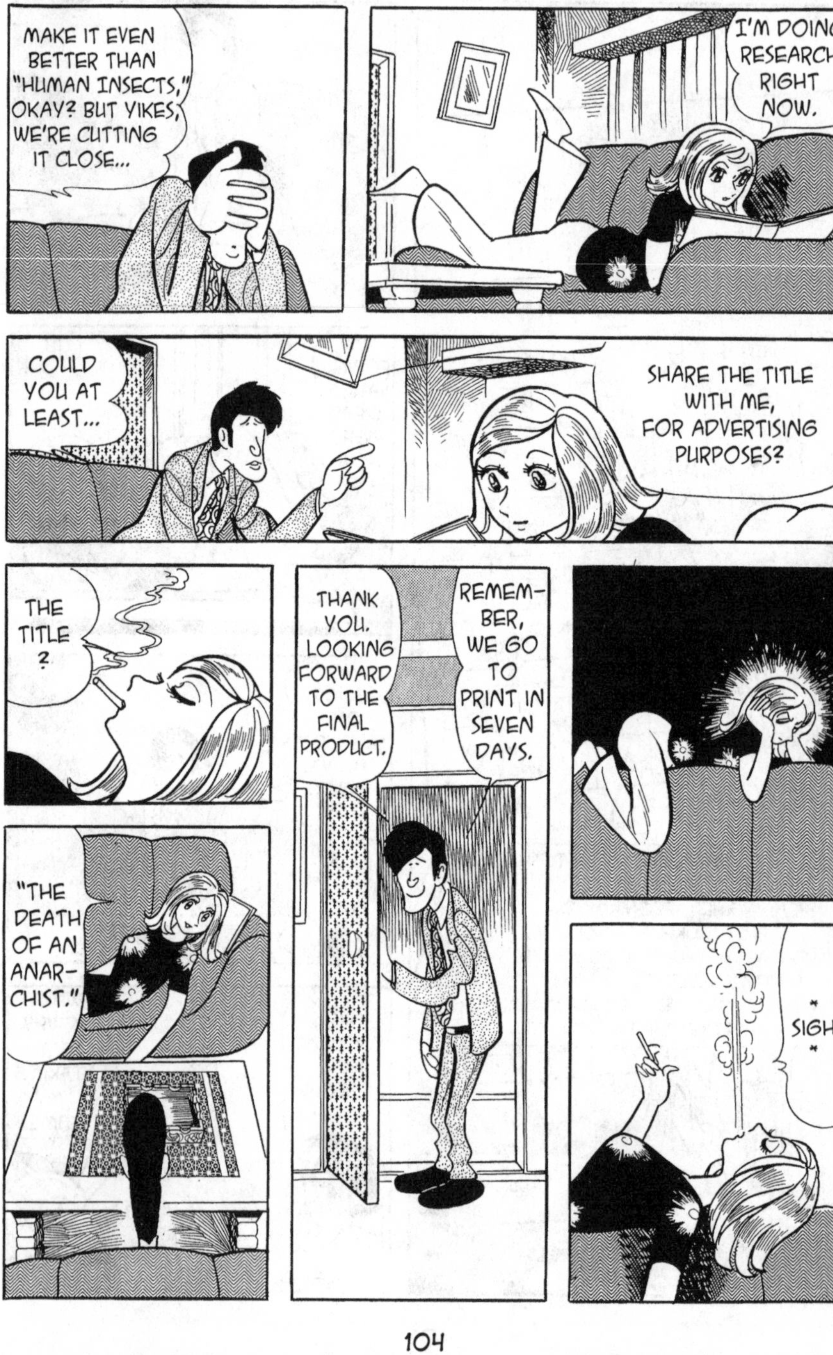
MAKE IT EVEN BETTER THAN "HUMAN INSECTS," OKAY? BUT YIKES, WE'RE CUTTING IT CLOSE...
I'M DOING RESEARCH RIGHT NOW.
COULD YOU AT LEAST...
SHARE THE TITLE WITH ME, FOR ADVERTISING PURPOSES?
THE TITLE?
THANK YOU. LOOKING FORWARD TO THE FINAL PRODUCT.
REMEMBER, WE GO TO PRINT IN SEVEN DAYS.
"THE DEATH OF AN ANARCHIST."
SIGH

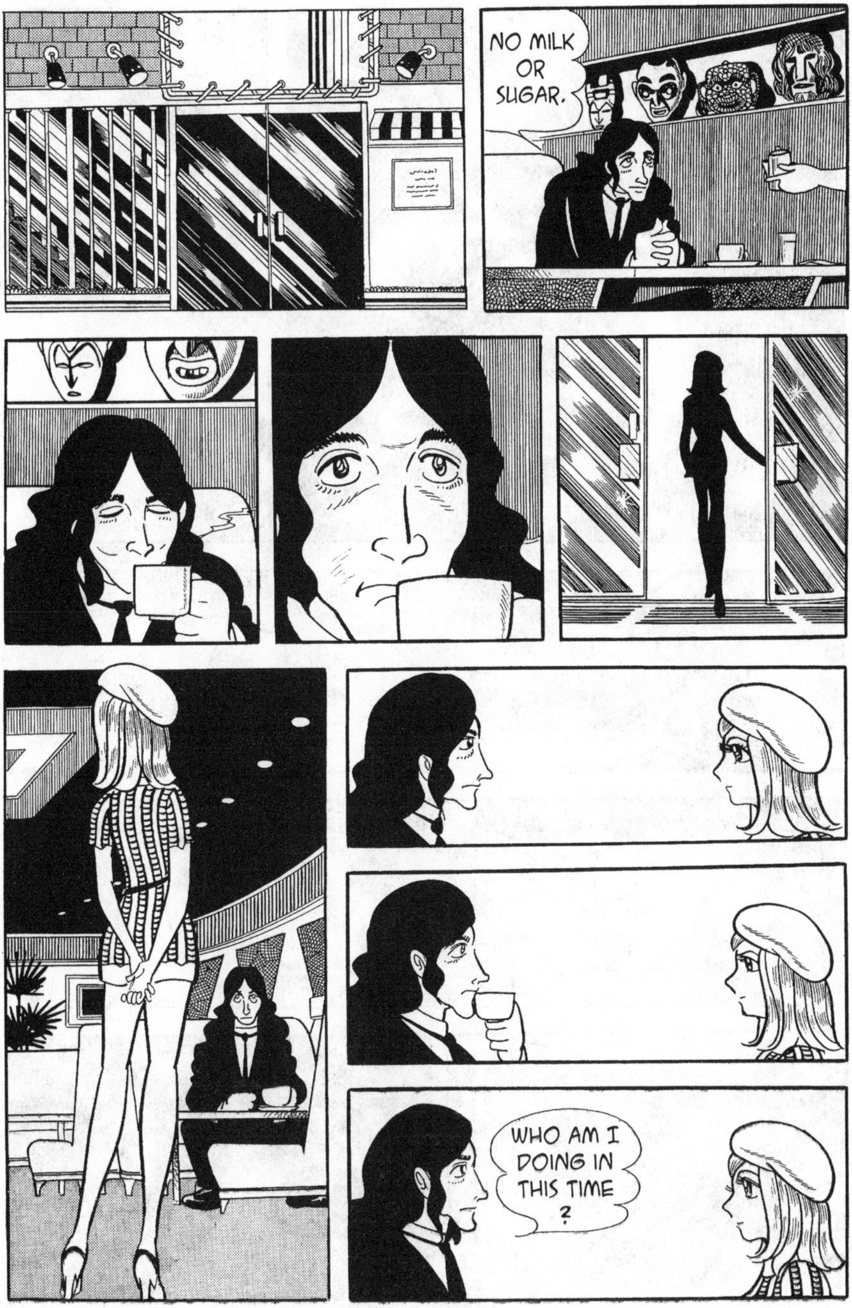
NO MILK OR SUGAR.
WHO AM I DOING IN THIS TIME ?

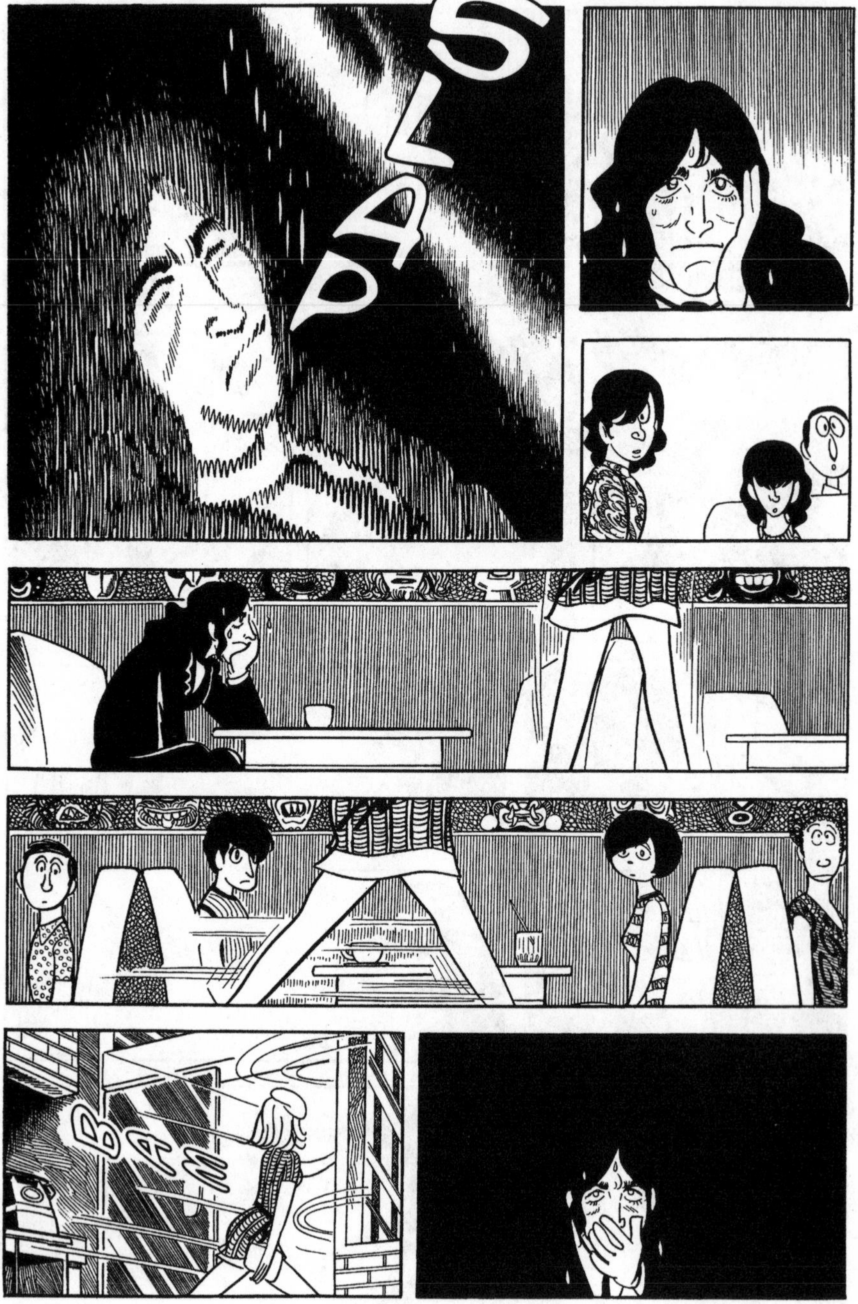
SLAP
BAM

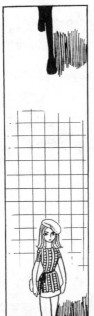

I'VE GOT SOME-THING TO SAY, TOO.

...

UNH!

107

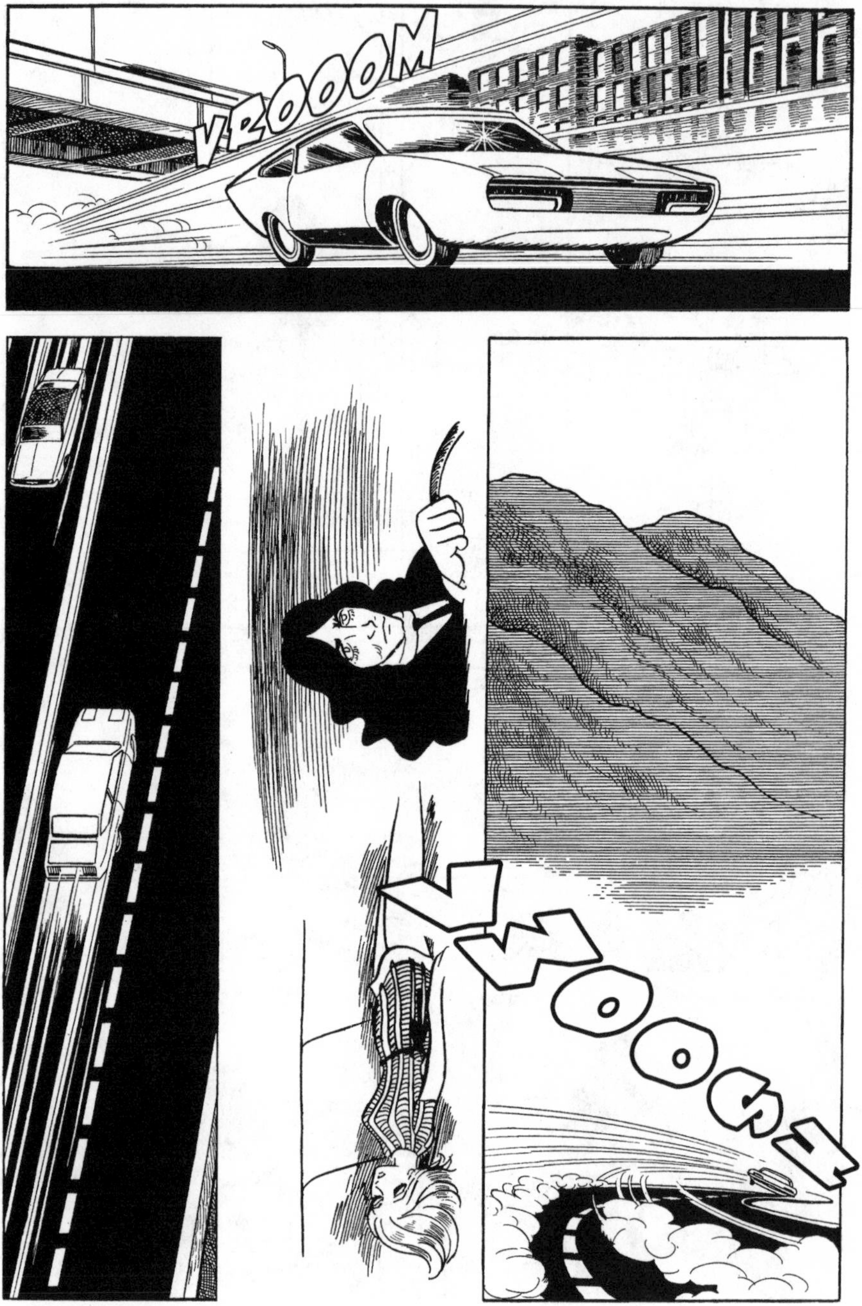
VROOOM

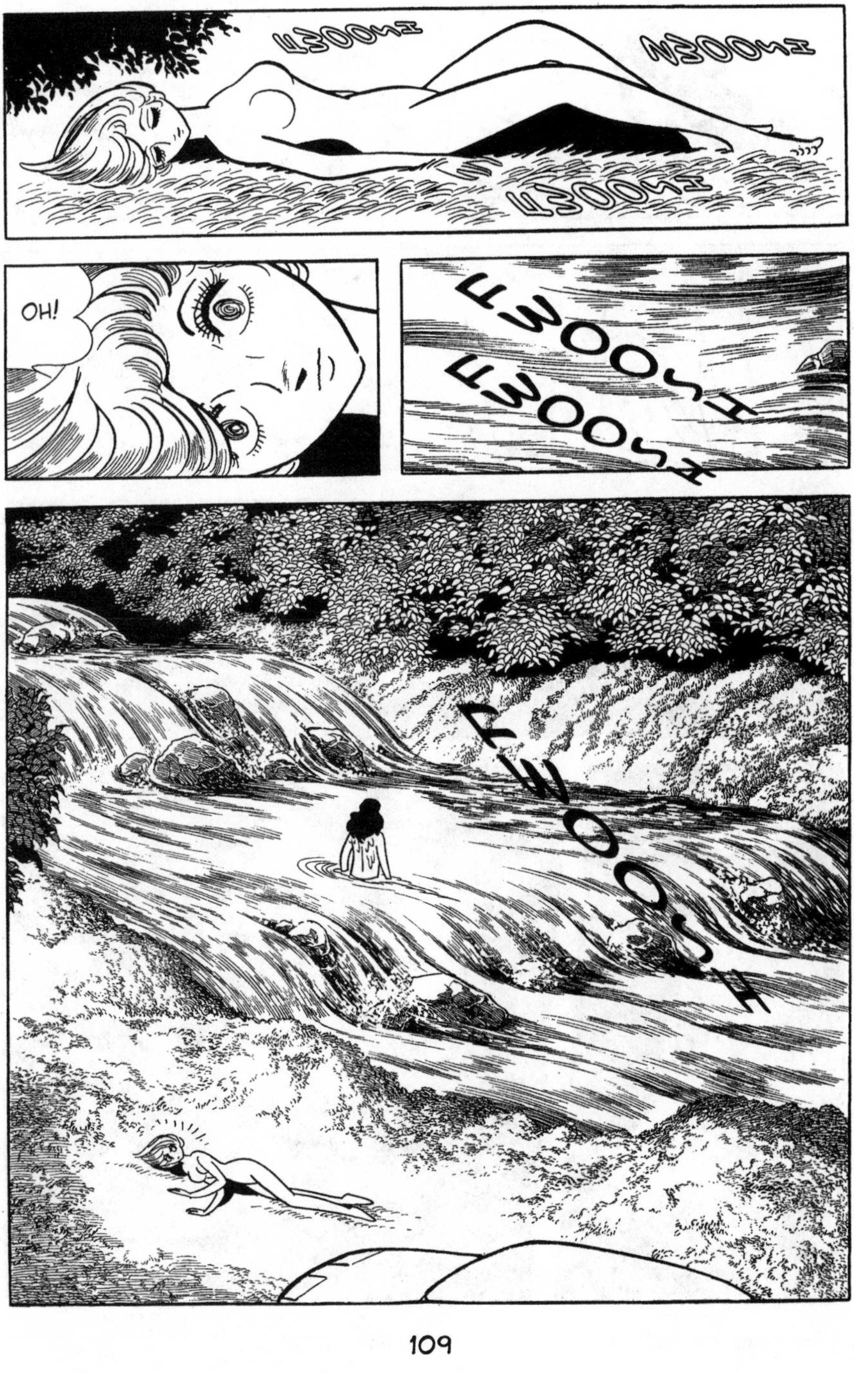
OH!

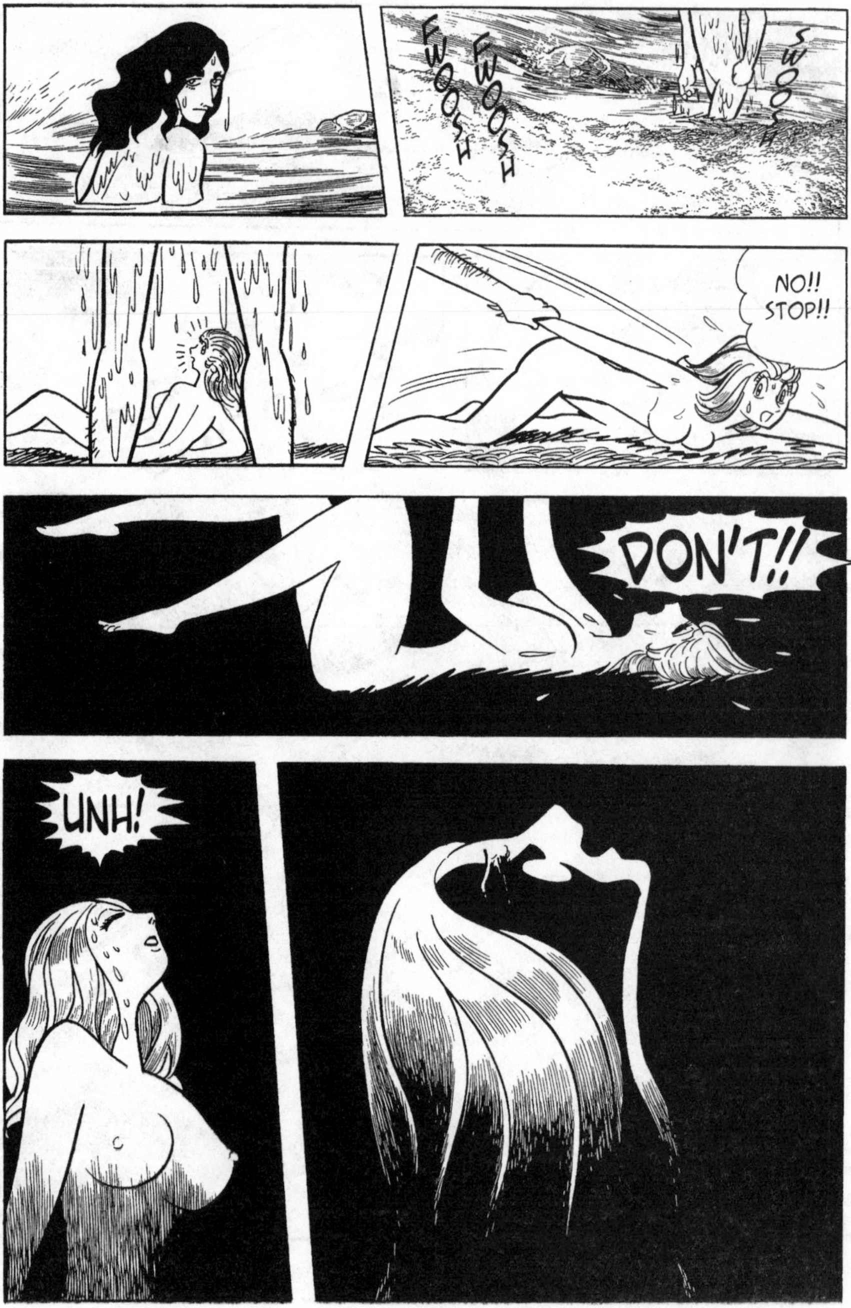
FWOOSH
FWOOSH
SWOOSH
NO!! STOP!!
DON'T!!
UNH!

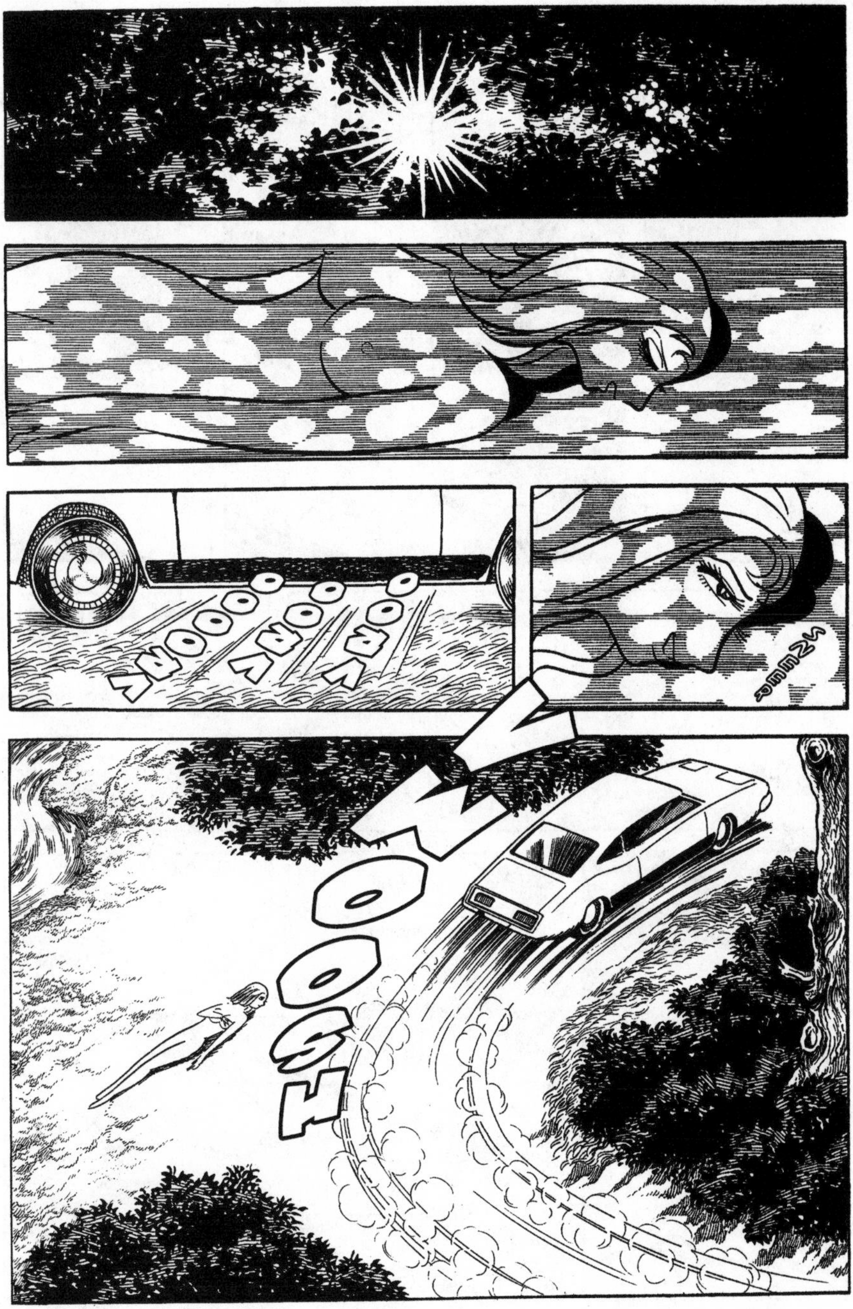
VROOOO
VROO
VROO
SNEER
WOOSH

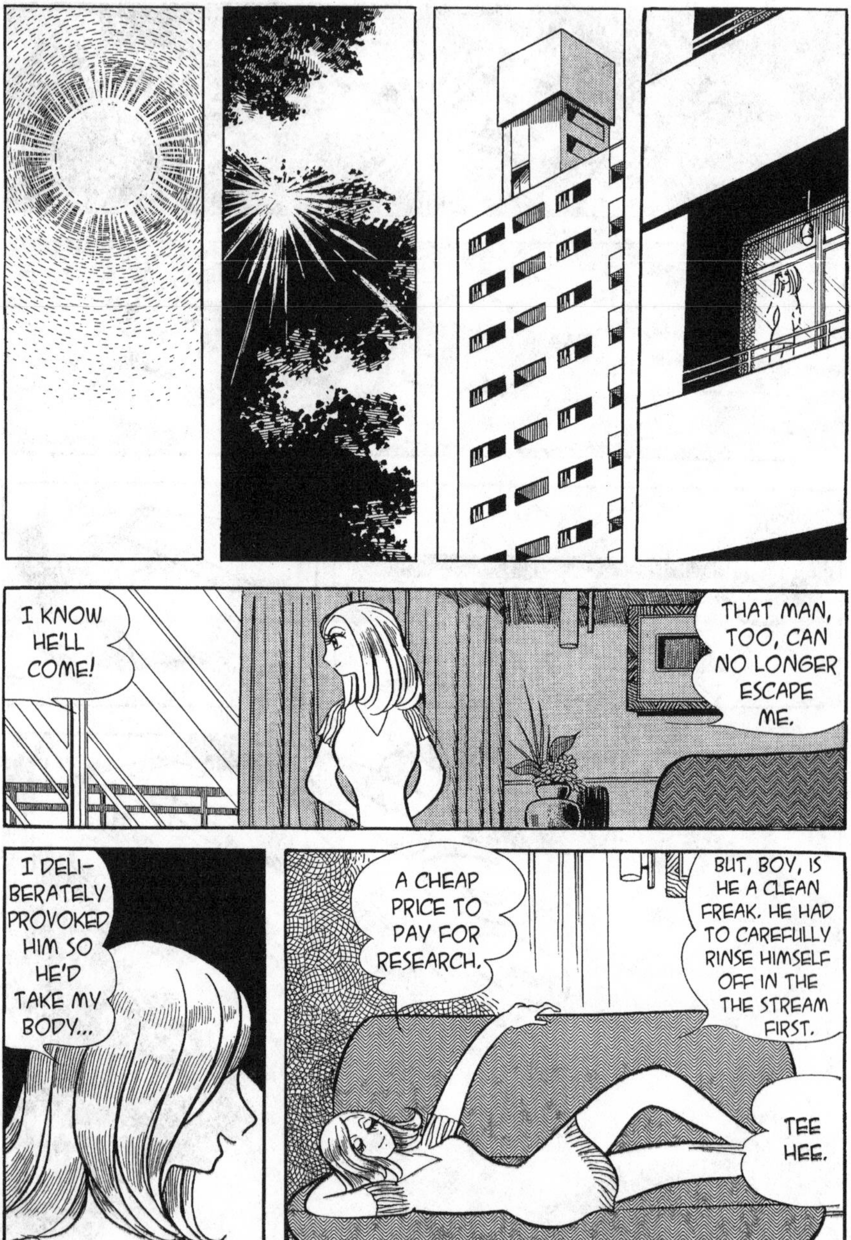

I KNOW HE'LL COME!
THAT MAN, TOO, CAN NO LONGER ESCAPE ME.
I DELI-BERATELY PROVOKED HIM SO HE'D TAKE MY BODY...
A CHEAP PRICE TO PAY FOR RESEARCH.
BUT, BOY, IS HE A CLEAN FREAK. HE HAD TO CAREFULLY RINSE HIMSELF OFF IN THE THE STREAM FIRST.
TEE HEE.

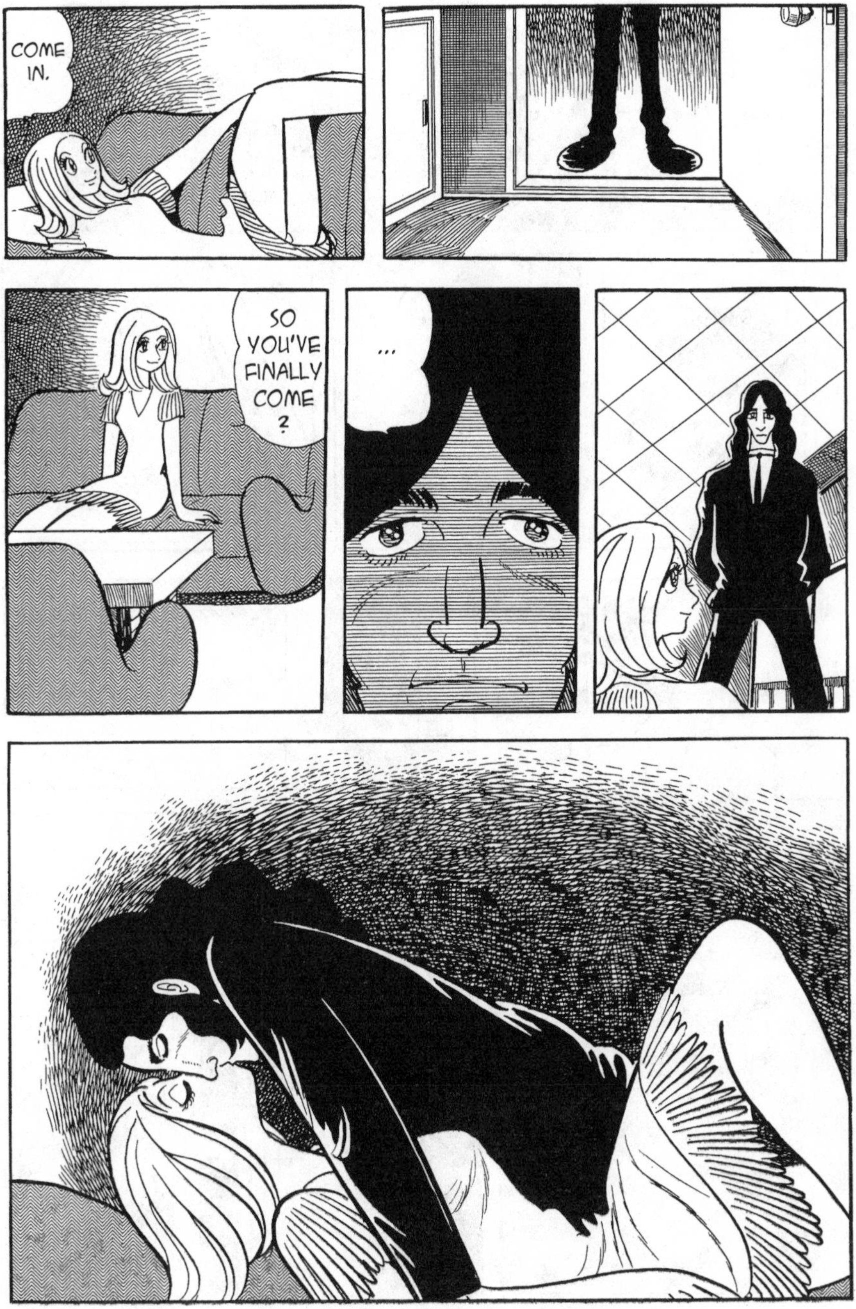
COME IN.
SO YOU'VE FINALLY COME?
...

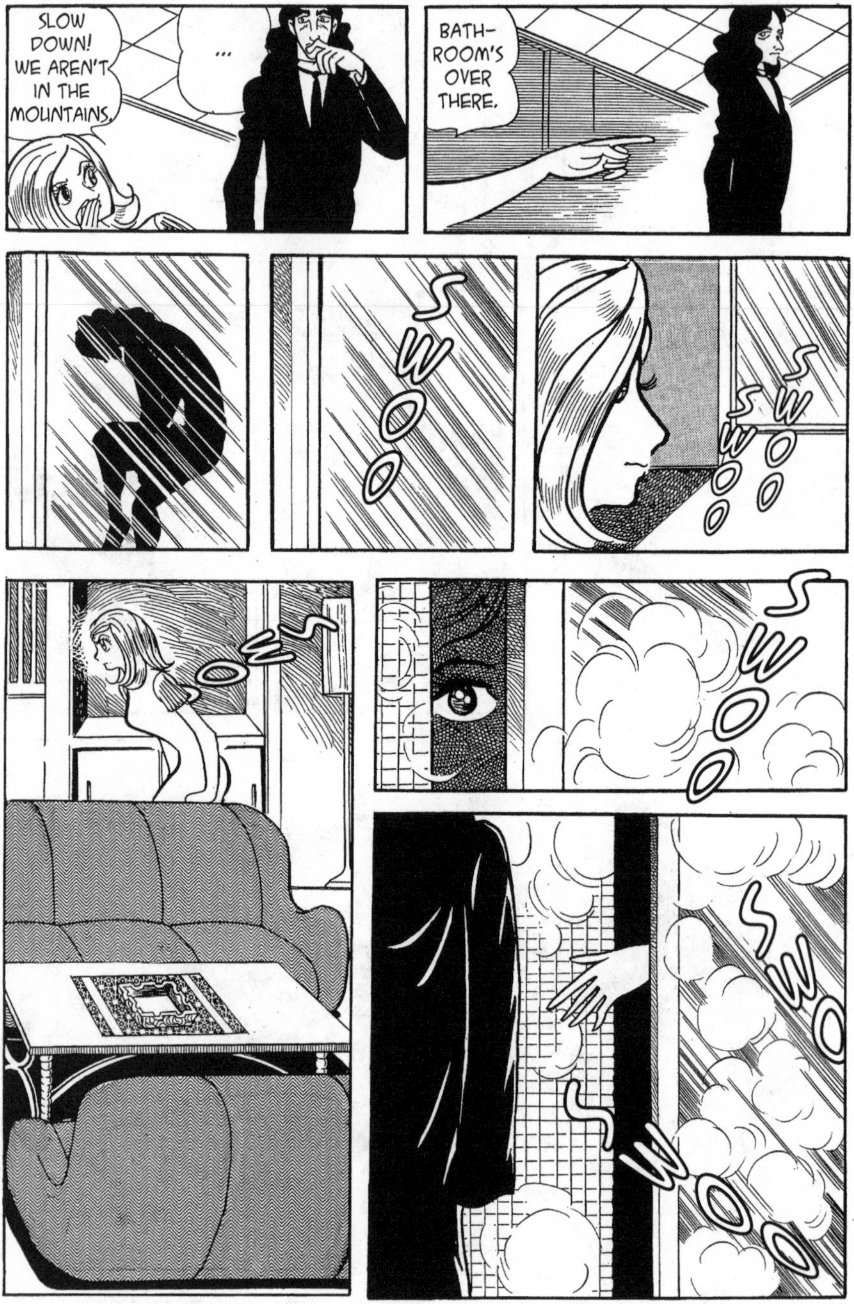
SLOW DOWN! WE AREN'T IN THE MOUNTAINS.
...
BATH-ROOM'S OVER THERE.
SWOOO
SWOOO
SWOOO
SWOO
SWOOO
SWOOO
SWOOO

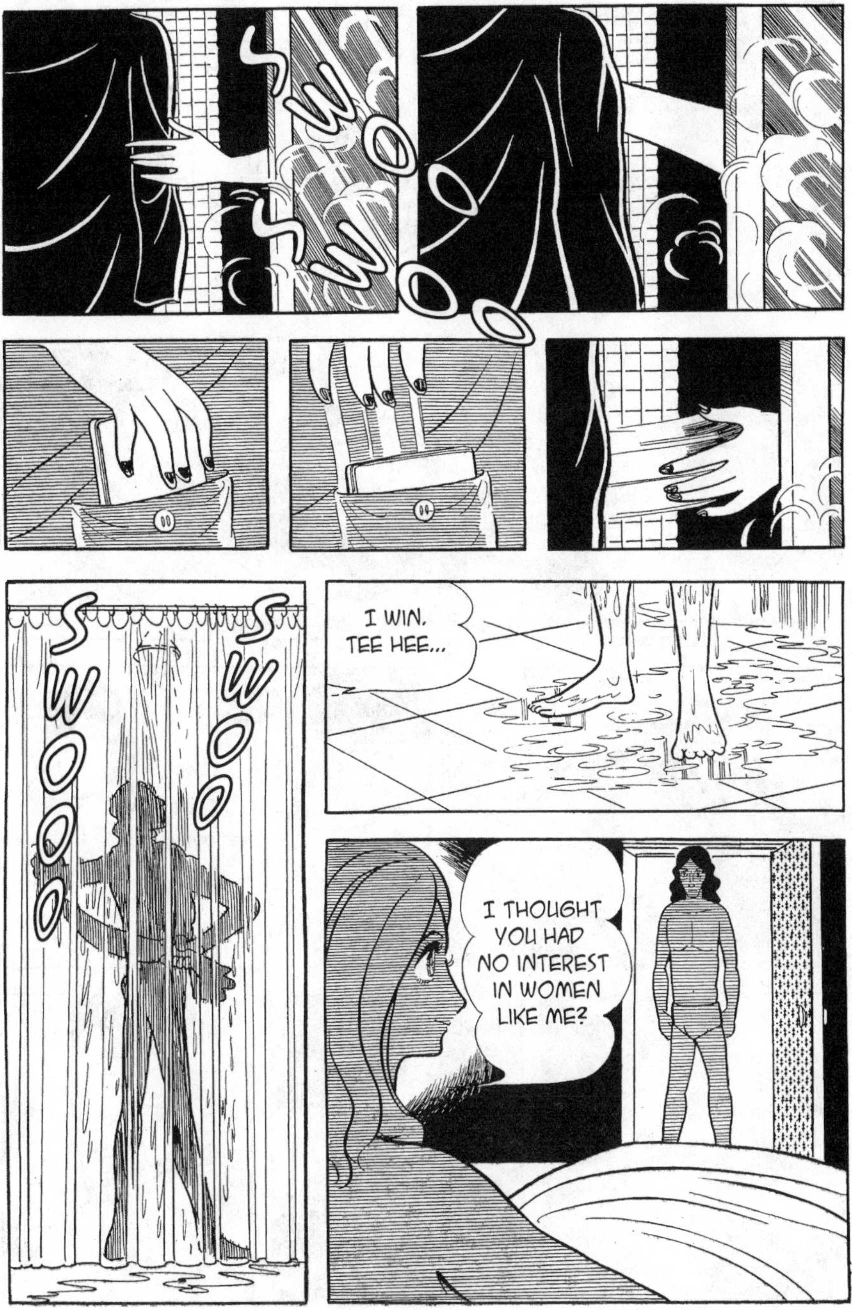
SWOOO
SWOOO
SWOOO
SWOOO
I WIN. TEE HEE...
I THOUGHT YOU HAD NO INTEREST IN WOMEN LIKE ME?

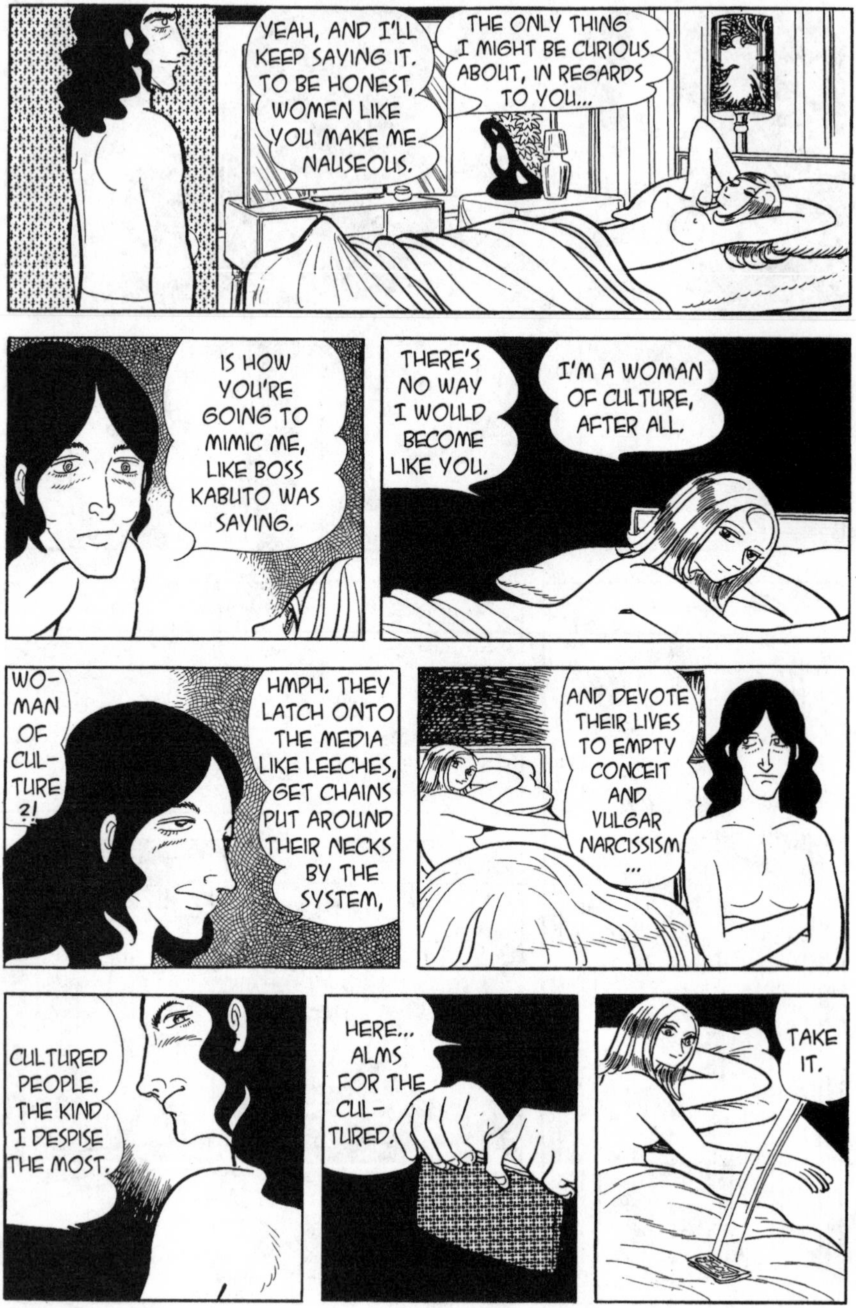
YEAH, AND I'LL KEEP SAYING IT. TO BE HONEST, WOMEN LIKE YOU MAKE ME NAUSEOUS.
THE ONLY THING I MIGHT BE CURIOUS ABOUT, IN REGARDS TO YOU...
IS HOW YOU'RE GOING TO MIMIC ME, LIKE BOSS KABUTO WAS SAYING.
THERE'S NO WAY I WOULD BECOME LIKE YOU.
I'M A WOMAN OF CULTURE, AFTER ALL.
WO-MAN OF CUL-TURE?!
HMPH. THEY LATCH ONTO THE MEDIA LIKE LEECHES, GET CHAINS PUT AROUND THEIR NECKS BY THE SYSTEM,
AND DEVOTE THEIR LIVES TO EMPTY CONCEIT AND VULGAR NARCISSISM...
CULTURED PEOPLE. THE KIND I DESPISE THE MOST.
HERE... ALMS FOR THE CUL-TURED.
TAKE IT.

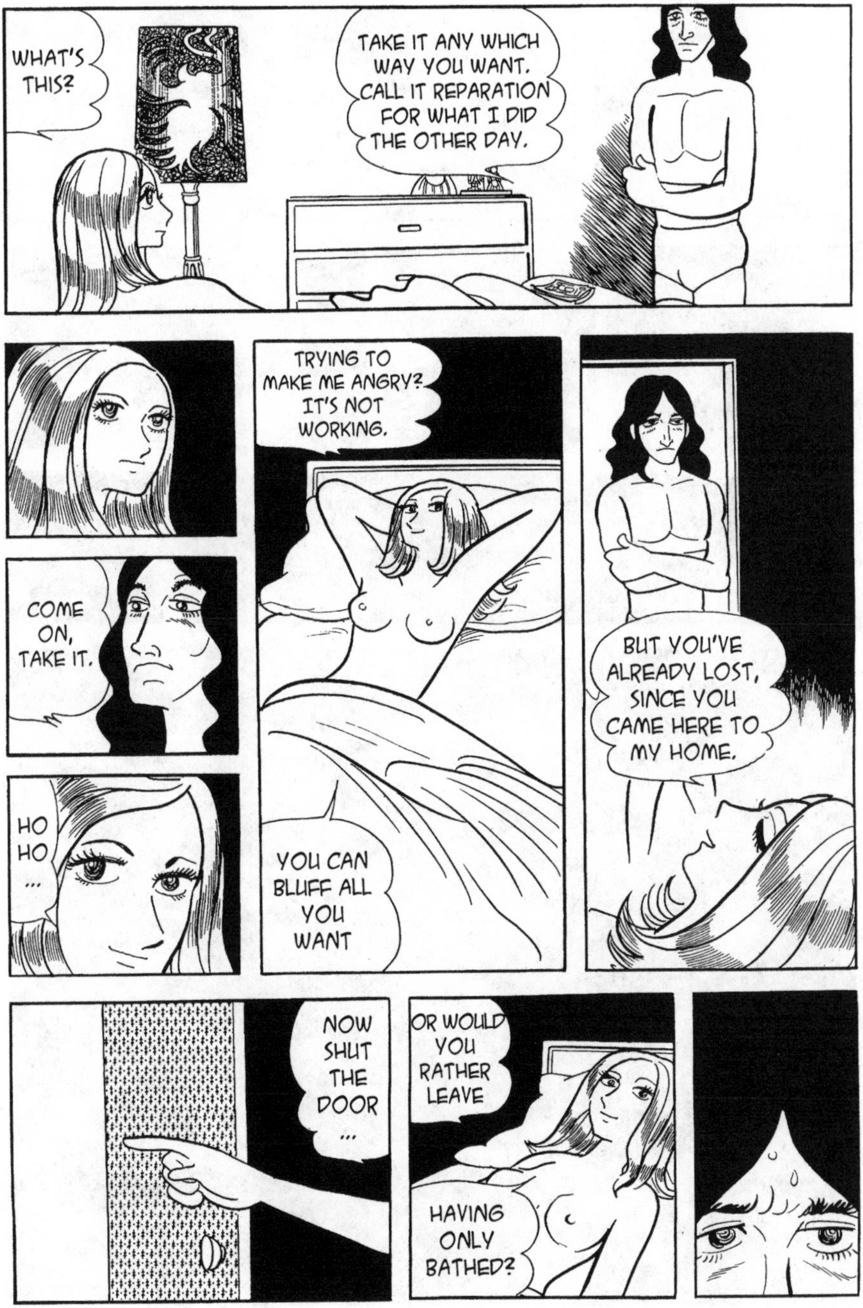
WHAT'S THIS?
TAKE IT ANY WHICH WAY YOU WANT. CALL IT REPARATION FOR WHAT I DID THE OTHER DAY.
COME ON, TAKE IT.
HO HO ...
TRYING TO MAKE ME ANGRY? IT'S NOT WORKING.
YOU CAN BLUFF ALL YOU WANT
BUT YOU'VE ALREADY LOST, SINCE YOU CAME HERE TO MY HOME.
NOW SHUT THE DOOR ...
OR WOULD YOU RATHER LEAVE
HAVING ONLY BATHED?

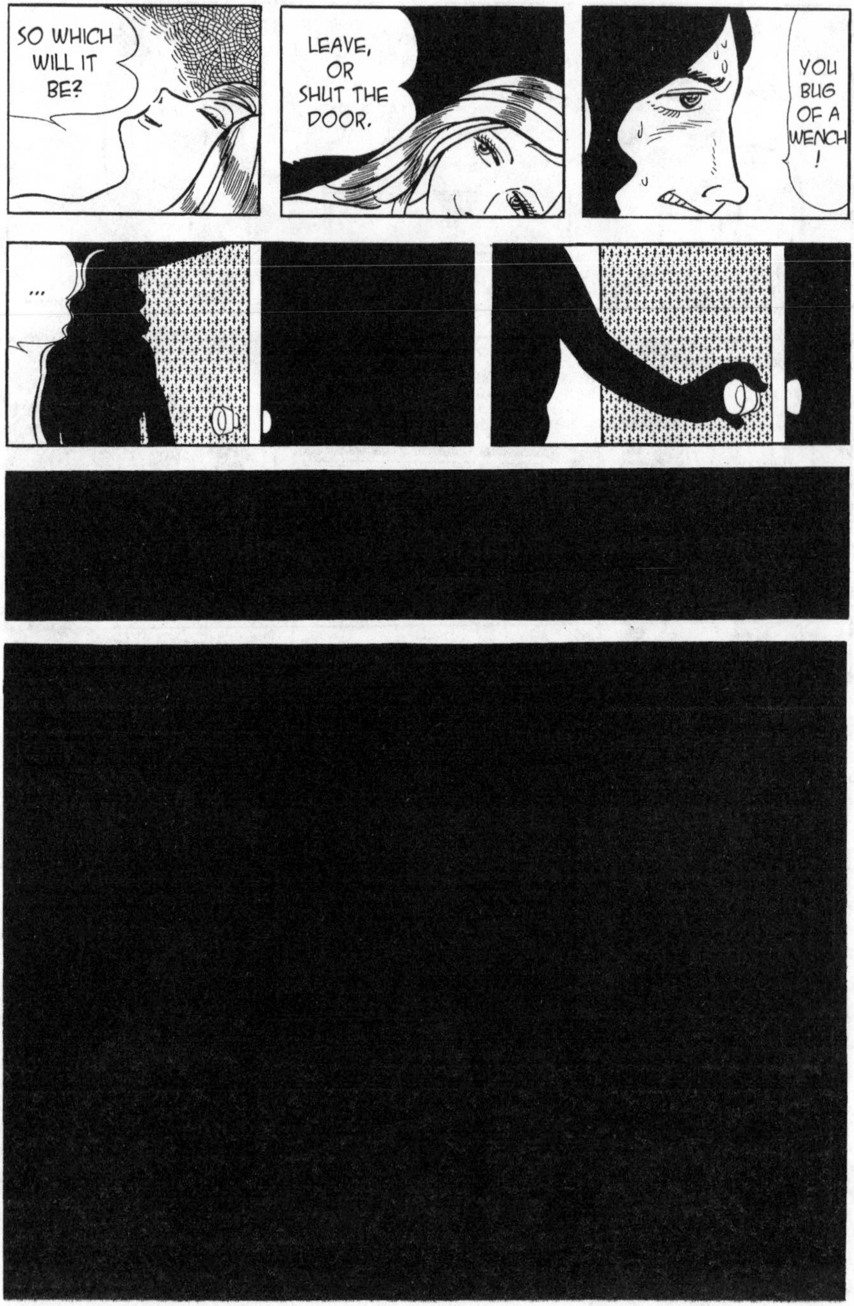
SO WHICH WILL IT BE?
LEAVE, OR SHUT THE DOOR.
YOU BUG OF A WENCH!
...

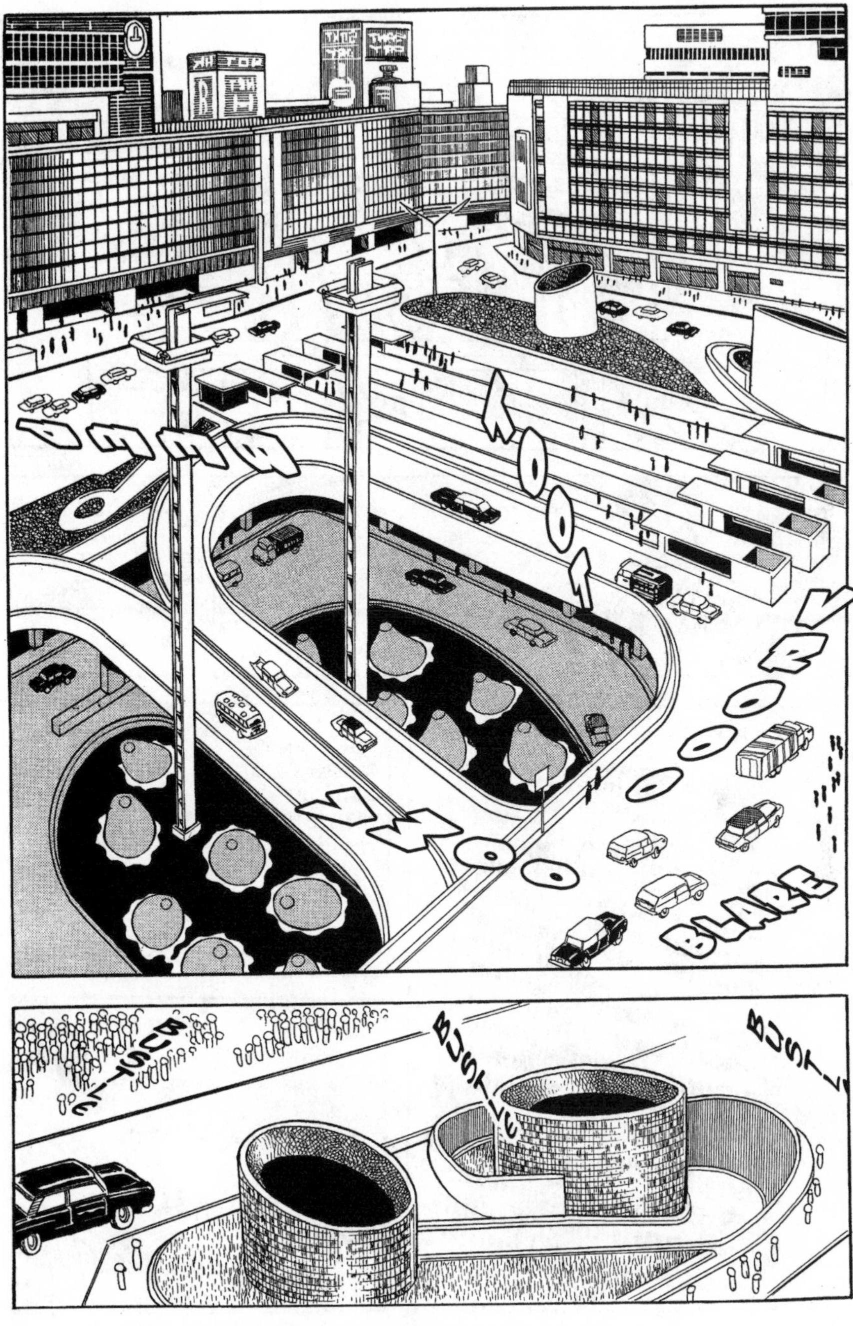
BLARE
BUSTLE
BUSTLE
BUSTLE

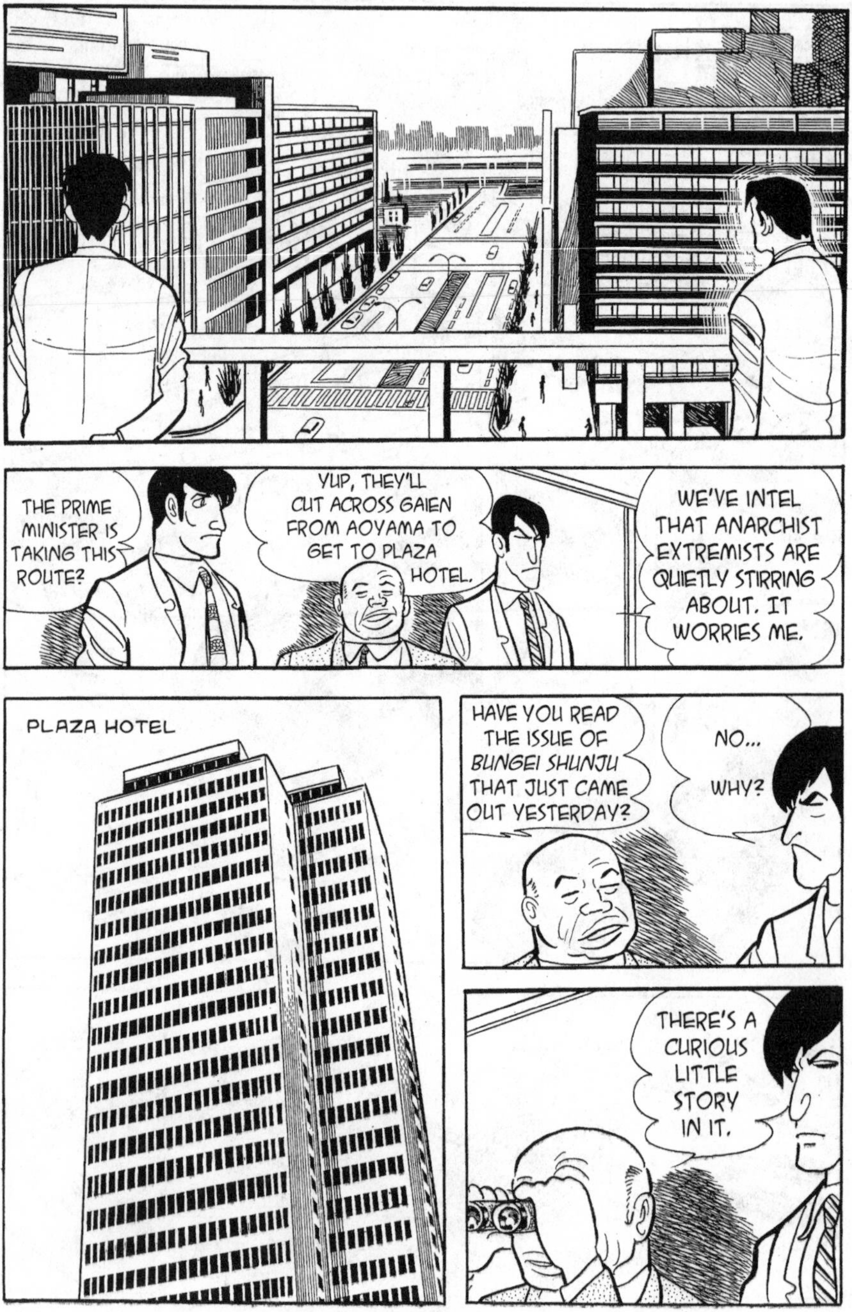
THE PRIME MINISTER IS TAKING THIS ROUTE?
YUP, THEY'LL CUT ACROSS GAIEN FROM AOYAMA TO GET TO PLAZA HOTEL.
WE'VE INTEL THAT ANARCHIST EXTREMISTS ARE QUIETLY STIRRING ABOUT. IT WORRIES ME.
PLAZA HOTEL
HAVE YOU READ THE ISSUE OF *BUNGEI SHUNJU* THAT JUST CAME OUT YESTERDAY?
NO... WHY?
THERE'S A CURIOUS LITTLE STORY IN IT.

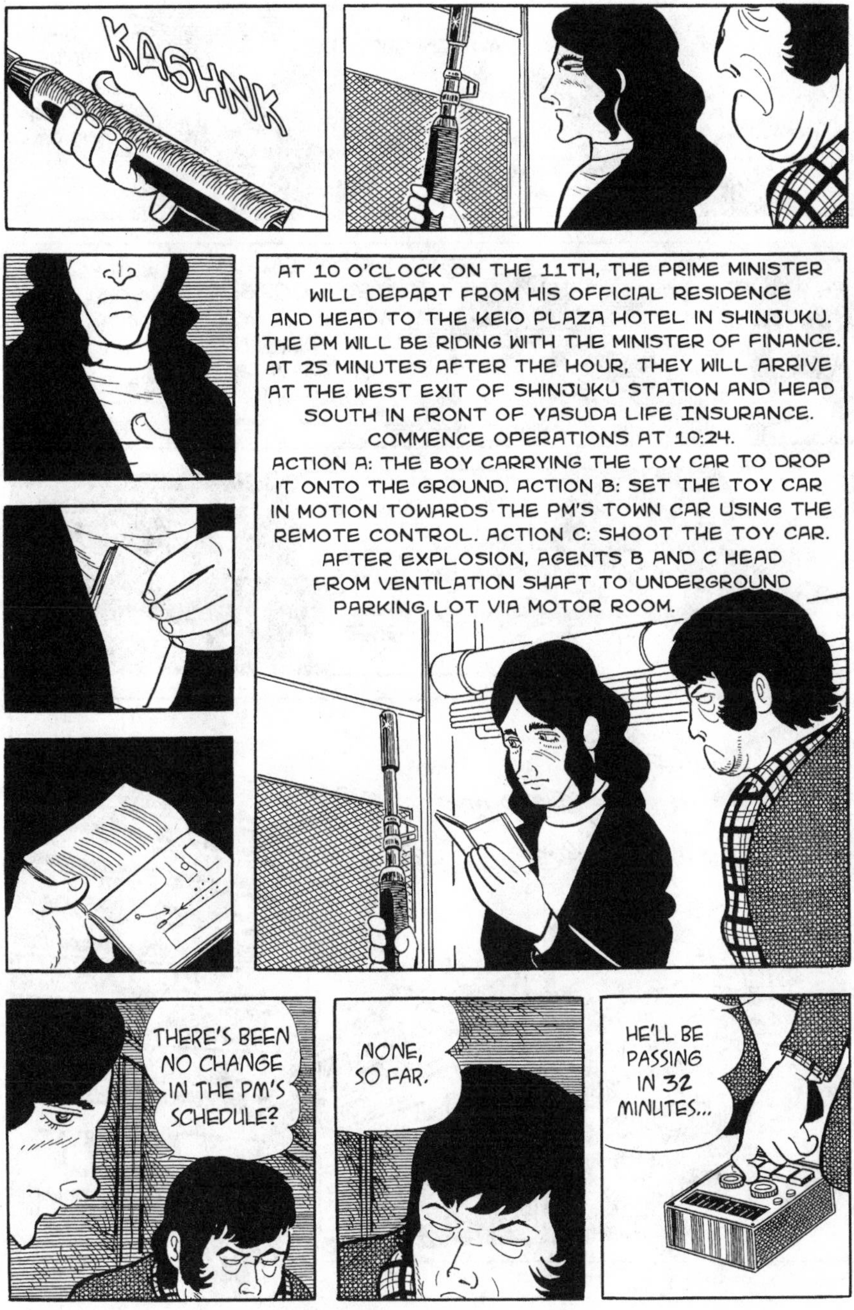
KASHNK
AT 10 O'CLOCK ON THE 11TH, THE PRIME MINISTER WILL DEPART FROM HIS OFFICIAL RESIDENCE AND HEAD TO THE KEIO PLAZA HOTEL IN SHINJUKU. THE PM WILL BE RIDING WITH THE MINISTER OF FINANCE. AT 25 MINUTES AFTER THE HOUR, THEY WILL ARRIVE AT THE WEST EXIT OF SHINJUKU STATION AND HEAD SOUTH IN FRONT OF YASUDA LIFE INSURANCE. COMMENCE OPERATIONS AT 10:24. ACTION A: THE BOY CARRYING THE TOY CAR TO DROP IT ONTO THE GROUND. ACTION B: SET THE TOY CAR IN MOTION TOWARDS THE PM'S TOWN CAR USING THE REMOTE CONTROL. ACTION C: SHOOT THE TOY CAR. AFTER EXPLOSION, AGENTS B AND C HEAD FROM VENTILATION SHAFT TO UNDERGROUND PARKING LOT VIA MOTOR ROOM.
THERE'S BEEN NO CHANGE IN THE PM'S SCHEDULE?
NONE, SO FAR.
HE'LL BE PASSING IN 32 MINUTES...

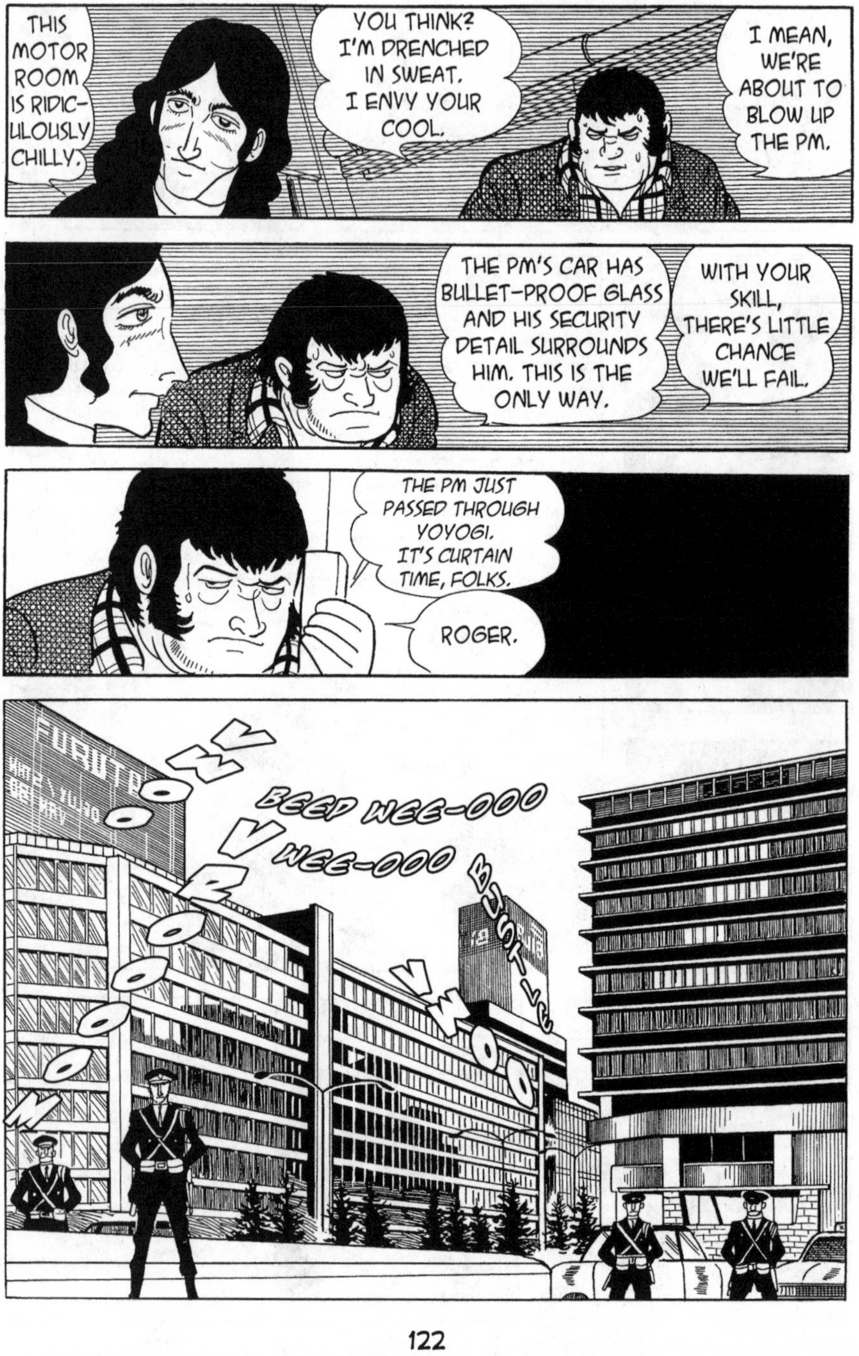
THIS MOTOR ROOM IS RIDICULOUSLY CHILLY.
YOU THINK? I'M DRENCHED IN SWEAT. I ENVY YOUR COOL.
I MEAN, WE'RE ABOUT TO BLOW UP THE PM.
THE PM'S CAR HAS BULLET-PROOF GLASS AND HIS SECURITY DETAIL SURROUNDS HIM. THIS IS THE ONLY WAY.
WITH YOUR SKILL, THERE'S LITTLE CHANCE WE'LL FAIL.
THE PM JUST PASSED THROUGH YOYOGI. IT'S CURTAIN TIME, FOLKS.
ROGER.
BEEP WEE-OOO
WEE-OOO

TIK
TIK
TIK
TIK

HUH? WHAT?

TOSHIKO TOMURA?

TH–THAT'S RIDICULOUS! I DON'T BELIEVE IT!!

WHAT IS IT? LET ME LISTEN.

THERE'S A STORY BY HER IN THE BUNGEI SHUNJU WHICH JUST CAME OUT YESTERDAY TITLED "THE DEATH OF AN ANARCHIST." IT'S ABOUT A PLOT JUST LIKE OUR OWN!

IT'S LIKE SHE'S LOOKED AT SOMEONE'S MEMO. SHE LISTS MINUTE DETAILS OF THE TIMETABLE AND OUR METHODS, AS IF SHE HAD A CARBON COPY!! IT'S ABOUT ASSASSINATING THE PM FROM INSIDE A VENT AT THE WEST EXIT OF SHINJUKU STATION!

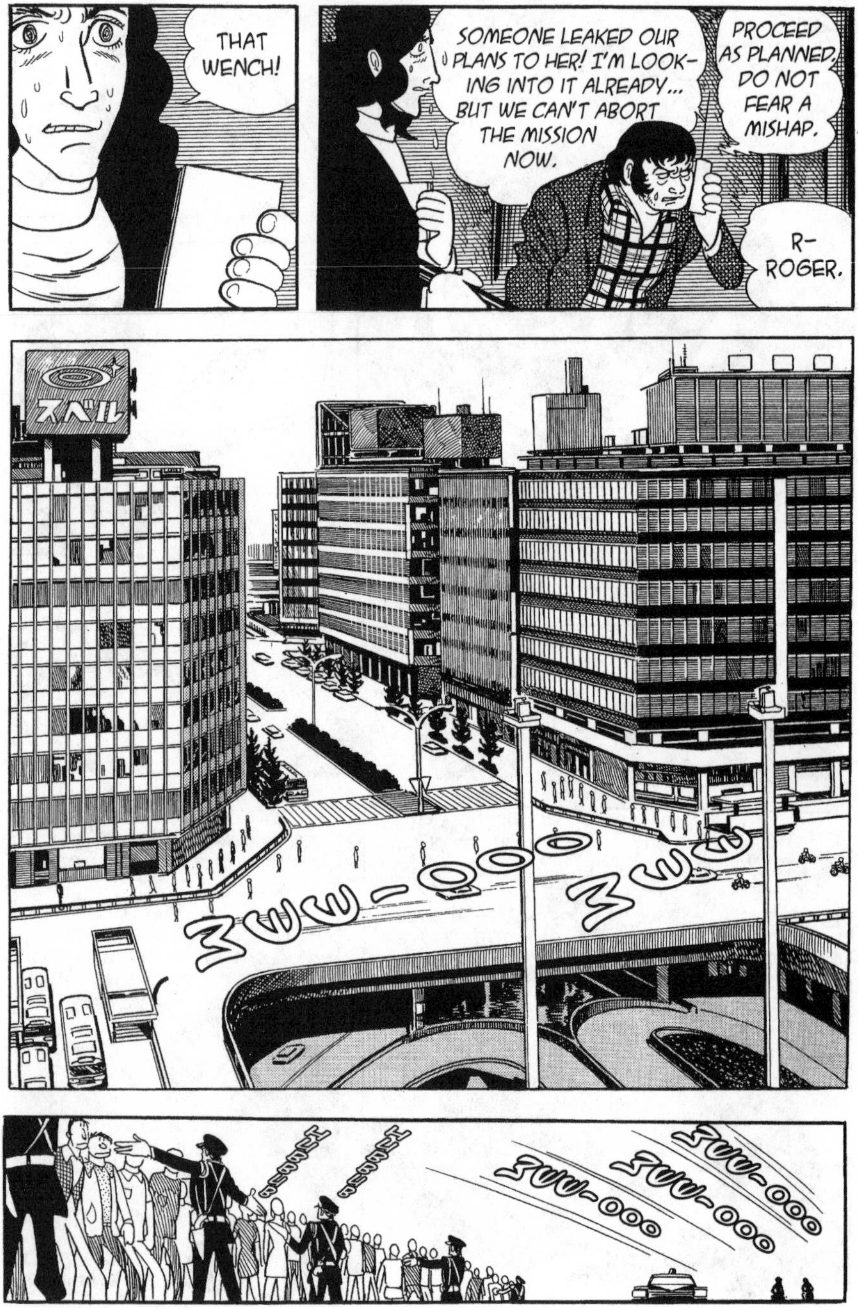
THAT WENCH!
SOMEONE LEAKED OUR PLANS TO HER! I'M LOOKING INTO IT ALREADY... BUT WE CAN'T ABORT THE MISSION NOW.
PROCEED AS PLANNED, DO NOT FEAR A MISHAP.
R-ROGER.
WEE-OOO WEE
HUBBUB
HUBBUB
WEE-OOO
WEE-OOO
WEE-OOO

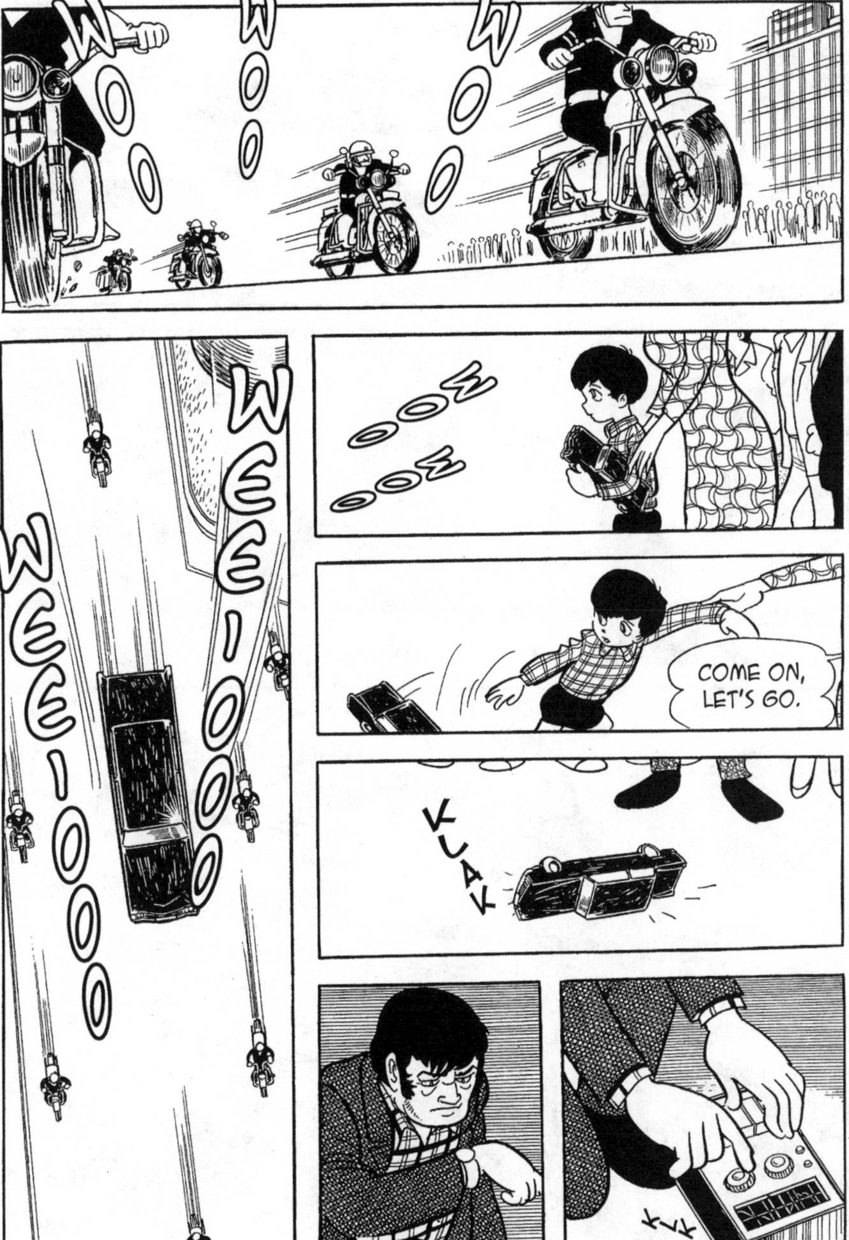
WOO
WOOO
WOOO
WEE-IOOO
WEE-IOOO
WOOO
WOOO
COME ON, LET'S GO.
KLAK
KAK
KAK

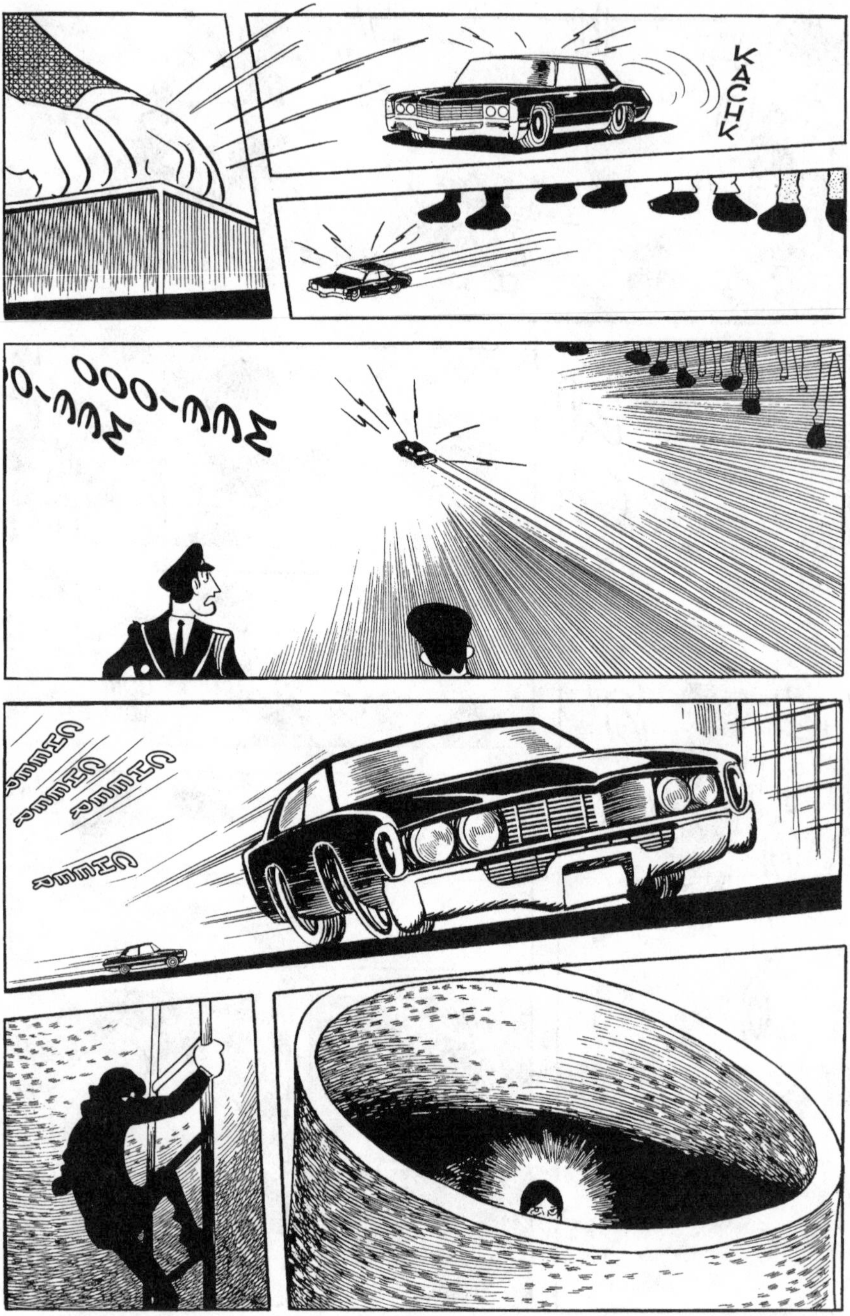
KACHK
WEE-OOO WEE-OO
CHEER CHEER CHEER CHEER

LOOK!

JUST LIKE THAT STORY'S PLOT!

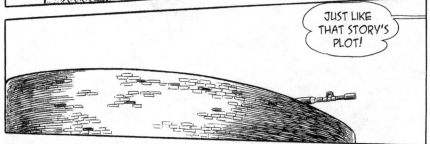

IT'S THAT VENT!

IT'S OUT OF PISTOL RANGE!! GET A RIFLE!

THAT GUN IS AIMING FOR A TOY CAR THAT'S PACKED WITH POWERFUL DYNAMITE!! HURRY!!

VOOSH

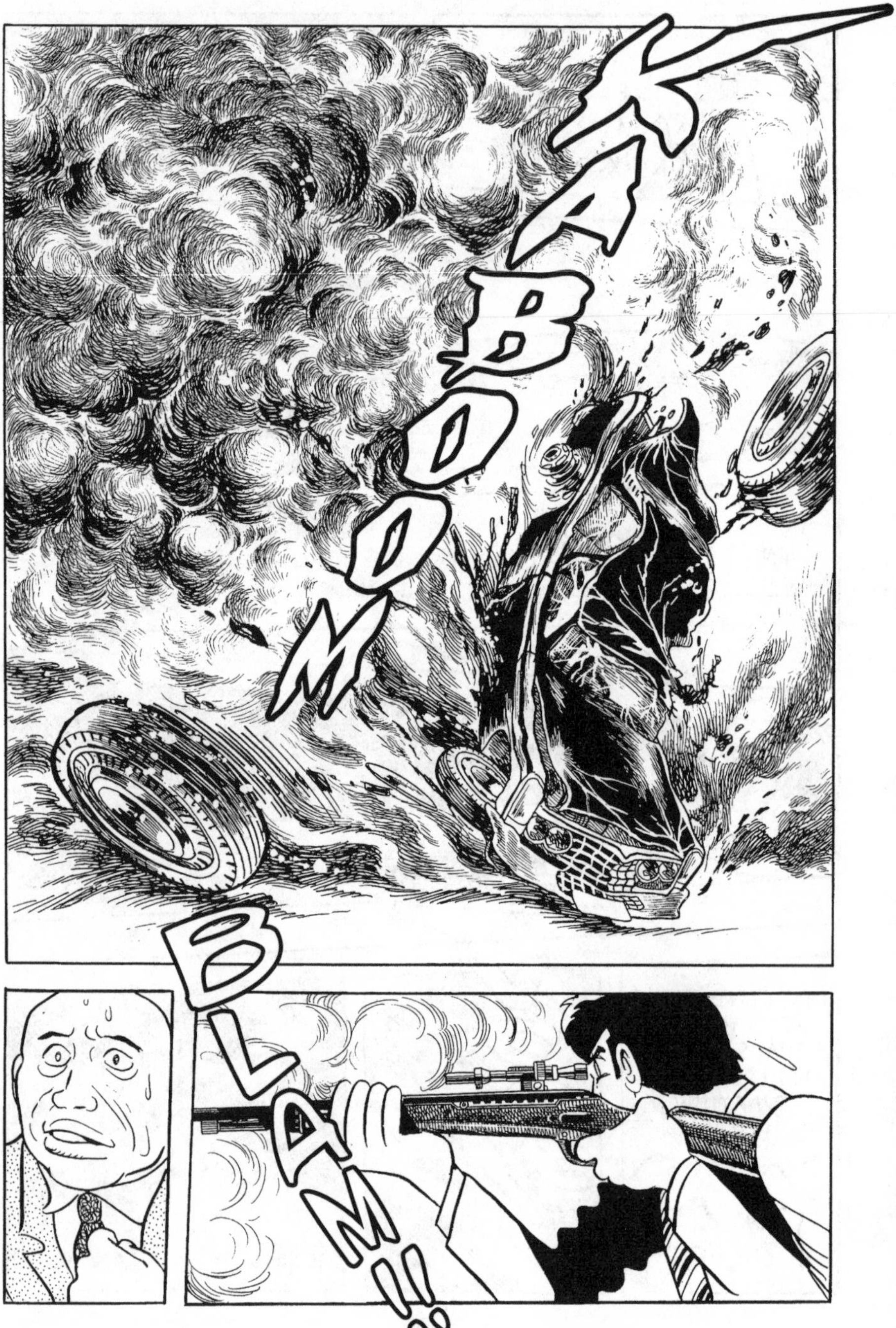
KABOOOM
BLAM!!

CHNNNG
FWEEEET
TMP
LET'S GET OUTTA HERE!

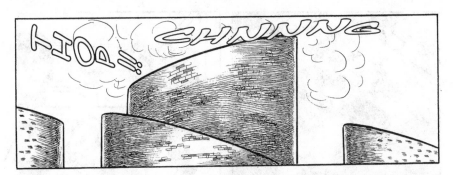

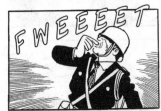

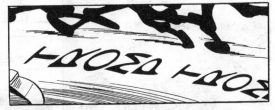

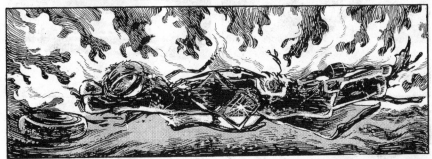

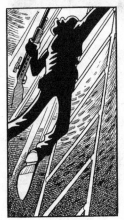

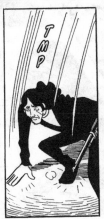

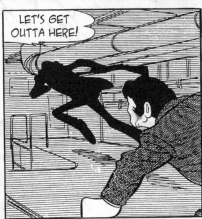

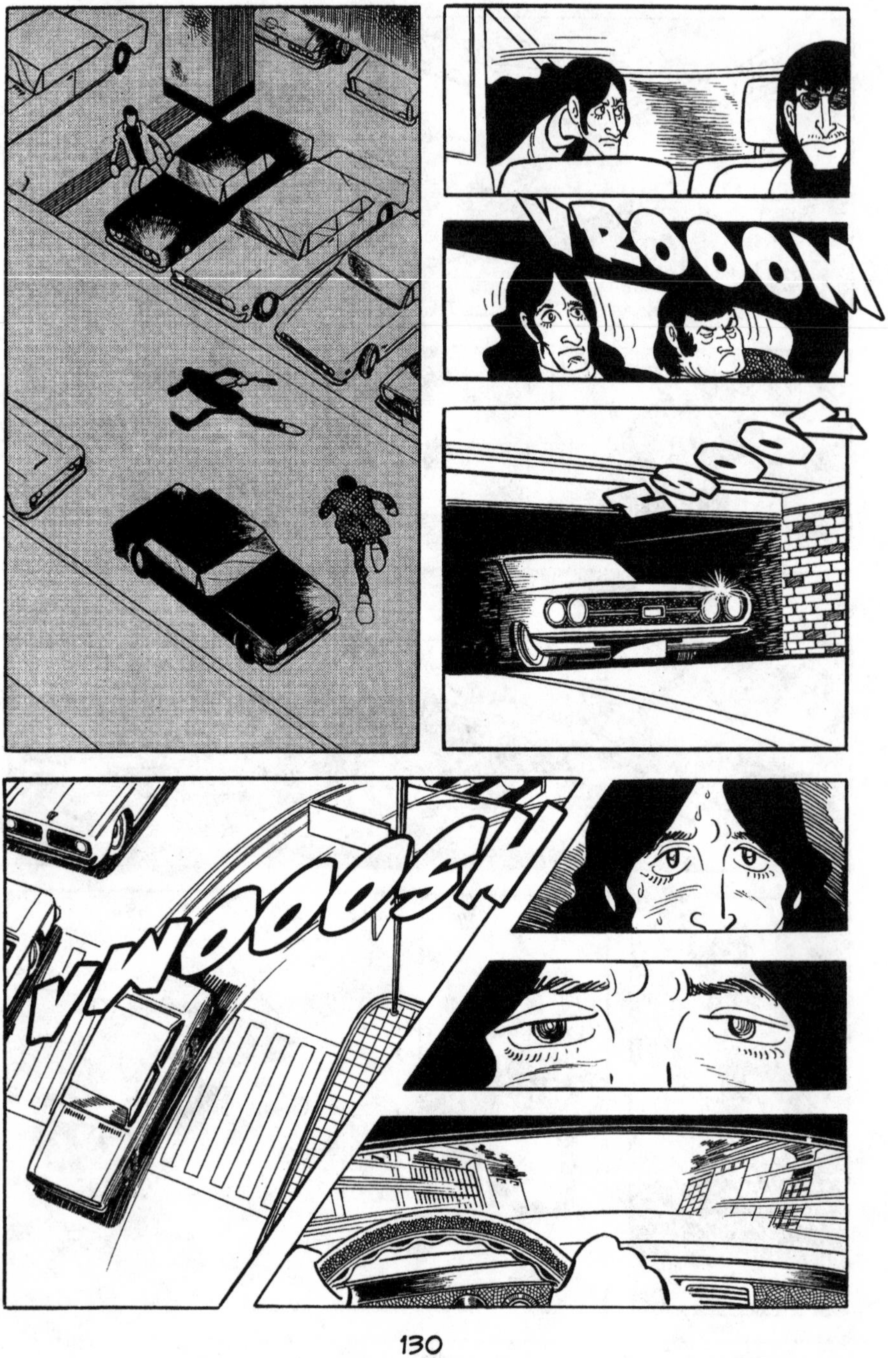
VROOOM
VROOOM
VWOOOOSH

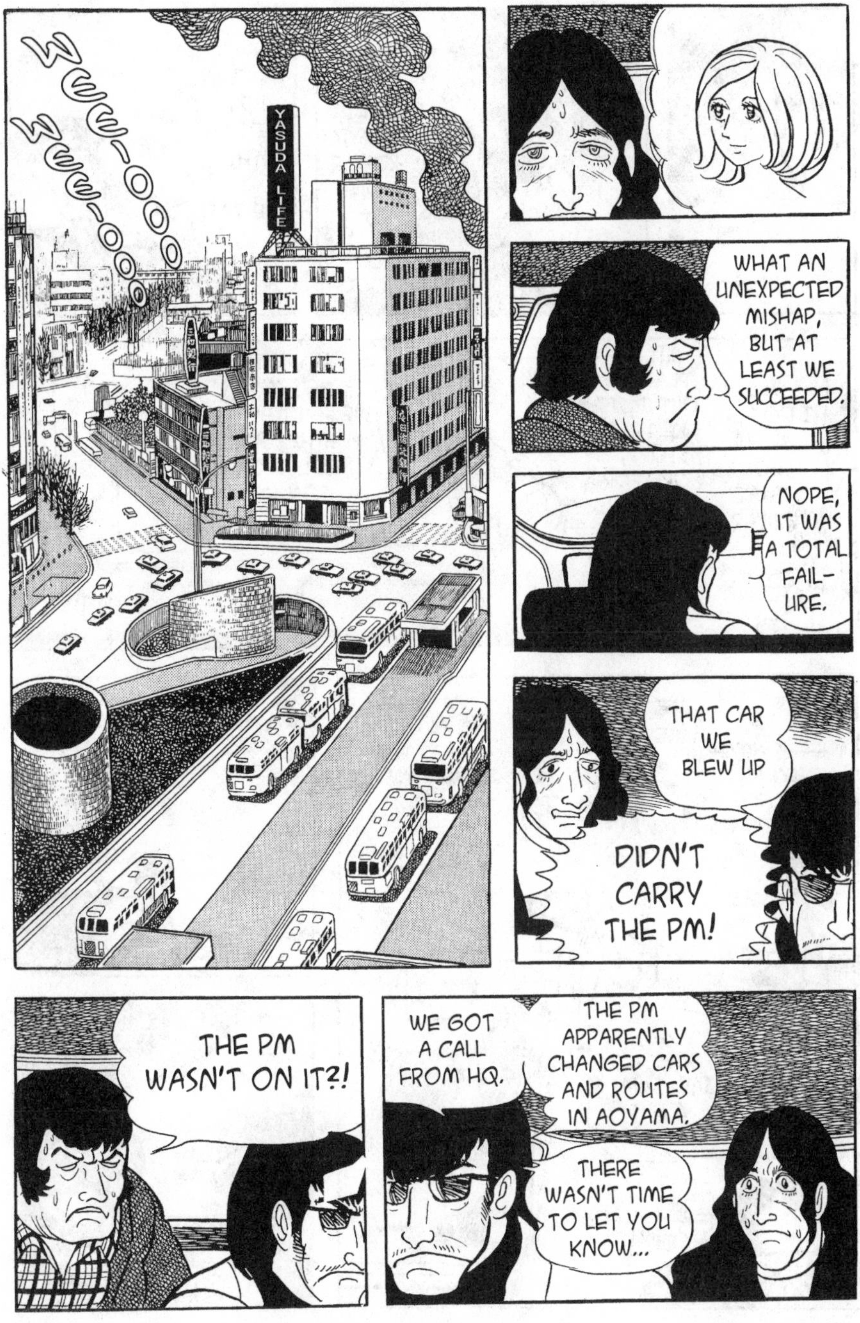
WEE-OOO
WEE-OOO
YASUDA LIFE
WHAT AN UNEXPECTED MISHAP, BUT AT LEAST WE SUCCEEDED.
NOPE, IT WAS A TOTAL FAIL-URE.
THAT CAR WE BLEW UP
DIDN'T CARRY THE PM!
THE PM WASN'T ON IT?!
WE GOT A CALL FROM HQ.
THE PM APPARENTLY CHANGED CARS AND ROUTES IN AOYAMA.
THERE WASN'T TIME TO LET YOU KNOW...

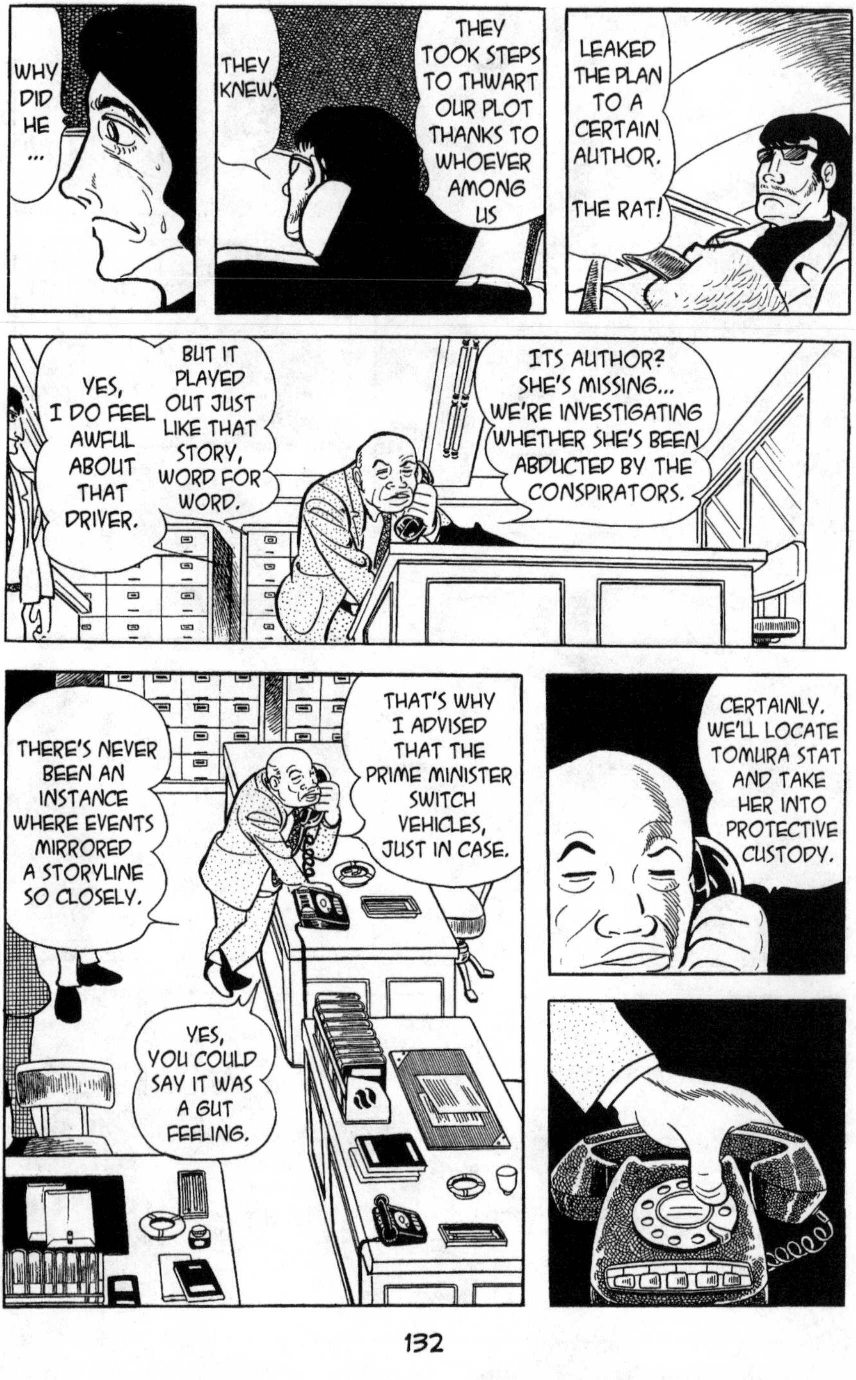
WHY DID HE ...
THEY KNEW.
THEY TOOK STEPS TO THWART OUR PLOT THANKS TO WHOEVER AMONG US
LEAKED THE PLAN TO A CERTAIN AUTHOR.
THE RAT!
YES, I DO FEEL AWFUL ABOUT THAT DRIVER.
BUT IT PLAYED OUT JUST LIKE THAT STORY, WORD FOR WORD.
ITS AUTHOR? SHE'S MISSING... WE'RE INVESTIGATING WHETHER SHE'S BEEN ABDUCTED BY THE CONSPIRATORS.
THERE'S NEVER BEEN AN INSTANCE WHERE EVENTS MIRRORED A STORYLINE SO CLOSELY.
THAT'S WHY I ADVISED THAT THE PRIME MINISTER SWITCH VEHICLES, JUST IN CASE.
YES, YOU COULD SAY IT WAS A GUT FEELING.
CERTAINLY. WE'LL LOCATE TOMURA STAT AND TAKE HER INTO PROTECTIVE CUSTODY.

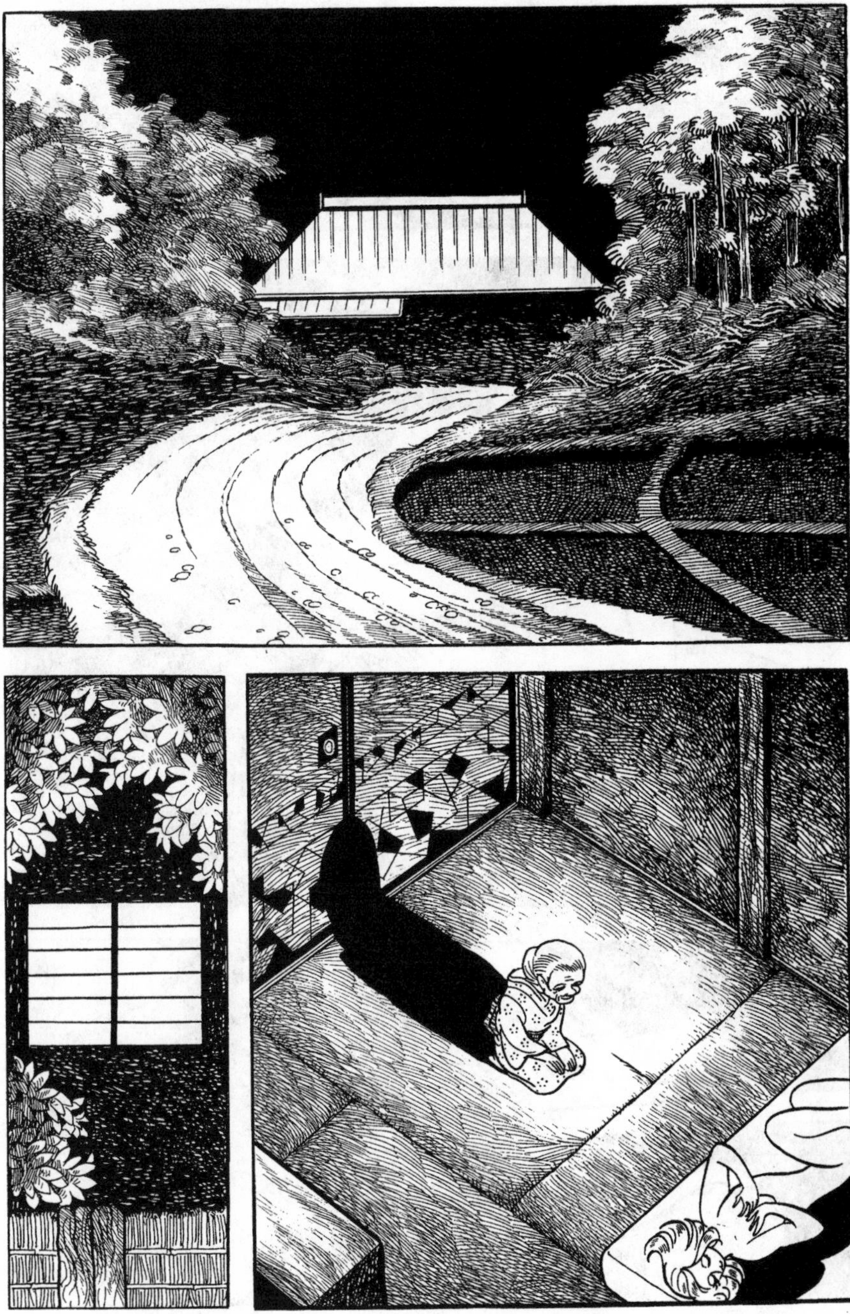

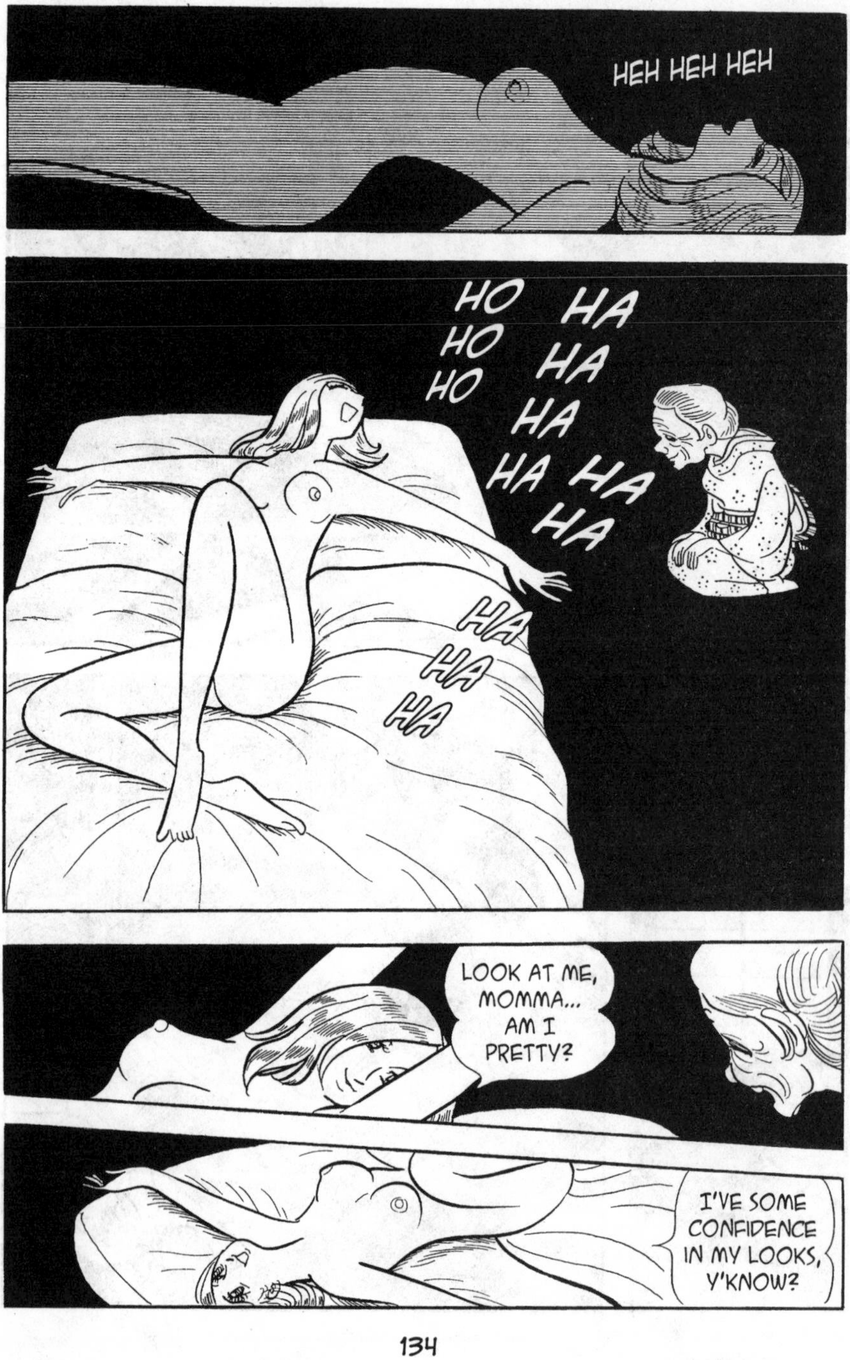
HEH HEH HEH
HO HO HO
HA HA HA HA HA HA
HA HA HA
LOOK AT ME, MOMMA... AM I PRETTY?
I'VE SOME CONFIDENCE IN MY LOOKS, Y'KNOW?

WHY ALL THE FUSS OVER THE PRIME MINISTER OR WHOEVER CROAKING?

HEY, MOMMA, I'M PLANNING TO GO ABROAD. YOU MIGHT HAVE TO WAIT HERE FOR YEARS, GATHERING DUST... BUT THAT'S OKAY, RIGHT, MOMMA?

MAYBE... I SHOULD BECOME A GYMNAST NEXT.

AH, I'M BORED. I CAN'T SEEM TO FEEL EXCITED ABOUT ANYTHING. JAPAN SUCKS.

I LIKE IT HERE. IT'S MY HOME. TEE HEE.

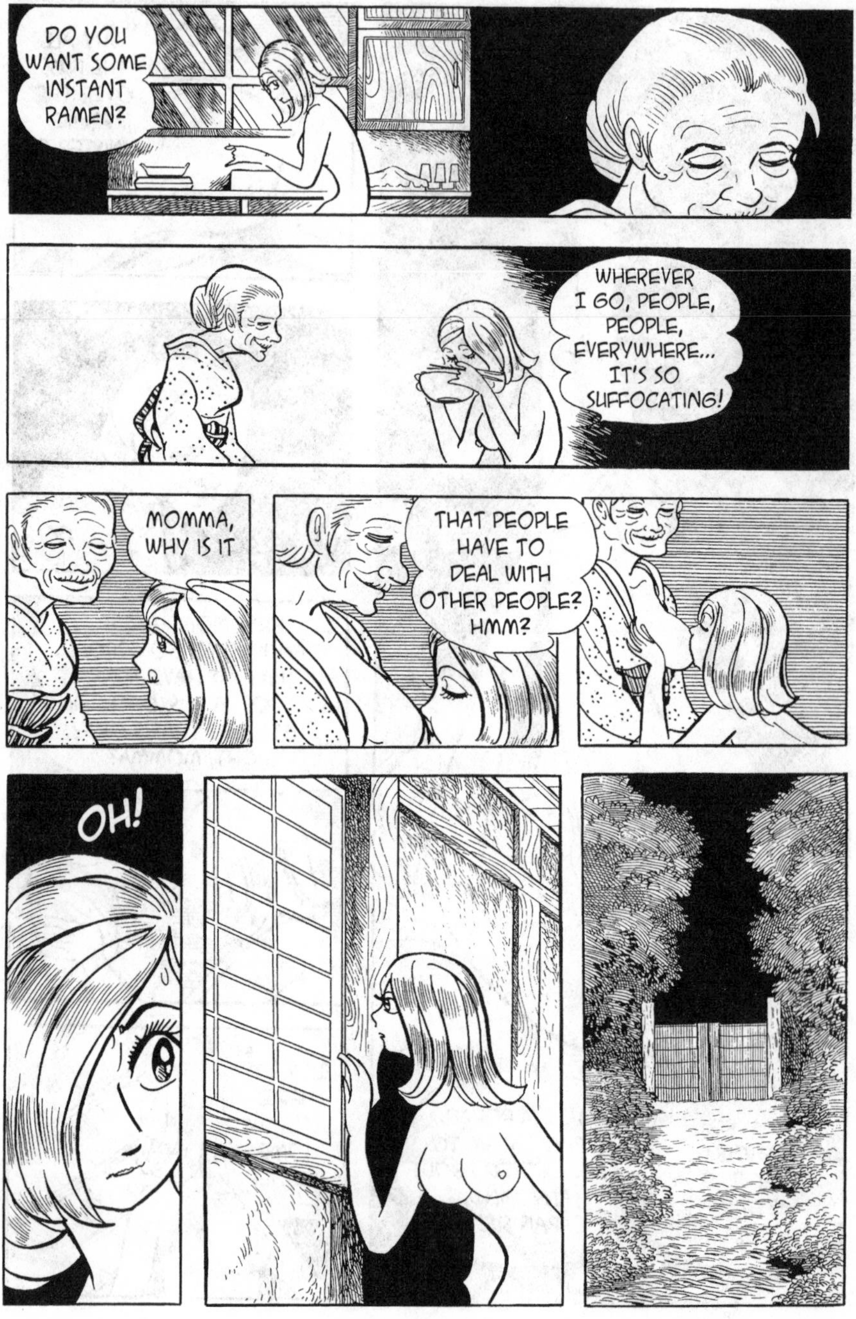
DO YOU WANT SOME INSTANT RAMEN?
WHEREVER I GO, PEOPLE, PEOPLE, EVERYWHERE... IT'S SO SUFFOCATING!
MOMMA, WHY IS IT
THAT PEOPLE HAVE TO DEAL WITH OTHER PEOPLE? HMM?
OH!

WHEW.
KLATTER

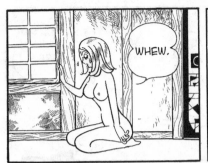

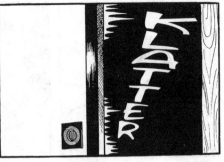

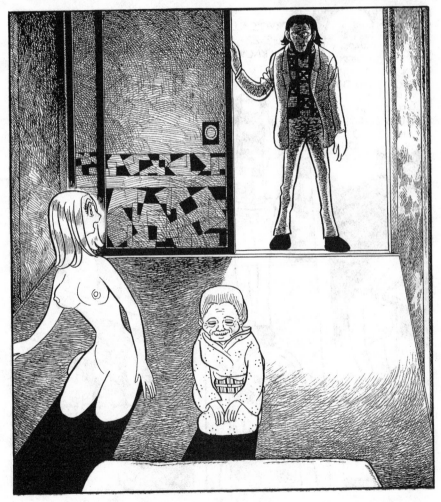

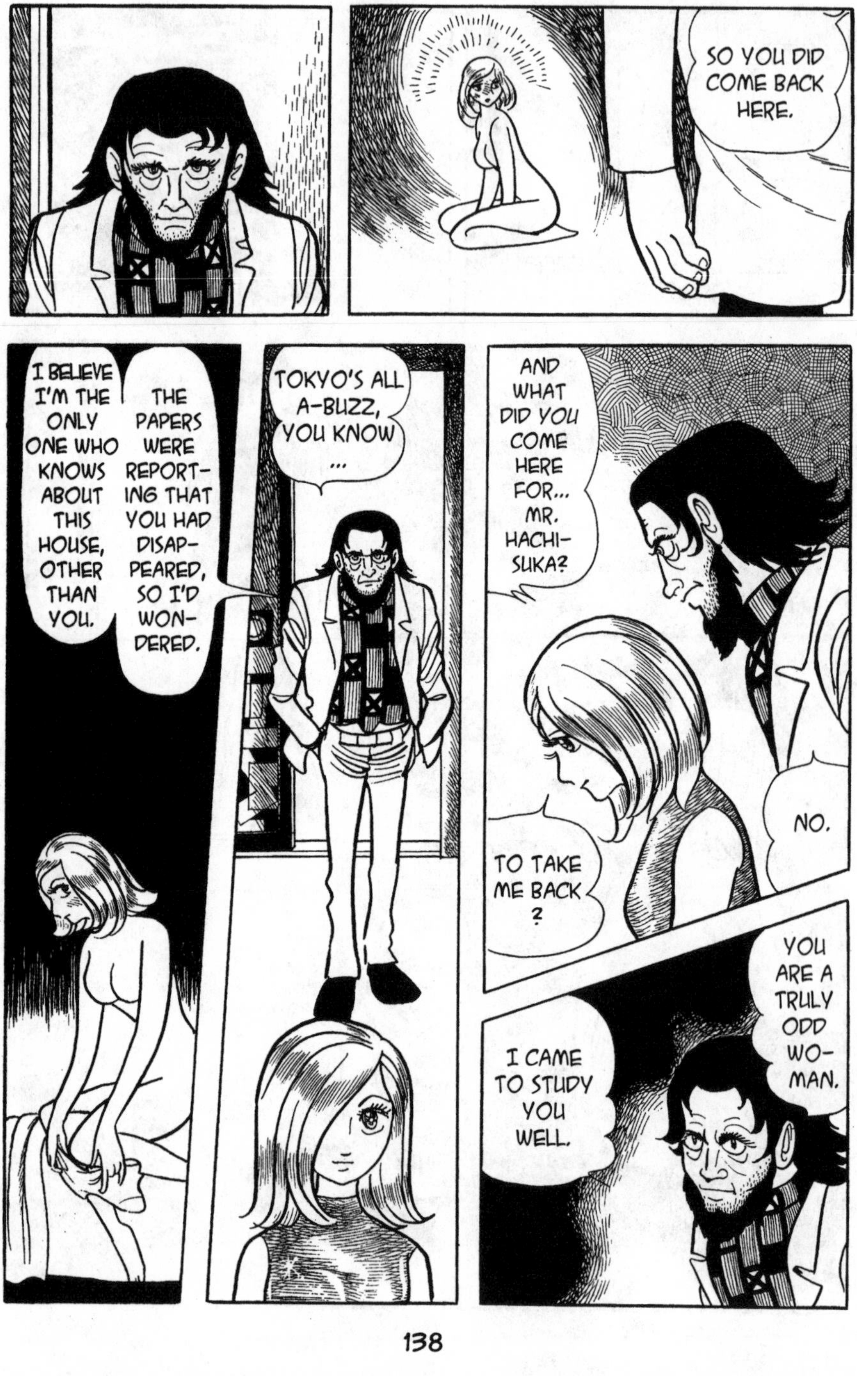
SO YOU DID COME BACK HERE.
I BELIEVE I'M THE ONLY ONE WHO KNOWS ABOUT THIS HOUSE, OTHER THAN YOU.
THE PAPERS WERE REPORTING THAT YOU HAD DISAPPEARED, SO I'D WONDERED.
TOKYO'S ALL A-BUZZ, YOU KNOW ...
AND WHAT DID YOU COME HERE FOR... MR. HACHISUKA?
TO TAKE ME BACK ?
NO.
I CAME TO STUDY YOU WELL.
YOU ARE A TRULY ODD WOMAN.

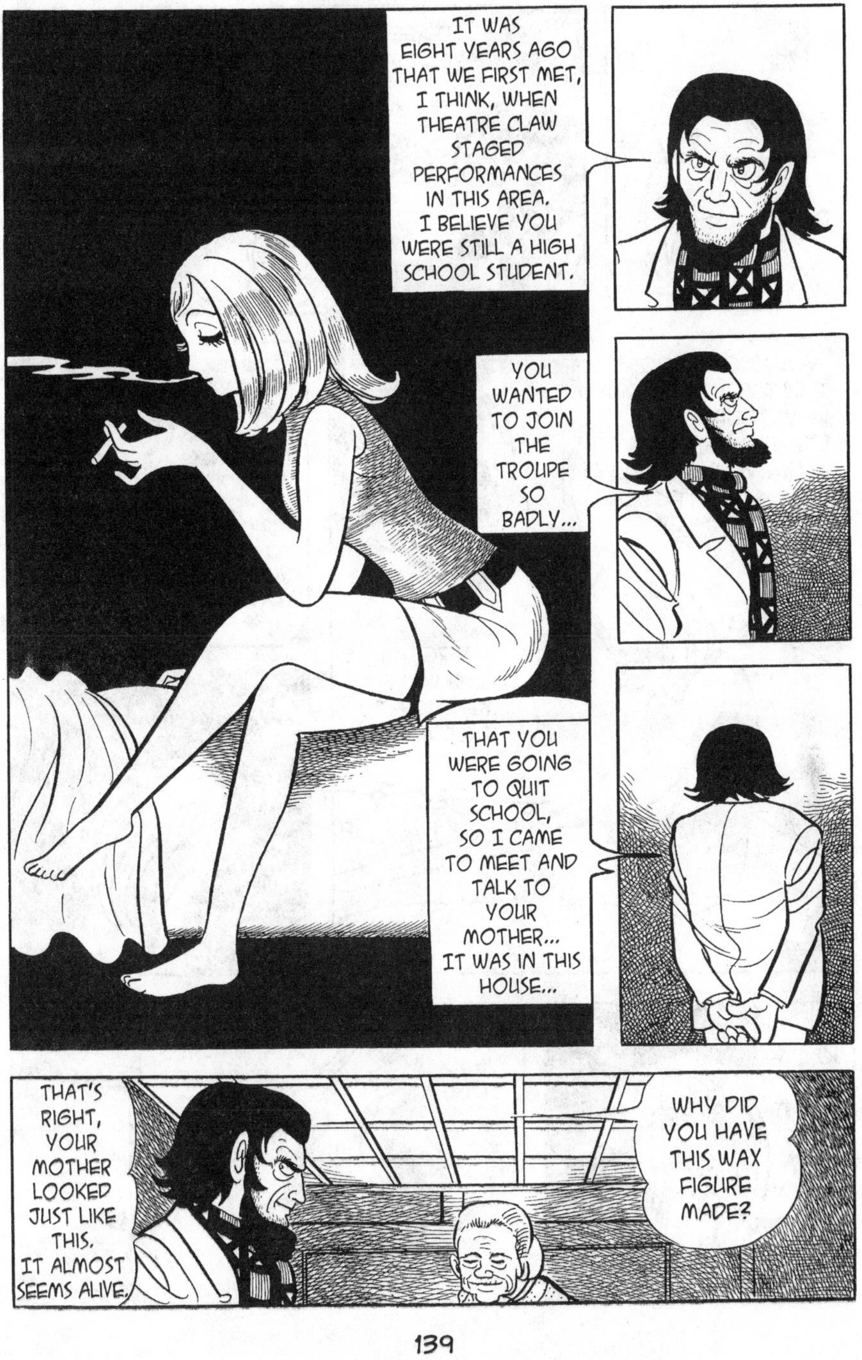
IT WAS EIGHT YEARS AGO THAT WE FIRST MET, I THINK, WHEN THEATRE CLAW STAGED PERFORMANCES IN THIS AREA. I BELIEVE YOU WERE STILL A HIGH SCHOOL STUDENT.
YOU WANTED TO JOIN THE TROUPE SO BADLY...
THAT YOU WERE GOING TO QUIT SCHOOL, SO I CAME TO MEET AND TALK TO YOUR MOTHER... IT WAS IN THIS HOUSE...
THAT'S RIGHT, YOUR MOTHER LOOKED JUST LIKE THIS. IT ALMOST SEEMS ALIVE.
WHY DID YOU HAVE THIS WAX FIGURE MADE?

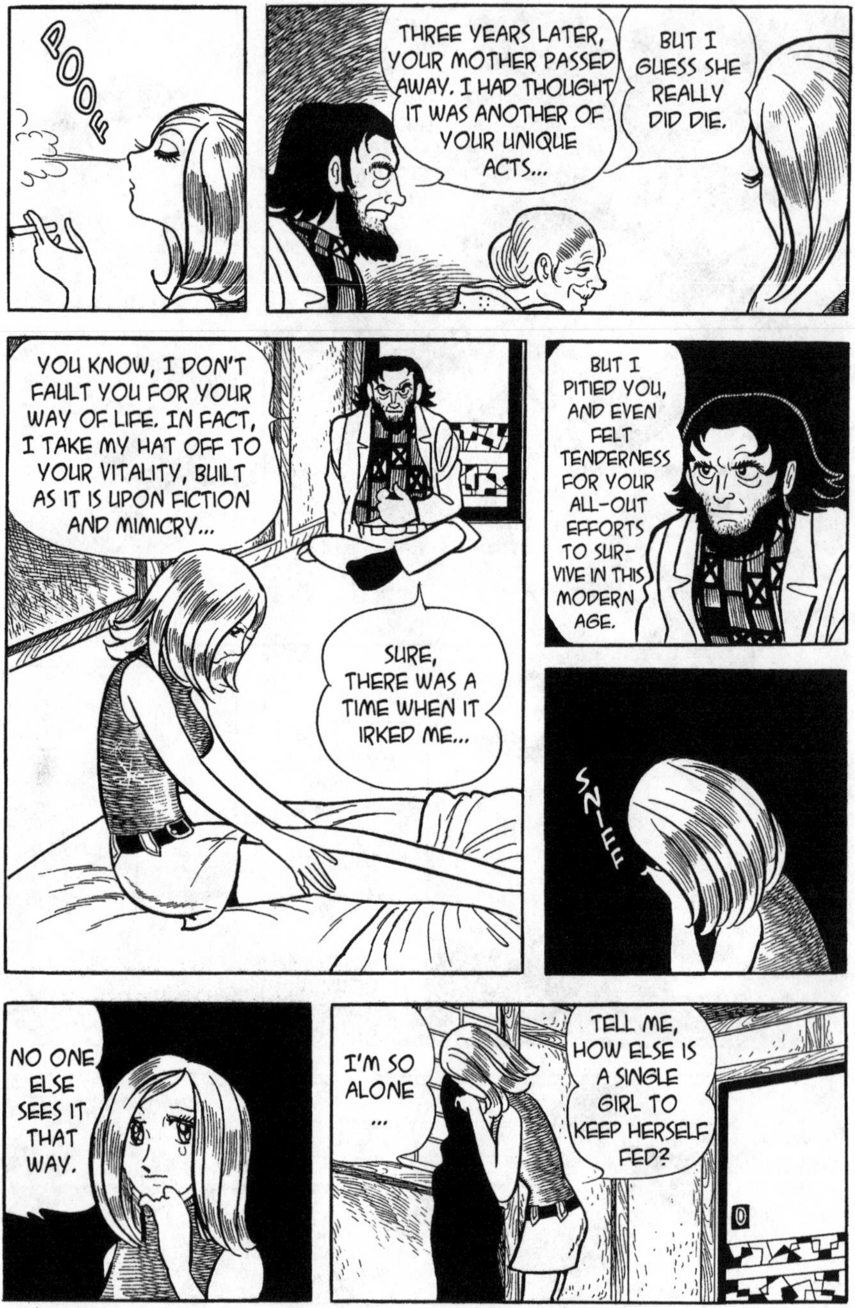
POOF
THREE YEARS LATER, YOUR MOTHER PASSED AWAY. I HAD THOUGHT IT WAS ANOTHER OF YOUR UNIQUE ACTS...
BUT I GUESS SHE REALLY DID DIE.
YOU KNOW, I DON'T FAULT YOU FOR YOUR WAY OF LIFE. IN FACT, I TAKE MY HAT OFF TO YOUR VITALITY, BUILT AS IT IS UPON FICTION AND MIMICRY...
SURE, THERE WAS A TIME WHEN IT IRKED ME...
BUT I PITIED YOU, AND EVEN FELT TENDERNESS FOR YOUR ALL-OUT EFFORTS TO SUR-VIVE IN THIS MODERN AGE.
SNIFF
NO ONE ELSE SEES IT THAT WAY.
I'M SO ALONE ...
TELL ME, HOW ELSE IS A SINGLE GIRL TO KEEP HERSELF FED?

YOU DON'T HAVE TO PUT ON AN ACT FOR ME.

A-HA HA HA HA HA!

YOU'RE RIGHT, ESPECIALLY SINCE WE'RE STRANGERS NOW.

I'VE BEEN THINKING ABOUT GOING ABROAD.

WHERE TO?

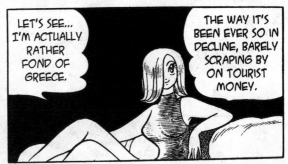

LET'S SEE... I'M ACTUALLY RATHER FOND OF GREECE.

THE WAY IT'S BEEN EVER SO IN DECLINE, BARELY SCRAPING BY ON TOURIST MONEY.

TEMPLES TO THE GODS DOTTING DESOLATE HILLTOPS LIKE BLEACHED BONES. I LIKE THAT SORT OF THING.

LIVING THERE WON'T BE WORTH A DIME TO YOU.

WELL THEN, WHAT ABOUT ANCHORAGE?

WHY SUCH OUT-OF-THE-WAY PLACES? YOU CRAVE GLORY IN THE BIG CITY, DON'T YOU?

HA HA HA, HA HA HA! YOU... STILL DON'T GET ME AT ALL.

141

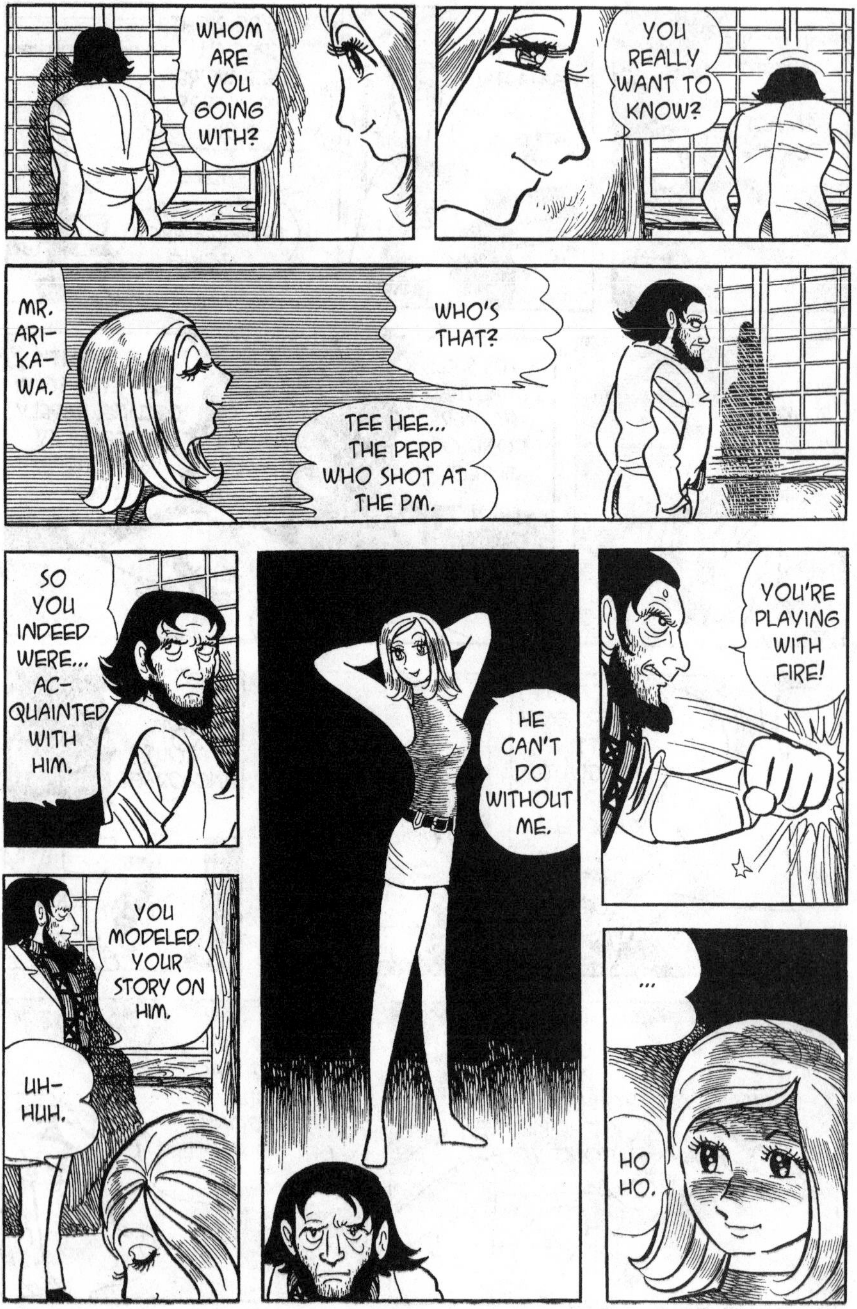
WHOM ARE YOU GOING WITH?
YOU REALLY WANT TO KNOW?
MR. ARI-KA-WA.
WHO'S THAT?
TEE HEE... THE PERP WHO SHOT AT THE PM.
SO YOU INDEED WERE... AC-QUAINTED WITH HIM.
HE CAN'T DO WITHOUT ME.
YOU'RE PLAYING WITH FIRE!
YOU MODELED YOUR STORY ON HIM.
UH-HUH.
...
HO HO.

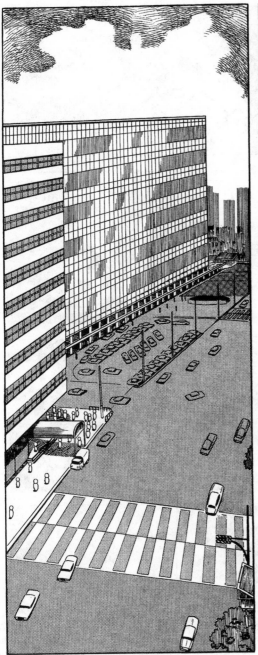

PEACE, ONE PACK.

TOBA

BOSS ...

HELP ME. I'VE BEEN TARGETED BY THE OR-GANIZATION.

PUTTERING ABOUT IN A TRAIN STATION? RISKY.

143

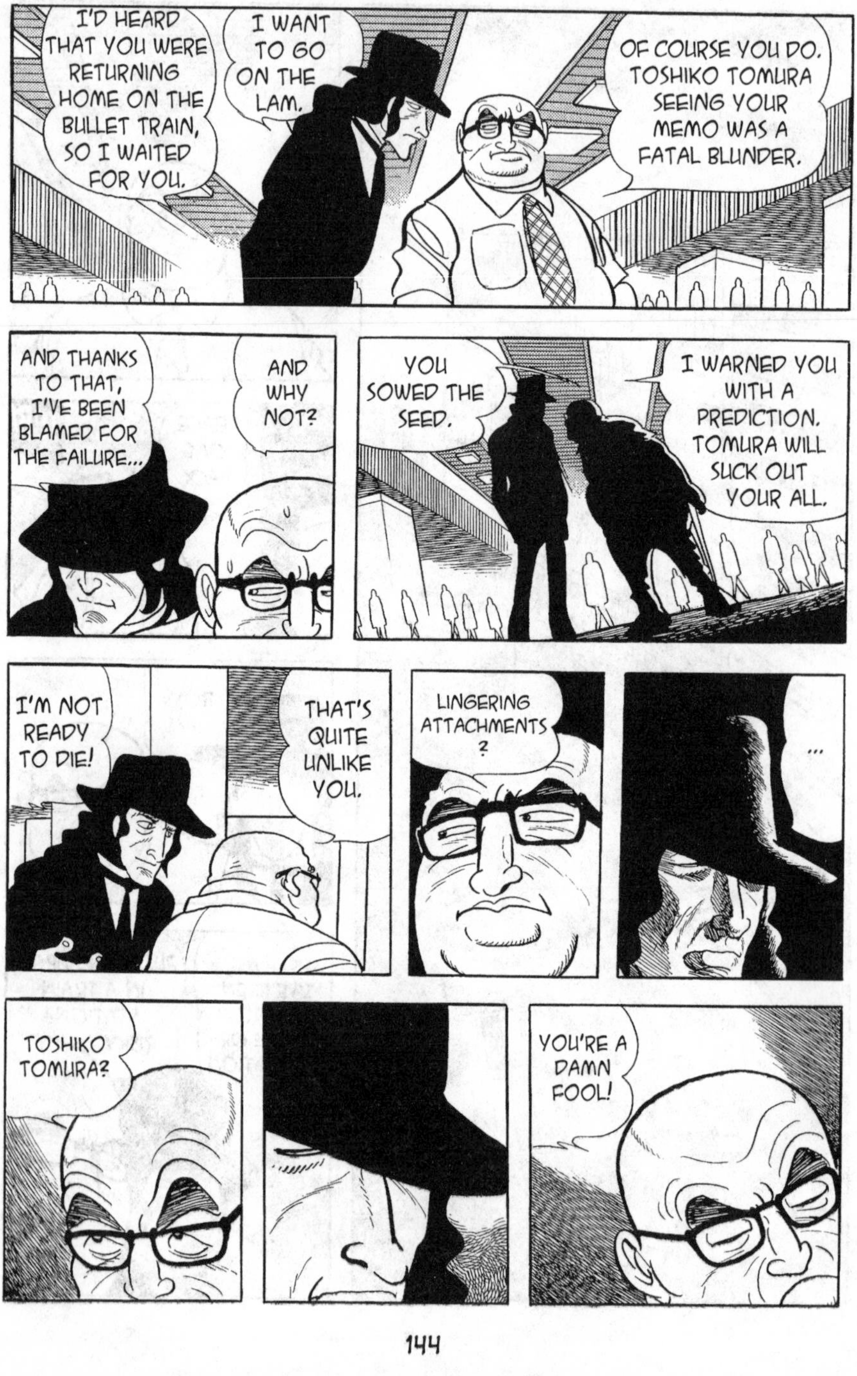
I'D HEARD THAT YOU WERE RETURNING HOME ON THE BULLET TRAIN, SO I WAITED FOR YOU.
I WANT TO GO ON THE LAM.
OF COURSE YOU DO. TOSHIKO TOMURA SEEING YOUR MEMO WAS A FATAL BLUNDER.
AND THANKS TO THAT, I'VE BEEN BLAMED FOR THE FAILURE...
AND WHY NOT?
YOU SOWED THE SEED.
I WARNED YOU WITH A PREDICTION. TOMURA WILL SUCK OUT YOUR ALL.
I'M NOT READY TO DIE!
THAT'S QUITE UNLIKE YOU.
LINGERING ATTACHMENTS?
...
TOSHIKO TOMURA?
YOU'RE A DAMN FOOL!

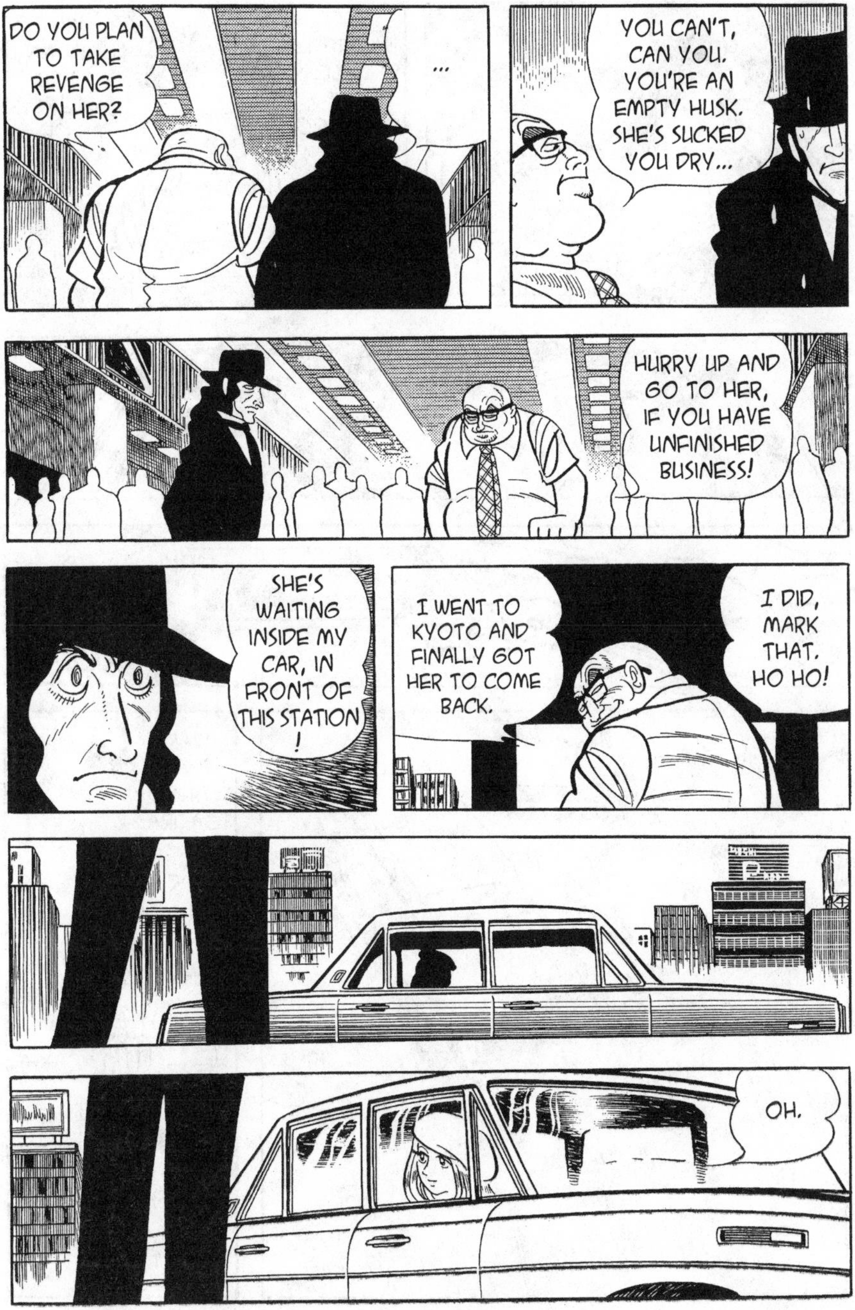
DO YOU PLAN TO TAKE REVENGE ON HER?
...
YOU CAN'T, CAN YOU. YOU'RE AN EMPTY HUSK. SHE'S SUCKED YOU DRY...
HURRY UP AND GO TO HER, IF YOU HAVE UNFINISHED BUSINESS!
SHE'S WAITING INSIDE MY CAR, IN FRONT OF THIS STATION!
I WENT TO KYOTO AND FINALLY GOT HER TO COME BACK.
I DID, MARK THAT. HO HO!
OH.

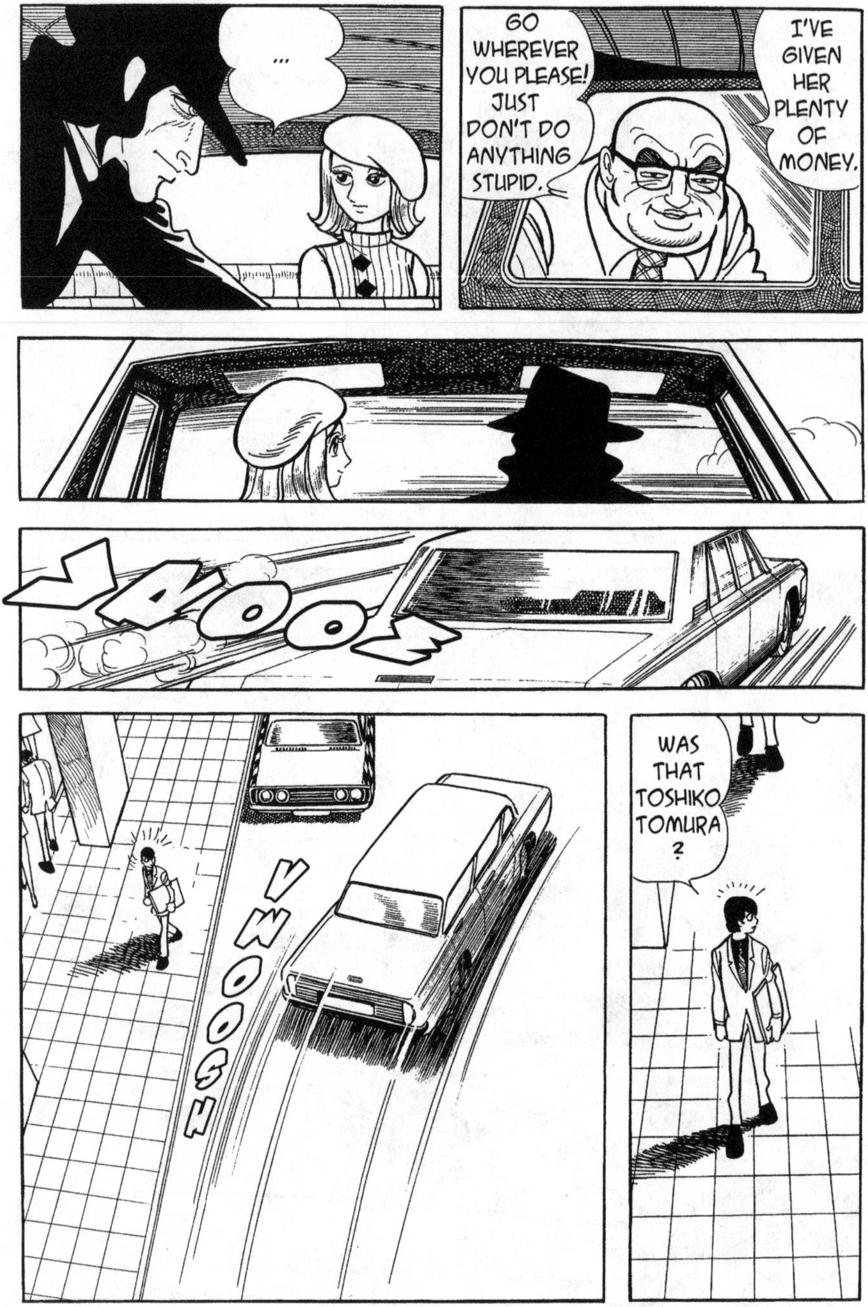
...
GO WHEREVER YOU PLEASE! JUST DON'T DO ANYTHING STUPID.
I'VE GIVEN HER PLENTY OF MONEY.
VROOM
VWOOOSH
WAS THAT TOSHIKO TOMURA?

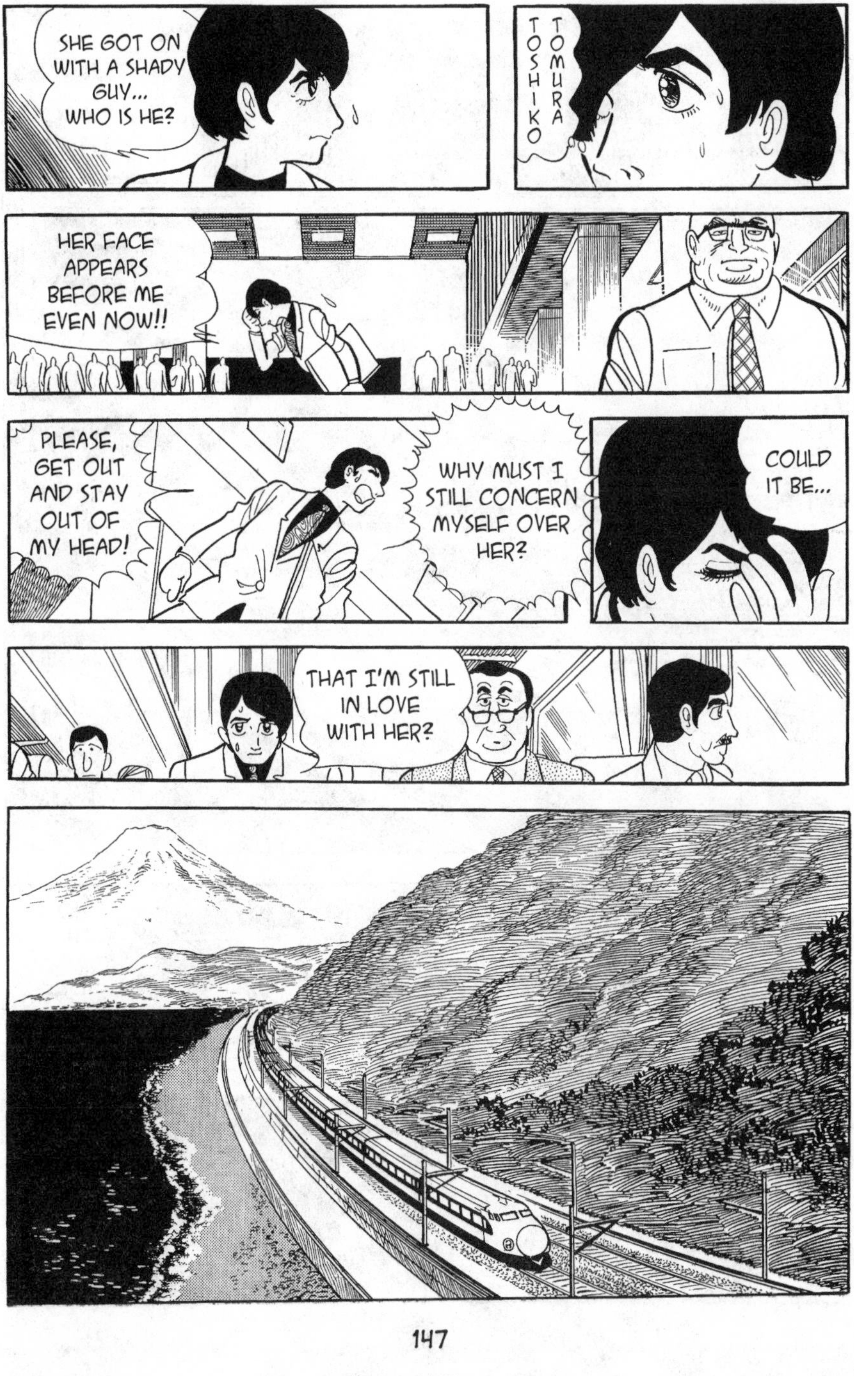
SHE GOT ON WITH A SHADY GUY... WHO IS HE?
TOSHIKO
TOMURA
HER FACE APPEARS BEFORE ME EVEN NOW!!
PLEASE, GET OUT AND STAY OUT OF MY HEAD!
WHY MUST I STILL CONCERN MYSELF OVER HER?
COULD IT BE...
THAT I'M STILL IN LOVE WITH HER?

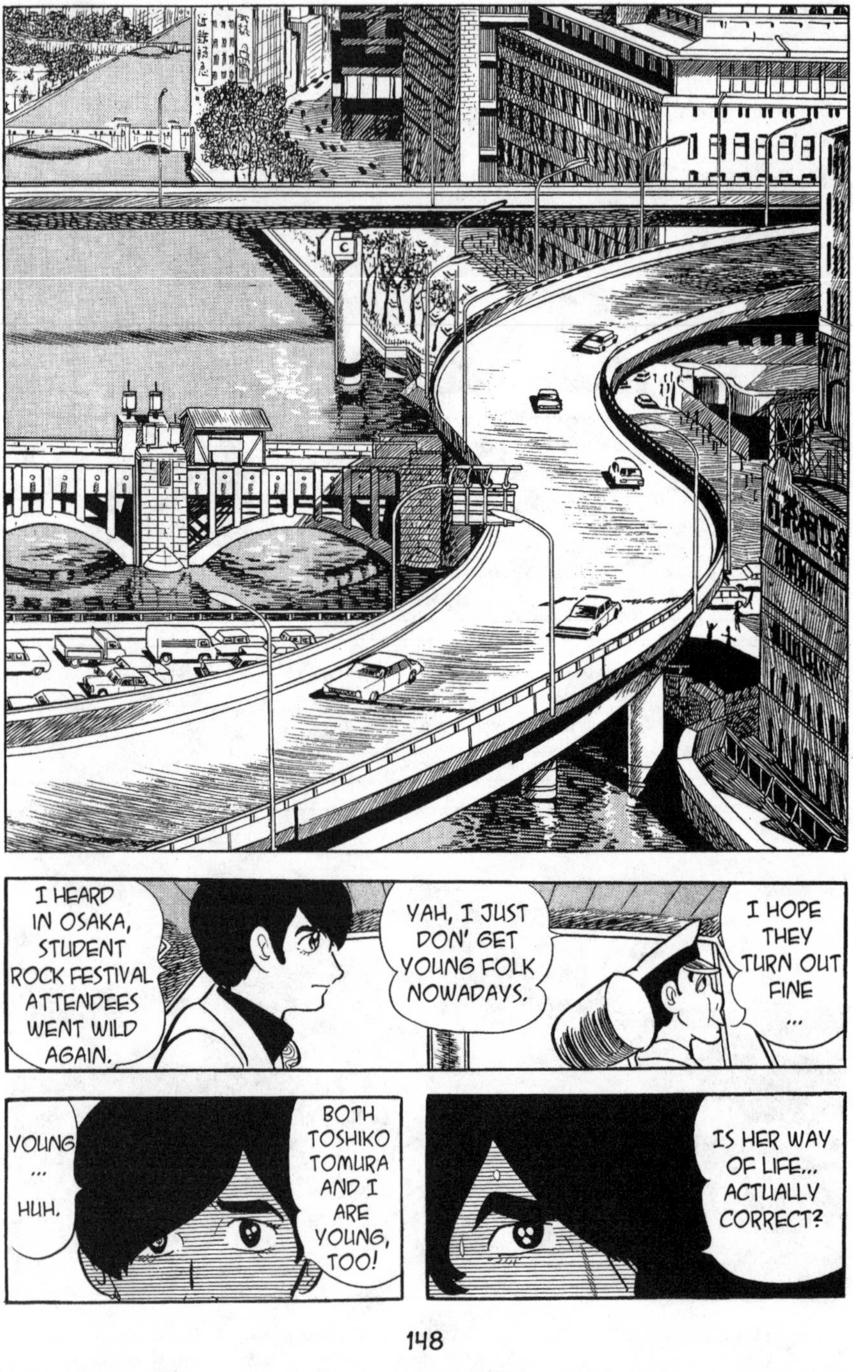
I HEARD IN OSAKA, STUDENT ROCK FESTIVAL ATTENDEES WENT WILD AGAIN.
YAH, I JUST DON' GET YOUNG FOLK NOWADAYS.
I HOPE THEY TURN OUT FINE ...
YOUNG ... HUH.
BOTH TOSHIKO TOMURA AND I ARE YOUNG, TOO!
IS HER WAY OF LIFE... ACTUALLY CORRECT?

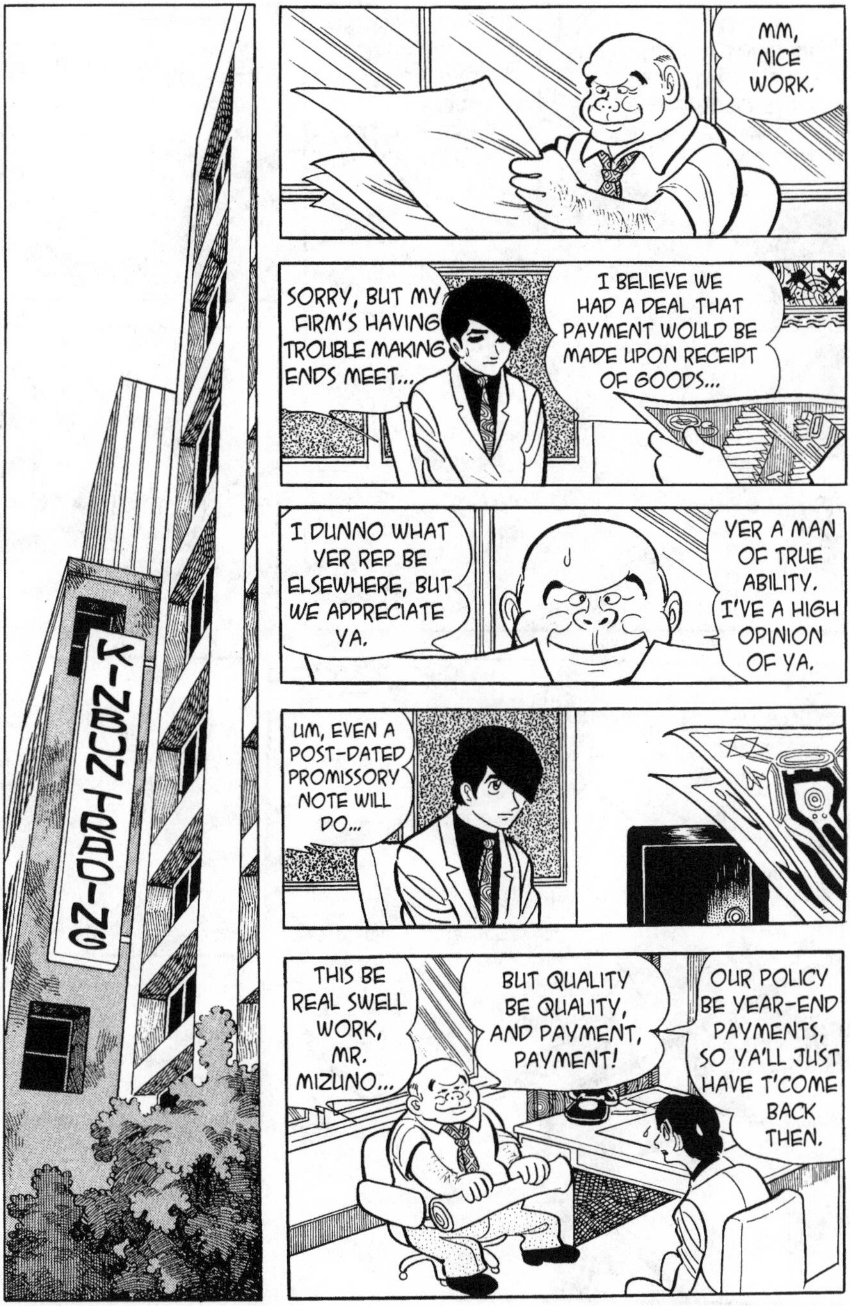
KINBUN TRADING
MM, NICE WORK.
SORRY, BUT MY FIRM'S HAVING TROUBLE MAKING ENDS MEET...
I BELIEVE WE HAD A DEAL THAT PAYMENT WOULD BE MADE UPON RECEIPT OF GOODS...
I DUNNO WHAT YER REP BE ELSEWHERE, BUT WE APPRECIATE YA.
YER A MAN OF TRUE ABILITY. I'VE A HIGH OPINION OF YA.
UM, EVEN A POST-DATED PROMISSORY NOTE WILL DO...
THIS BE REAL SWELL WORK, MR. MIZUNO...
BUT QUALITY BE QUALITY, AND PAYMENT, PAYMENT!
OUR POLICY BE YEAR-END PAYMENTS, SO YA'LL JUST HAVE T'COME BACK THEN.

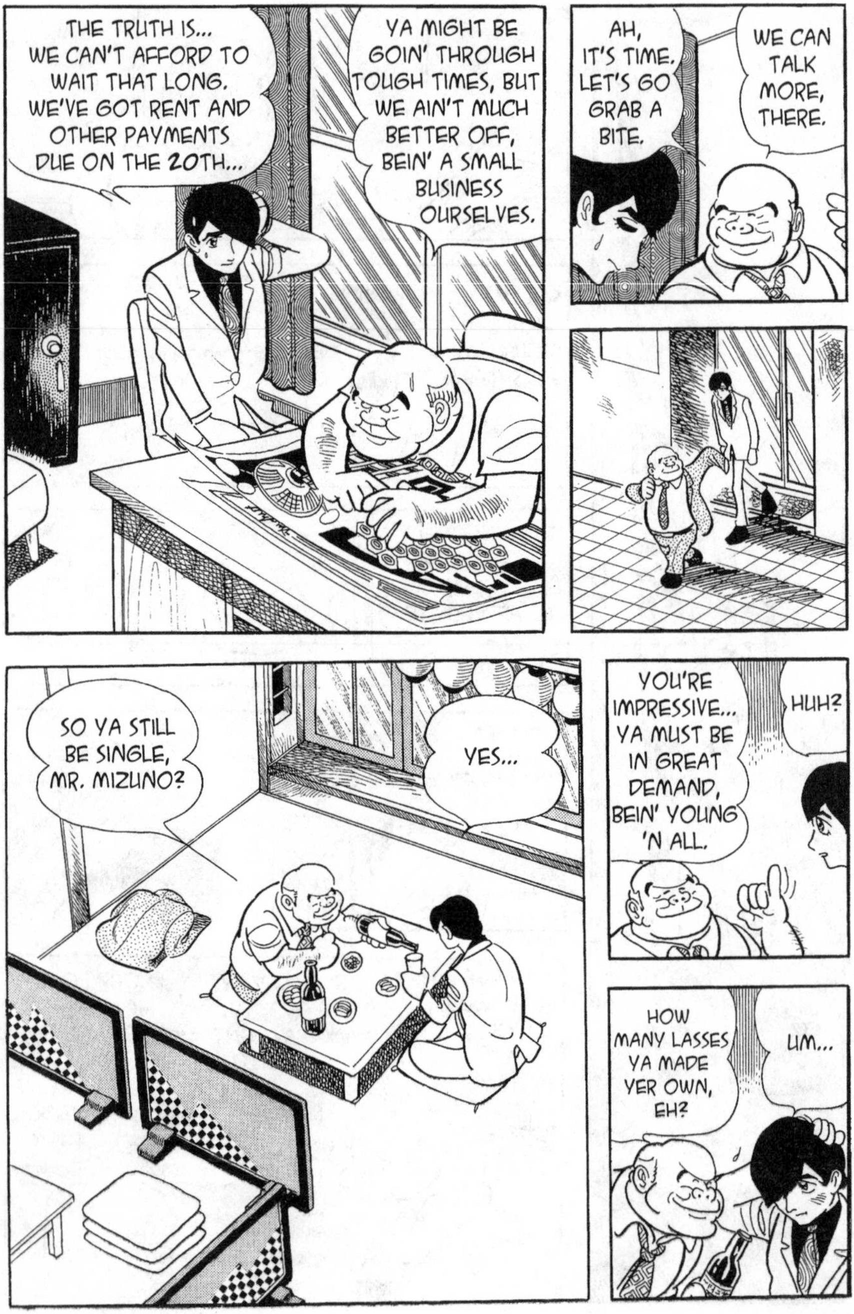
THE TRUTH IS... WE CAN'T AFFORD TO WAIT THAT LONG. WE'VE GOT RENT AND OTHER PAYMENTS DUE ON THE 20TH...
YA MIGHT BE GOIN' THROUGH TOUGH TIMES, BUT WE AIN'T MUCH BETTER OFF, BEIN' A SMALL BUSINESS OURSELVES.
AH, IT'S TIME. LET'S GO GRAB A BITE.
WE CAN TALK MORE, THERE.
SO YA STILL BE SINGLE, MR. MIZUNO?
YES...
YOU'RE IMPRESSIVE... YA MUST BE IN GREAT DEMAND, BEIN' YOUNG 'N ALL.
HUH?
HOW MANY LASSES YA MADE YER OWN, EH?
UM...

MORE IMPORTANTLY, ABOUT THAT PROMISED PAYMENT...

HAVE YA EVER BEEN ENGAGED AT ALL?

YES, I WAS ...

BUT WE SPLIT UP. IT WAS A DISSATISFYING SEPARATION.

THAT BE WOUNDS OF YOUTH. YA OUGHTA SETTLE DOWN 'N TAKE A WIFE. THAT'LL HELP YA FERGET HER COMPLETELY. IT BE TRUE.

UM... HOW ABOUT A CHECK?

I KNOW A REAL SWEET GIRL.

IF SHE'S A CLUB HOSTESS ... NO THANKS.

NAH! SHE BE RESPECTABLE.

ONE O' MY EMPLOYEES.

IS IT OKAY TO CALL ON HER THIS LATE AT NIGHT?

RELAX, RELAX ...

151

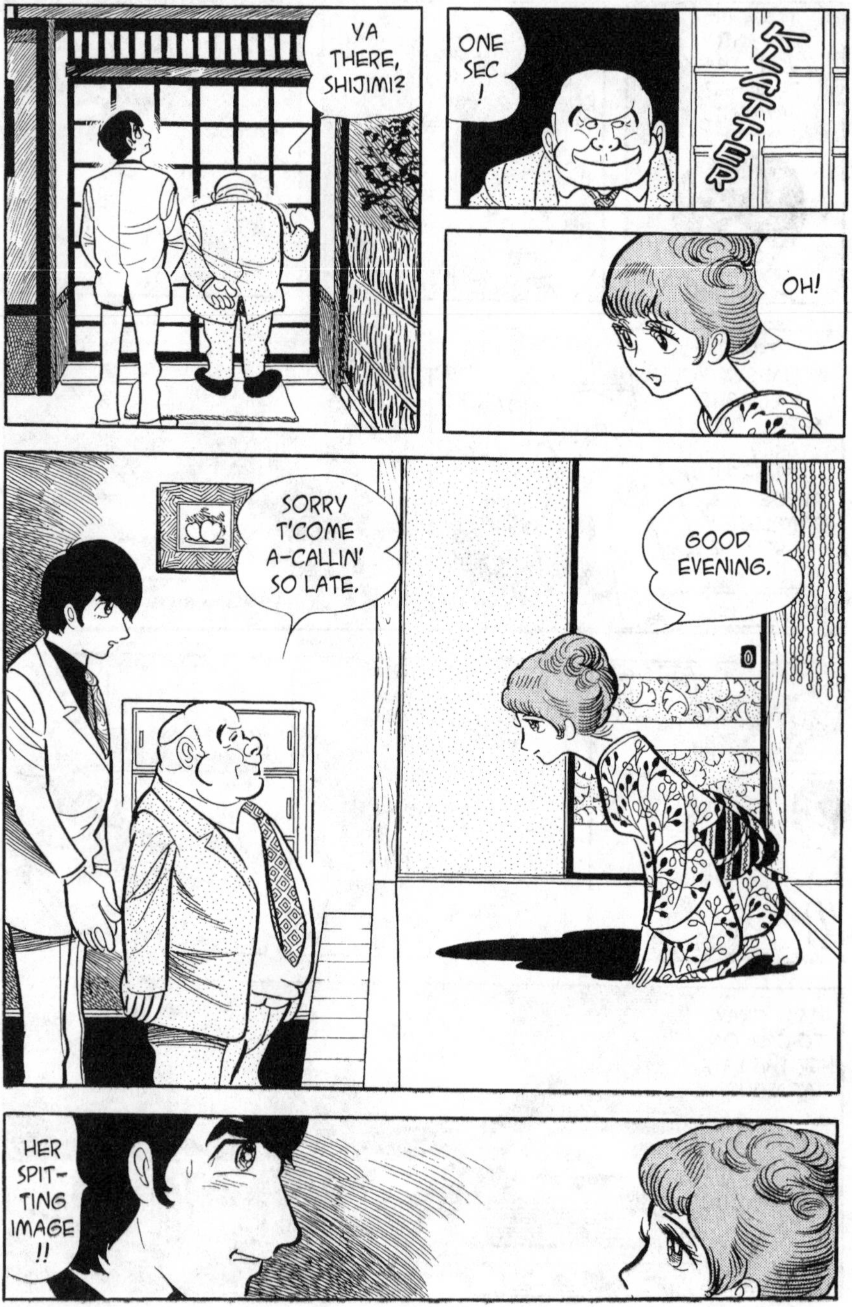

YA THERE, SHIJIMI?
ONE SEC!
KLATTER
OH!
SORRY T'COME A-CALLIN' SO LATE.
GOOD EVENING.
HER SPIT-TING IMAGE!!

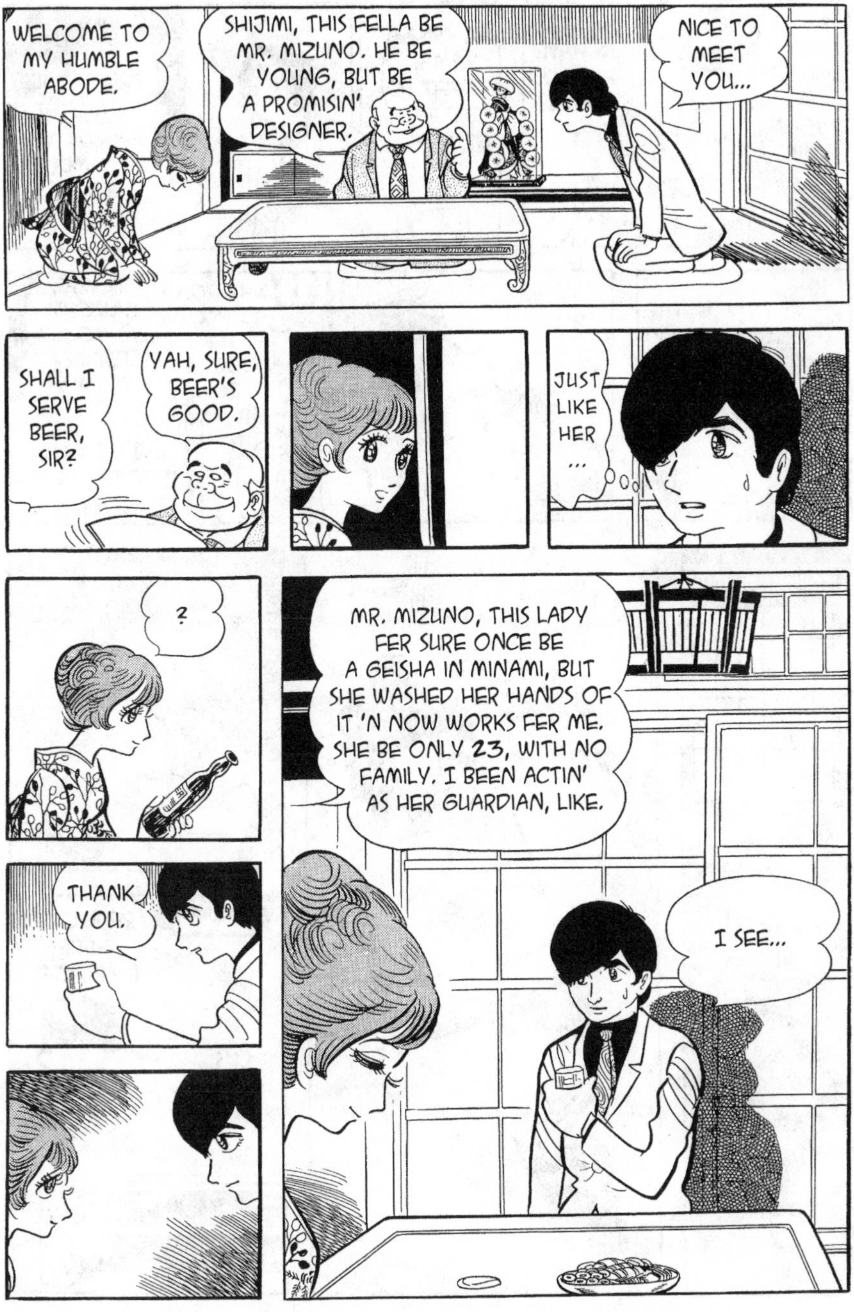
WELCOME TO MY HUMBLE ABODE.
SHIJIMI, THIS FELLA BE MR. MIZUNO. HE BE YOUNG, BUT BE A PROMISIN' DESIGNER.
NICE TO MEET YOU...
SHALL I SERVE BEER, SIR?
YAH, SURE, BEER'S GOOD.
JUST LIKE HER ...
?
MR. MIZUNO, THIS LADY FER SURE ONCE BE A GEISHA IN MINAMI, BUT SHE WASHED HER HANDS OF IT 'N NOW WORKS FER ME. SHE BE ONLY 23, WITH NO FAMILY. I BEEN ACTIN' AS HER GUARDIAN, LIKE.
THANK YOU.
I SEE...

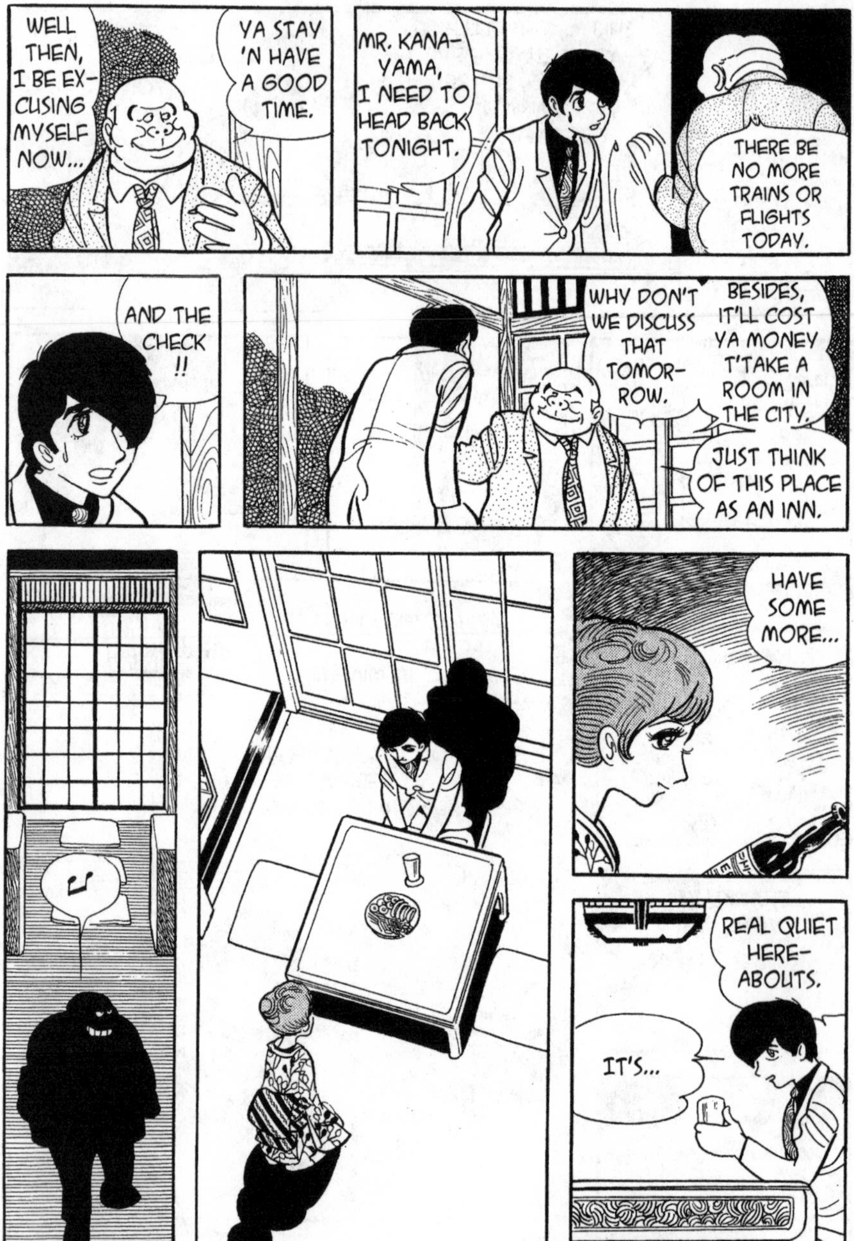
WELL THEN, I BE EX-CUSING MYSELF NOW...
YA STAY 'N HAVE A GOOD TIME.
MR. KANA-YAMA, I NEED TO HEAD BACK TONIGHT.
THERE BE NO MORE TRAINS OR FLIGHTS TODAY.
AND THE CHECK !!
WHY DON'T WE DISCUSS THAT TOMOR-ROW.
BESIDES, IT'LL COST YA MONEY T'TAKE A ROOM IN THE CITY.
JUST THINK OF THIS PLACE AS AN INN.
HAVE SOME MORE...
REAL QUIET HERE-ABOUTS.
IT'S...

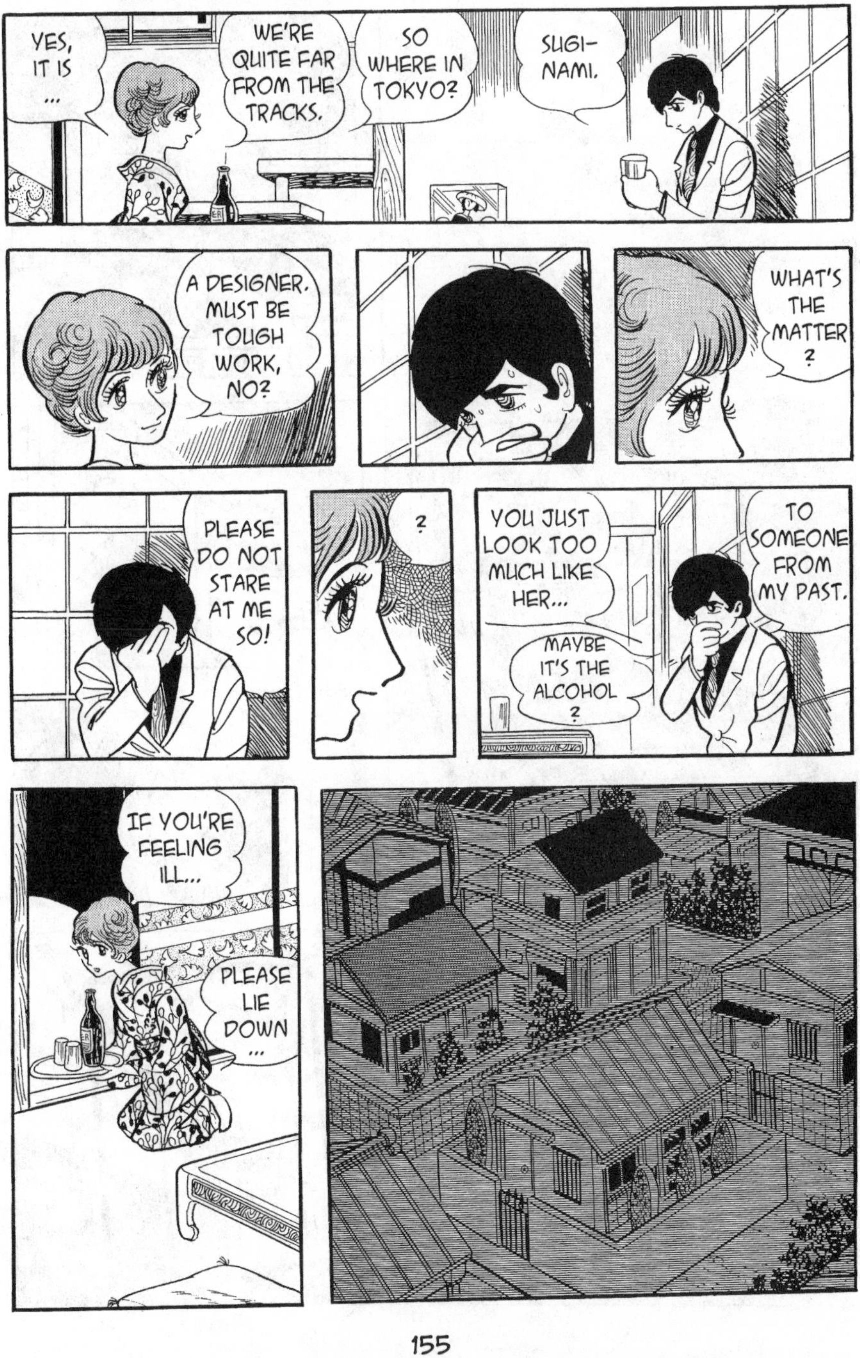
YES, IT IS ...
WE'RE QUITE FAR FROM THE TRACKS.
SO WHERE IN TOKYO?
SUGI-NAMI.
A DESIGNER. MUST BE TOUGH WORK, NO?
WHAT'S THE MATTER ?
PLEASE DO NOT STARE AT ME SO!
?
YOU JUST LOOK TOO MUCH LIKE HER...
TO SOMEONE FROM MY PAST.
MAYBE IT'S THE ALCOHOL ?
IF YOU'RE FEELING ILL...
PLEASE LIE DOWN ...

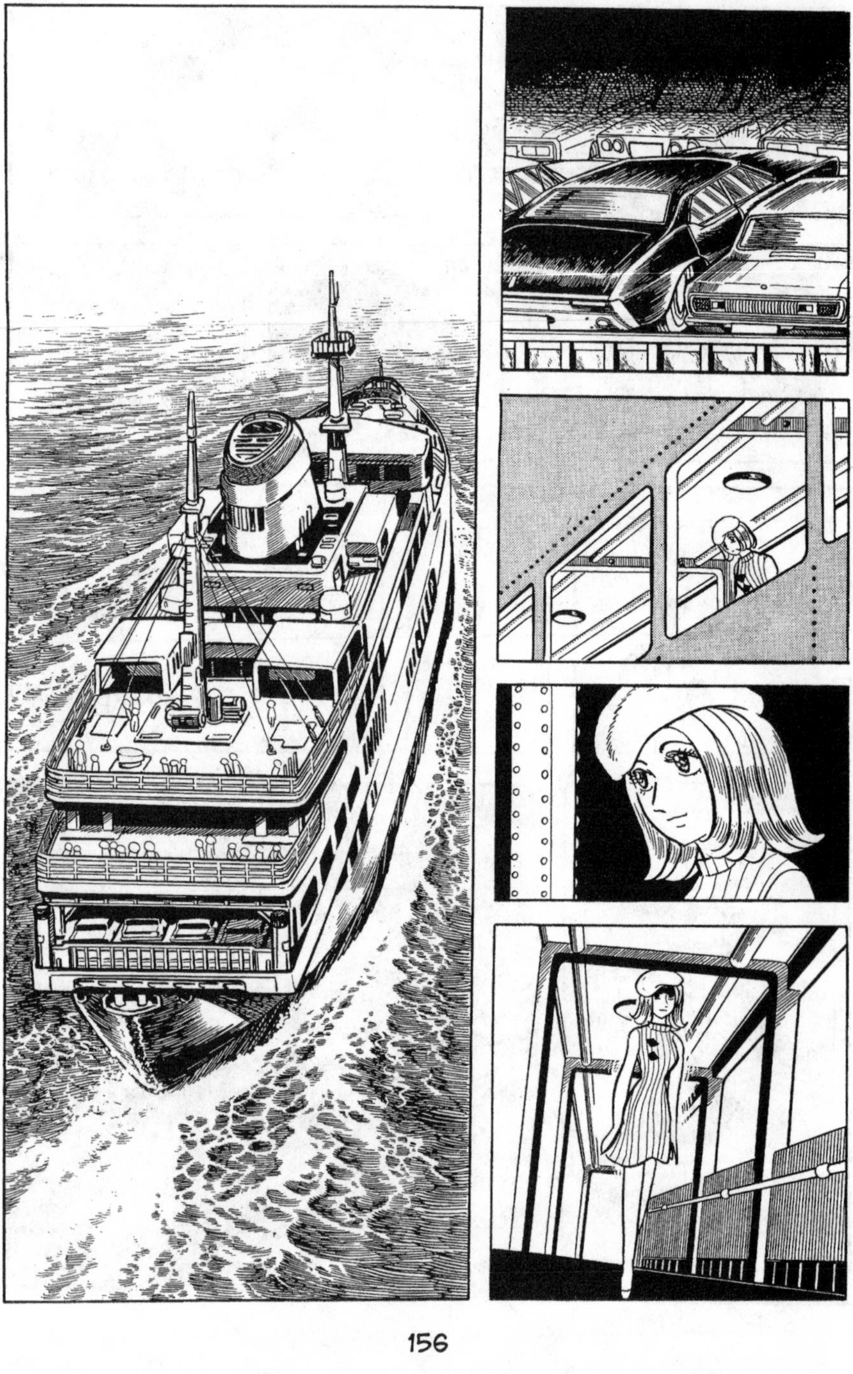

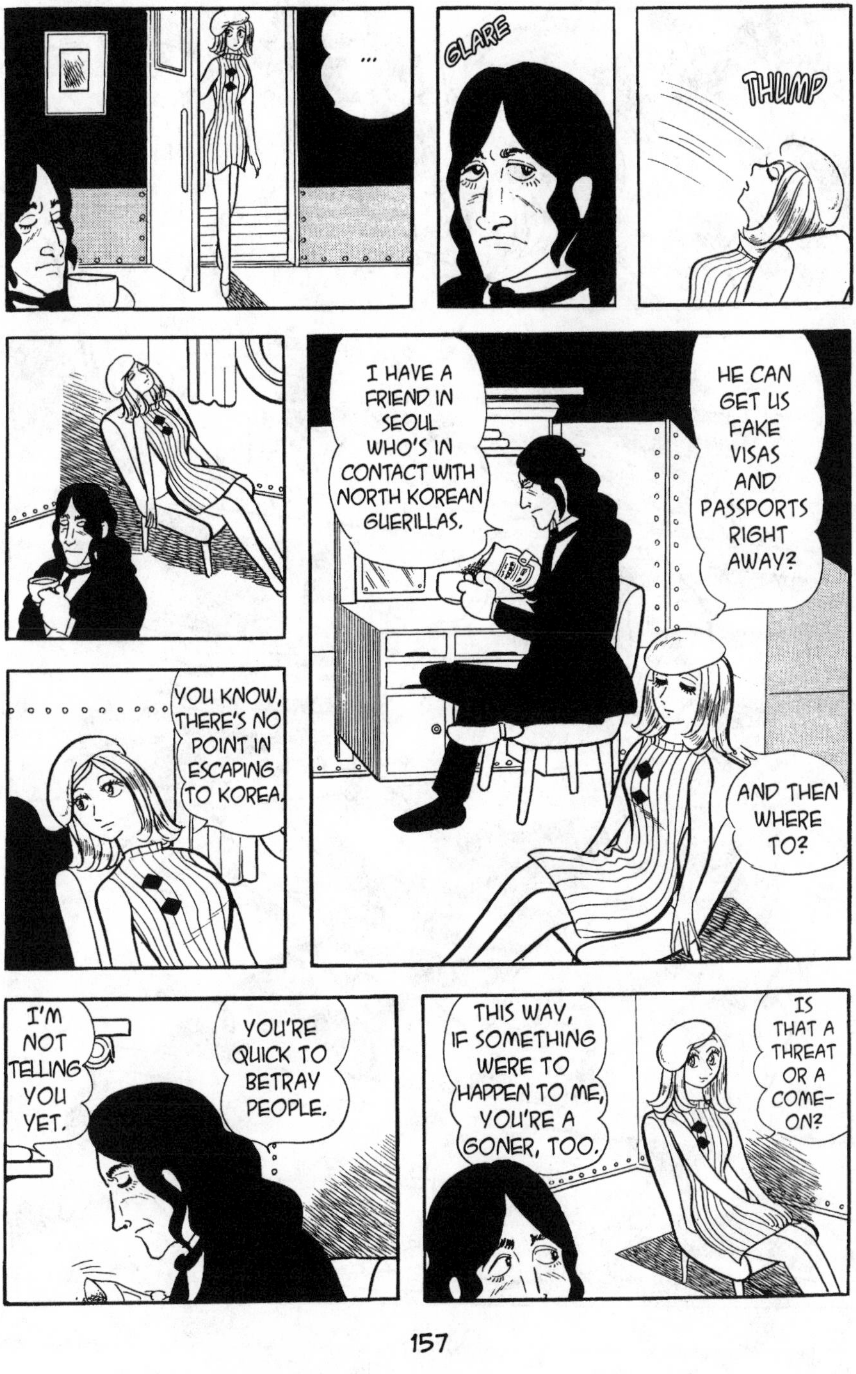
...
GLARE
THUMP
YOU KNOW, THERE'S NO POINT IN ESCAPING TO KOREA.
I HAVE A FRIEND IN SEOUL WHO'S IN CONTACT WITH NORTH KOREAN GUERILLAS.
HE CAN GET US FAKE VISAS AND PASSPORTS RIGHT AWAY?
AND THEN WHERE TO?
I'M NOT TELLING YOU YET.
YOU'RE QUICK TO BETRAY PEOPLE.
THIS WAY, IF SOMETHING WERE TO HAPPEN TO ME, YOU'RE A GONER, TOO.
IS THAT A THREAT OR A COME-ON?

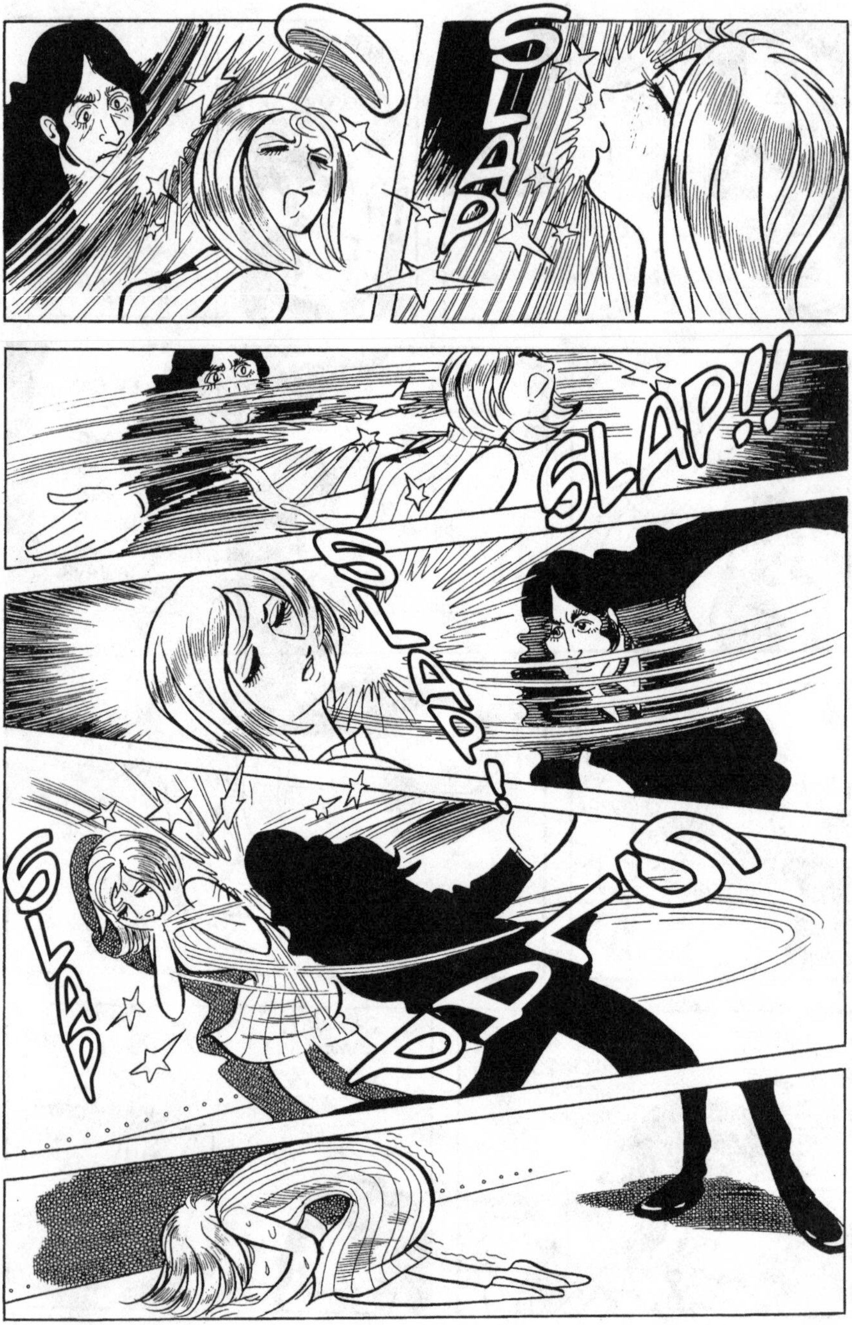
SLAP
SLAP!!
SLAP!
SLAP
SLAP

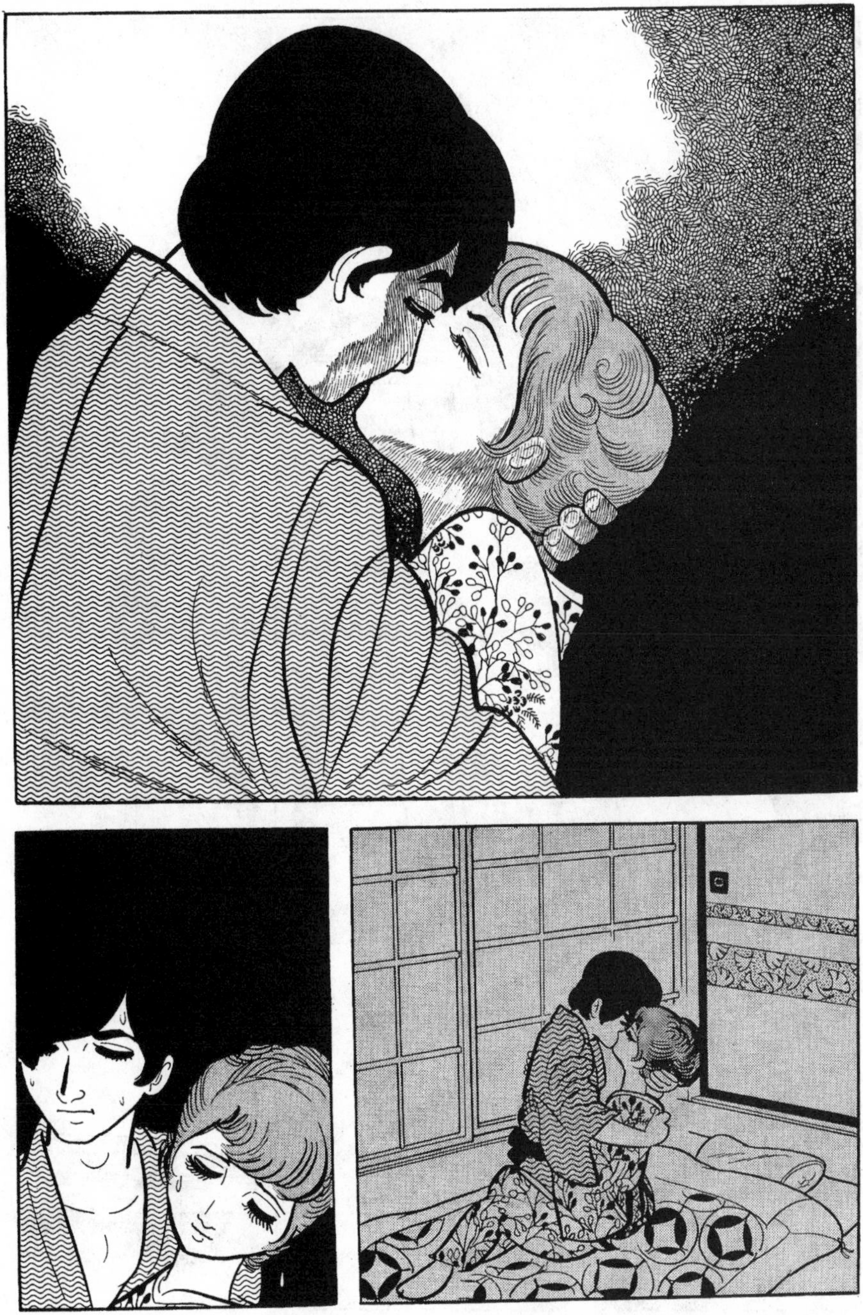

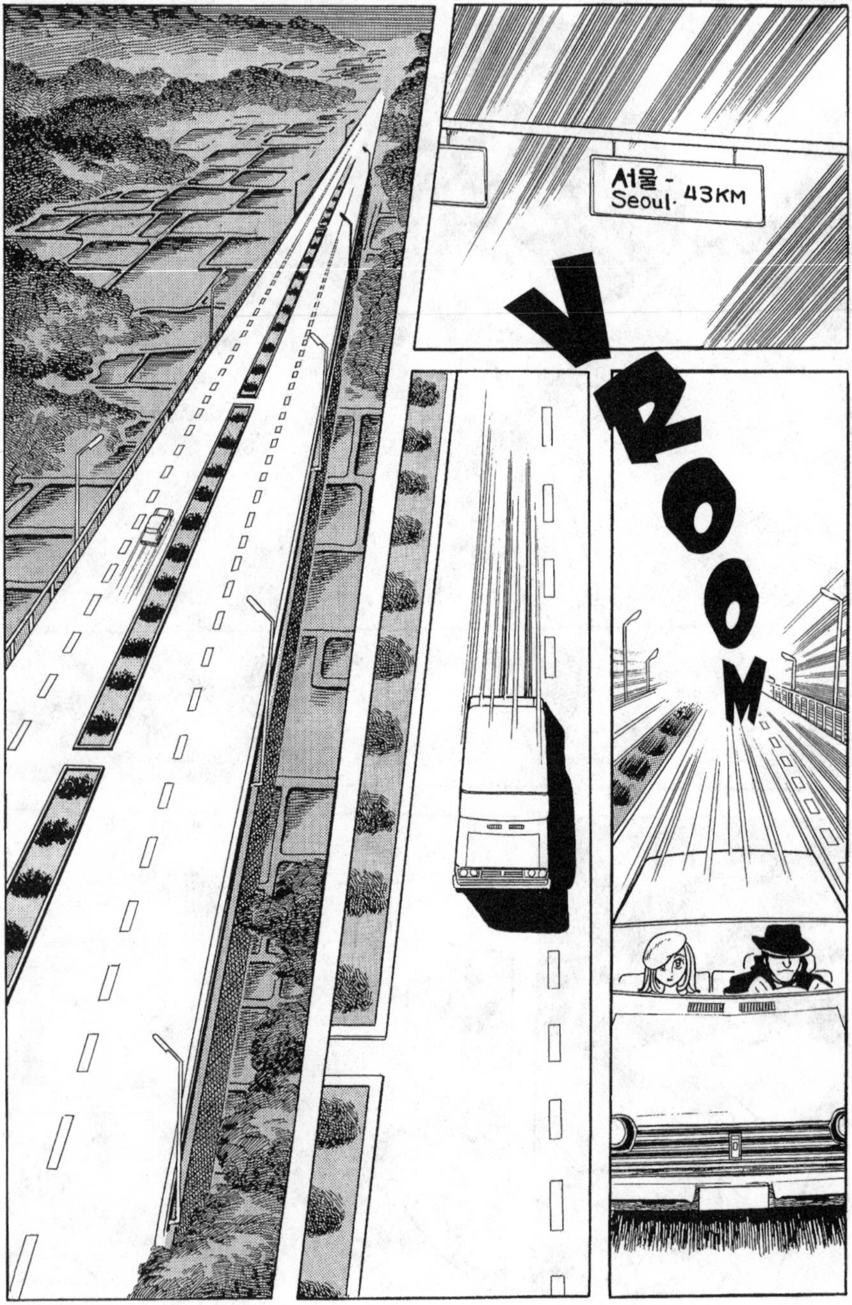
서울 - Seoul · 43KM
VROOM

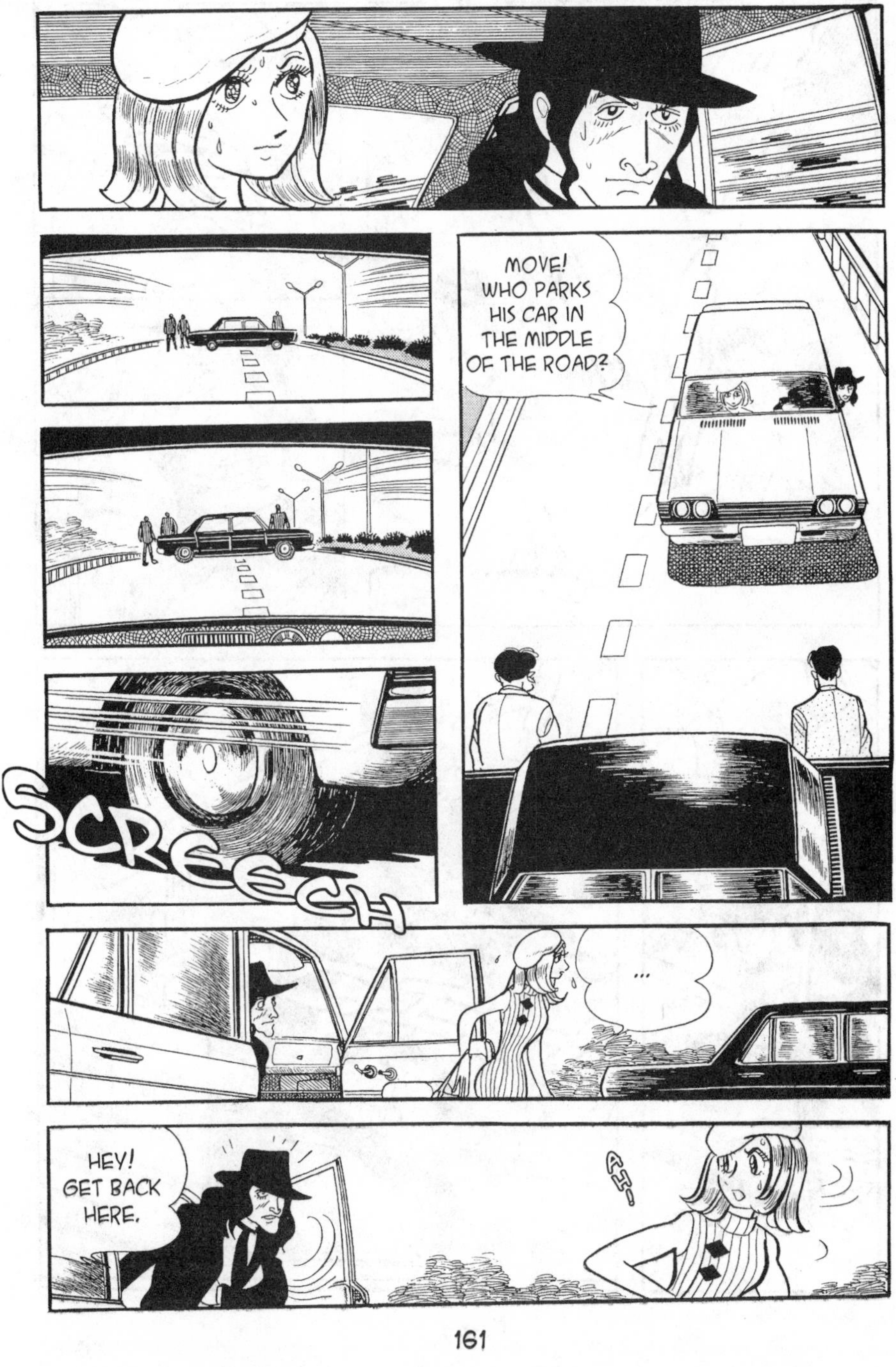

MOVE! WHO PARKS HIS CAR IN THE MIDDLE OF THE ROAD?
SCREECH
...
HEY! GET BACK HERE.
AH!

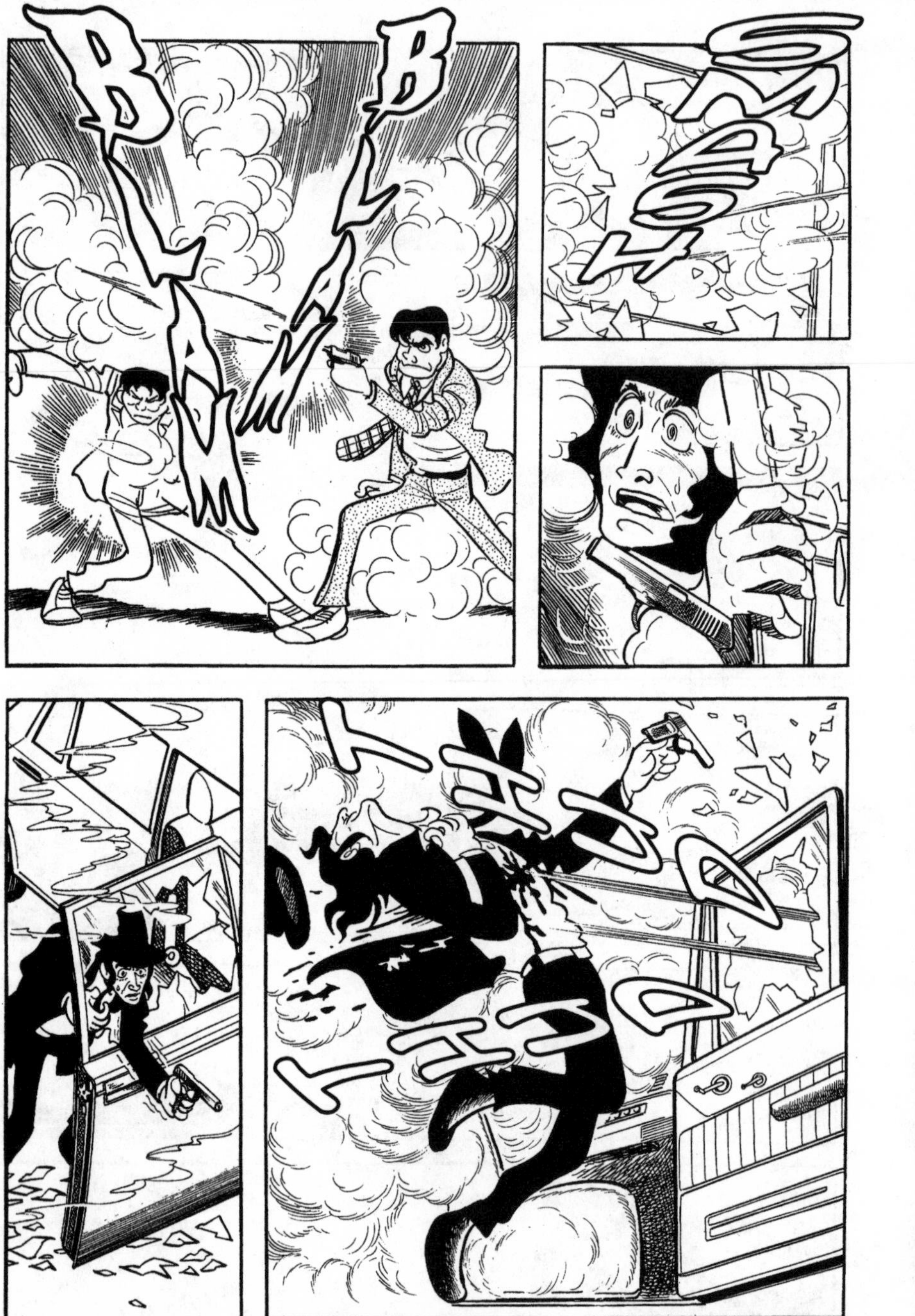
BLAM
BLAM
SMASH

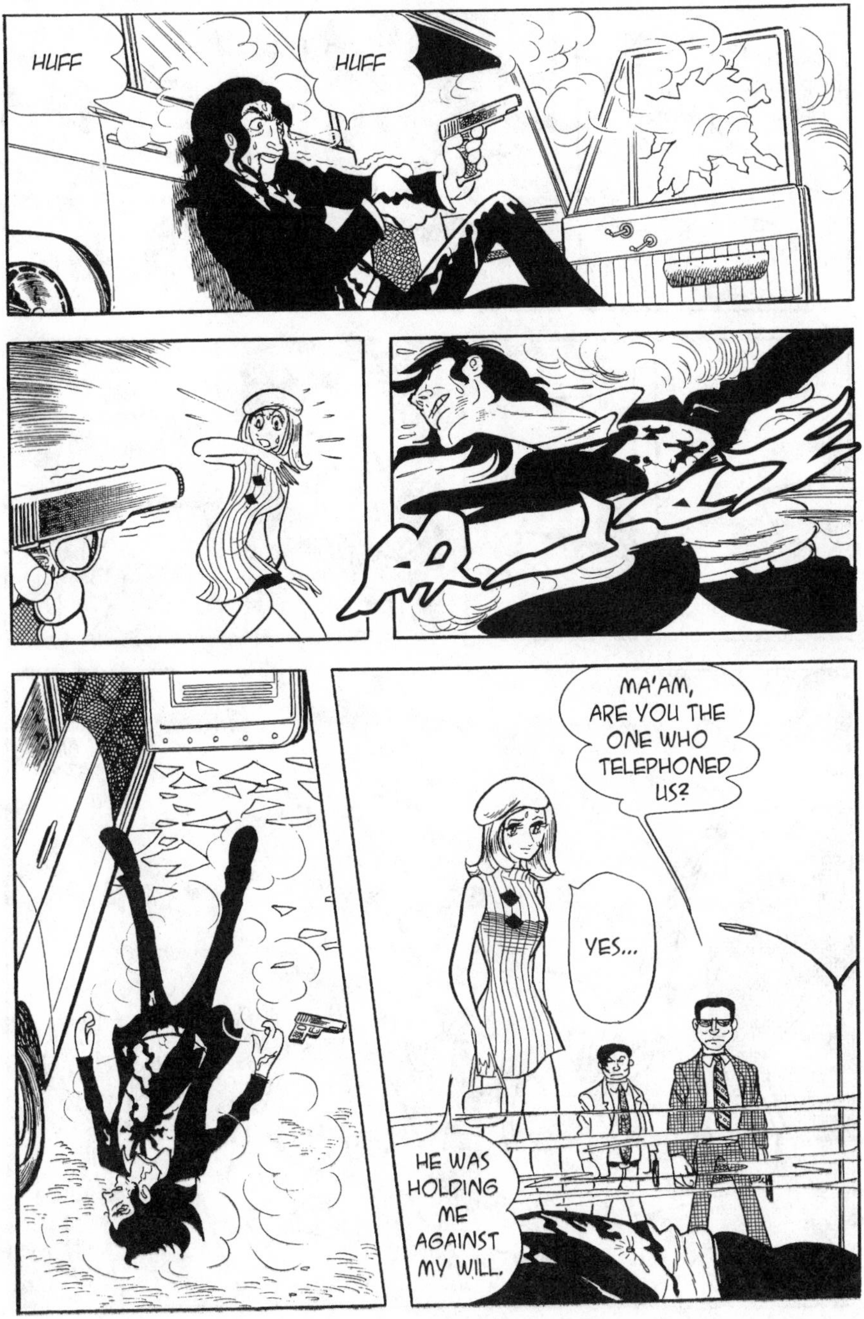
HUFF
HUFF
MA'AM, ARE YOU THE ONE WHO TELEPHONED US?
YES...
HE WAS HOLDING ME AGAINST MY WILL.

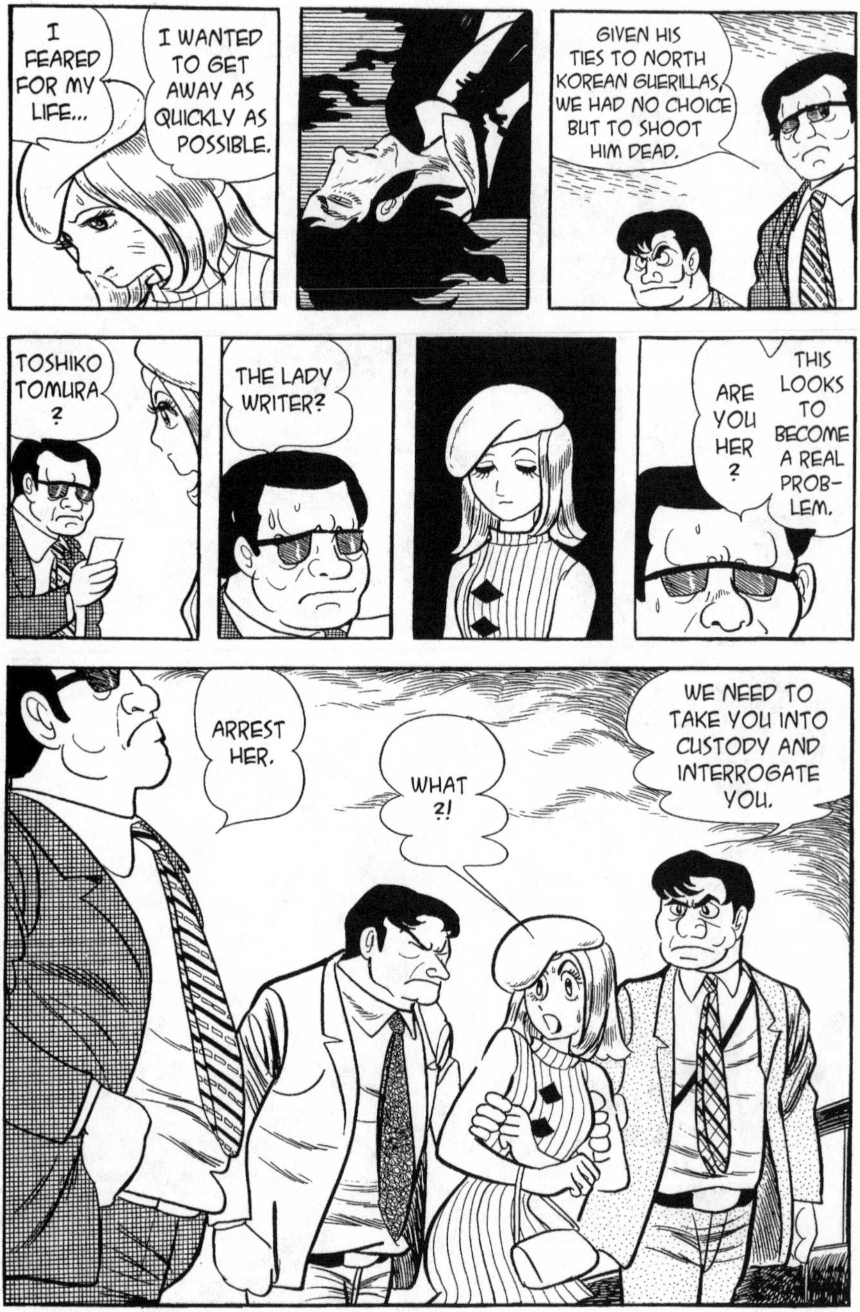
I FEARED FOR MY LIFE...
I WANTED TO GET AWAY AS QUICKLY AS POSSIBLE.
GIVEN HIS TIES TO NORTH KOREAN GUERILLAS, WE HAD NO CHOICE BUT TO SHOOT HIM DEAD.
TOSHIKO TOMURA?
THE LADY WRITER?
ARE YOU HER?
THIS LOOKS TO BECOME A REAL PROB-LEM.
ARREST HER.
WHAT?!
WE NEED TO TAKE YOU INTO CUSTODY AND INTERROGATE YOU.

LONGHORN BEETLE

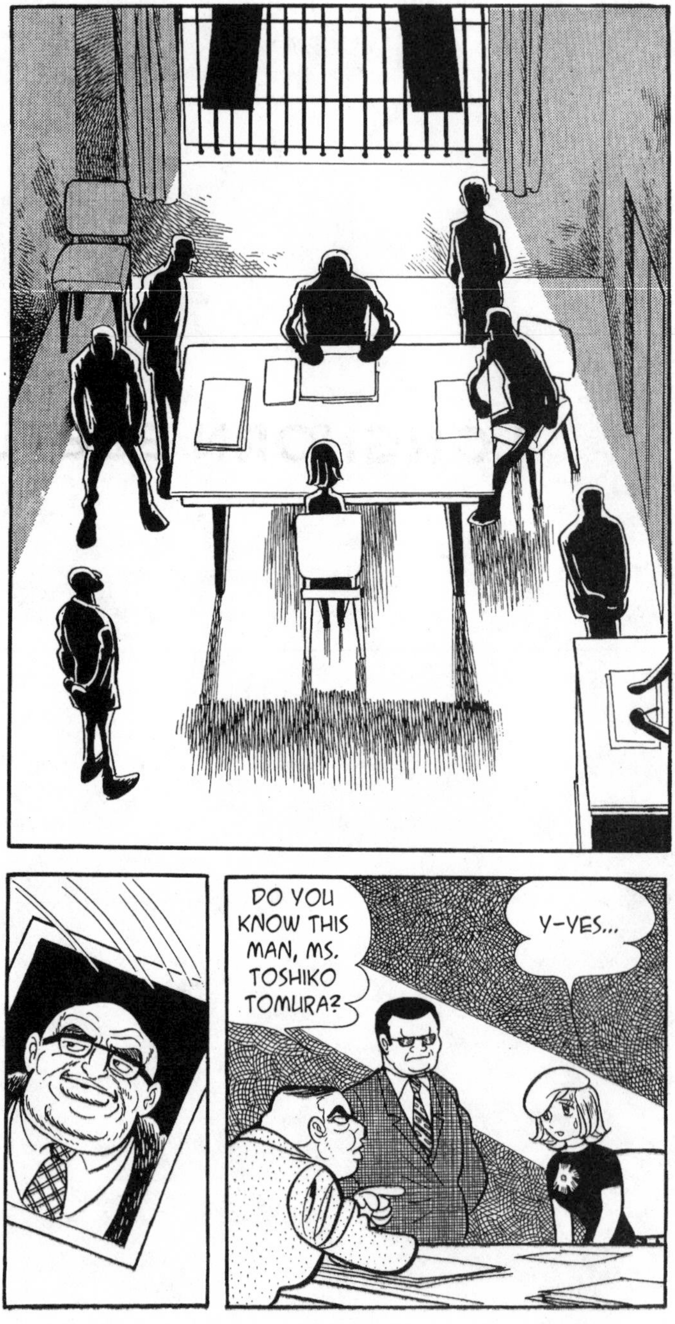
DO YOU KNOW THIS MAN, MS. TOSHIKO TOMURA?
Y-YES...

SESSON KABUTO, HEAD OF THE RIGHT-WING TOUSAN GANG, ISN'T THAT RIGHT?

YOU'VE BEEN SEEN FREQUENTING HIS RESIDENCE.

FREQUENTING? I'D MERELY MADE HIS ACQUAINTANCE IN GINZA...

THIS KABUTO FELLOW IS A VERY DANGEROUS CHARACTER.

TO BE FRANK, HE IS AN INDIVIDUAL THAT THE REPUBLIC OF KOREA ABHORS.

?

SHE KNOWS NOTHING.

I FEARED AS MUCH.

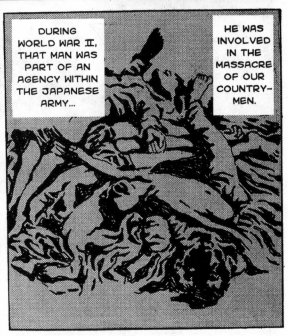

DURING WORLD WAR II, THAT MAN WAS PART OF AN AGENCY WITHIN THE JAPANESE ARMY...

HE WAS INVOLVED IN THE MASSACRE OF OUR COUNTRYMEN.

KABUTO PRESIDED OVER OUR BRETHREN'S SLAUGHTER SEVERAL TIMES.

IN FACT, HE SEEMS TO HAVE GIVEN THE ORDERS.

HE'S A DANGEROUS MAN WHO STILL ESPOUSES THE EXPANSIONIST IDEOLOGY.

B-BUT THAT HAS NOTHING TO DO WITH ME! I WAS BORN IN 1947!

IT DOESN'T MATTER WHEN YOU WERE BORN!!

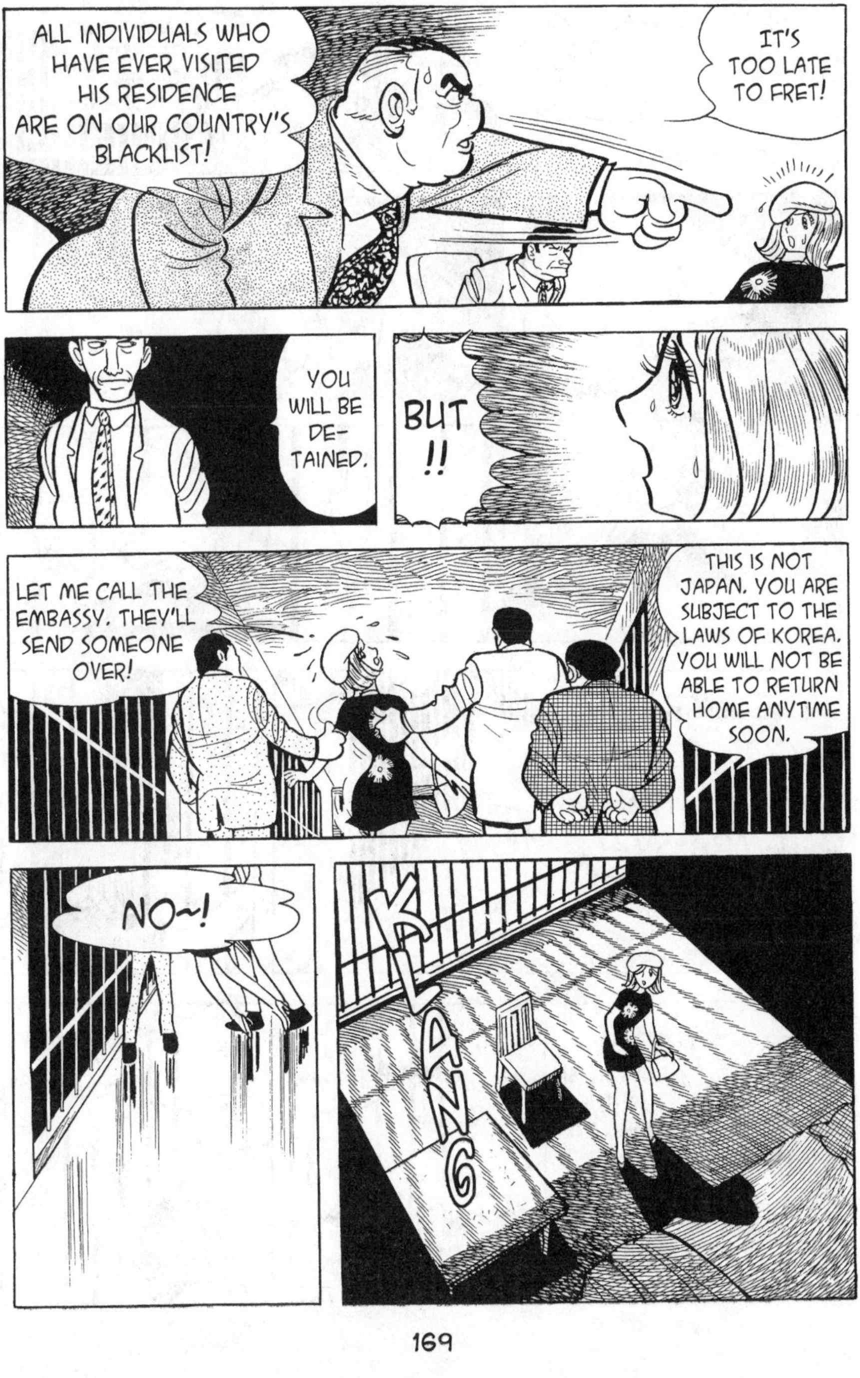
ALL INDIVIDUALS WHO HAVE EVER VISITED HIS RESIDENCE ARE ON OUR COUNTRY'S BLACKLIST!
IT'S TOO LATE TO FRET!
YOU WILL BE DE-TAINED.
BUT !!
LET ME CALL THE EMBASSY. THEY'LL SEND SOMEONE OVER!
THIS IS NOT JAPAN. YOU ARE SUBJECT TO THE LAWS OF KOREA. YOU WILL NOT BE ABLE TO RETURN HOME ANYTIME SOON.
NO~!
KLANG

SHE'S JUST A LI'L YOUNG THING.

THAT IGNORANT TYPE IS THE HARDEST TO HANDLE.

I'LL ADMIT SHE'S ONE CUTE JAPANESE WOMAN.

THE EMBASSY, COULD YOU CALL THE EMBASSY?!

KLAK

KLAK

UNFORTUNATELY, IT'S SATURDAY TODAY.

I DOUBT ANYONE'S AT THE EMBASSY.

THEN TOMORROW!!

IT'LL BE SUNDAY.

THEN... THE DAY AFTER!!

A HOLIDAY IN OUR COUNTRY.

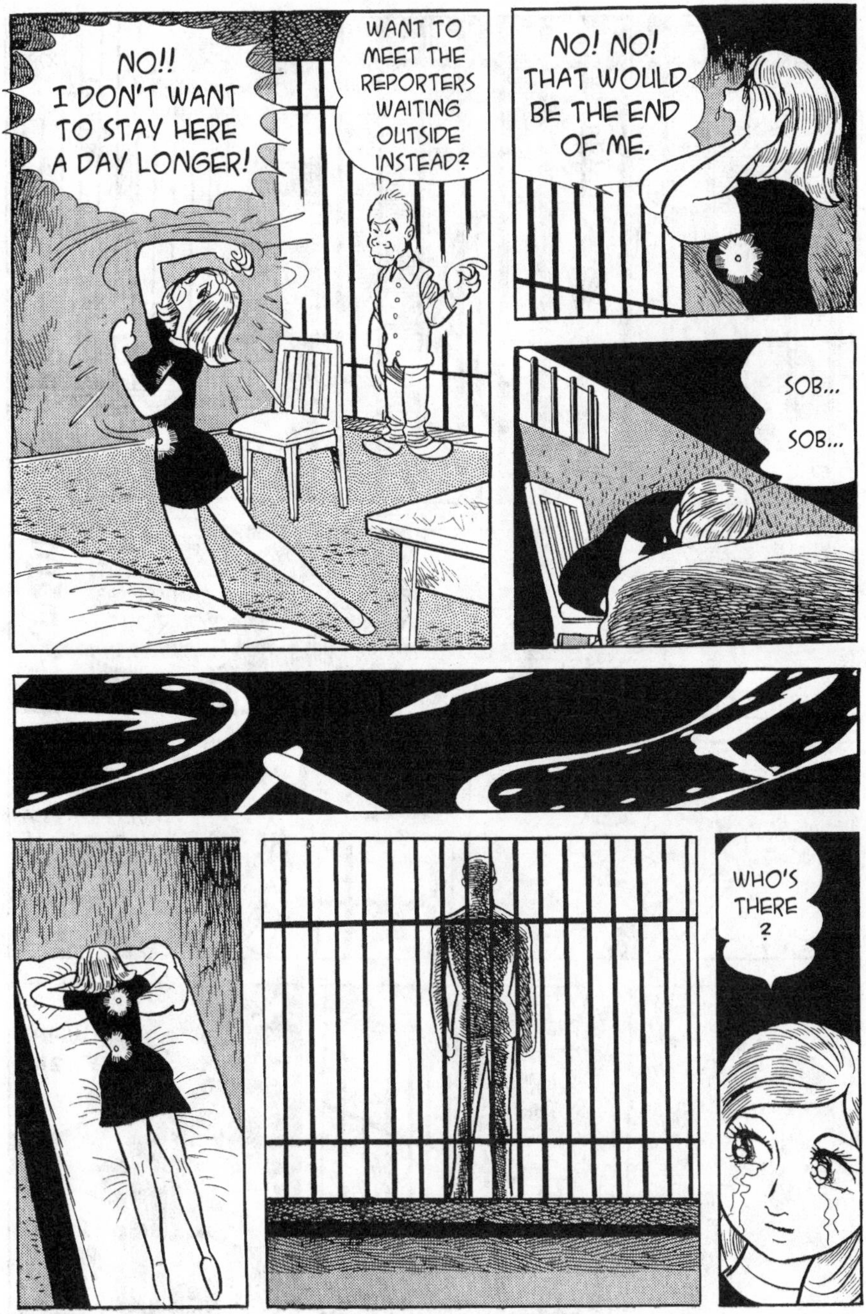
NO!! I DON'T WANT TO STAY HERE A DAY LONGER!
WANT TO MEET THE REPORTERS WAITING OUTSIDE INSTEAD?
NO! NO! THAT WOULD BE THE END OF ME.
SOB... SOB...
WHO'S THERE ?

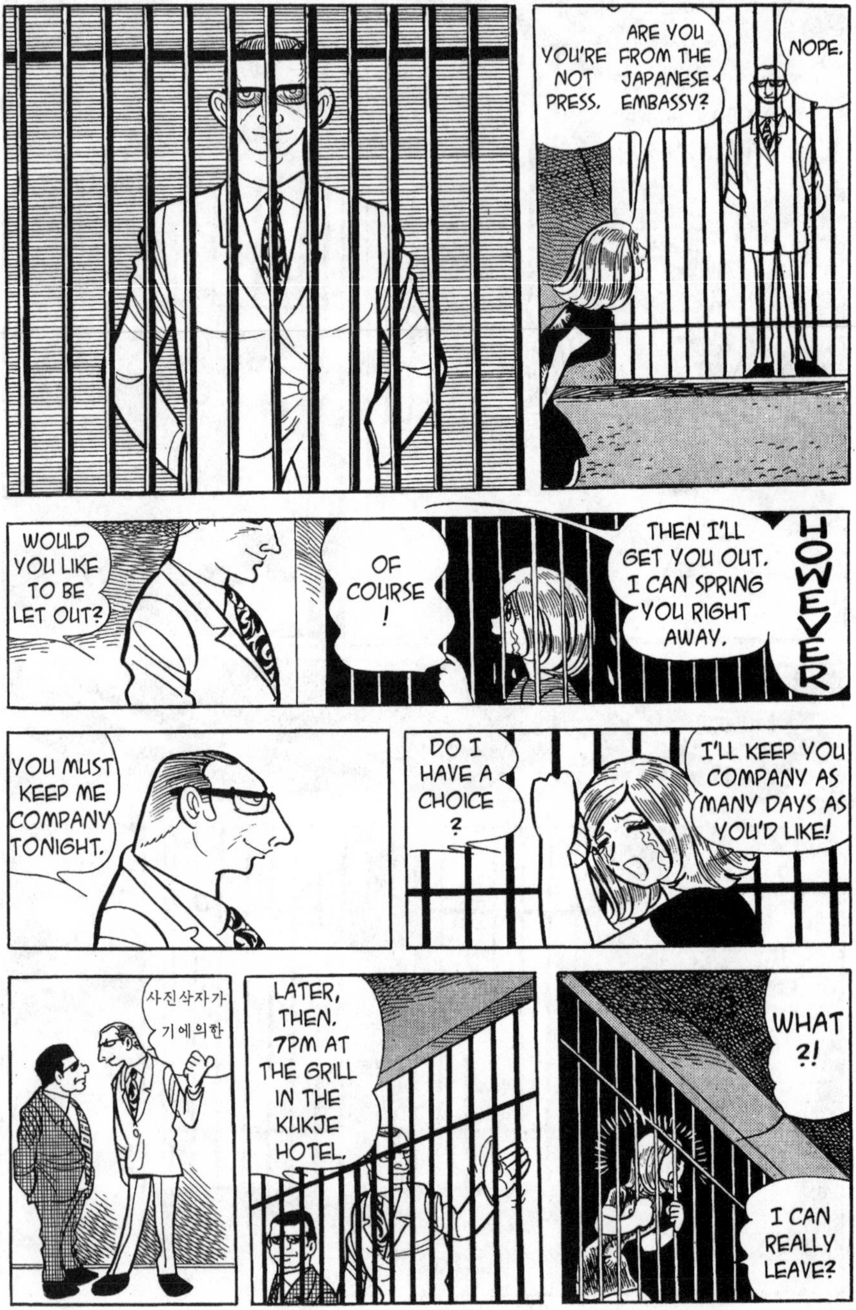
YOU'RE NOT PRESS.
ARE YOU FROM THE JAPANESE EMBASSY?
NOPE.
WOULD YOU LIKE TO BE LET OUT?
OF COURSE!
THEN I'LL GET YOU OUT. I CAN SPRING YOU RIGHT AWAY.
HOWEVER
YOU MUST KEEP ME COMPANY TONIGHT.
DO I HAVE A CHOICE?
I'LL KEEP YOU COMPANY AS MANY DAYS AS YOU'D LIKE!
사진삭자가 기예의한
LATER, THEN. 7PM AT THE GRILL IN THE KUKJE HOTEL.
WHAT?!
I CAN REALLY LEAVE?

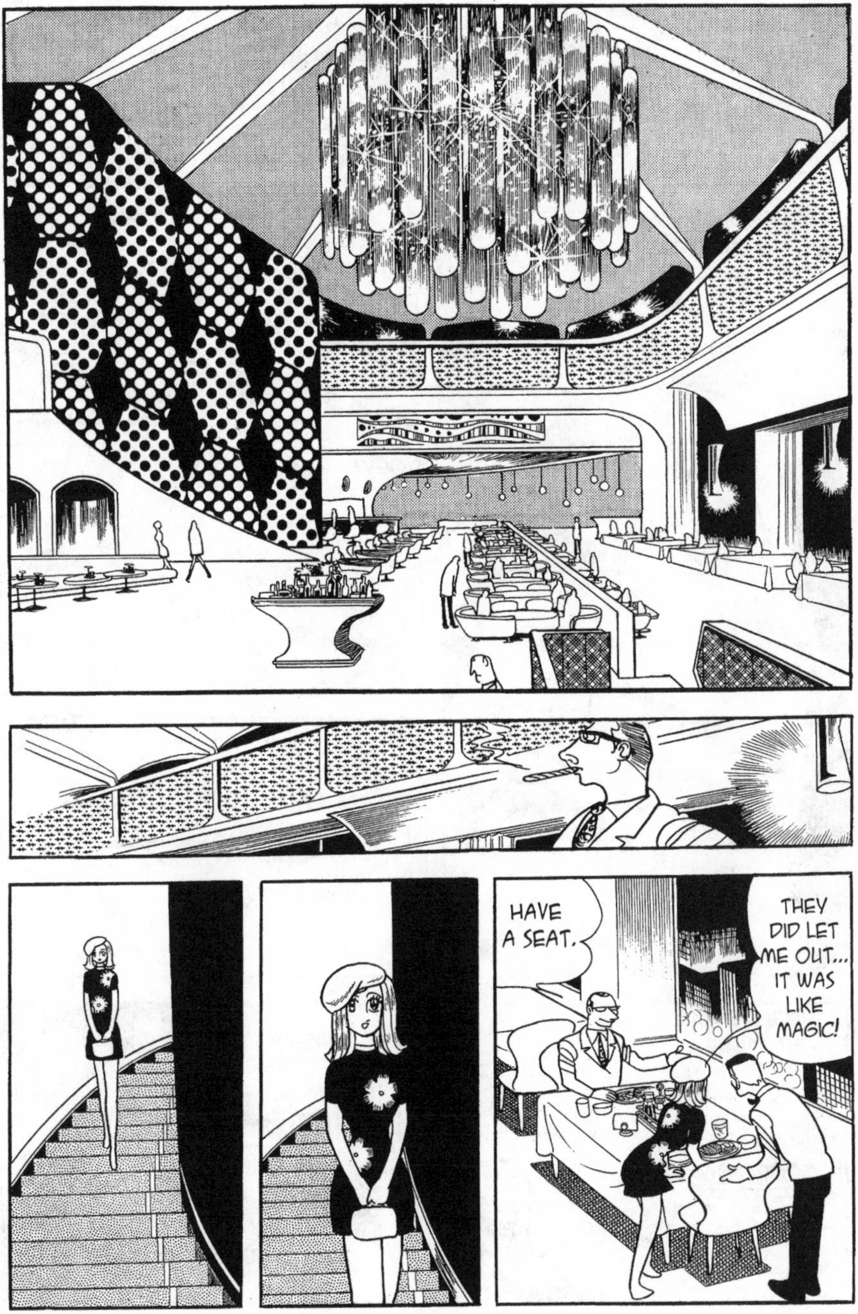
HAVE A SEAT.
THEY DID LET ME OUT... IT WAS LIKE MAGIC!

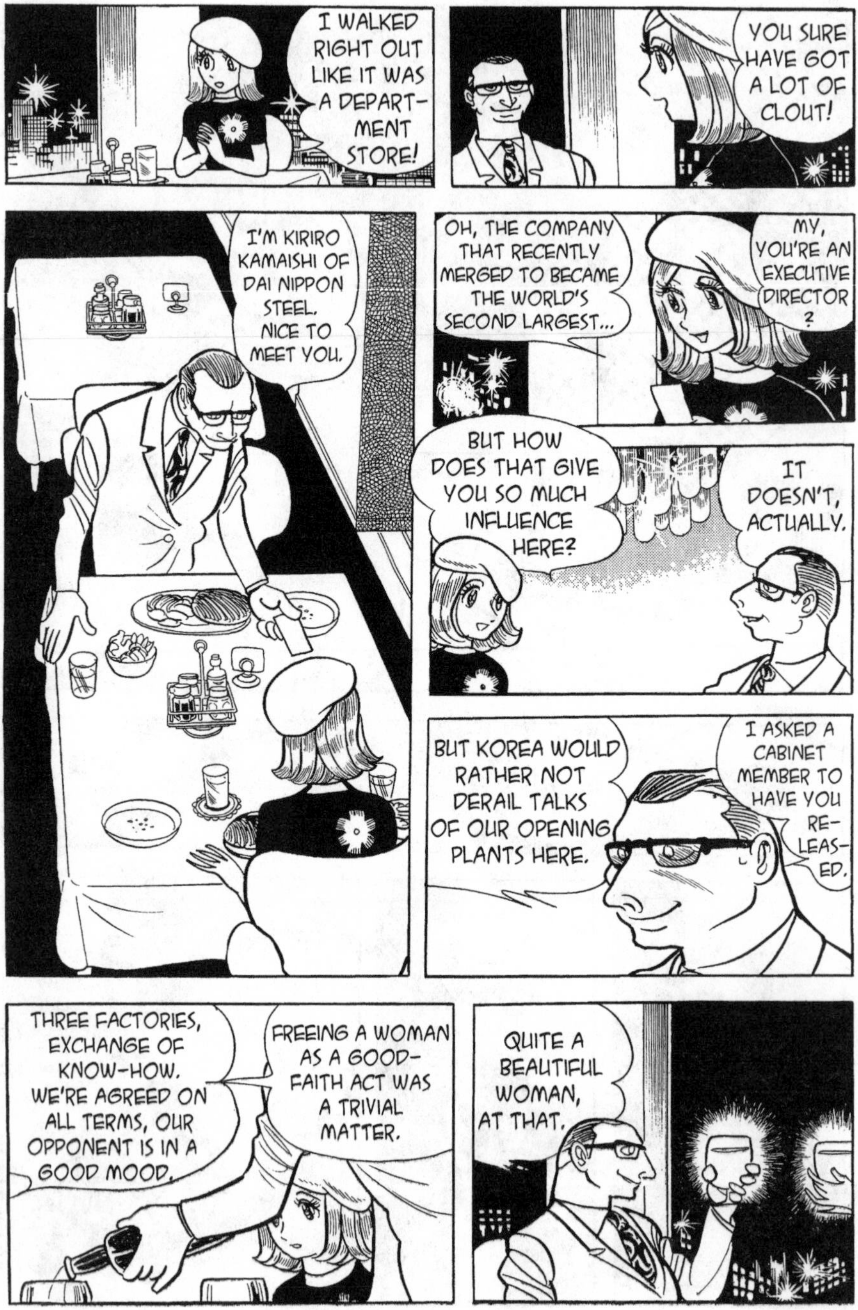
I WALKED RIGHT OUT LIKE IT WAS A DEPARTMENT STORE!
YOU SURE HAVE GOT A LOT OF CLOUT!
I'M KIRIRO KAMAISHI OF DAI NIPPON STEEL. NICE TO MEET YOU.
OH, THE COMPANY THAT RECENTLY MERGED TO BECAME THE WORLD'S SECOND LARGEST...
MY, YOU'RE AN EXECUTIVE DIRECTOR?
BUT HOW DOES THAT GIVE YOU SO MUCH INFLUENCE HERE?
IT DOESN'T, ACTUALLY.
BUT KOREA WOULD RATHER NOT DERAIL TALKS OF OUR OPENING PLANTS HERE.
I ASKED A CABINET MEMBER TO HAVE YOU RELEASED.
THREE FACTORIES, EXCHANGE OF KNOW-HOW. WE'RE AGREED ON ALL TERMS, OUR OPPONENT IS IN A GOOD MOOD.
FREEING A WOMAN AS A GOOD-FAITH ACT WAS A TRIVIAL MATTER.
QUITE A BEAUTIFUL WOMAN, AT THAT.

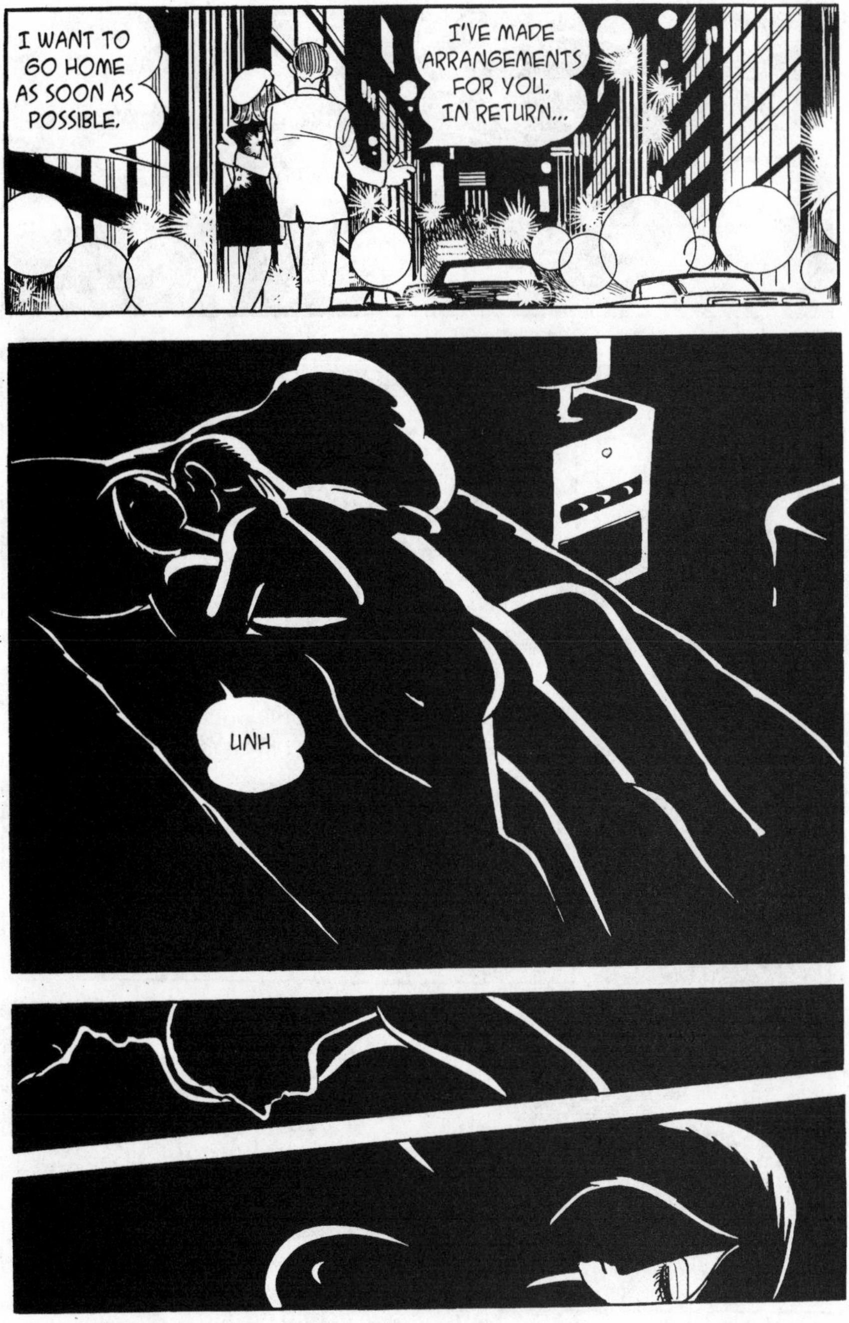
I WANT TO GO HOME AS SOON AS POSSIBLE.
I'VE MADE ARRANGEMENTS FOR YOU. IN RETURN...
UNH

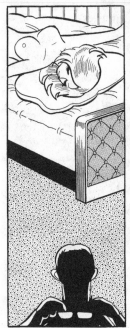

I'VE NEVER MET ANYONE LIKE YOU BEFORE.

...
REALLY?

ARE YOU EXPECTING MORE WINING AND DINING?

DON'T. WE'RE DONE HERE.

THIS IS GOODBYE FOR US.

176

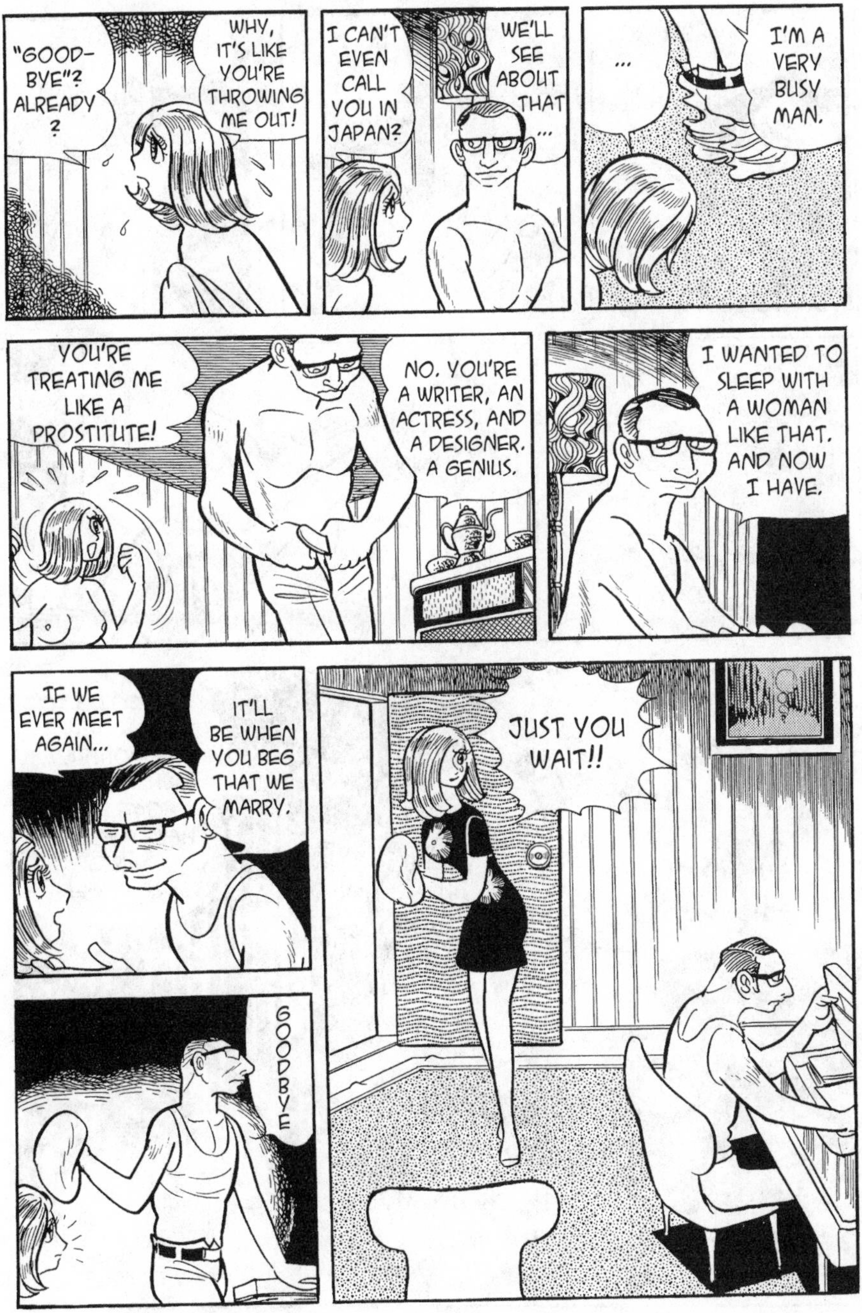
"GOOD-BYE"? ALREADY?
WHY, IT'S LIKE YOU'RE THROWING ME OUT!
I CAN'T EVEN CALL YOU IN JAPAN?
WE'LL SEE ABOUT THAT ...
...
I'M A VERY BUSY MAN.
YOU'RE TREATING ME LIKE A PROSTITUTE!
NO. YOU'RE A WRITER, AN ACTRESS, AND A DESIGNER. A GENIUS.
I WANTED TO SLEEP WITH A WOMAN LIKE THAT. AND NOW I HAVE.
IF WE EVER MEET AGAIN...
IT'LL BE WHEN YOU BEG THAT WE MARRY.
GOODBYE
JUST YOU WAIT!!

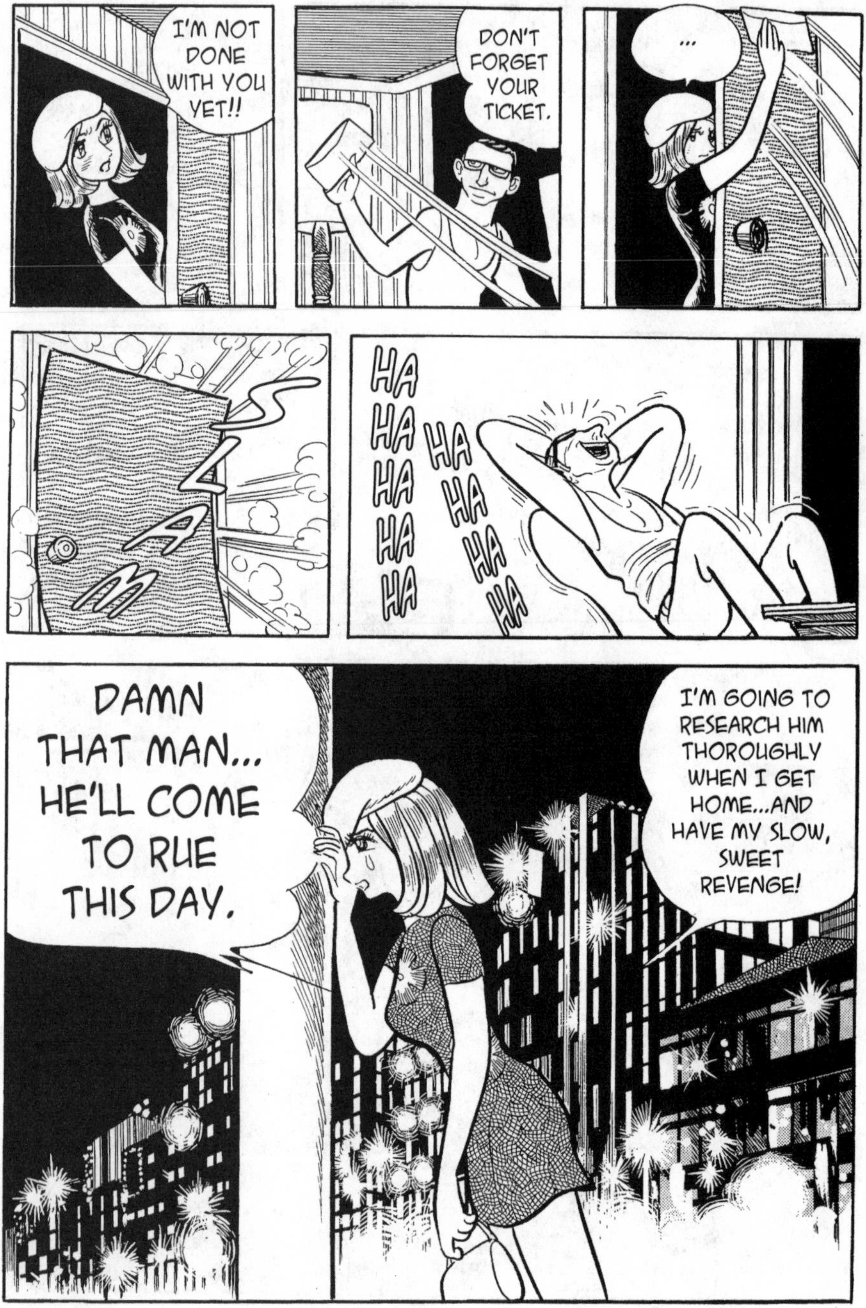
I'M NOT DONE WITH YOU YET!!
DON'T FORGET YOUR TICKET.
...
SLAM
HA HA HA HA HA HA
HA HA HA HA HA
DAMN THAT MAN... HE'LL COME TO RUE THIS DAY.
I'M GOING TO RESEARCH HIM THOROUGHLY WHEN I GET HOME...AND HAVE MY SLOW, SWEET REVENGE!

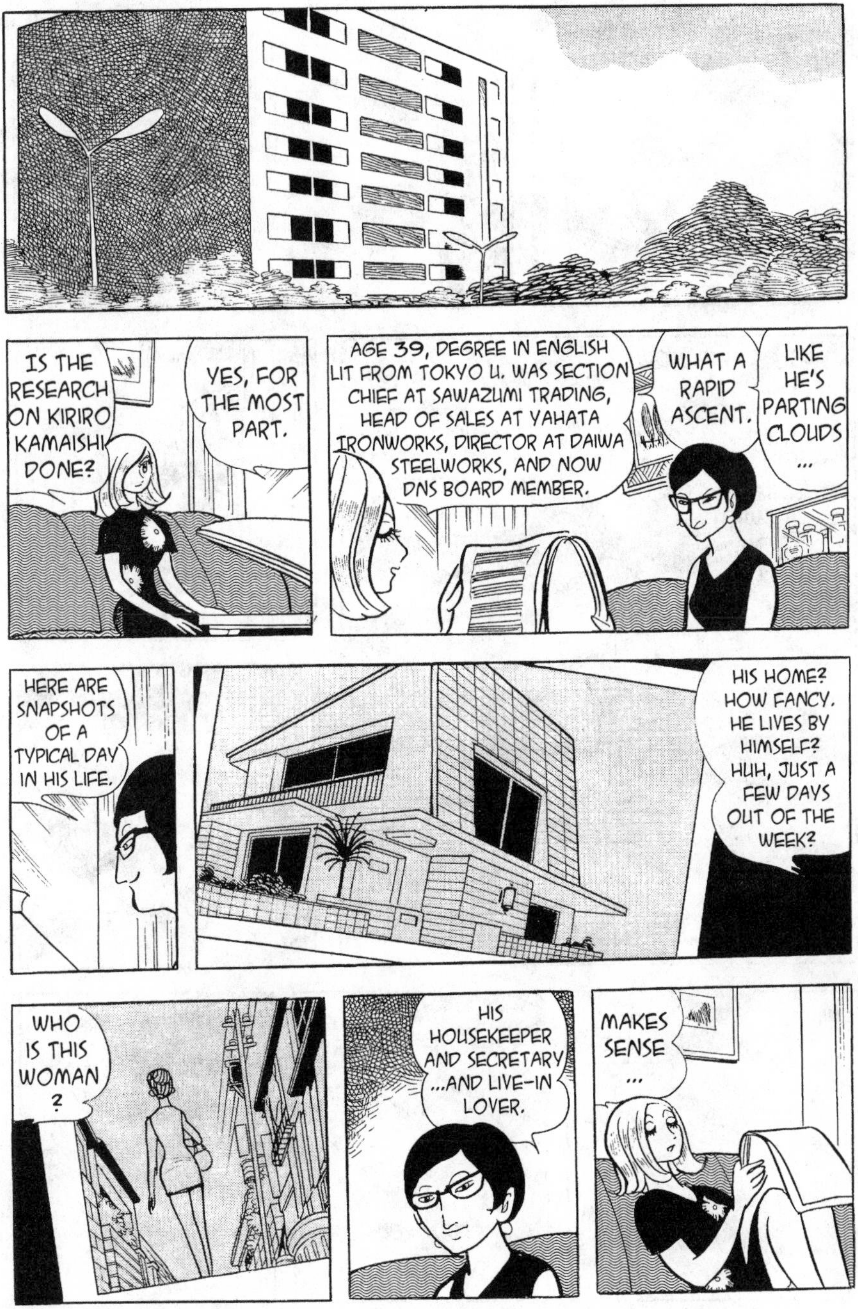
IS THE RESEARCH ON KIRIRO KAMAISHI DONE?
YES, FOR THE MOST PART.
AGE 39, DEGREE IN ENGLISH LIT FROM TOKYO U. WAS SECTION CHIEF AT SAWAZUMI TRADING, HEAD OF SALES AT YAHATA IRONWORKS, DIRECTOR AT DAIWA STEELWORKS, AND NOW DNS BOARD MEMBER.
WHAT A RAPID ASCENT.
LIKE HE'S PARTING CLOUDS ...
HERE ARE SNAPSHOTS OF A TYPICAL DAY IN HIS LIFE.
HIS HOME? HOW FANCY. HE LIVES BY HIMSELF? HUH, JUST A FEW DAYS OUT OF THE WEEK?
WHO IS THIS WOMAN ?
HIS HOUSEKEEPER AND SECRETARY ...AND LIVE-IN LOVER.
MAKES SENSE ...

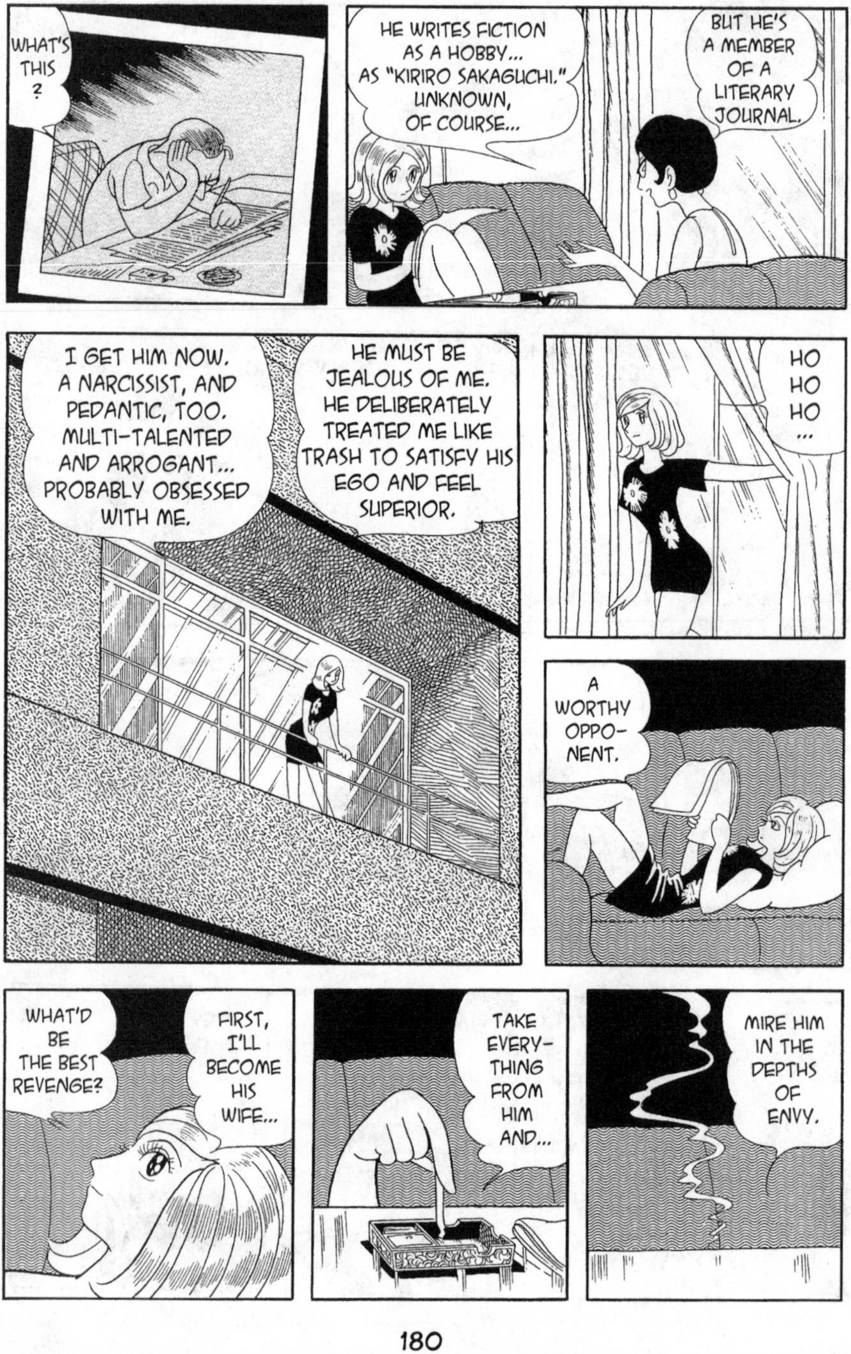
WHAT'S THIS ?
HE WRITES FICTION AS A HOBBY... AS "KIRIRO SAKAGUCHI." UNKNOWN, OF COURSE...
BUT HE'S A MEMBER OF A LITERARY JOURNAL.
I GET HIM NOW. A NARCISSIST, AND PEDANTIC, TOO. MULTI-TALENTED AND ARROGANT... PROBABLY OBSESSED WITH ME.
HE MUST BE JEALOUS OF ME. HE DELIBERATELY TREATED ME LIKE TRASH TO SATISFY HIS EGO AND FEEL SUPERIOR.
HO HO HO ...
A WORTHY OPPO-NENT.
WHAT'D BE THE BEST REVENGE?
FIRST, I'LL BECOME HIS WIFE...
TAKE EVERY-THING FROM HIM AND...
MIRE HIM IN THE DEPTHS OF ENVY.

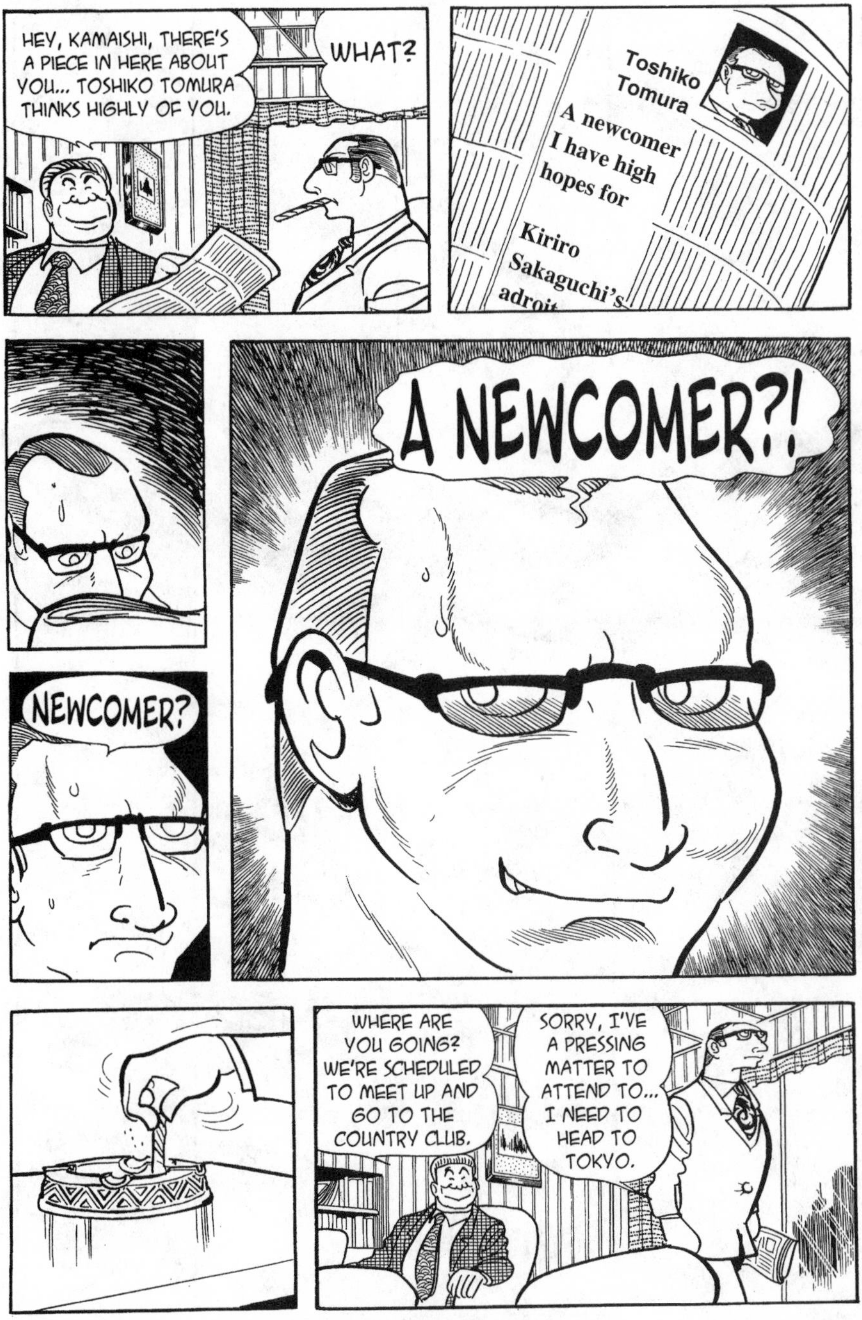
HEY, KAMAISHI, THERE'S A PIECE IN HERE ABOUT YOU... TOSHIKO TOMURA THINKS HIGHLY OF YOU.
WHAT?
Toshiko Tomura
A newcomer I have high hopes for
Kiriro Sakaguchi's adroit
A NEWCOMER?!
NEWCOMER?
WHERE ARE YOU GOING? WE'RE SCHEDULED TO MEET UP AND GO TO THE COUNTRY CLUB.
SORRY, I'VE A PRESSING MATTER TO ATTEND TO... I NEED TO HEAD TO TOKYO.

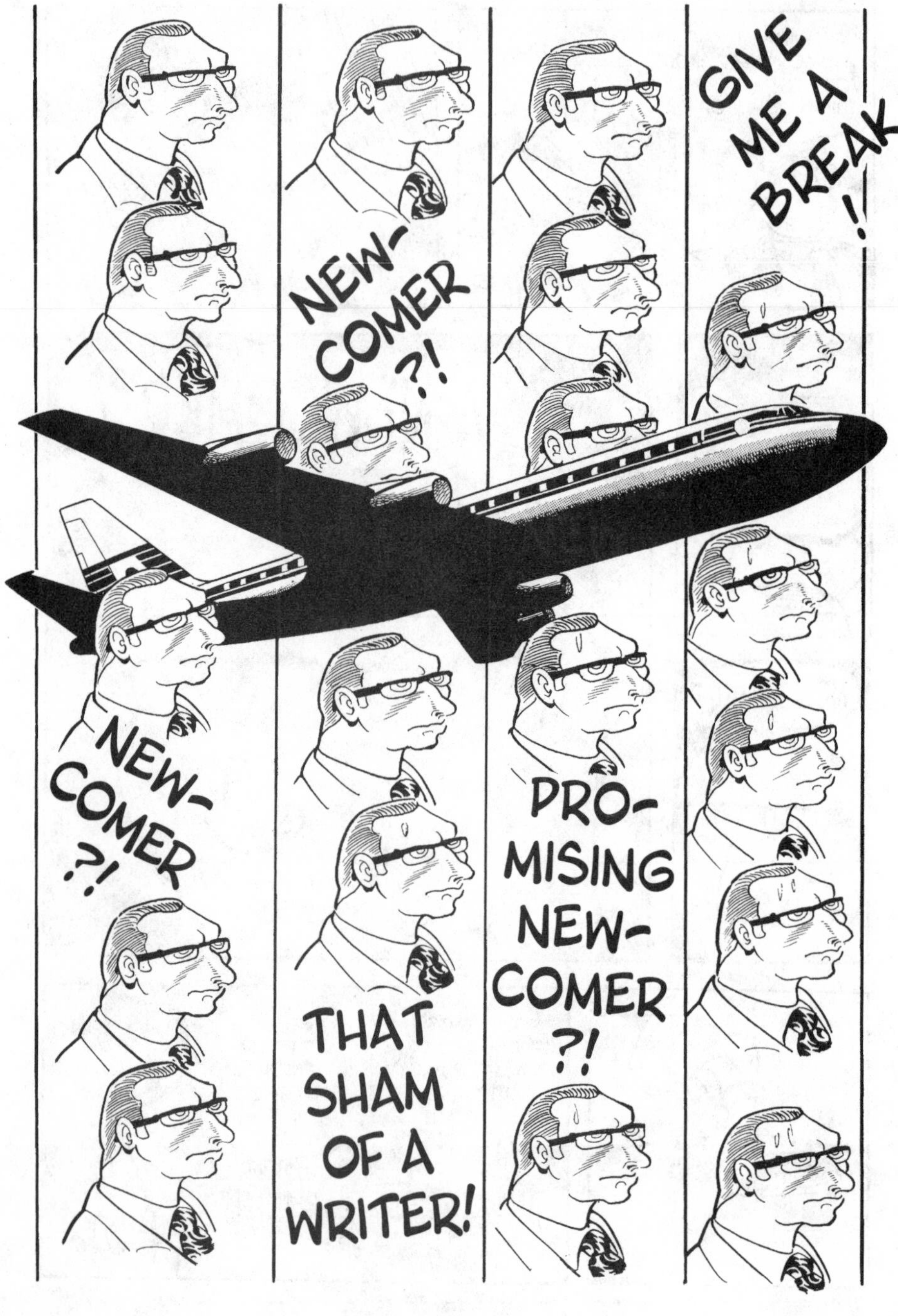
NEW-COMER ?!
NEW-COMER ?!
THAT SHAM OF A WRITER!
PRO-MISING NEW-COMER ?!
GIVE ME A BREAK !!

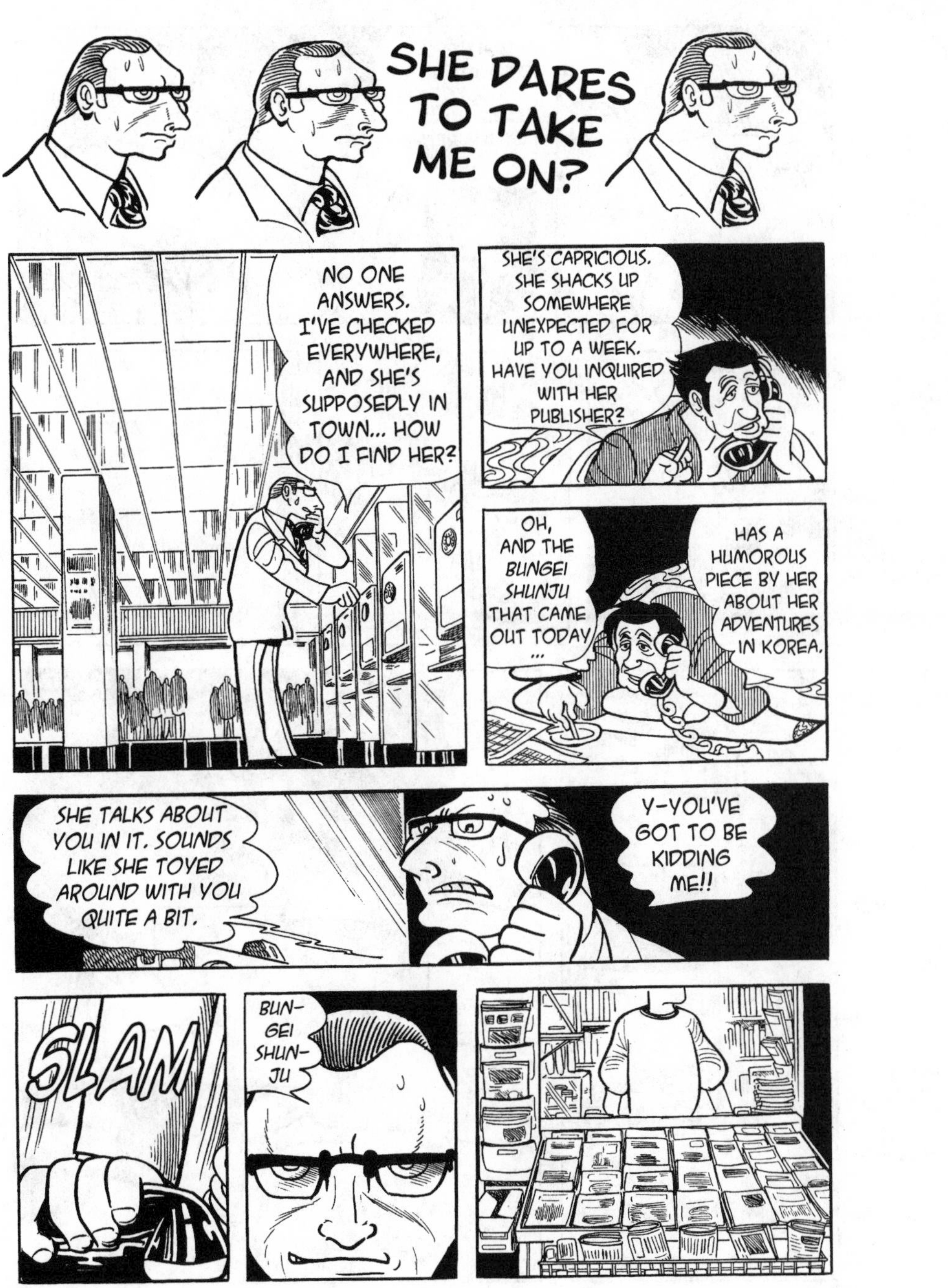
SHE DARES TO TAKE ME ON?
NO ONE ANSWERS. I'VE CHECKED EVERYWHERE, AND SHE'S SUPPOSEDLY IN TOWN... HOW DO I FIND HER?
SHE'S CAPRICIOUS. SHE SHACKS UP SOMEWHERE UNEXPECTED FOR UP TO A WEEK. HAVE YOU INQUIRED WITH HER PUBLISHER?
OH, AND THE BUNGEI SHUNJU THAT CAME OUT TODAY ...
HAS A HUMOROUS PIECE BY HER ABOUT HER ADVENTURES IN KOREA.
SHE TALKS ABOUT YOU IN IT. SOUNDS LIKE SHE TOYED AROUND WITH YOU QUITE A BIT.
Y-YOU'VE GOT TO BE KIDDING ME!!
SLAM
BUN-GEI SHUN-JU

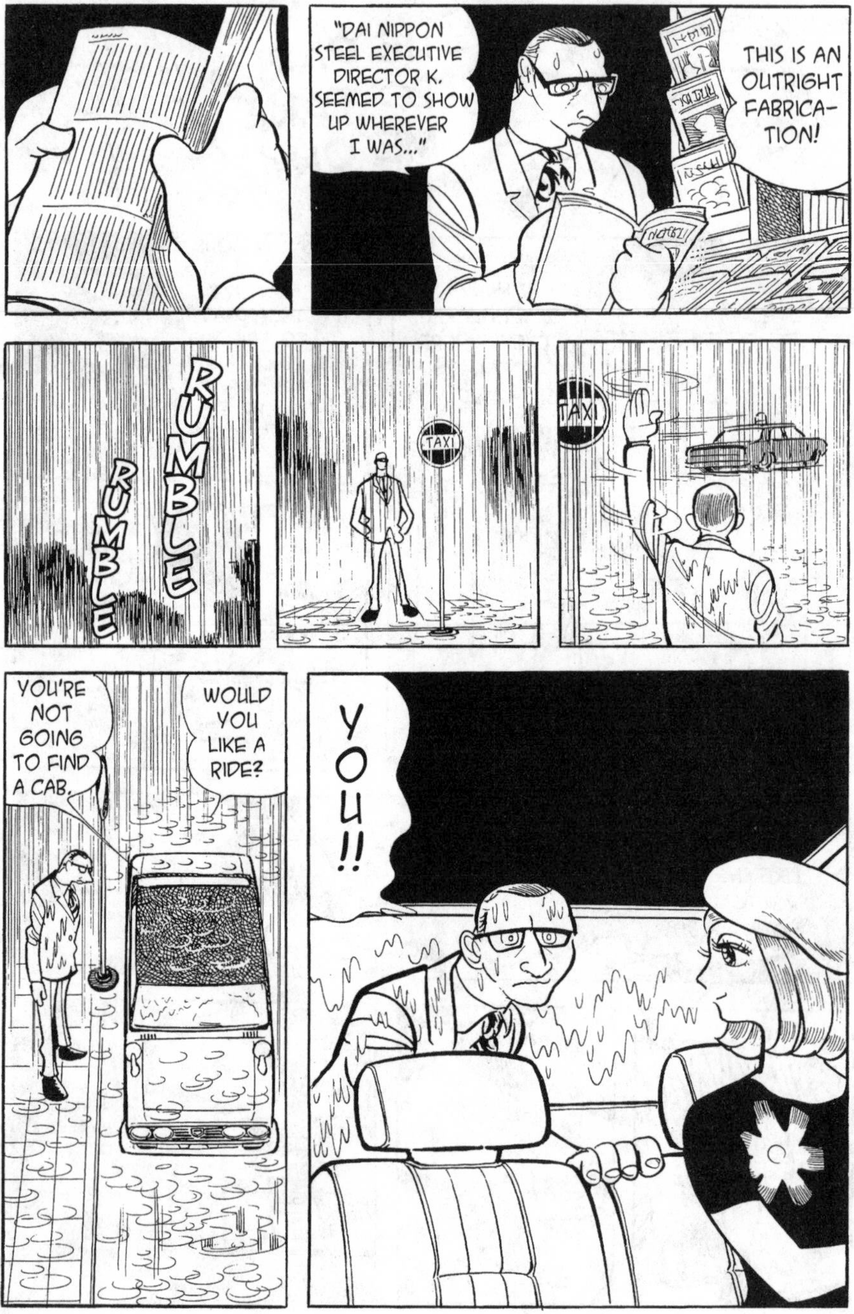
"DAI NIPPON STEEL EXECUTIVE DIRECTOR K. SEEMED TO SHOW UP WHEREVER I WAS..."
THIS IS AN OUTRIGHT FABRICATION!
RUMBLE
RUMBLE
TAXI
TAXI
YOU'RE NOT GOING TO FIND A CAB.
WOULD YOU LIKE A RIDE?
YOU!!

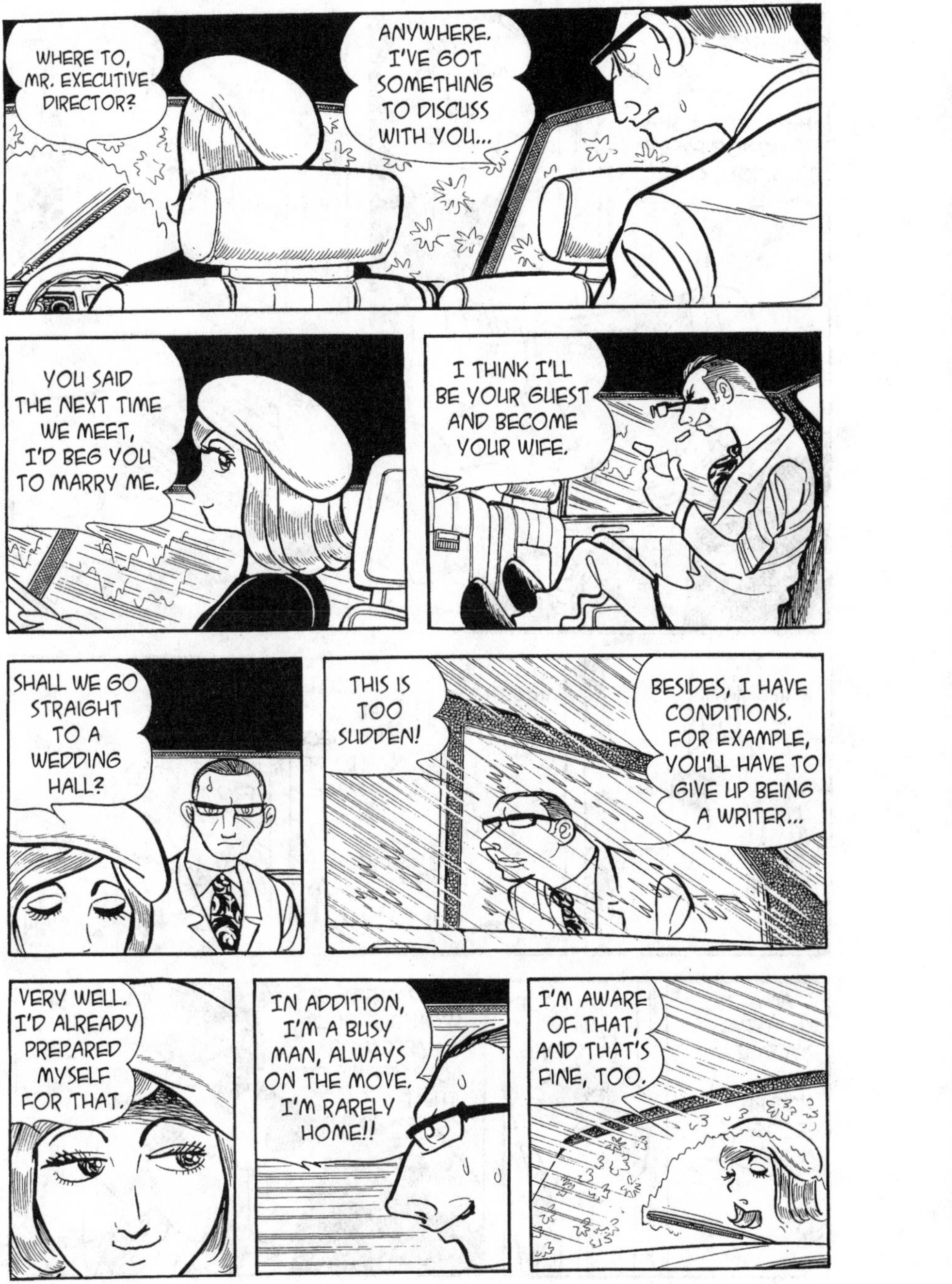
WHERE TO, MR. EXECUTIVE DIRECTOR?
ANYWHERE. I'VE GOT SOMETHING TO DISCUSS WITH YOU...
YOU SAID THE NEXT TIME WE MEET, I'D BEG YOU TO MARRY ME.
I THINK I'LL BE YOUR GUEST AND BECOME YOUR WIFE.
SHALL WE GO STRAIGHT TO A WEDDING HALL?
THIS IS TOO SUDDEN!
BESIDES, I HAVE CONDITIONS. FOR EXAMPLE, YOU'LL HAVE TO GIVE UP BEING A WRITER...
VERY WELL. I'D ALREADY PREPARED MYSELF FOR THAT.
IN ADDITION, I'M A BUSY MAN, ALWAYS ON THE MOVE. I'M RARELY HOME!!
I'M AWARE OF THAT, AND THAT'S FINE, TOO.

PLEASE WRITE DOWN ALL OF THE TERMS YOU DESIRE, HERE, AND I SHALL HONOR EVERY SINGLE ONE.

ARE YOU MOCKING ME? YOU'LL REGRET IT.

...

HERE.

THIS IS IT?

YEAH, THAT'S ALL.

YOU'LL BE KEPT IN CHECK ALL LIFE LONG.

THERE'S ONE HUGE THING MISSING FROM HERE.

ALLOW ME TO WRITE IT IN.

"ANY UNILATERAL DIVORCE WILL NOT BE RECOGNIZED."

THAT GOES WITHOUT SAYING.

"AND IF EITHER SPOUSE SHOULD HAPPEN TO VIOLATE ANY OF THESE TERMS...

ALL OF THEIR ASSETS SHALL BE TRANSFERRED TO THE OTHER."

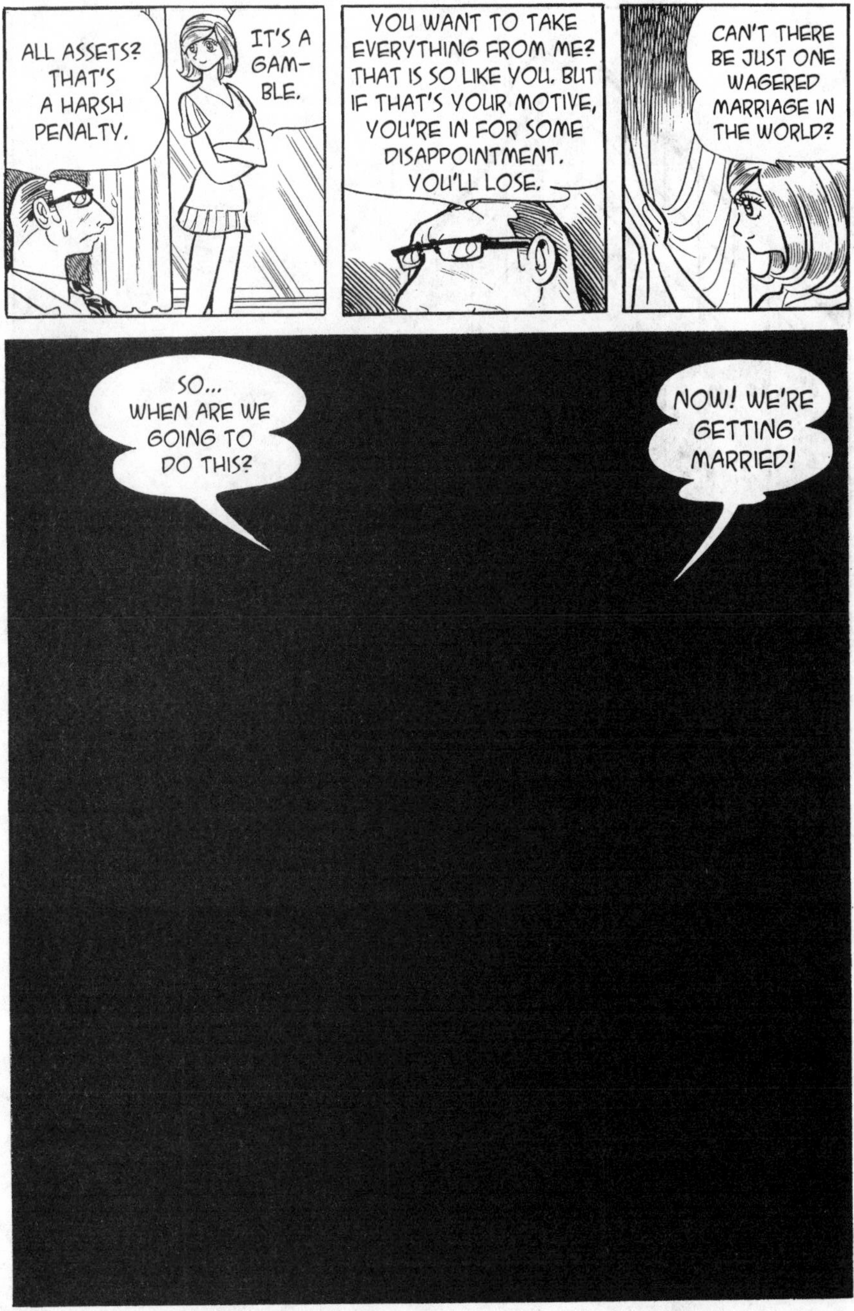
ALL ASSETS? THAT'S A HARSH PENALTY.
IT'S A GAMBLE.
YOU WANT TO TAKE EVERYTHING FROM ME? THAT IS SO LIKE YOU. BUT IF THAT'S YOUR MOTIVE, YOU'RE IN FOR SOME DISAPPOINTMENT. YOU'LL LOSE.
CAN'T THERE BE JUST ONE WAGERED MARRIAGE IN THE WORLD?
SO... WHEN ARE WE GOING TO DO THIS?
NOW! WE'RE GETTING MARRIED!

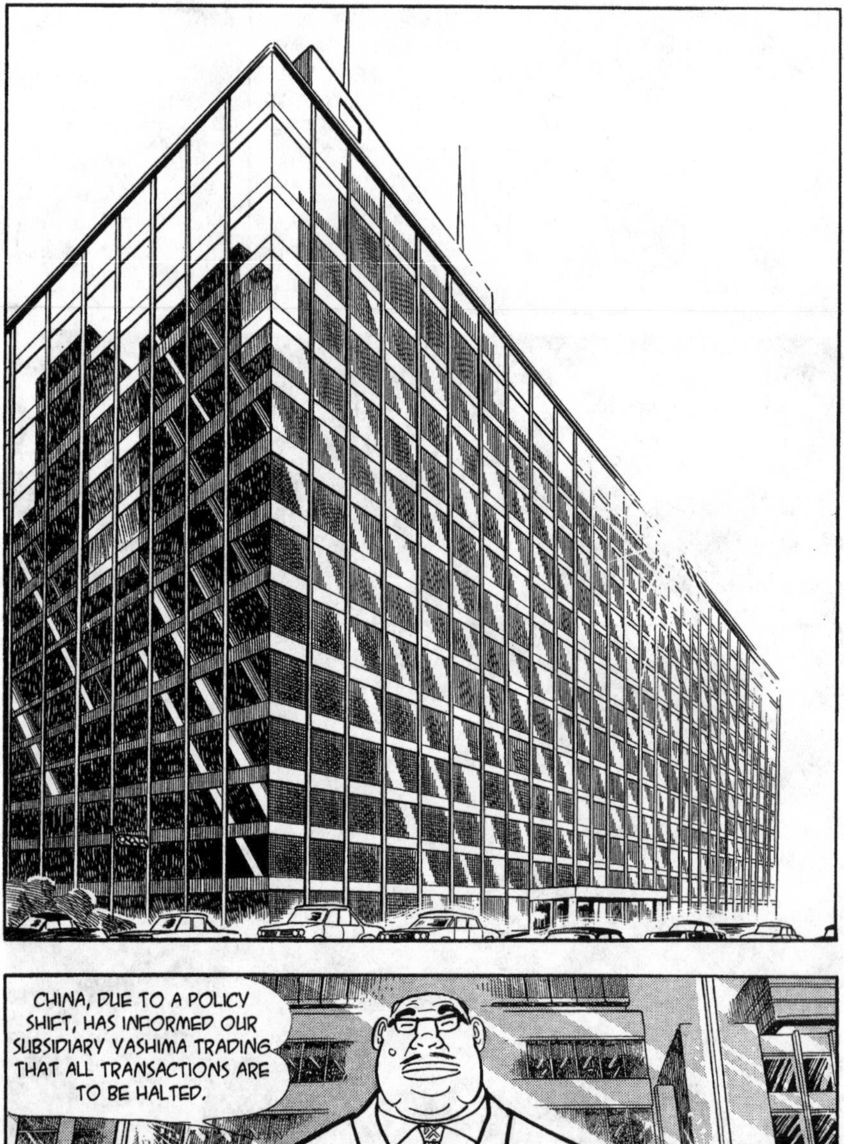

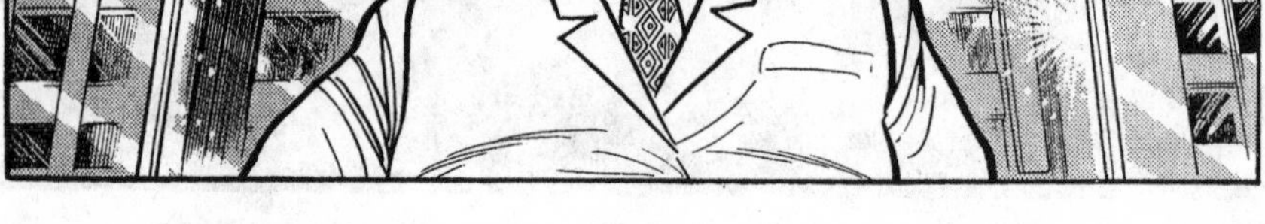
CHINA, DUE TO A POLICY SHIFT, HAS INFORMED OUR SUBSIDIARY YASHIMA TRADING THAT ALL TRANSACTIONS ARE TO BE HALTED.

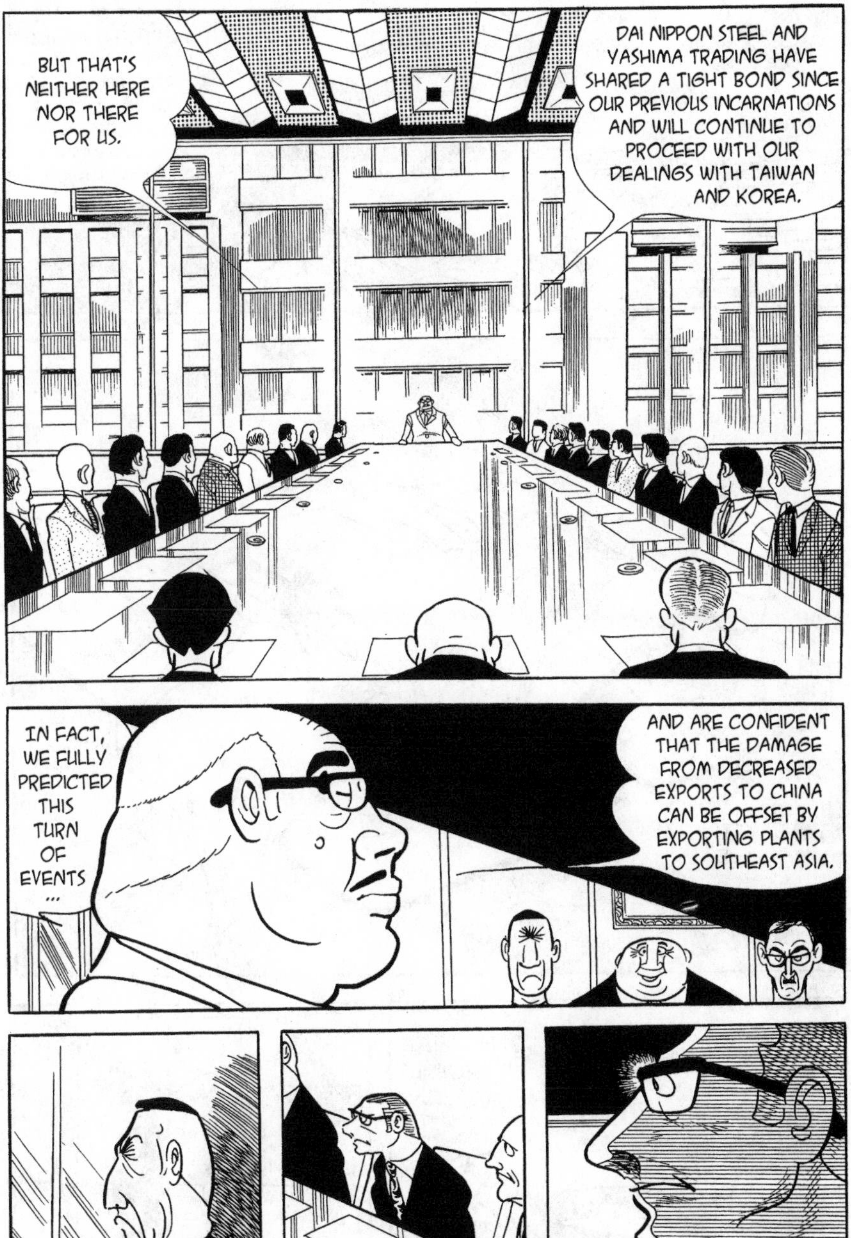
BUT THAT'S NEITHER HERE NOR THERE FOR US.
DAI NIPPON STEEL AND YASHIMA TRADING HAVE SHARED A TIGHT BOND SINCE OUR PREVIOUS INCARNATIONS AND WILL CONTINUE TO PROCEED WITH OUR DEALINGS WITH TAIWAN AND KOREA.
IN FACT, WE FULLY PREDICTED THIS TURN OF EVENTS ...
AND ARE CONFIDENT THAT THE DAMAGE FROM DECREASED EXPORTS TO CHINA CAN BE OFFSET BY EXPORTING PLANTS TO SOUTHEAST ASIA.

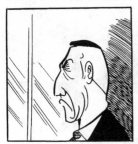

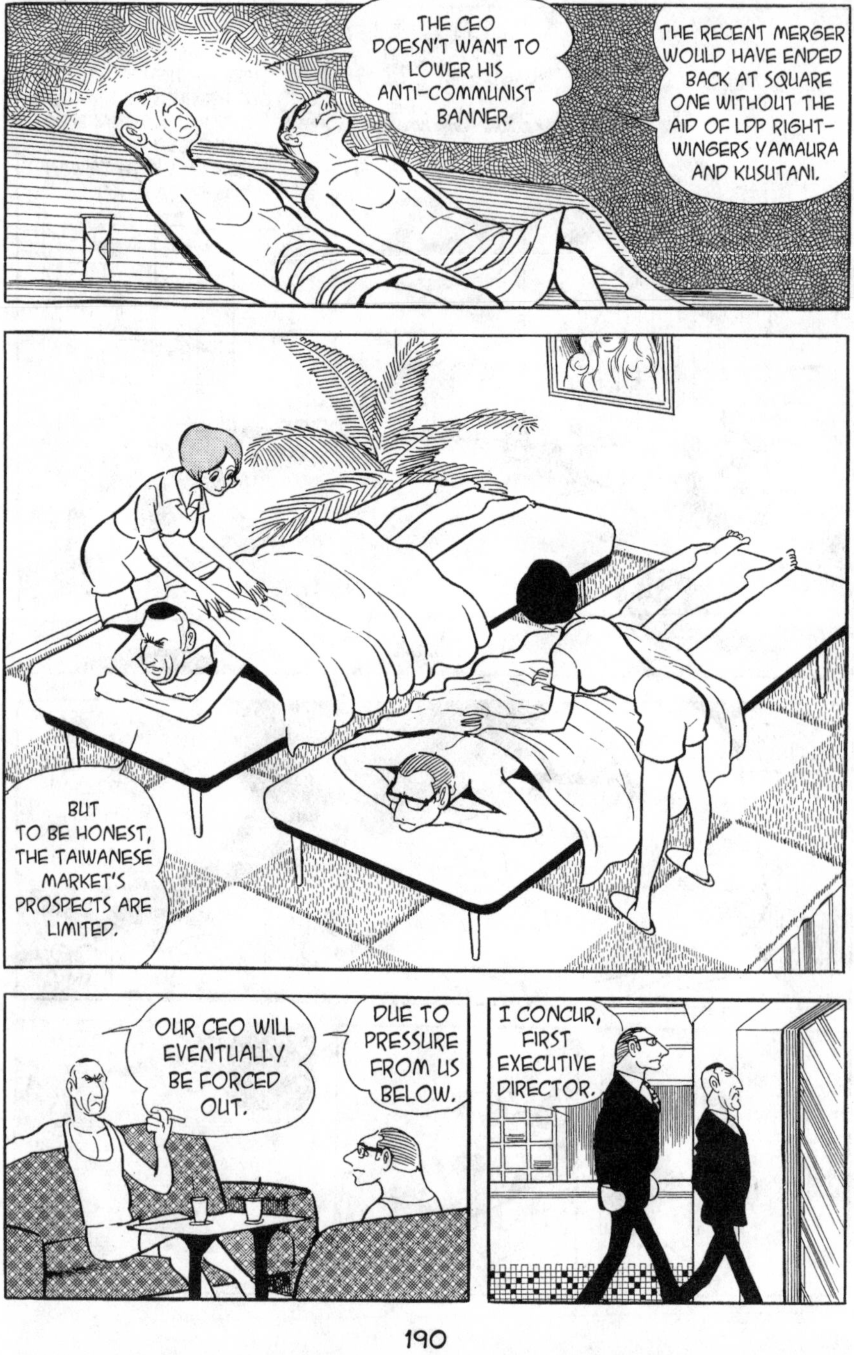
THE CEO DOESN'T WANT TO LOWER HIS ANTI-COMMUNIST BANNER.
THE RECENT MERGER WOULD HAVE ENDED BACK AT SQUARE ONE WITHOUT THE AID OF LDP RIGHT-WINGERS YAMAURA AND KUSUTANI.
BUT TO BE HONEST, THE TAIWANESE MARKET'S PROSPECTS ARE LIMITED.
OUR CEO WILL EVENTUALLY BE FORCED OUT.
DUE TO PRESSURE FROM US BELOW.
I CONCUR, FIRST EXECUTIVE DIRECTOR.

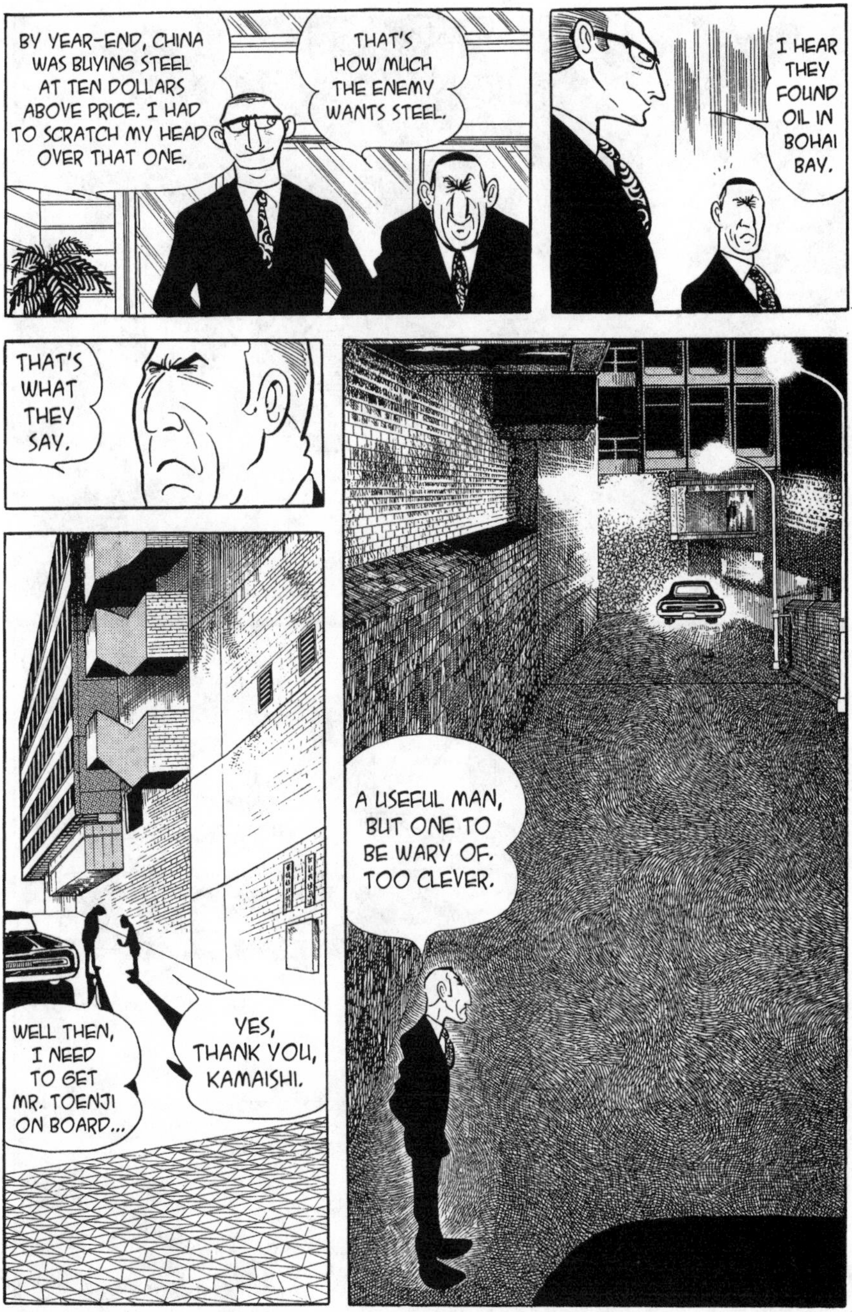
BY YEAR-END, CHINA WAS BUYING STEEL AT TEN DOLLARS ABOVE PRICE. I HAD TO SCRATCH MY HEAD OVER THAT ONE.
THAT'S HOW MUCH THE ENEMY WANTS STEEL.
I HEAR THEY FOUND OIL IN BOHAI BAY.
THAT'S WHAT THEY SAY.
WELL THEN, I NEED TO GET MR. TOENJI ON BOARD...
YES, THANK YOU, KAMAISHI.
A USEFUL MAN, BUT ONE TO BE WARY OF. TOO CLEVER.

AH, THE 1ST DIRECTOR...

DURING THE MERGER, HE WAS HUMILIATED BY THE CURRENT CEO... HE'LL OPPOSE THE CEO AT ANY COST. A MAN WORTH CULTIVATING...

STOP THE CAR !

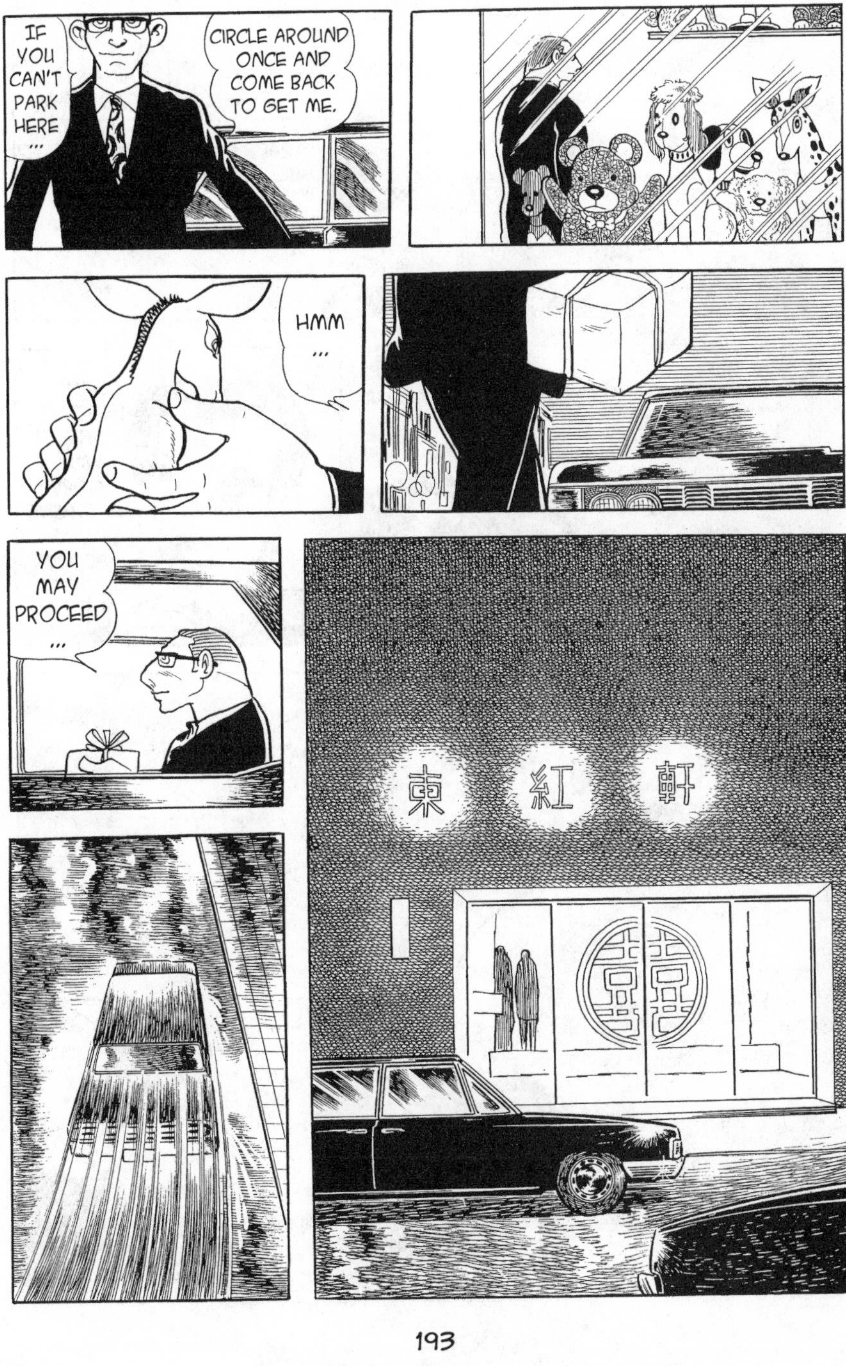
IF YOU CAN'T PARK HERE ...
CIRCLE AROUND ONCE AND COME BACK TO GET ME.
HMM ...
YOU MAY PROCEED ...
東 紅 軒

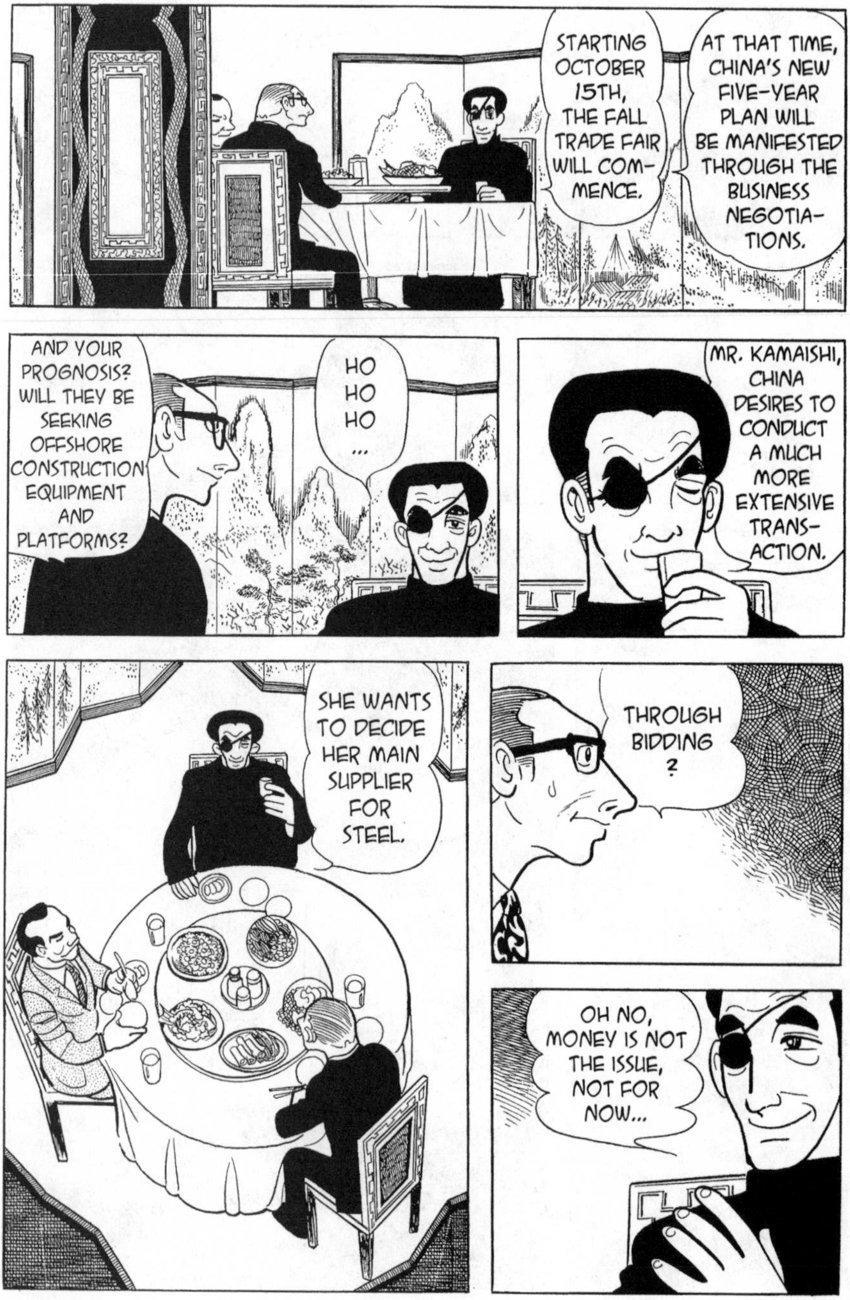
STARTING OCTOBER 15TH, THE FALL TRADE FAIR WILL COMMENCE.
AT THAT TIME, CHINA'S NEW FIVE-YEAR PLAN WILL BE MANIFESTED THROUGH THE BUSINESS NEGOTIATIONS.
AND YOUR PROGNOSIS? WILL THEY BE SEEKING OFFSHORE CONSTRUCTION EQUIPMENT AND PLATFORMS?
HO HO HO ...
MR. KAMAISHI, CHINA DESIRES TO CONDUCT A MUCH MORE EXTENSIVE TRANSACTION.
SHE WANTS TO DECIDE HER MAIN SUPPLIER FOR STEEL.
THROUGH BIDDING ?
OH NO, MONEY IS NOT THE ISSUE, NOT FOR NOW...

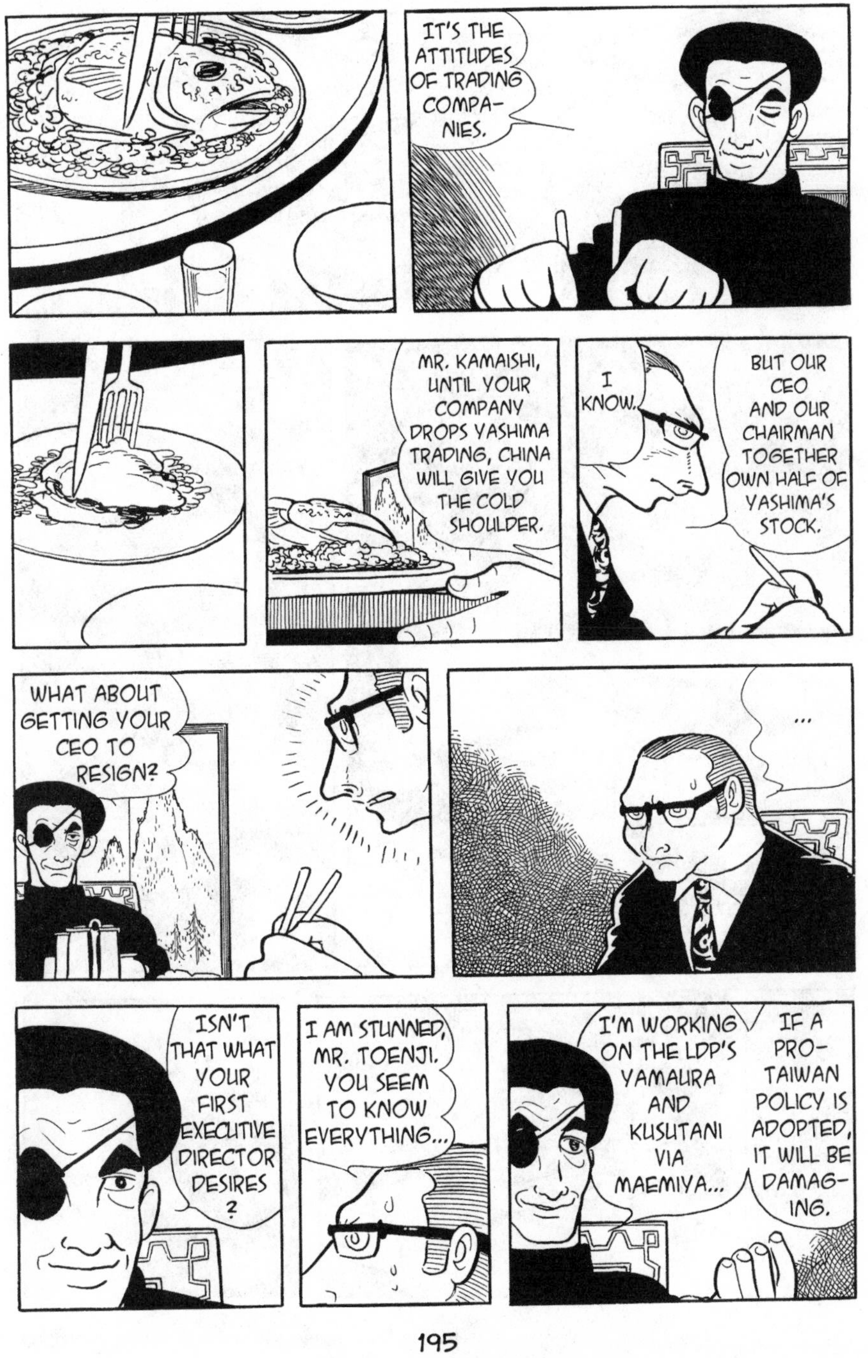
IT'S THE ATTITUDES OF TRADING COMPA-NIES.
MR. KAMAISHI, UNTIL YOUR COMPANY DROPS YASHIMA TRADING, CHINA WILL GIVE YOU THE COLD SHOULDER.
I KNOW.
BUT OUR CEO AND OUR CHAIRMAN TOGETHER OWN HALF OF YASHIMA'S STOCK.
WHAT ABOUT GETTING YOUR CEO TO RESIGN?
...
ISN'T THAT WHAT YOUR FIRST EXECUTIVE DIRECTOR DESIRES ?
I AM STUNNED, MR. TOENJI. YOU SEEM TO KNOW EVERYTHING...
I'M WORKING ON THE LDP'S YAMAURA AND KUSUTANI VIA MAEMIYA...
IF A PRO-TAIWAN POLICY IS ADOPTED, IT WILL BE DAMAG-ING.

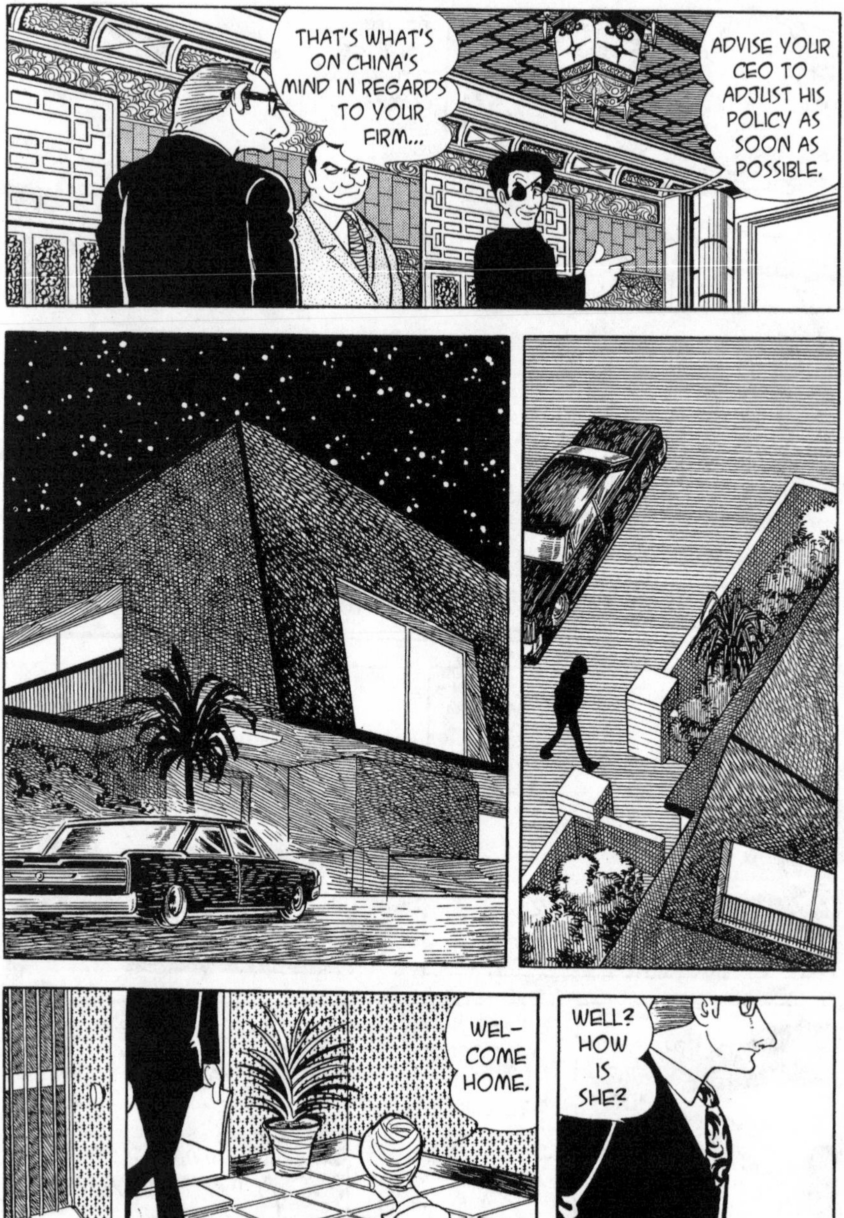
THAT'S WHAT'S ON CHINA'S MIND IN REGARDS TO YOUR FIRM...
ADVISE YOUR CEO TO ADJUST HIS POLICY AS SOON AS POSSIBLE.
WEL-COME HOME.
WELL? HOW IS SHE?

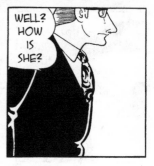

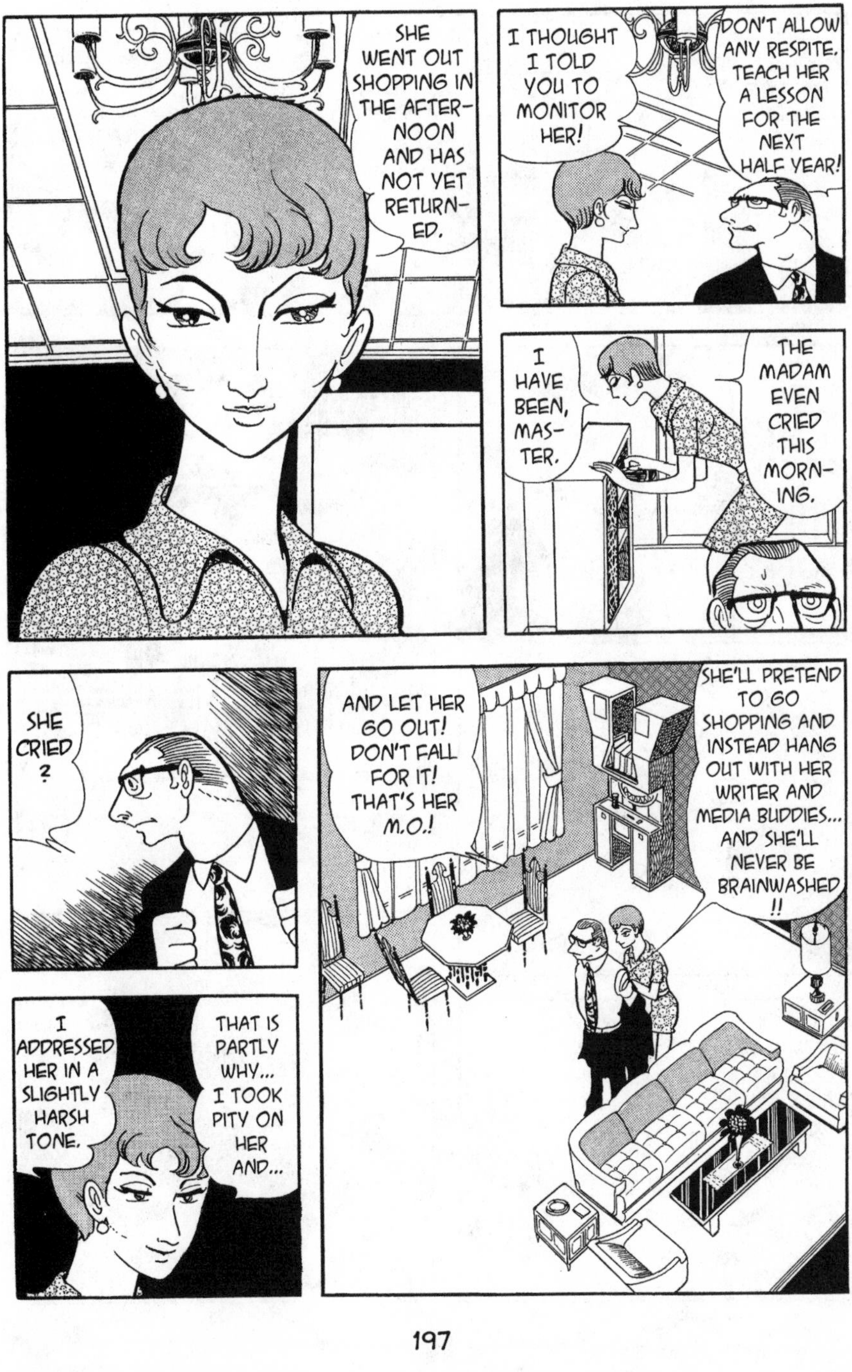
SHE WENT OUT SHOPPING IN THE AFTER-NOON AND HAS NOT YET RETURN-ED.
I THOUGHT I TOLD YOU TO MONITOR HER!
DON'T ALLOW ANY RESPITE. TEACH HER A LESSON FOR THE NEXT HALF YEAR!
I HAVE BEEN, MAS-TER.
THE MADAM EVEN CRIED THIS MORN-ING.
SHE CRIED ?
I ADDRESSED HER IN A SLIGHTLY HARSH TONE.
THAT IS PARTLY WHY... I TOOK PITY ON HER AND...
AND LET HER GO OUT! DON'T FALL FOR IT! THAT'S HER M.O.!
SHE'LL PRETEND TO GO SHOPPING AND INSTEAD HANG OUT WITH HER WRITER AND MEDIA BUDDIES... AND SHE'LL NEVER BE BRAINWASHED !!

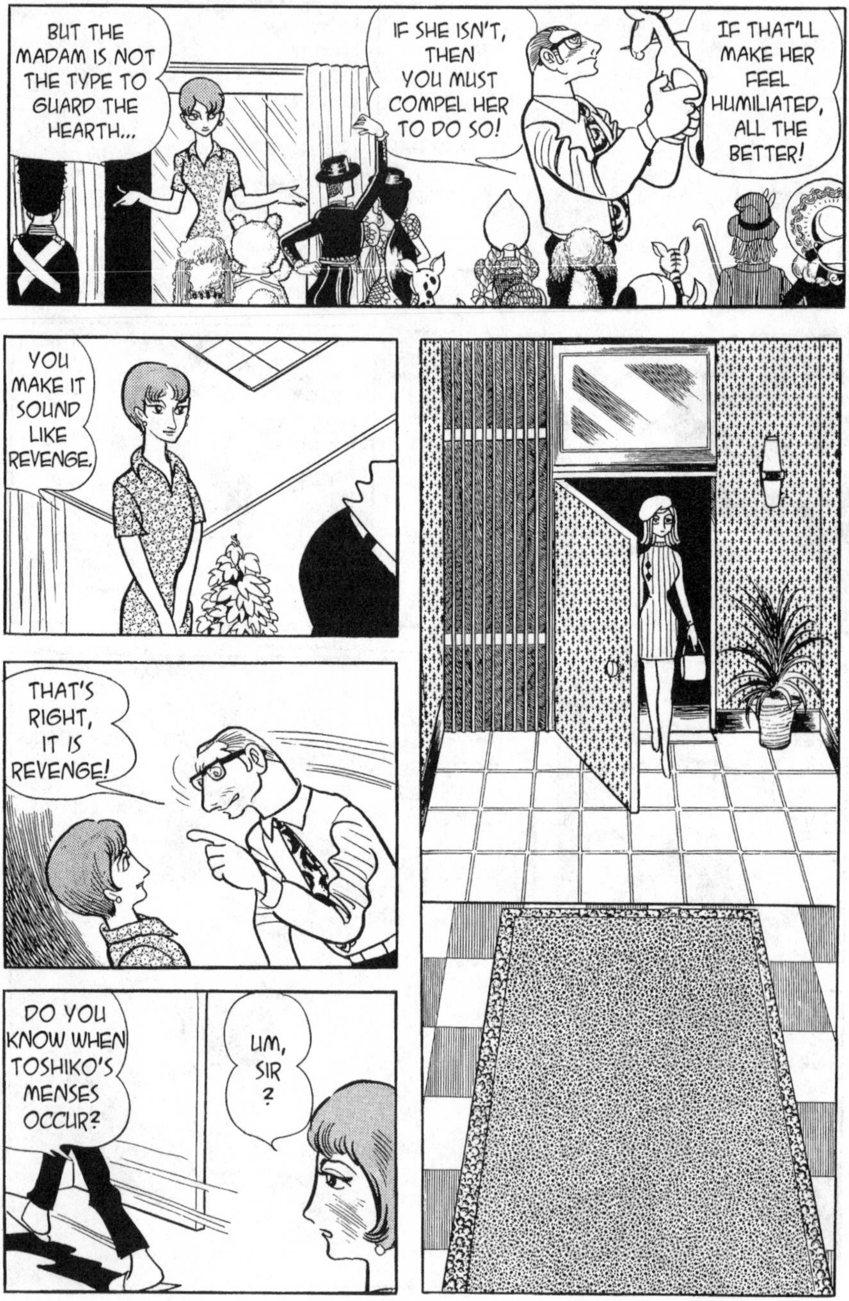

BUT THE MADAM IS NOT THE TYPE TO GUARD THE HEARTH...
IF SHE ISN'T, THEN YOU MUST COMPEL HER TO DO SO!
IF THAT'LL MAKE HER FEEL HUMILIATED, ALL THE BETTER!
YOU MAKE IT SOUND LIKE REVENGE.
THAT'S RIGHT, IT IS REVENGE!
DO YOU KNOW WHEN TOSHIKO'S MENSES OCCUR?
UM, SIR?

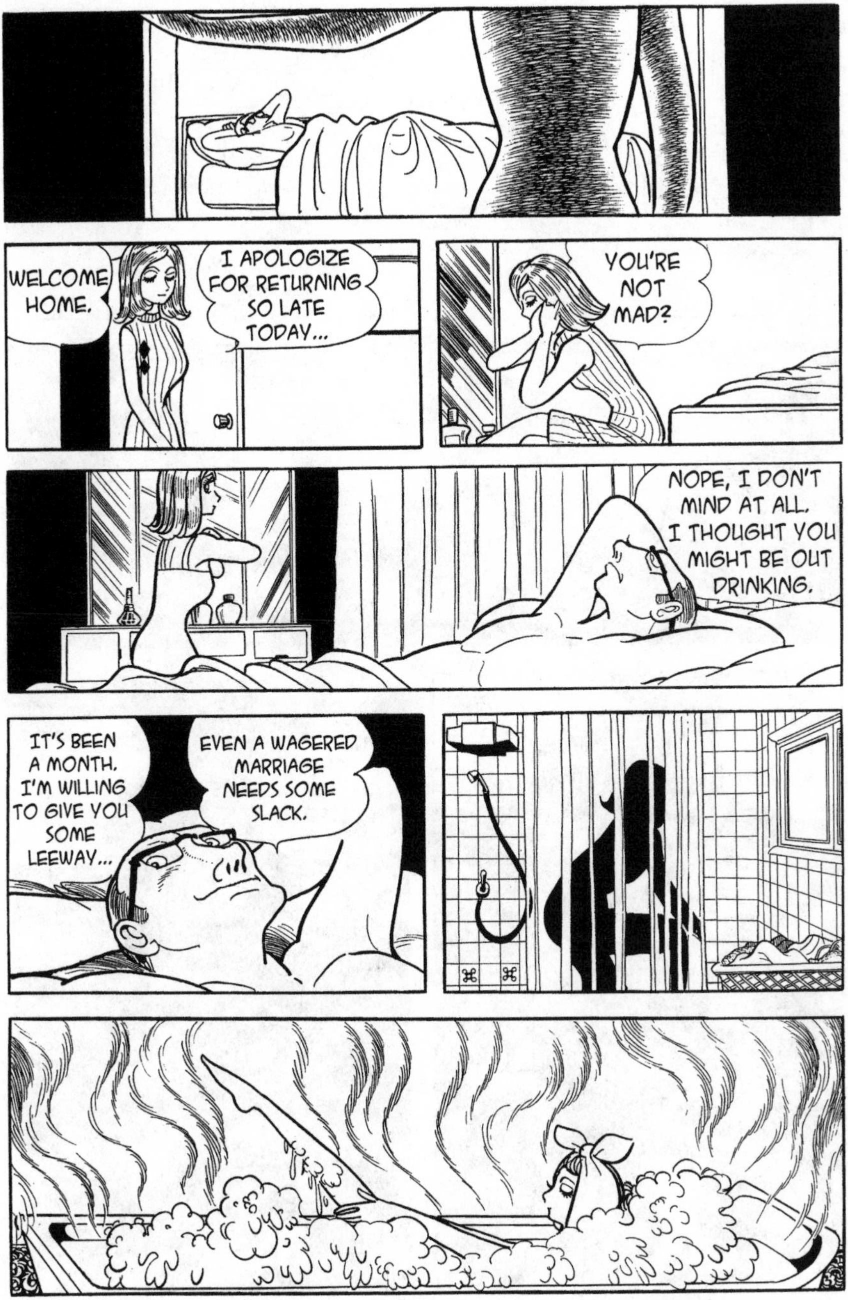
WELCOME HOME.
I APOLOGIZE FOR RETURNING SO LATE TODAY...
YOU'RE NOT MAD?
NOPE, I DON'T MIND AT ALL. I THOUGHT YOU MIGHT BE OUT DRINKING.
IT'S BEEN A MONTH. I'M WILLING TO GIVE YOU SOME LEEWAY...
EVEN A WAGERED MARRIAGE NEEDS SOME SLACK.

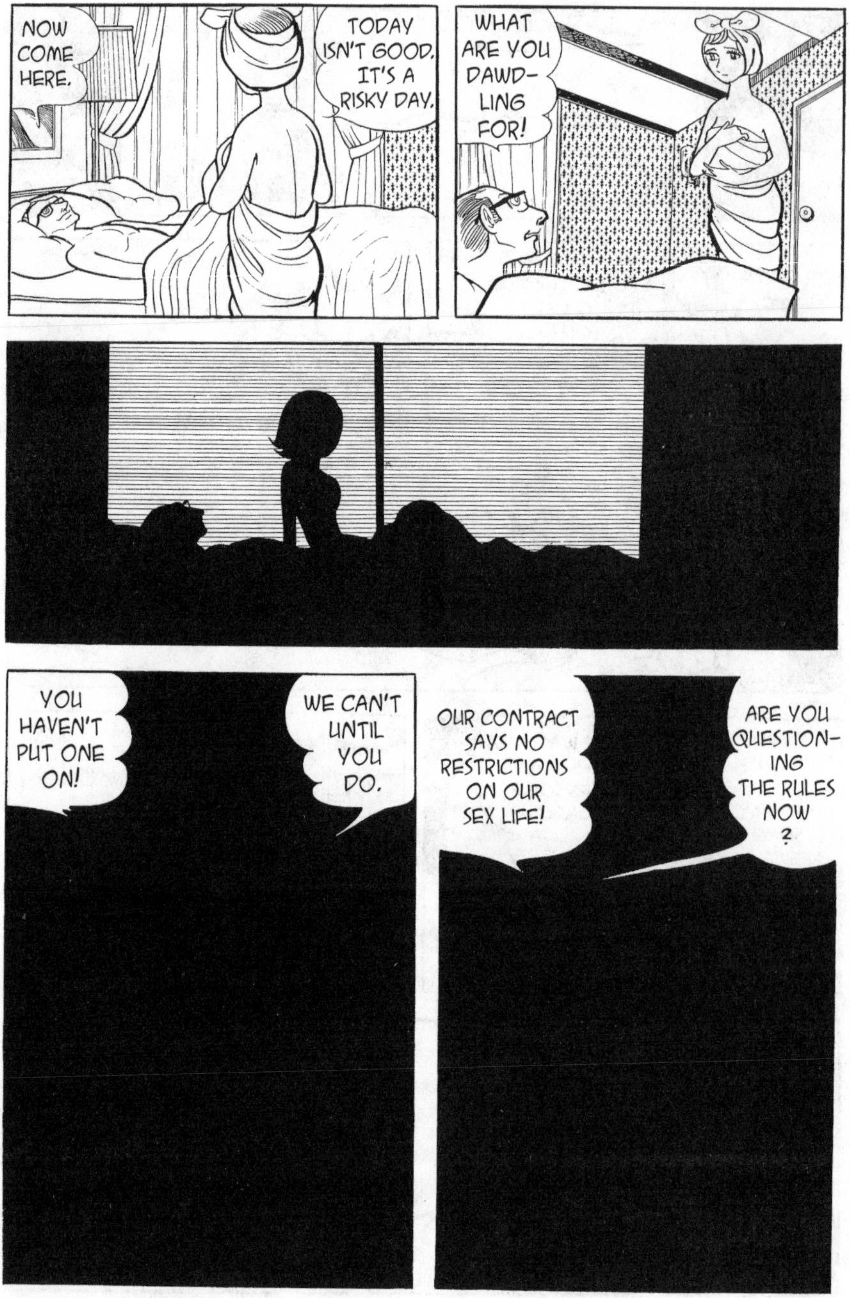
NOW COME HERE.
TODAY ISN'T GOOD. IT'S A RISKY DAY.
WHAT ARE YOU DAWDLING FOR!
YOU HAVEN'T PUT ONE ON!
WE CAN'T UNTIL YOU DO.
OUR CONTRACT SAYS NO RESTRICTIONS ON OUR SEX LIFE!
ARE YOU QUESTIONING THE RULES NOW?

BUT...
I'LL GET
PREGNANT
!

YES!
GET KNOCKED
UP AND HAVE
A BABY!

I WANT
CHILDREN.

I WANT YOU TO
GIVE BIRTH TO
A BABY JUST LIKE
ME AND STRUGGLE
TO RAISE IT!

FUNNY, BUT
SEEING A CHILD
OF MINE IS THE
ONLY THING
THAT COULD
RESTORE MY
HUMANITY!

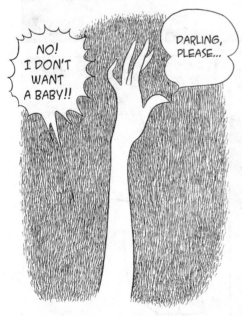

NO!
I DON'T
WANT
A BABY!!

DARLING,
PLEASE...

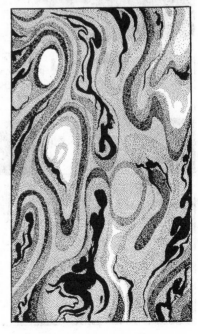

201

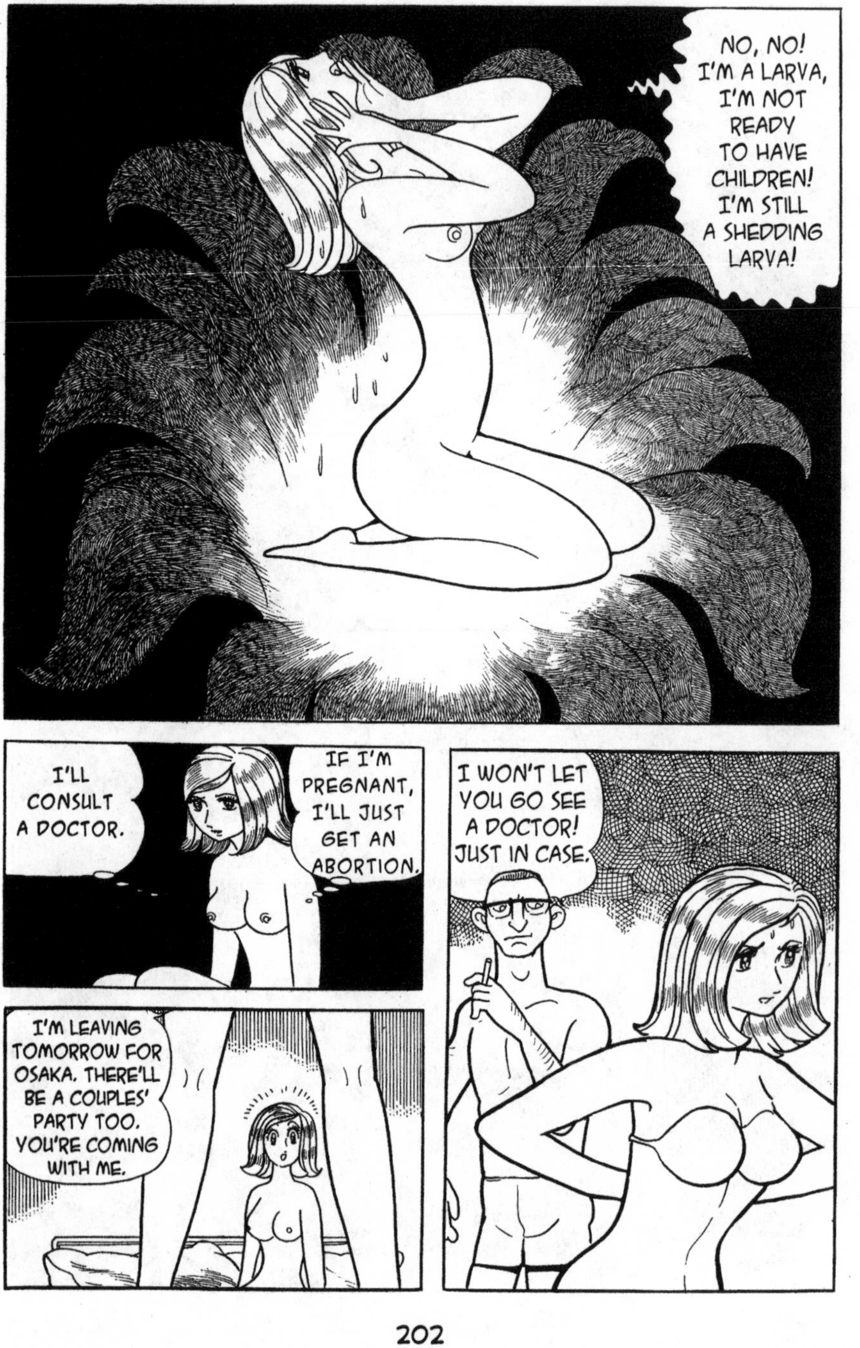
NO, NO! I'M A LARVA, I'M NOT READY TO HAVE CHILDREN! I'M STILL A SHEDDING LARVA!
I'LL CONSULT A DOCTOR.
IF I'M PREGNANT, I'LL JUST GET AN ABORTION.
I'M LEAVING TOMORROW FOR OSAKA. THERE'LL BE A COUPLES' PARTY TOO. YOU'RE COMING WITH ME.
I WON'T LET YOU GO SEE A DOCTOR! JUST IN CASE.

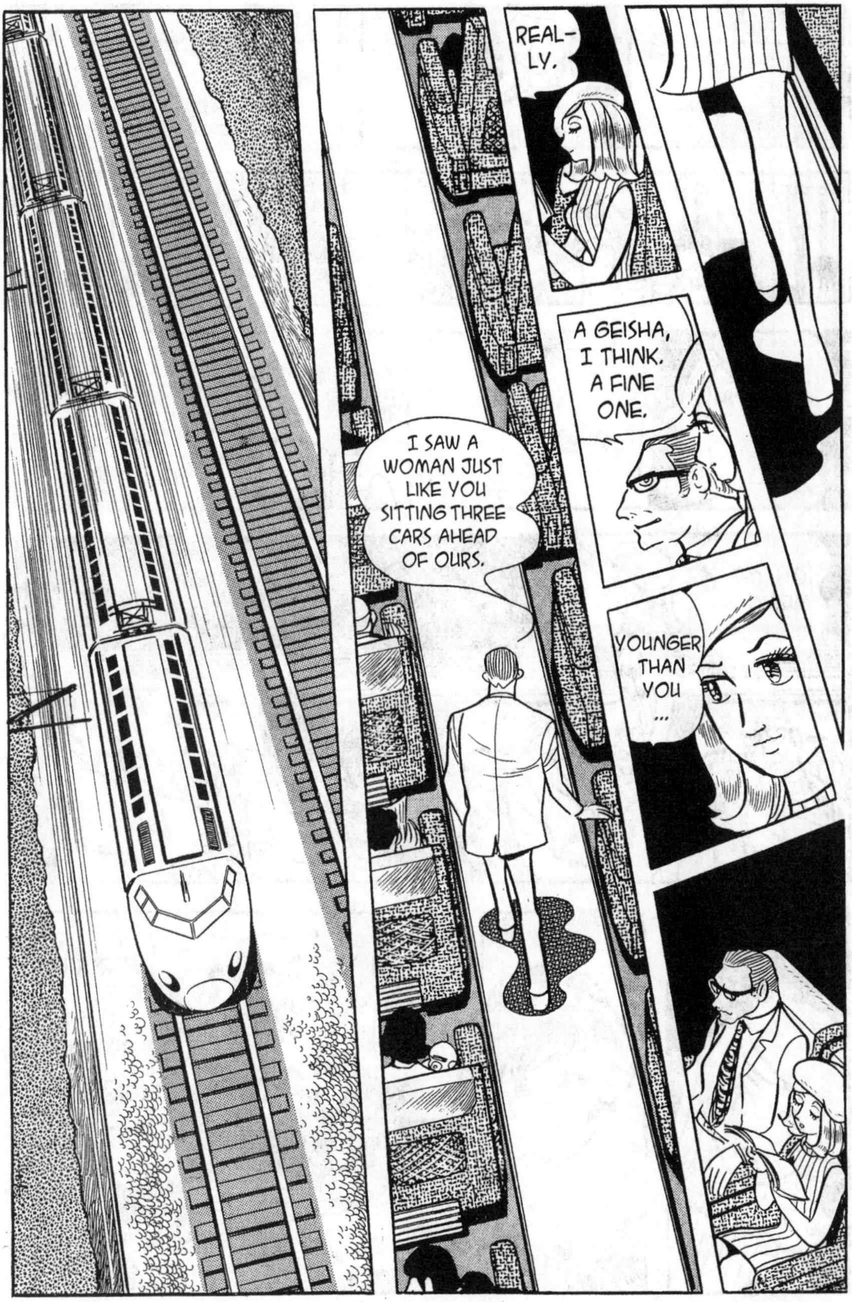
I SAW A WOMAN JUST LIKE YOU SITTING THREE CARS AHEAD OF OURS.
REAL-LY.
A GEISHA, I THINK. A FINE ONE.
YOUNGER THAN YOU ...

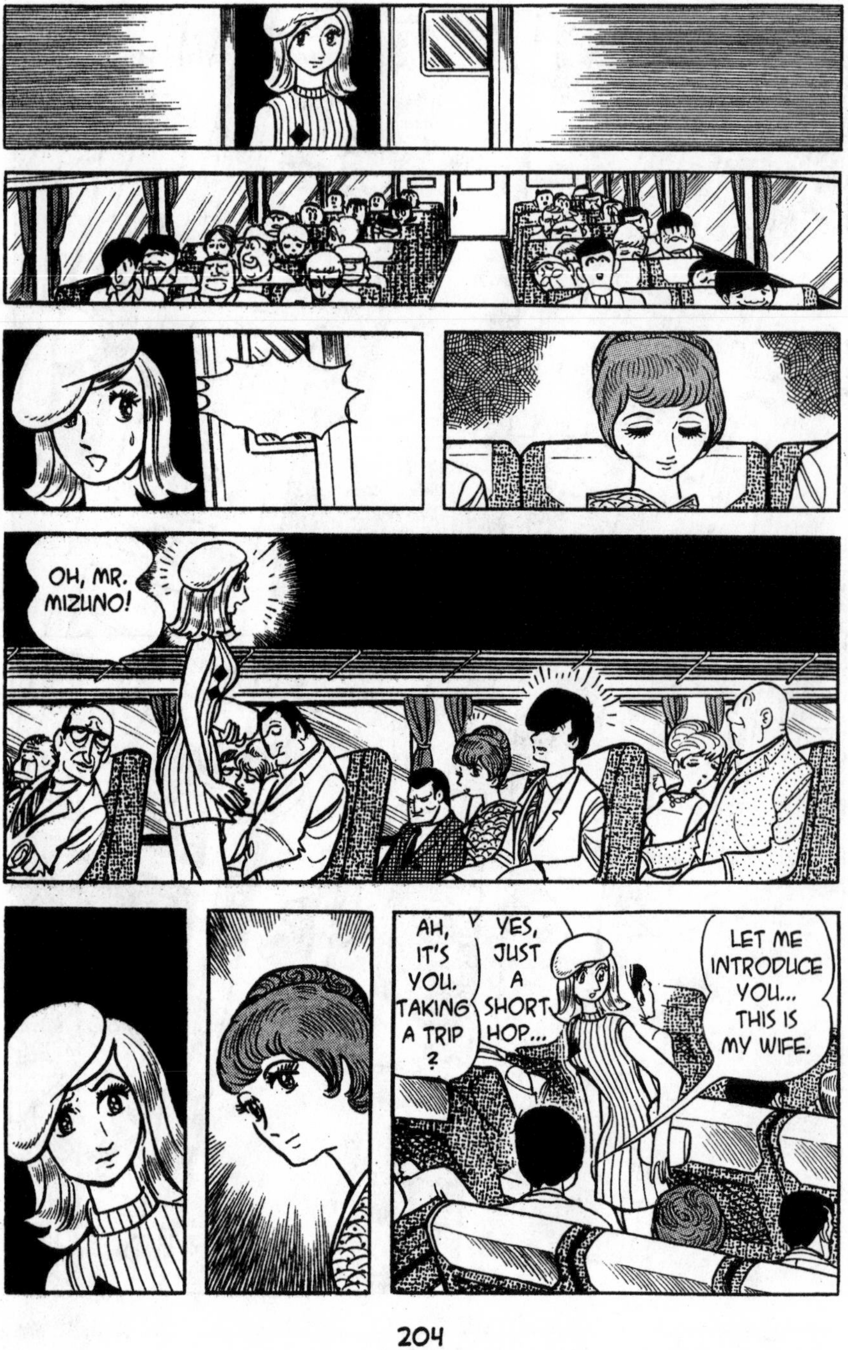

OH, MR. MIZUNO!
AH, IT'S YOU. TAKING A TRIP ?
YES, JUST A SHORT HOP...
LET ME INTRODUCE YOU... THIS IS MY WIFE.

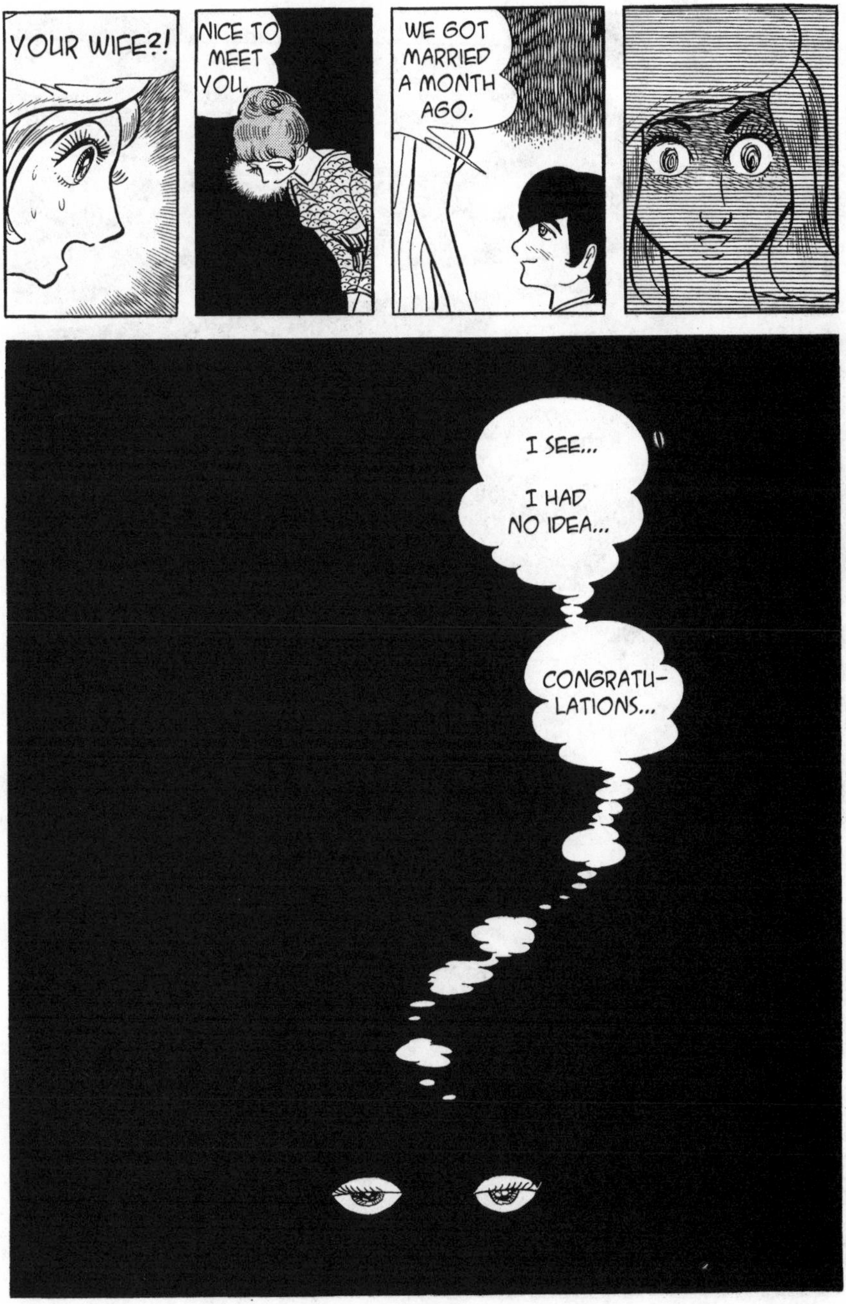
YOUR WIFE?!
NICE TO MEET YOU.
WE GOT MARRIED A MONTH AGO.
I SEE... I HAD NO IDEA...
CONGRATU-LATIONS...

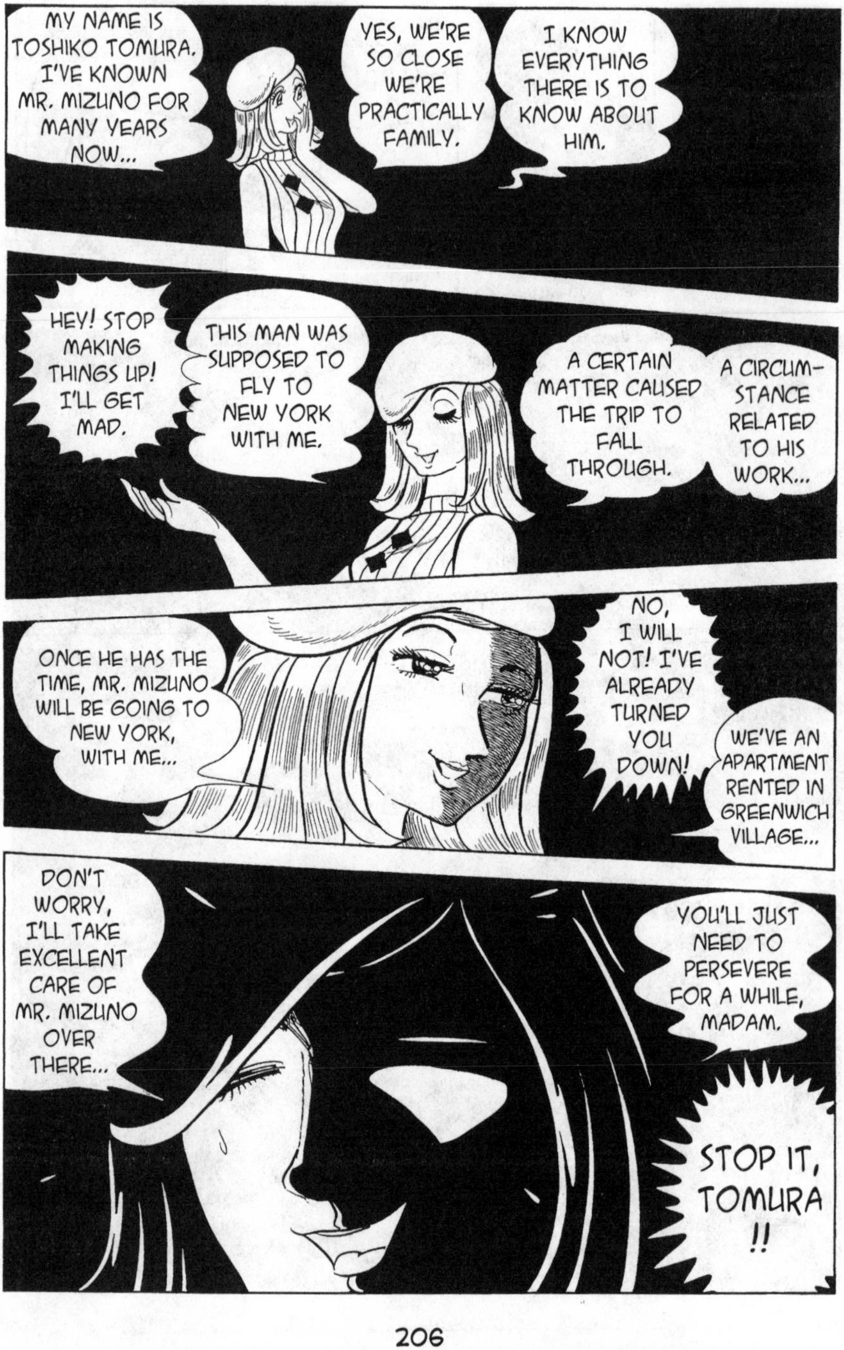
MY NAME IS TOSHIKO TOMURA. I'VE KNOWN MR. MIZUNO FOR MANY YEARS NOW...
YES, WE'RE SO CLOSE WE'RE PRACTICALLY FAMILY.
I KNOW EVERYTHING THERE IS TO KNOW ABOUT HIM.
HEY! STOP MAKING THINGS UP! I'LL GET MAD.
THIS MAN WAS SUPPOSED TO FLY TO NEW YORK WITH ME.
A CERTAIN MATTER CAUSED THE TRIP TO FALL THROUGH.
A CIRCUM-STANCE RELATED TO HIS WORK...
ONCE HE HAS THE TIME, MR. MIZUNO WILL BE GOING TO NEW YORK, WITH ME...
NO, I WILL NOT! I'VE ALREADY TURNED YOU DOWN!
WE'VE AN APARTMENT RENTED IN GREENWICH VILLAGE...
DON'T WORRY, I'LL TAKE EXCELLENT CARE OF MR. MIZUNO OVER THERE...
YOU'LL JUST NEED TO PERSEVERE FOR A WHILE, MADAM.
STOP IT, TOMURA !!

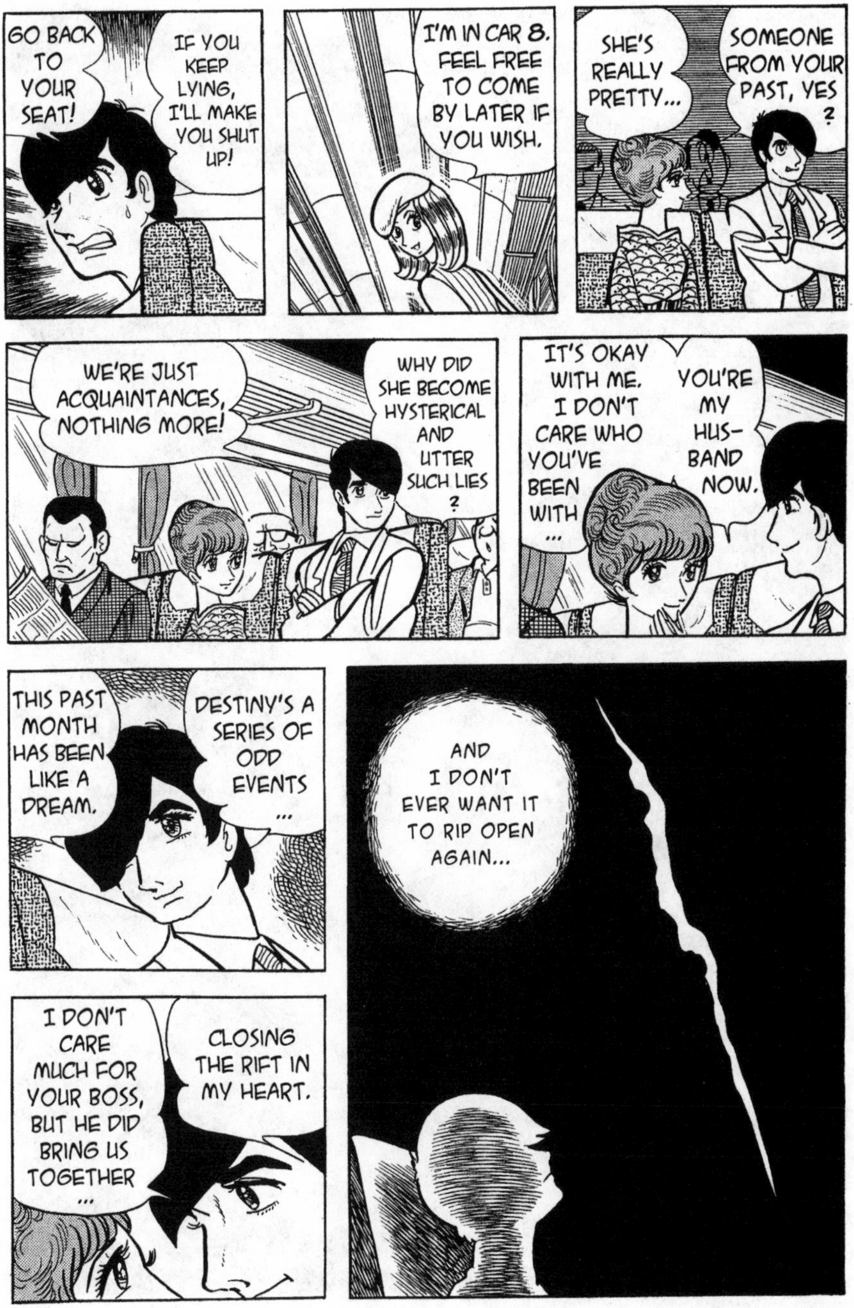
GO BACK TO YOUR SEAT!
IF YOU KEEP LYING, I'LL MAKE YOU SHUT UP!
I'M IN CAR 8. FEEL FREE TO COME BY LATER IF YOU WISH.
SHE'S REALLY PRETTY...
SOMEONE FROM YOUR PAST, YES?
WE'RE JUST ACQUAINTANCES, NOTHING MORE!
WHY DID SHE BECOME HYSTERICAL AND UTTER SUCH LIES?
IT'S OKAY WITH ME. I DON'T CARE WHO YOU'VE BEEN WITH...
YOU'RE MY HUS-BAND NOW.
THIS PAST MONTH HAS BEEN LIKE A DREAM.
DESTINY'S A SERIES OF ODD EVENTS...
AND I DON'T EVER WANT IT TO RIP OPEN AGAIN...
I DON'T CARE MUCH FOR YOUR BOSS, BUT HE DID BRING US TOGETHER...
CLOSING THE RIFT IN MY HEART.

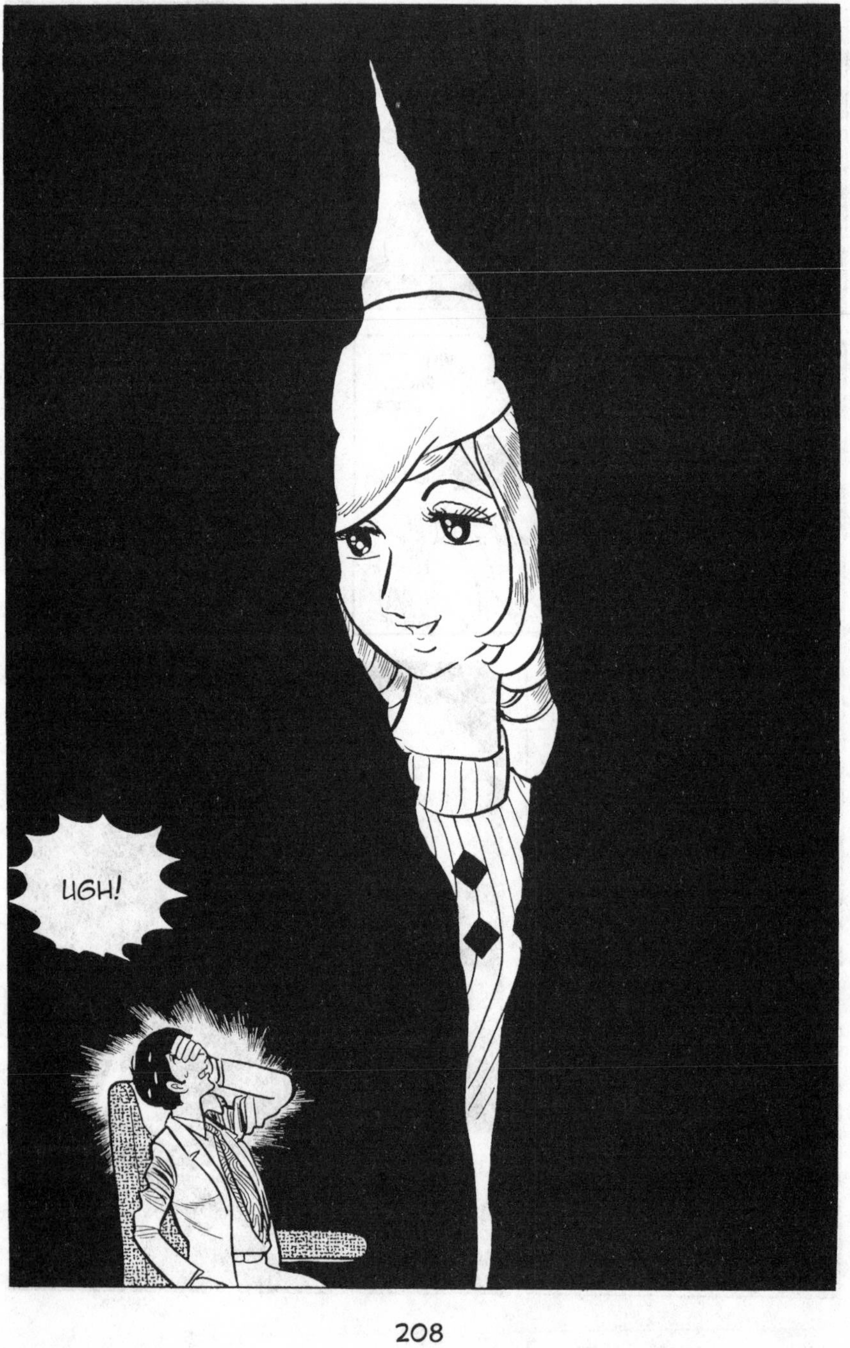
UGH!

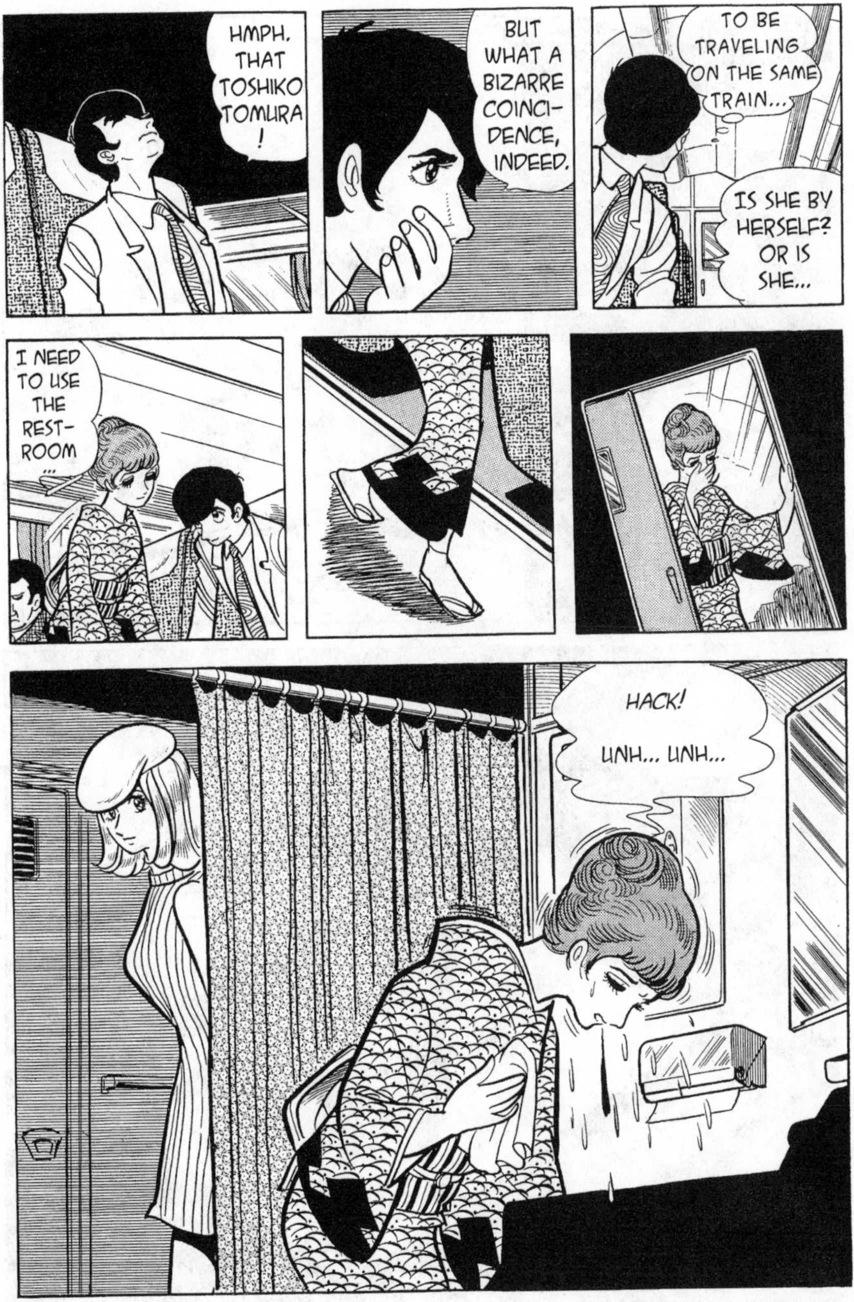
HMPH. THAT TOSHIKO TOMURA !
BUT WHAT A BIZARRE COINCIDENCE, INDEED.
TO BE TRAVELING ON THE SAME TRAIN...
IS SHE BY HERSELF? OR IS SHE...
I NEED TO USE THE REST-ROOM ...
HACK!
UNH... UNH...

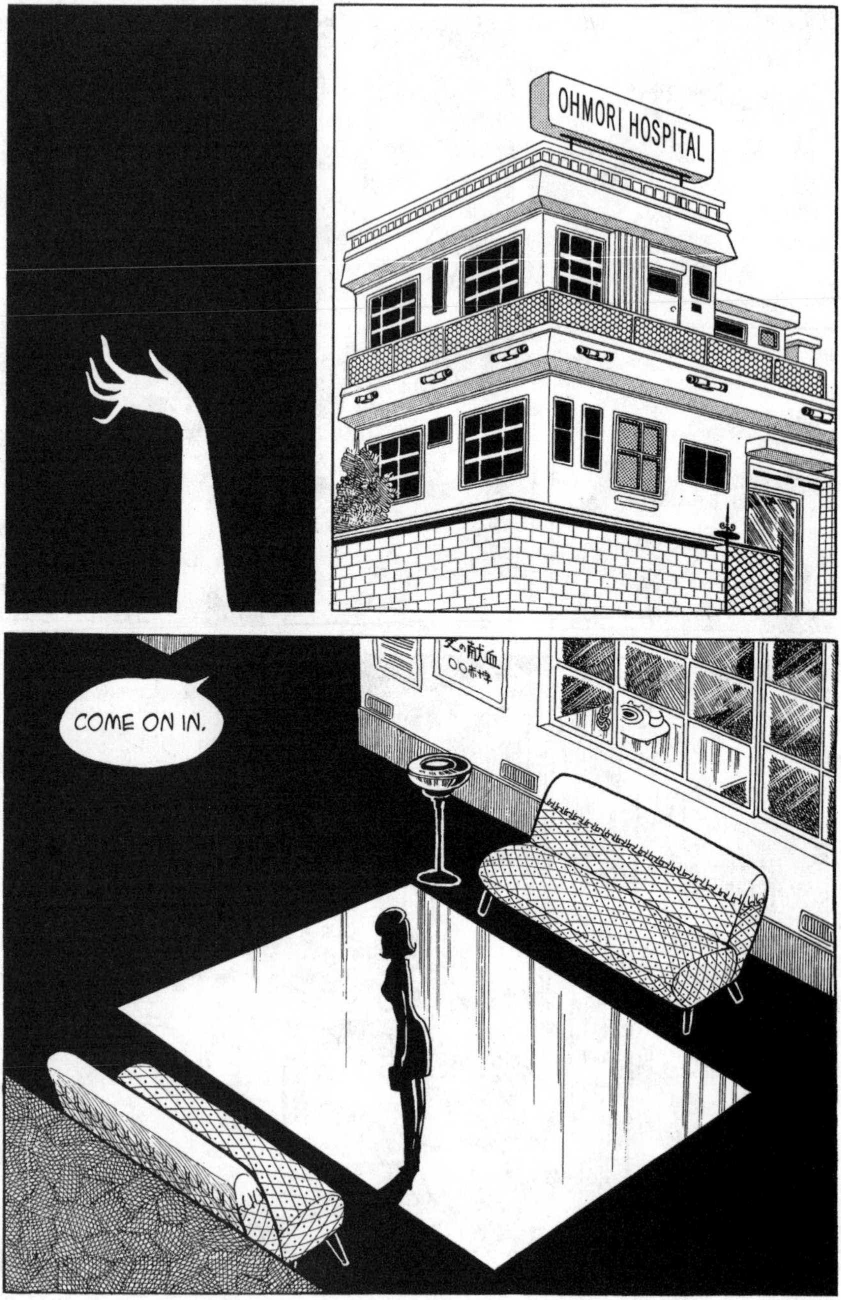
OHMORI HOSPITAL
COME ON IN.

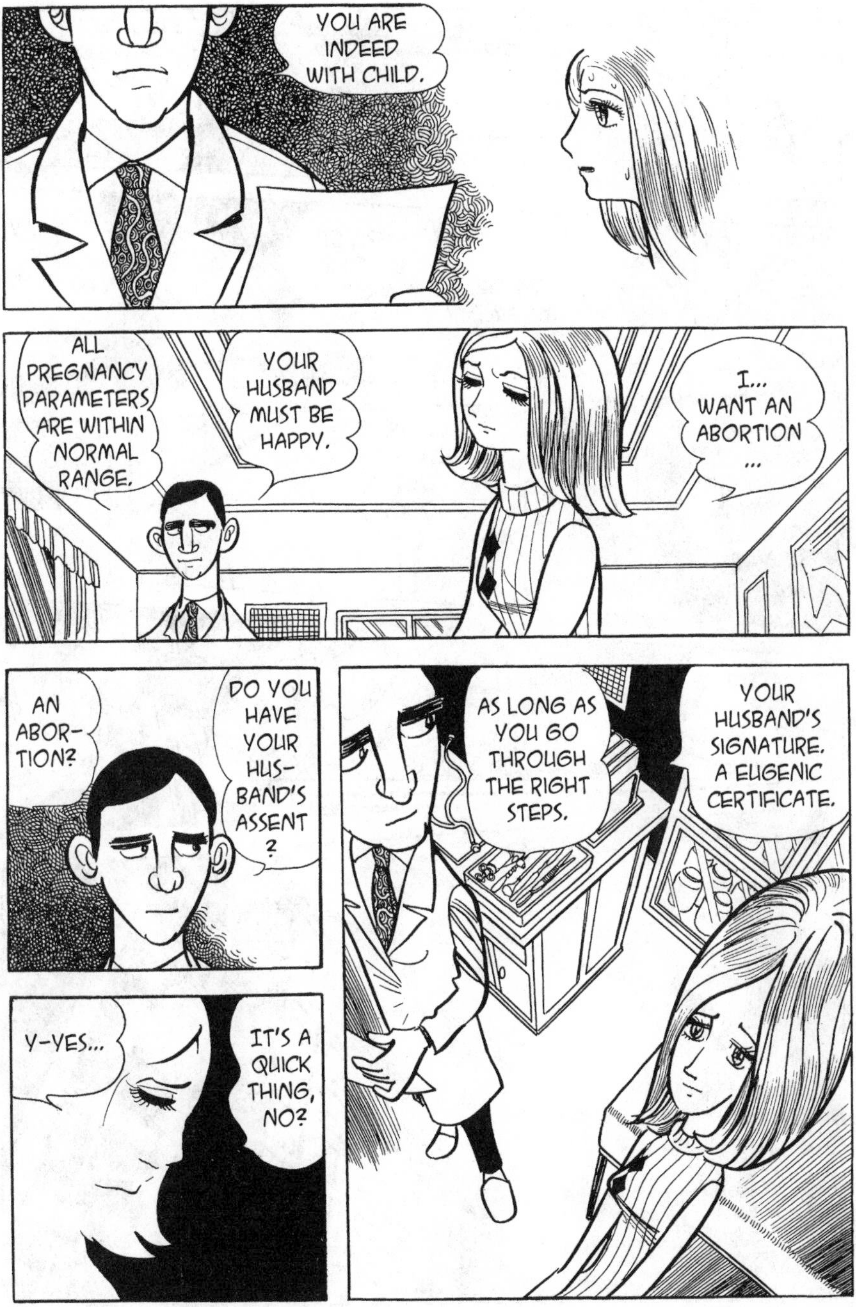
YOU ARE INDEED WITH CHILD.
ALL PREGNANCY PARAMETERS ARE WITHIN NORMAL RANGE.
YOUR HUSBAND MUST BE HAPPY.
I... WANT AN ABORTION ...
AN ABOR-TION?
DO YOU HAVE YOUR HUS-BAND'S ASSENT ?
Y-YES...
IT'S A QUICK THING, NO?
AS LONG AS YOU GO THROUGH THE RIGHT STEPS.
YOUR HUSBAND'S SIGNATURE. A EUGENIC CERTIFICATE.

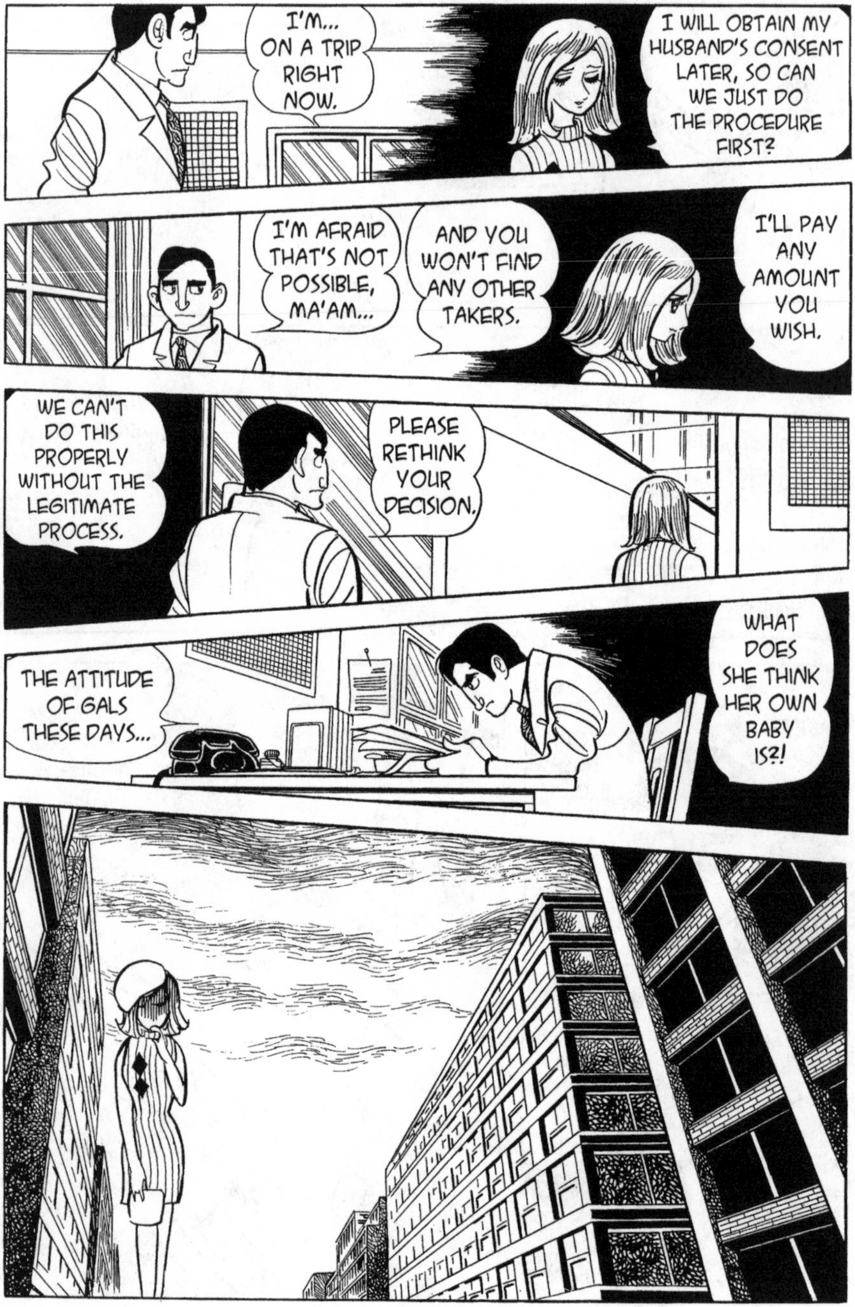
I'M... ON A TRIP RIGHT NOW.
I WILL OBTAIN MY HUSBAND'S CONSENT LATER, SO CAN WE JUST DO THE PROCEDURE FIRST?
I'M AFRAID THAT'S NOT POSSIBLE, MA'AM...
AND YOU WON'T FIND ANY OTHER TAKERS.
I'LL PAY ANY AMOUNT YOU WISH.
WE CAN'T DO THIS PROPERLY WITHOUT THE LEGITIMATE PROCESS.
PLEASE RETHINK YOUR DECISION.
THE ATTITUDE OF GALS THESE DAYS...
WHAT DOES SHE THINK HER OWN BABY IS?!

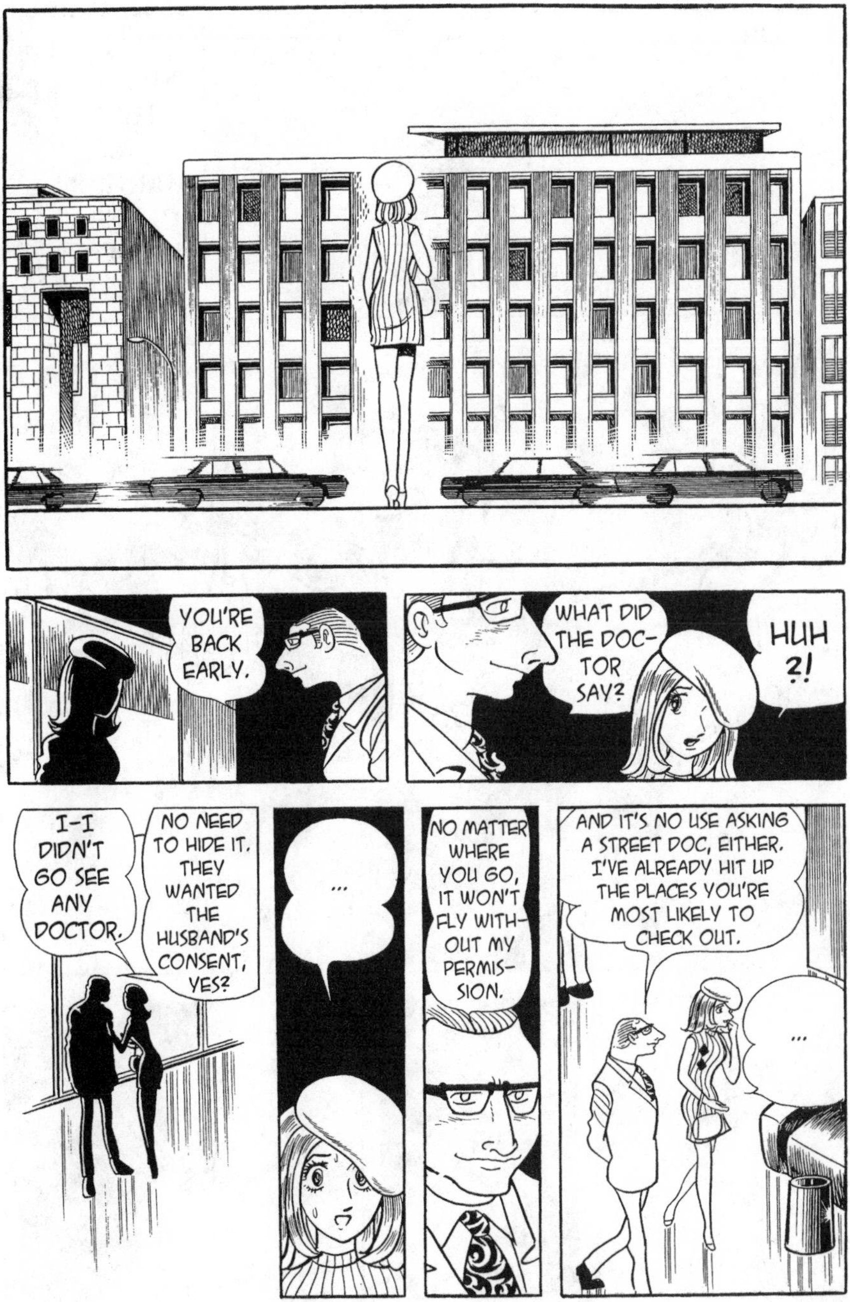
YOU'RE BACK EARLY.
WHAT DID THE DOC-TOR SAY?
HUH ?!
I-I DIDN'T GO SEE ANY DOCTOR.
NO NEED TO HIDE IT. THEY WANTED THE HUSBAND'S CONSENT, YES?
...
NO MATTER WHERE YOU GO, IT WON'T FLY WITH-OUT MY PERMIS-SION.
AND IT'S NO USE ASKING A STREET DOC, EITHER. I'VE ALREADY HIT UP THE PLACES YOU'RE MOST LIKELY TO CHECK OUT.
...

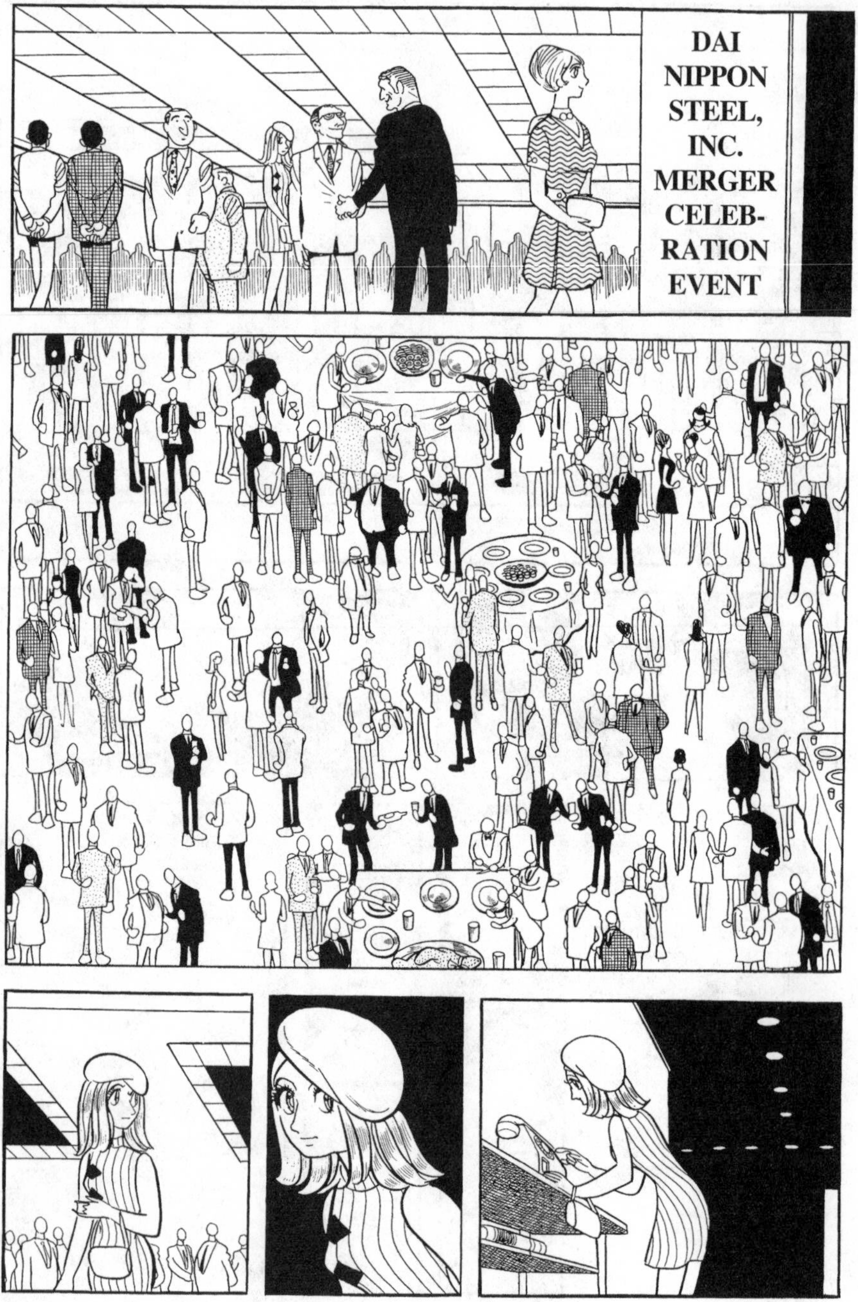
DAI NIPPON STEEL, INC. MERGER CELEB-RATION EVENT

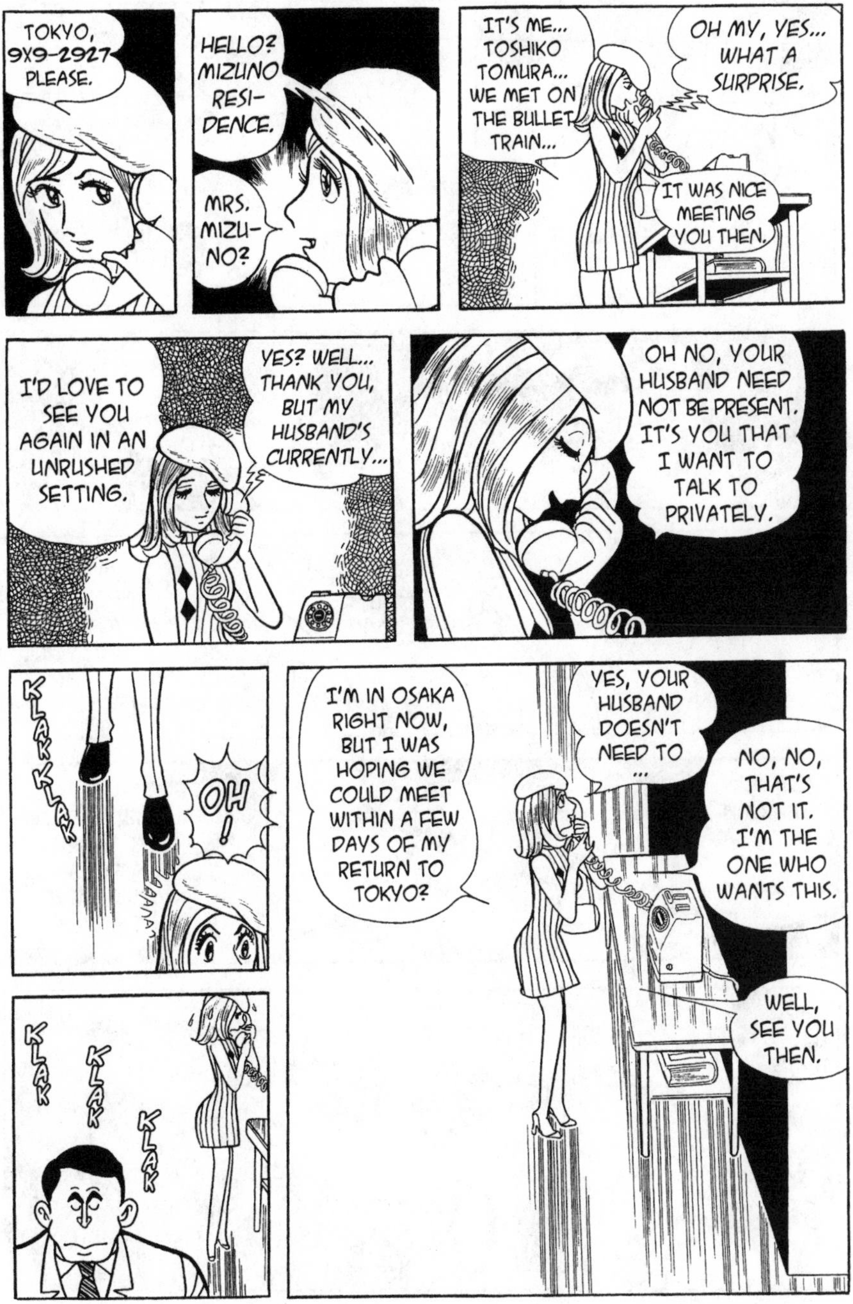
TOKYO, 9X9-2927 PLEASE.
HELLO? MIZUNO RESI-DENCE.
MRS. MIZU-NO?
IT'S ME... TOSHIKO TOMURA... WE MET ON THE BULLET TRAIN...
OH MY, YES... WHAT A SURPRISE.
IT WAS NICE MEETING YOU THEN.
I'D LOVE TO SEE YOU AGAIN IN AN UNRUSHED SETTING.
YES? WELL... THANK YOU, BUT MY HUSBAND'S CURRENTLY...
OH NO, YOUR HUSBAND NEED NOT BE PRESENT. IT'S YOU THAT I WANT TO TALK TO PRIVATELY.
KLAK KLAK KLAK
OH!
I'M IN OSAKA RIGHT NOW, BUT I WAS HOPING WE COULD MEET WITHIN A FEW DAYS OF MY RETURN TO TOKYO?
YES, YOUR HUSBAND DOESN'T NEED TO ...
NO, NO, THAT'S NOT IT. I'M THE ONE WHO WANTS THIS.
WELL, SEE YOU THEN.
KLAK KLAK KLAK

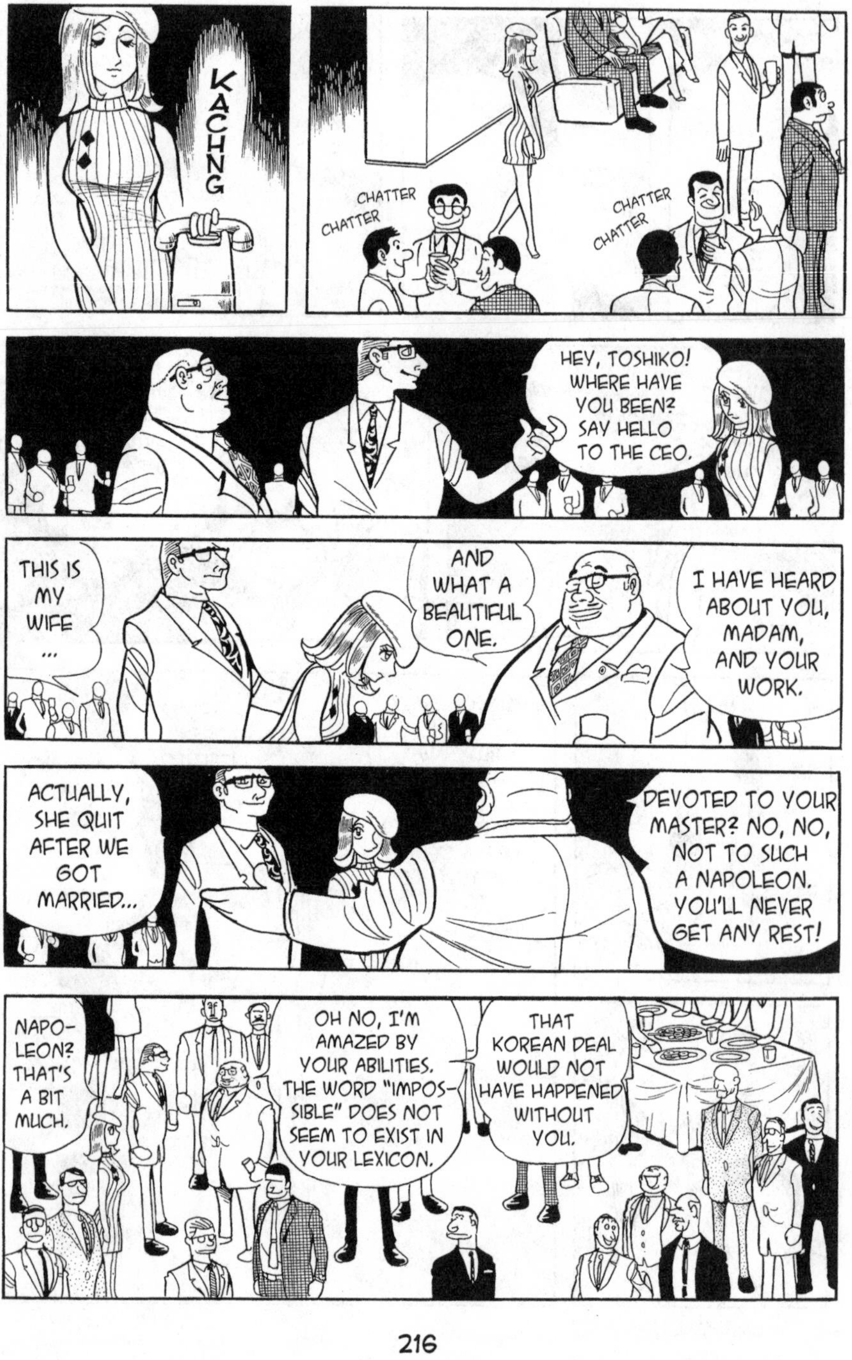
KACHNG
CHATTER CHATTER
CHATTER CHATTER
HEY, TOSHIKO! WHERE HAVE YOU BEEN? SAY HELLO TO THE CEO.
THIS IS MY WIFE ...
AND WHAT A BEAUTIFUL ONE.
I HAVE HEARD ABOUT YOU, MADAM, AND YOUR WORK.
ACTUALLY, SHE QUIT AFTER WE GOT MARRIED...
DEVOTED TO YOUR MASTER? NO, NO, NOT TO SUCH A NAPOLEON. YOU'LL NEVER GET ANY REST!
NAPOLEON? THAT'S A BIT MUCH.
OH NO, I'M AMAZED BY YOUR ABILITIES. THE WORD "IMPOSSIBLE" DOES NOT SEEM TO EXIST IN YOUR LEXICON.
THAT KOREAN DEAL WOULD NOT HAVE HAPPENED WITHOUT YOU.

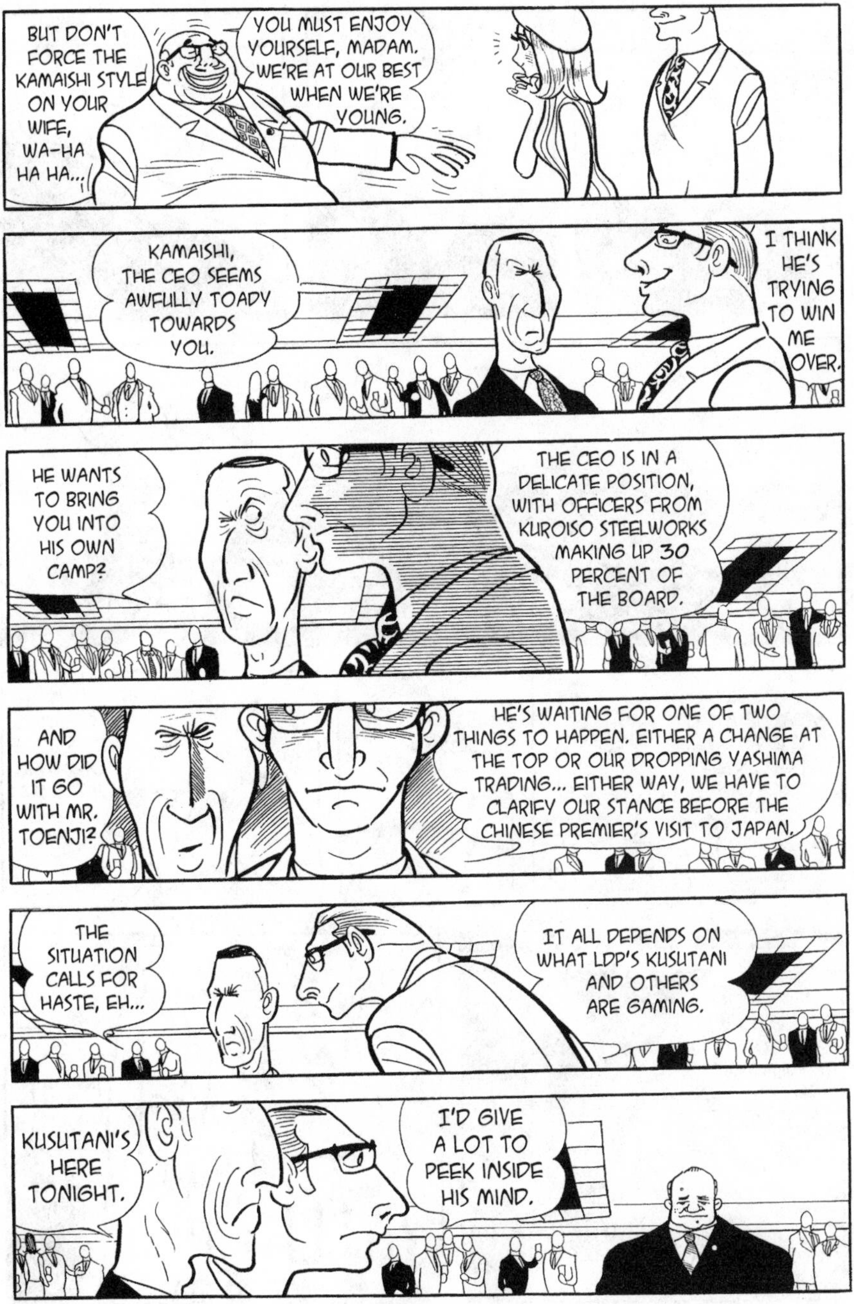
BUT DON'T FORCE THE KAMAISHI STYLE ON YOUR WIFE, WA-HA HA HA...!
YOU MUST ENJOY YOURSELF, MADAM. WE'RE AT OUR BEST WHEN WE'RE YOUNG.
KAMAISHI, THE CEO SEEMS AWFULLY TOADY TOWARDS YOU.
I THINK HE'S TRYING TO WIN ME OVER.
HE WANTS TO BRING YOU INTO HIS OWN CAMP?
THE CEO IS IN A DELICATE POSITION, WITH OFFICERS FROM KUROISO STEELWORKS MAKING UP 30 PERCENT OF THE BOARD.
AND HOW DID IT GO WITH MR. TOENJI?
HE'S WAITING FOR ONE OF TWO THINGS TO HAPPEN. EITHER A CHANGE AT THE TOP OR OUR DROPPING YASHIMA TRADING... EITHER WAY, WE HAVE TO CLARIFY OUR STANCE BEFORE THE CHINESE PREMIER'S VISIT TO JAPAN.
THE SITUATION CALLS FOR HASTE, EH...
IT ALL DEPENDS ON WHAT LDP'S KUSUTANI AND OTHERS ARE GAMING.
KUSUTANI'S HERE TONIGHT.
I'D GIVE A LOT TO PEEK INSIDE HIS MIND.

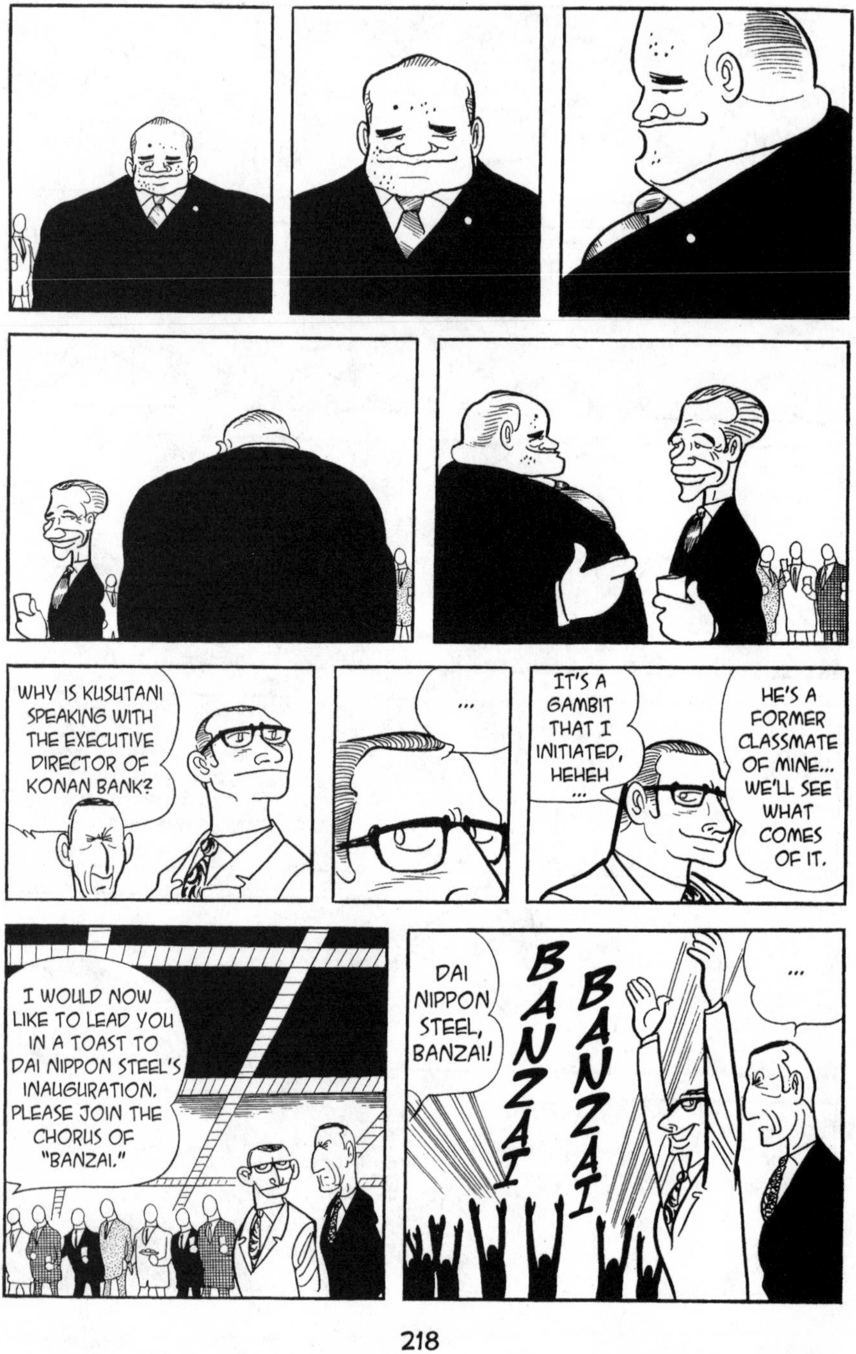
WHY IS KUSUTANI SPEAKING WITH THE EXECUTIVE DIRECTOR OF KONAN BANK?
...
IT'S A GAMBIT THAT I INITIATED, HEHEH ...
HE'S A FORMER CLASSMATE OF MINE... WE'LL SEE WHAT COMES OF IT.
I WOULD NOW LIKE TO LEAD YOU IN A TOAST TO DAI NIPPON STEEL'S INAUGURATION. PLEASE JOIN THE CHORUS OF "BANZAI."
DAI NIPPON STEEL, BANZAI!
BANZAI
BANZAI
...

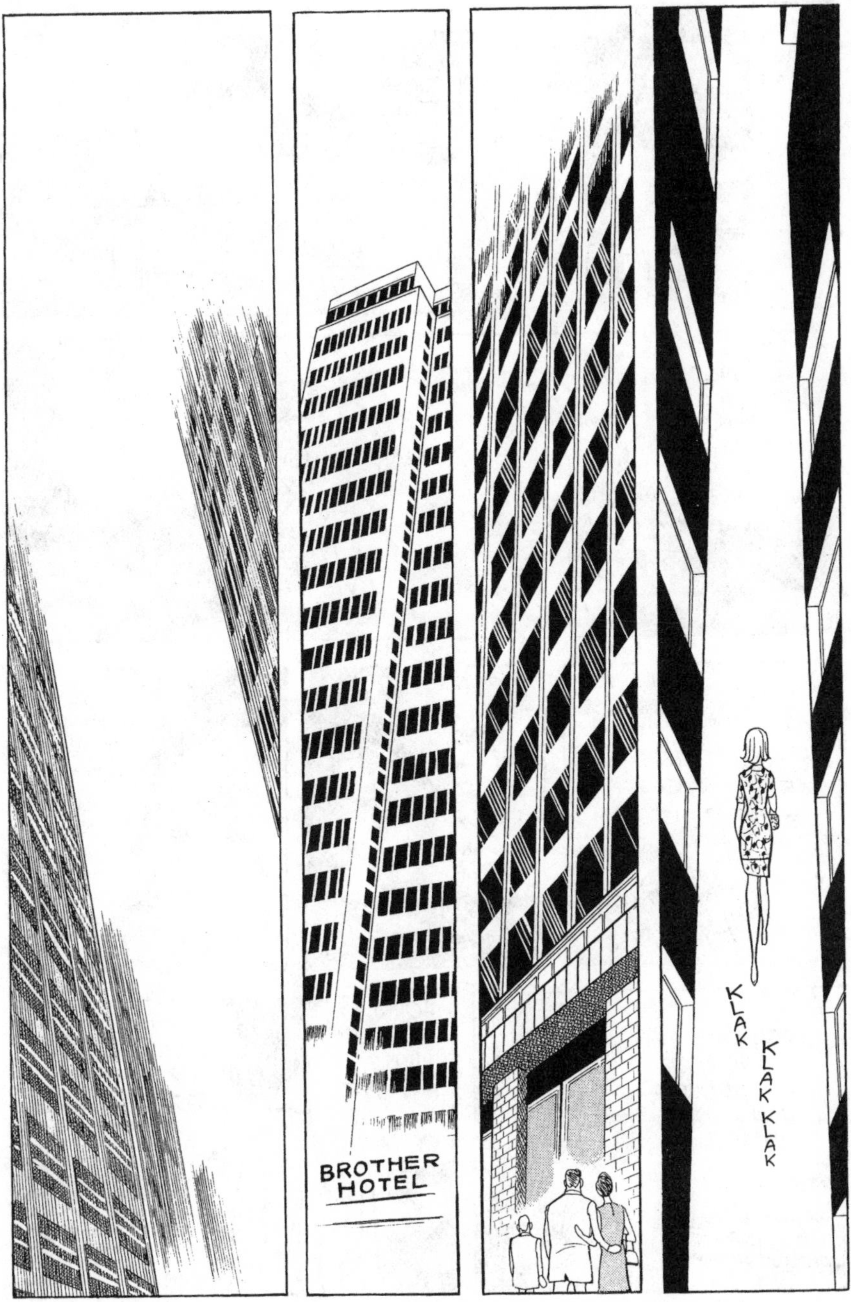
BROTHER HOTEL
KLAK
KLAK KLAK KLAK

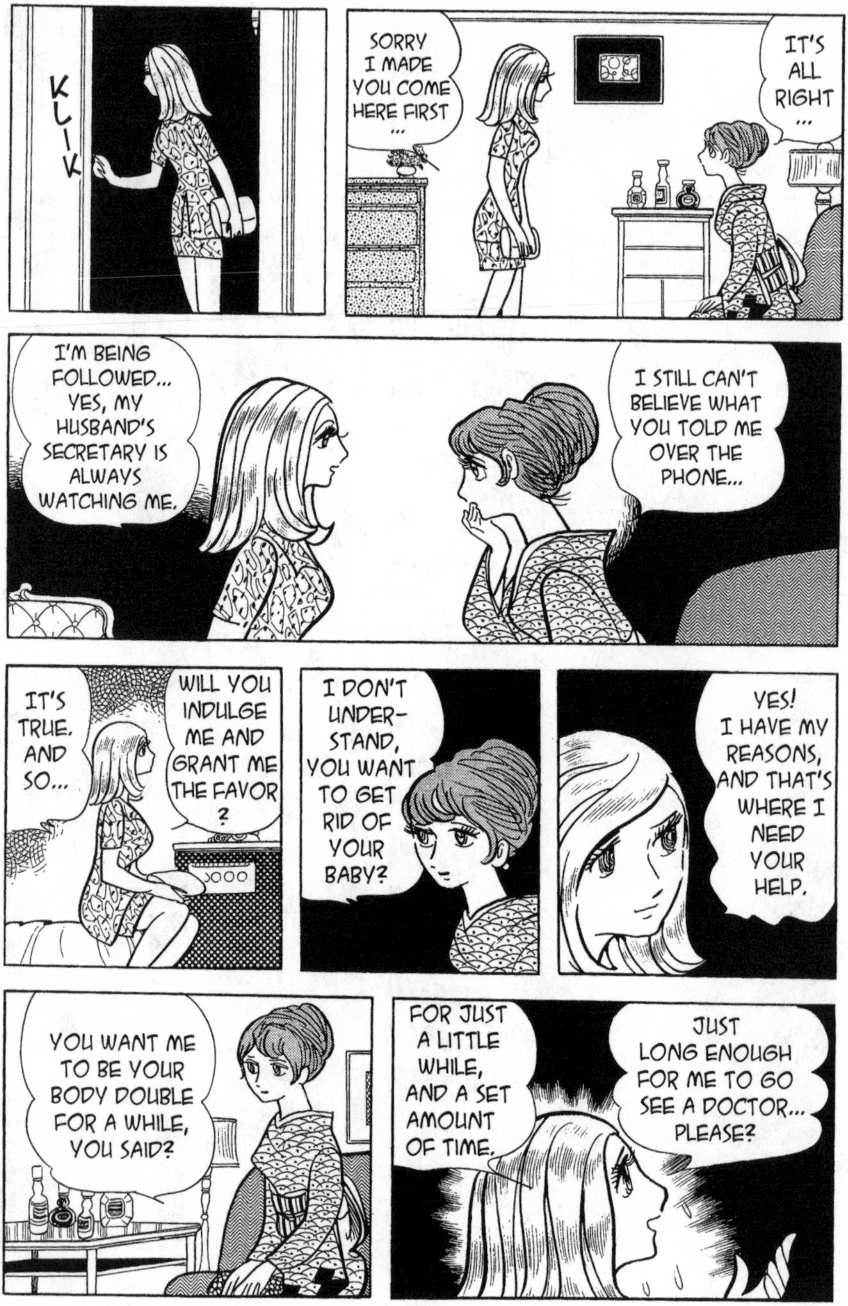
KLIK
SORRY I MADE YOU COME HERE FIRST ...
IT'S ALL RIGHT ...
I'M BEING FOLLOWED... YES, MY HUSBAND'S SECRETARY IS ALWAYS WATCHING ME.
I STILL CAN'T BELIEVE WHAT YOU TOLD ME OVER THE PHONE...
IT'S TRUE. AND SO...
WILL YOU INDULGE ME AND GRANT ME THE FAVOR?
I DON'T UNDER-STAND, YOU WANT TO GET RID OF YOUR BABY?
YES! I HAVE MY REASONS, AND THAT'S WHERE I NEED YOUR HELP.
YOU WANT ME TO BE YOUR BODY DOUBLE FOR A WHILE, YOU SAID?
FOR JUST A LITTLE WHILE, AND A SET AMOUNT OF TIME.
JUST LONG ENOUGH FOR ME TO GO SEE A DOCTOR... PLEASE?

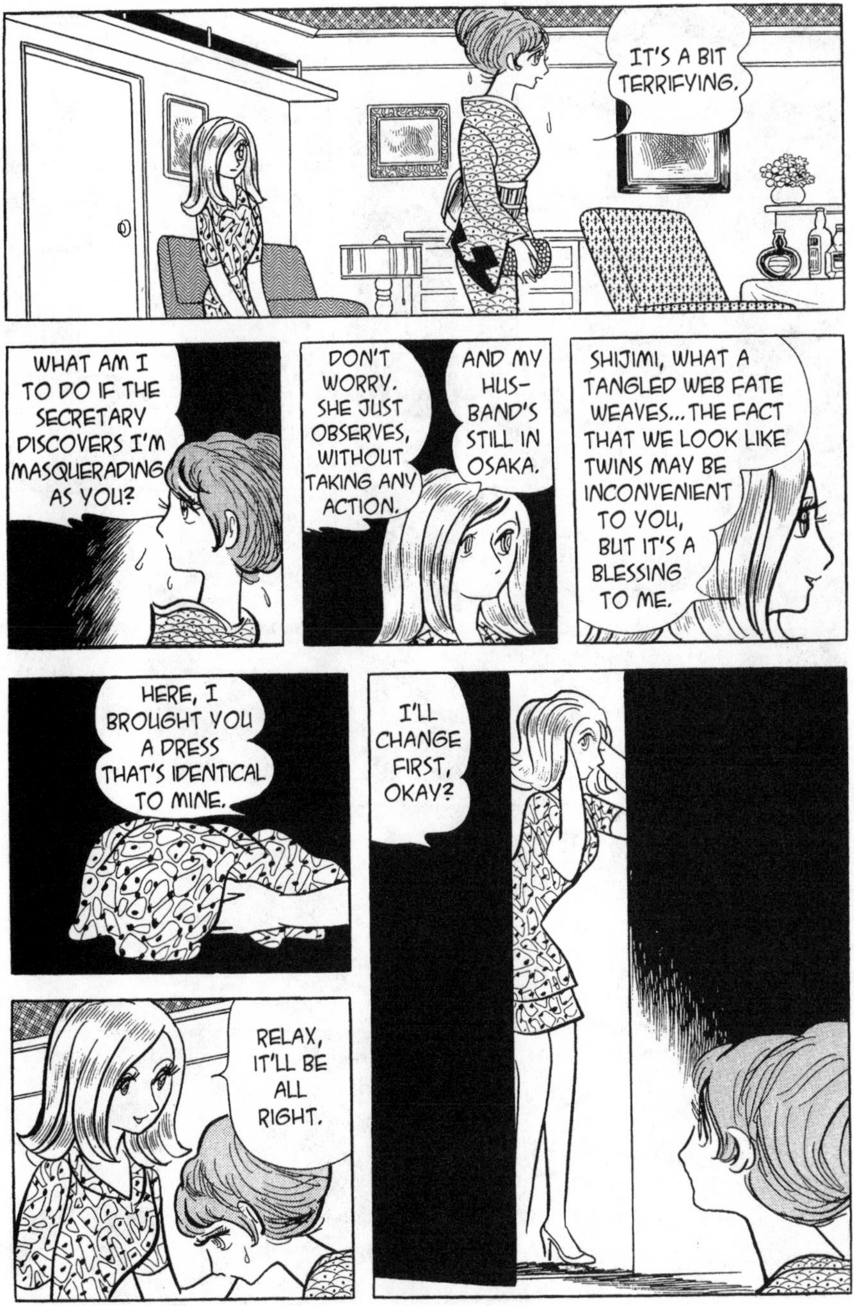
IT'S A BIT TERRIFYING.
WHAT AM I TO DO IF THE SECRETARY DISCOVERS I'M MASQUERADING AS YOU?
DON'T WORRY. SHE JUST OBSERVES, WITHOUT TAKING ANY ACTION.
AND MY HUS-BAND'S STILL IN OSAKA.
SHIJIMI, WHAT A TANGLED WEB FATE WEAVES... THE FACT THAT WE LOOK LIKE TWINS MAY BE INCONVENIENT TO YOU, BUT IT'S A BLESSING TO ME.
HERE, I BROUGHT YOU A DRESS THAT'S IDENTICAL TO MINE.
RELAX, IT'LL BE ALL RIGHT.
I'LL CHANGE FIRST, OKAY?

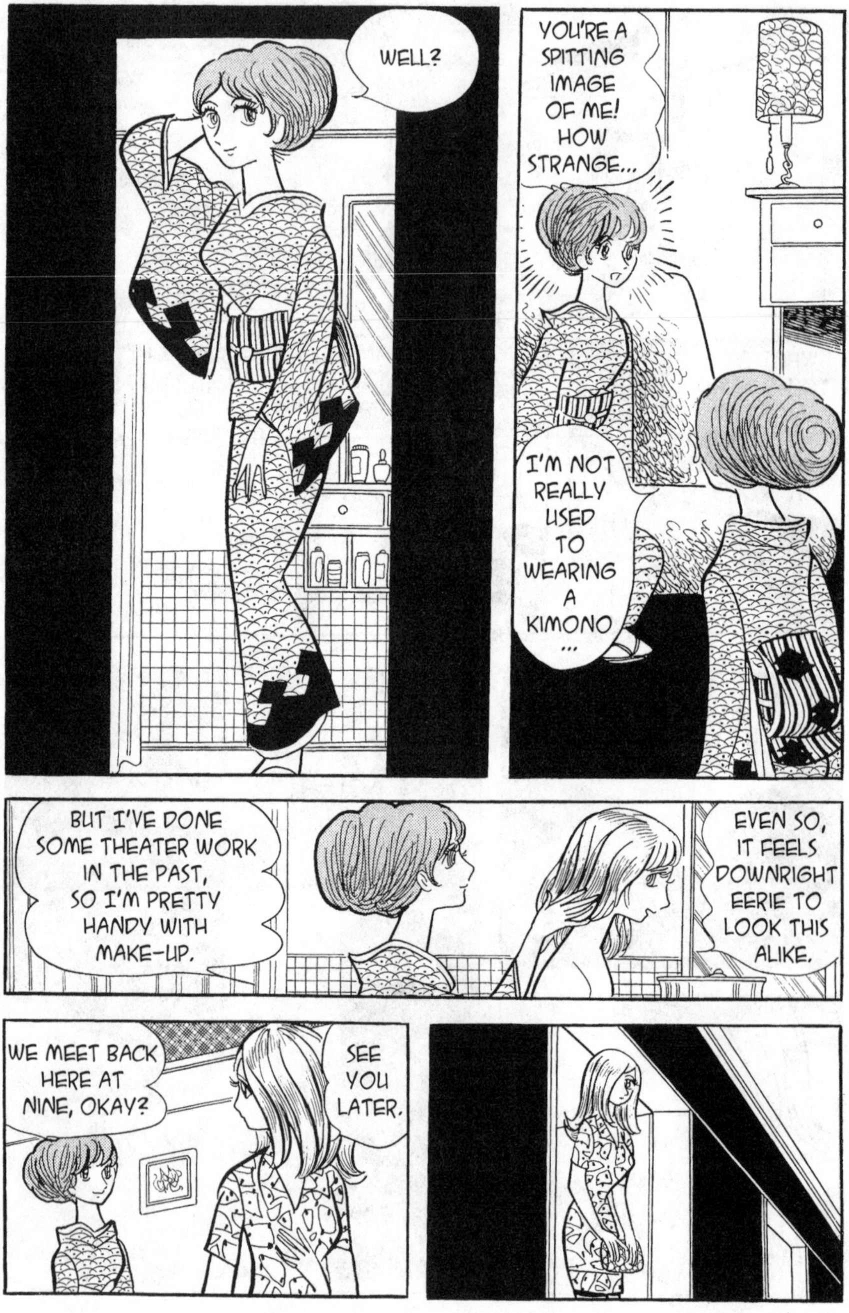
WELL?
YOU'RE A SPITTING IMAGE OF ME! HOW STRANGE...
I'M NOT REALLY USED TO WEARING A KIMONO ...
BUT I'VE DONE SOME THEATER WORK IN THE PAST, SO I'M PRETTY HANDY WITH MAKE-UP.
EVEN SO, IT FEELS DOWNRIGHT EERIE TO LOOK THIS ALIKE.
WE MEET BACK HERE AT NINE, OKAY?
SEE YOU LATER.

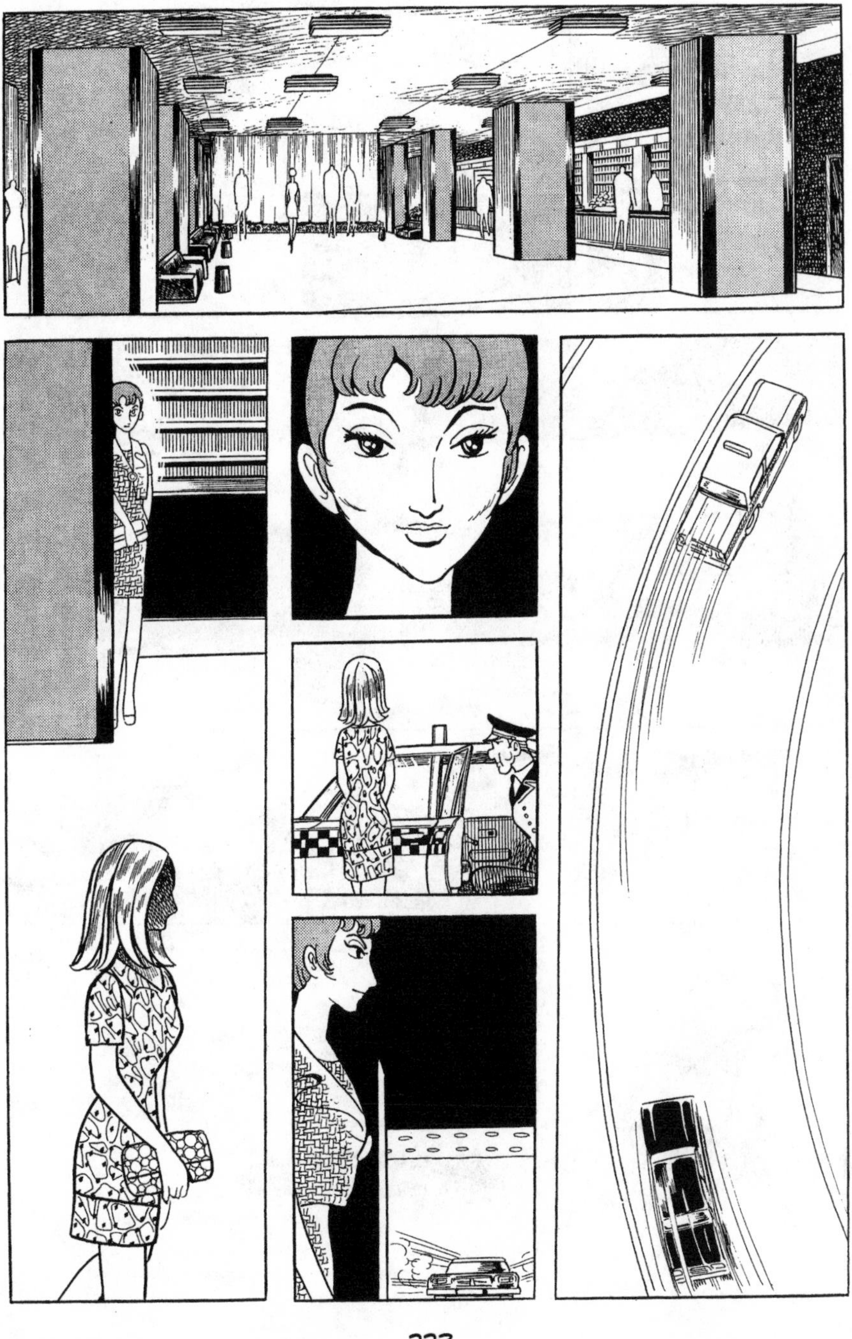

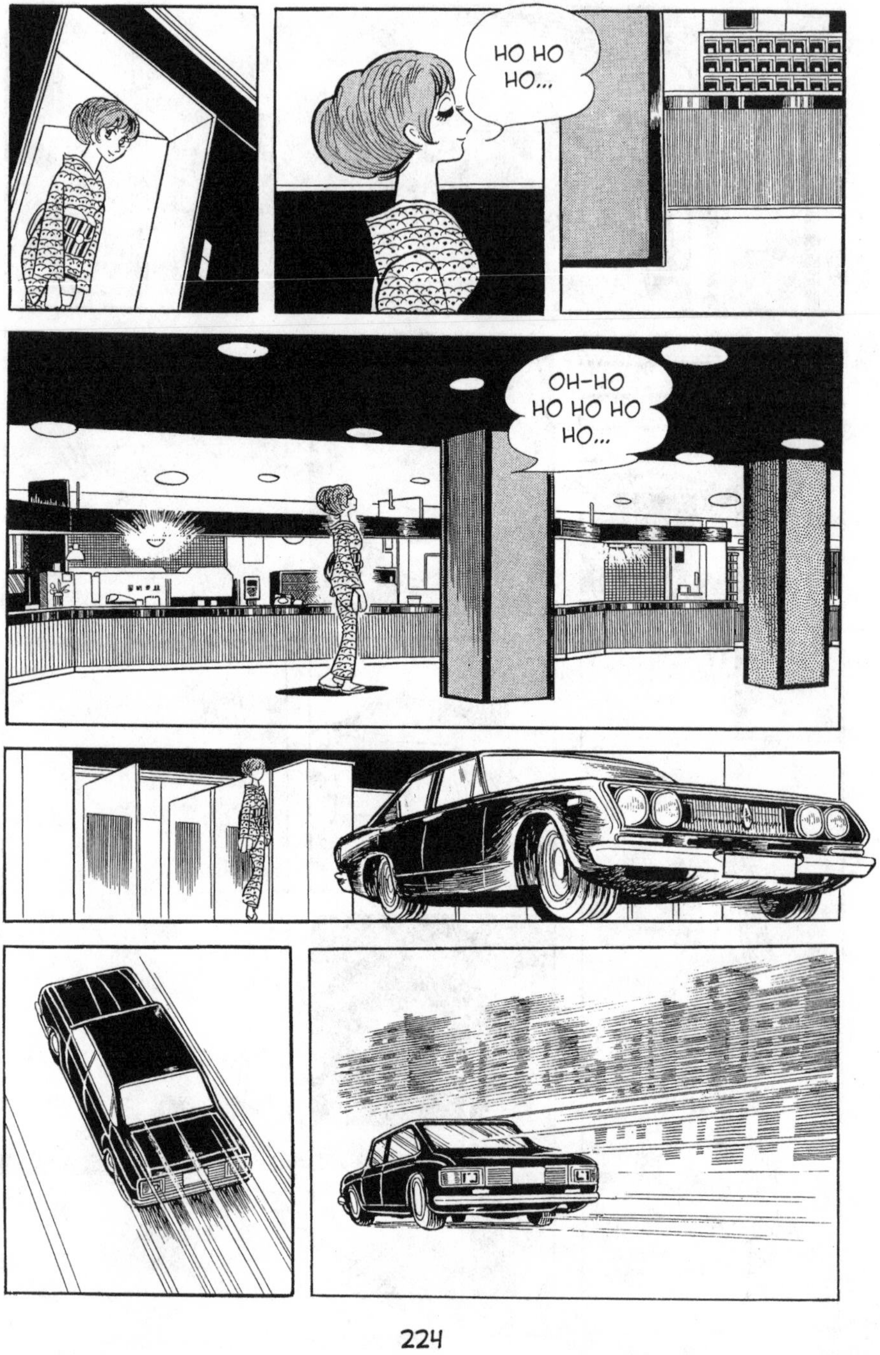
HO HO HO...
OH-HO HO HO HO HO...

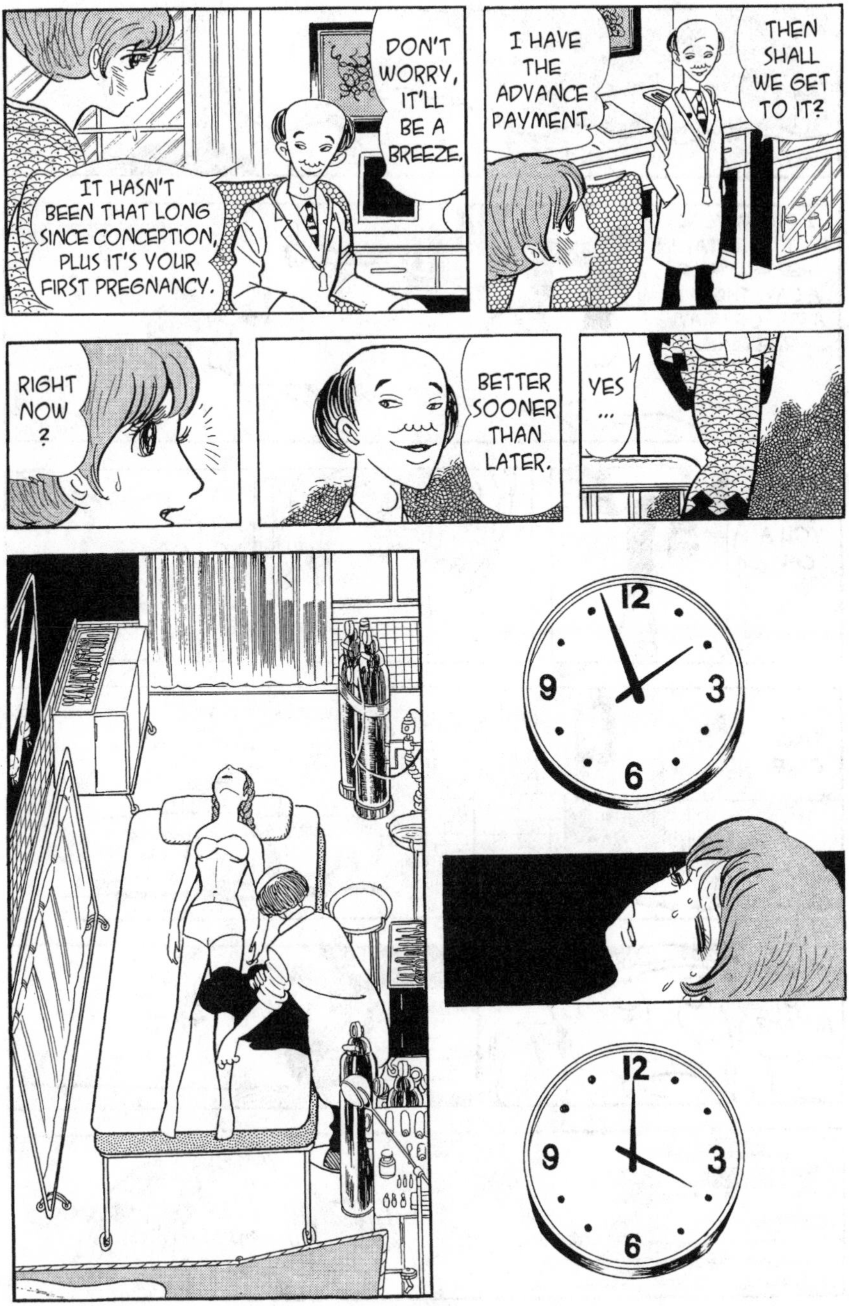
IT HASN'T BEEN THAT LONG SINCE CONCEPTION, PLUS IT'S YOUR FIRST PREGNANCY.
DON'T WORRY, IT'LL BE A BREEZE.
I HAVE THE ADVANCE PAYMENT.
THEN SHALL WE GET TO IT?
RIGHT NOW?
BETTER SOONER THAN LATER.
YES...

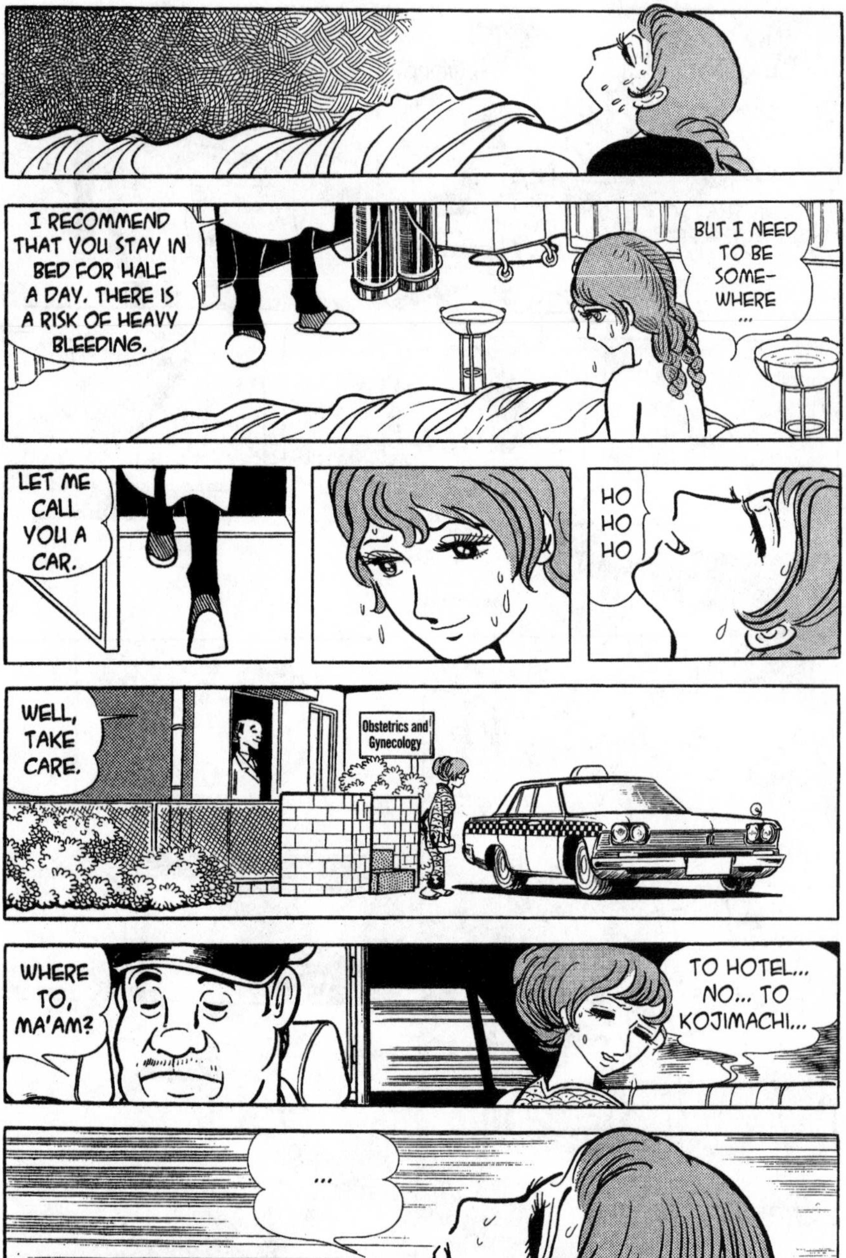
I RECOMMEND THAT YOU STAY IN BED FOR HALF A DAY. THERE IS A RISK OF HEAVY BLEEDING.
BUT I NEED TO BE SOME-WHERE ...
LET ME CALL YOU A CAR.
HO HO HO
WELL, TAKE CARE.
Obstetrics and Gynecology
WHERE TO, MA'AM?
TO HOTEL... NO... TO KOJIMACHI...
...

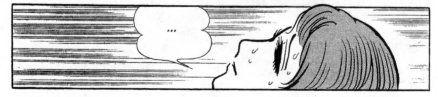

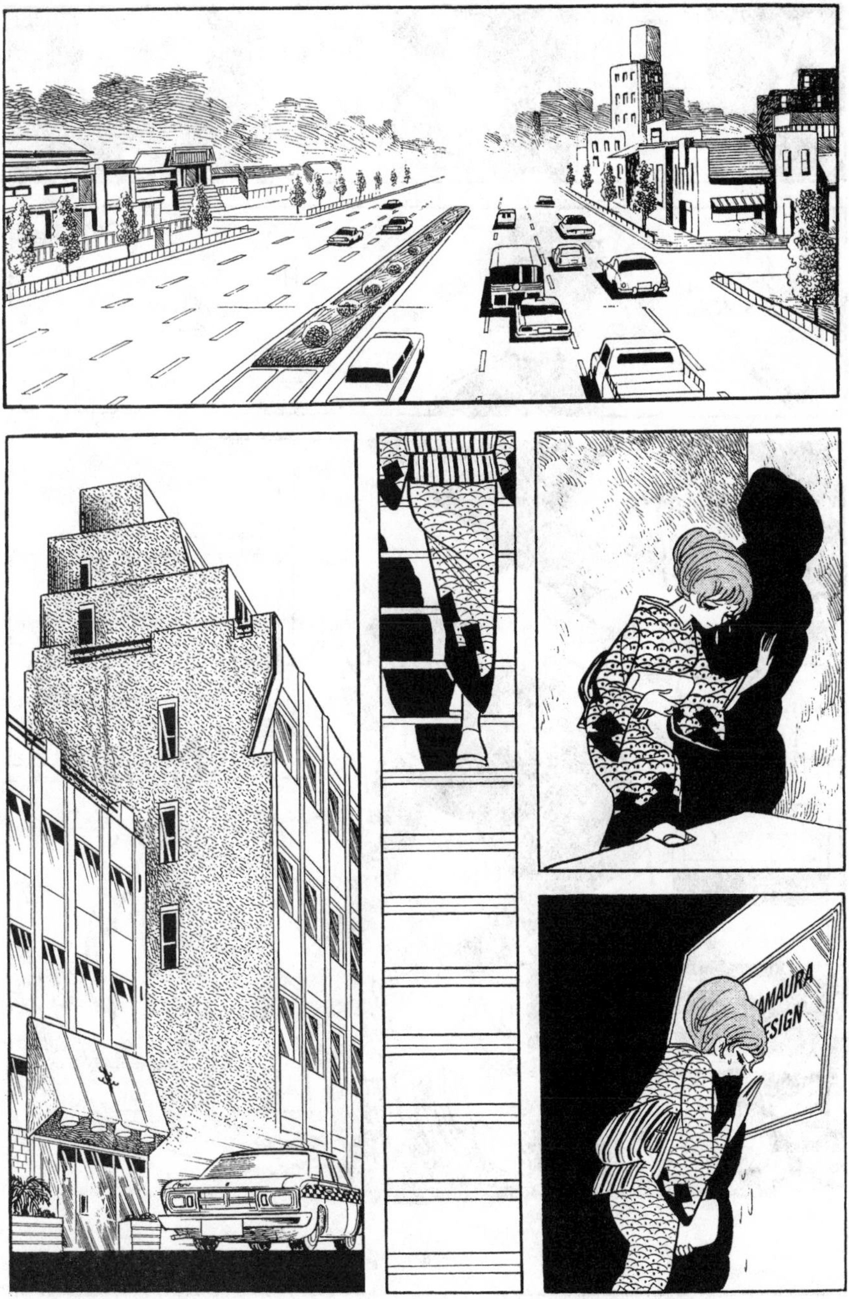
AMAURA
ESIGN

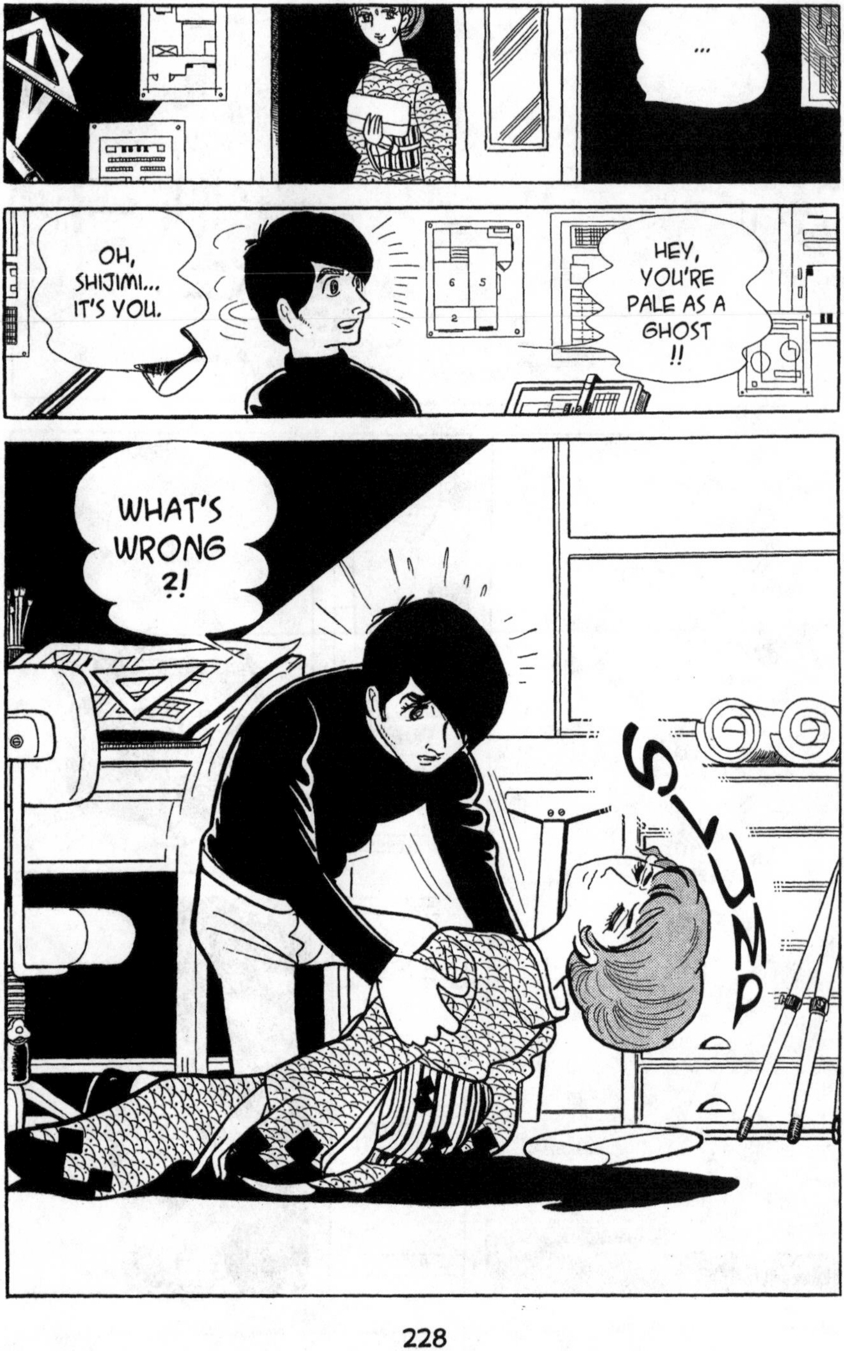
...
OH, SHIJIMI... IT'S YOU.
HEY, YOU'RE PALE AS A GHOST !!
WHAT'S WRONG ?!
SLUMP

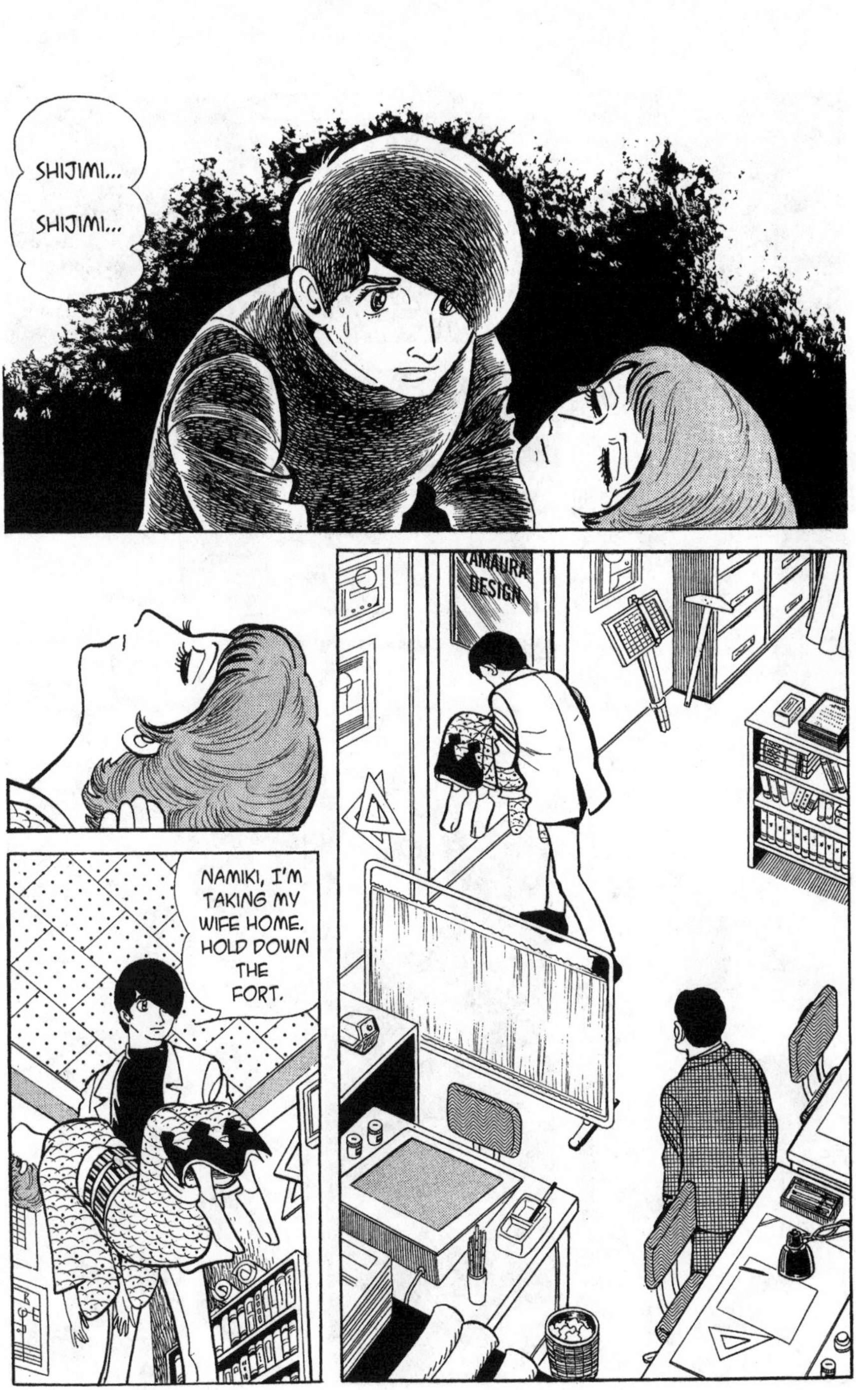
SHIJIMI...
SHIJIMI...
YAMAURA DESIGN
NAMIKI, I'M TAKING MY WIFE HOME. HOLD DOWN THE FORT.

SHE'S NOT MY WIFE !!

IT'S TOSHIKO TOMURA ...

WHY DID SHE SHOW UP DRESSED AS SHIJIMI ?

WHAT'S GOING ON?

TRYING TO INFLICT PAIN ON ME AGAIN ?

FINE, LET ME TAKE HER HOME.

WHAT THE HECK ?

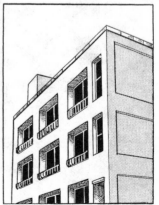

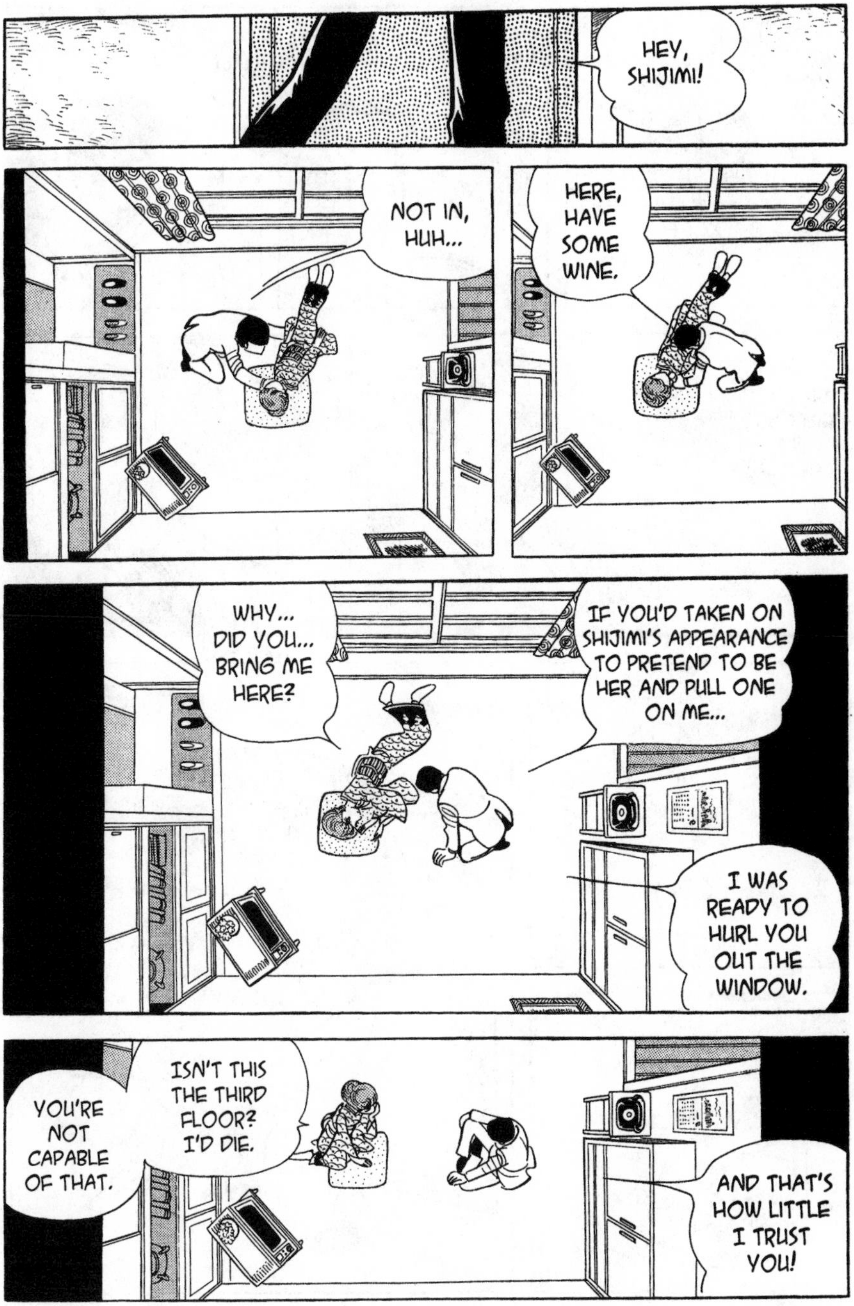
HEY, SHIJIMI!
NOT IN, HUH...
HERE, HAVE SOME WINE.
WHY... DID YOU... BRING ME HERE?
IF YOU'D TAKEN ON SHIJIMI'S APPEARANCE TO PRETEND TO BE HER AND PULL ONE ON ME...
I WAS READY TO HURL YOU OUT THE WINDOW.
YOU'RE NOT CAPABLE OF THAT.
ISN'T THIS THE THIRD FLOOR? I'D DIE.
AND THAT'S HOW LITTLE I TRUST YOU!

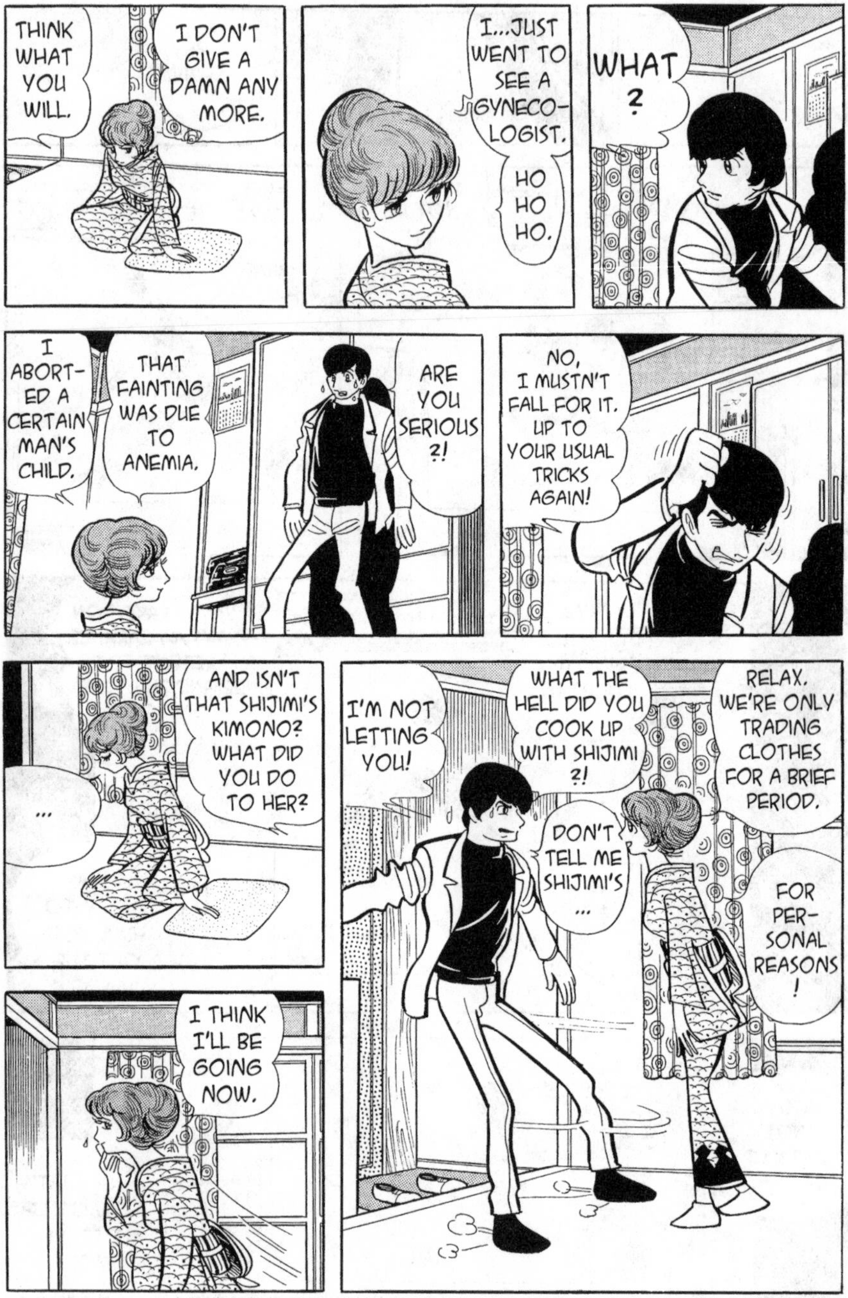

THINK WHAT YOU WILL.
I DON'T GIVE A DAMN ANY MORE.
I...JUST WENT TO SEE A GYNECO-LOGIST.
HO HO HO.
WHAT?
I ABORT-ED A CERTAIN MAN'S CHILD.
THAT FAINTING WAS DUE TO ANEMIA.
ARE YOU SERIOUS?!
NO, I MUSTN'T FALL FOR IT. UP TO YOUR USUAL TRICKS AGAIN!
...
AND ISN'T THAT SHIJIMI'S KIMONO? WHAT DID YOU DO TO HER?
I THINK I'LL BE GOING NOW.
I'M NOT LETTING YOU!
WHAT THE HELL DID YOU COOK UP WITH SHIJIMI?!
RELAX, WE'RE ONLY TRADING CLOTHES FOR A BRIEF PERIOD.
DON'T TELL ME SHIJIMI'S...
FOR PER-SONAL REASONS!

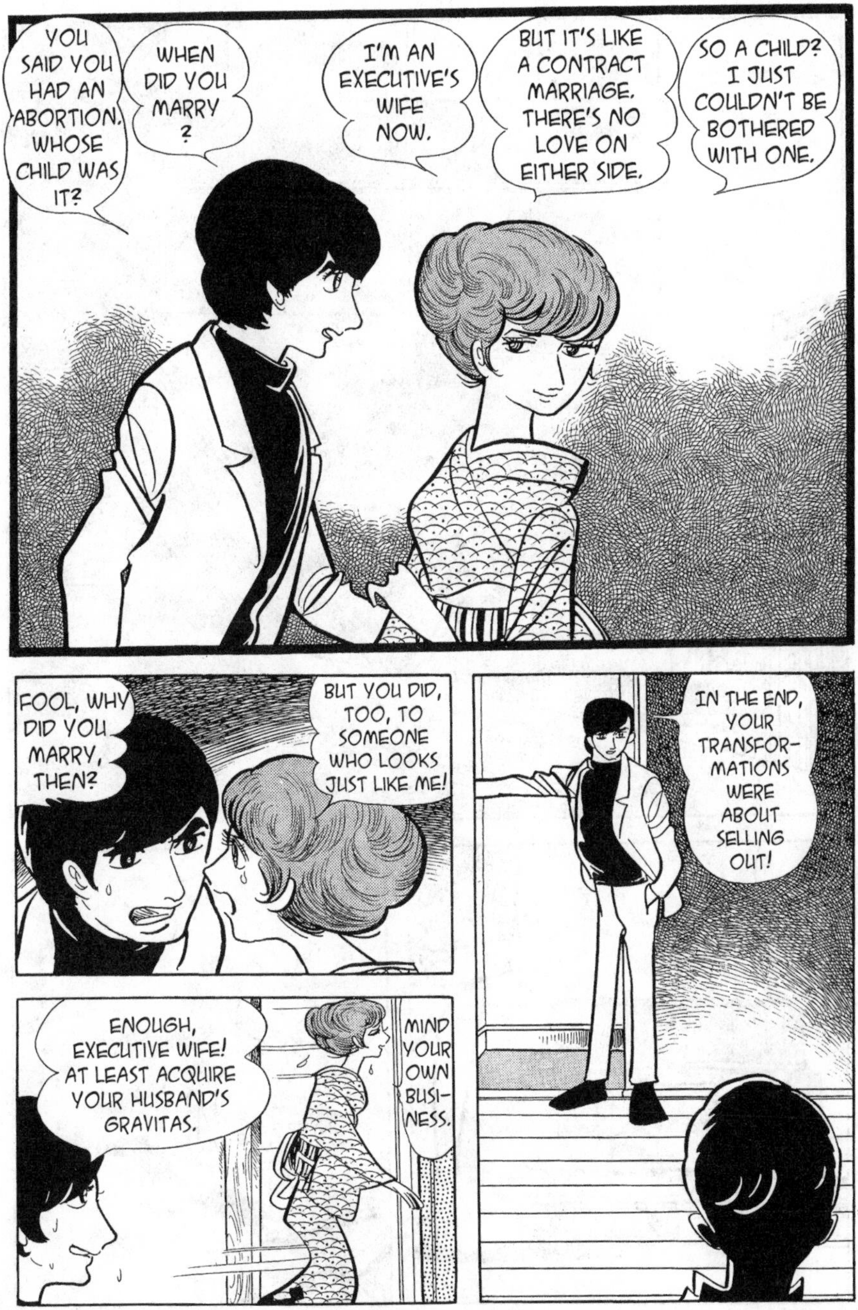
YOU SAID YOU HAD AN ABORTION. WHOSE CHILD WAS IT?
WHEN DID YOU MARRY?
I'M AN EXECUTIVE'S WIFE NOW.
BUT IT'S LIKE A CONTRACT MARRIAGE. THERE'S NO LOVE ON EITHER SIDE.
SO A CHILD? I JUST COULDN'T BE BOTHERED WITH ONE.
FOOL, WHY DID YOU MARRY, THEN?
BUT YOU DID, TOO, TO SOMEONE WHO LOOKS JUST LIKE ME!
IN THE END, YOUR TRANSFOR-MATIONS WERE ABOUT SELLING OUT!
ENOUGH, EXECUTIVE WIFE! AT LEAST ACQUIRE YOUR HUSBAND'S GRAVITAS.
MIND YOUR OWN BUSI-NESS.

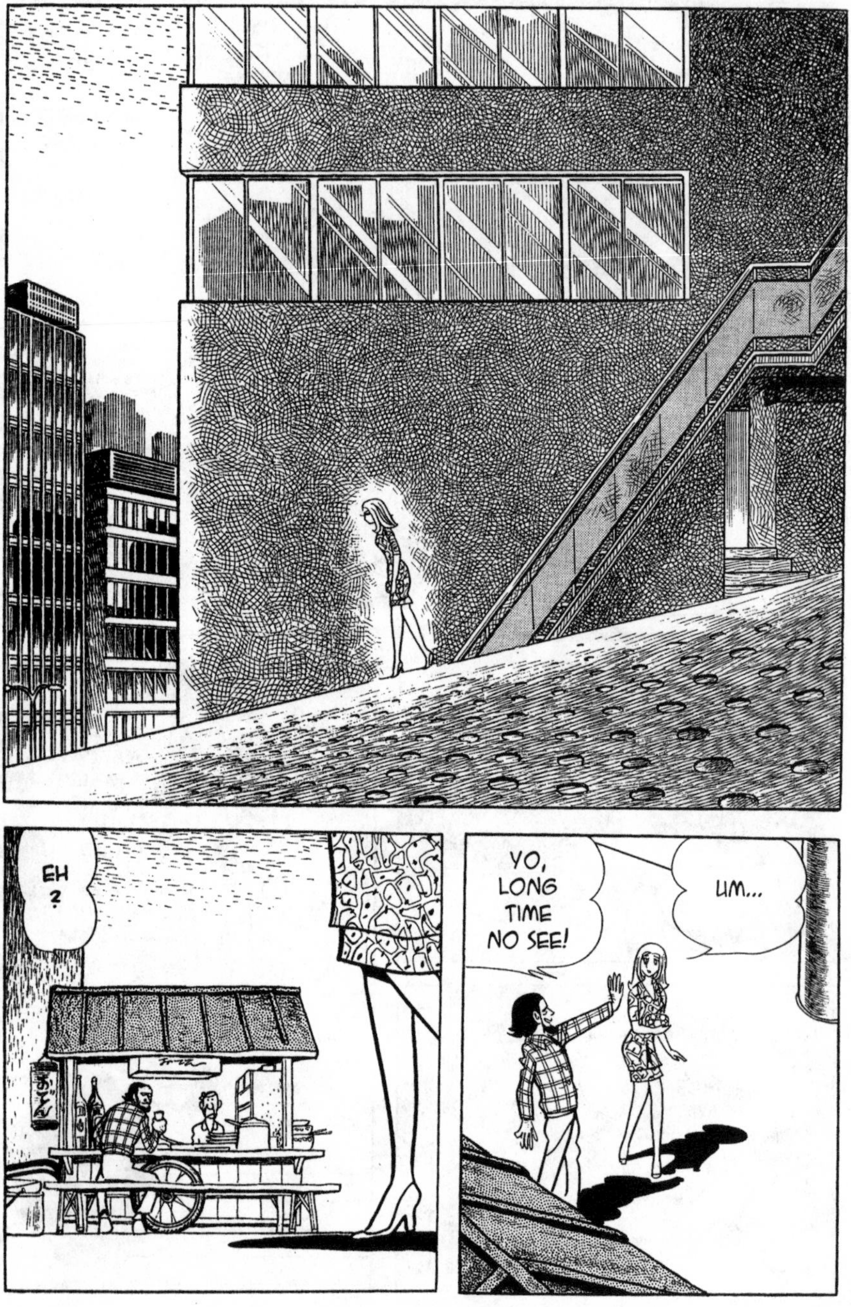
EH ?
YO, LONG TIME NO SEE!
UM...

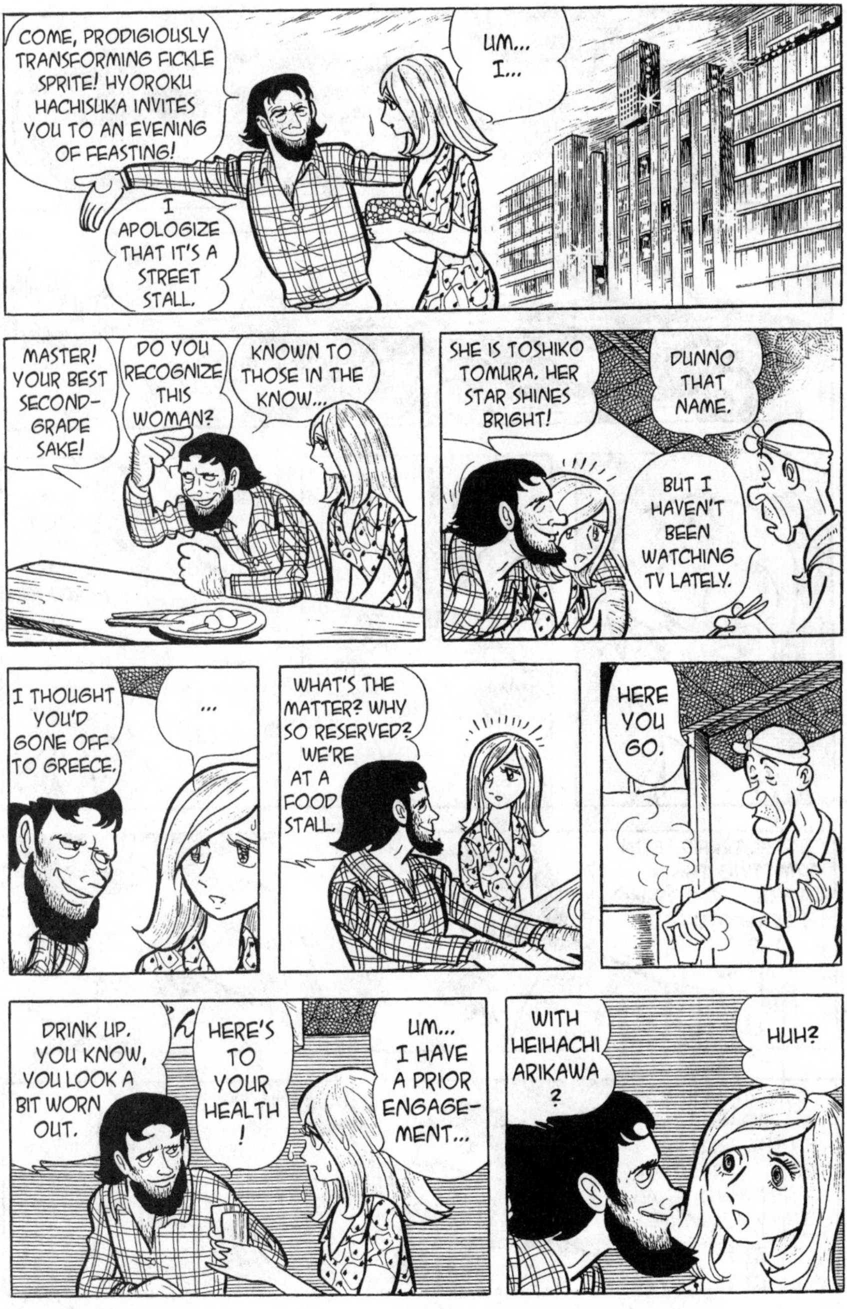
COME, PRODIGIOUSLY TRANSFORMING FICKLE SPRITE! HYOROKU HACHISUKA INVITES YOU TO AN EVENING OF FEASTING!
I APOLOGIZE THAT IT'S A STREET STALL.
UM... I...
MASTER! YOUR BEST SECOND-GRADE SAKE!
DO YOU RECOGNIZE THIS WOMAN?
KNOWN TO THOSE IN THE KNOW...
SHE IS TOSHIKO TOMURA. HER STAR SHINES BRIGHT!
DUNNO THAT NAME.
BUT I HAVEN'T BEEN WATCHING TV LATELY.
I THOUGHT YOU'D GONE OFF TO GREECE.
...
WHAT'S THE MATTER? WHY SO RESERVED? WE'RE AT A FOOD STALL.
HERE YOU GO.
DRINK UP. YOU KNOW, YOU LOOK A BIT WORN OUT.
HERE'S TO YOUR HEALTH!
UM... I HAVE A PRIOR ENGAGE-MENT...
WITH HEIHACHI ARIKAWA?
HUH?

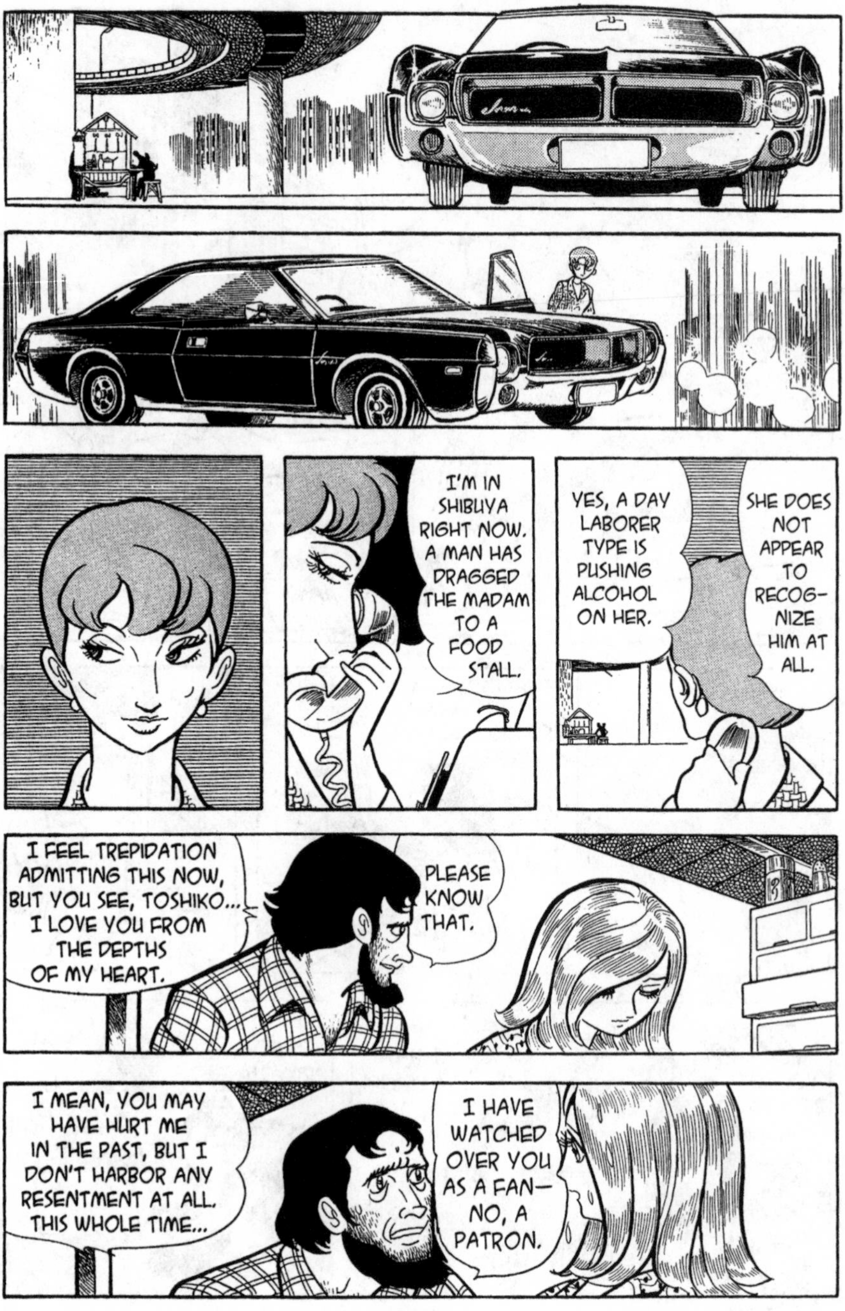
I'M IN SHIBUYA RIGHT NOW. A MAN HAS DRAGGED THE MADAM TO A FOOD STALL.
YES, A DAY LABORER TYPE IS PUSHING ALCOHOL ON HER.
SHE DOES NOT APPEAR TO RECOG-NIZE HIM AT ALL.
I FEEL TREPIDATION ADMITTING THIS NOW, BUT YOU SEE, TOSHIKO... I LOVE YOU FROM THE DEPTHS OF MY HEART.
PLEASE KNOW THAT.
I MEAN, YOU MAY HAVE HURT ME IN THE PAST, BUT I DON'T HARBOR ANY RESENTMENT AT ALL. THIS WHOLE TIME...
I HAVE WATCHED OVER YOU AS A FAN— NO, A PATRON.

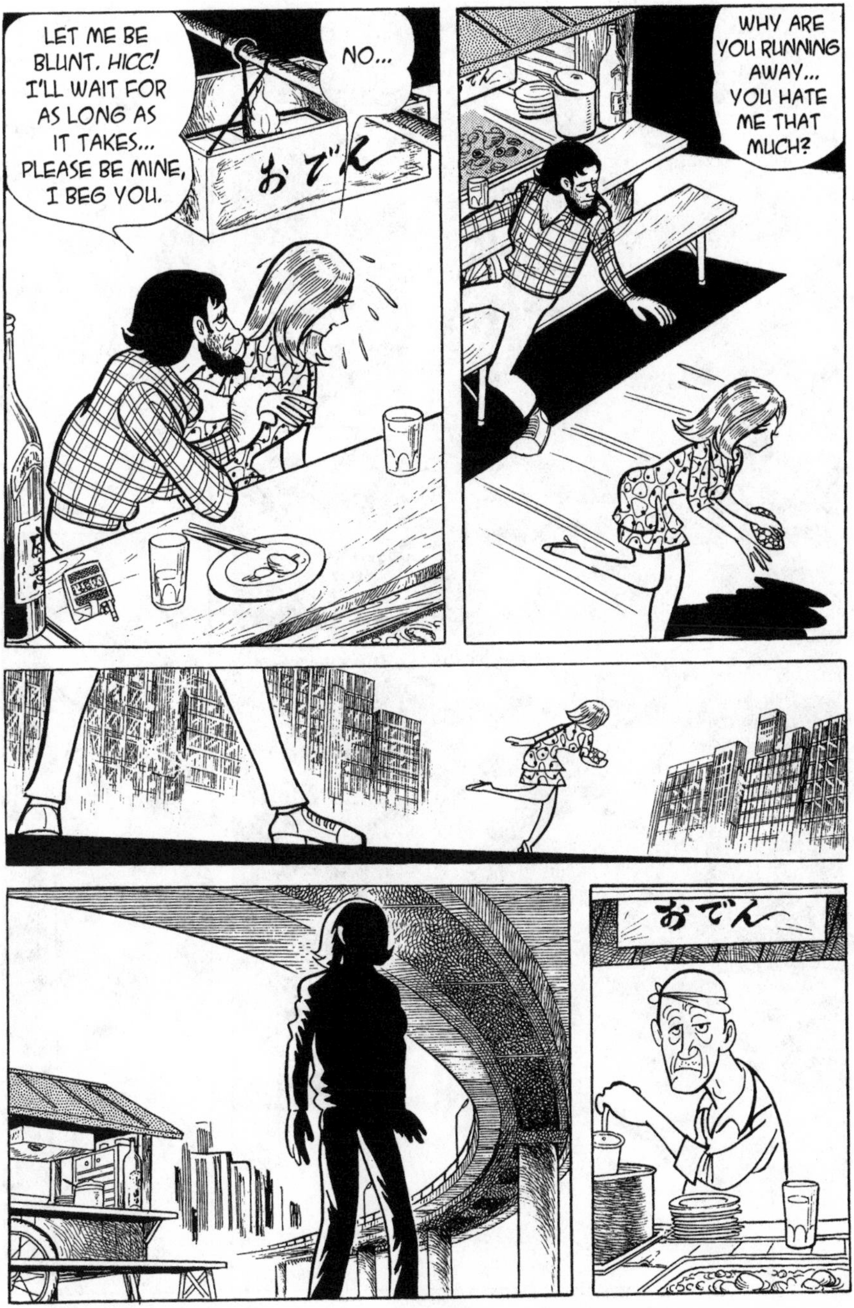
LET ME BE BLUNT. *HICC!* I'LL WAIT FOR AS LONG AS IT TAKES... PLEASE BE MINE, I BEG YOU.
NO...
おでん
WHY ARE YOU RUNNING AWAY... YOU HATE ME THAT MUCH?
おでん

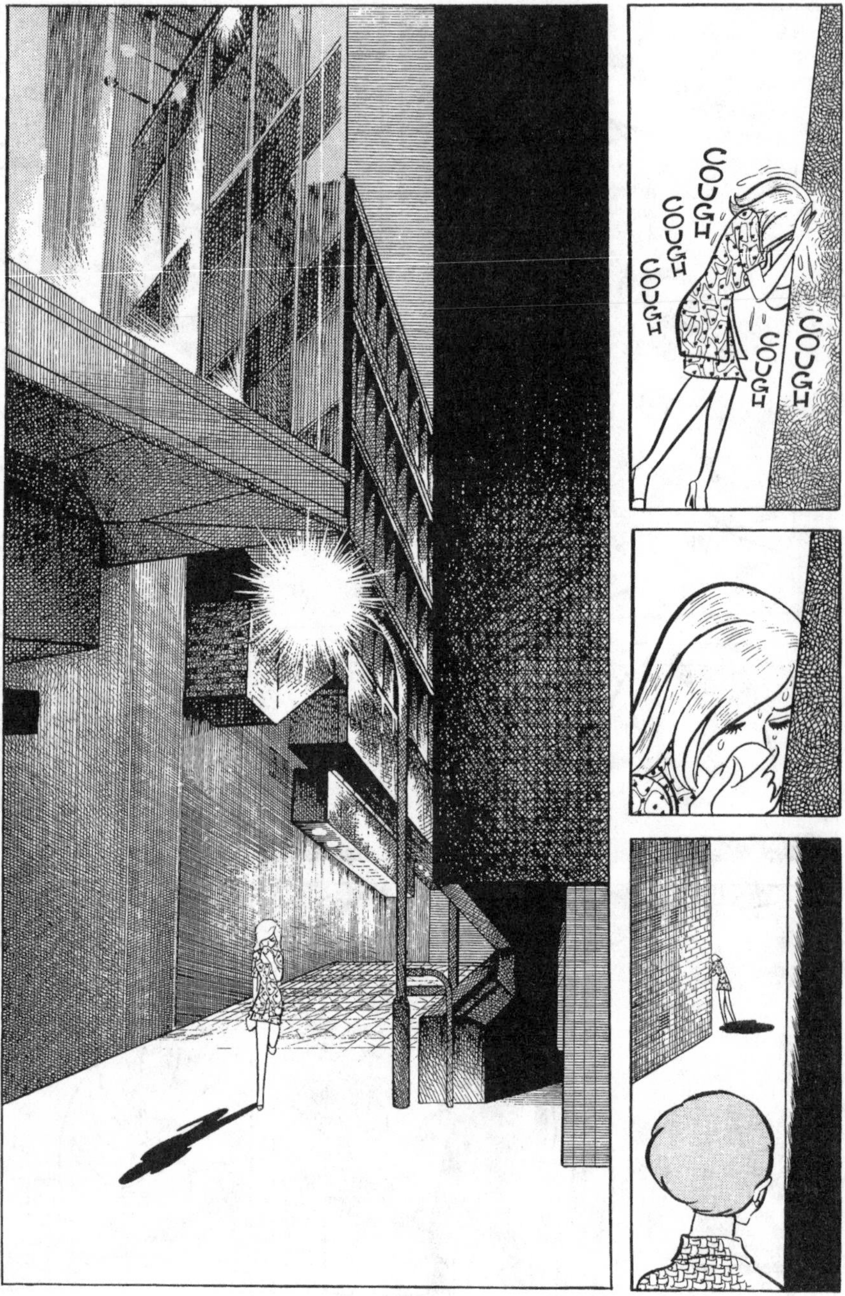
COUGH
COUGH
COUGH
COUGH
COUGH

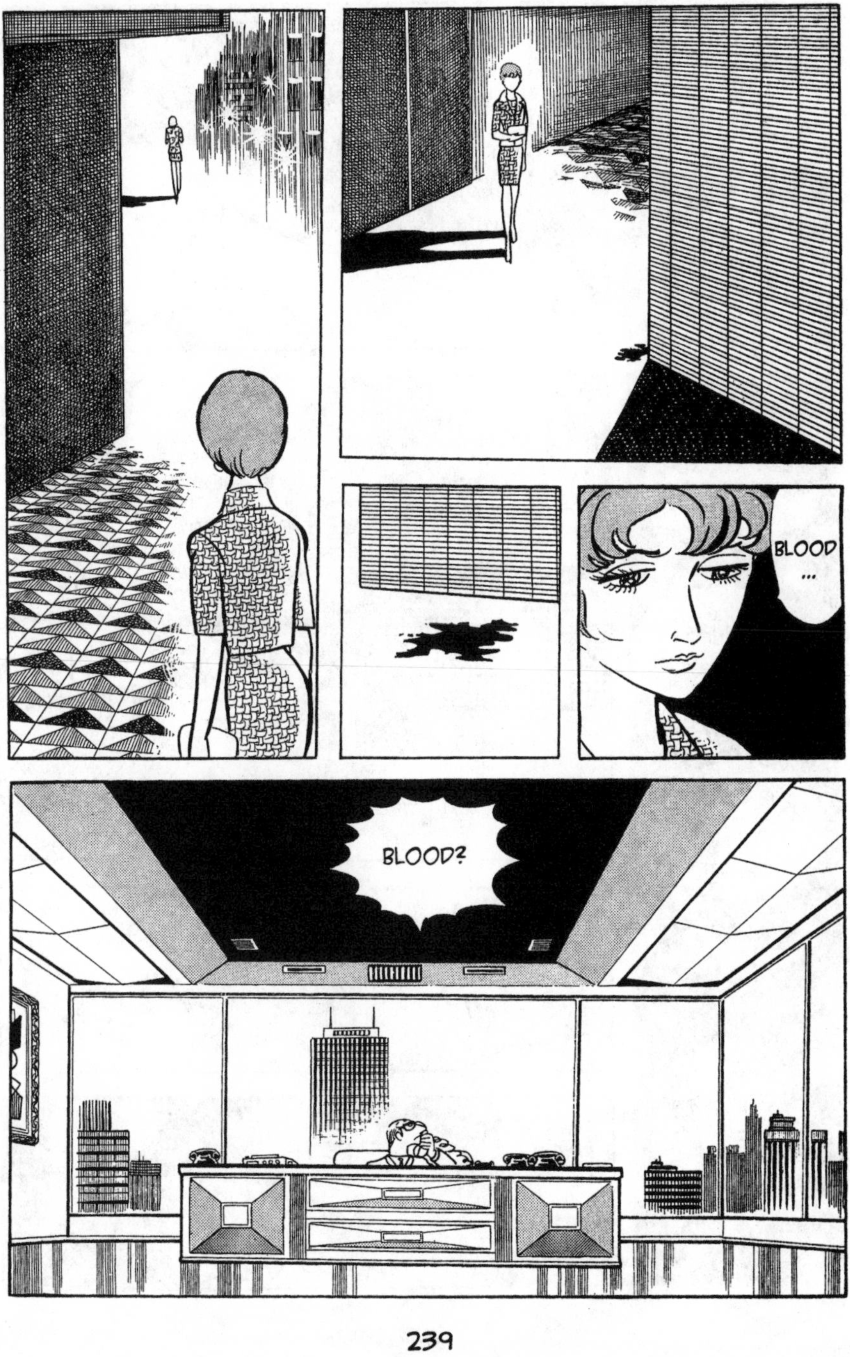
BLOOD
...
BLOOD?

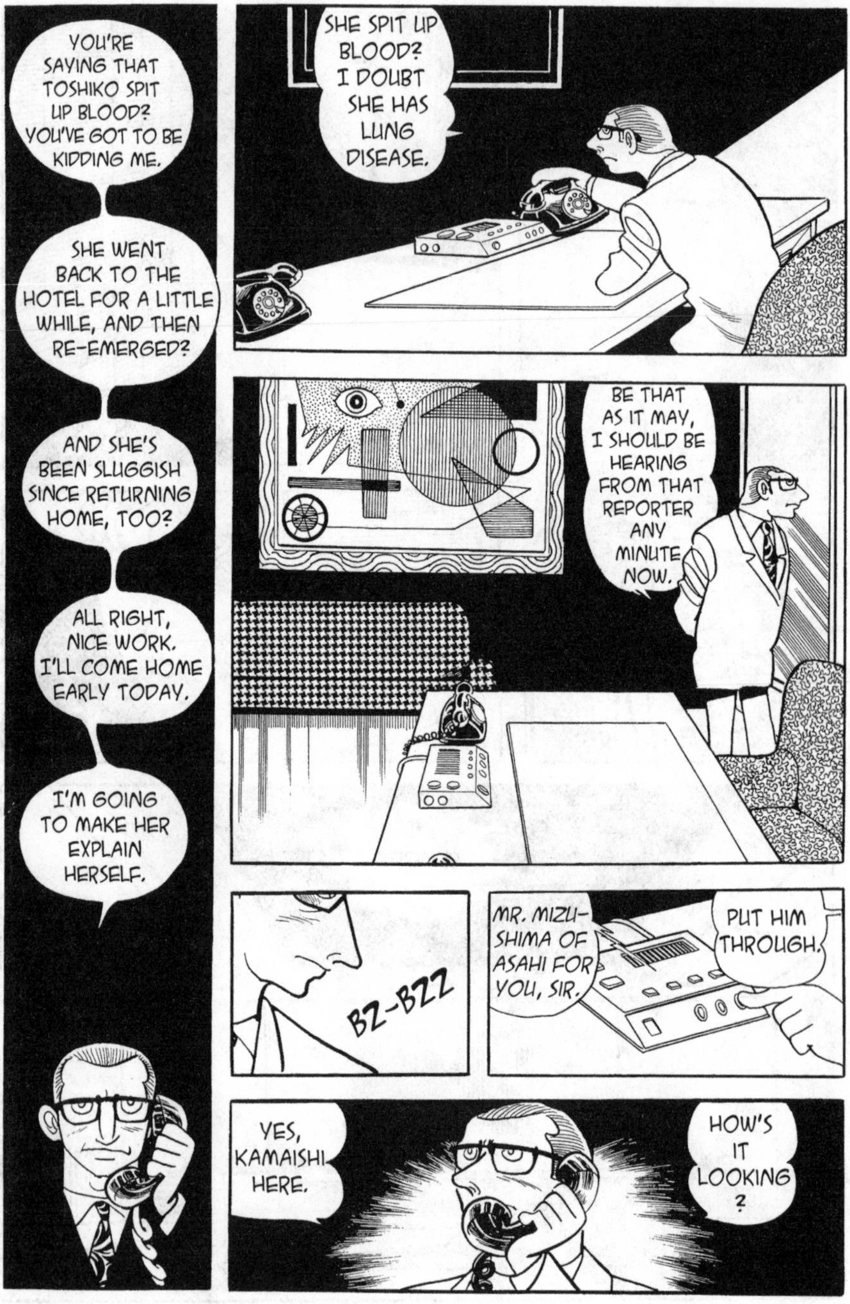
YOU'RE SAYING THAT TOSHIKO SPIT UP BLOOD? YOU'VE GOT TO BE KIDDING ME.
SHE WENT BACK TO THE HOTEL FOR A LITTLE WHILE, AND THEN RE-EMERGED?
AND SHE'S BEEN SLUGGISH SINCE RETURNING HOME, TOO?
ALL RIGHT, NICE WORK. I'LL COME HOME EARLY TODAY.
I'M GOING TO MAKE HER EXPLAIN HERSELF.
SHE SPIT UP BLOOD? I DOUBT SHE HAS LUNG DISEASE.
BE THAT AS IT MAY, I SHOULD BE HEARING FROM THAT REPORTER ANY MINUTE NOW.
BZ-BZZ
MR. MIZU-SHIMA OF ASAHI FOR YOU, SIR.
PUT HIM THROUGH.
YES, KAMAISHI HERE.
HOW'S IT LOOKING?

ACCORDING TO TAIPEI AP, FOR THE CONSTRUCTION OF OIL RIGS IN THE TAIWAN STRAIT AS WELL AS NORTHERN TAIWANESE WATERS, THE ROC MINISTRY OF FINANCIAL AFFAIRS WILL BE SIGNING AN AGREEMENT WITH U.S. STEEL AND BETHLEHEM STEEL, BOTH OF AMERICA, TO SECURE ANNUAL IMPORTS OF APPROXIMATELY 8 MILLION TONS.

ARE YOU CERTAIN?

WHEN IS THIS BREAKING?

THE ARTICLE SHOULD APPEAR TOMORROW MORNING.

THANKS

GET ME KONAN BANK HQ.

IS MR. IWABUCHI IN?

IMMEDIATELY, PLEASE. IT'S KAMAISHI OF DNS.

HEY, IWABUCHI?

BUY! TORA, TORA, TORA!

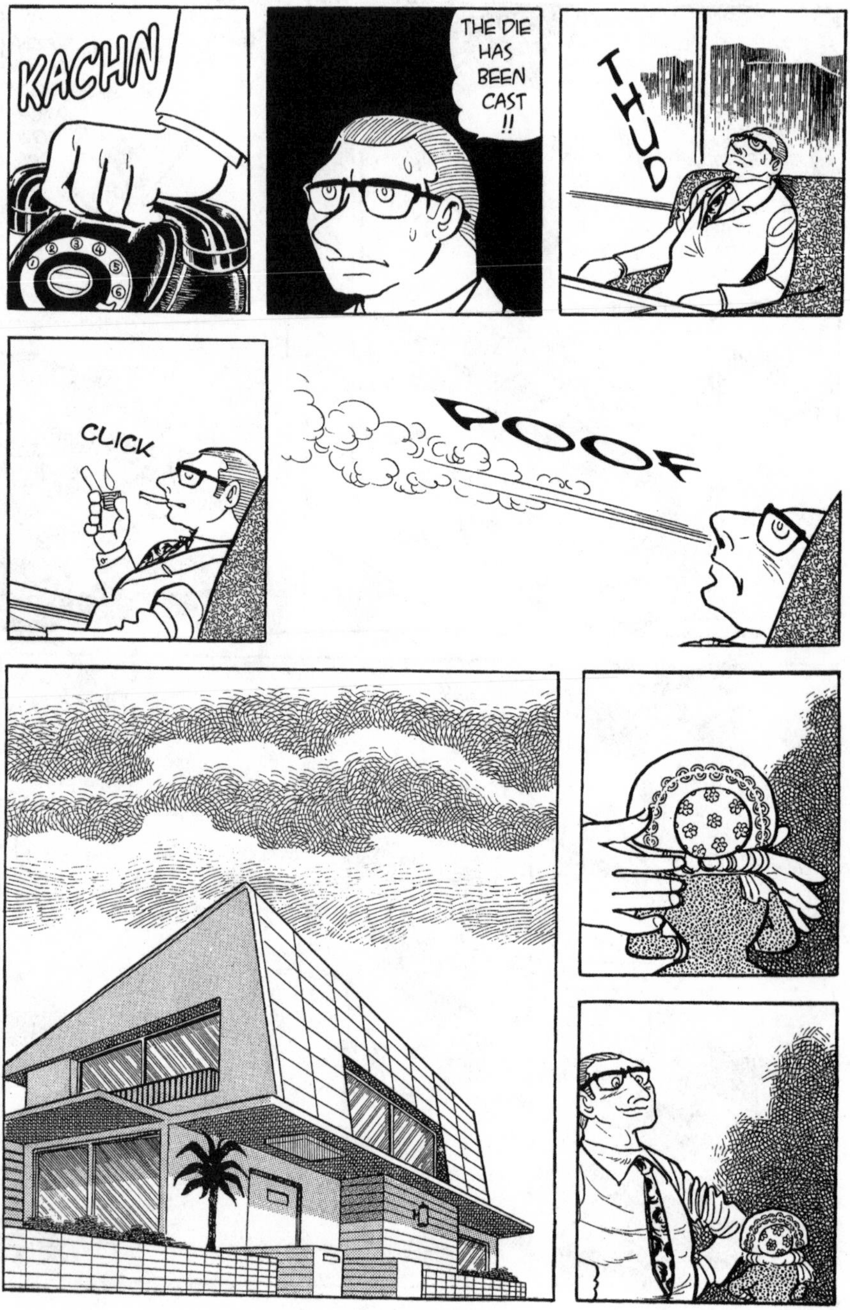
KACHN
THE DIE HAS BEEN CAST !!
THUD
CLICK
POOF

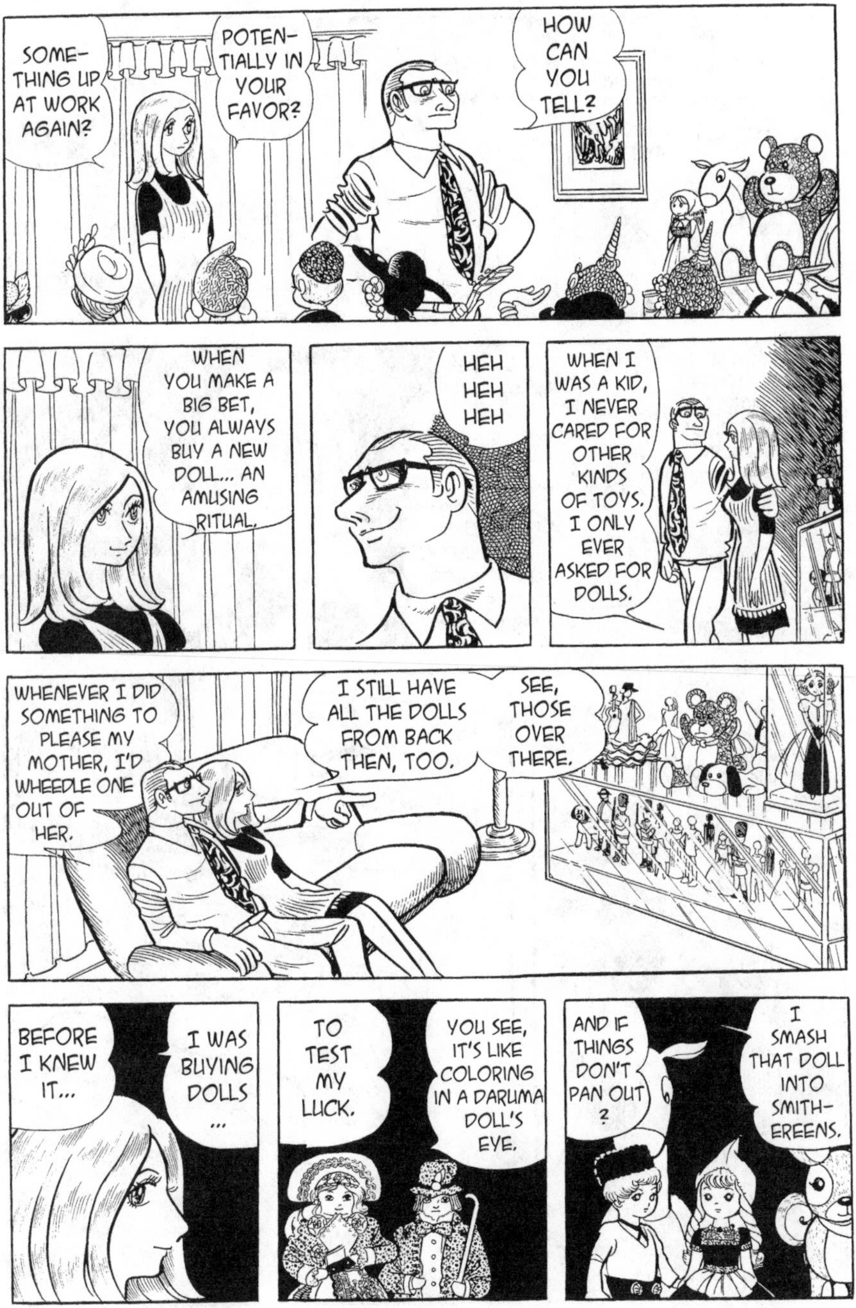
SOME-THING UP AT WORK AGAIN?
POTEN-TIALLY IN YOUR FAVOR?
HOW CAN YOU TELL?
WHEN YOU MAKE A BIG BET, YOU ALWAYS BUY A NEW DOLL... AN AMUSING RITUAL.
HEH HEH HEH
WHEN I WAS A KID, I NEVER CARED FOR OTHER KINDS OF TOYS. I ONLY EVER ASKED FOR DOLLS.
WHENEVER I DID SOMETHING TO PLEASE MY MOTHER, I'D WHEEDLE ONE OUT OF HER.
I STILL HAVE ALL THE DOLLS FROM BACK THEN, TOO.
SEE, THOSE OVER THERE.
BEFORE I KNEW IT...
I WAS BUYING DOLLS ...
TO TEST MY LUCK.
YOU SEE, IT'S LIKE COLORING IN A DARUMA DOLL'S EYE.
AND IF THINGS DON'T PAN OUT ?
I SMASH THAT DOLL INTO SMITH-EREENS.

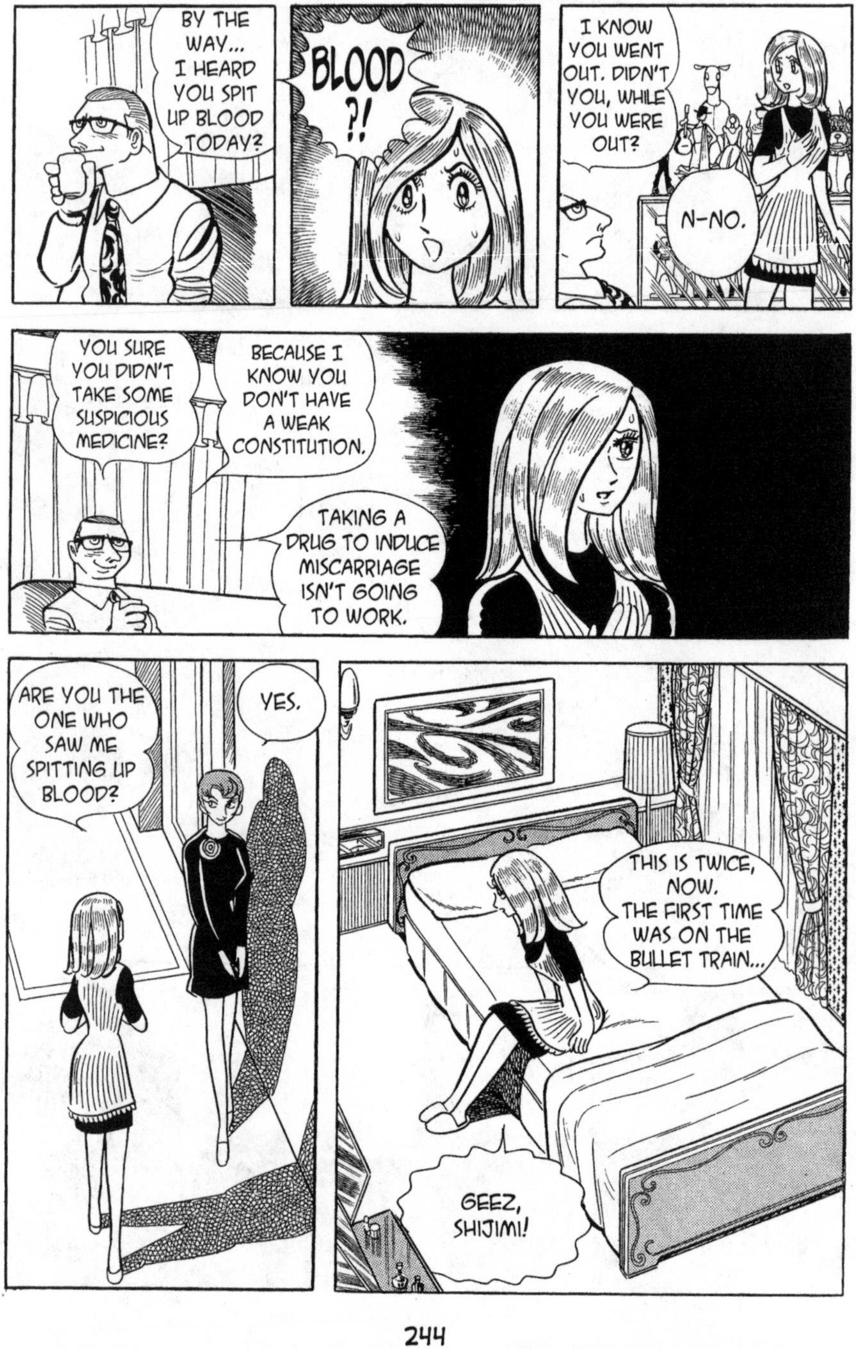
BY THE WAY... I HEARD YOU SPIT UP BLOOD TODAY?
BLOOD ?!
I KNOW YOU WENT OUT. DIDN'T YOU, WHILE YOU WERE OUT?
N-NO.
YOU SURE YOU DIDN'T TAKE SOME SUSPICIOUS MEDICINE?
BECAUSE I KNOW YOU DON'T HAVE A WEAK CONSTITUTION.
TAKING A DRUG TO INDUCE MISCARRIAGE ISN'T GOING TO WORK.
ARE YOU THE ONE WHO SAW ME SPITTING UP BLOOD?
YES.
THIS IS TWICE, NOW. THE FIRST TIME WAS ON THE BULLET TRAIN...
GEEZ, SHIJIMI!

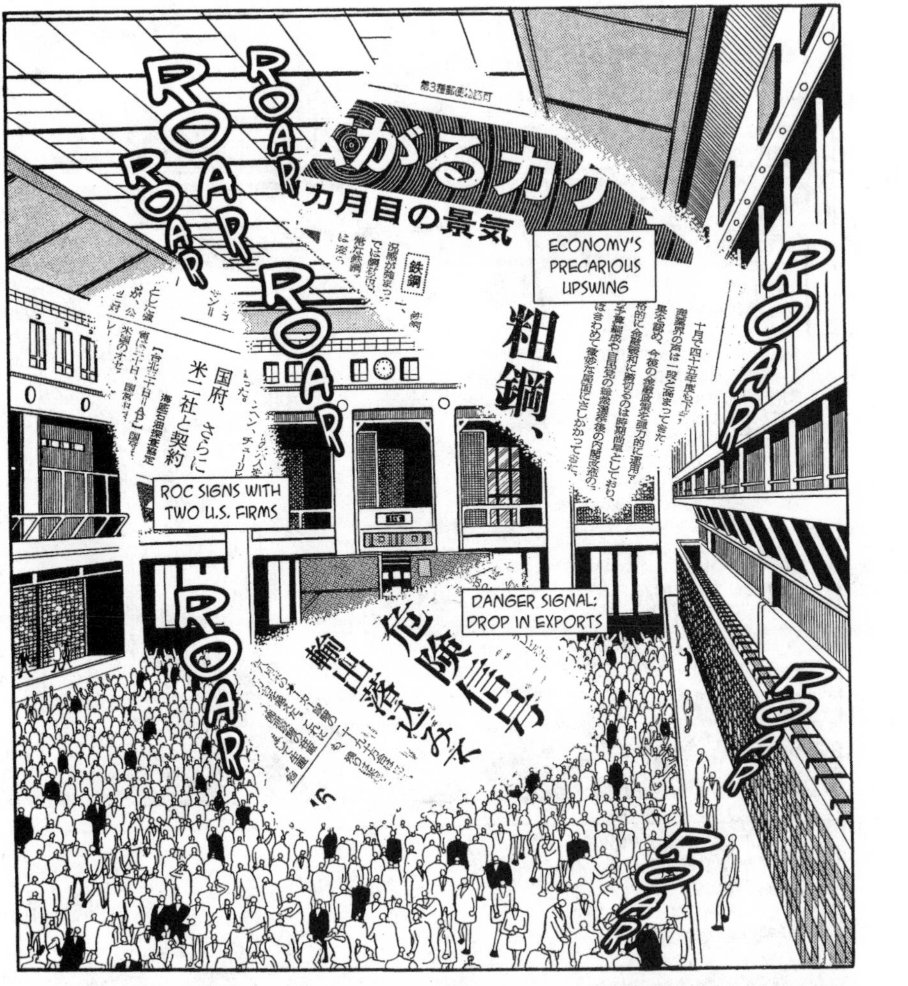
ROAR
ROAR
ROAR
ROAR
ROAR
ECONOMY'S PRECARIOUS UPSWING
ROAR
ROC SIGNS WITH TWO U.S. FIRMS
ROAR
DANGER SIGNAL: DROP IN EXPORTS
ROAR
ROAR

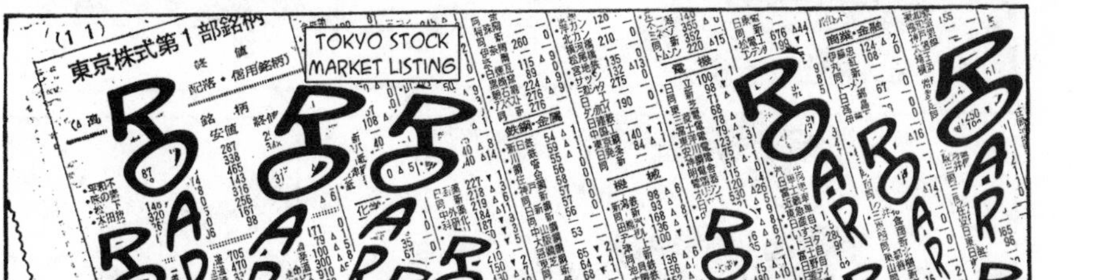
TOKYO STOCK MARKET LISTING
ROAR
ROAR
ROAR
ROAR
ROAR
ROAR
ROAR
ROAR
ROAR
ROAR

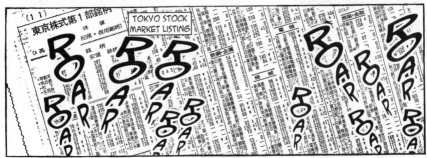

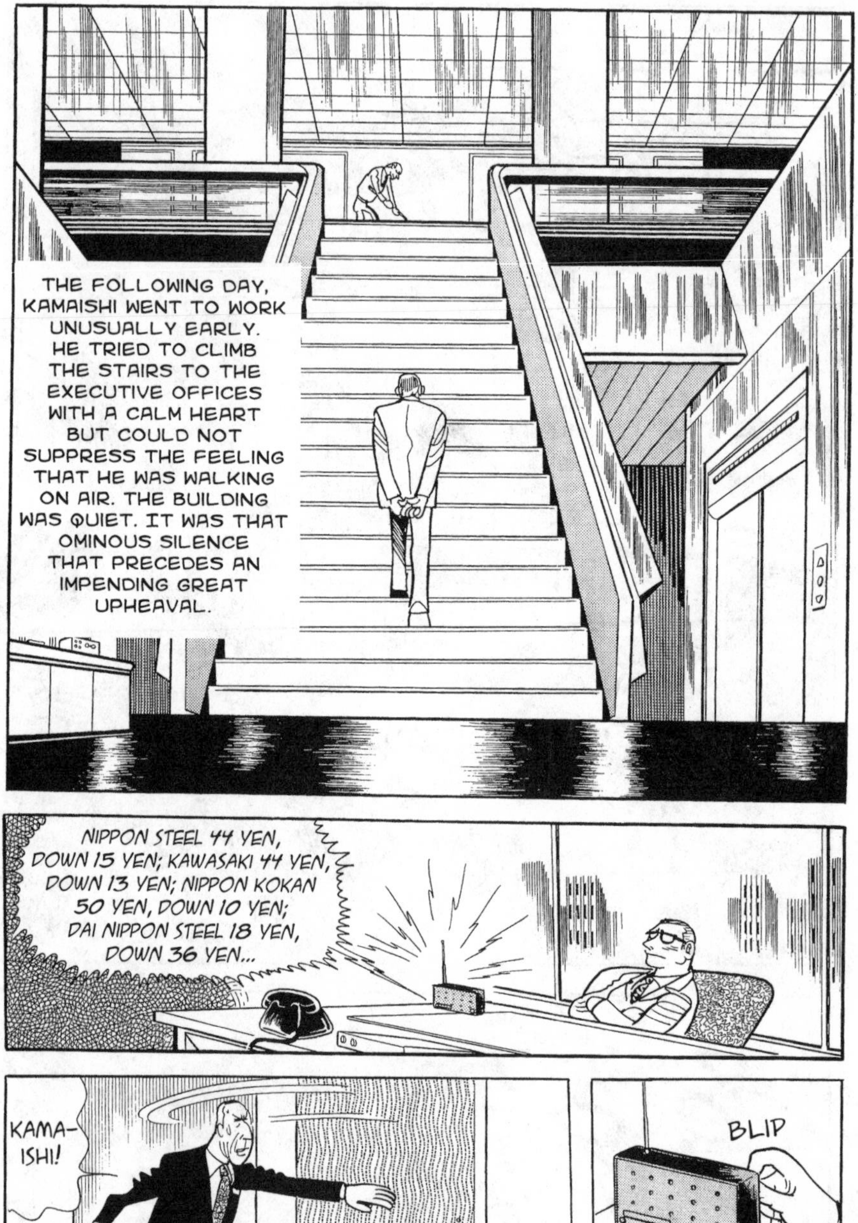
THE FOLLOWING DAY, KAMAISHI WENT TO WORK UNUSUALLY EARLY. HE TRIED TO CLIMB THE STAIRS TO THE EXECUTIVE OFFICES WITH A CALM HEART BUT COULD NOT SUPPRESS THE FEELING THAT HE WAS WALKING ON AIR. THE BUILDING WAS QUIET. IT WAS THAT OMINOUS SILENCE THAT PRECEDES AN IMPENDING GREAT UPHEAVAL.
NIPPON STEEL 44 YEN, DOWN 15 YEN; KAWASAKI 44 YEN, DOWN 13 YEN; NIPPON KOKAN 50 YEN, DOWN 10 YEN; DAI NIPPON STEEL 18 YEN, DOWN 36 YEN...
KAMA-ISHI!
BLIP

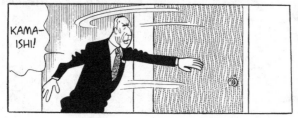

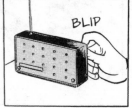

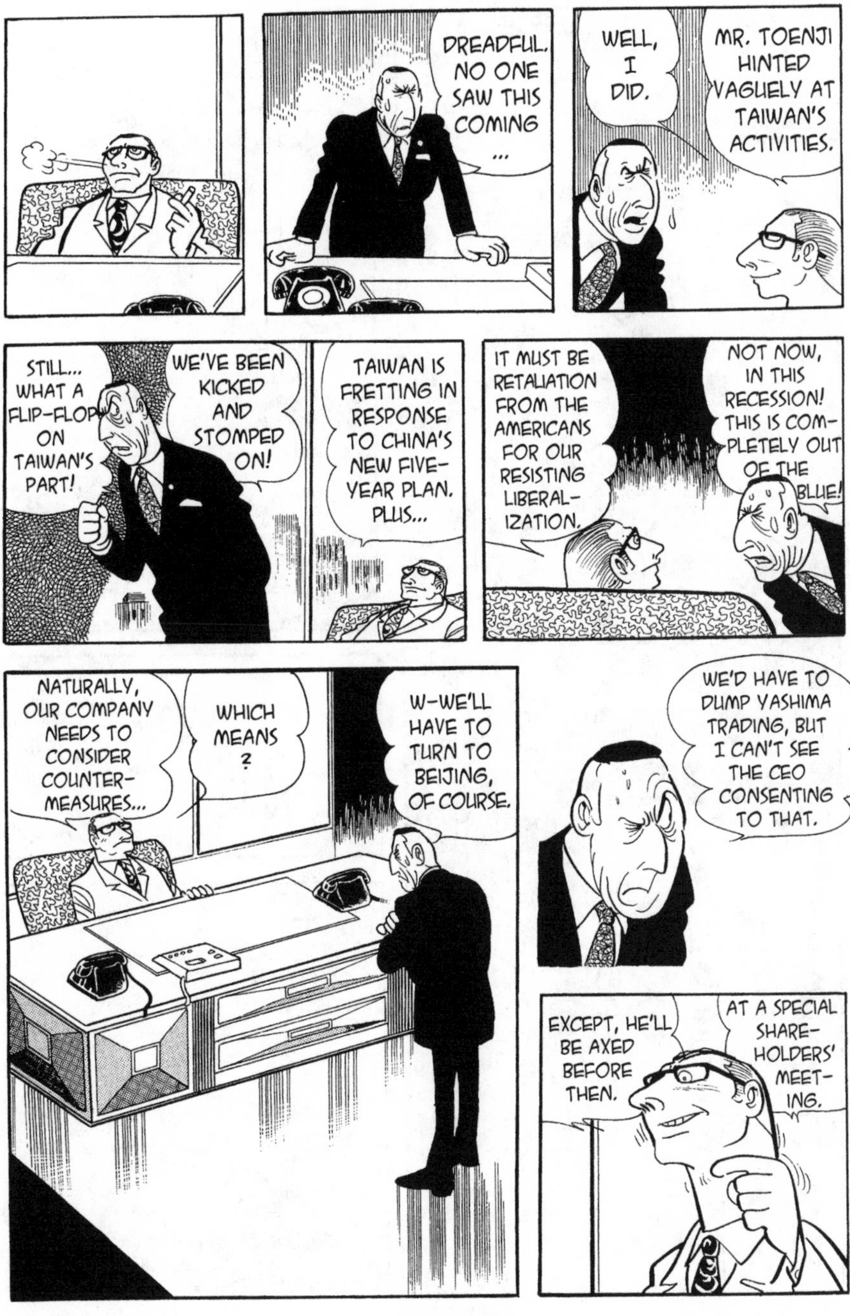
DREADFUL. NO ONE SAW THIS COMING ...
WELL, I DID.
MR. TOENJI HINTED VAGUELY AT TAIWAN'S ACTIVITIES.
STILL... WHAT A FLIP-FLOP ON TAIWAN'S PART!
WE'VE BEEN KICKED AND STOMPED ON!
TAIWAN IS FRETTING IN RESPONSE TO CHINA'S NEW FIVE-YEAR PLAN. PLUS...
IT MUST BE RETALIATION FROM THE AMERICANS FOR OUR RESISTING LIBERAL-IZATION.
NOT NOW, IN THIS RECESSION! THIS IS COM-PLETELY OUT OF THE BLUE!
NATURALLY, OUR COMPANY NEEDS TO CONSIDER COUNTER-MEASURES...
WHICH MEANS ?
W-WE'LL HAVE TO TURN TO BEIJING, OF COURSE.
WE'D HAVE TO DUMP YASHIMA TRADING, BUT I CAN'T SEE THE CEO CONSENTING TO THAT.
EXCEPT, HE'LL BE AXED BEFORE THEN.
AT A SPECIAL SHARE-HOLDERS' MEET-ING.

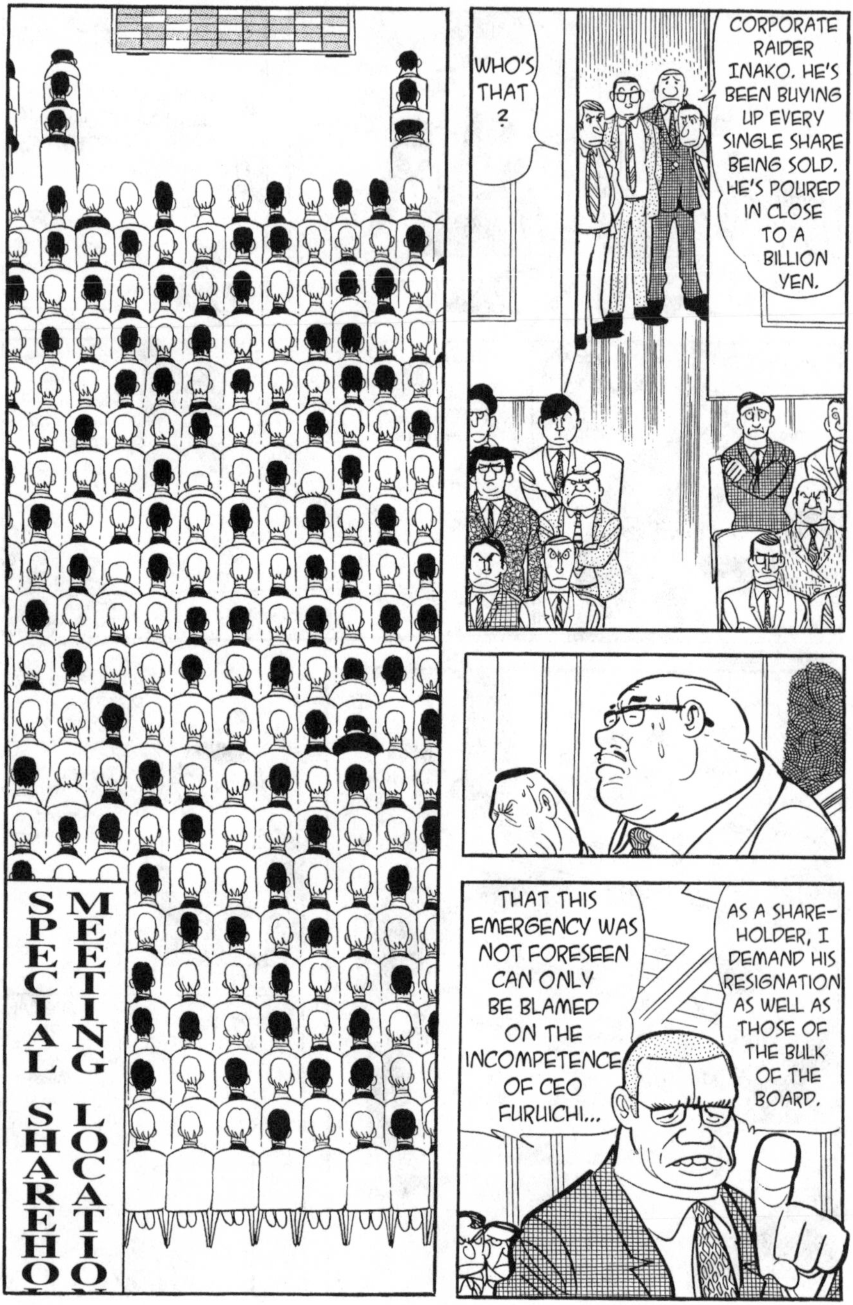
SPECIAL SHAREHO
MEETING LOCATIO
WHO'S THAT?
CORPORATE RAIDER INAKO. HE'S BEEN BUYING UP EVERY SINGLE SHARE BEING SOLD. HE'S POURED IN CLOSE TO A BILLION YEN.
THAT THIS EMERGENCY WAS NOT FORESEEN CAN ONLY BE BLAMED ON THE INCOMPETENCE OF CEO FURUICHI...
AS A SHARE-HOLDER, I DEMAND HIS RESIGNATION AS WELL AS THOSE OF THE BULK OF THE BOARD.

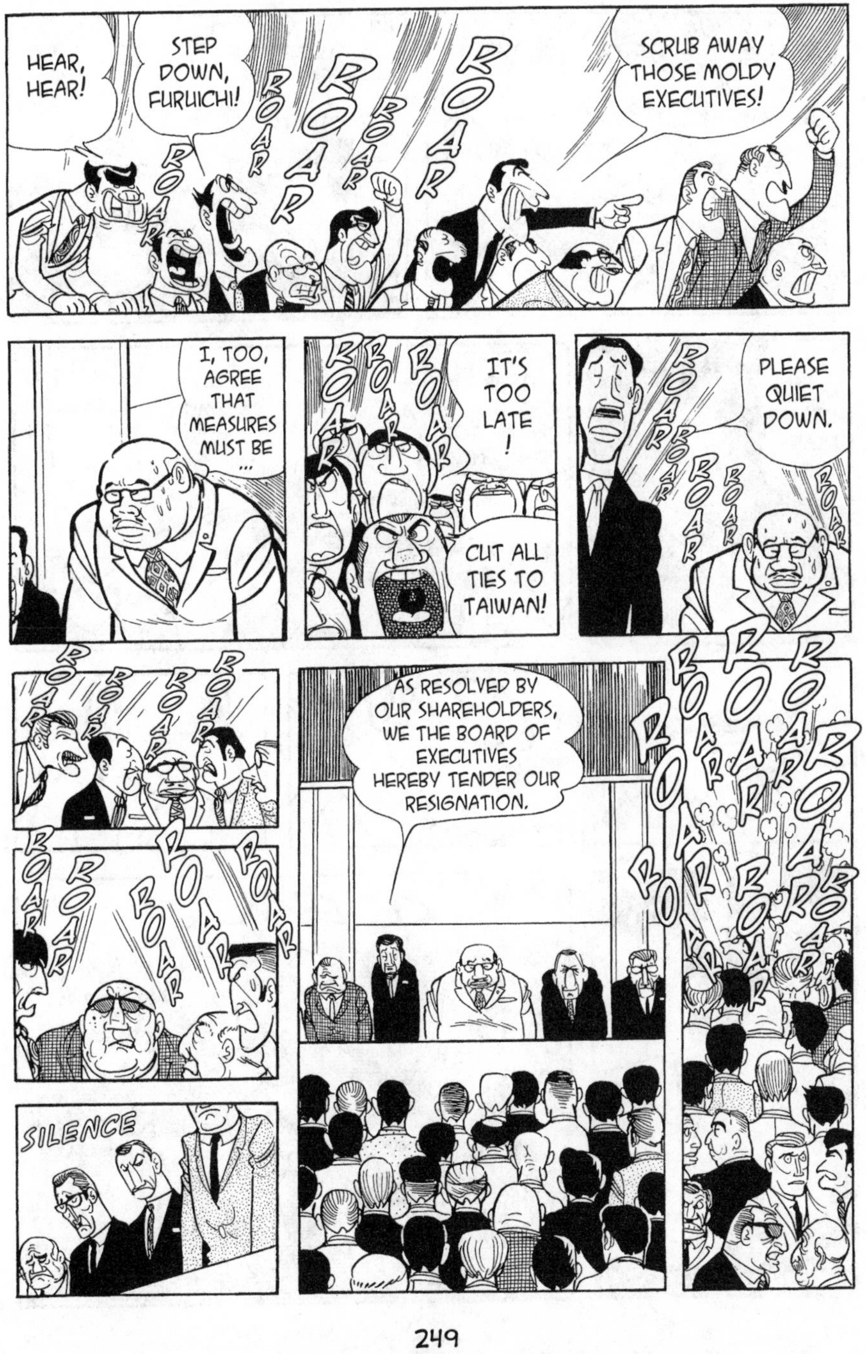
HEAR, HEAR!
STEP DOWN, FURUICHI!
ROAR
SCRUB AWAY THOSE MOLDY EXECUTIVES!
I, TOO, AGREE THAT MEASURES MUST BE ...
ROAR
IT'S TOO LATE!
CUT ALL TIES TO TAIWAN!
ROAR
PLEASE QUIET DOWN.
ROAR
ROAR
SILENCE
AS RESOLVED BY OUR SHAREHOLDERS, WE THE BOARD OF EXECUTIVES HEREBY TENDER OUR RESIGNATION.
ROAR

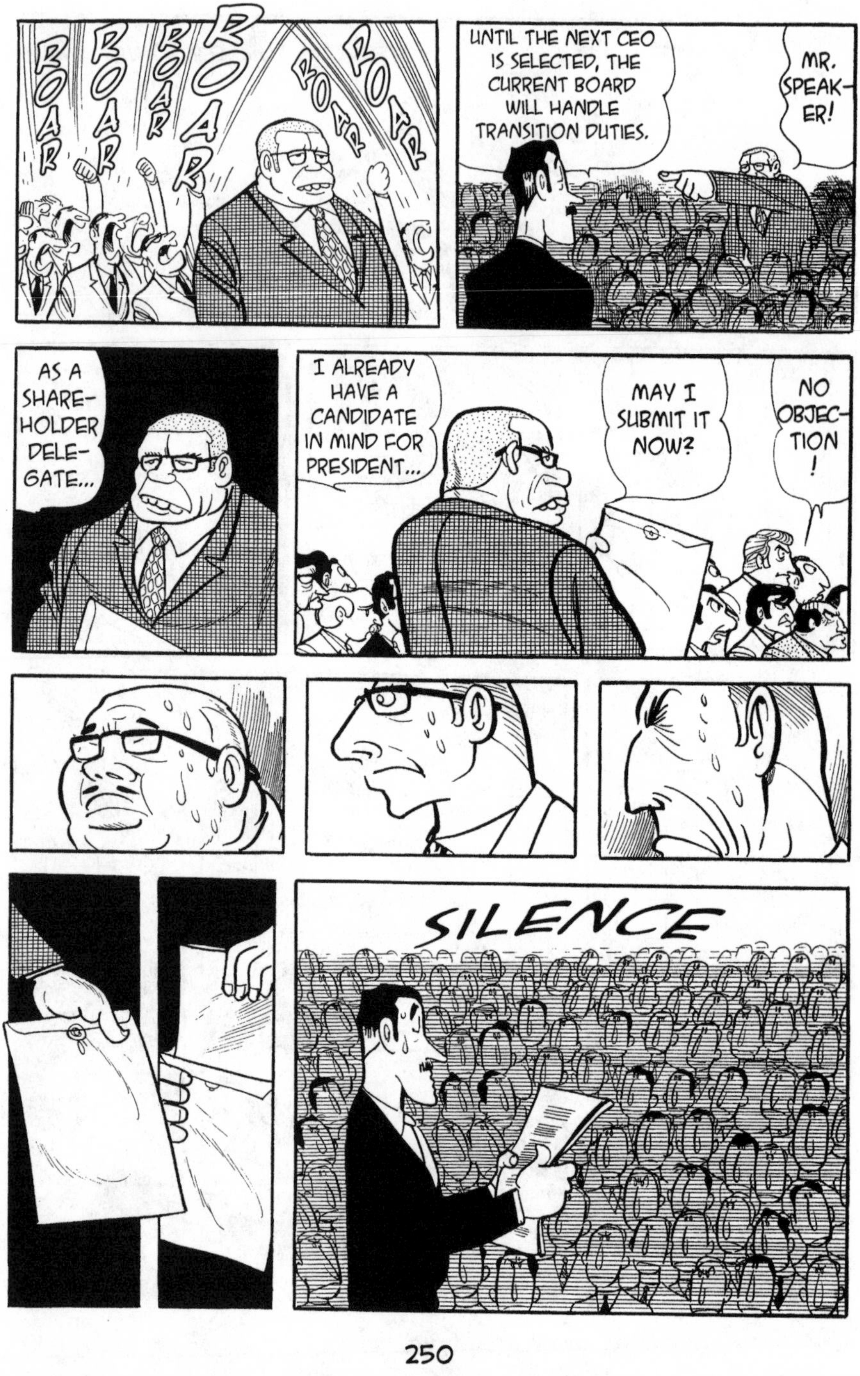
ROAR ROAR ROAR ROAR ROAR ROAR
UNTIL THE NEXT CEO IS SELECTED, THE CURRENT BOARD WILL HANDLE TRANSITION DUTIES.
MR. SPEAK-ER!
AS A SHARE-HOLDER DELE-GATE...
I ALREADY HAVE A CANDIDATE IN MIND FOR PRESIDENT...
MAY I SUBMIT IT NOW?
NO OBJEC-TION!
SILENCE

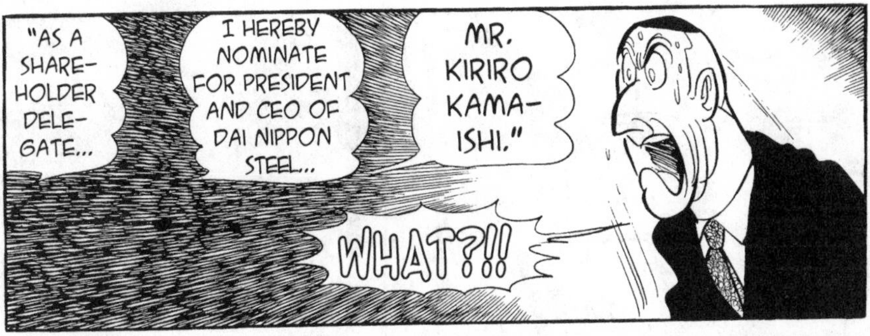
"AS A SHARE-HOLDER DELE-GATE...
I HEREBY NOMINATE FOR PRESIDENT AND CEO OF DAI NIPPON STEEL...
MR. KIRIRO KAMA-ISHI."
WHAT?!!

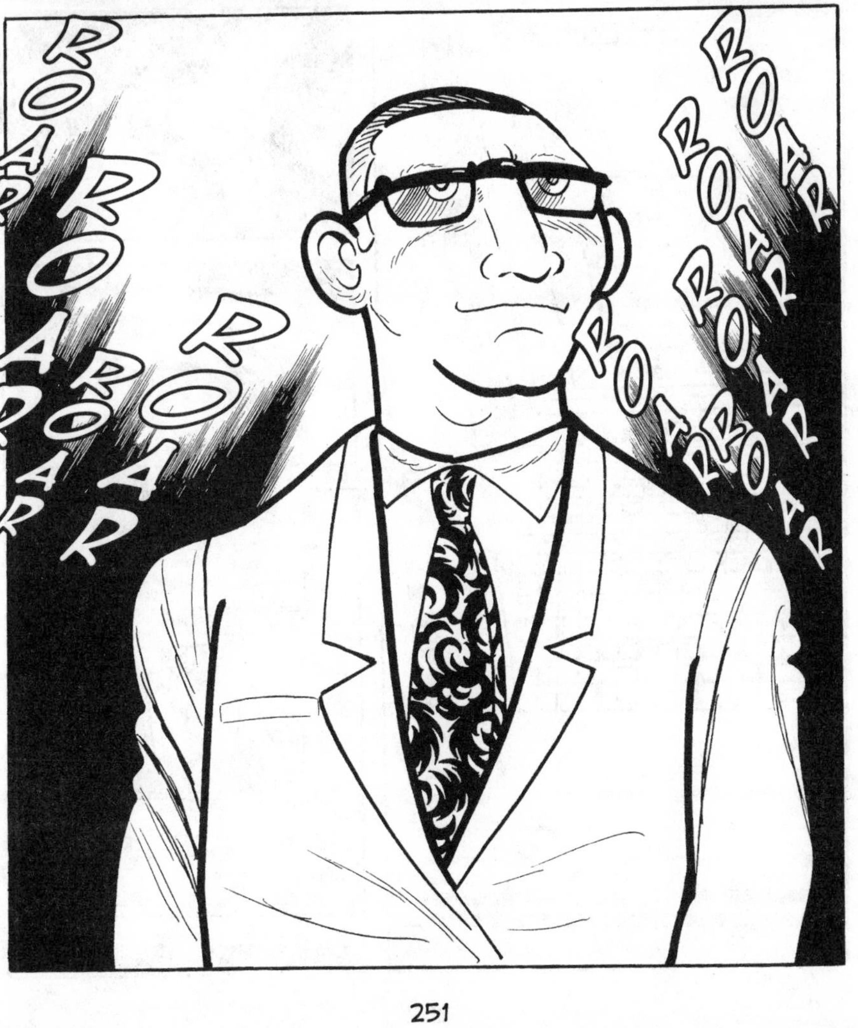
ROAR ROAR ROAR
ROAR ROAR
ROAR ROAR ROAR ROAR

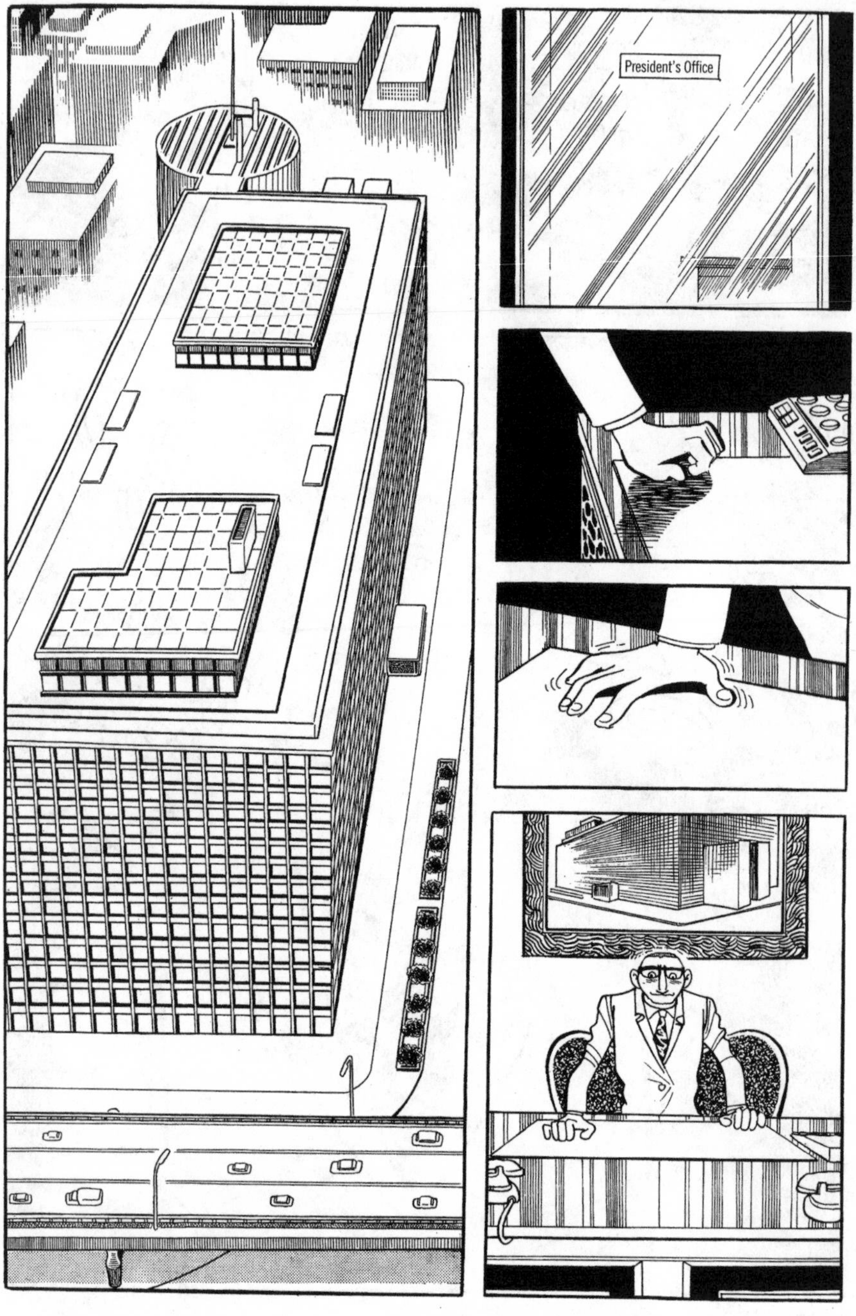
President's Office

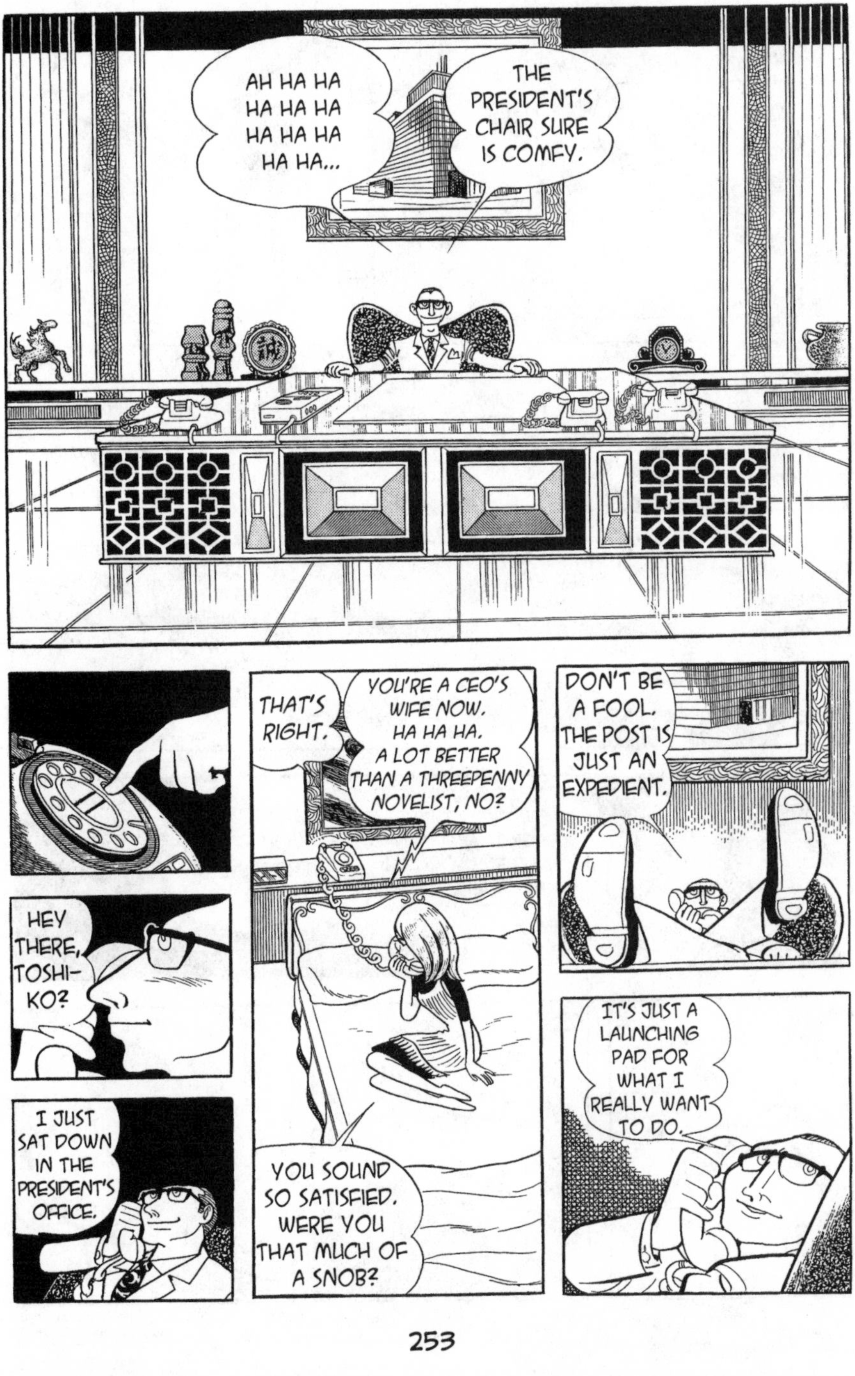
AH HA HA HA HA HA HA HA HA HA HA...
THE PRESIDENT'S CHAIR SURE IS COMFY.
HEY THERE, TOSHI-KO?
I JUST SAT DOWN IN THE PRESIDENT'S OFFICE.
THAT'S RIGHT.
YOU'RE A CEO'S WIFE NOW. HA HA HA. A LOT BETTER THAN A THREEPENNY NOVELIST, NO?
YOU SOUND SO SATISFIED. WERE YOU THAT MUCH OF A SNOB?
DON'T BE A FOOL. THE POST IS JUST AN EXPEDIENT.
IT'S JUST A LAUNCHING PAD FOR WHAT I REALLY WANT TO DO.

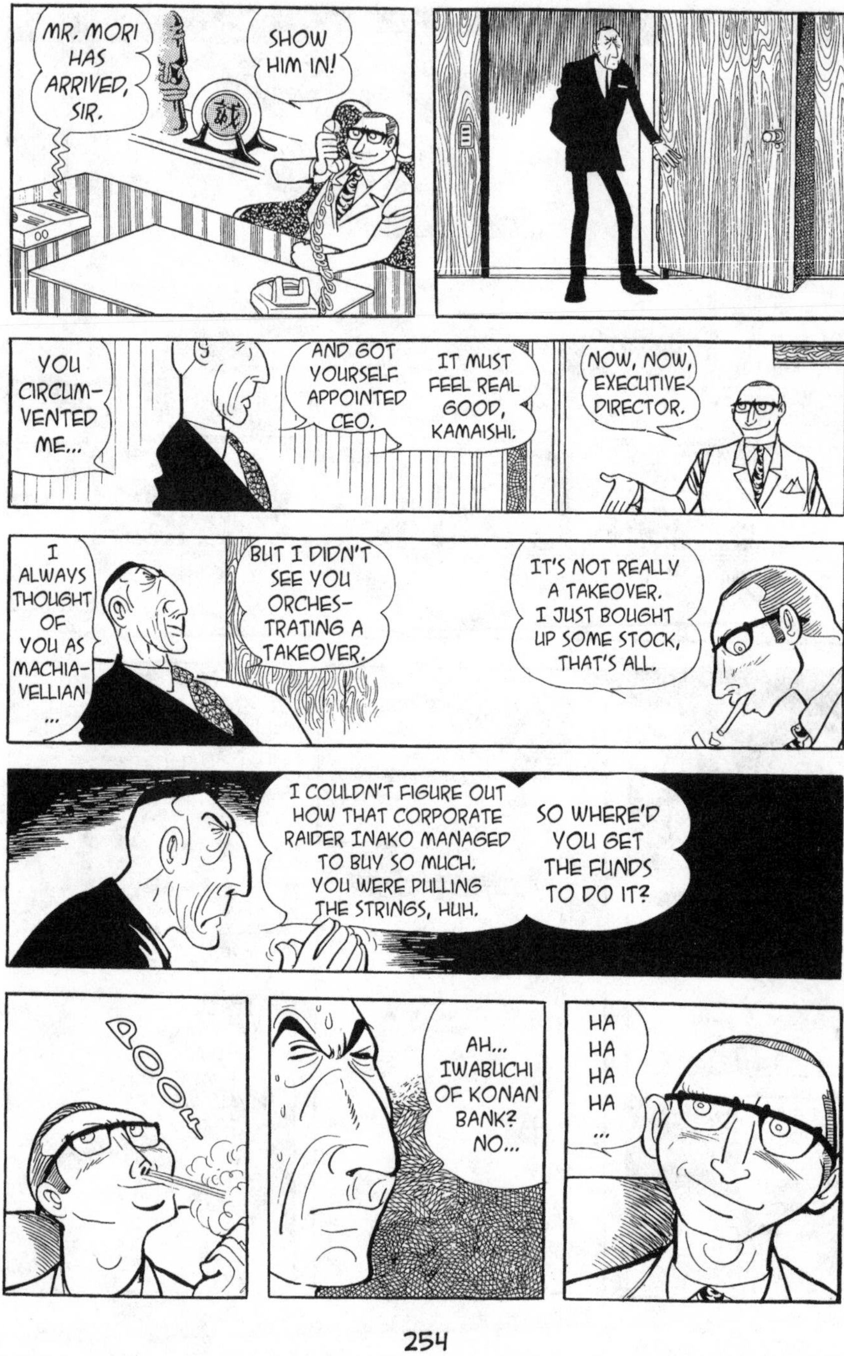
MR. MORI HAS ARRIVED, SIR.
SHOW HIM IN!
YOU CIRCUMVENTED ME...
AND GOT YOURSELF APPOINTED CEO.
IT MUST FEEL REAL GOOD, KAMAISHI.
NOW, NOW, EXECUTIVE DIRECTOR.
I ALWAYS THOUGHT OF YOU AS MACHIAVELLIAN ...
BUT I DIDN'T SEE YOU ORCHESTRATING A TAKEOVER.
IT'S NOT REALLY A TAKEOVER. I JUST BOUGHT UP SOME STOCK, THAT'S ALL.
I COULDN'T FIGURE OUT HOW THAT CORPORATE RAIDER INAKO MANAGED TO BUY SO MUCH. YOU WERE PULLING THE STRINGS, HUH.
SO WHERE'D YOU GET THE FUNDS TO DO IT?
POOF
AH... IWABUCHI OF KONAN BANK? NO...
HA HA HA HA ...

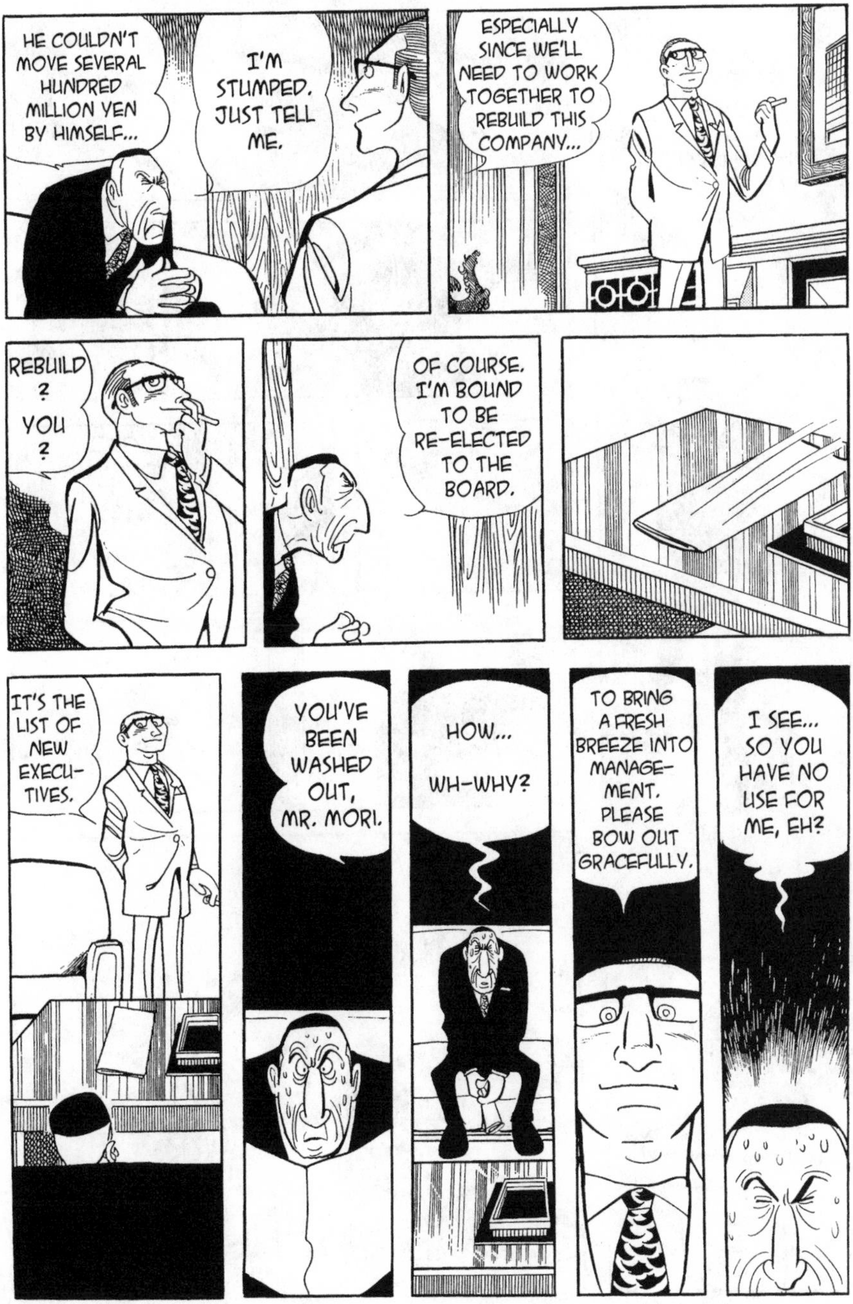
HE COULDN'T MOVE SEVERAL HUNDRED MILLION YEN BY HIMSELF...
I'M STUMPED. JUST TELL ME.
ESPECIALLY SINCE WE'LL NEED TO WORK TOGETHER TO REBUILD THIS COMPANY...
REBUILD? YOU?
OF COURSE. I'M BOUND TO BE RE-ELECTED TO THE BOARD.
IT'S THE LIST OF NEW EXECU-TIVES.
YOU'VE BEEN WASHED OUT, MR. MORI.
HOW...
WH-WHY?
TO BRING A FRESH BREEZE INTO MANAGE-MENT. PLEASE BOW OUT GRACEFULLY.
I SEE... SO YOU HAVE NO USE FOR ME, EH?

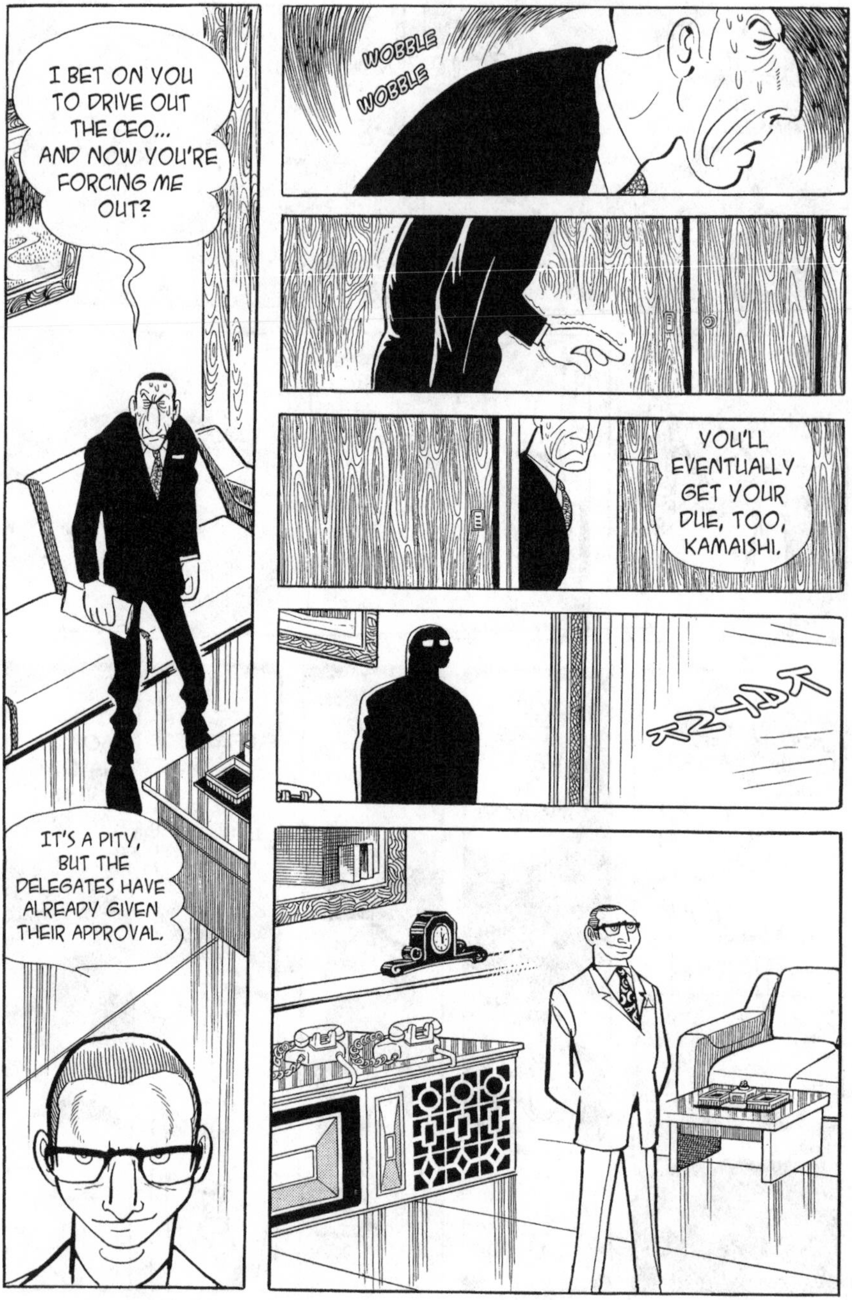
I BET ON YOU TO DRIVE OUT THE CEO... AND NOW YOU'RE FORCING ME OUT?
IT'S A PITY, BUT THE DELEGATES HAVE ALREADY GIVEN THEIR APPROVAL.
WOBBLE WOBBLE
YOU'LL EVENTUALLY GET YOUR DUE, TOO, KAMAISHI.

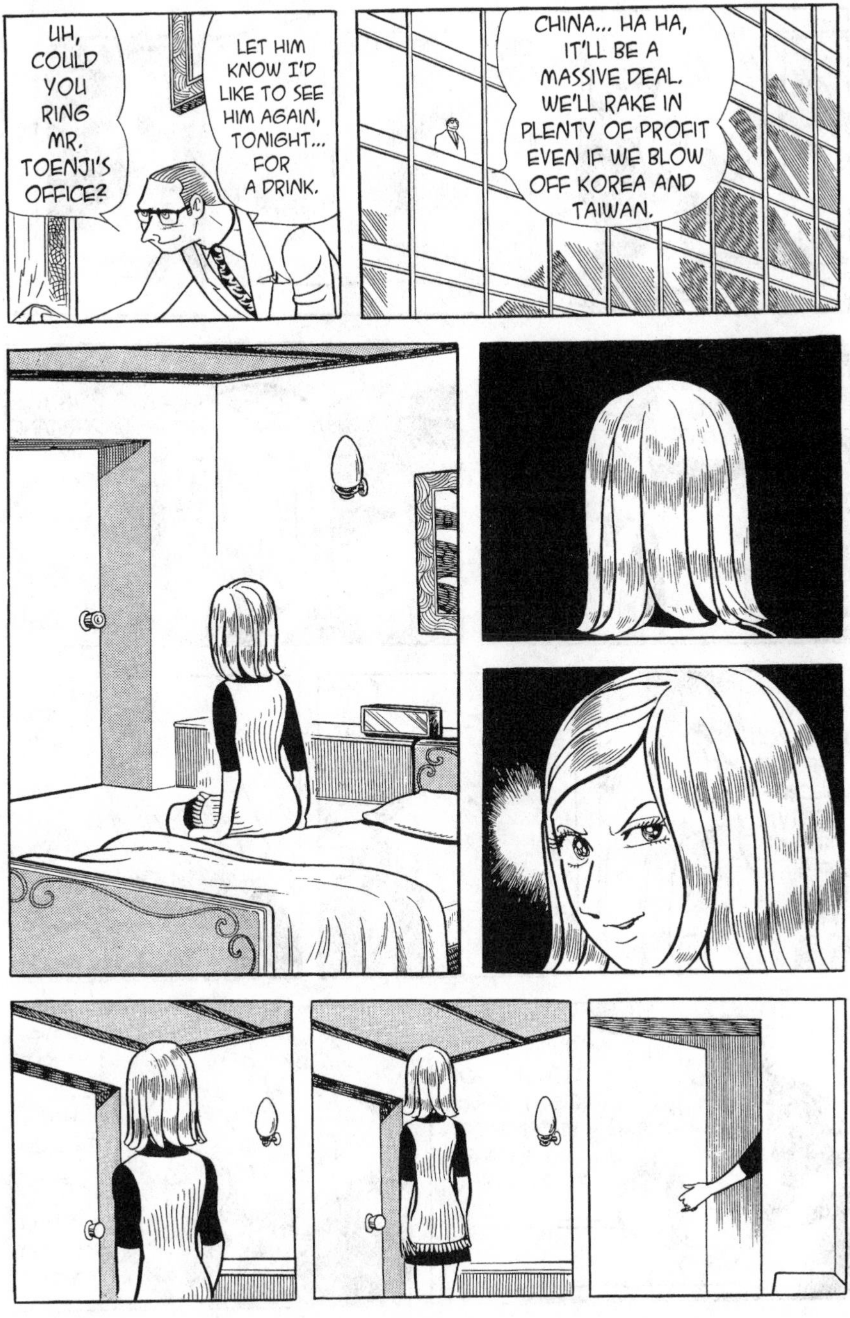
UH, COULD YOU RING MR. TOENJI'S OFFICE?
LET HIM KNOW I'D LIKE TO SEE HIM AGAIN, TONIGHT... FOR A DRINK.
CHINA... HA HA, IT'LL BE A MASSIVE DEAL. WE'LL RAKE IN PLENTY OF PROFIT EVEN IF WE BLOW OFF KOREA AND TAIWAN.

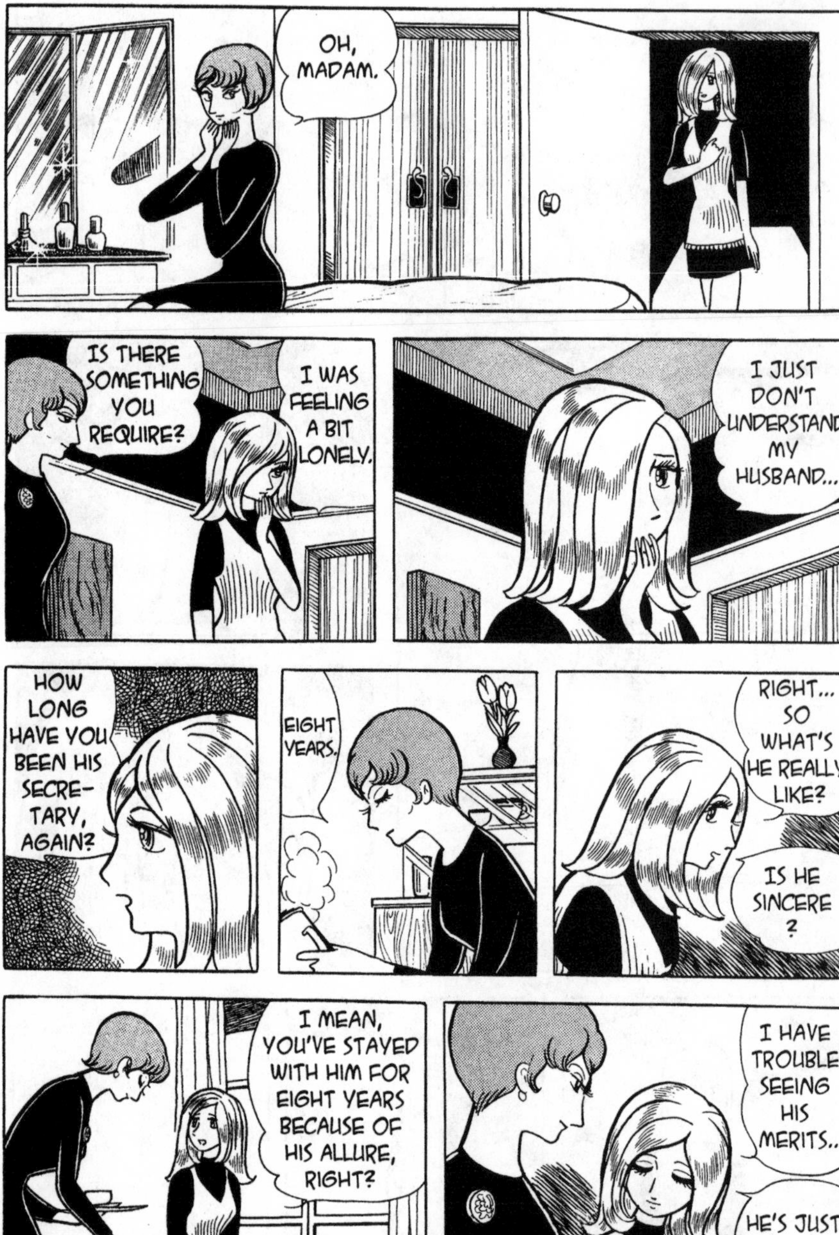
OH, MADAM.
IS THERE SOMETHING YOU REQUIRE?
I WAS FEELING A BIT LONELY.
I JUST DON'T UNDERSTAND MY HUSBAND...
HOW LONG HAVE YOU BEEN HIS SECRE-TARY, AGAIN?
EIGHT YEARS.
RIGHT... SO WHAT'S HE REALLY LIKE?
IS HE SINCERE?
I MEAN, YOU'VE STAYED WITH HIM FOR EIGHT YEARS BECAUSE OF HIS ALLURE, RIGHT?
I HAVE TROUBLE SEEING HIS MERITS...
HE'S JUST COLD TO ME.

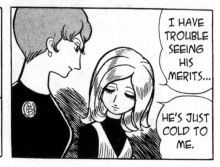

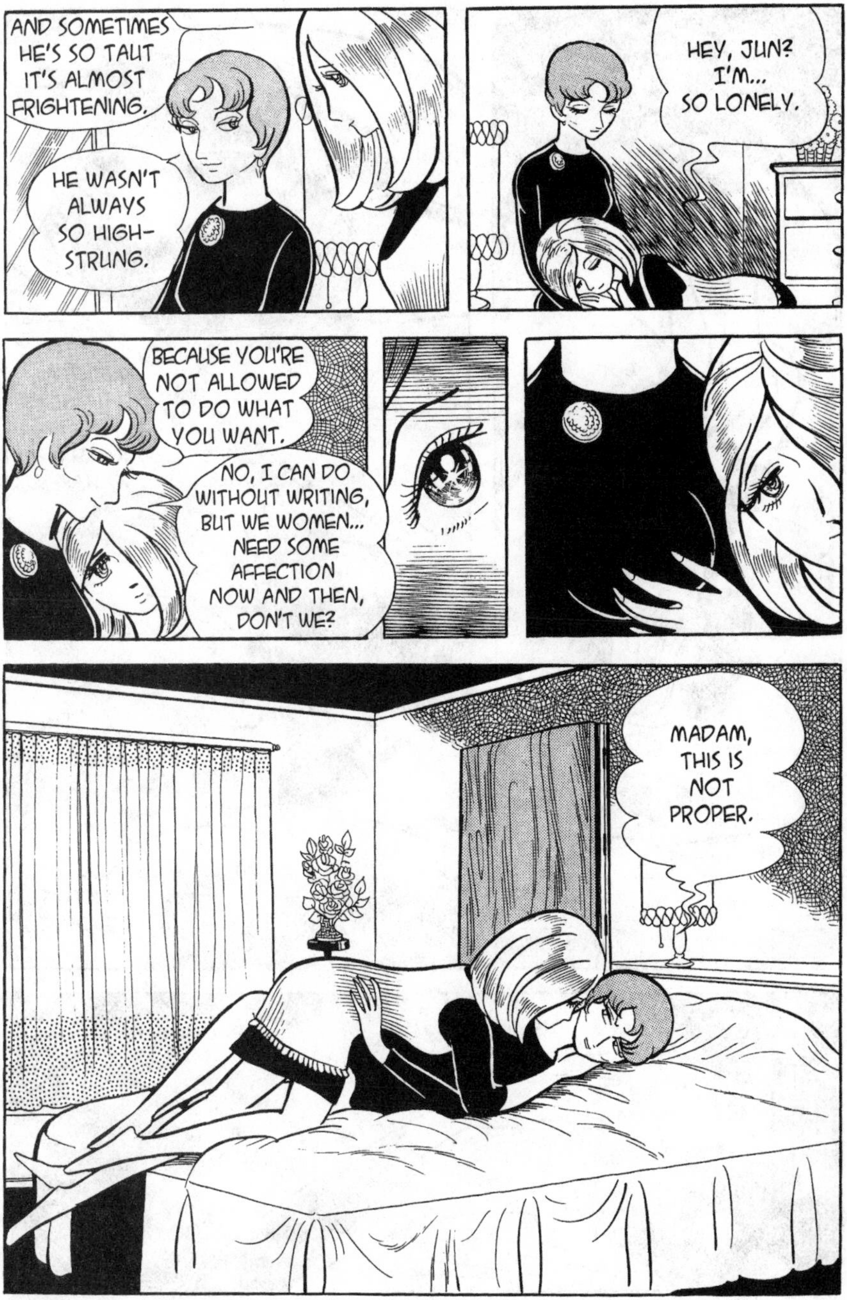
AND SOMETIMES HE'S SO TAUT IT'S ALMOST FRIGHTENING.
HE WASN'T ALWAYS SO HIGH-STRUNG.
HEY, JUN? I'M... SO LONELY.
BECAUSE YOU'RE NOT ALLOWED TO DO WHAT YOU WANT.
NO, I CAN DO WITHOUT WRITING, BUT WE WOMEN... NEED SOME AFFECTION NOW AND THEN, DON'T WE?
MADAM, THIS IS NOT PROPER.

HOLD ME TIGHT. IT WOULD... MAKE ME SO HAPPY.

NO... WE MUSTN'T... WE CAN'T...

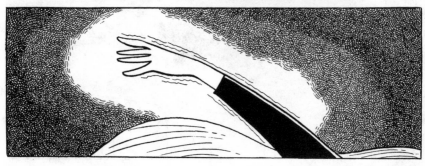

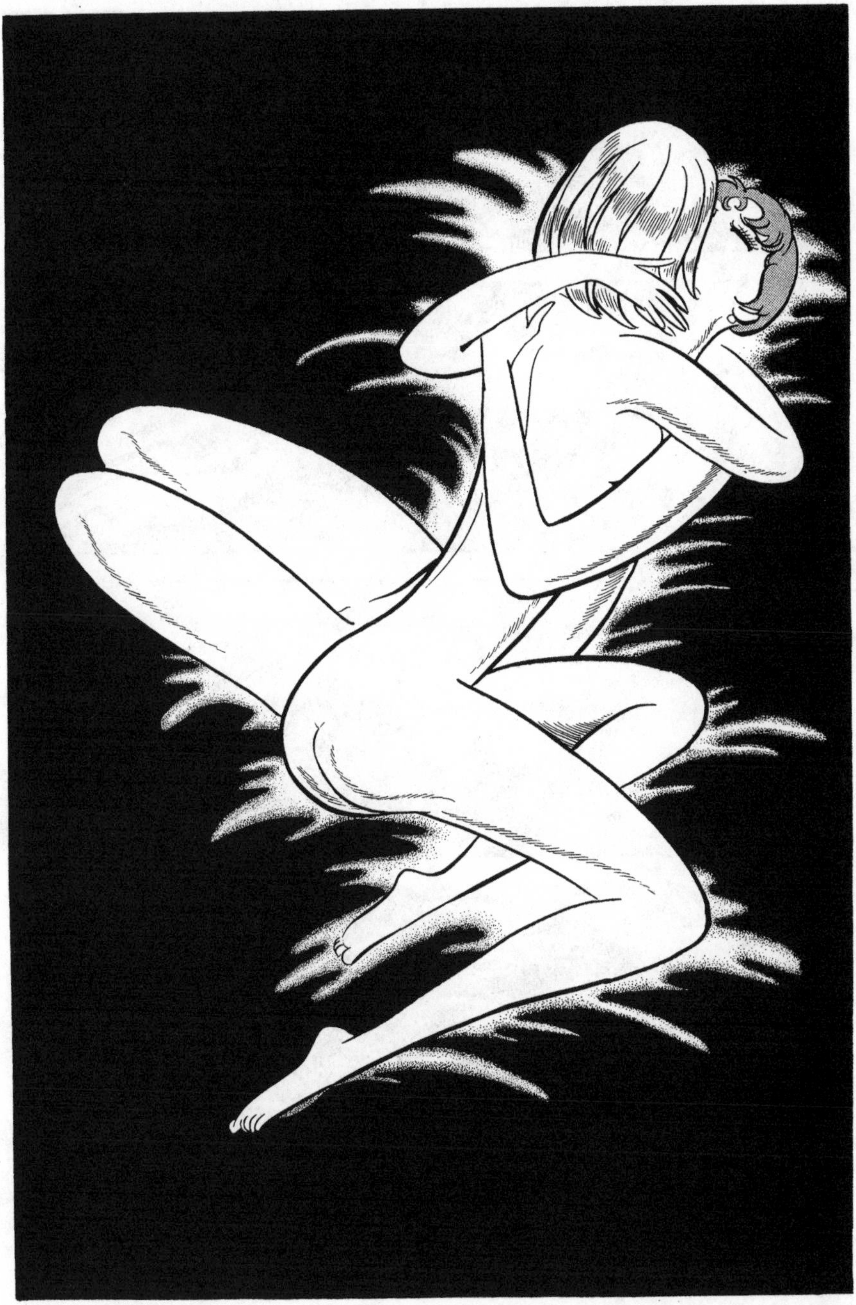

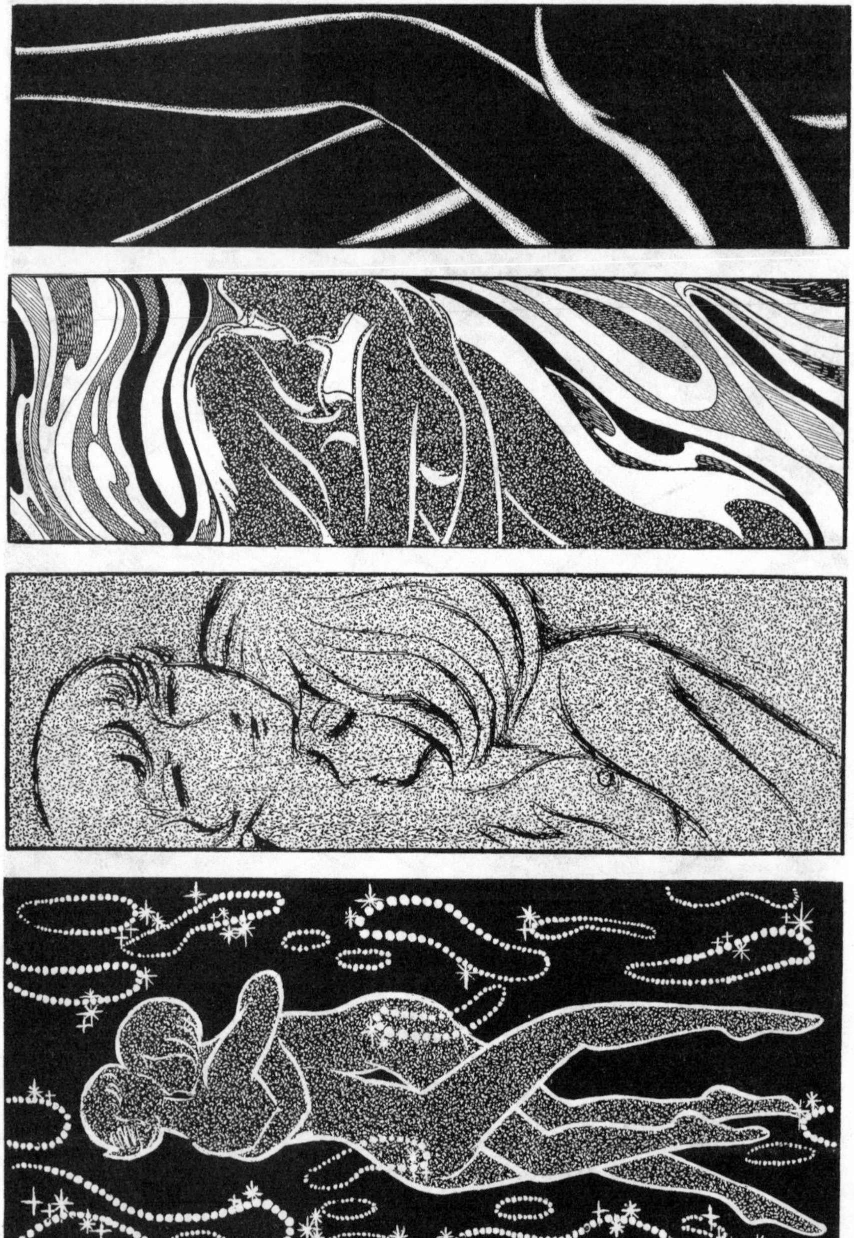

WEL-COME HOME.

DID SHE GO OUT ANYWHERE?

NO...

YES, SIR.

THESE ARE IMPORTANT DOCUMENTS. LOCK THEM IN THE SAFE.

WELCOME HOME.

AN-OTHER DOLL?

YEAH, I BOUGHT A SPECIAL ONE TODAY.

YOU'VE ATTAINED THE STATUS AND POWER YOU SOUGHT.

I KNEW YOU'D BUY ONE!

HAH, THE REAL GAME IS JUST BEGINNING.

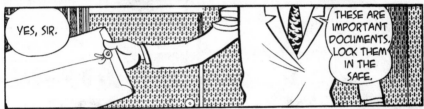

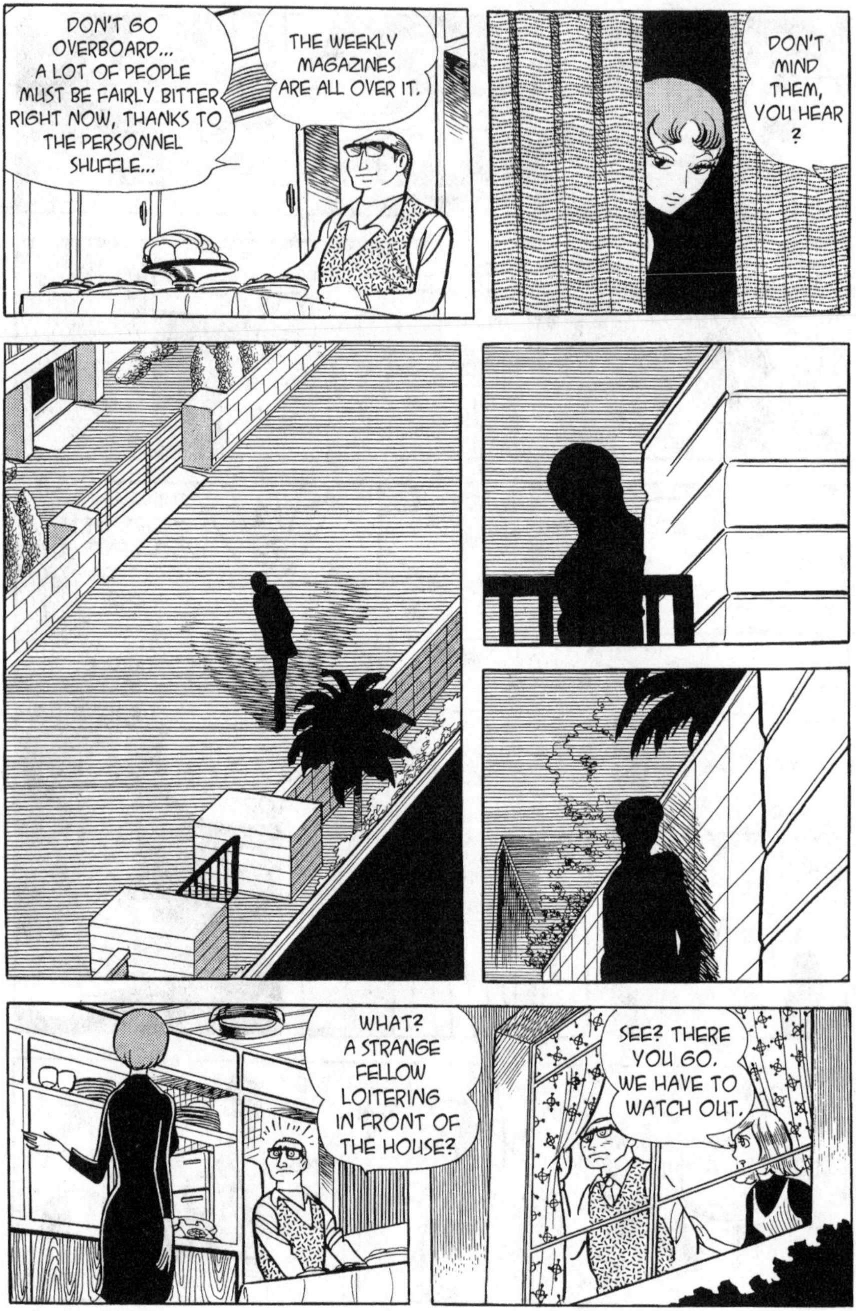
DON'T GO OVERBOARD... A LOT OF PEOPLE MUST BE FAIRLY BITTER RIGHT NOW, THANKS TO THE PERSONNEL SHUFFLE...
THE WEEKLY MAGAZINES ARE ALL OVER IT.
DON'T MIND THEM, YOU HEAR?
WHAT? A STRANGE FELLOW LOITERING IN FRONT OF THE HOUSE?
SEE? THERE YOU GO. WE HAVE TO WATCH OUT.

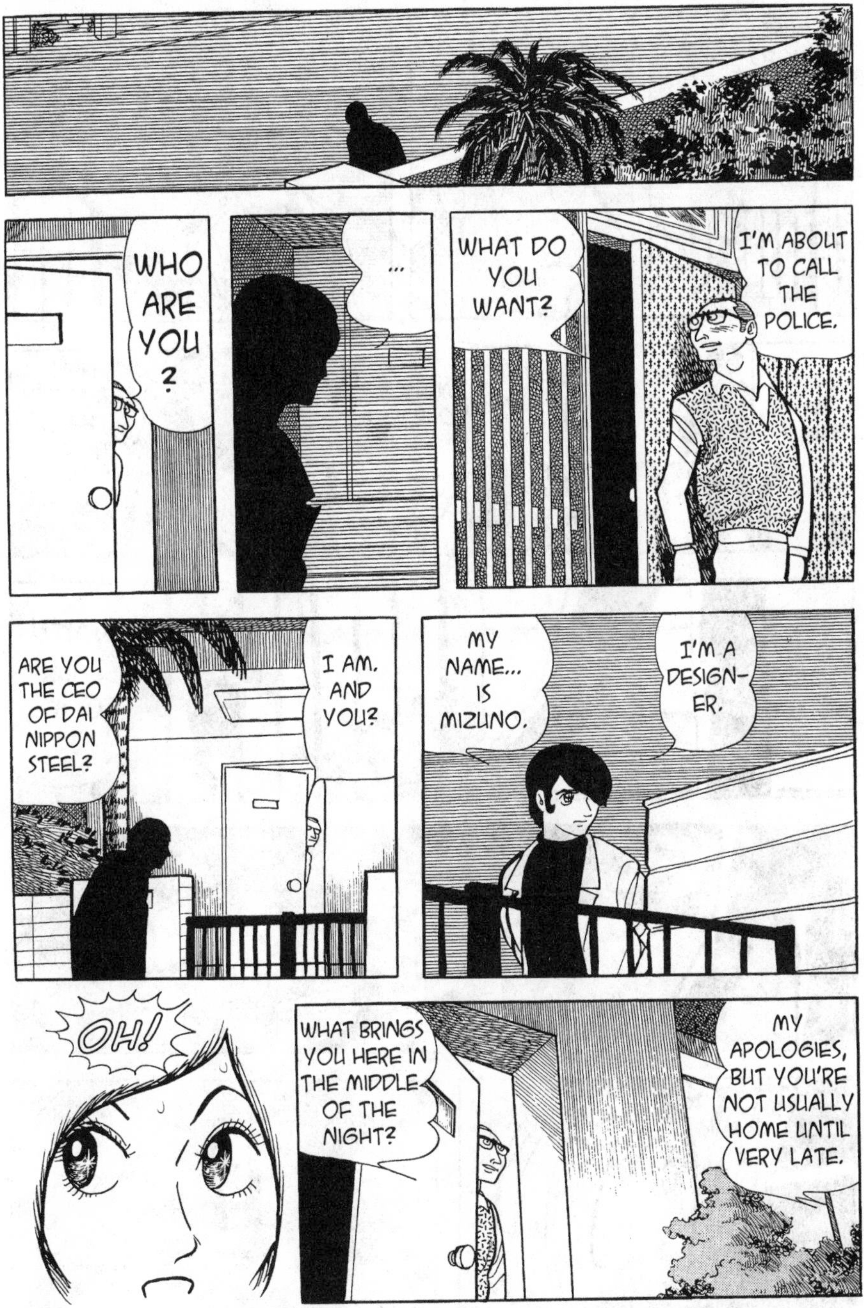
WHO ARE YOU?
...
WHAT DO YOU WANT?
I'M ABOUT TO CALL THE POLICE.
ARE YOU THE CEO OF DAI NIPPON STEEL?
I AM. AND YOU?
MY NAME... IS MIZUNO.
I'M A DESIGNER.
OH!
WHAT BRINGS YOU HERE IN THE MIDDLE OF THE NIGHT?
MY APOLOGIES, BUT YOU'RE NOT USUALLY HOME UNTIL VERY LATE.

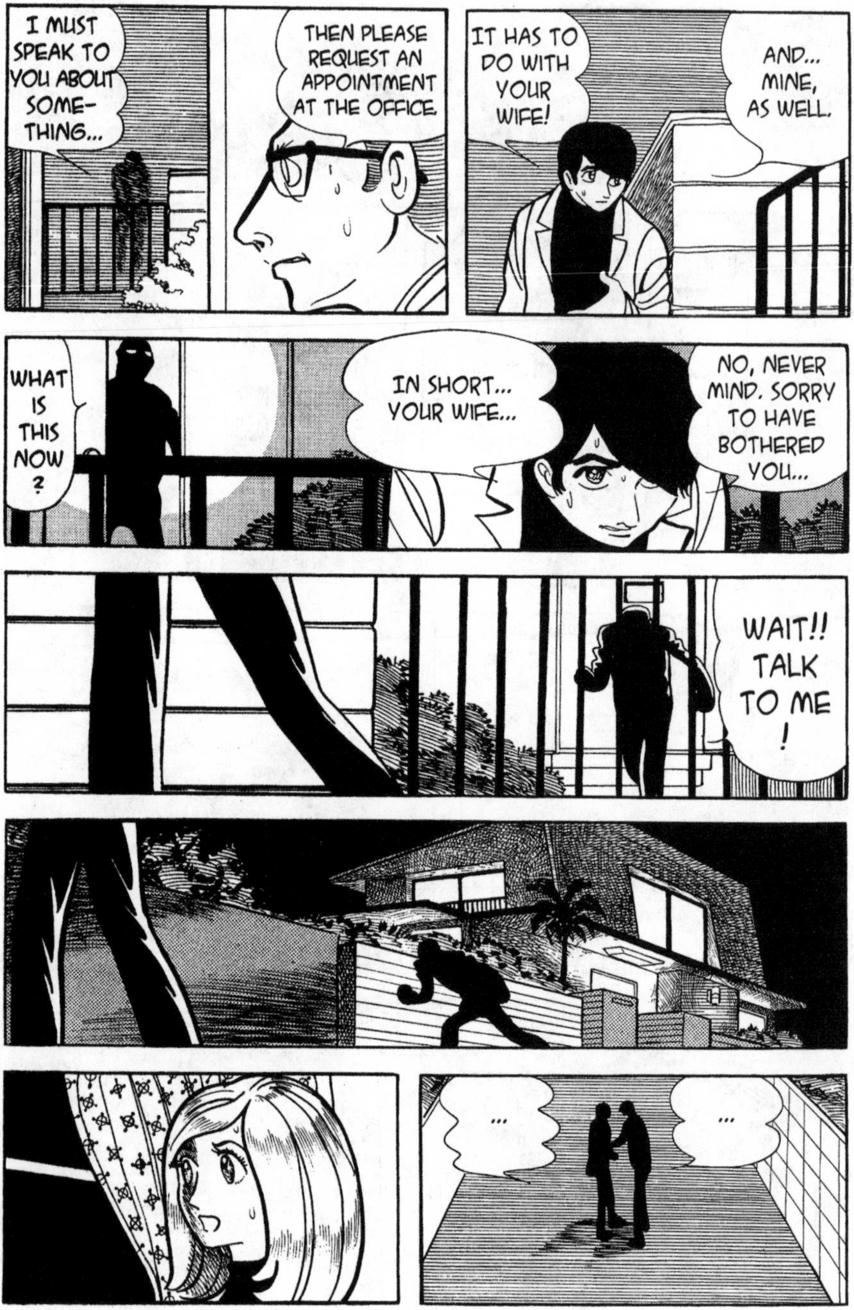
I MUST SPEAK TO YOU ABOUT SOME-THING...
THEN PLEASE REQUEST AN APPOINTMENT AT THE OFFICE.
IT HAS TO DO WITH YOUR WIFE!
AND... MINE, AS WELL.
WHAT IS THIS NOW ?
IN SHORT... YOUR WIFE...
NO, NEVER MIND. SORRY TO HAVE BOTHERED YOU...
WAIT!! TALK TO ME !
...
...

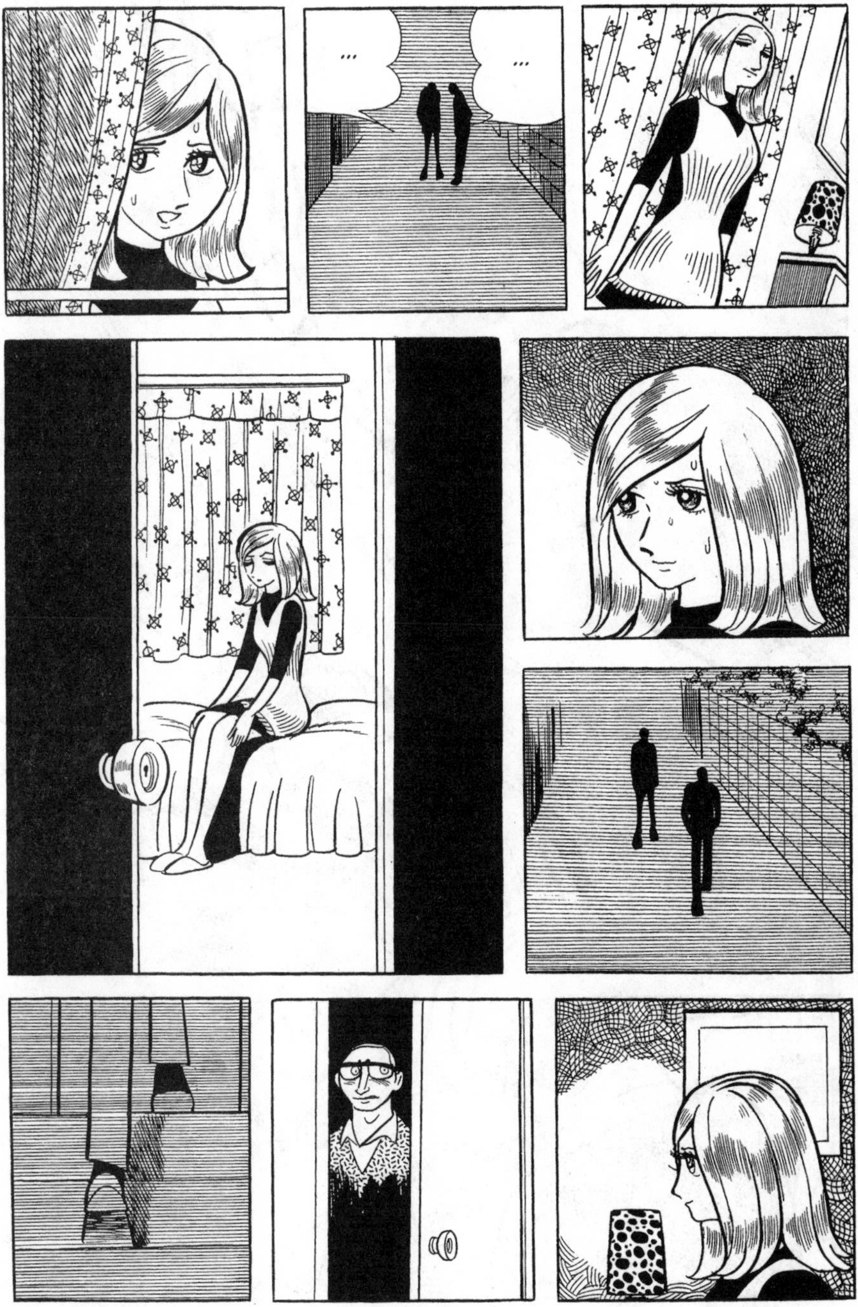
...
...

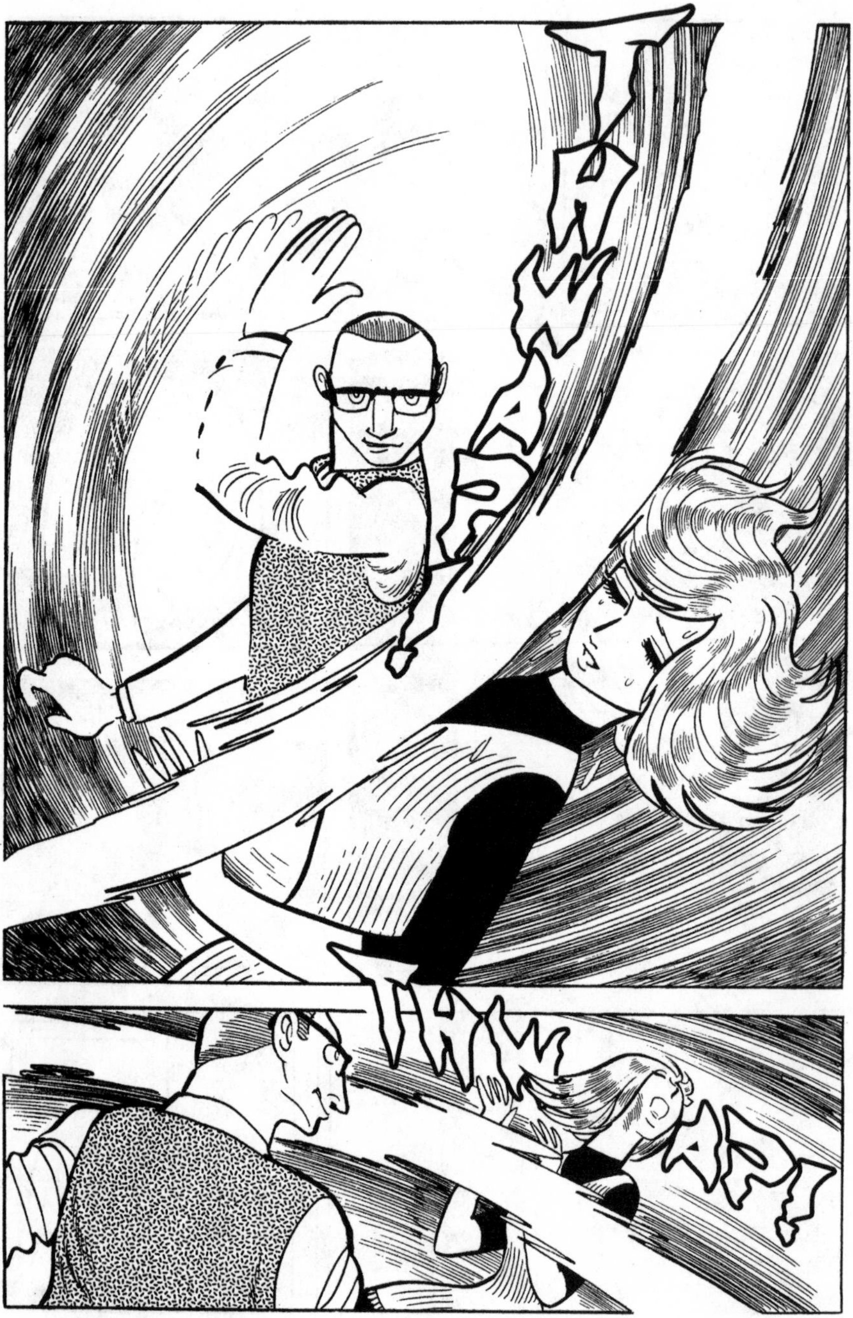
THWAP!
THWAP!

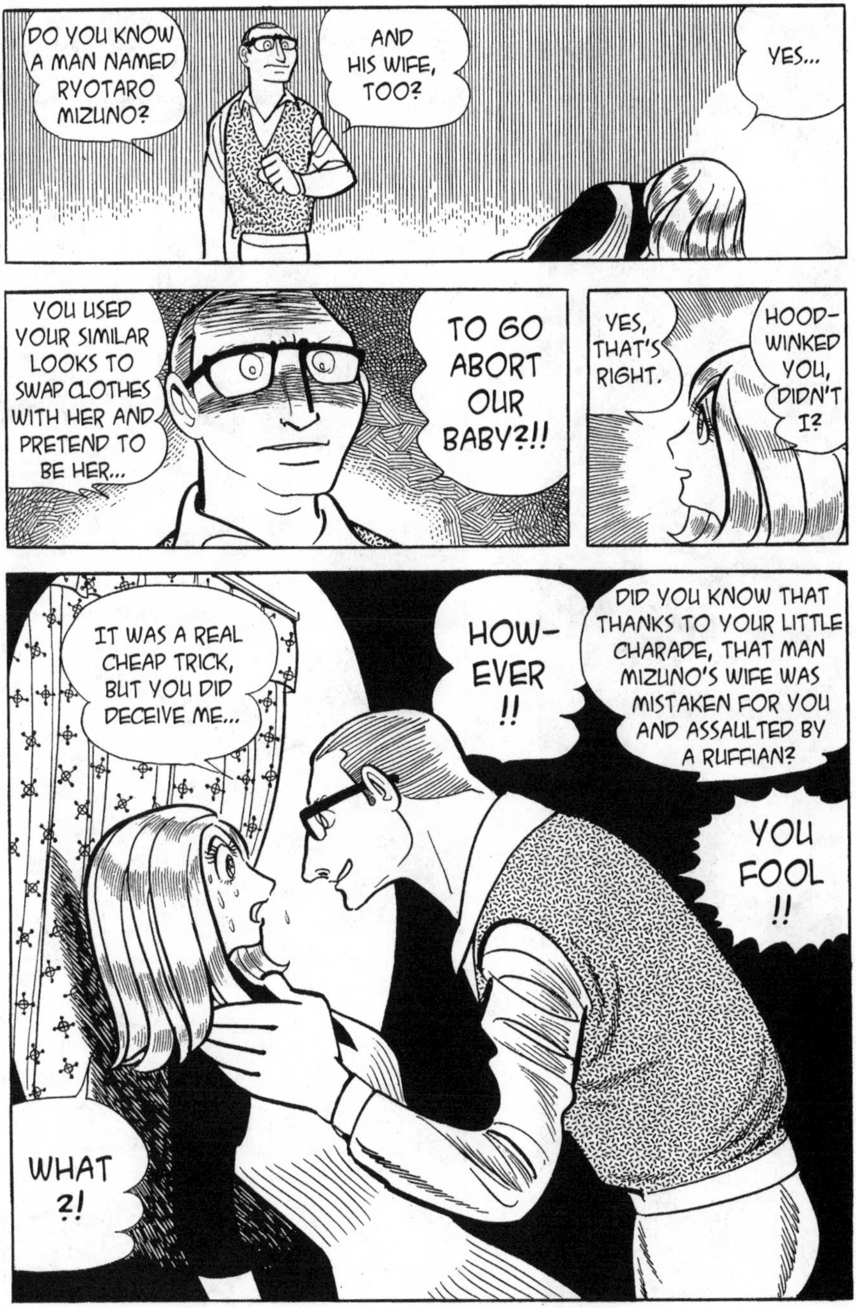
DO YOU KNOW A MAN NAMED RYOTARO MIZUNO?
AND HIS WIFE, TOO?
YES...
YOU USED YOUR SIMILAR LOOKS TO SWAP CLOTHES WITH HER AND PRETEND TO BE HER...
TO GO ABORT OUR BABY?!!
YES, THAT'S RIGHT.
HOOD-WINKED YOU, DIDN'T I?
IT WAS A REAL CHEAP TRICK, BUT YOU DID DECEIVE ME...
HOW-EVER !!
DID YOU KNOW THAT THANKS TO YOUR LITTLE CHARADE, THAT MAN MIZUNO'S WIFE WAS MISTAKEN FOR YOU AND ASSAULTED BY A RUFFIAN?
YOU FOOL !!
WHAT ?!

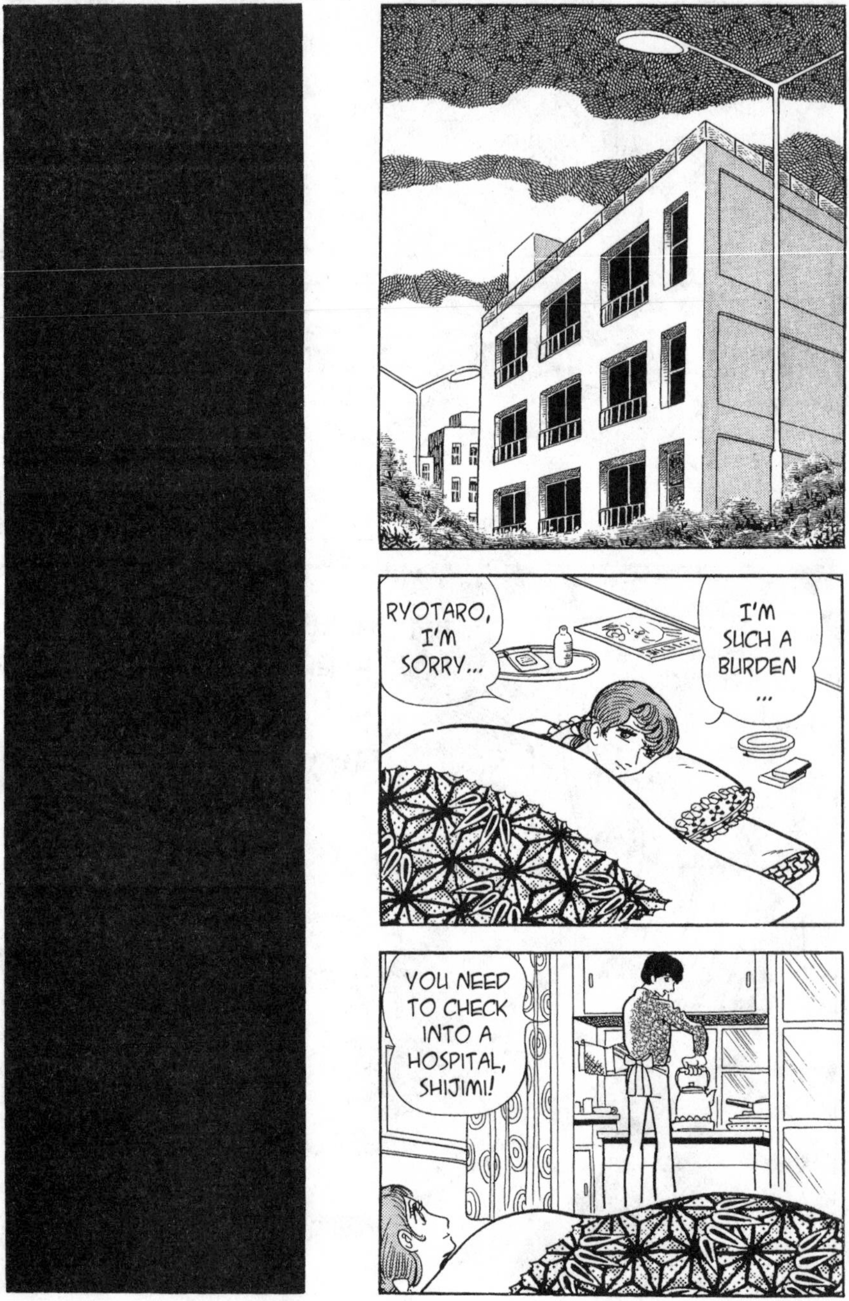
RYOTARO, I'M SORRY...
I'M SUCH A BURDEN ...
YOU NEED TO CHECK INTO A HOSPITAL, SHIJIMI!

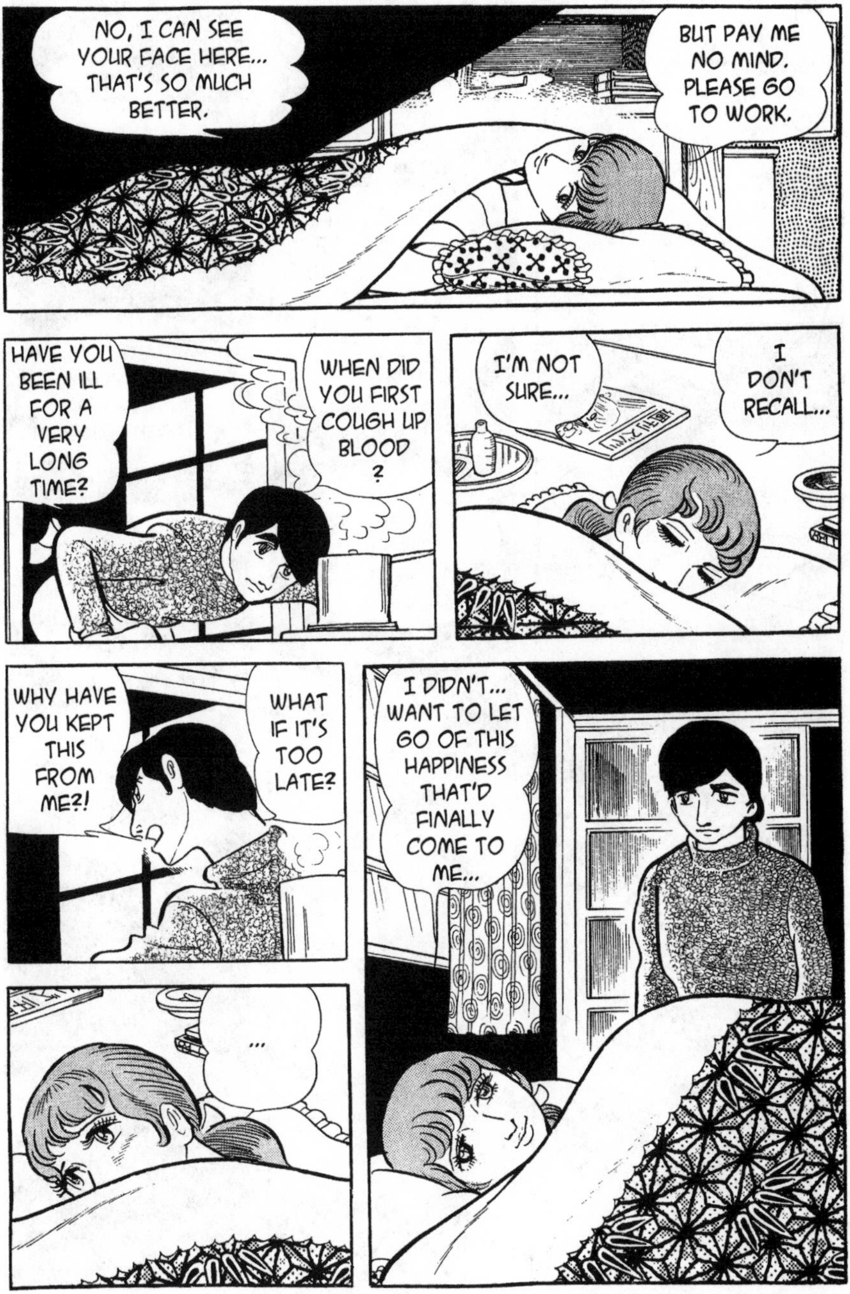
NO, I CAN SEE YOUR FACE HERE... THAT'S SO MUCH BETTER.
BUT PAY ME NO MIND. PLEASE GO TO WORK.
HAVE YOU BEEN ILL FOR A VERY LONG TIME?
WHEN DID YOU FIRST COUGH UP BLOOD?
I'M NOT SURE...
I DON'T RECALL...
WHY HAVE YOU KEPT THIS FROM ME?!
WHAT IF IT'S TOO LATE?
I DIDN'T... WANT TO LET GO OF THIS HAPPINESS THAT'D FINALLY COME TO ME...
...

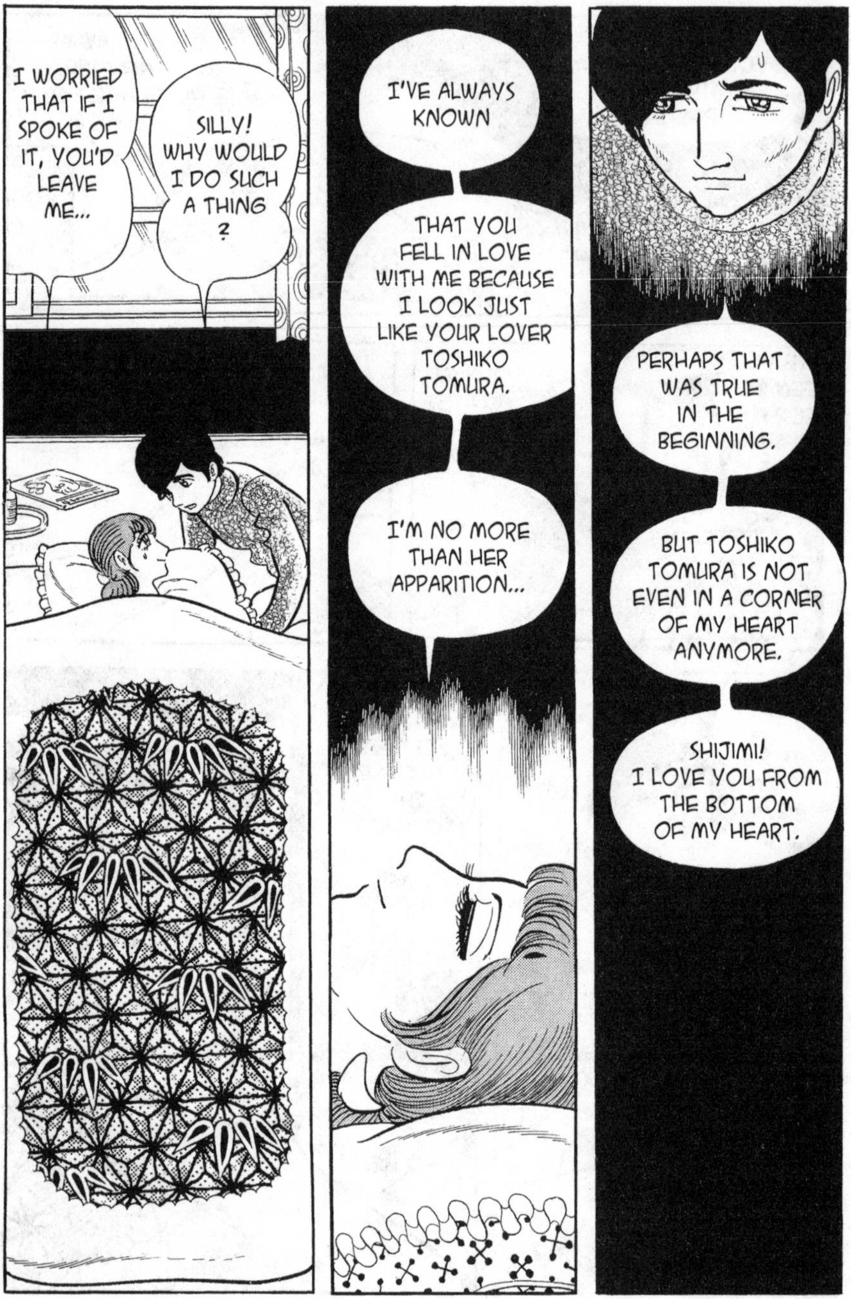
I WORRIED THAT IF I SPOKE OF IT, YOU'D LEAVE ME...
SILLY! WHY WOULD I DO SUCH A THING ?
I'VE ALWAYS KNOWN
THAT YOU FELL IN LOVE WITH ME BECAUSE I LOOK JUST LIKE YOUR LOVER TOSHIKO TOMURA.
I'M NO MORE THAN HER APPARITION...
PERHAPS THAT WAS TRUE IN THE BEGINNING.
BUT TOSHIKO TOMURA IS NOT EVEN IN A CORNER OF MY HEART ANYMORE.
SHIJIMI! I LOVE YOU FROM THE BOTTOM OF MY HEART.

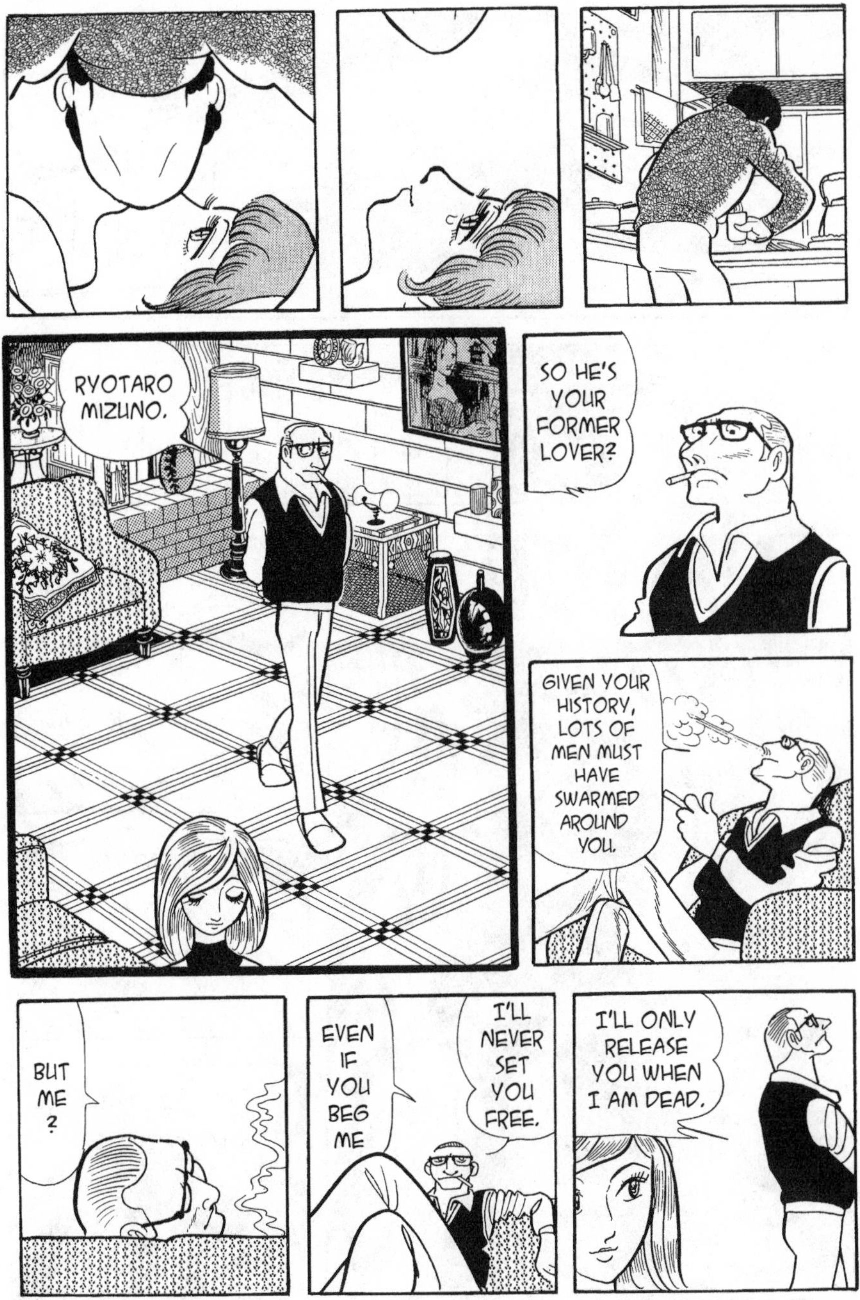

RYOTARO MIZUNO.
SO HE'S YOUR FORMER LOVER?
GIVEN YOUR HISTORY, LOTS OF MEN MUST HAVE SWARMED AROUND YOU.
BUT ME?
EVEN IF YOU BEG ME
I'LL NEVER SET YOU FREE.
I'LL ONLY RELEASE YOU WHEN I AM DEAD.

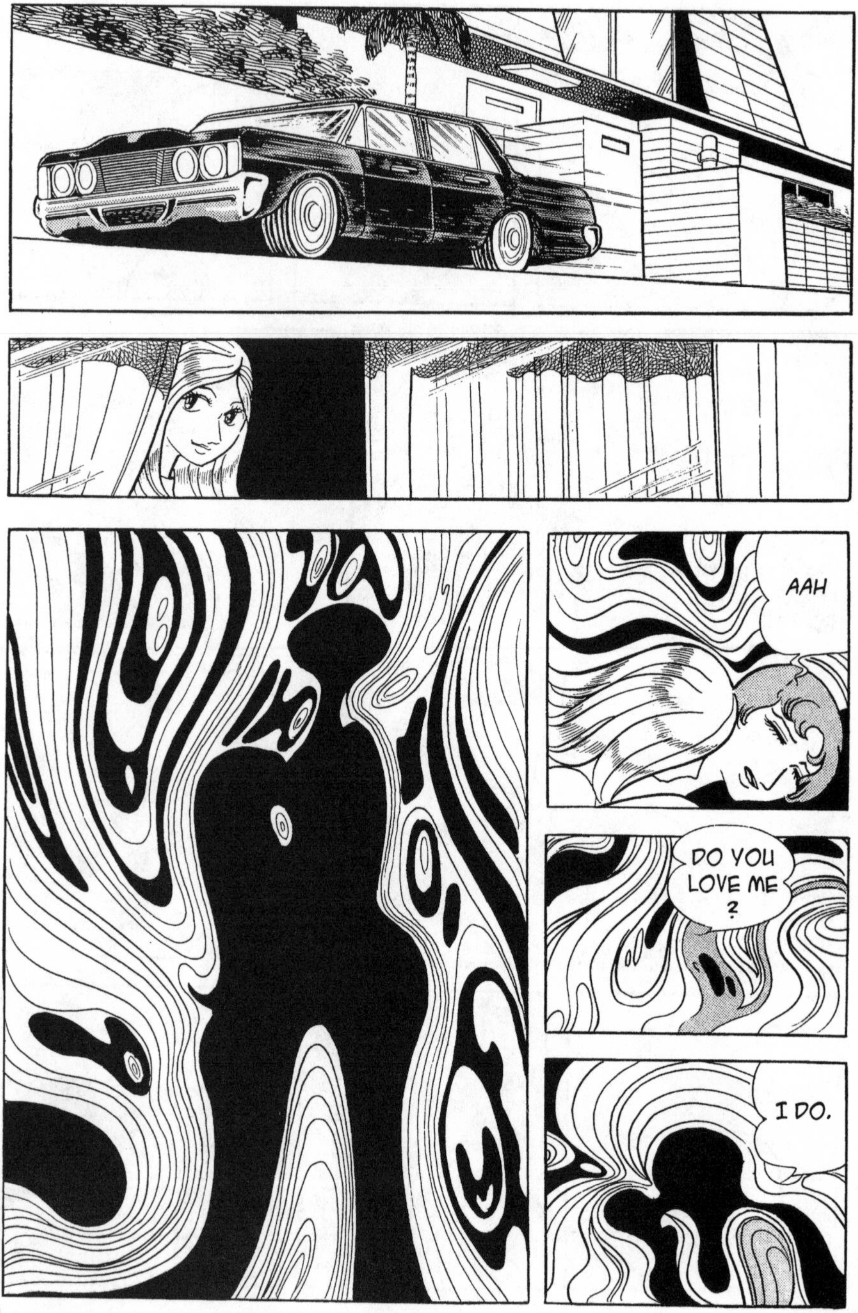
AAH
DO YOU LOVE ME ?
I DO.

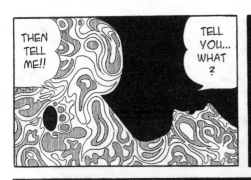

THEN TELL ME!!

TELL YOU... WHAT?

THE COMBINATION TO THE SAFE. ONLY YOU KNOW IT...

I BEG YOU.

AAAH

OH

UNH

SET IT TO "6"... THREE TIMES CLOCKWISE... SIX COUNTER-CLOCKWISE...

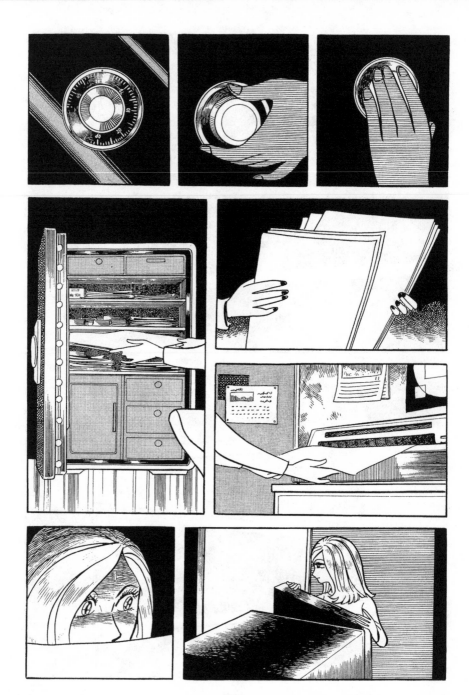

KABUTO

MY, MY, LONG TIME NO SEE,

LADY TOSHIKO TOMURA.

KNOW-ING YOU...

I FIGURED YOU'D DROP BY AGAIN SOME DAY, WA-HA HA HA...

I HAVE SOMETHING THAT I WANT YOU TO BUY.

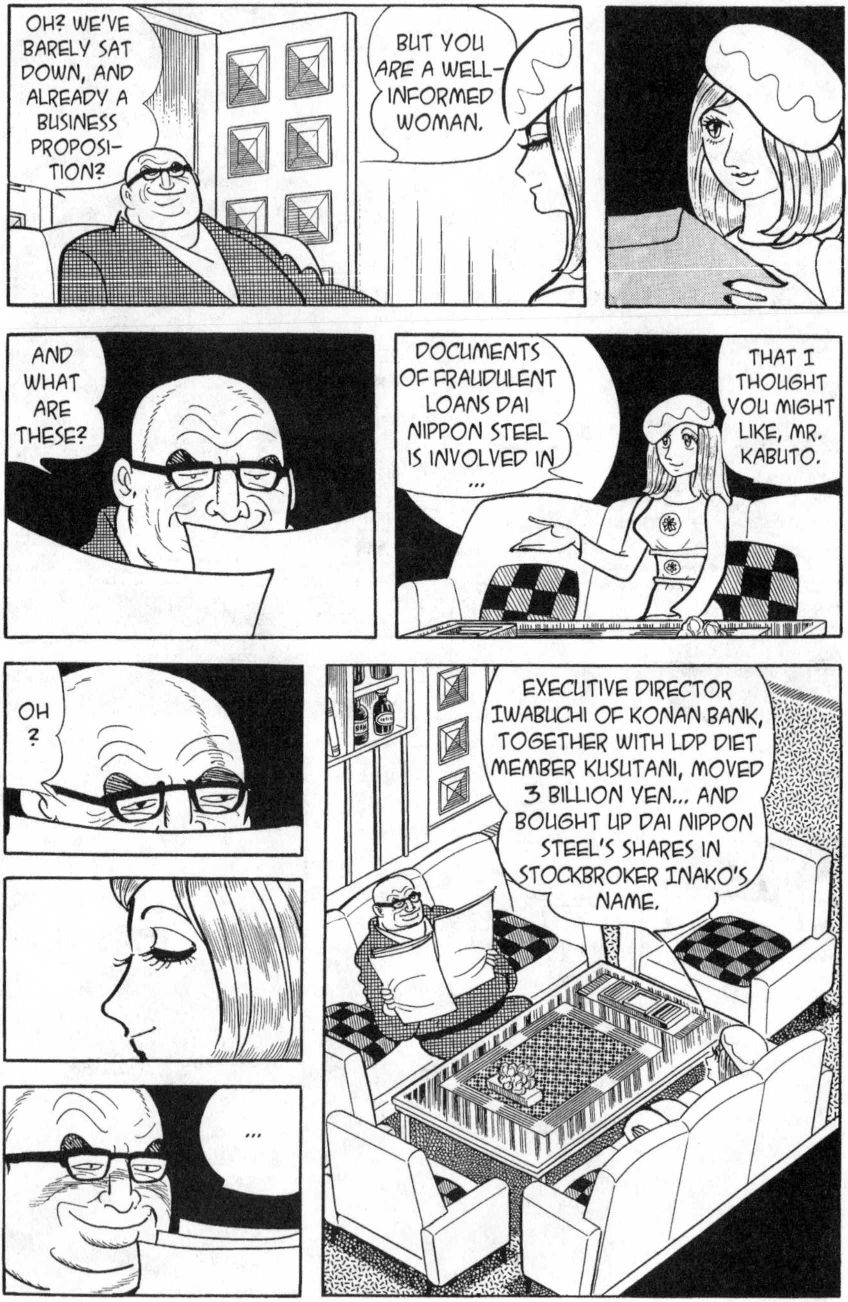
OH? WE'VE BARELY SAT DOWN, AND ALREADY A BUSINESS PROPOSI-TION?
BUT YOU ARE A WELL-INFORMED WOMAN.
AND WHAT ARE THESE?
DOCUMENTS OF FRAUDULENT LOANS DAI NIPPON STEEL IS INVOLVED IN ...
THAT I THOUGHT YOU MIGHT LIKE, MR. KABUTO.
OH ?
...
EXECUTIVE DIRECTOR IWABUCHI OF KONAN BANK, TOGETHER WITH LDP DIET MEMBER KUSUTANI, MOVED 3 BILLION YEN... AND BOUGHT UP DAI NIPPON STEEL'S SHARES IN STOCKBROKER INAKO'S NAME.

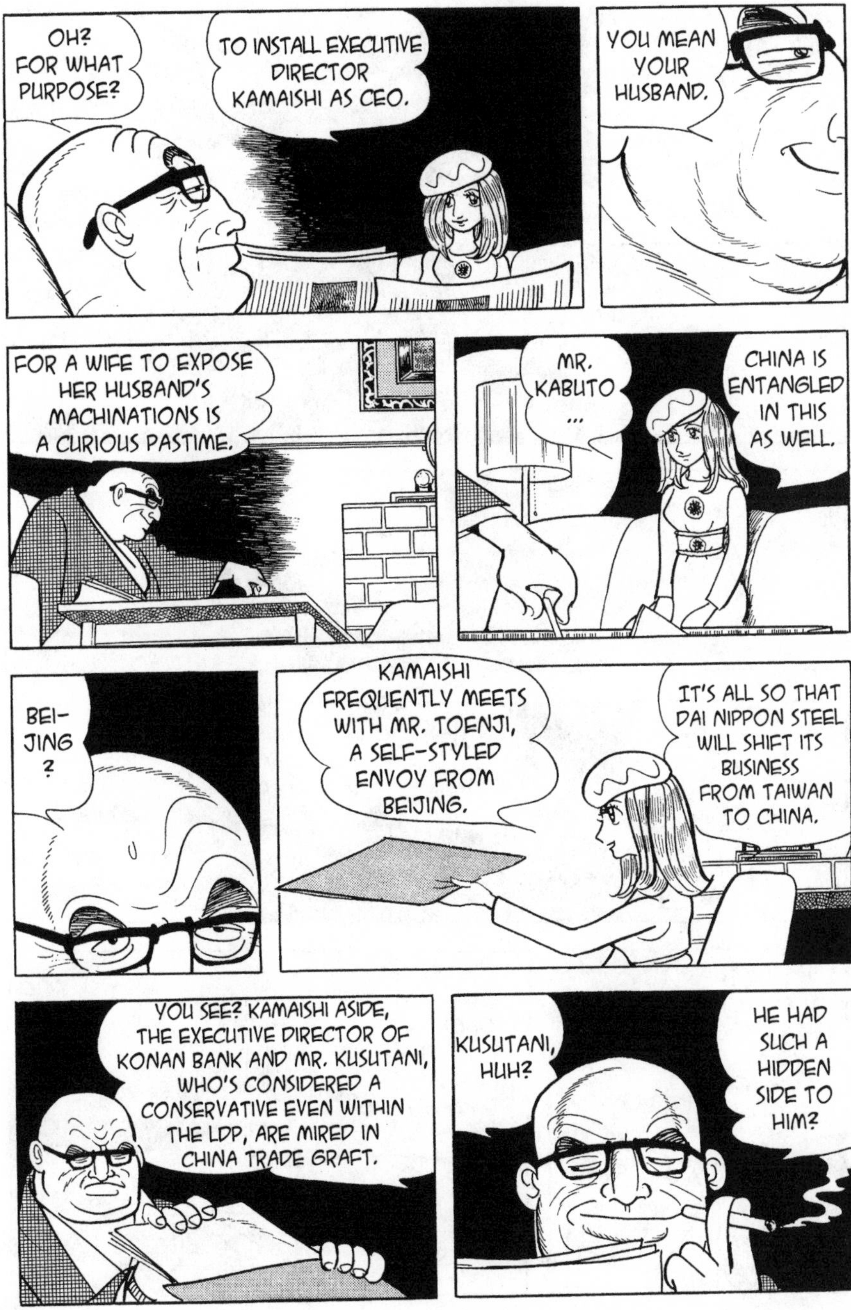
OH? FOR WHAT PURPOSE?
TO INSTALL EXECUTIVE DIRECTOR KAMAISHI AS CEO.
YOU MEAN YOUR HUSBAND.
FOR A WIFE TO EXPOSE HER HUSBAND'S MACHINATIONS IS A CURIOUS PASTIME.
MR. KABUTO ...
CHINA IS ENTANGLED IN THIS AS WELL.
BEI-JING ?
KAMAISHI FREQUENTLY MEETS WITH MR. TOENJI, A SELF-STYLED ENVOY FROM BEIJING.
IT'S ALL SO THAT DAI NIPPON STEEL WILL SHIFT ITS BUSINESS FROM TAIWAN TO CHINA.
YOU SEE? KAMAISHI ASIDE, THE EXECUTIVE DIRECTOR OF KONAN BANK AND MR. KUSUTANI, WHO'S CONSIDERED A CONSERVATIVE EVEN WITHIN THE LDP, ARE MIRED IN CHINA TRADE GRAFT.
KUSUTANI, HUH?
HE HAD SUCH A HIDDEN SIDE TO HIM?

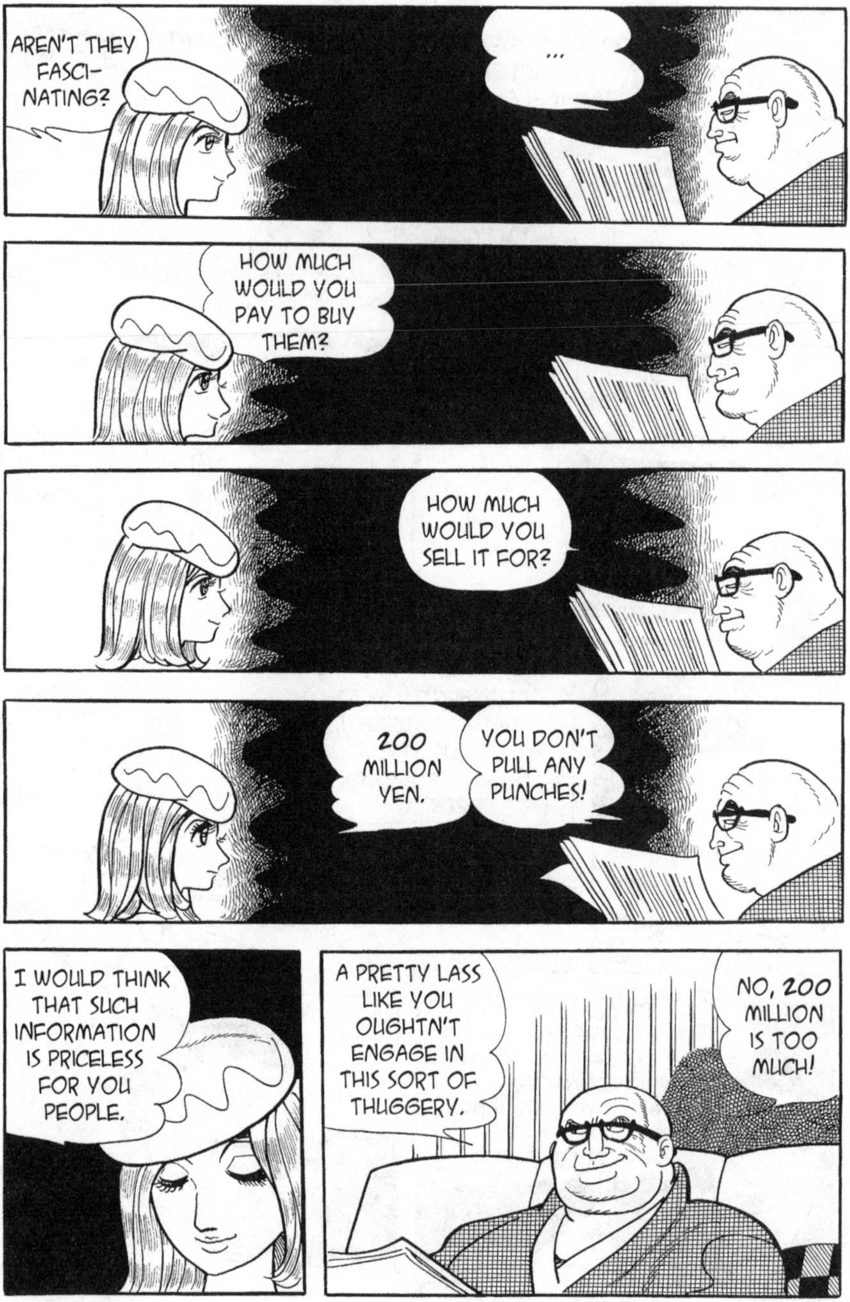
AREN'T THEY FASCI- NATING?
...
HOW MUCH WOULD YOU PAY TO BUY THEM?
HOW MUCH WOULD YOU SELL IT FOR?
200 MILLION YEN.
YOU DON'T PULL ANY PUNCHES!
I WOULD THINK THAT SUCH INFORMATION IS PRICELESS FOR YOU PEOPLE.
A PRETTY LASS LIKE YOU OUGHTN'T ENGAGE IN THIS SORT OF THUGGERY.
NO, 200 MILLION IS TOO MUCH!

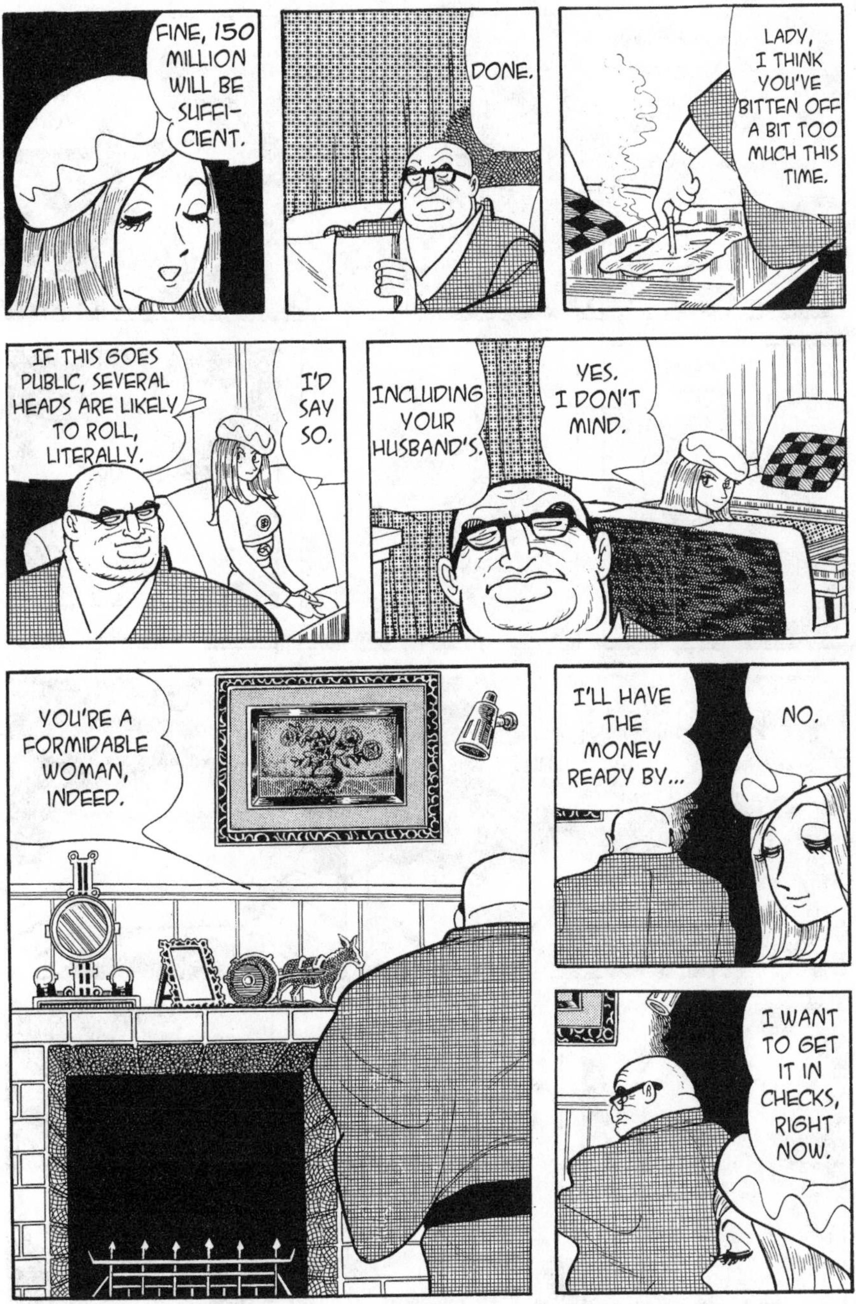

FINE, 150 MILLION WILL BE SUFFI-CIENT.
DONE.
LADY, I THINK YOU'VE BITTEN OFF A BIT TOO MUCH THIS TIME.
IF THIS GOES PUBLIC, SEVERAL HEADS ARE LIKELY TO ROLL, LITERALLY.
I'D SAY SO.
INCLUDING YOUR HUSBAND'S.
YES. I DON'T MIND.
YOU'RE A FORMIDABLE WOMAN, INDEED.
I'LL HAVE THE MONEY READY BY...
NO.
I WANT TO GET IT IN CHECKS, RIGHT NOW.

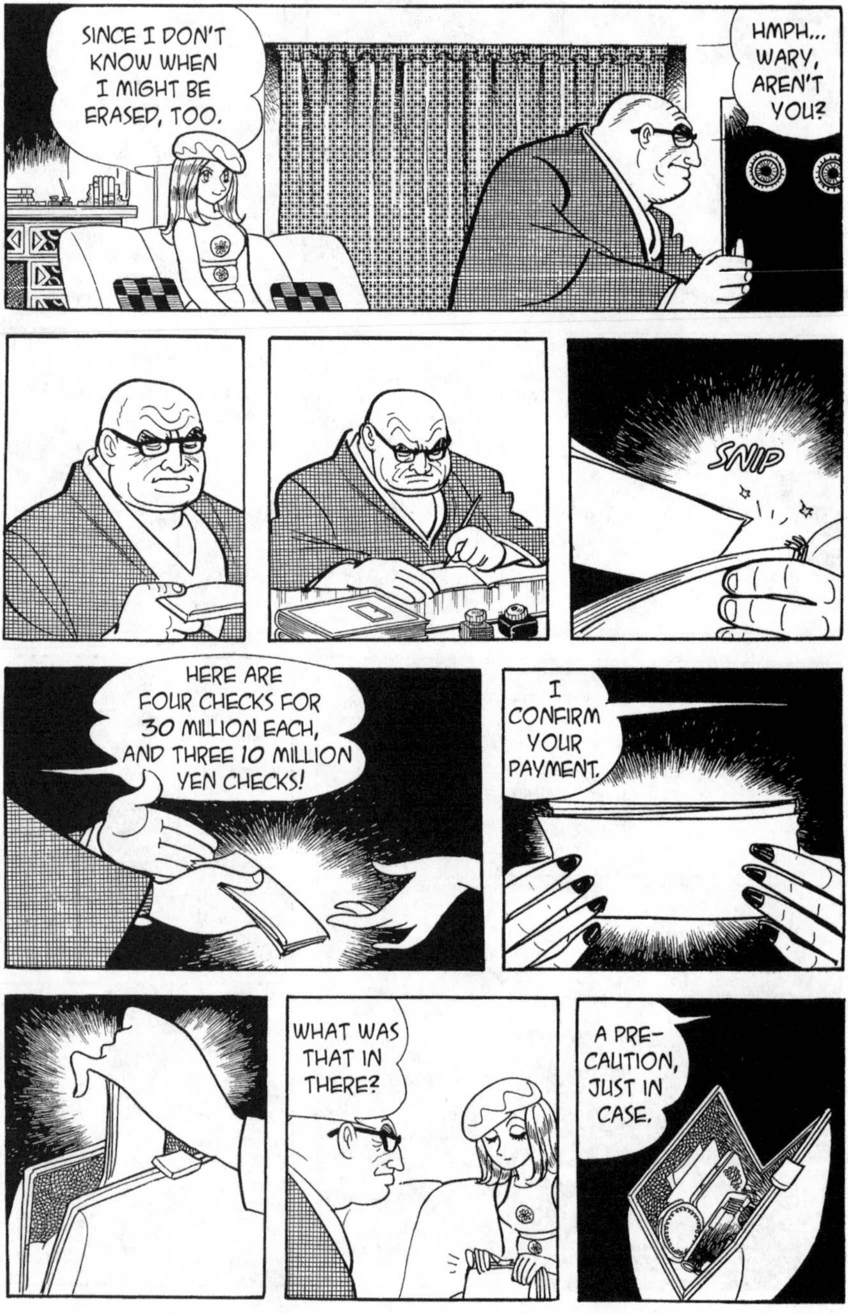
SINCE I DON'T KNOW WHEN I MIGHT BE ERASED, TOO.
HMPH... WARY, AREN'T YOU?
SNIP
HERE ARE FOUR CHECKS FOR 30 MILLION EACH, AND THREE 10 MILLION YEN CHECKS!
I CONFIRM YOUR PAYMENT.
WHAT WAS THAT IN THERE?
A PRE-CAUTION, JUST IN CASE.

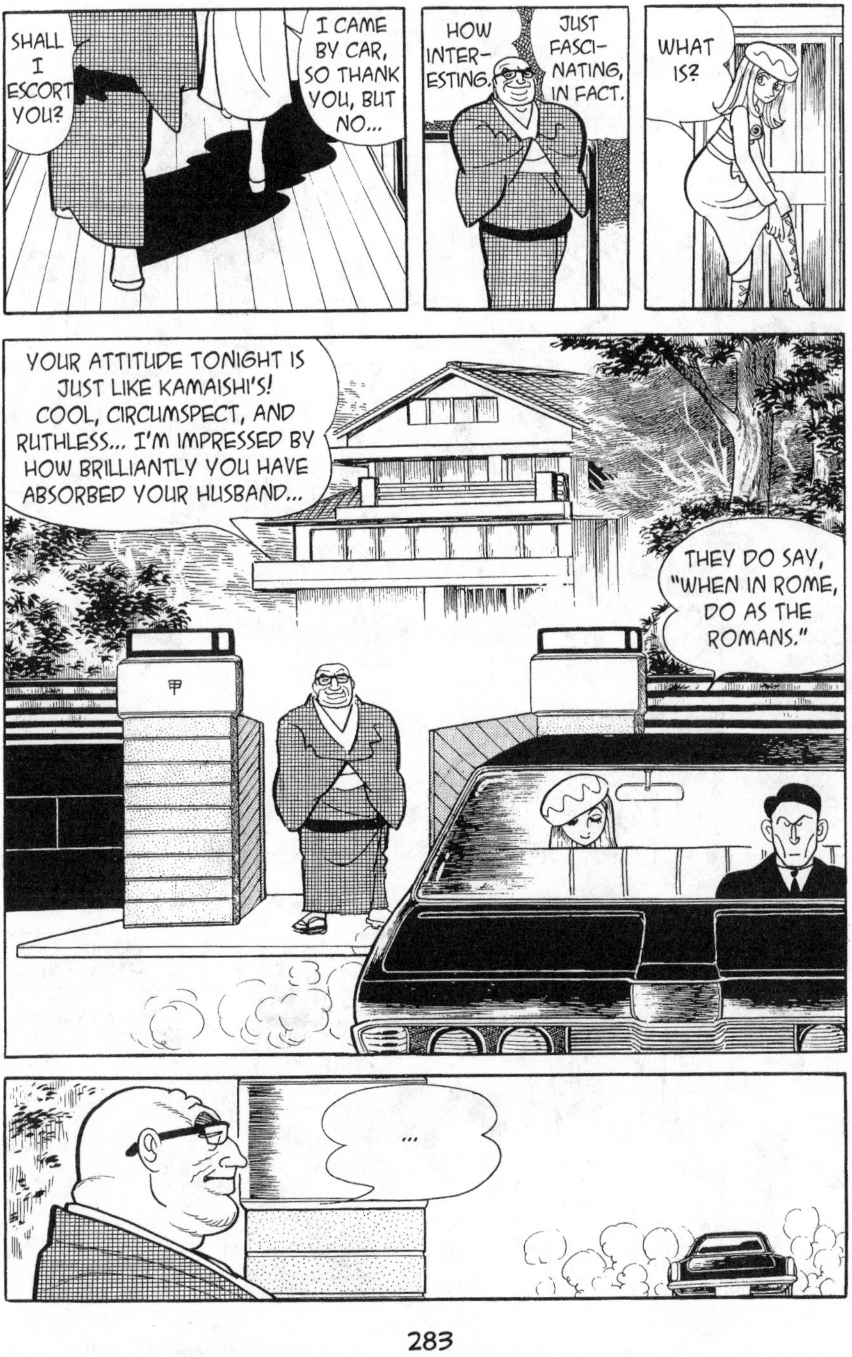
SHALL I ESCORT YOU?
I CAME BY CAR, SO THANK YOU, BUT NO...
HOW INTERESTING.
JUST FASCINATING, IN FACT.
WHAT IS?
YOUR ATTITUDE TONIGHT IS JUST LIKE KAMAISHI'S! COOL, CIRCUMSPECT, AND RUTHLESS... I'M IMPRESSED BY HOW BRILLIANTLY YOU HAVE ABSORBED YOUR HUSBAND...
THEY DO SAY, "WHEN IN ROME, DO AS THE ROMANS."
...

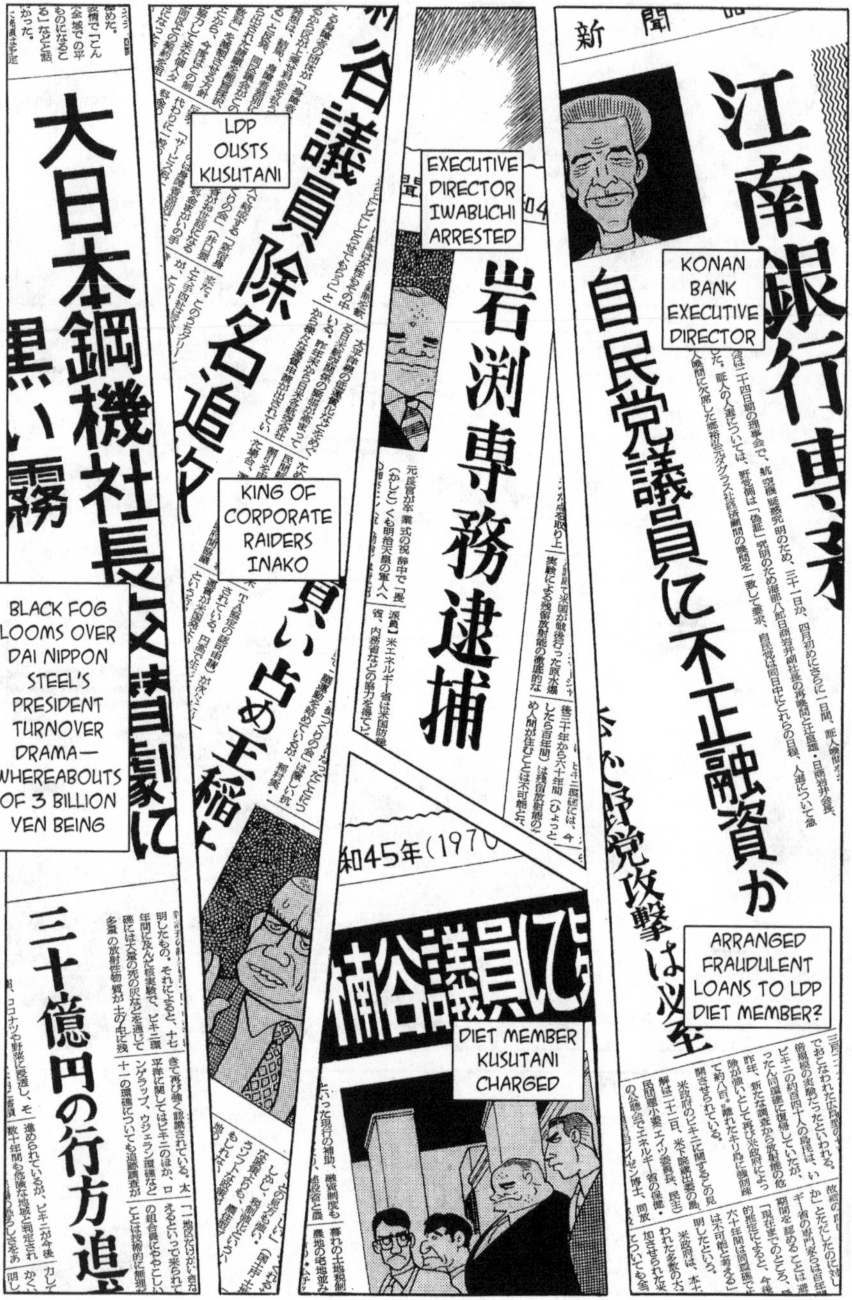
大日本鋼機社長交替劇に
三十億円の行方追
BLACK FOG LOOMS OVER DAI NIPPON STEEL'S PRESIDENT TURNOVER DRAMA—WHEREABOUTS OF 3 BILLION YEN BEING
LDP OUSTS KUSUTANI
KING OF CORPORATE RAIDERS INAKO
EXECUTIVE DIRECTOR IWABUCHI ARRESTED
岩渕専務逮捕
DIET MEMBER KUSUTANI CHARGED
KONAN BANK EXECUTIVE DIRECTOR
自民党議員に不正融資か
ARRANGED FRAUDULENT LOANS TO LDP DIET MEMBER?

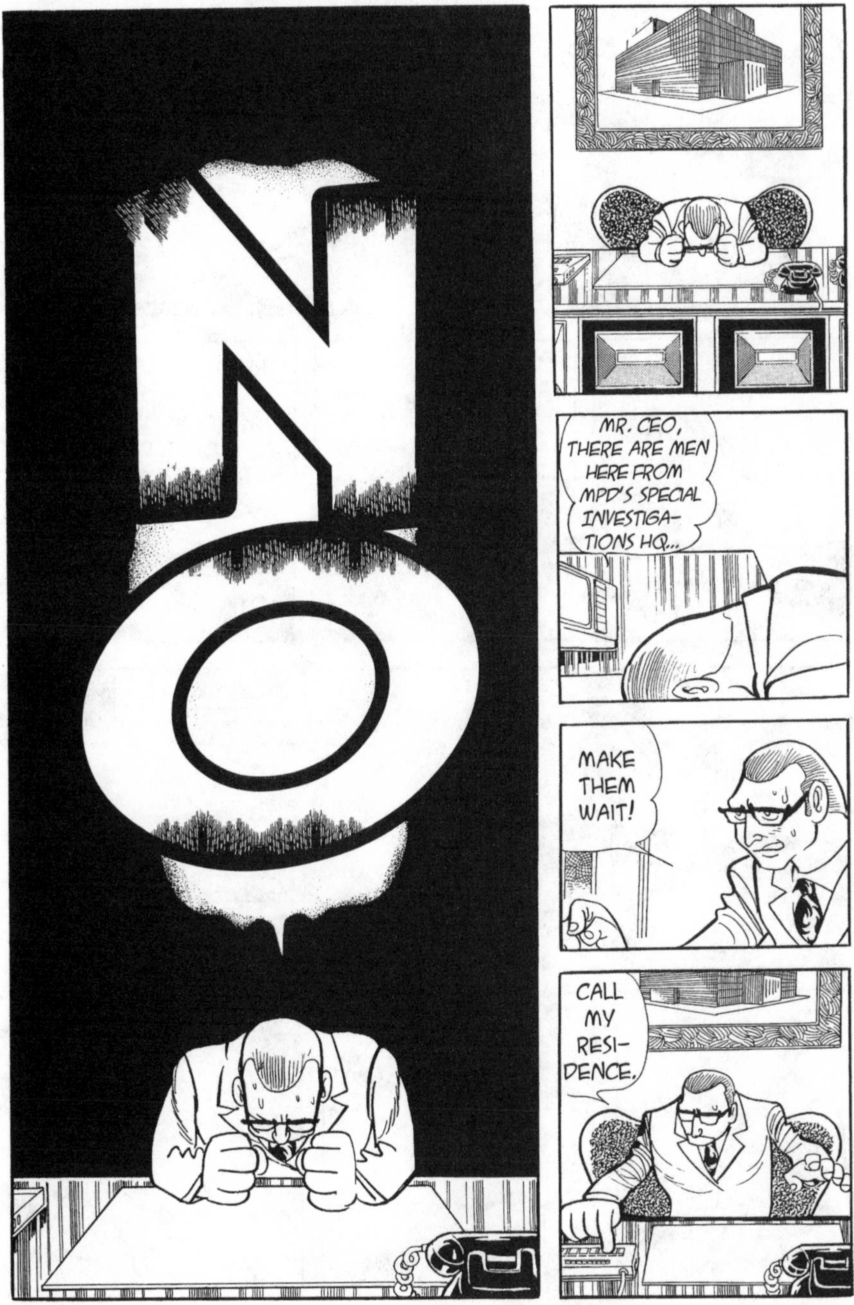
NO
MR. CEO, THERE ARE MEN HERE FROM MPD'S SPECIAL INVESTIGA- TIONS HQ...
MAKE THEM WAIT!
CALL MY RESI- DENCE.

HEY THERE!

NO... IT'S NOTHING, REALLY.

THOSE DOLLS IN THE LIVING ROOM... I DON'T NEED THEM ANYMORE.

BURN THEM ALL IN THE YARD.

I'LL BE GETTING HOME LATE...

YEAH, I MAY NOT AT ALL.

BY THE WAY, SINCE WE GOT MARRIED, YOU'VE NEVER ONCE SAID YOU LOVED ME.

WON'T YOU SAY IT JUST ONCE?

WELL, IT FEELS ODD TO STAND ON CEREMONY, BUT I LOVE YOU.

BYE NOW...

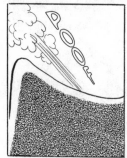
POOF

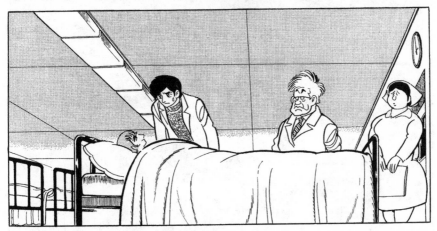

IT'S ADVANCED CANCER OF THE PYLORUS... PROBABLY METASTASIZED.

SHE HAS TWO WEEKS AT MOST.

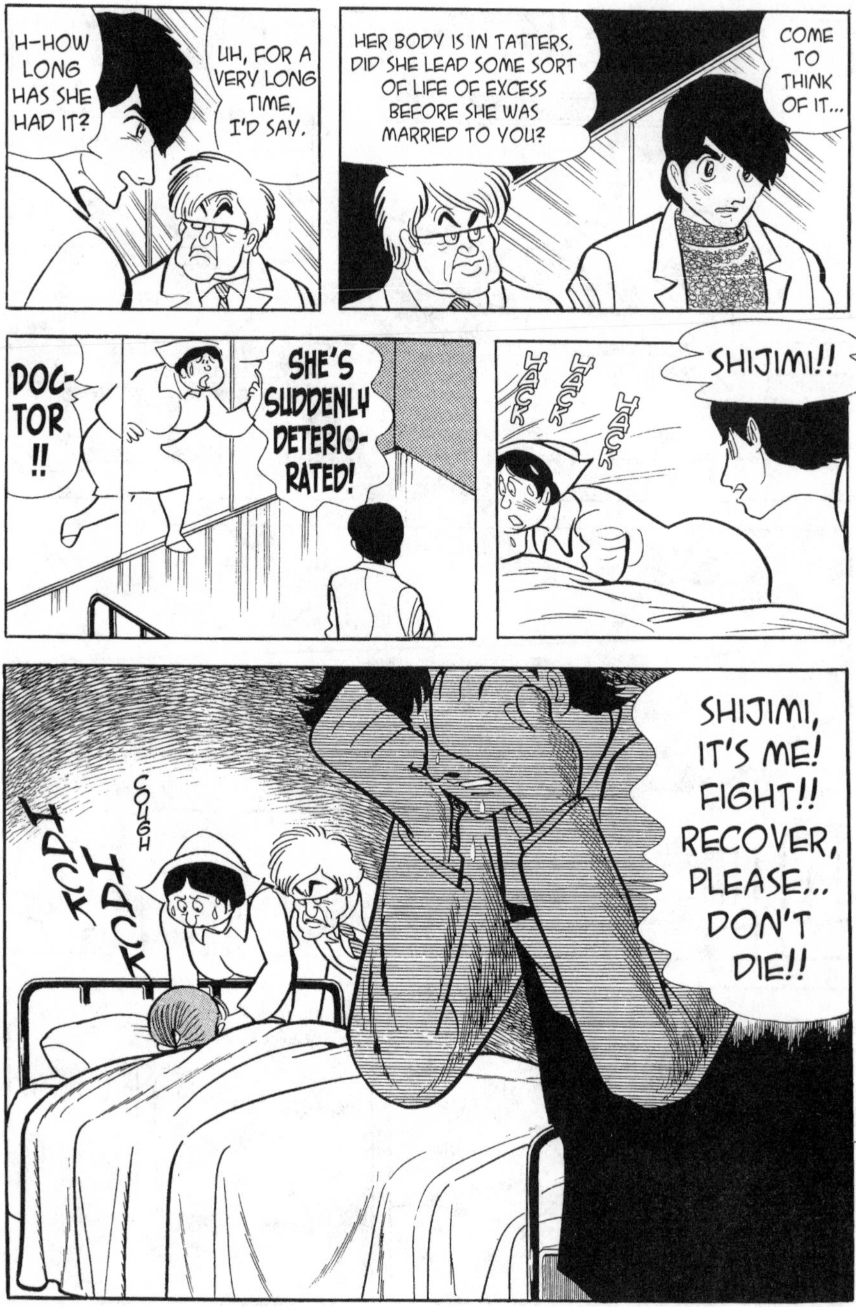
H-HOW LONG HAS SHE HAD IT?
UH, FOR A VERY LONG TIME, I'D SAY.
HER BODY IS IN TATTERS. DID SHE LEAD SOME SORT OF LIFE OF EXCESS BEFORE SHE WAS MARRIED TO YOU?
COME TO THINK OF IT...
DOCTOR!!
SHE'S SUDDENLY DETERIORATED!
HACK HACK HACK
SHIJIMI!!
HACK HACK
COUGH
SHIJIMI, IT'S ME! FIGHT!! RECOVER, PLEASE... DON'T DIE!!

KATYDID

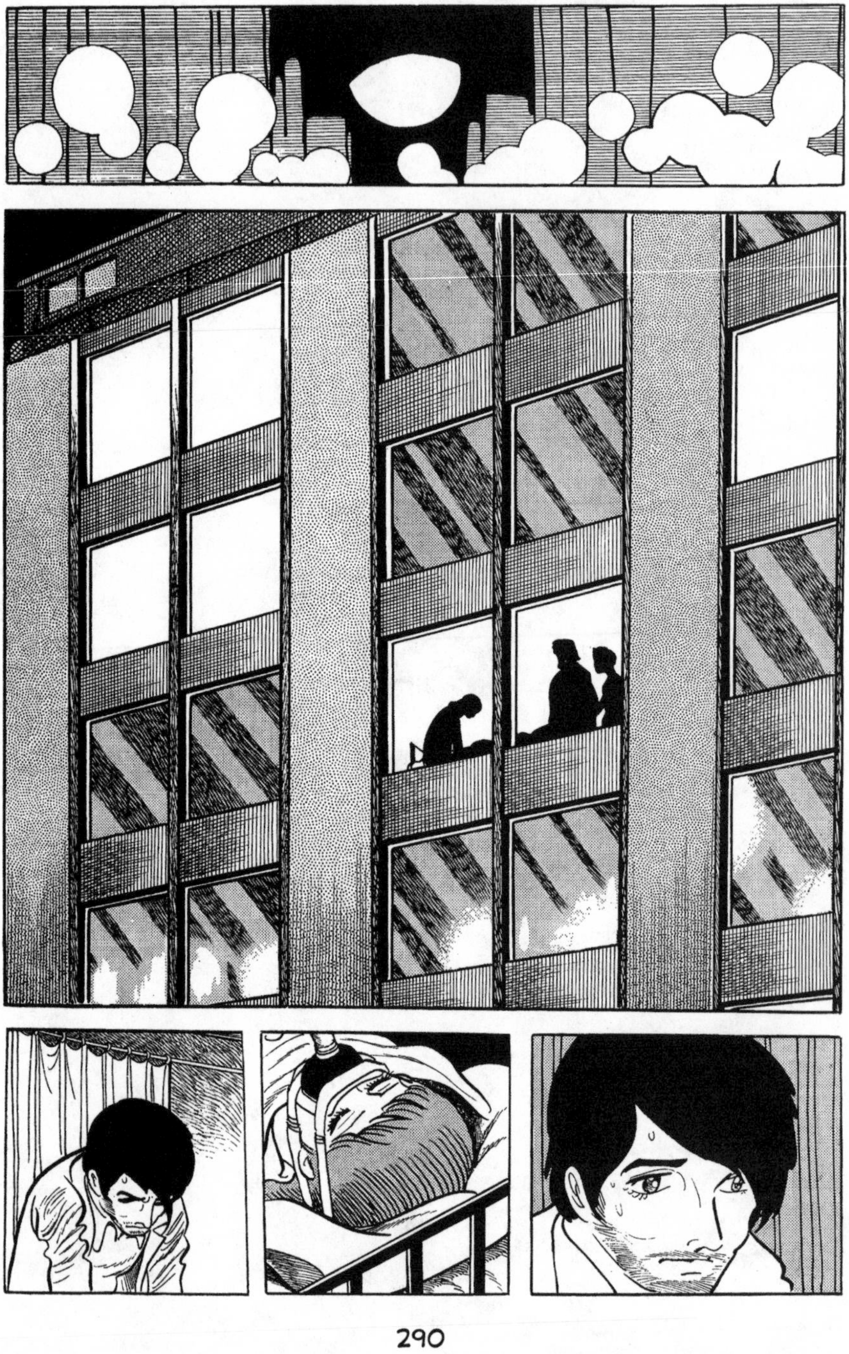

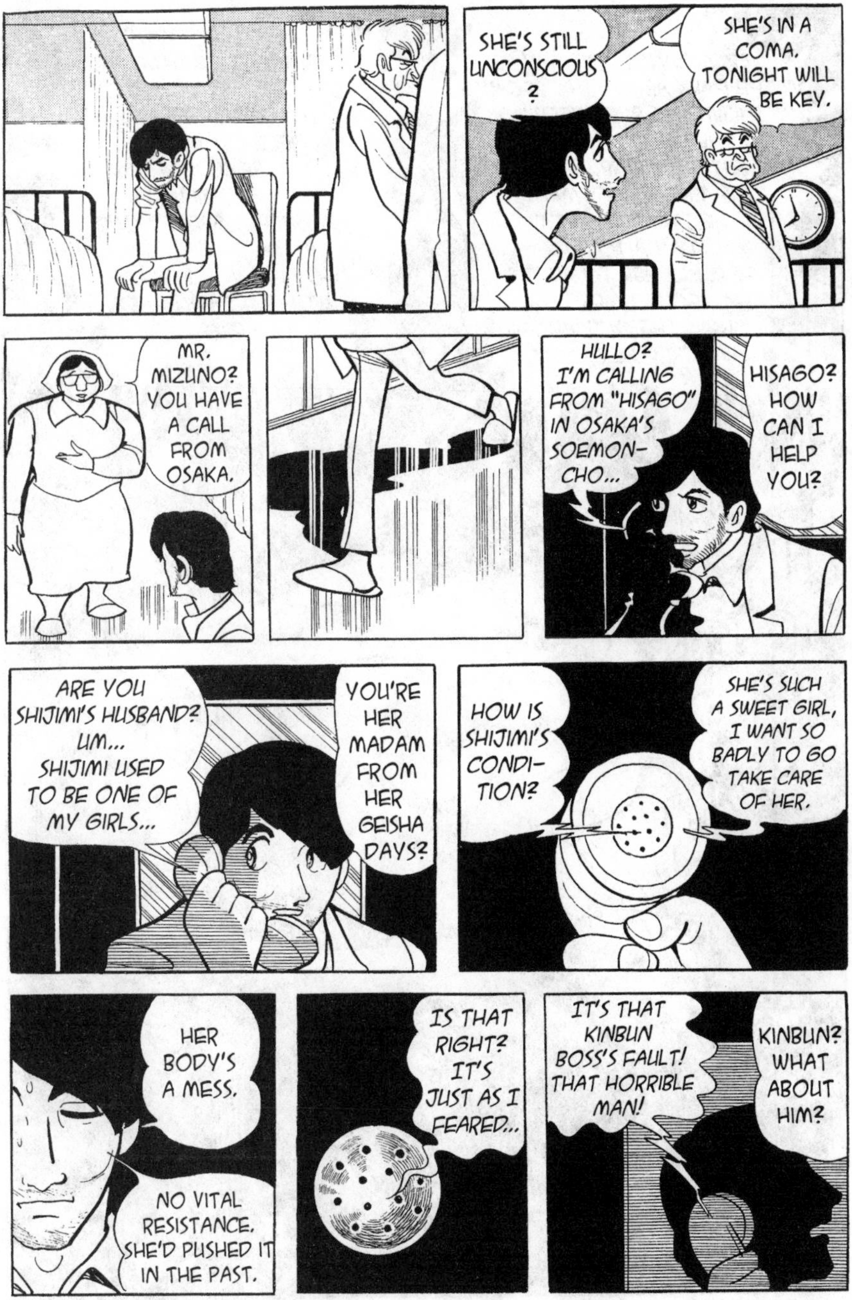
SHE'S STILL UNCONSCIOUS?
SHE'S IN A COMA. TONIGHT WILL BE KEY.
MR. MIZUNO? YOU HAVE A CALL FROM OSAKA.
HULLO? I'M CALLING FROM "HISAGO" IN OSAKA'S SOEMON-CHO...
HISAGO? HOW CAN I HELP YOU?
ARE YOU SHIJIMI'S HUSBAND? UM... SHIJIMI USED TO BE ONE OF MY GIRLS...
YOU'RE HER MADAM FROM HER GEISHA DAYS?
HOW IS SHIJIMI'S CONDITION?
SHE'S SUCH A SWEET GIRL, I WANT SO BADLY TO GO TAKE CARE OF HER.
HER BODY'S A MESS.
NO VITAL RESISTANCE. SHE'D PUSHED IT IN THE PAST.
IS THAT RIGHT? IT'S JUST AS I FEARED...
IT'S THAT KINBUN BOSS'S FAULT! THAT HORRIBLE MAN!
KINBUN? WHAT ABOUT HIM?

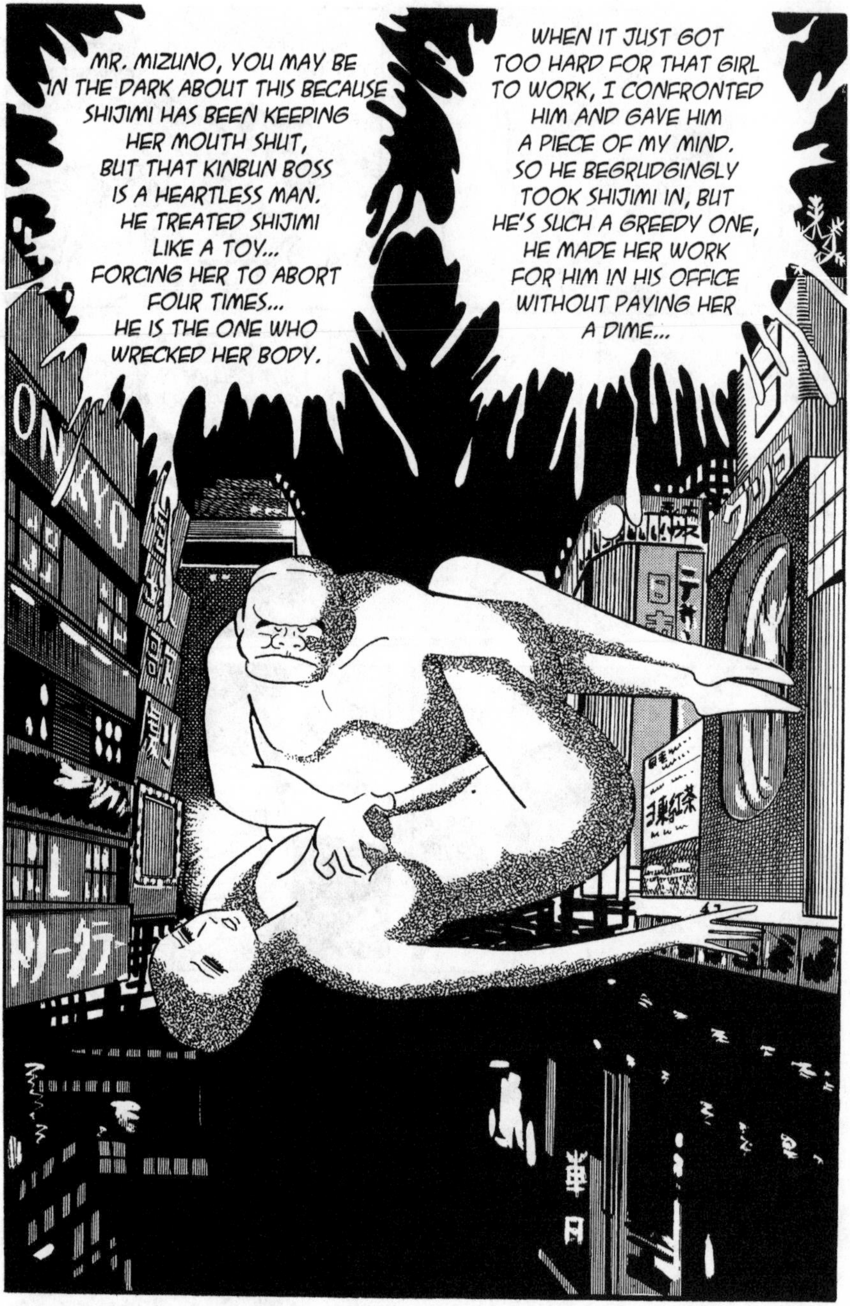
MR. MIZUNO, YOU MAY BE IN THE DARK ABOUT THIS BECAUSE SHIJIMI HAS BEEN KEEPING HER MOUTH SHUT, BUT THAT KINBUN BOSS IS A HEARTLESS MAN. HE TREATED SHIJIMI LIKE A TOY... FORCING HER TO ABORT FOUR TIMES... HE IS THE ONE WHO WRECKED HER BODY.
WHEN IT JUST GOT TOO HARD FOR THAT GIRL TO WORK, I CONFRONTED HIM AND GAVE HIM A PIECE OF MY MIND. SO HE BEGRUDGINGLY TOOK SHIJIMI IN, BUT HE'S SUCH A GREEDY ONE, HE MADE HER WORK FOR HIM IN HIS OFFICE WITHOUT PAYING HER A DIME...

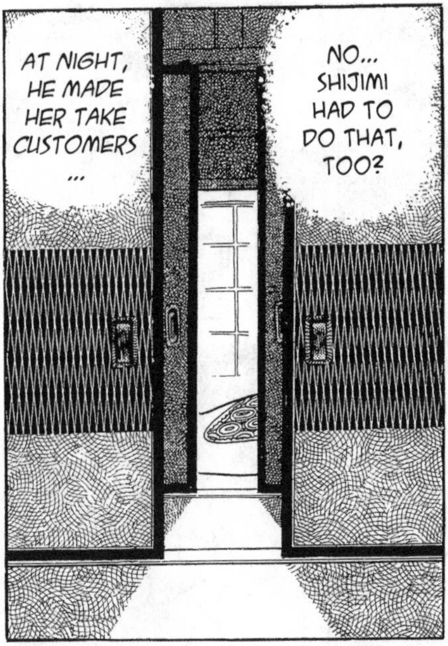
AT NIGHT, HE MADE HER TAKE CUSTOMERS ...
NO... SHIJIMI HAD TO DO THAT, TOO?
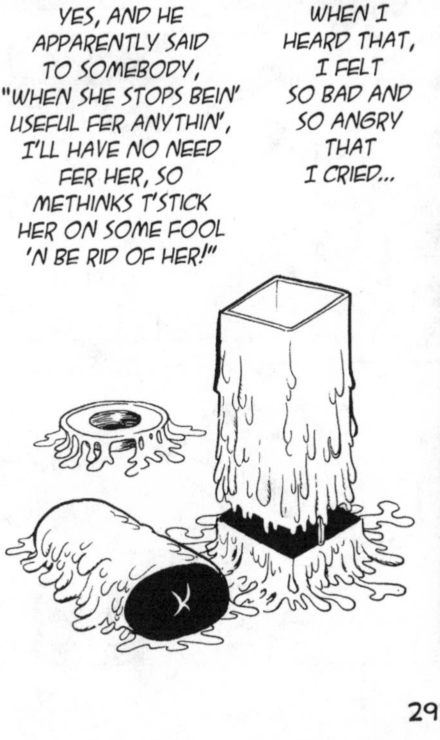
YES, AND HE APPARENTLY SAID TO SOMEBODY, "WHEN SHE STOPS BEIN' USEFUL FER ANYTHIN', I'LL HAVE NO NEED FER HER, SO METHINKS T'STICK HER ON SOME FOOL 'N BE RID OF HER!"
WHEN I HEARD THAT, I FELT SO BAD AND SO ANGRY THAT I CRIED...
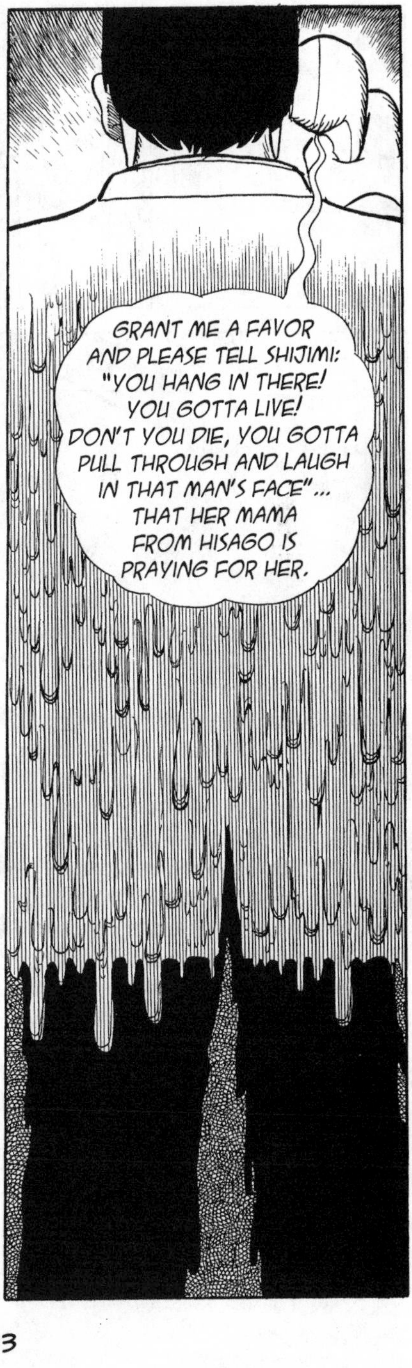
GRANT ME A FAVOR AND PLEASE TELL SHIJIMI: "YOU HANG IN THERE! YOU GOTTA LIVE! DON'T YOU DIE, YOU GOTTA PULL THROUGH AND LAUGH IN THAT MAN'S FACE"... THAT HER MAMA FROM HISAGO IS PRAYING FOR HER.

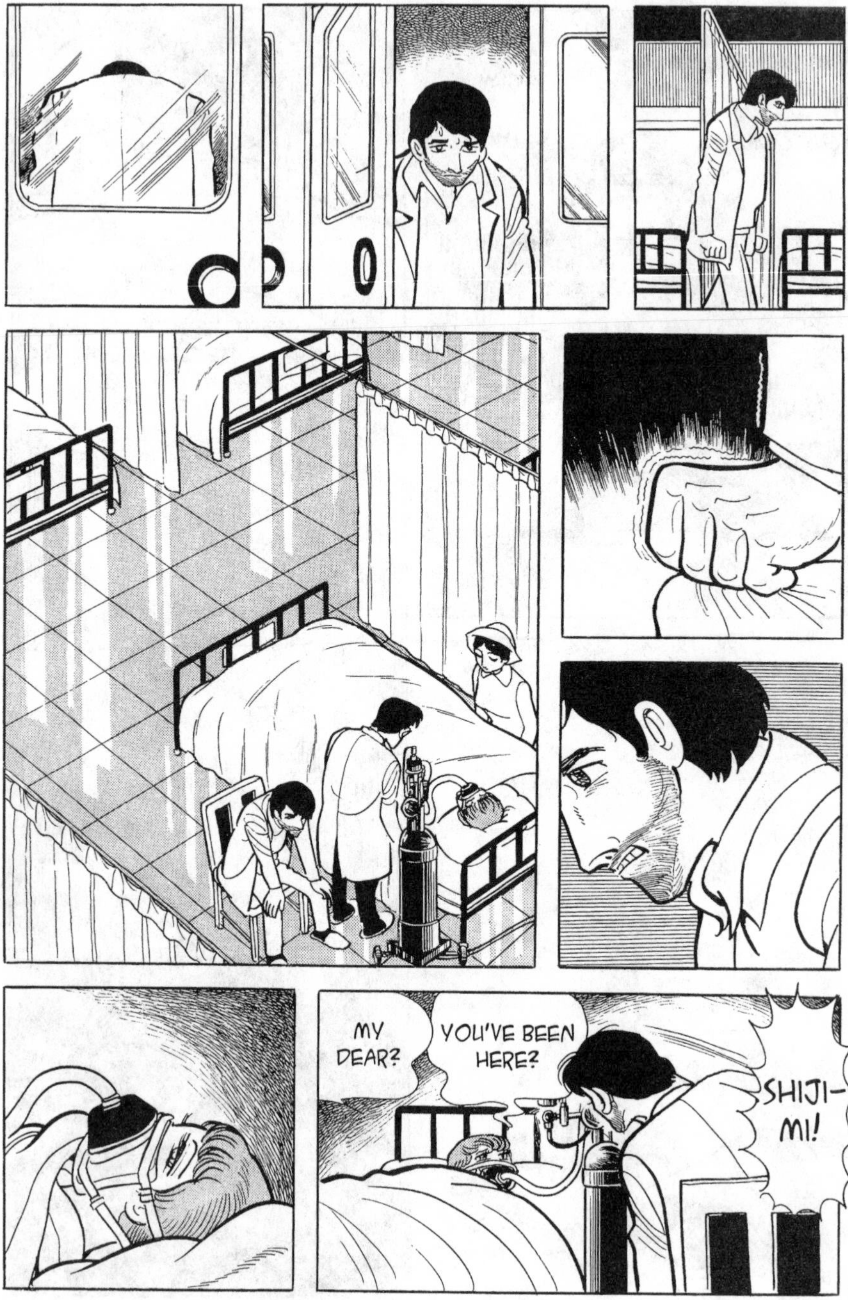
MY DEAR?
YOU'VE BEEN HERE?
SHIJI-MI!

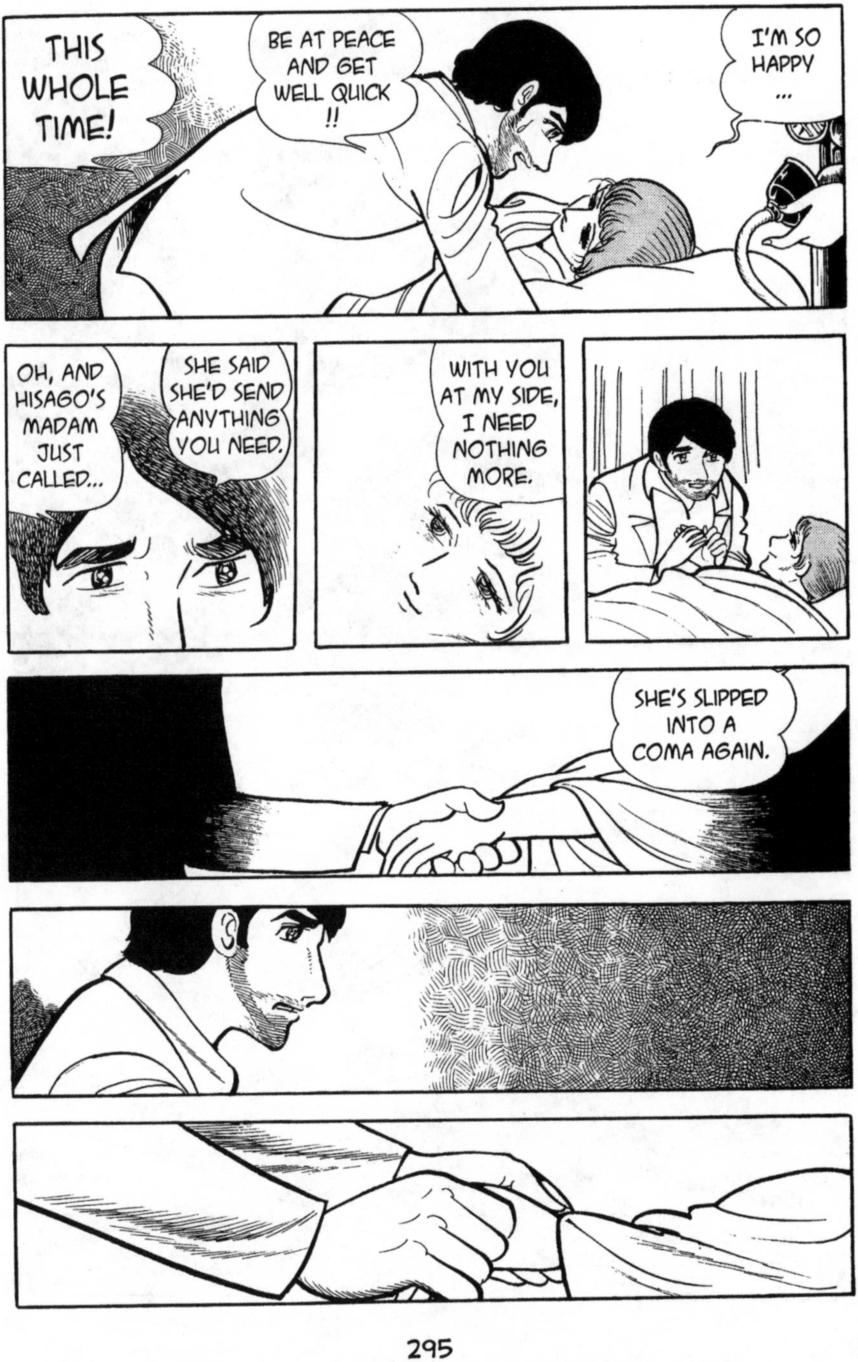
THIS WHOLE TIME!
BE AT PEACE AND GET WELL QUICK !!
I'M SO HAPPY ...
OH, AND HISAGO'S MADAM JUST CALLED...
SHE SAID SHE'D SEND ANYTHING YOU NEED.
WITH YOU AT MY SIDE, I NEED NOTHING MORE.
SHE'S SLIPPED INTO A COMA AGAIN.

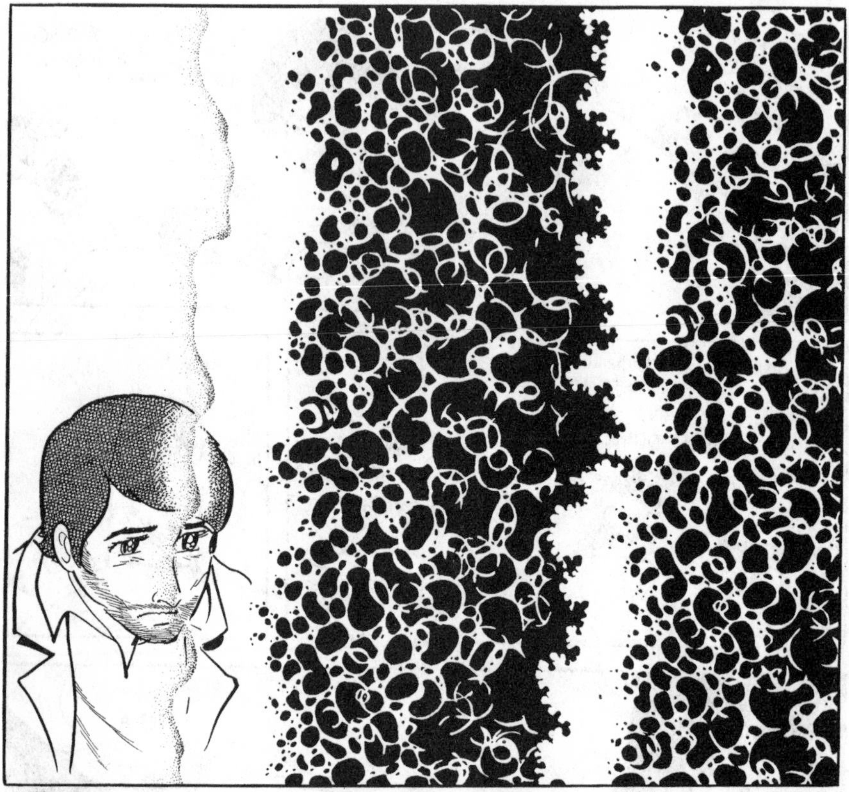

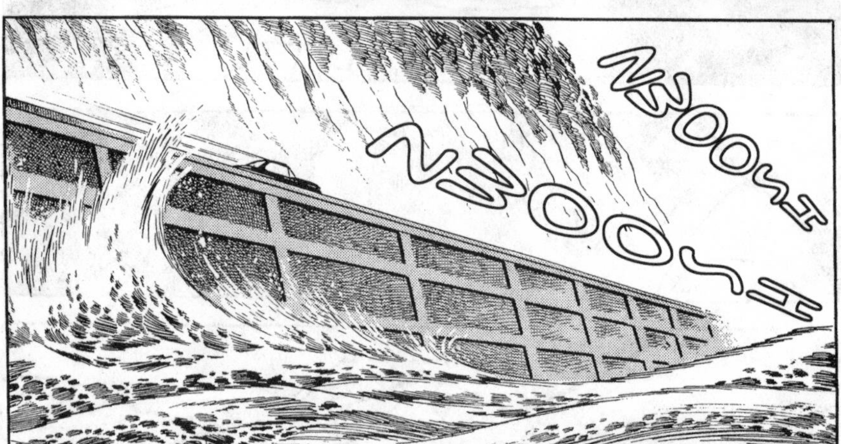

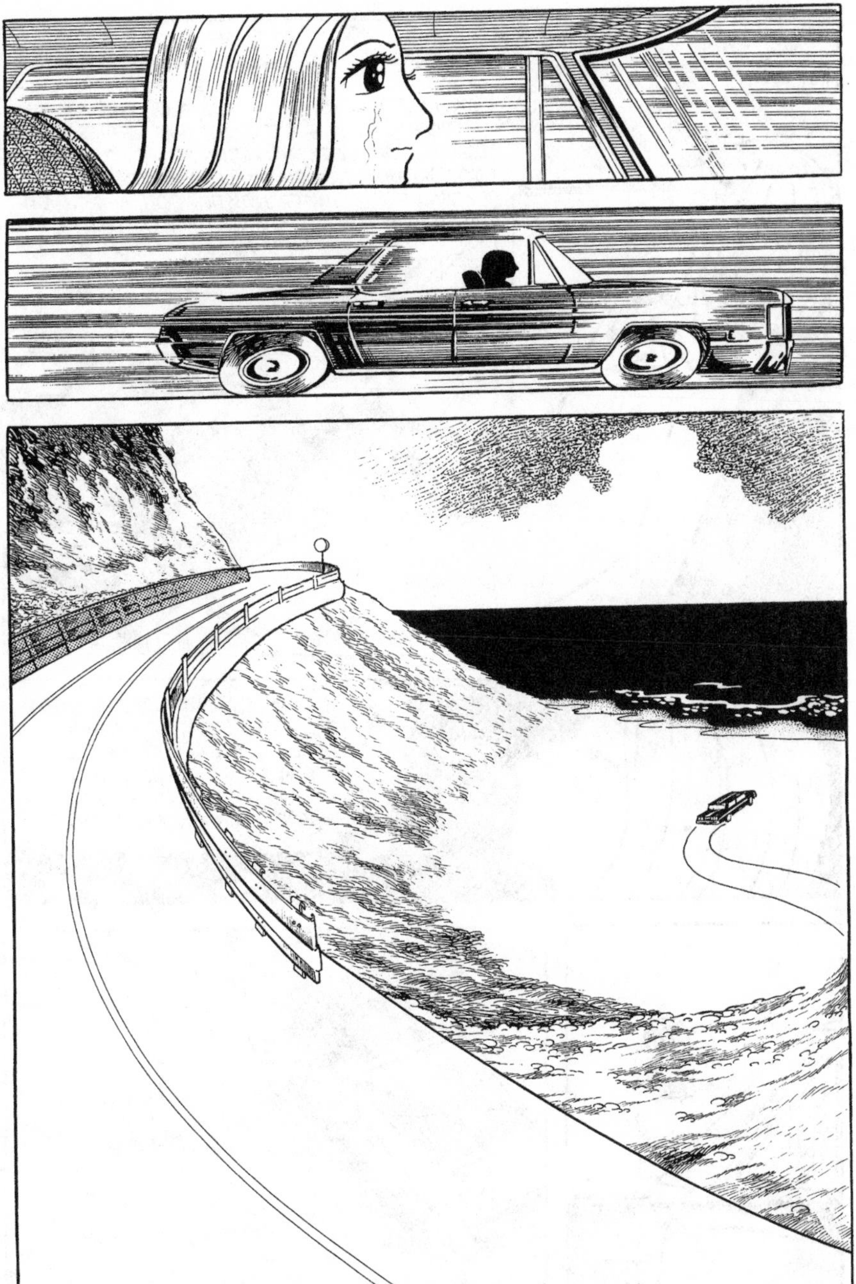

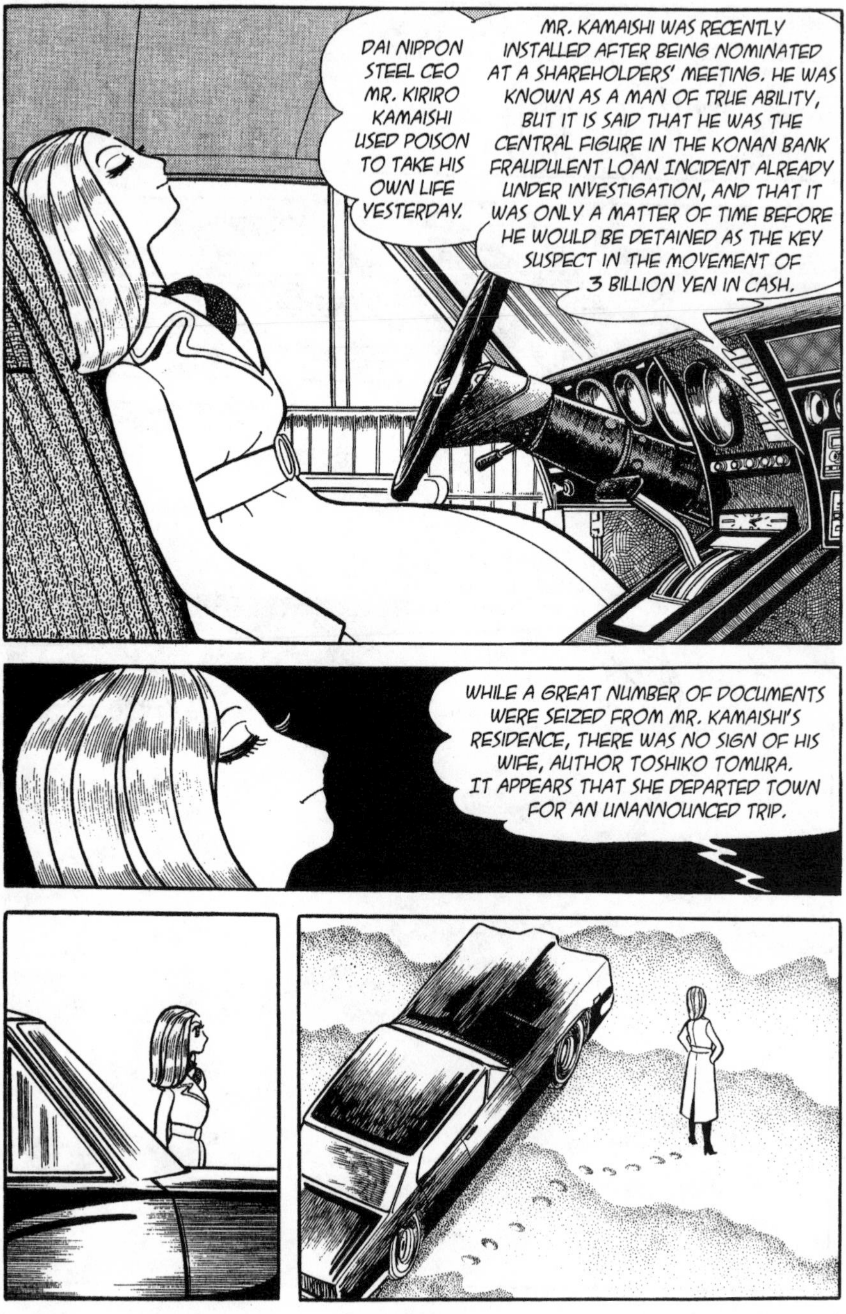
DAI NIPPON STEEL CEO MR. KIRIRO KAMAISHI USED POISON TO TAKE HIS OWN LIFE YESTERDAY.
MR. KAMAISHI WAS RECENTLY INSTALLED AFTER BEING NOMINATED AT A SHAREHOLDERS' MEETING. HE WAS KNOWN AS A MAN OF TRUE ABILITY, BUT IT IS SAID THAT HE WAS THE CENTRAL FIGURE IN THE KONAN BANK FRAUDULENT LOAN INCIDENT ALREADY UNDER INVESTIGATION, AND THAT IT WAS ONLY A MATTER OF TIME BEFORE HE WOULD BE DETAINED AS THE KEY SUSPECT IN THE MOVEMENT OF 3 BILLION YEN IN CASH.
WHILE A GREAT NUMBER OF DOCUMENTS WERE SEIZED FROM MR. KAMAISHI'S RESIDENCE, THERE WAS NO SIGN OF HIS WIFE, AUTHOR TOSHIKO TOMURA. IT APPEARS THAT SHE DEPARTED TOWN FOR AN UNANNOUNCED TRIP.

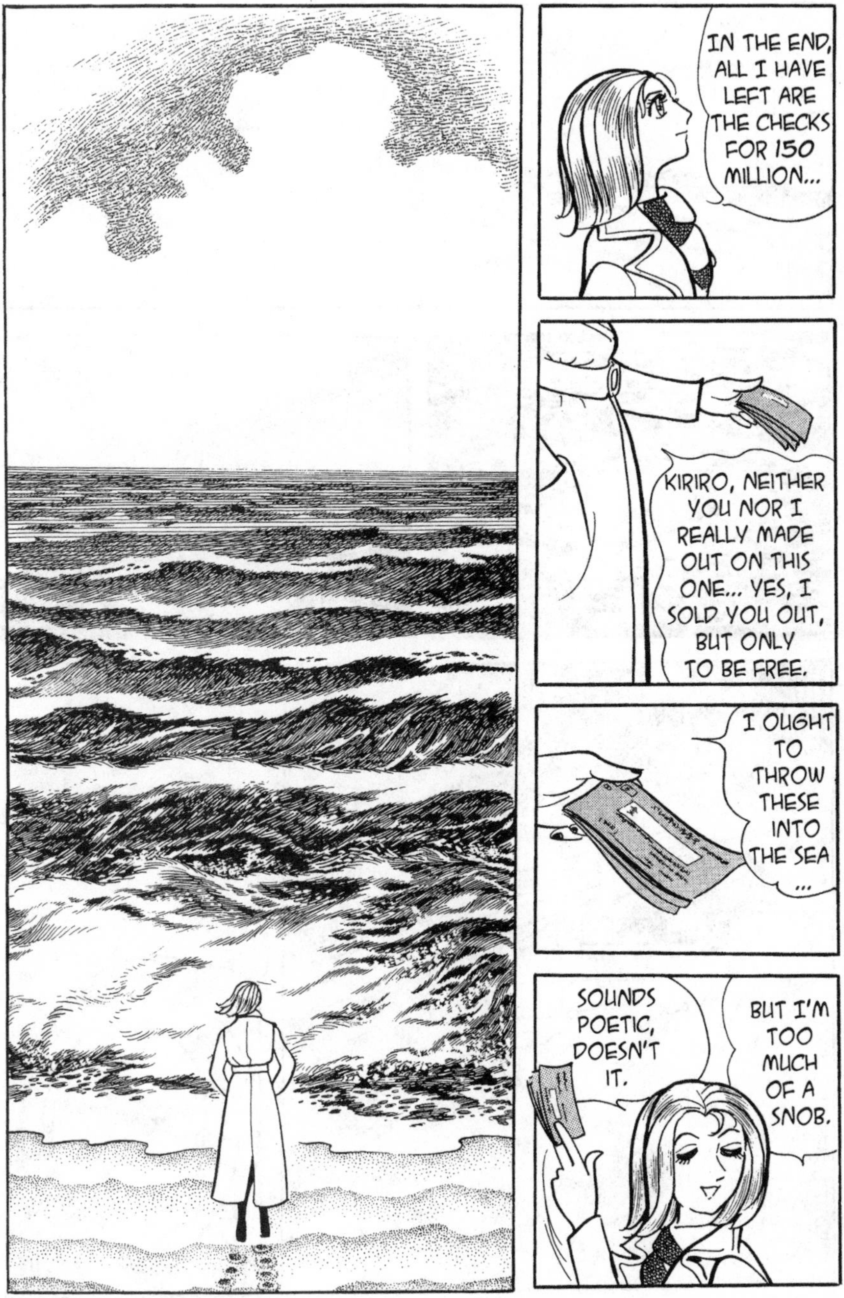
IN THE END, ALL I HAVE LEFT ARE THE CHECKS FOR 150 MILLION...
KIRIRO, NEITHER YOU NOR I REALLY MADE OUT ON THIS ONE... YES, I SOLD YOU OUT, BUT ONLY TO BE FREE.
I OUGHT TO THROW THESE INTO THE SEA ...
SOUNDS POETIC, DOESN'T IT.
BUT I'M TOO MUCH OF A SNOB.

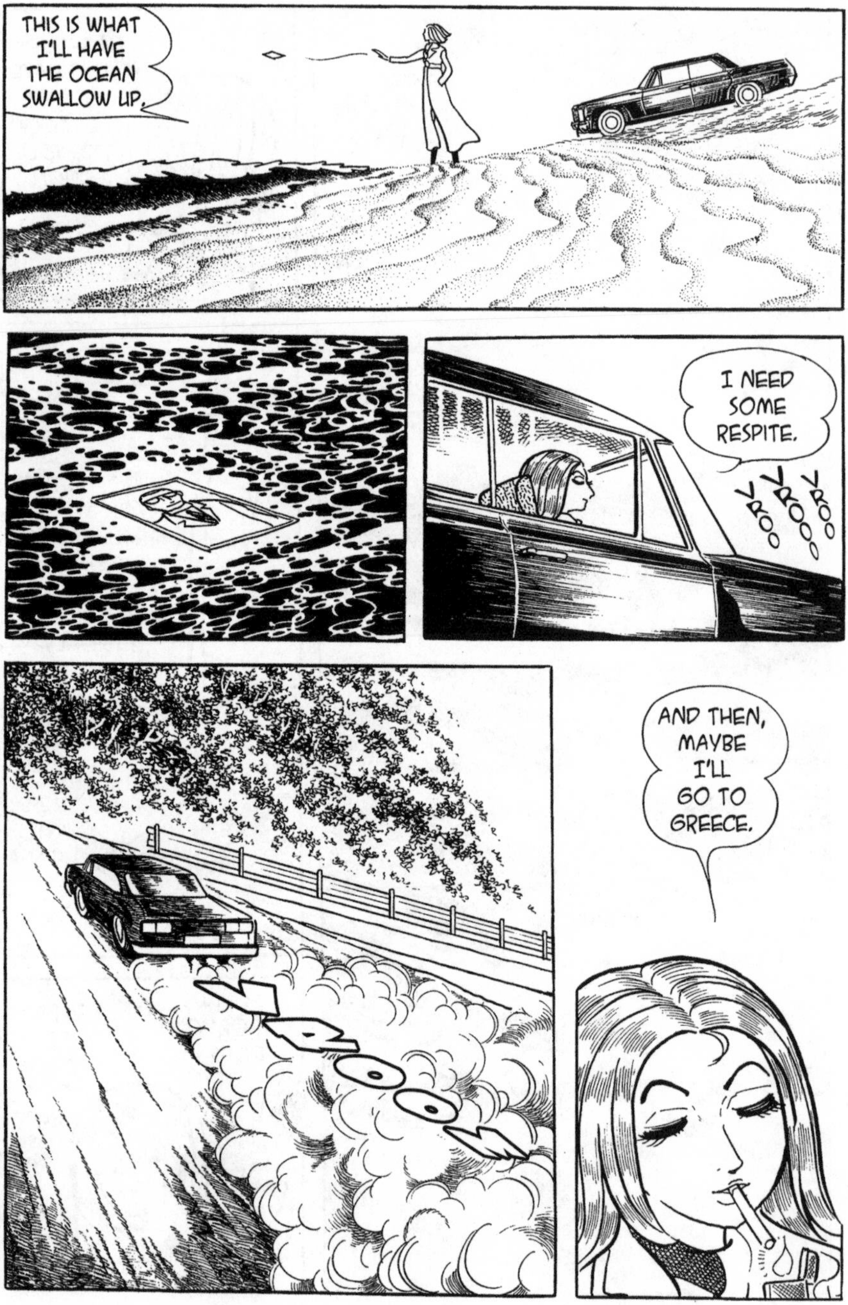
THIS IS WHAT I'LL HAVE THE OCEAN SWALLOW UP.
I NEED SOME RESPITE.
VROO
VROOOO
VROOO
AND THEN, MAYBE I'LL GO TO GREECE.
VROOOM

WELL-PLAYED, TOSHIKO.

THIS ROUND, I ADMIT DEFEAT.

MOMMA, I'M HOME.

YOU KNOW, I GOT PREGNANT, BUT I GOT RID OF IT.

A LOT HAPPENED THIS LAST TIME.

HERE, 150 MILLION IN CHECKS!

EVER SEEN SUCH A THING BEFORE, MOMMA?

AAH, I'M SO TIRED...

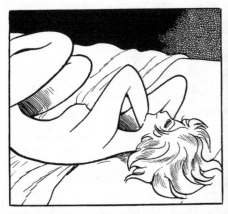

I FEEL SO EMPTY...

WHY SHOULD A WOMAN LIVING LIFE TO THE FULLEST ON HER OWN FEEL SO EMPTY?

MOMMA, I WANT... MR. MIZUNO !!

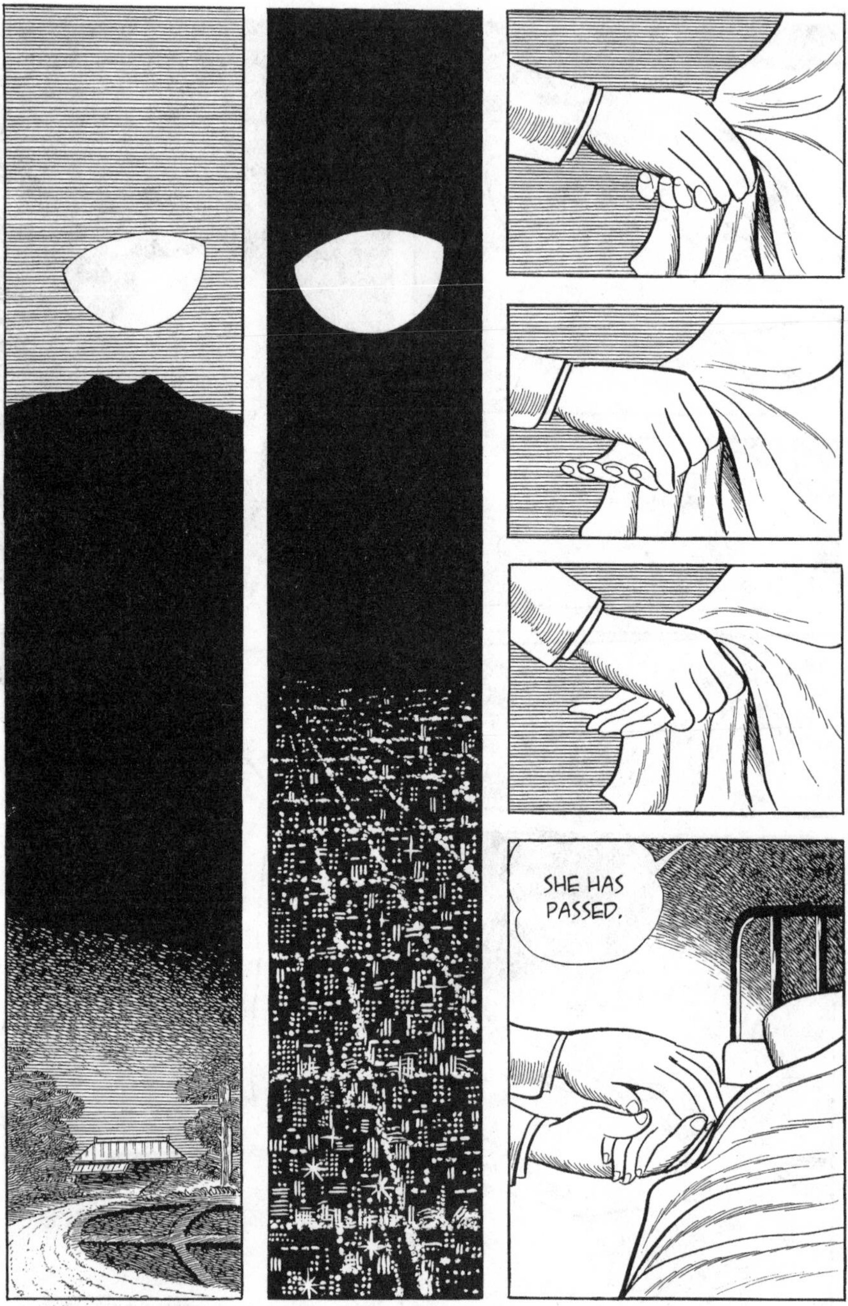
SHE HAS PASSED.

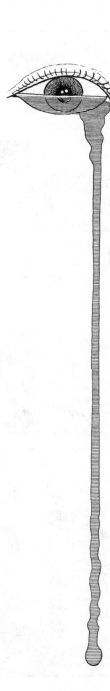

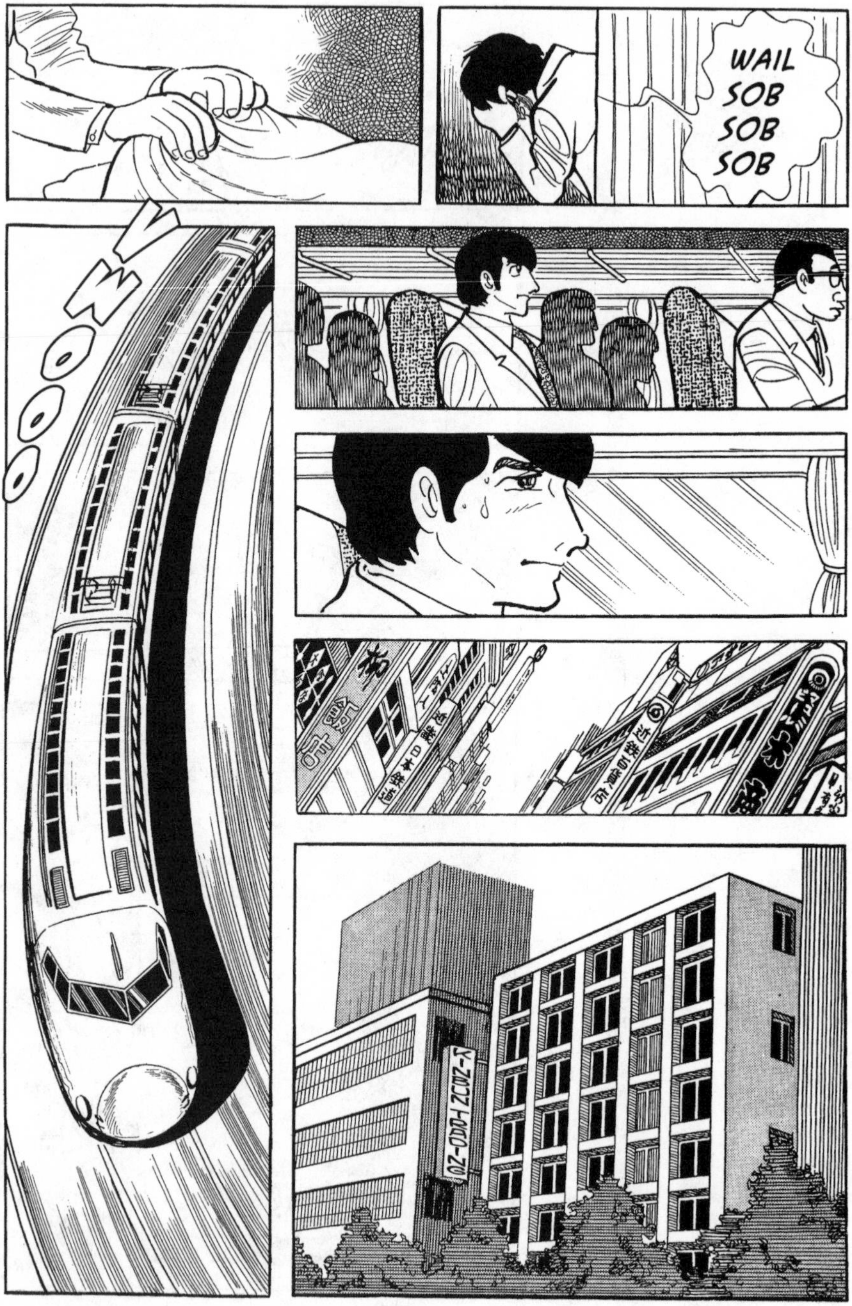
WAIL SOB SOB SOB
VWOOOO

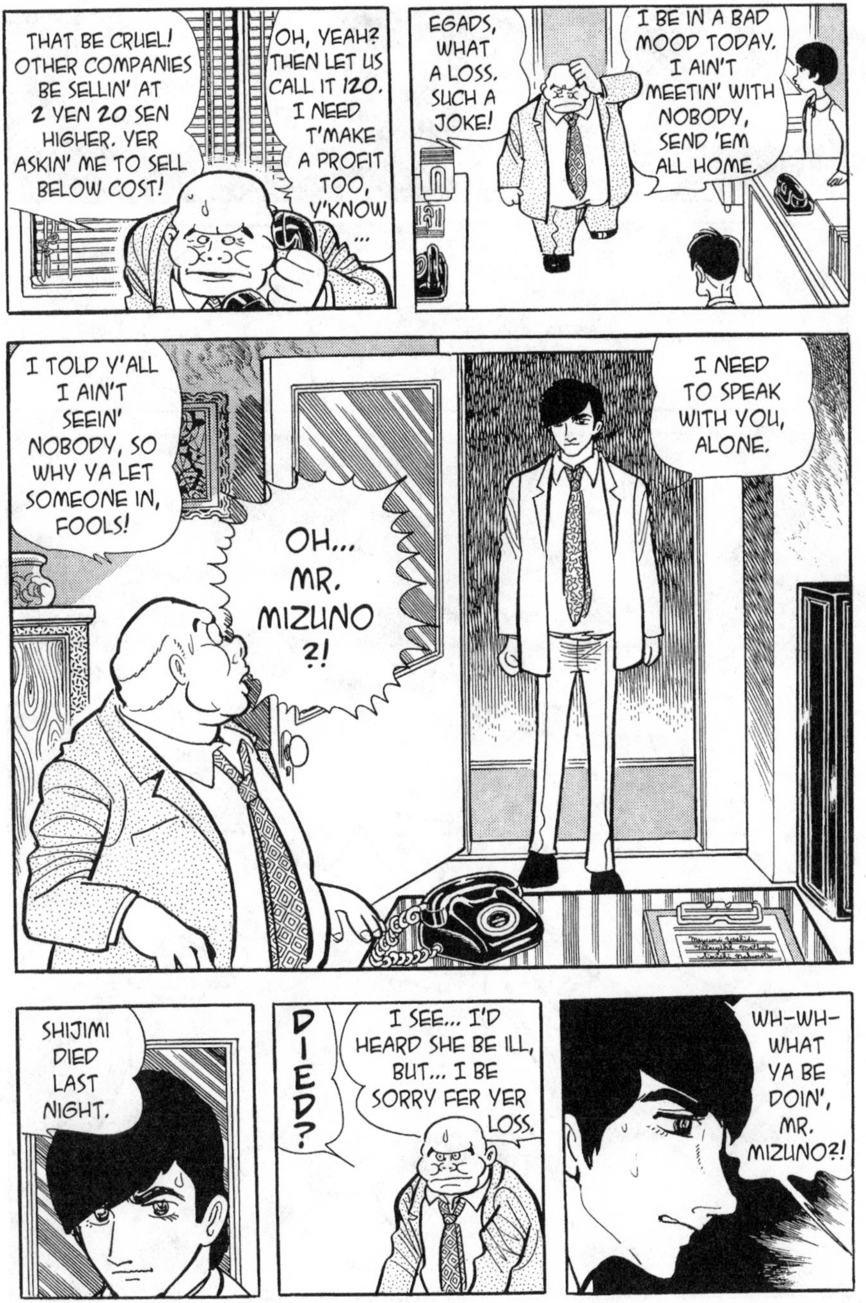
THAT BE CRUEL! OTHER COMPANIES BE SELLIN' AT 2 YEN 20 SEN HIGHER. YER ASKIN' ME TO SELL BELOW COST!
OH, YEAH? THEN LET US CALL IT 120. I NEED T'MAKE A PROFIT TOO, Y'KNOW ...
EGADS, WHAT A LOSS. SUCH A JOKE!
I BE IN A BAD MOOD TODAY. I AIN'T MEETIN' WITH NOBODY, SEND 'EM ALL HOME.
I TOLD Y'ALL I AIN'T SEEIN' NOBODY, SO WHY YA LET SOMEONE IN, FOOLS!
OH... MR. MIZUNO?!
I NEED TO SPEAK WITH YOU, ALONE.
SHIJIMI DIED LAST NIGHT.
DIED?
I SEE... I'D HEARD SHE BE ILL, BUT... I BE SORRY FER YER LOSS.
WH-WH-WHAT YA BE DOIN', MR. MIZUNO?!

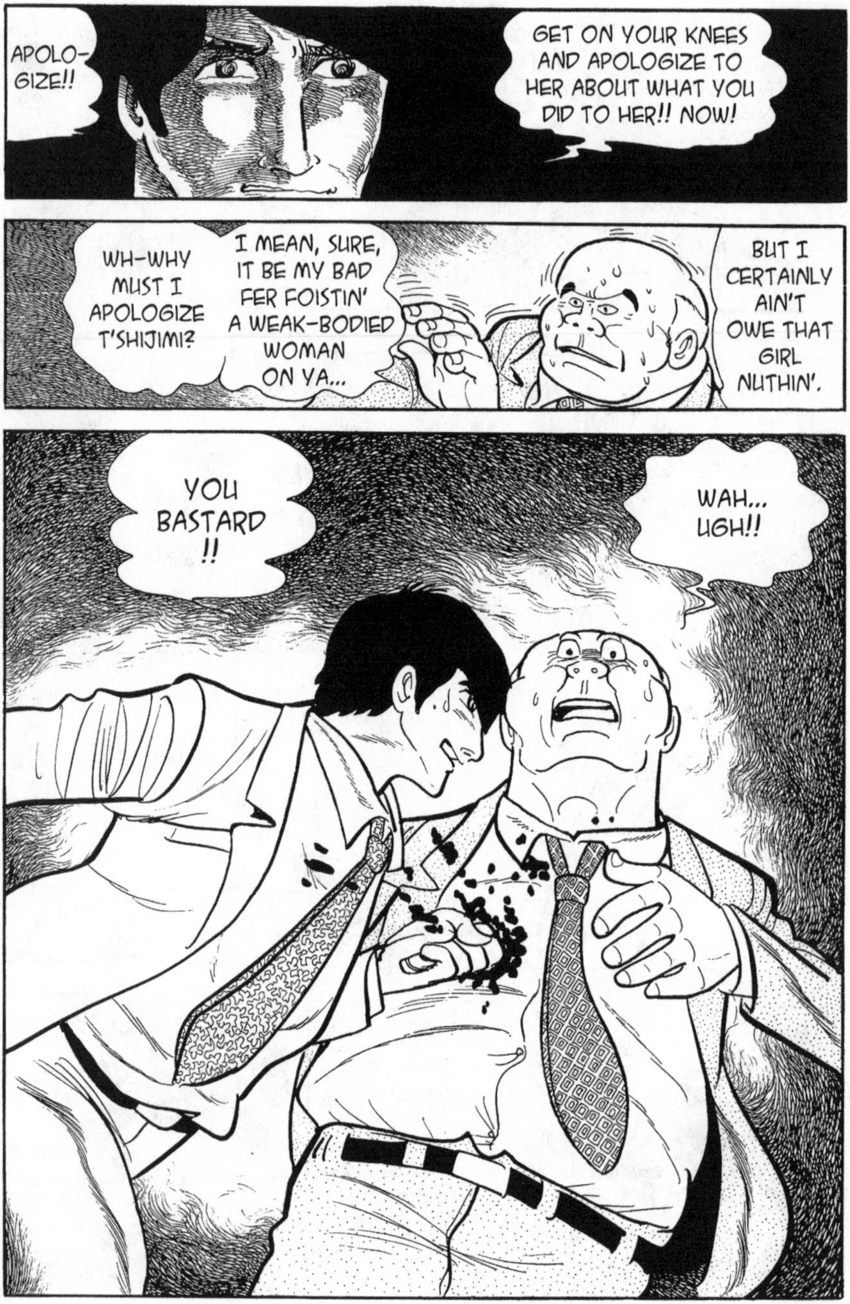
APOLOGIZE!!
GET ON YOUR KNEES AND APOLOGIZE TO HER ABOUT WHAT YOU DID TO HER!! NOW!
WH-WHY MUST I APOLOGIZE T'SHIJIMI?
I MEAN, SURE, IT BE MY BAD FER FOISTIN' A WEAK-BODIED WOMAN ON YA...
BUT I CERTAINLY AIN'T OWE THAT GIRL NUTHIN'.
YOU BASTARD!!
WAH... UGH!!

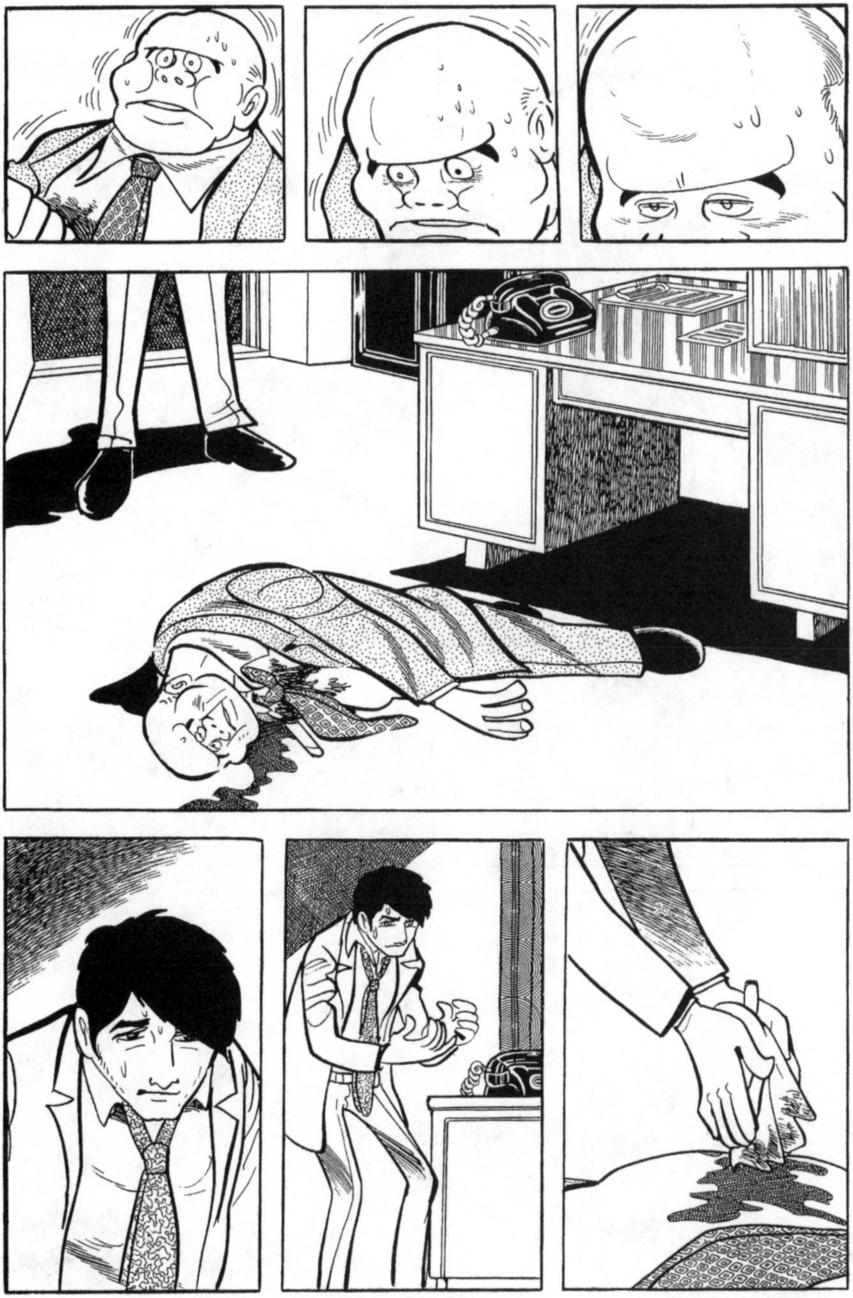

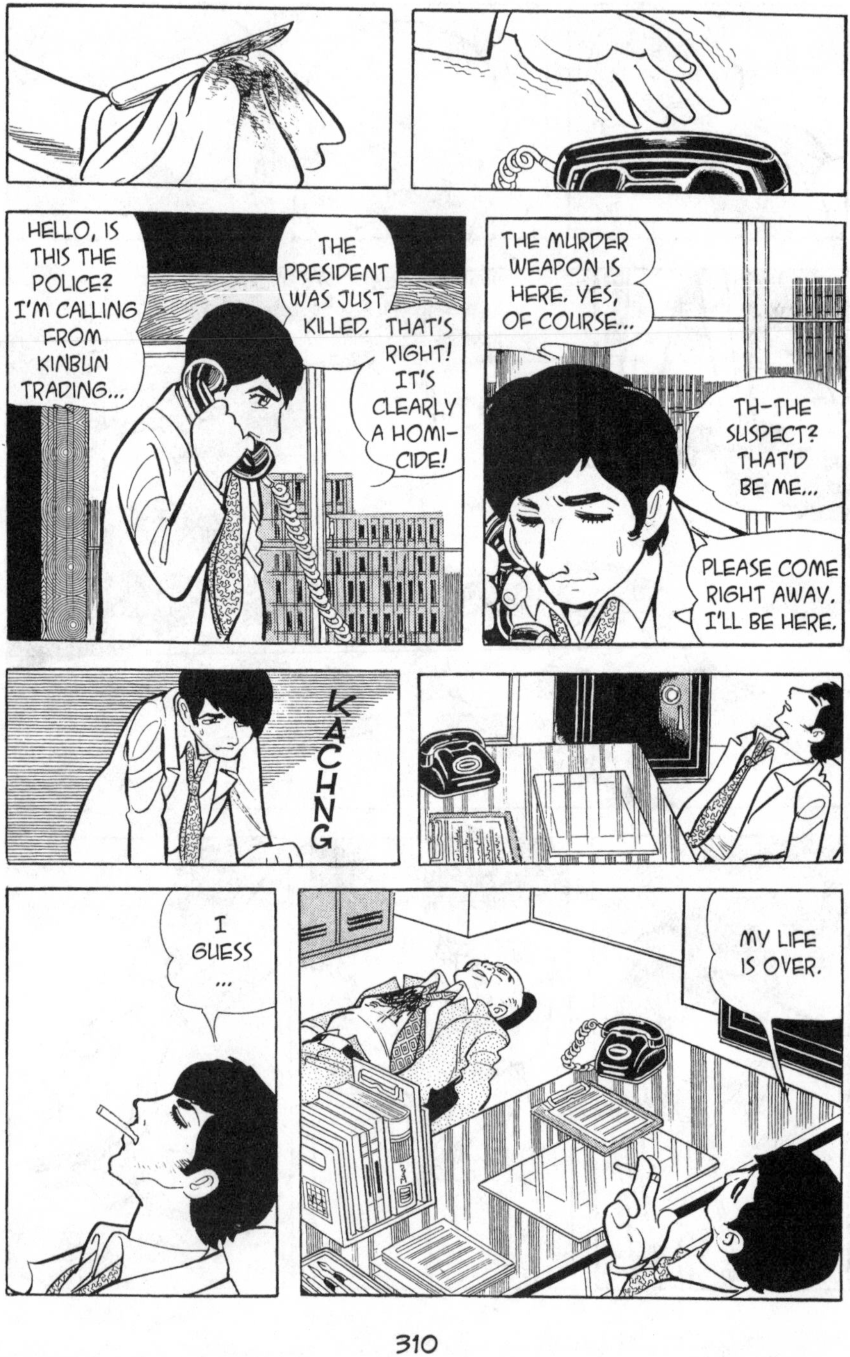

HELLO, IS THIS THE POLICE? I'M CALLING FROM KINBUN TRADING...
THE PRESIDENT WAS JUST KILLED.
THAT'S RIGHT! IT'S CLEARLY A HOMI-CIDE!
THE MURDER WEAPON IS HERE. YES, OF COURSE...
TH-THE SUSPECT? THAT'D BE ME...
PLEASE COME RIGHT AWAY. I'LL BE HERE.
KACHNG
I GUESS ...
MY LIFE IS OVER.

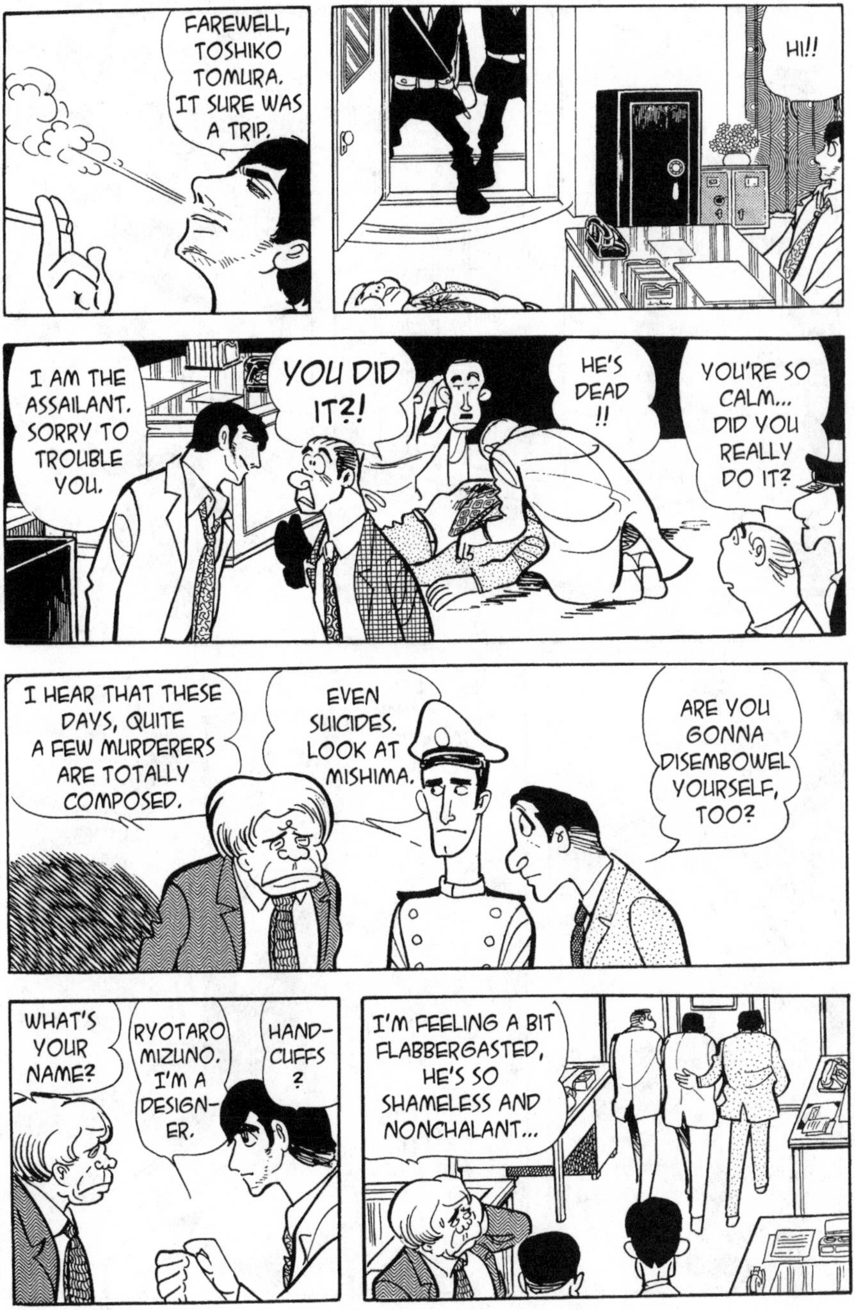
FAREWELL, TOSHIKO TOMURA. IT SURE WAS A TRIP.
HI!!
I AM THE ASSAILANT. SORRY TO TROUBLE YOU.
YOU DID IT?!
HE'S DEAD !!
YOU'RE SO CALM... DID YOU REALLY DO IT?
I HEAR THAT THESE DAYS, QUITE A FEW MURDERERS ARE TOTALLY COMPOSED.
EVEN SUICIDES. LOOK AT MISHIMA.
ARE YOU GONNA DISEMBOWEL YOURSELF, TOO?
WHAT'S YOUR NAME?
RYOTARO MIZUNO. I'M A DESIGNER.
HANDCUFFS ?
I'M FEELING A BIT FLABBERGASTED, HE'S SO SHAMELESS AND NONCHALANT...

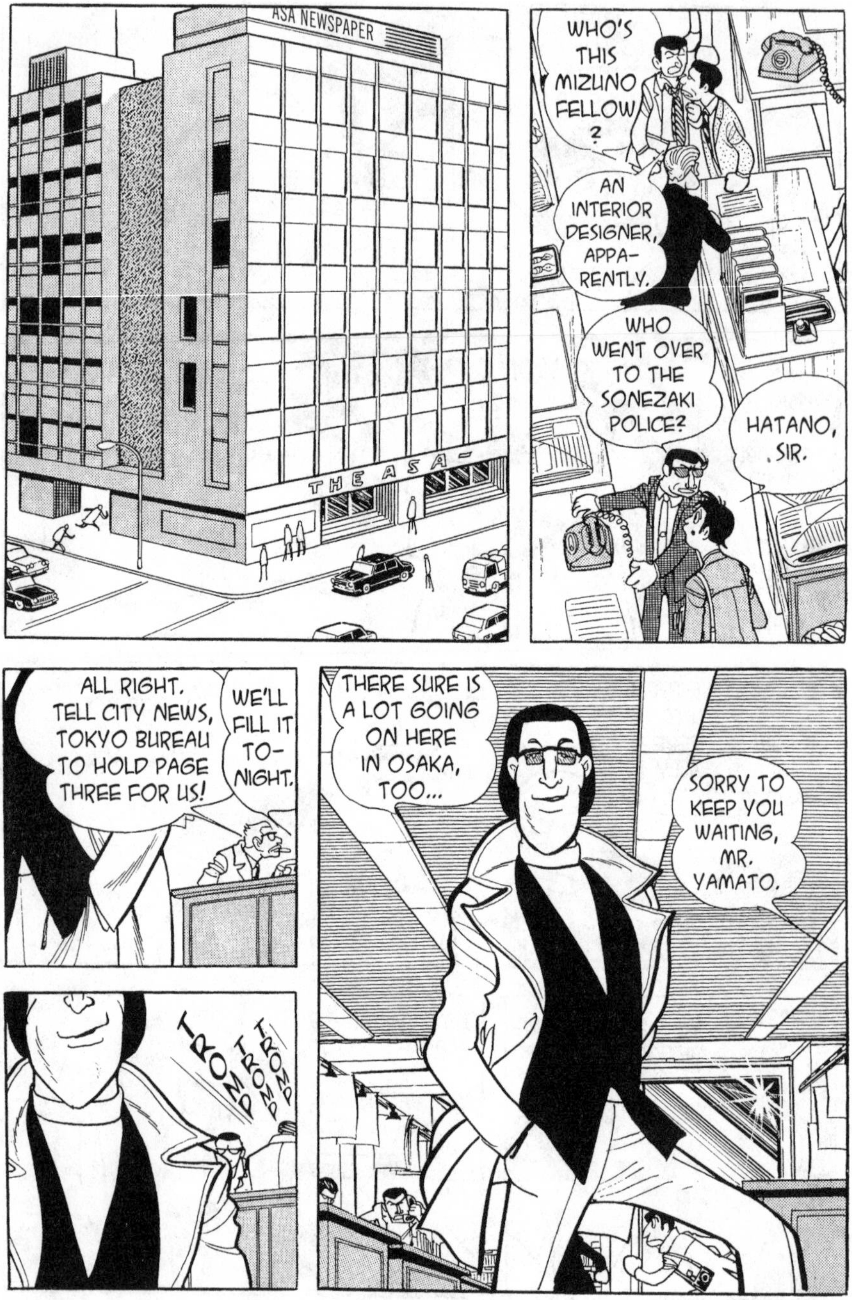
ASA NEWSPAPER
THE ASA–
WHO'S THIS MIZUNO FELLOW?
AN INTERIOR DESIGNER, APPA-RENTLY.
WHO WENT OVER TO THE SONEZAKI POLICE?
HATANO, SIR.
ALL RIGHT. TELL CITY NEWS, TOKYO BUREAU TO HOLD PAGE THREE FOR US!
WE'LL FILL IT TO-NIGHT.
TROMP
TROMP
TROMP
THERE SURE IS A LOT GOING ON HERE IN OSAKA, TOO...
SORRY TO KEEP YOU WAITING, MR. YAMATO.

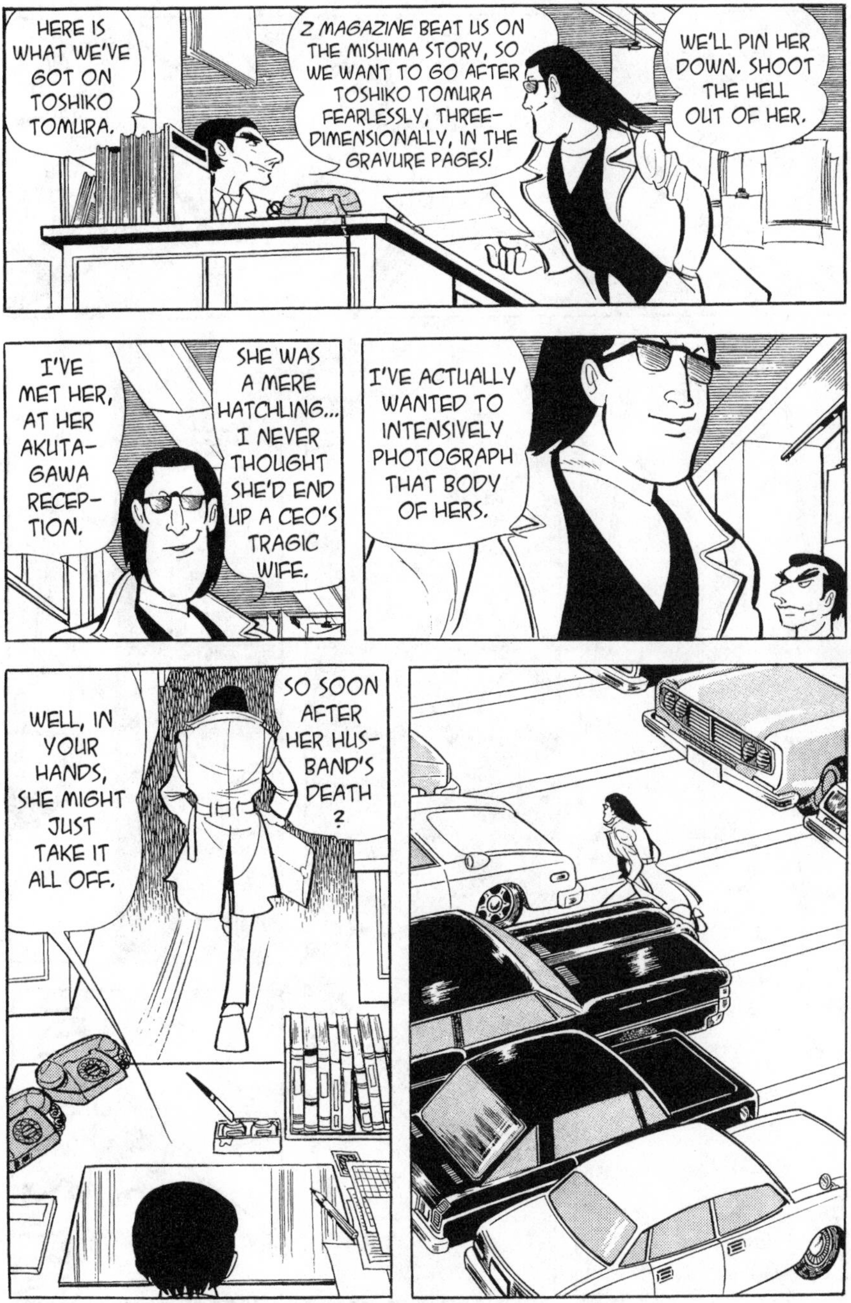
HERE IS WHAT WE'VE GOT ON TOSHIKO TOMURA.
Z MAGAZINE BEAT US ON THE MISHIMA STORY, SO WE WANT TO GO AFTER TOSHIKO TOMURA FEARLESSLY, THREE-DIMENSIONALLY, IN THE GRAVURE PAGES!
WE'LL PIN HER DOWN. SHOOT THE HELL OUT OF HER.
I'VE MET HER, AT HER AKUTA-GAWA RECEP-TION.
SHE WAS A MERE HATCHLING... I NEVER THOUGHT SHE'D END UP A CEO'S TRAGIC WIFE.
I'VE ACTUALLY WANTED TO INTENSIVELY PHOTOGRAPH THAT BODY OF HERS.
WELL, IN YOUR HANDS, SHE MIGHT JUST TAKE IT ALL OFF.
SO SOON AFTER HER HUS-BAND'S DEATH ?

MY GUT'S NOT FAILED ME THESE TEN-PLUS YEARS.
I GOTTA GO CHECK OUT HER BIRTHPLACE...
SHE SAYS SHE'S ON A TRIP, BUT SHE MAY BE HIDING THERE...
DAILY NEWS

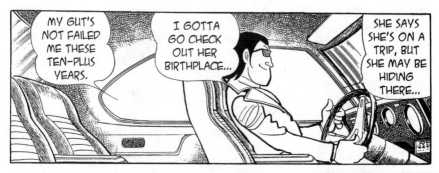

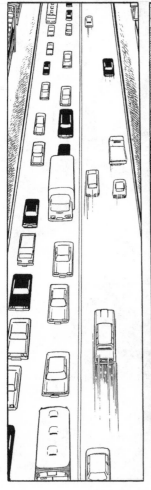

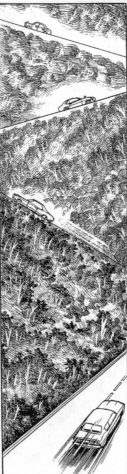

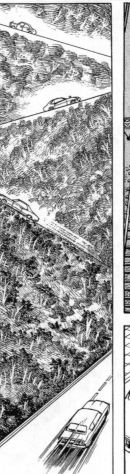

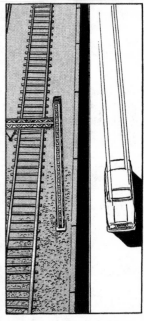

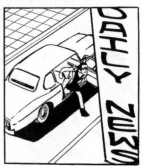

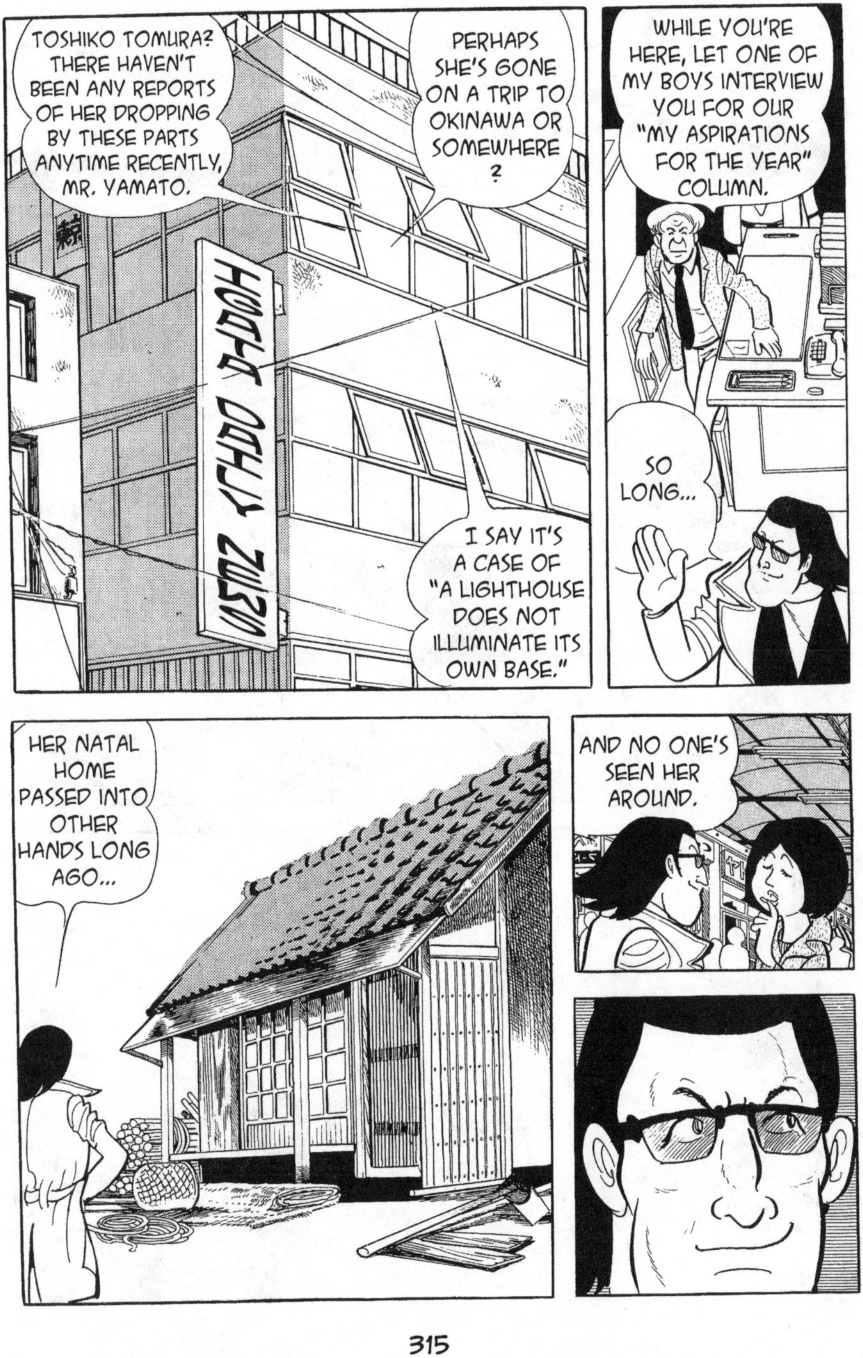
TOSHIKO TOMURA? THERE HAVEN'T BEEN ANY REPORTS OF HER DROPPING BY THESE PARTS ANYTIME RECENTLY, MR. YAMATO.
PERHAPS SHE'S GONE ON A TRIP TO OKINAWA OR SOMEWHERE ?
I SAY IT'S A CASE OF "A LIGHTHOUSE DOES NOT ILLUMINATE ITS OWN BASE."
WHILE YOU'RE HERE, LET ONE OF MY BOYS INTERVIEW YOU FOR OUR "MY ASPIRATIONS FOR THE YEAR" COLUMN.
SO LONG...
HER NATAL HOME PASSED INTO OTHER HANDS LONG AGO...
AND NO ONE'S SEEN HER AROUND.

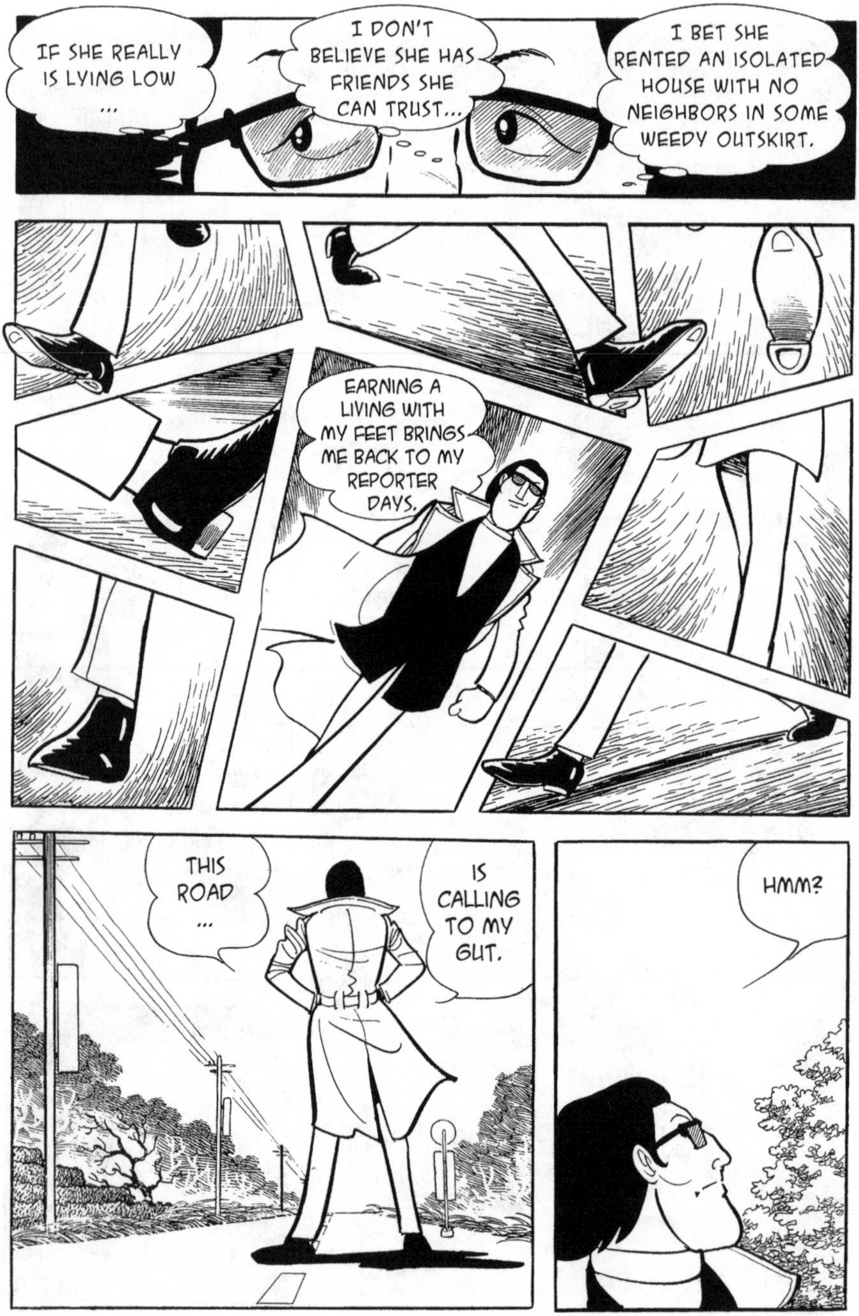
IF SHE REALLY IS LYING LOW ...
I DON'T BELIEVE SHE HAS FRIENDS SHE CAN TRUST...
I BET SHE RENTED AN ISOLATED HOUSE WITH NO NEIGHBORS IN SOME WEEDY OUTSKIRT.
EARNING A LIVING WITH MY FEET BRINGS ME BACK TO MY REPORTER DAYS.
THIS ROAD ...
IS CALLING TO MY GUT.
HMM?

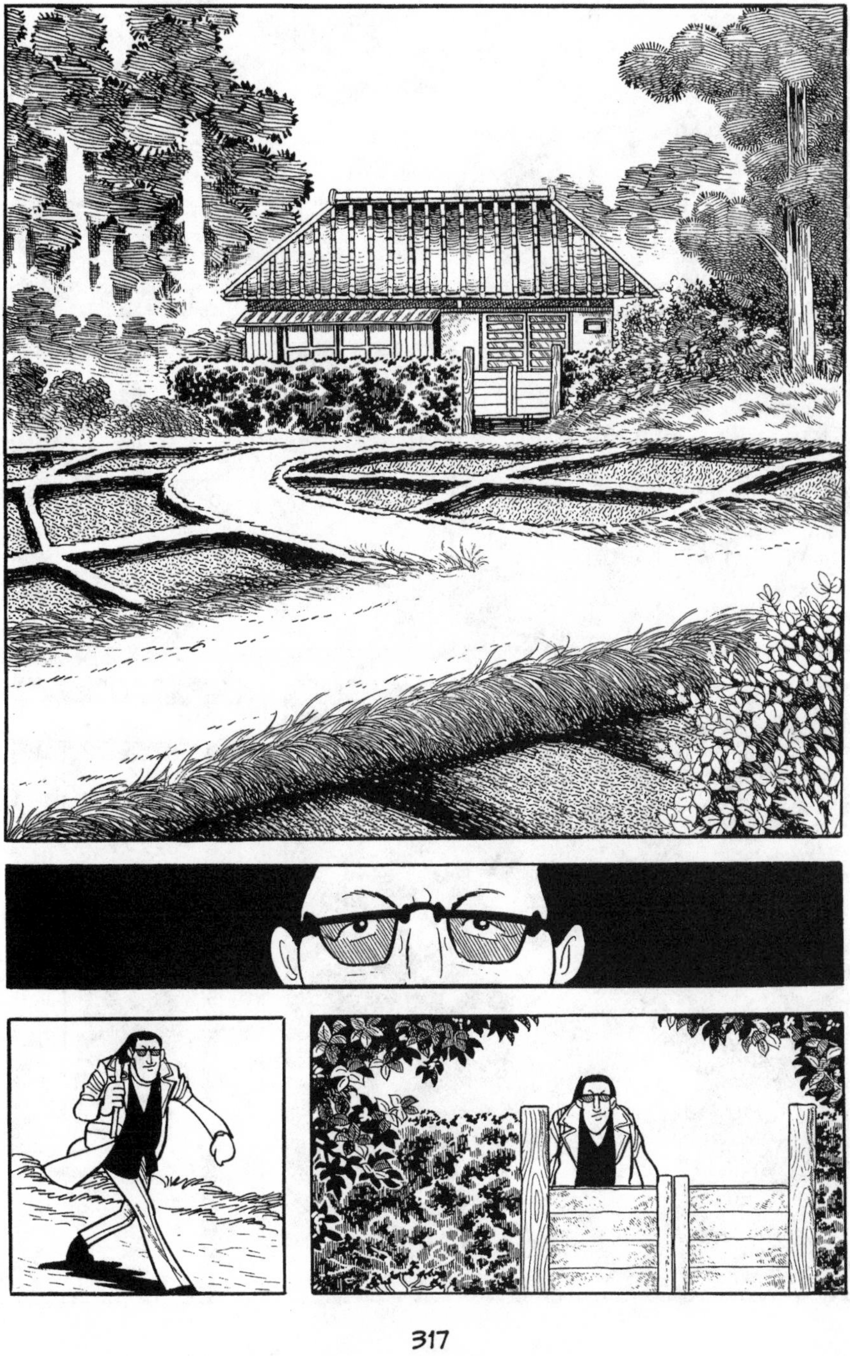

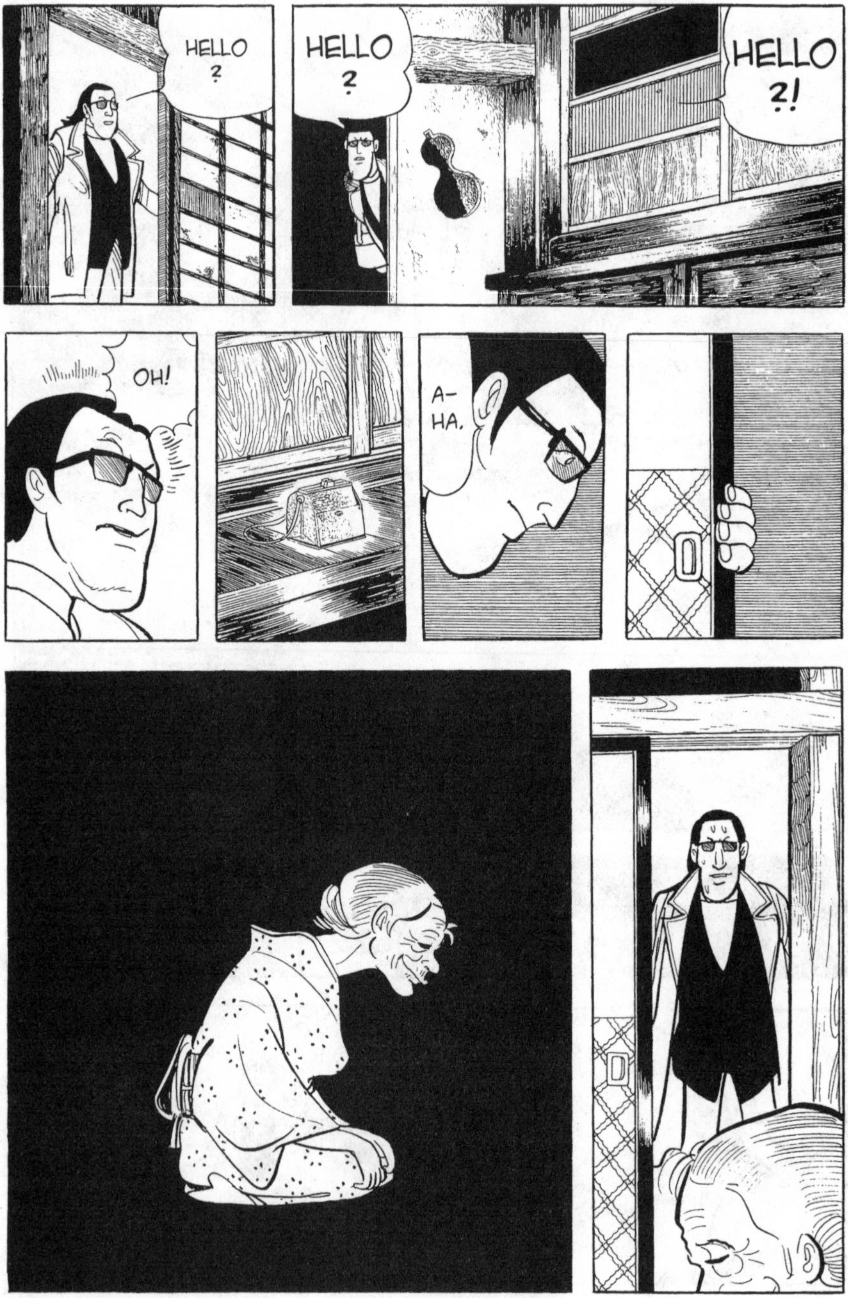
HELLO ?
HELLO ?
HELLO ?!
OH!
A-HA.

GEEZ
...

IT'S JUST A WAX FIGURE.

WHAT'S THIS DOING HERE?

A MAT-TRESS AND BLANKET ...

AND THE OUTLINE OF A PERSON.

BIN-GO!

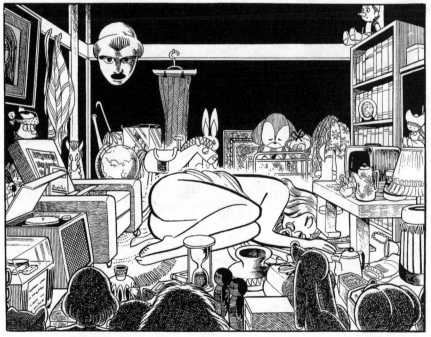

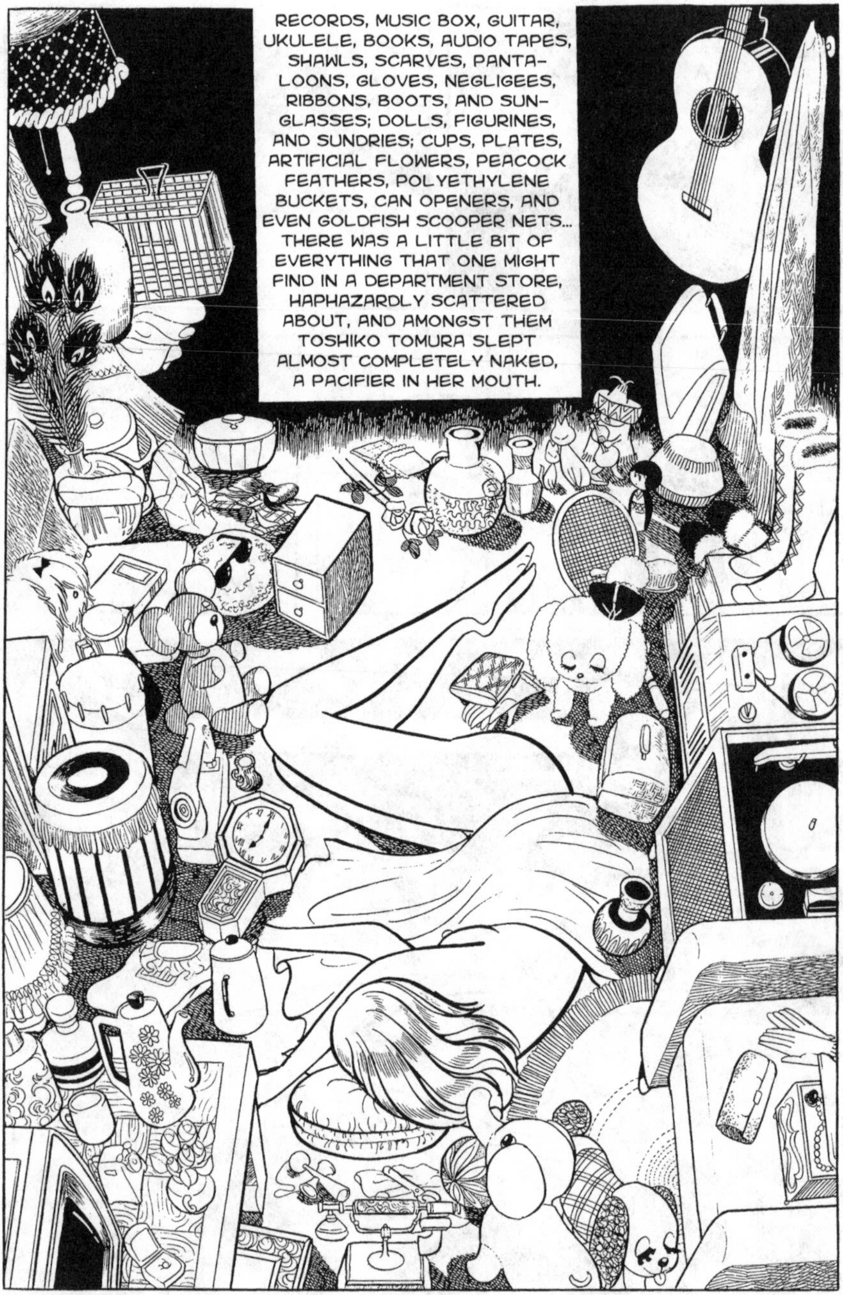
RECORDS, MUSIC BOX, GUITAR, UKULELE, BOOKS, AUDIO TAPES, SHAWLS, SCARVES, PANTA-LOONS, GLOVES, NEGLIGEES, RIBBONS, BOOTS, AND SUN-GLASSES; DOLLS, FIGURINES, AND SUNDRIES; CUPS, PLATES, ARTIFICIAL FLOWERS, PEACOCK FEATHERS, POLYETHYLENE BUCKETS, CAN OPENERS, AND EVEN GOLDFISH SCOOPER NETS... THERE WAS A LITTLE BIT OF EVERYTHING THAT ONE MIGHT FIND IN A DEPARTMENT STORE, HAPHAZARDLY SCATTERED ABOUT, AND AMONGST THEM TOSHIKO TOMURA SLEPT ALMOST COMPLETELY NAKED, A PACIFIER IN HER MOUTH.

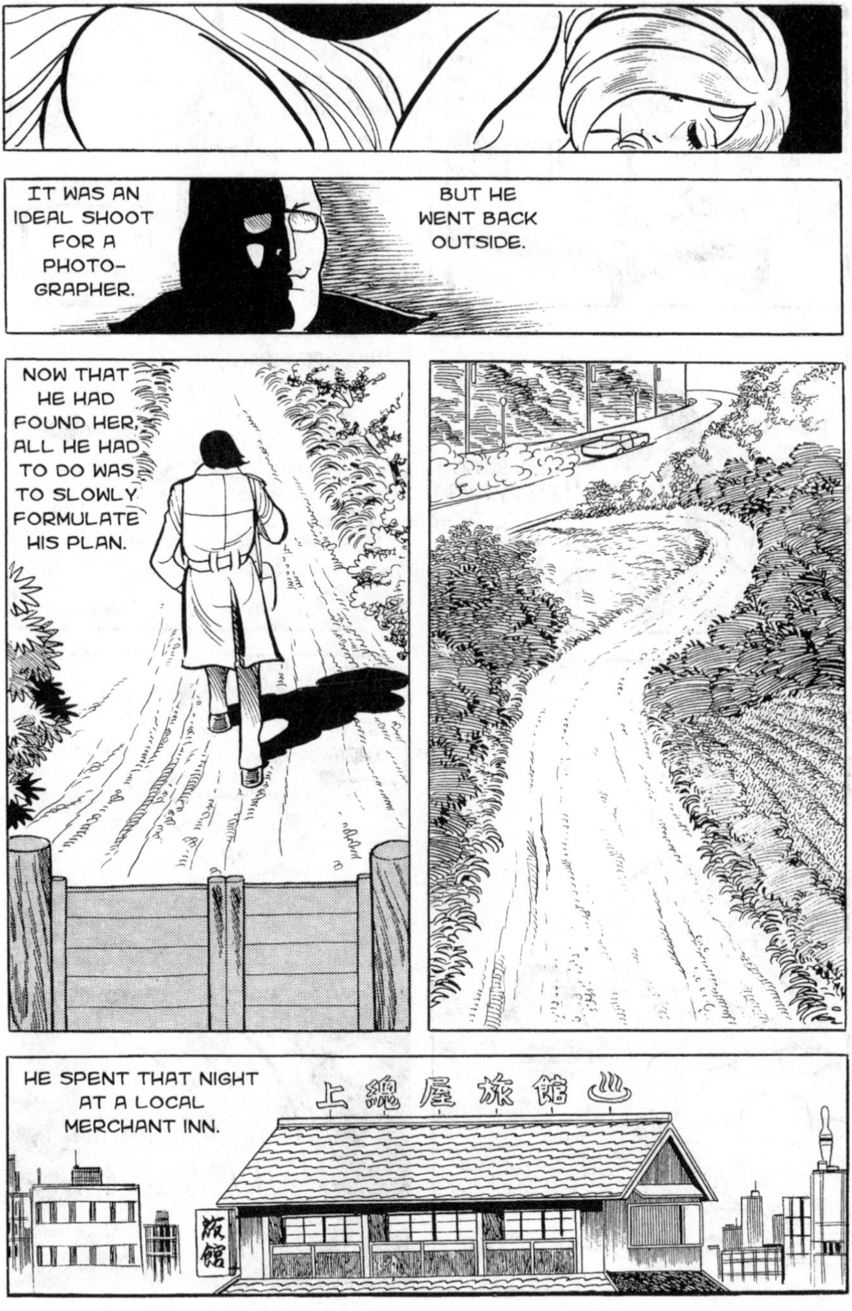
IT WAS AN IDEAL SHOOT FOR A PHOTO-GRAPHER.
BUT HE WENT BACK OUTSIDE.
NOW THAT HE HAD FOUND HER, ALL HE HAD TO DO WAS TO SLOWLY FORMULATE HIS PLAN.
HE SPENT THAT NIGHT AT A LOCAL MERCHANT INN.
上総屋旅館
旅館

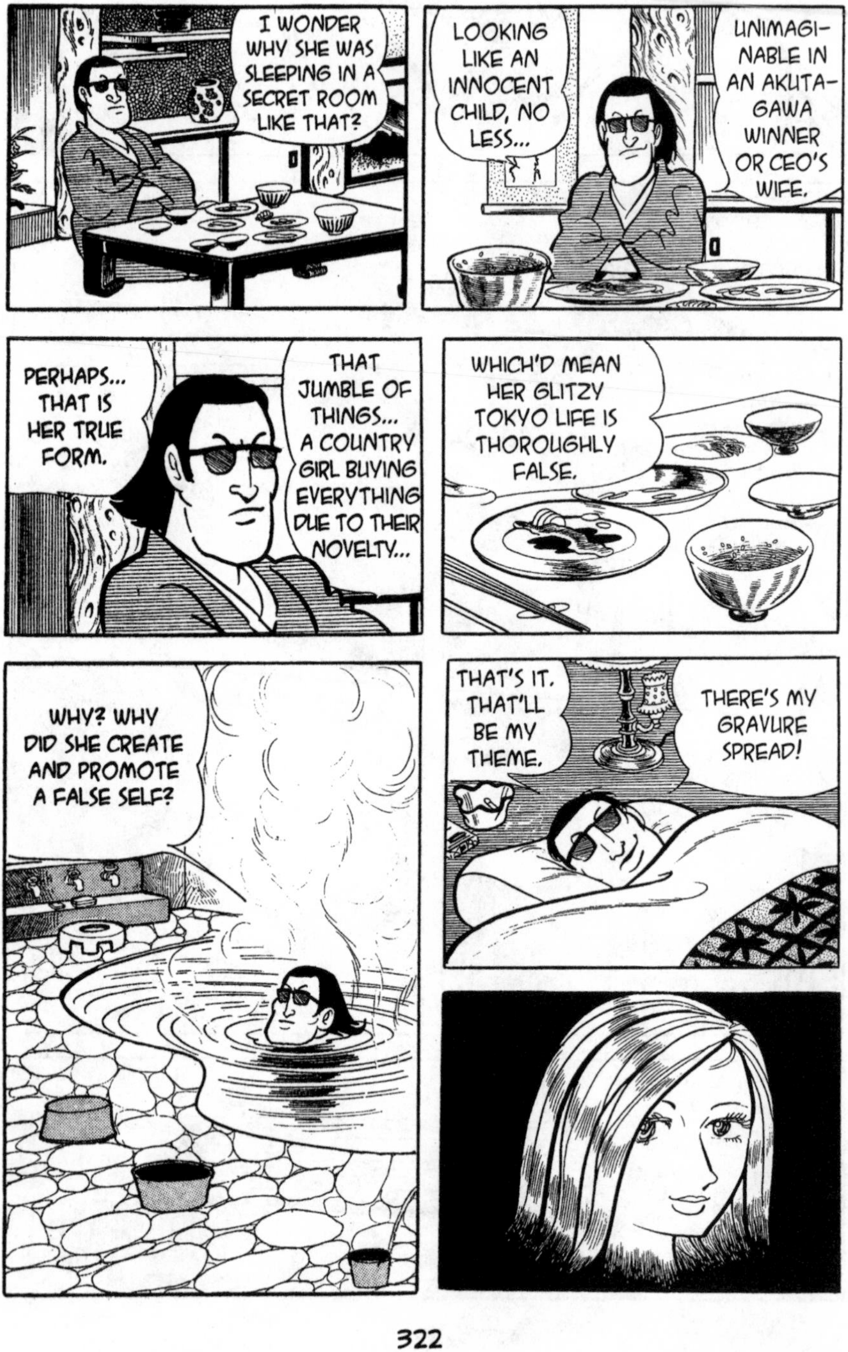
I WONDER WHY SHE WAS SLEEPING IN A SECRET ROOM LIKE THAT?
LOOKING LIKE AN INNOCENT CHILD, NO LESS...
UNIMAGINABLE IN AN AKUTAGAWA WINNER OR CEO'S WIFE.
PERHAPS... THAT IS HER TRUE FORM.
THAT JUMBLE OF THINGS... A COUNTRY GIRL BUYING EVERYTHING DUE TO THEIR NOVELTY...
WHICH'D MEAN HER GLITZY TOKYO LIFE IS THOROUGHLY FALSE.
WHY? WHY DID SHE CREATE AND PROMOTE A FALSE SELF?
THAT'S IT. THAT'LL BE MY THEME.
THERE'S MY GRAVURE SPREAD!

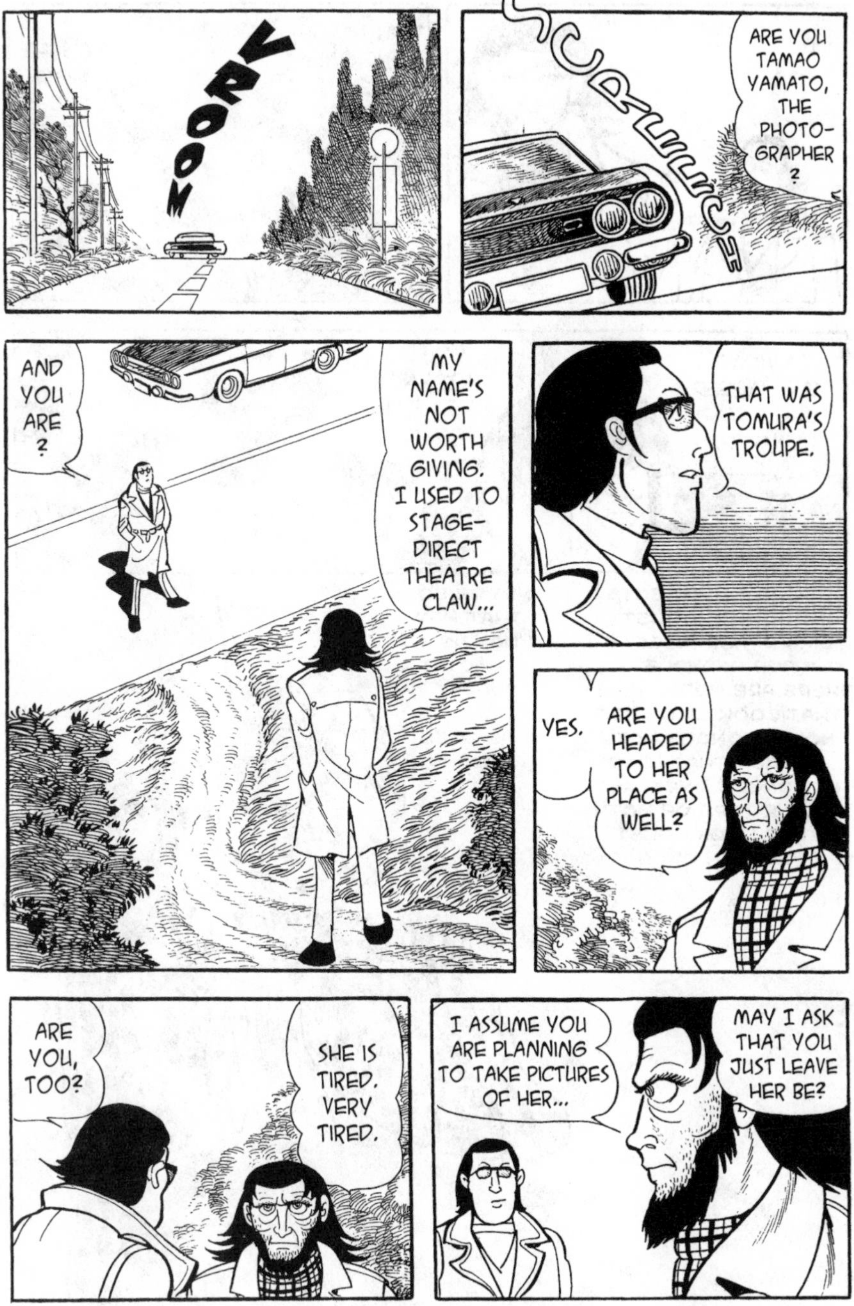
VROOOM
ARE YOU TAMAO YAMATO, THE PHOTO-GRAPHER?
AND YOU ARE?
MY NAME'S NOT WORTH GIVING. I USED TO STAGE-DIRECT THEATRE CLAW...
THAT WAS TOMURA'S TROUPE.
YES.
ARE YOU HEADED TO HER PLACE AS WELL?
ARE YOU, TOO?
SHE IS TIRED. VERY TIRED.
I ASSUME YOU ARE PLANNING TO TAKE PICTURES OF HER...
MAY I ASK THAT YOU JUST LEAVE HER BE?

WHY ?

THAT HOUSE IS THE ONLY PLACE SHE CAN RELAX,

A SAFE SPACE LIKE A WOMB.

A WOMB... AND INDEED, SHE IS STARK NAKED.

YOU DO NOT KNOW HER TRUE FORM...

THERE ARE INSECTS THAT LOOK JUST LIKE OTHER INSECTS. FOR EXAMPLE, THERE ARE HORSE FLIES THAT LOOK LIKE BEES, NONPOISONOUS MOTH SPECIES THAT MIMIC POISONOUS ONES, AND EVEN A TYPE OF MOTH THAT LOOKS JUST LIKE AN OWL!

THEY'RE BORN THAT WAY, KNOWING TO MIMIC TO SURVIVE...

AS DOES SHE!

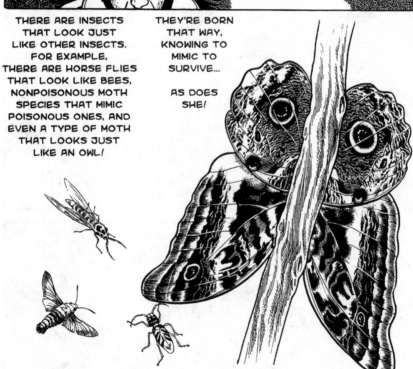

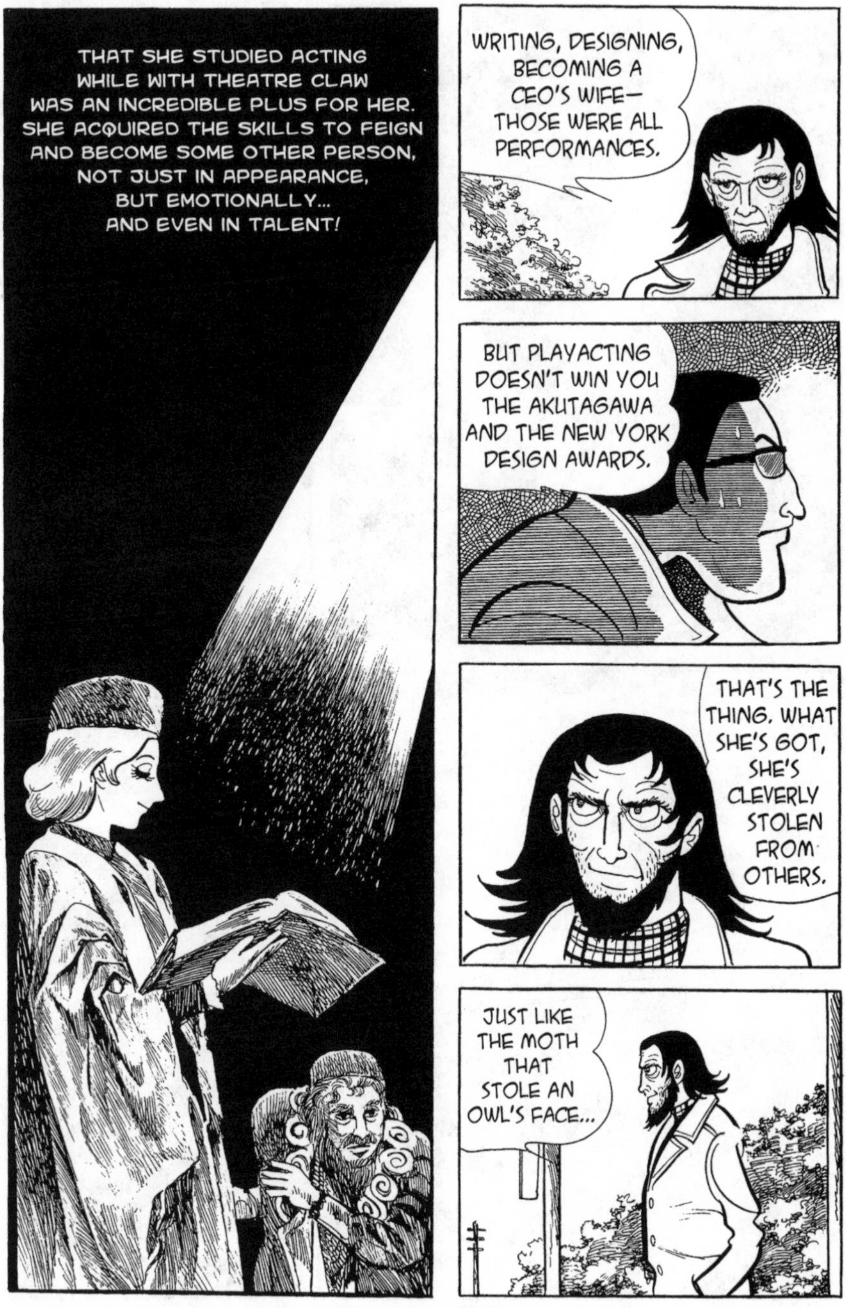
THAT SHE STUDIED ACTING WHILE WITH THEATRE CLAW WAS AN INCREDIBLE PLUS FOR HER. SHE ACQUIRED THE SKILLS TO FEIGN AND BECOME SOME OTHER PERSON, NOT JUST IN APPEARANCE, BUT EMOTIONALLY... AND EVEN IN TALENT!
WRITING, DESIGNING, BECOMING A CEO'S WIFE— THOSE WERE ALL PERFORMANCES.
BUT PLAYACTING DOESN'T WIN YOU THE AKUTAGAWA AND THE NEW YORK DESIGN AWARDS.
THAT'S THE THING. WHAT SHE'S GOT, SHE'S CLEVERLY STOLEN FROM OTHERS.
JUST LIKE THE MOTH THAT STOLE AN OWL'S FACE...

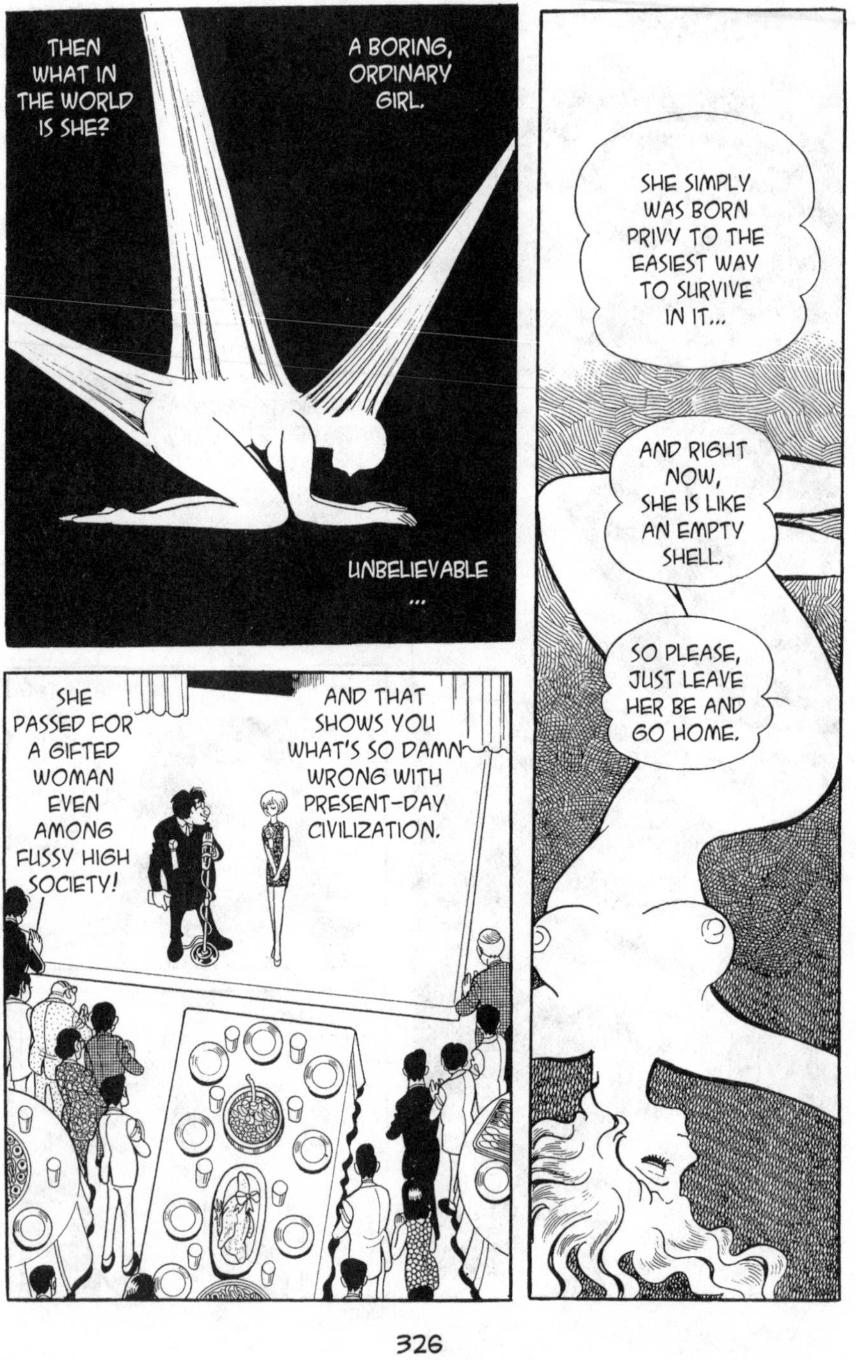
THEN WHAT IN THE WORLD IS SHE?
A BORING, ORDINARY GIRL.
UNBELIEVABLE ...
SHE PASSED FOR A GIFTED WOMAN EVEN AMONG FUSSY HIGH SOCIETY!
AND THAT SHOWS YOU WHAT'S SO DAMN WRONG WITH PRESENT-DAY CIVILIZATION.
SHE SIMPLY WAS BORN PRIVY TO THE EASIEST WAY TO SURVIVE IN IT...
AND RIGHT NOW, SHE IS LIKE AN EMPTY SHELL.
SO PLEASE, JUST LEAVE HER BE AND GO HOME.

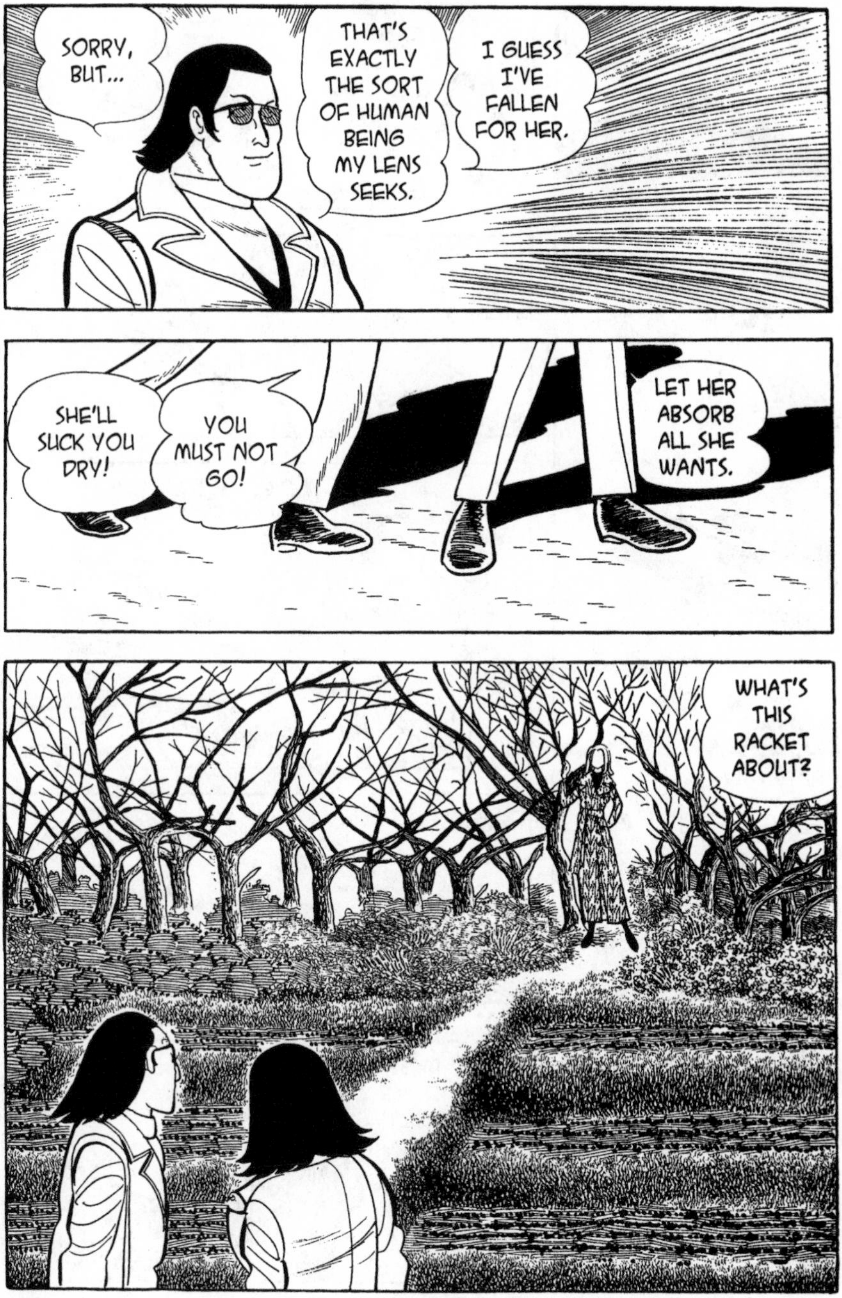

SORRY, BUT...
THAT'S EXACTLY THE SORT OF HUMAN BEING MY LENS SEEKS.
I GUESS I'VE FALLEN FOR HER.
SHE'LL SUCK YOU DRY!
YOU MUST NOT GO!
LET HER ABSORB ALL SHE WANTS.
WHAT'S THIS RACKET ABOUT?

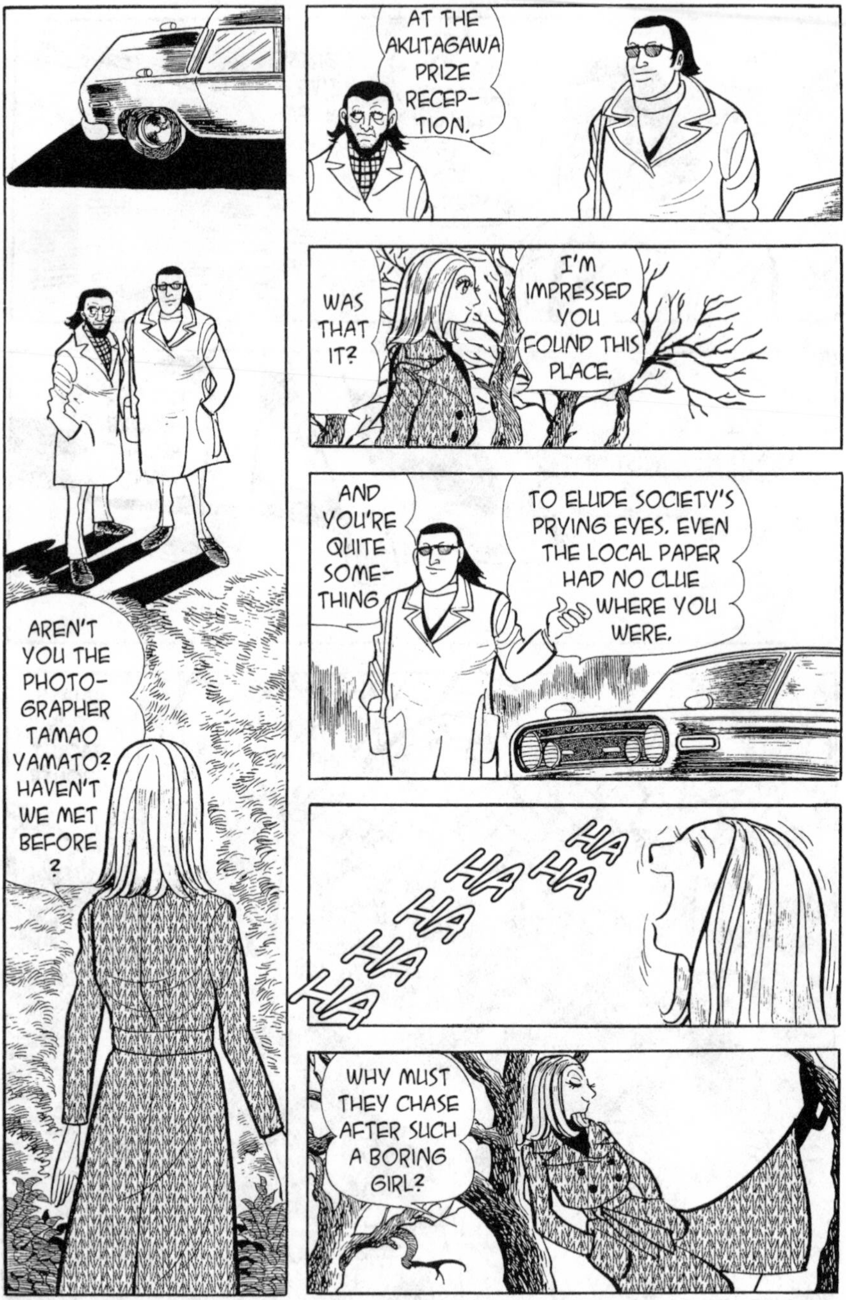
AREN'T YOU THE PHOTOGRAPHER TAMAO YAMATO? HAVEN'T WE MET BEFORE?
AT THE AKUTAGAWA PRIZE RECEPTION.
WAS THAT IT?
I'M IMPRESSED YOU FOUND THIS PLACE.
AND YOU'RE QUITE SOMETHING
TO ELUDE SOCIETY'S PRYING EYES. EVEN THE LOCAL PAPER HAD NO CLUE WHERE YOU WERE.
HA HA HA HA HA HA HA
WHY MUST THEY CHASE AFTER SUCH A BORING GIRL?

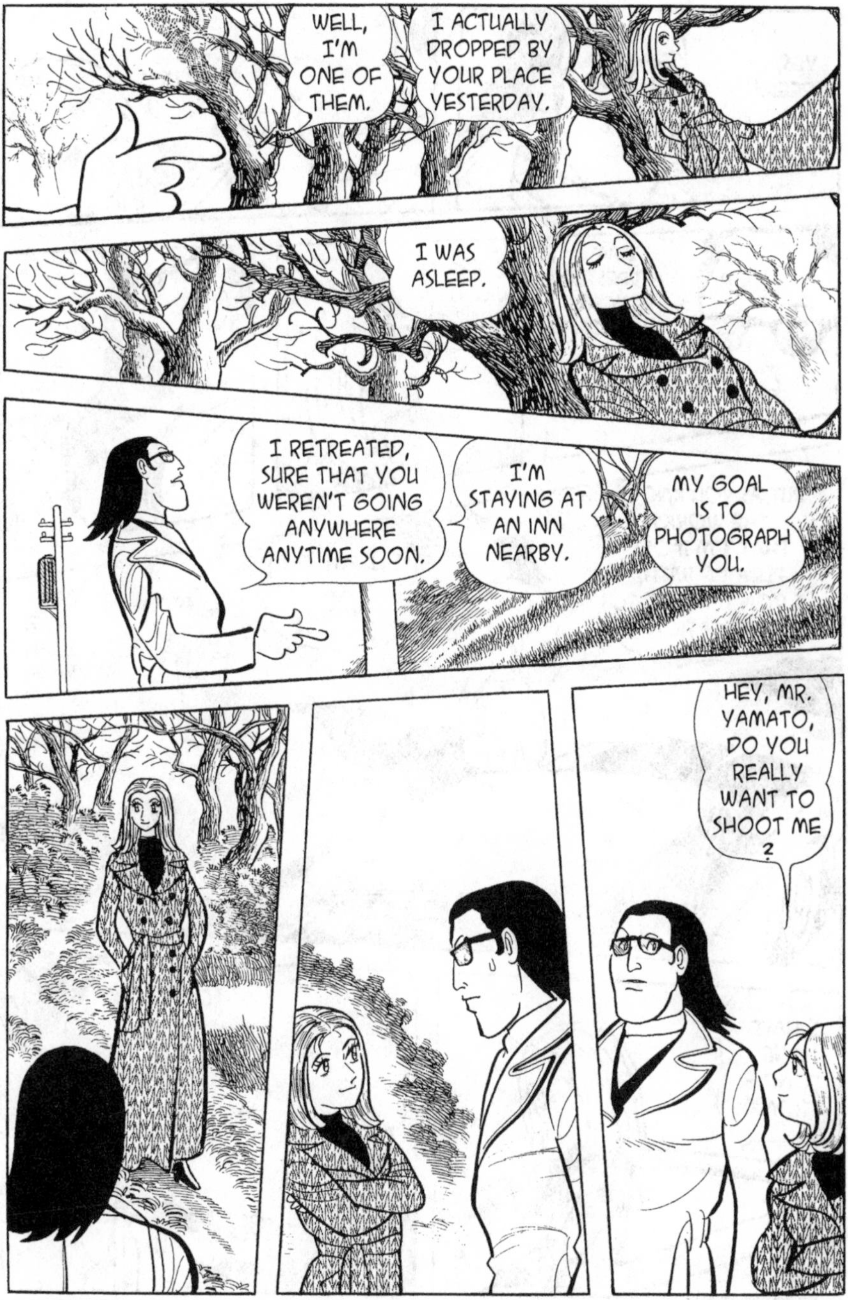
WELL, I'M ONE OF THEM.
I ACTUALLY DROPPED BY YOUR PLACE YESTERDAY.
I WAS ASLEEP.
I RETREATED, SURE THAT YOU WEREN'T GOING ANYWHERE ANYTIME SOON.
I'M STAYING AT AN INN NEARBY.
MY GOAL IS TO PHOTOGRAPH YOU.
HEY, MR. YAMATO, DO YOU REALLY WANT TO SHOOT ME?

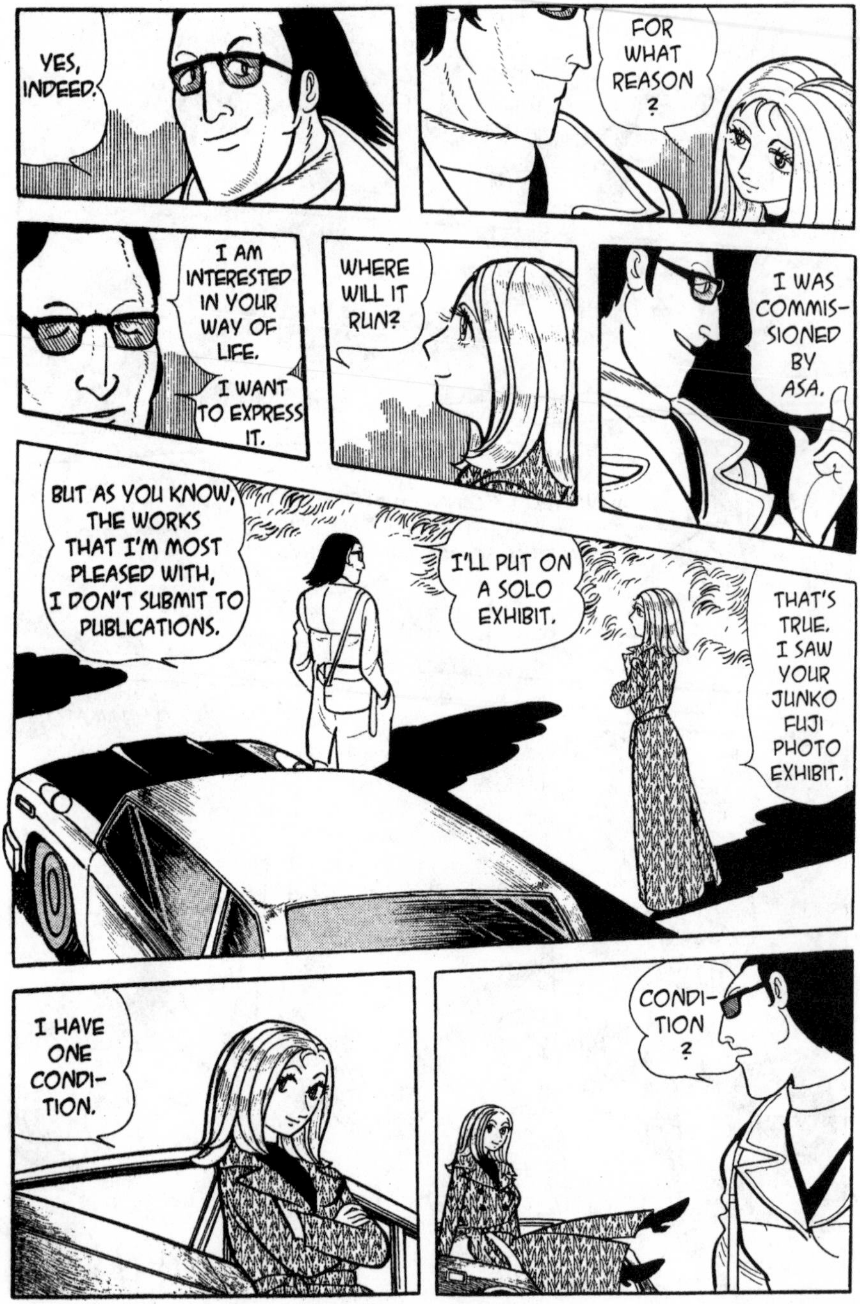
YES, INDEED.
FOR WHAT REASON?
I AM INTERESTED IN YOUR WAY OF LIFE.
I WANT TO EXPRESS IT.
WHERE WILL IT RUN?
I WAS COMMISSIONED BY ASA.
BUT AS YOU KNOW, THE WORKS THAT I'M MOST PLEASED WITH, I DON'T SUBMIT TO PUBLICATIONS.
I'LL PUT ON A SOLO EXHIBIT.
THAT'S TRUE. I SAW YOUR JUNKO FUJI PHOTO EXHIBIT.
I HAVE ONE CONDITION.
CONDITION?

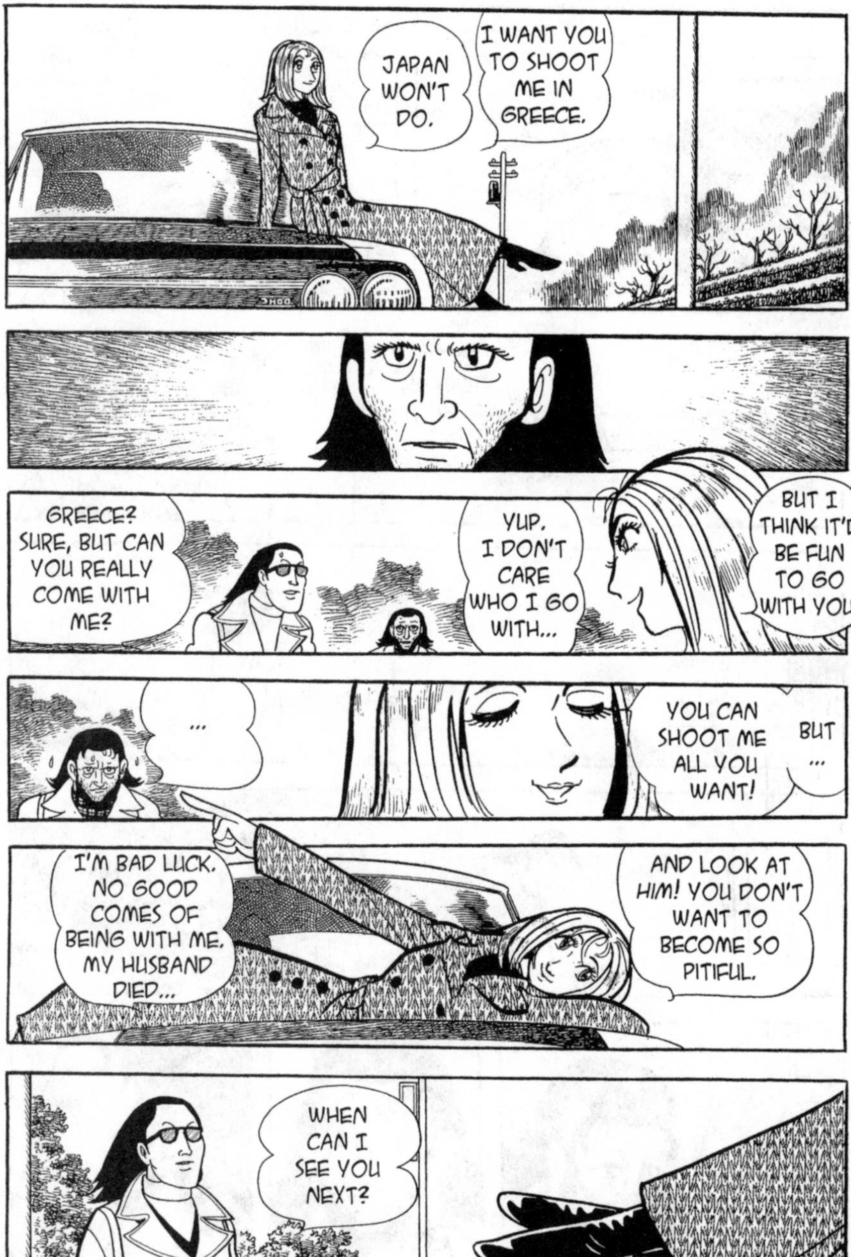
JAPAN WON'T DO.
I WANT YOU TO SHOOT ME IN GREECE.
GREECE? SURE, BUT CAN YOU REALLY COME WITH ME?
YUP. I DON'T CARE WHO I GO WITH...
BUT I THINK IT'D BE FUN TO GO WITH YOU.
...
YOU CAN SHOOT ME ALL YOU WANT!
BUT ...
I'M BAD LUCK. NO GOOD COMES OF BEING WITH ME. MY HUSBAND DIED...
AND LOOK AT HIM! YOU DON'T WANT TO BECOME SO PITIFUL.
WHEN CAN I SEE YOU NEXT?

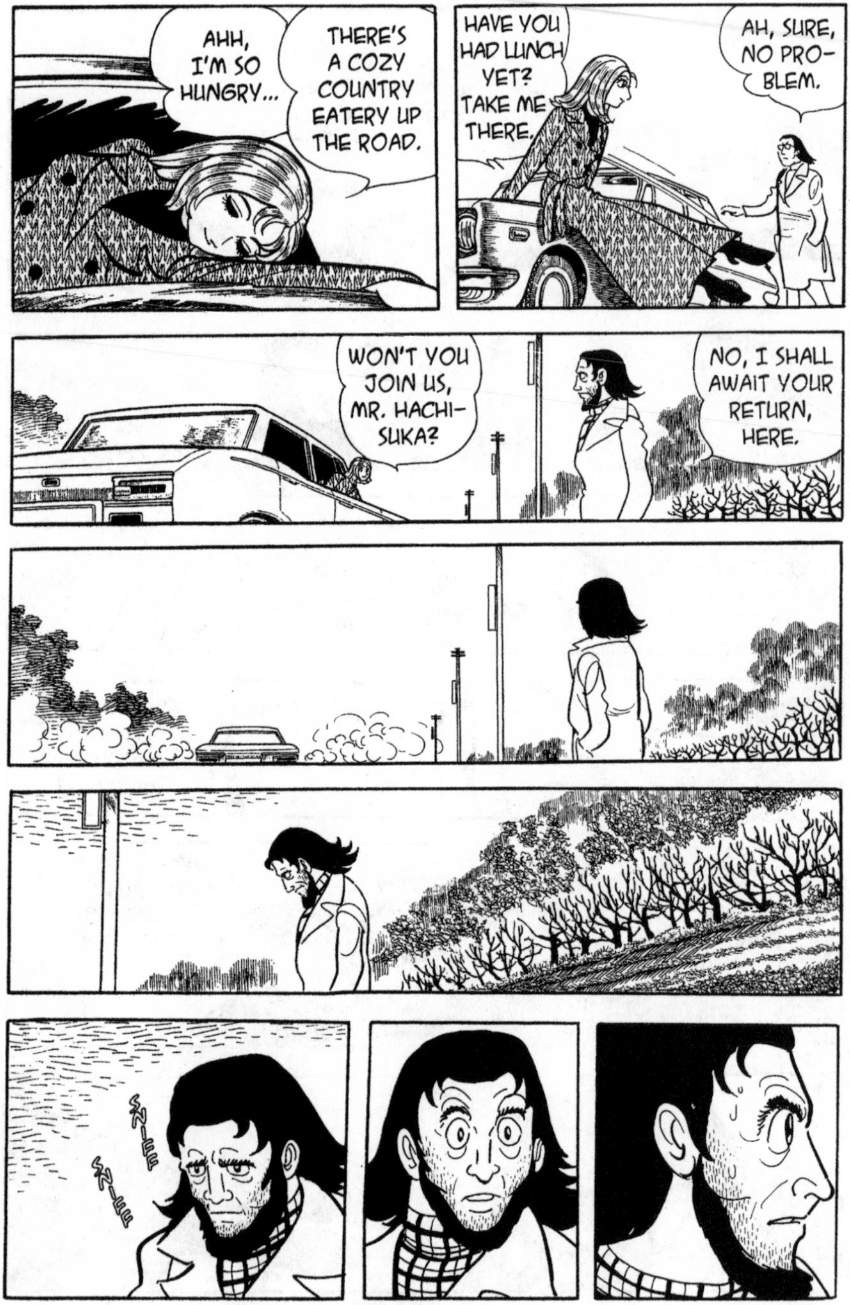
AHH, I'M SO HUNGRY...
THERE'S A COZY COUNTRY EATERY UP THE ROAD.
HAVE YOU HAD LUNCH YET? TAKE ME THERE.
AH, SURE, NO PRO-BLEM.
WON'T YOU JOIN US, MR. HACHI-SUKA?
NO, I SHALL AWAIT YOUR RETURN, HERE.
SNIFF
SNIFF

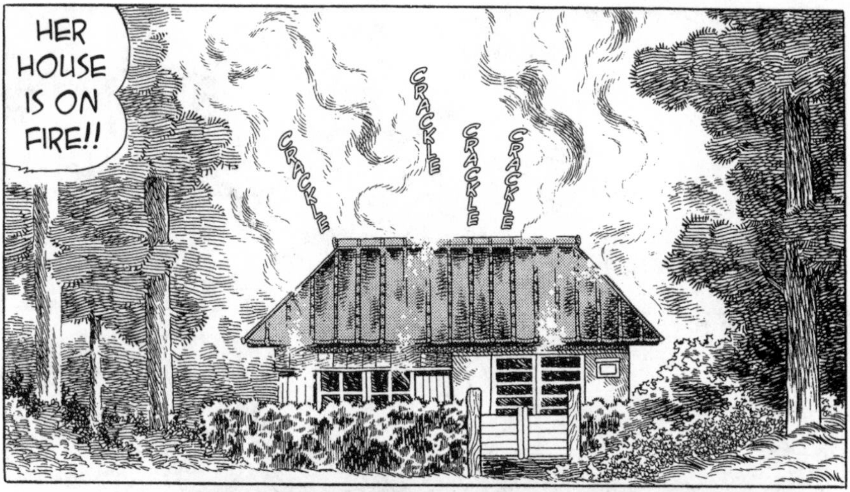
HER HOUSE IS ON FIRE!!
CRACKLE
CRACKLE
CRACKLE
CRACKLE

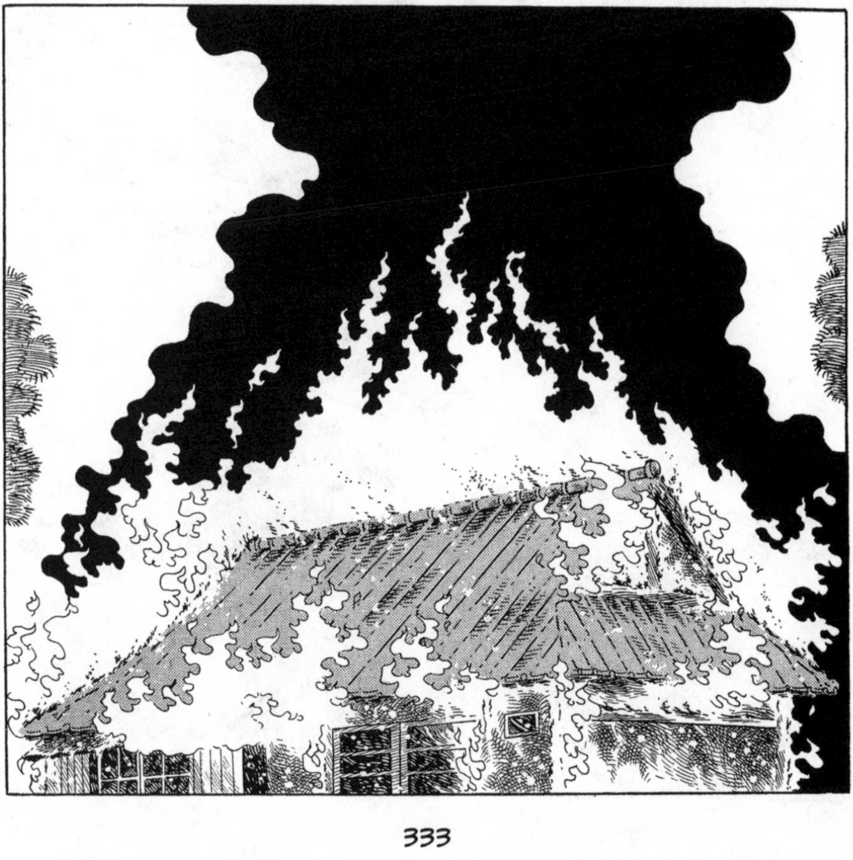

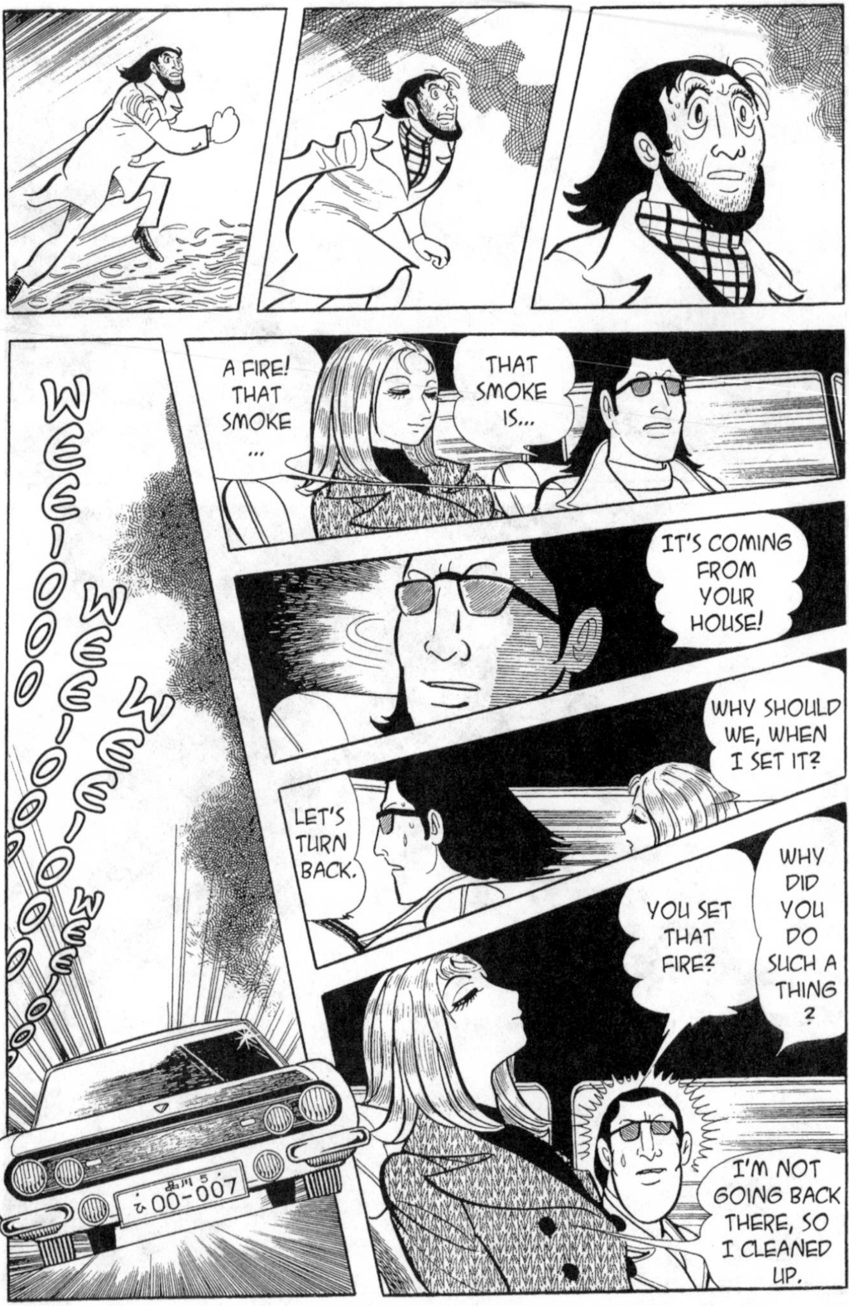
WEE-OOOO
WEE-OOOOOOOO
WEE-O WEE-OOO
A FIRE! THAT SMOKE ...
THAT SMOKE IS...
IT'S COMING FROM YOUR HOUSE!
WHY SHOULD WE, WHEN I SET IT?
LET'S TURN BACK.
WHY DID YOU DO SUCH A THING?
YOU SET THAT FIRE?
I'M NOT GOING BACK THERE, SO I CLEANED UP.

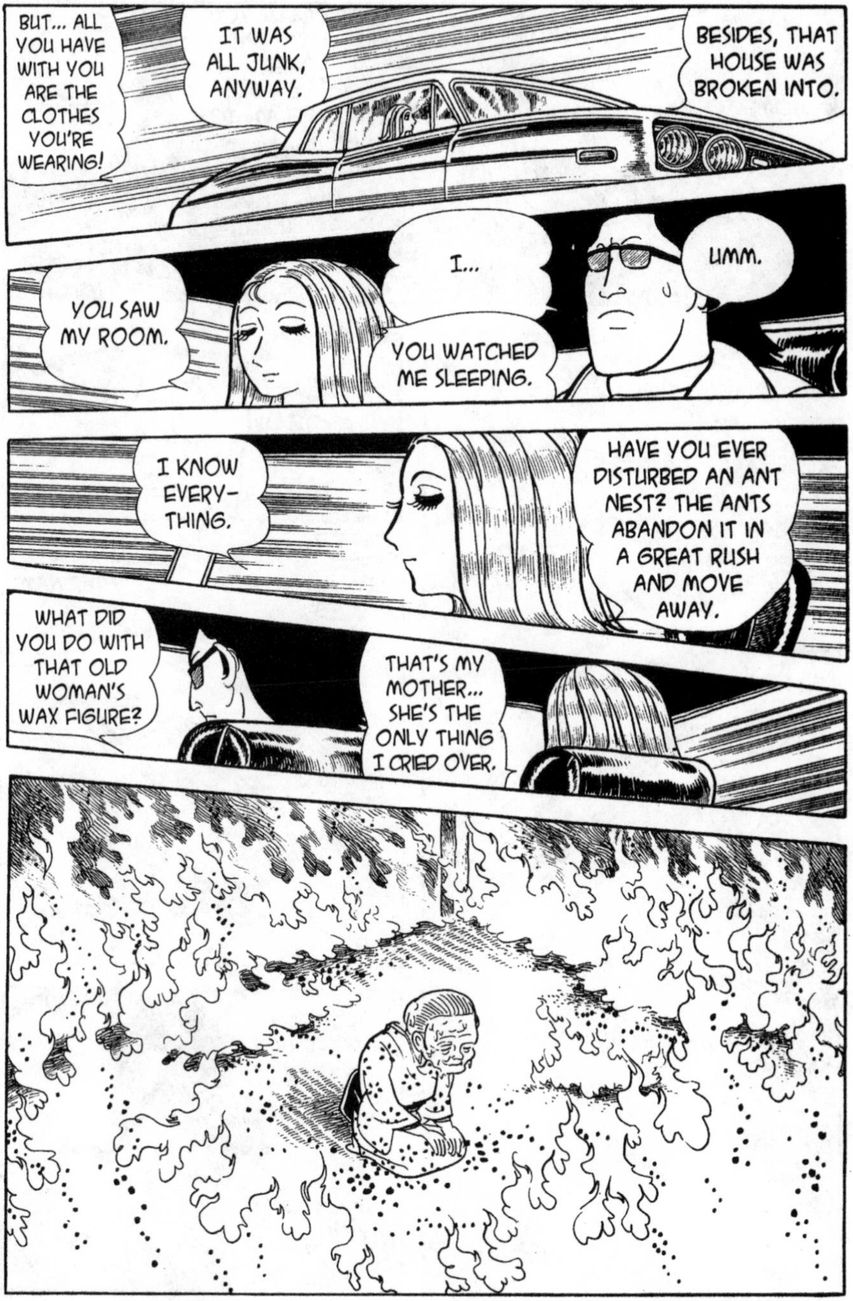
BUT... ALL YOU HAVE WITH YOU ARE THE CLOTHES YOU'RE WEARING!
IT WAS ALL JUNK, ANYWAY.
BESIDES, THAT HOUSE WAS BROKEN INTO.
YOU SAW MY ROOM.
I...
YOU WATCHED ME SLEEPING.
UMM.
I KNOW EVERY-THING.
HAVE YOU EVER DISTURBED AN ANT NEST? THE ANTS ABANDON IT IN A GREAT RUSH AND MOVE AWAY.
WHAT DID YOU DO WITH THAT OLD WOMAN'S WAX FIGURE?
THAT'S MY MOTHER... SHE'S THE ONLY THING I CRIED OVER.

I HAVE NOWHERE TO GO HOME TO NOW.

THERE'S ONE THING I MUST ATTEND TO BEFORE I LEAVE JAPAN.

COULD YOU LOOK INTO SOMETHING FOR ME, MR. YAMATO?

I WANT THE WHEREABOUTS OF A CERTAIN SOMEONE.

MIZU-NO?

A DESIGNER CALLED MIZUNO...

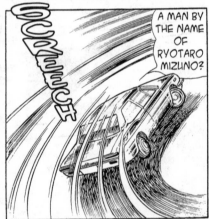

A MAN BY THE NAME OF RYOTARO MIZUNO?

HE'S BEEN INDICTED FOR MURDER.

WHAT?!

336

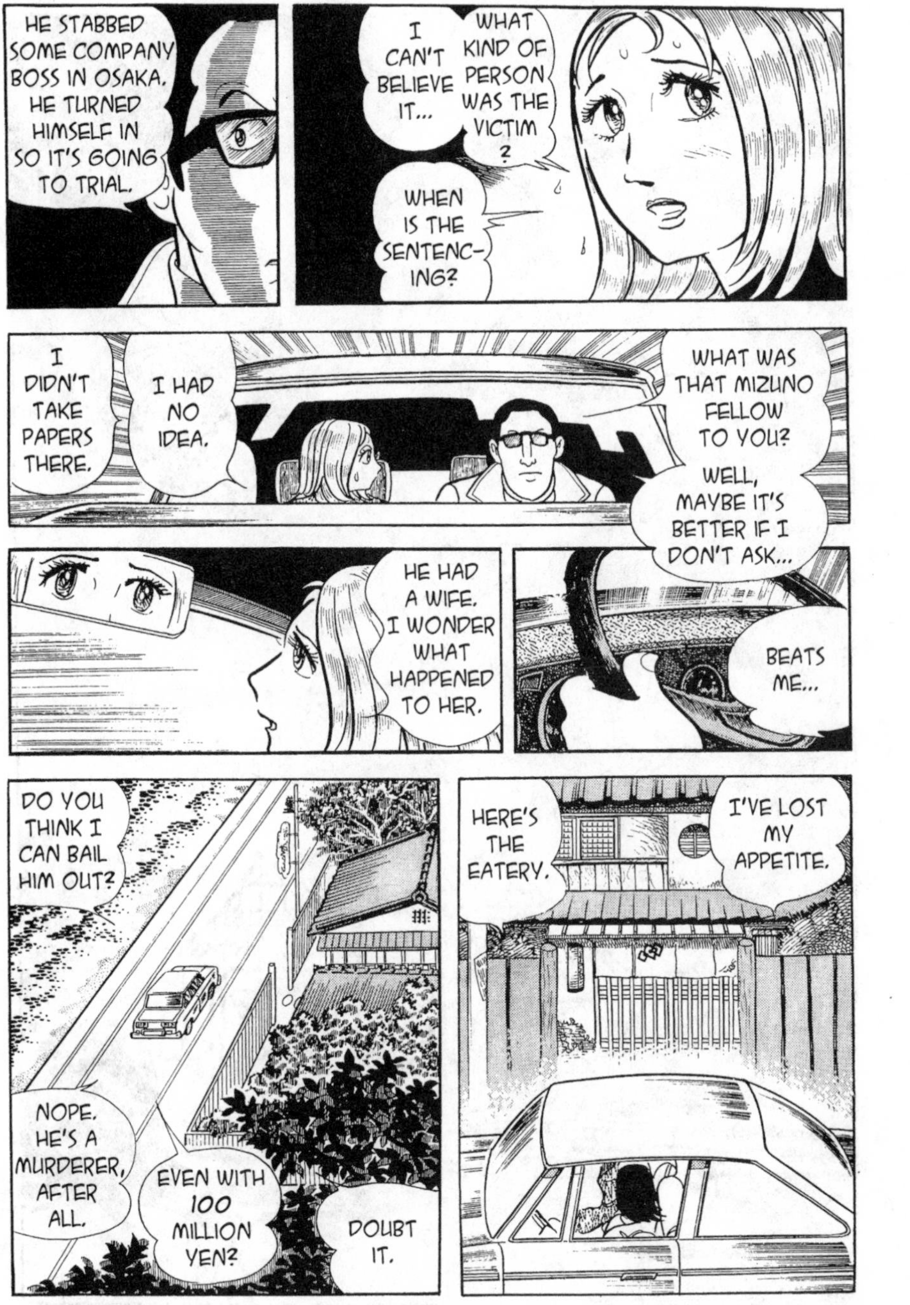
HE STABBED SOME COMPANY BOSS IN OSAKA. HE TURNED HIMSELF IN SO IT'S GOING TO TRIAL.
I CAN'T BELIEVE IT...
WHAT KIND OF PERSON WAS THE VICTIM ?
WHEN IS THE SENTENC-ING?
I DIDN'T TAKE PAPERS THERE.
I HAD NO IDEA.
WHAT WAS THAT MIZUNO FELLOW TO YOU?
WELL, MAYBE IT'S BETTER IF I DON'T ASK...
HE HAD A WIFE. I WONDER WHAT HAPPENED TO HER.
BEATS ME...
DO YOU THINK I CAN BAIL HIM OUT?
NOPE. HE'S A MURDERER, AFTER ALL.
EVEN WITH 100 MILLION YEN?
DOUBT IT.
HERE'S THE EATERY.
I'VE LOST MY APPETITE.

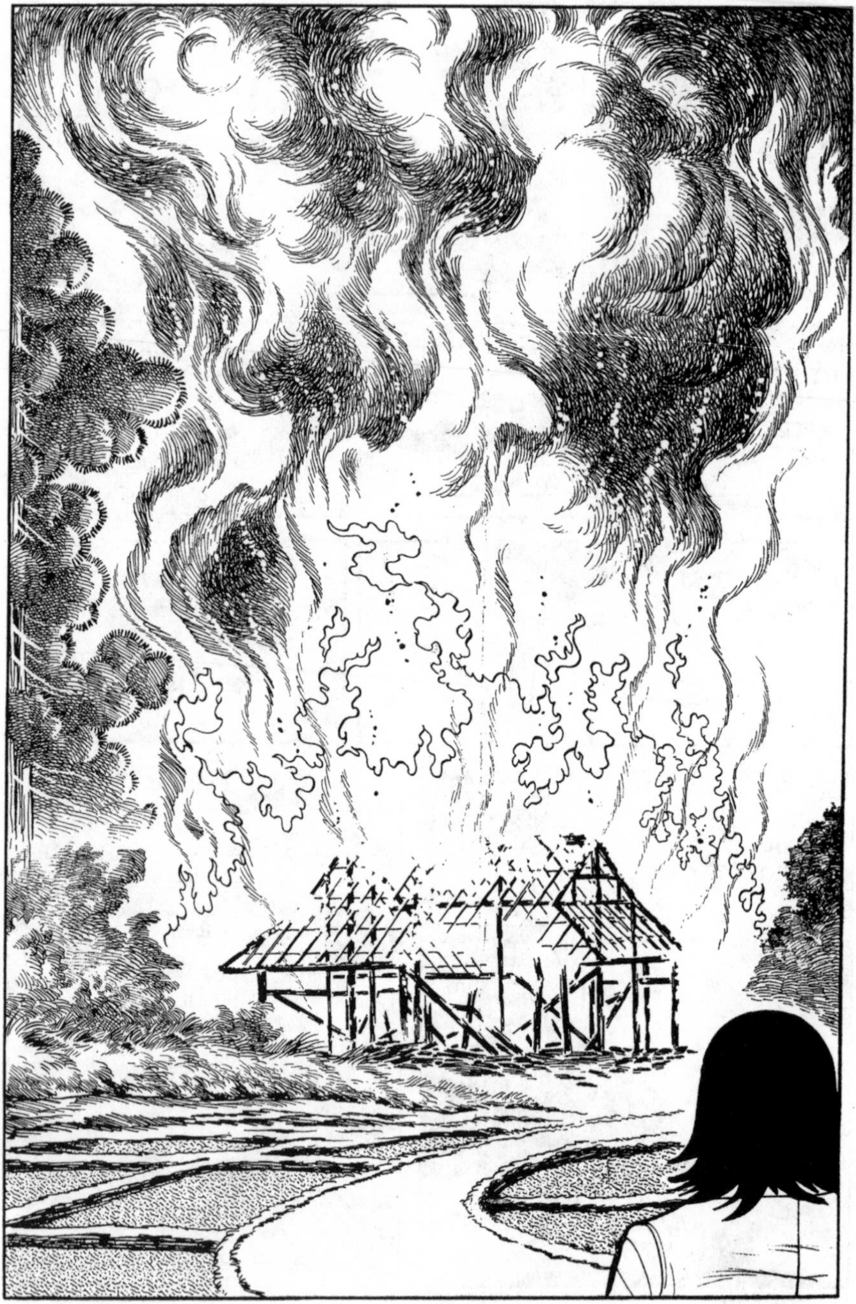

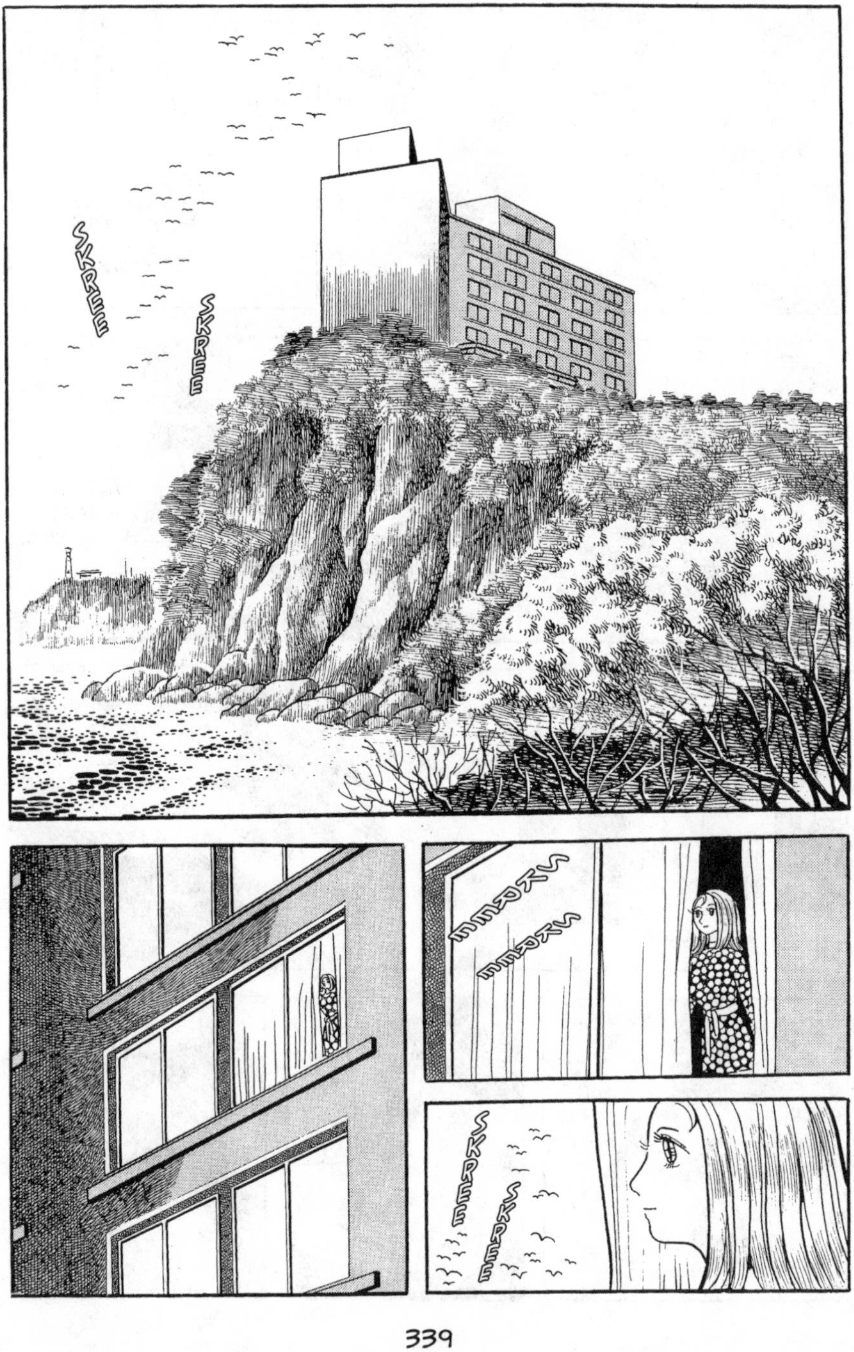
SKREE
SKREE
SKREE
SKREE
SKREE
SKREE

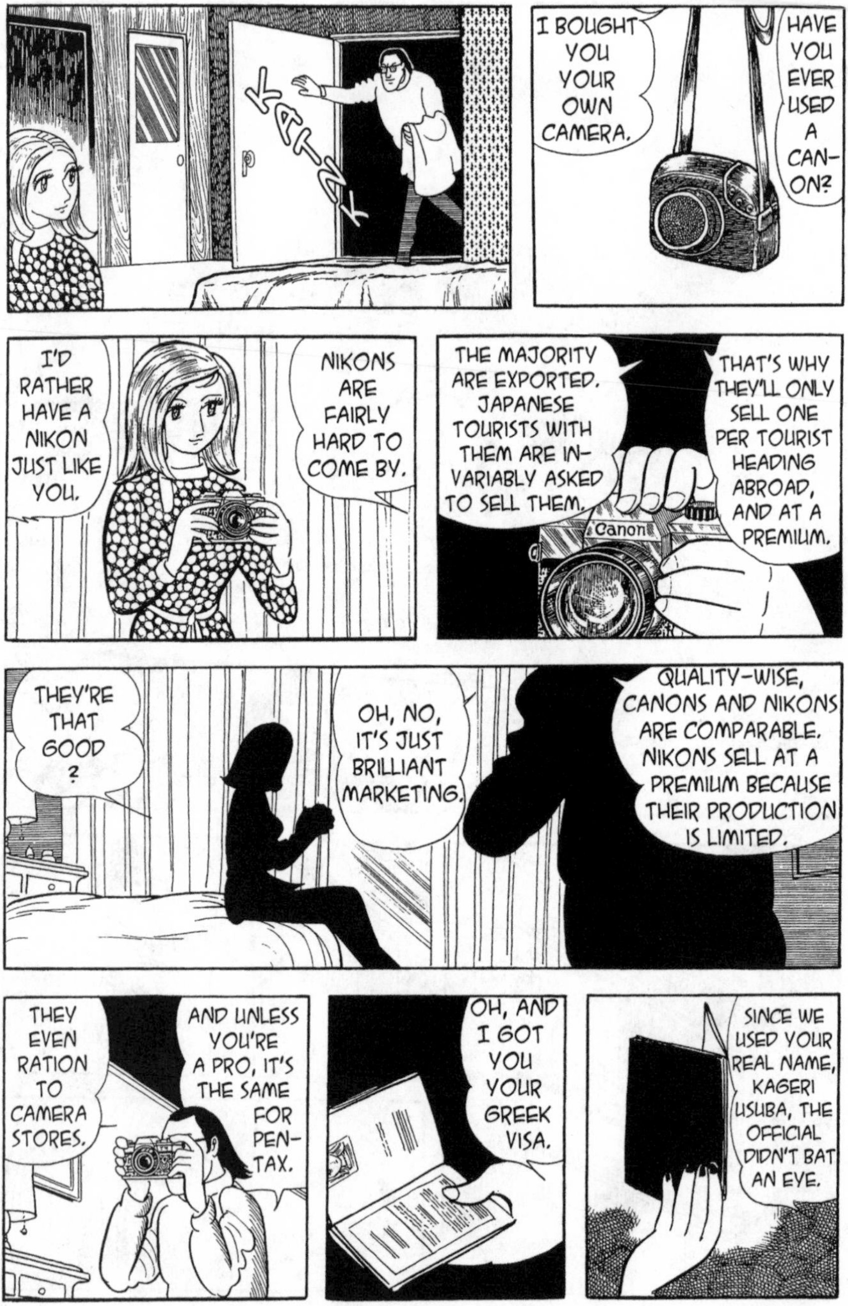
KATNK
I BOUGHT YOU YOUR OWN CAMERA.
HAVE YOU EVER USED A CAN-ON?
I'D RATHER HAVE A NIKON JUST LIKE YOU.
NIKONS ARE FAIRLY HARD TO COME BY.
THE MAJORITY ARE EXPORTED. JAPANESE TOURISTS WITH THEM ARE IN-VARIABLY ASKED TO SELL THEM.
Canon
THAT'S WHY THEY'LL ONLY SELL ONE PER TOURIST HEADING ABROAD, AND AT A PREMIUM.
THEY'RE THAT GOOD ?
OH, NO, IT'S JUST BRILLIANT MARKETING.
QUALITY-WISE, CANONS AND NIKONS ARE COMPARABLE. NIKONS SELL AT A PREMIUM BECAUSE THEIR PRODUCTION IS LIMITED.
THEY EVEN RATION TO CAMERA STORES.
AND UNLESS YOU'RE A PRO, IT'S THE SAME FOR PEN-TAX.
OH, AND I GOT YOU YOUR GREEK VISA.
SINCE WE USED YOUR REAL NAME, KAGERI USUBA, THE OFFICIAL DIDN'T BAT AN EYE.

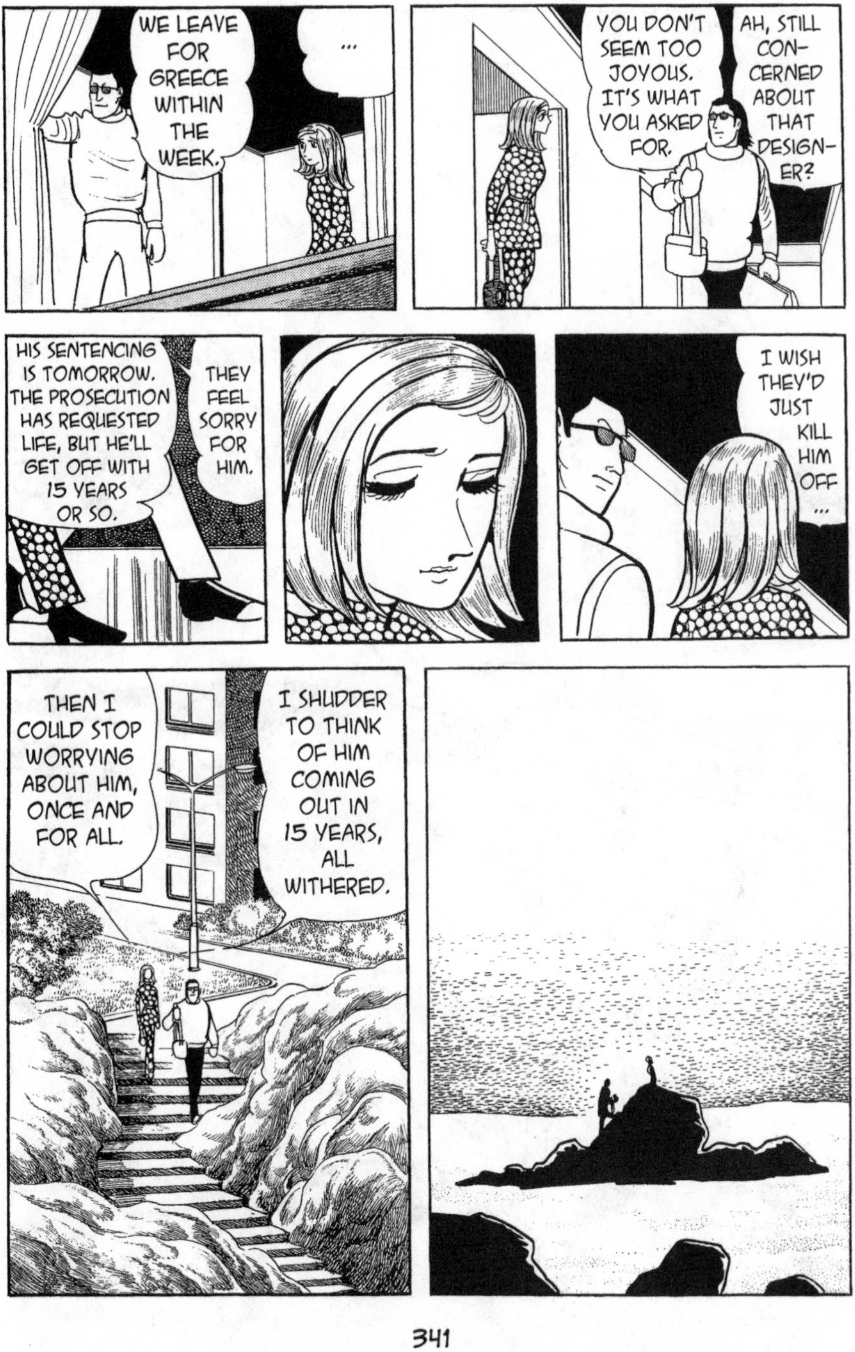
WE LEAVE FOR GREECE WITHIN THE WEEK.
...
YOU DON'T SEEM TOO JOYOUS. IT'S WHAT YOU ASKED FOR.
AH, STILL CON-CERNED ABOUT THAT DESIGN-ER?
HIS SENTENCING IS TOMORROW. THE PROSECUTION HAS REQUESTED LIFE, BUT HE'LL GET OFF WITH 15 YEARS OR SO.
THEY FEEL SORRY FOR HIM.
I WISH THEY'D JUST KILL HIM OFF ...
THEN I COULD STOP WORRYING ABOUT HIM, ONCE AND FOR ALL.
I SHUDDER TO THINK OF HIM COMING OUT IN 15 YEARS, ALL WITHERED.
...

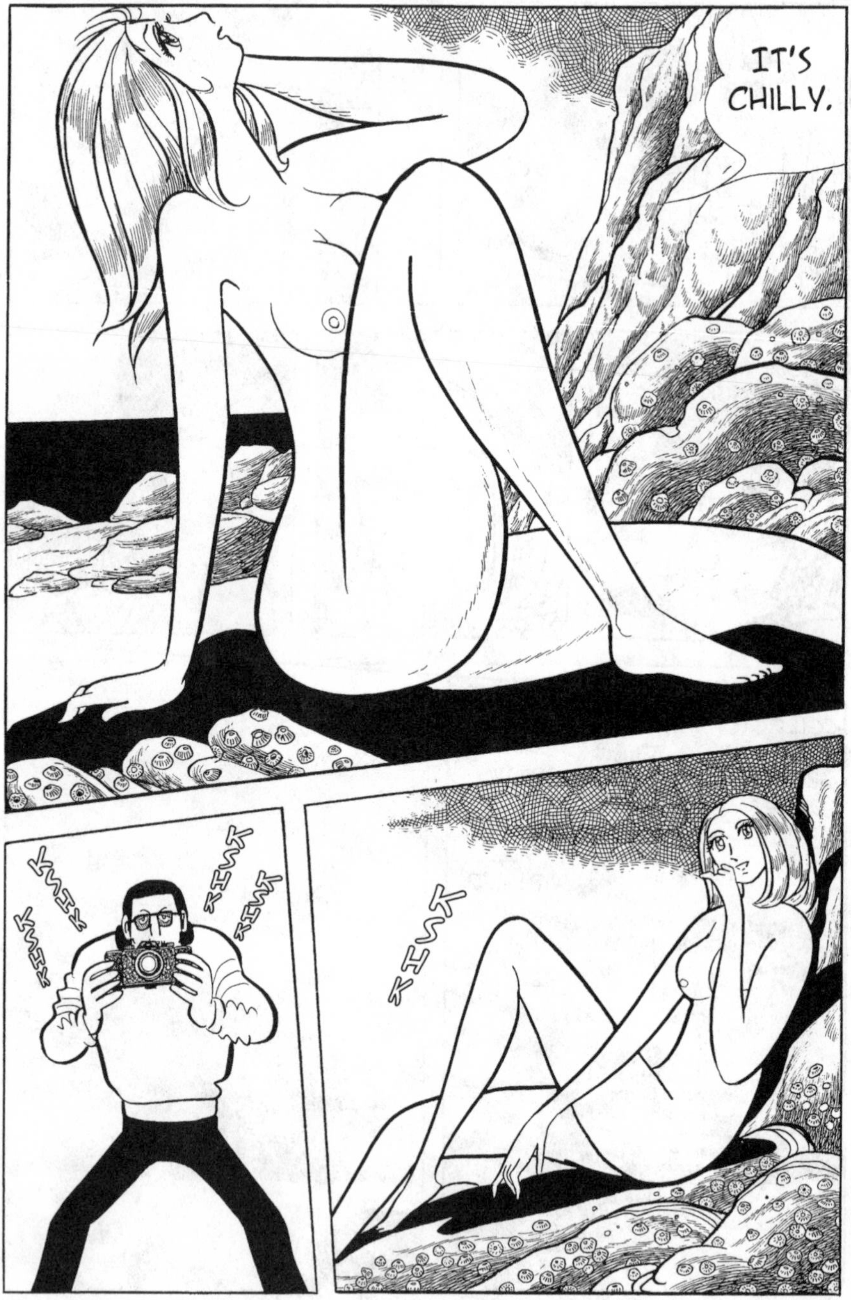
IT'S CHILLY.

IT'S THAT MAN AGAIN!!

NO BIGGIE!

COME ON OVER, MR. HACHISUKA!

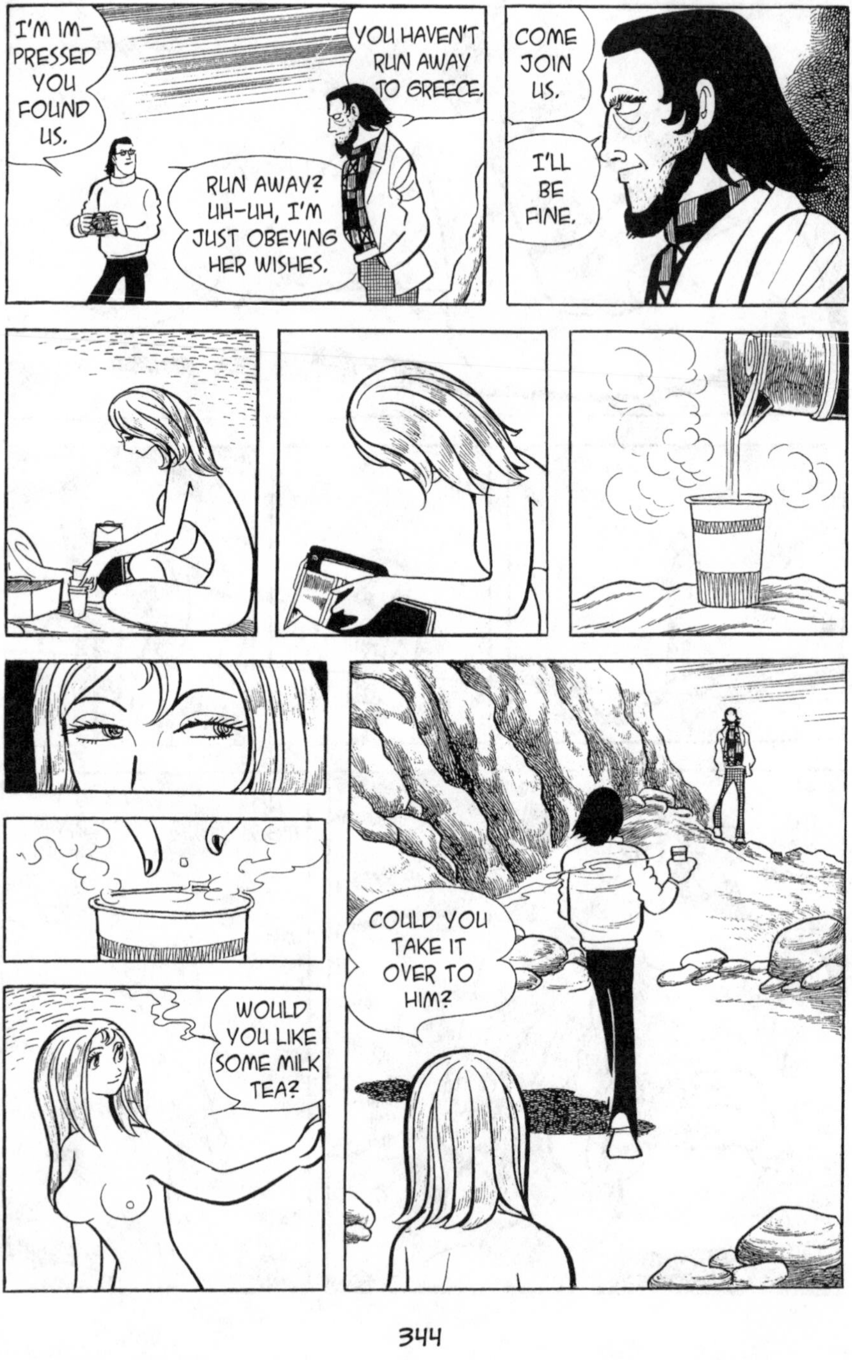
I'M IM-PRESSED YOU FOUND US.
YOU HAVEN'T RUN AWAY TO GREECE.
RUN AWAY? UH-UH, I'M JUST OBEYING HER WISHES.
COME JOIN US.
I'LL BE FINE.
WOULD YOU LIKE SOME MILK TEA?
COULD YOU TAKE IT OVER TO HIM?

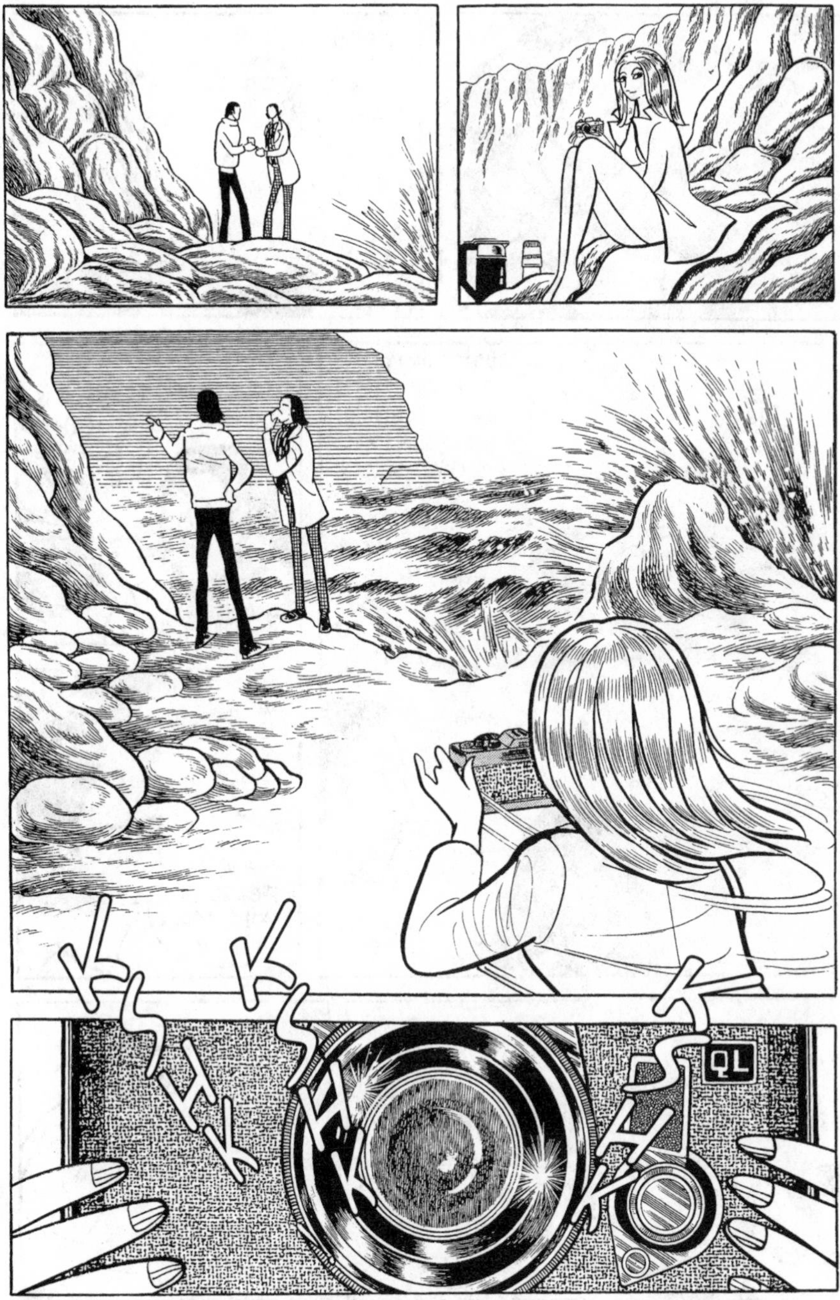
KSHK
KSHK
KSHK

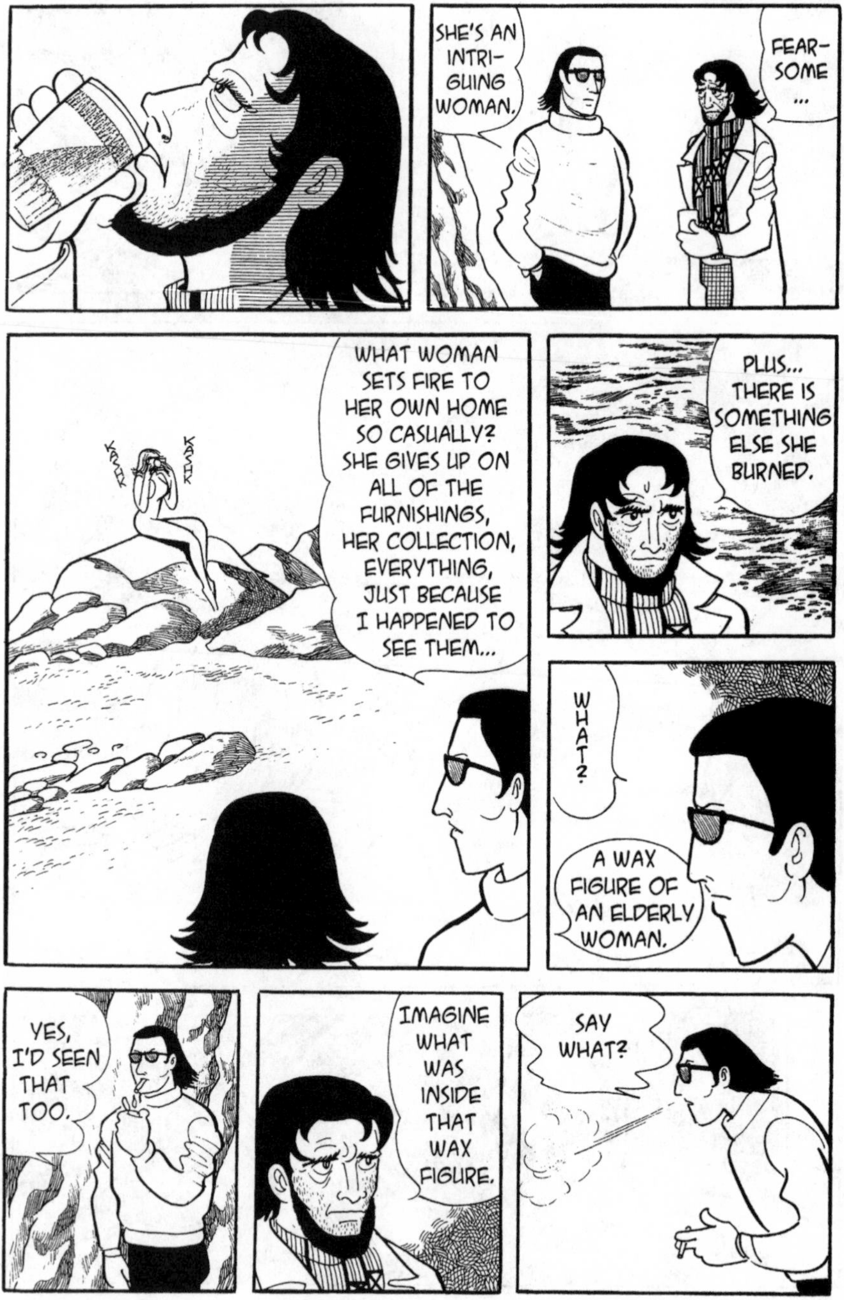
SHE'S AN INTRI-GUING WOMAN.
FEAR-SOME ...
WHAT WOMAN SETS FIRE TO HER OWN HOME SO CASUALLY? SHE GIVES UP ON ALL OF THE FURNISHINGS, HER COLLECTION, EVERYTHING, JUST BECAUSE I HAPPENED TO SEE THEM...
KASHK
KASHK
PLUS... THERE IS SOMETHING ELSE SHE BURNED.
WHAT?
A WAX FIGURE OF AN ELDERLY WOMAN.
YES, I'D SEEN THAT TOO.
IMAGINE WHAT WAS INSIDE THAT WAX FIGURE.
SAY WHAT?

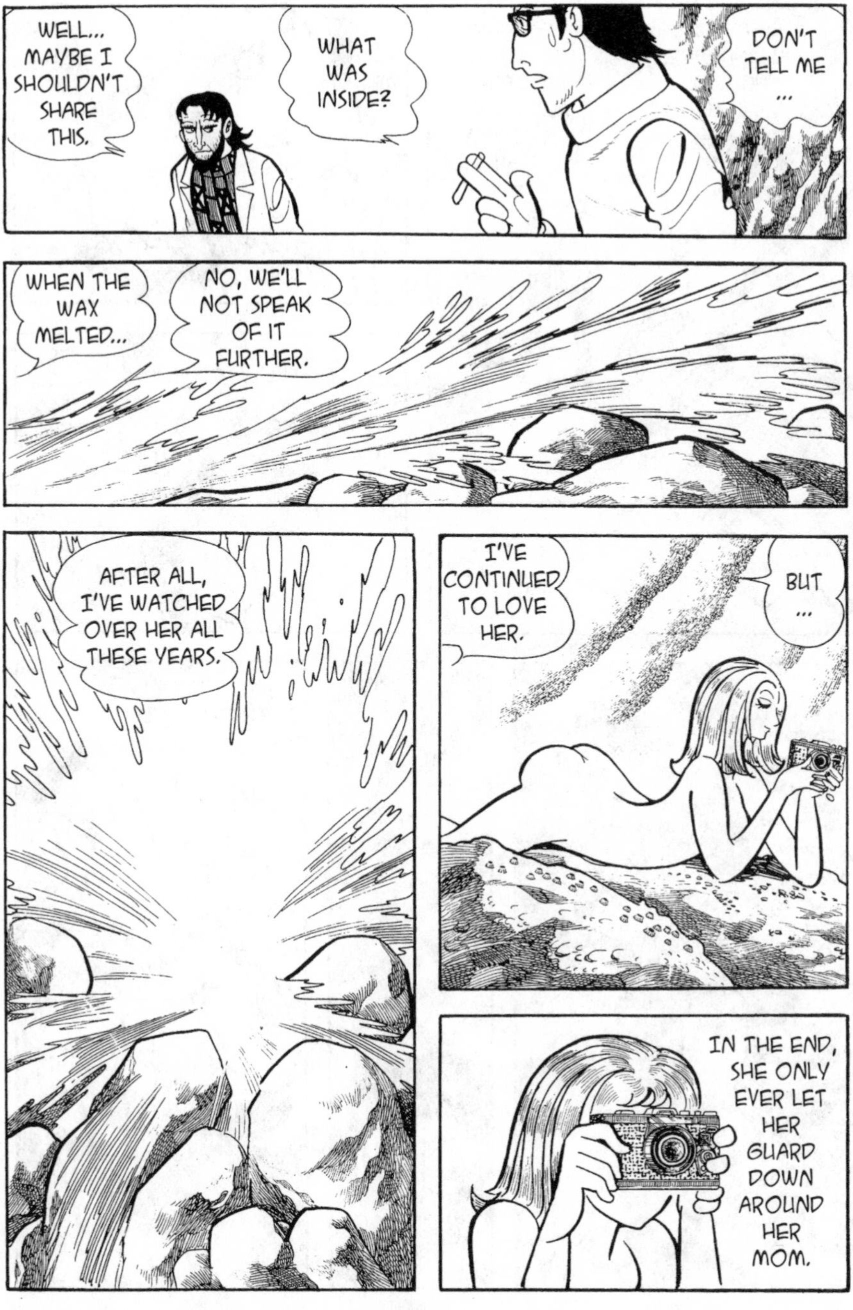
WELL... MAYBE I SHOULDN'T SHARE THIS.
WHAT WAS INSIDE?
DON'T TELL ME ...
WHEN THE WAX MELTED...
NO, WE'LL NOT SPEAK OF IT FURTHER.
AFTER ALL, I'VE WATCHED OVER HER ALL THESE YEARS.
I'VE CONTINUED TO LOVE HER.
BUT ...
IN THE END, SHE ONLY EVER LET HER GUARD DOWN AROUND HER MOM.

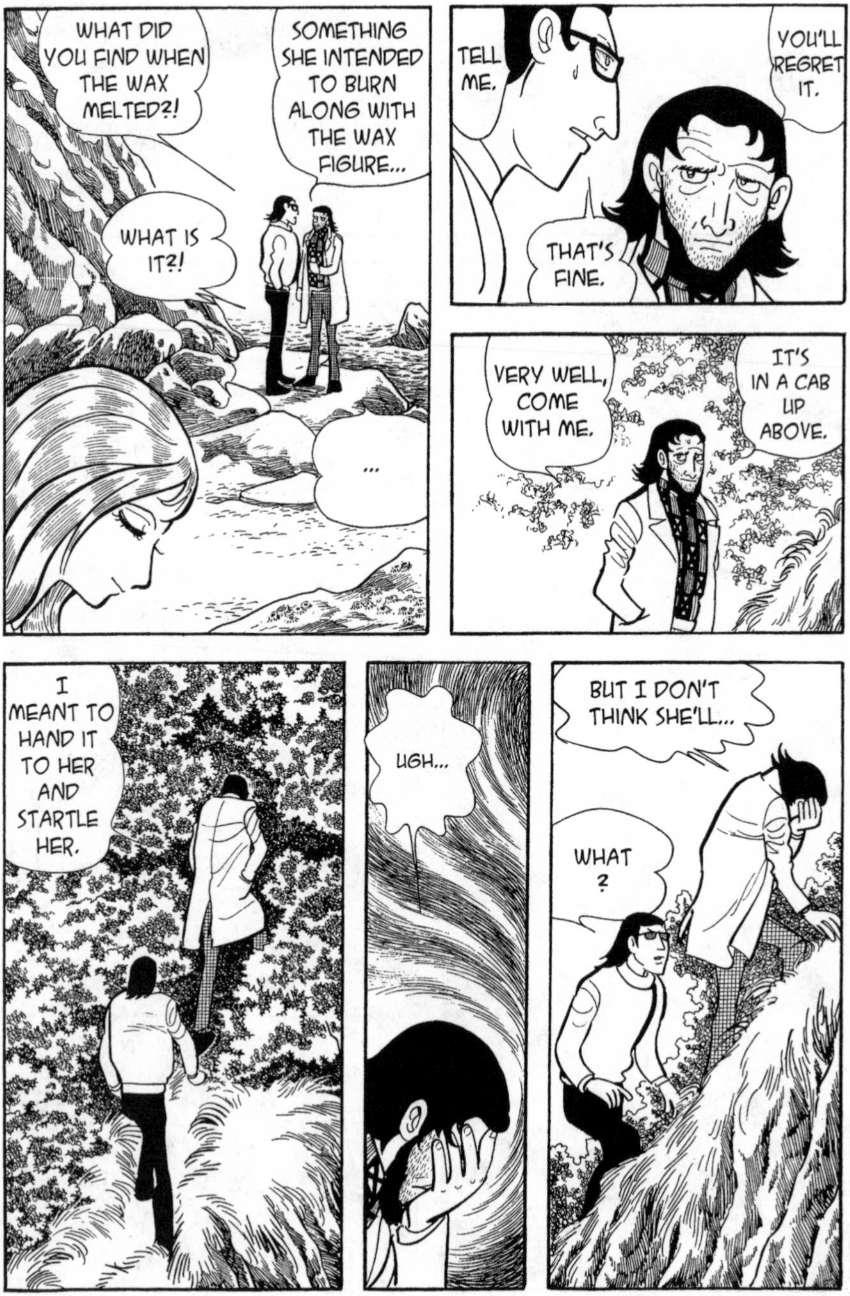
WHAT DID YOU FIND WHEN THE WAX MELTED?!
SOMETHING SHE INTENDED TO BURN ALONG WITH THE WAX FIGURE...
WHAT IS IT?!
...
TELL ME.
YOU'LL REGRET IT.
THAT'S FINE.
VERY WELL, COME WITH ME.
IT'S IN A CAB UP ABOVE.
I MEANT TO HAND IT TO HER AND STARTLE HER.
UGH...
BUT I DON'T THINK SHE'LL...
WHAT?

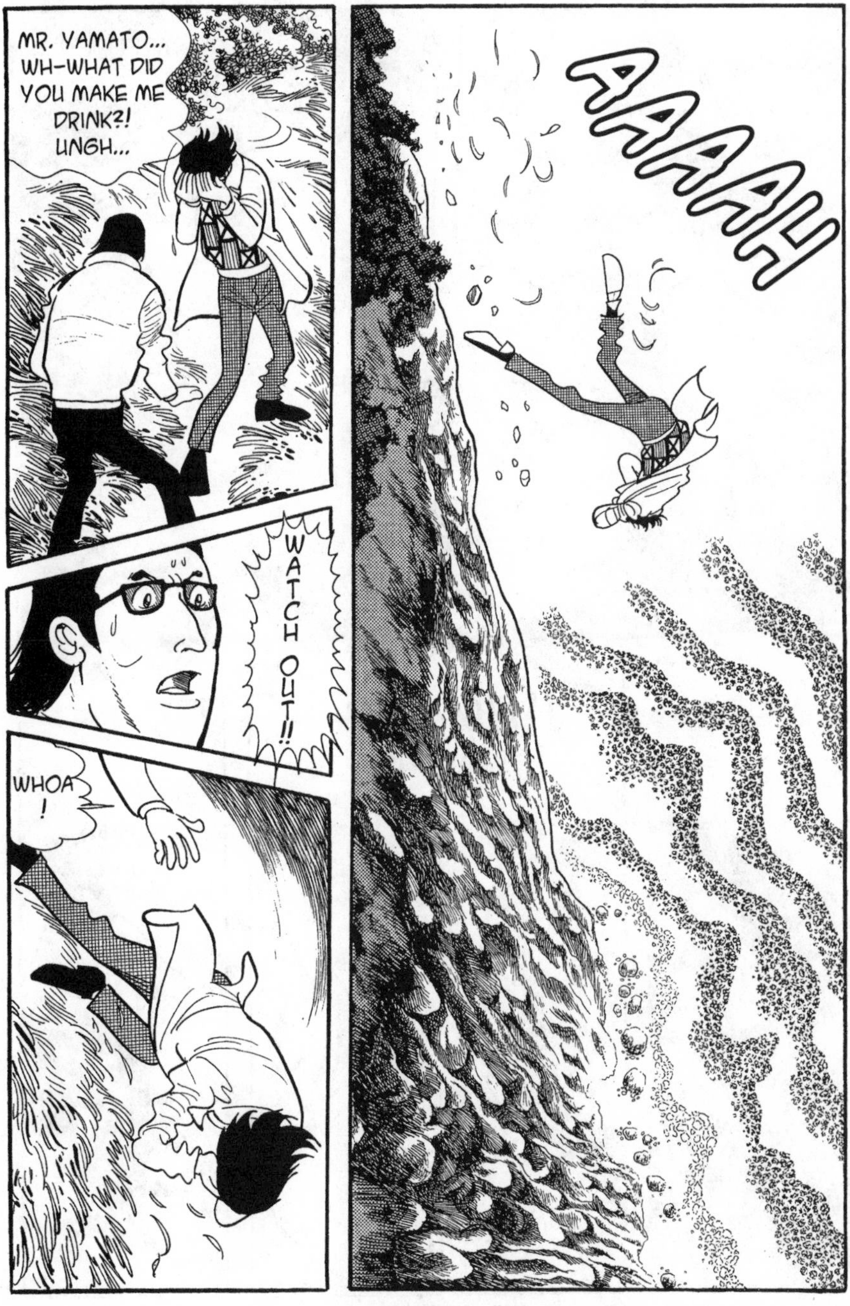
MR. YAMATO... WH-WHAT DID YOU MAKE ME DRINK?! UNGH...
WATCH OUT!!
WHOA!
AAAAAH

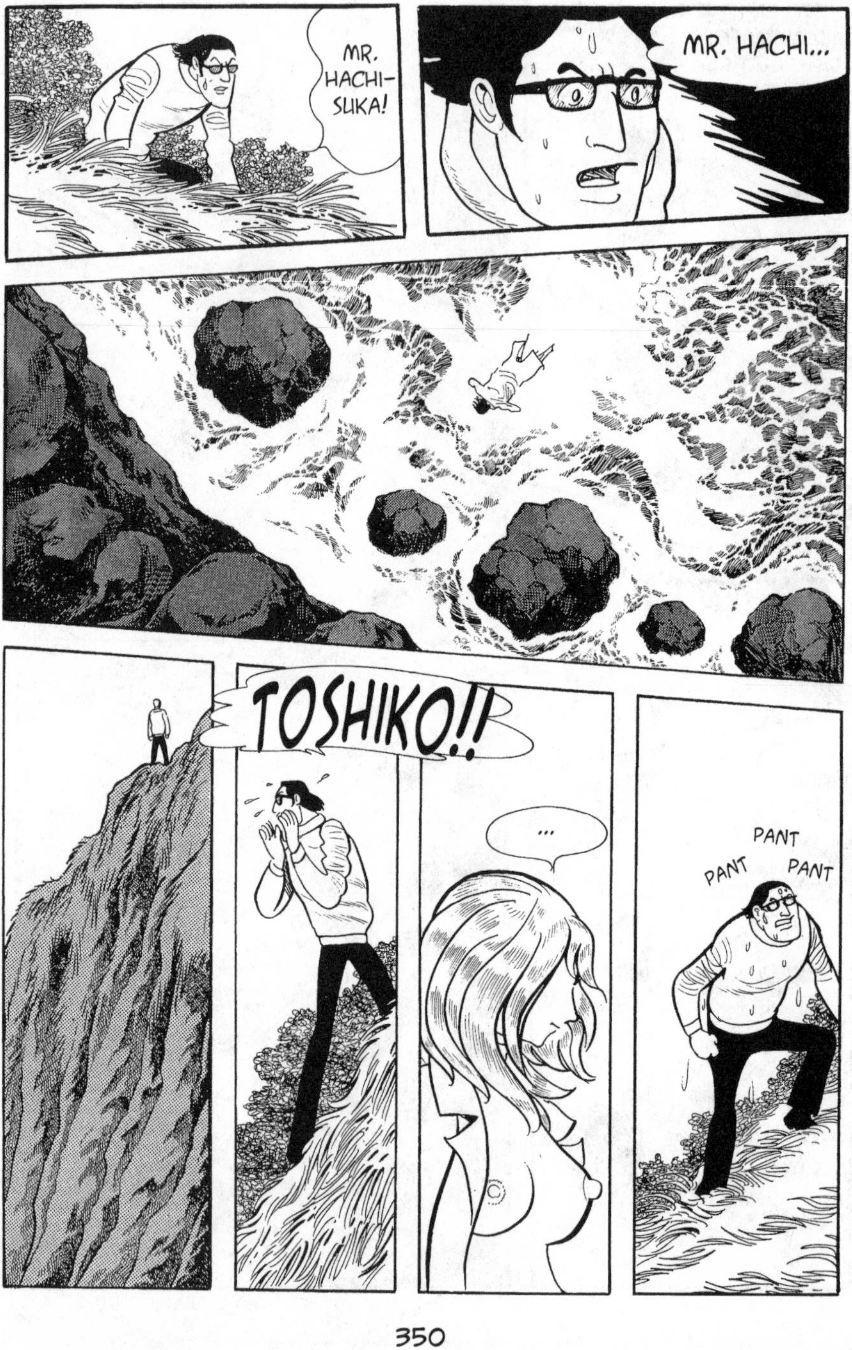
MR. HACHI-SUKA!
MR. HACHI...
TOSHIKO!!
...
PANT
PANT
PANT

YOUR FARE FELL OFF THE CLIFF! GO TELL THE HOTEL!!

WHAT ?!

JUST A SEC.

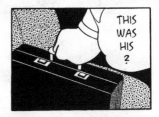

THIS WAS HIS?

I'LL HOLD ONTO IT.

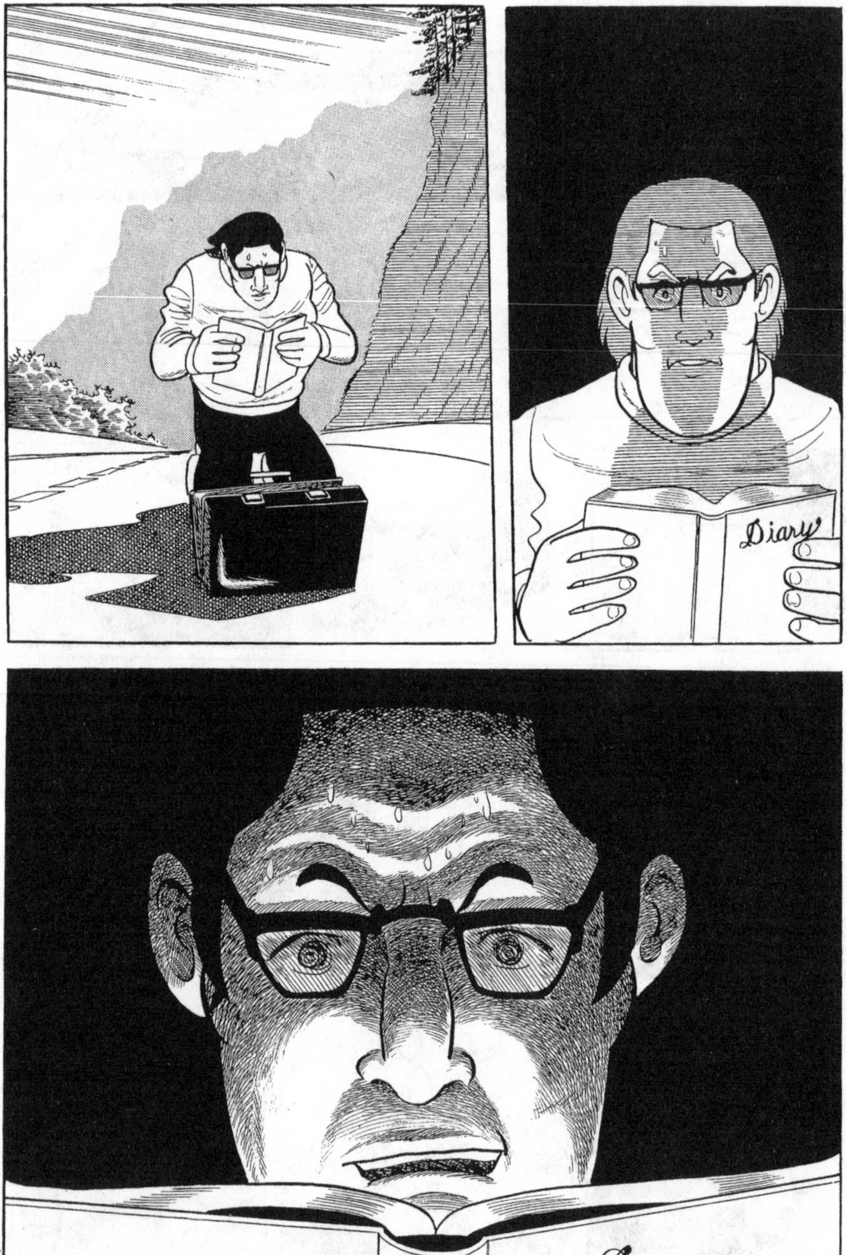
Diary
Diary

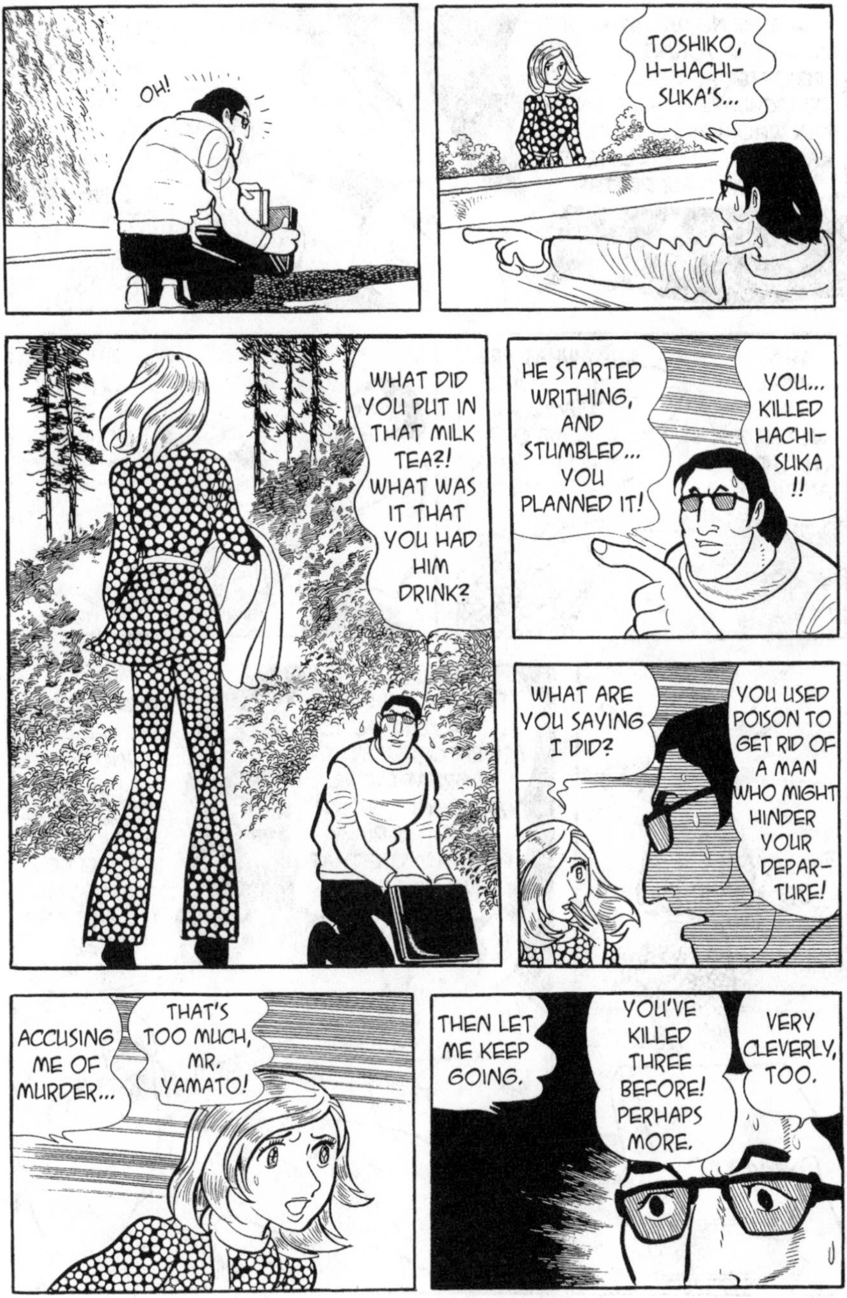
OH!
TOSHIKO, H-HACHI-SUKA'S...
WHAT DID YOU PUT IN THAT MILK TEA?! WHAT WAS IT THAT YOU HAD HIM DRINK?
HE STARTED WRITHING, AND STUMBLED... YOU PLANNED IT!
YOU... KILLED HACHI-SUKA !!
WHAT ARE YOU SAYING I DID?
YOU USED POISON TO GET RID OF A MAN WHO MIGHT HINDER YOUR DEPAR-TURE!
ACCUSING ME OF MURDER...
THAT'S TOO MUCH, MR. YAMATO!
THEN LET ME KEEP GOING.
YOU'VE KILLED THREE BEFORE! PERHAPS MORE.
VERY CLEVERLY, TOO.

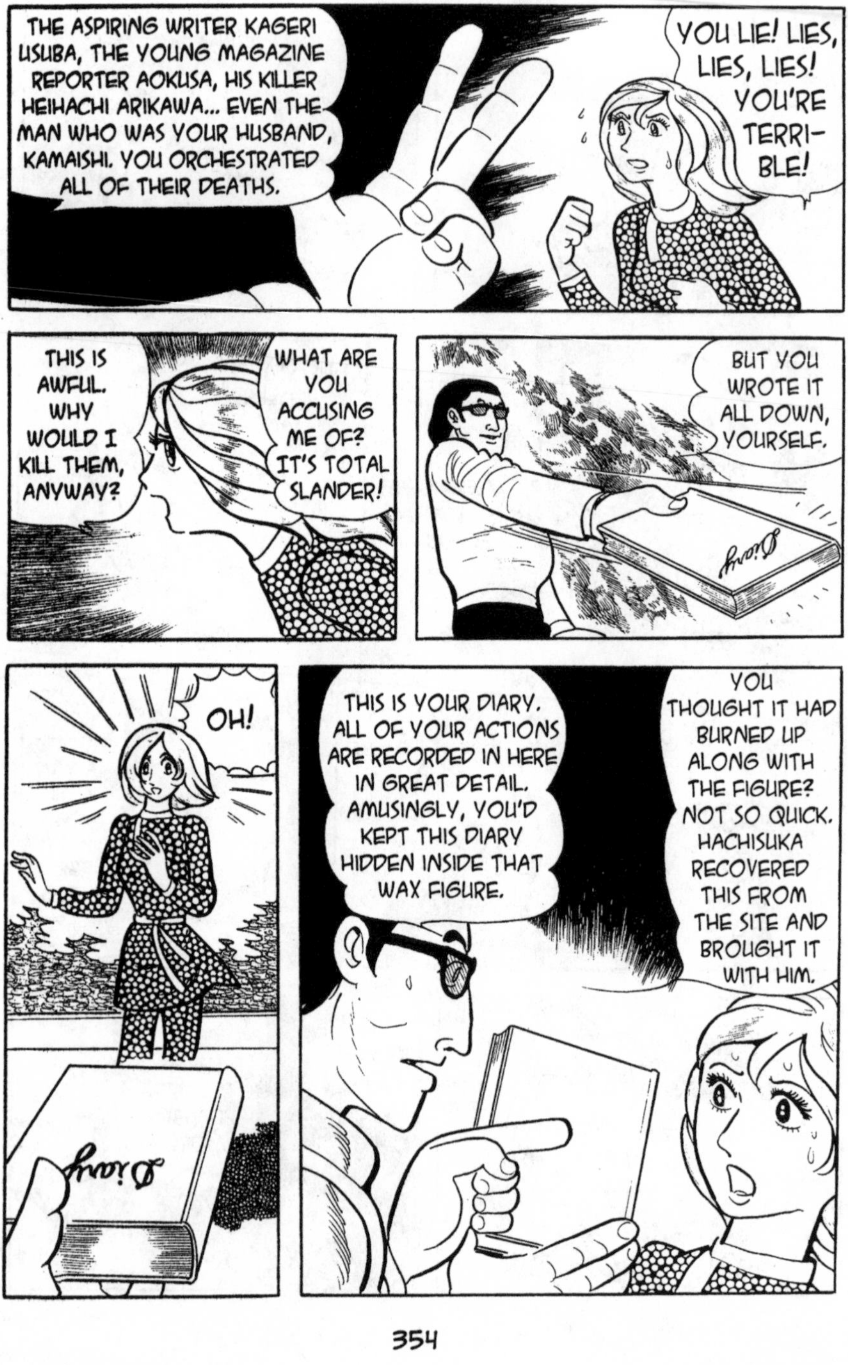
THE ASPIRING WRITER KAGERI USUBA, THE YOUNG MAGAZINE REPORTER AOKUSA, HIS KILLER HEIHACHI ARIKAWA... EVEN THE MAN WHO WAS YOUR HUSBAND, KAMAISHI. YOU ORCHESTRATED ALL OF THEIR DEATHS.
YOU LIE! LIES, LIES, LIES! YOU'RE TERRIBLE!
THIS IS AWFUL. WHY WOULD I KILL THEM, ANYWAY?
WHAT ARE YOU ACCUSING ME OF? IT'S TOTAL SLANDER!
BUT YOU WROTE IT ALL DOWN, YOURSELF.
Diary
OH!
Diary
THIS IS YOUR DIARY. ALL OF YOUR ACTIONS ARE RECORDED IN HERE IN GREAT DETAIL. AMUSINGLY, YOU'D KEPT THIS DIARY HIDDEN INSIDE THAT WAX FIGURE.
YOU THOUGHT IT HAD BURNED UP ALONG WITH THE FIGURE? NOT SO QUICK. HACHISUKA RECOVERED THIS FROM THE SITE AND BROUGHT IT WITH HIM.

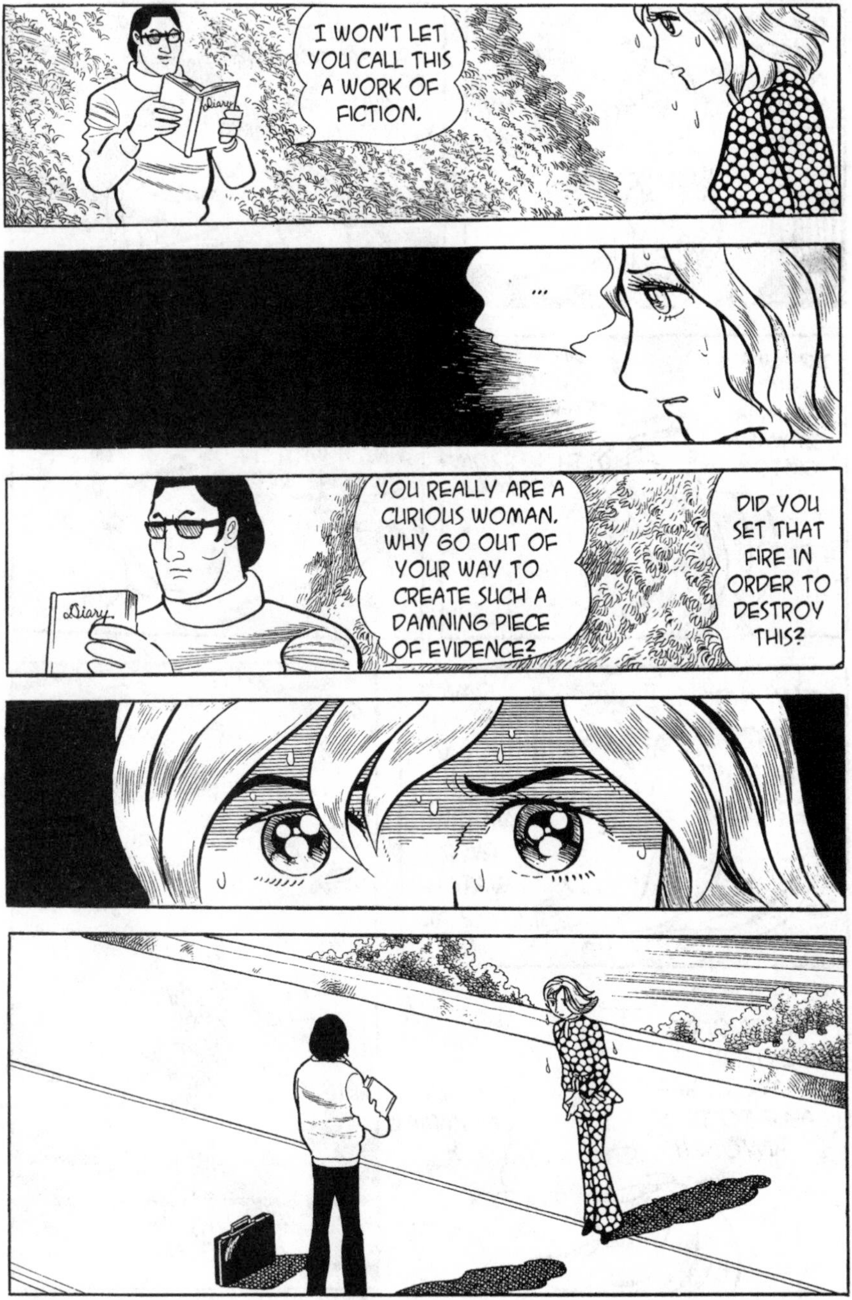
I WON'T LET YOU CALL THIS A WORK OF FICTION.
Diary
...
YOU REALLY ARE A CURIOUS WOMAN. WHY GO OUT OF YOUR WAY TO CREATE SUCH A DAMNING PIECE OF EVIDENCE?
DID YOU SET THAT FIRE IN ORDER TO DESTROY THIS?
Diary

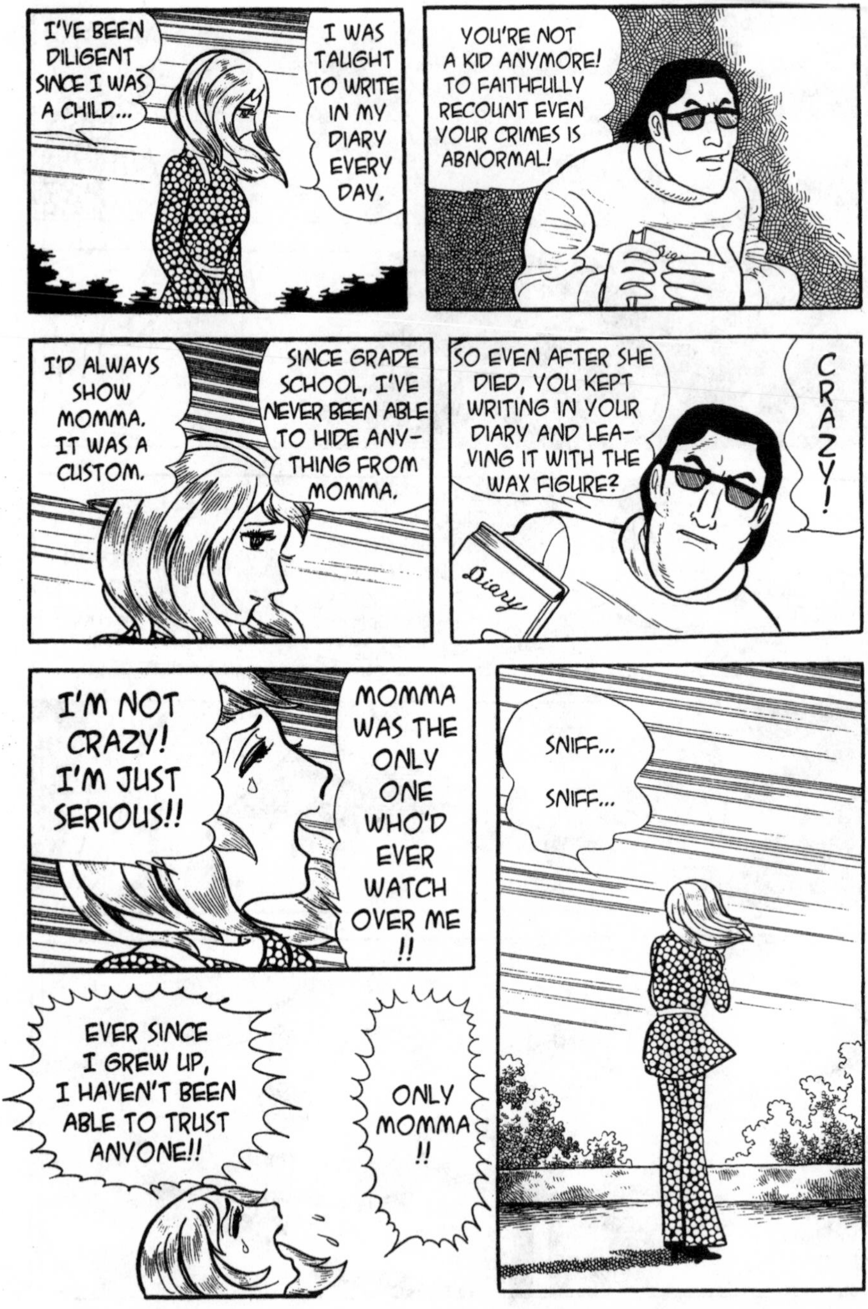
I'VE BEEN DILIGENT SINCE I WAS A CHILD...
I WAS TAUGHT TO WRITE IN MY DIARY EVERY DAY.
YOU'RE NOT A KID ANYMORE! TO FAITHFULLY RECOUNT EVEN YOUR CRIMES IS ABNORMAL!
I'D ALWAYS SHOW MOMMA. IT WAS A CUSTOM.
SINCE GRADE SCHOOL, I'VE NEVER BEEN ABLE TO HIDE ANY-THING FROM MOMMA.
SO EVEN AFTER SHE DIED, YOU KEPT WRITING IN YOUR DIARY AND LEA-VING IT WITH THE WAX FIGURE?
Diary
CRAZY!
I'M NOT CRAZY! I'M JUST SERIOUS!!
MOMMA WAS THE ONLY ONE WHO'D EVER WATCH OVER ME !!
EVER SINCE I GREW UP, I HAVEN'T BEEN ABLE TO TRUST ANYONE!!
ONLY MOMMA !!
SNIFF...
SNIFF...

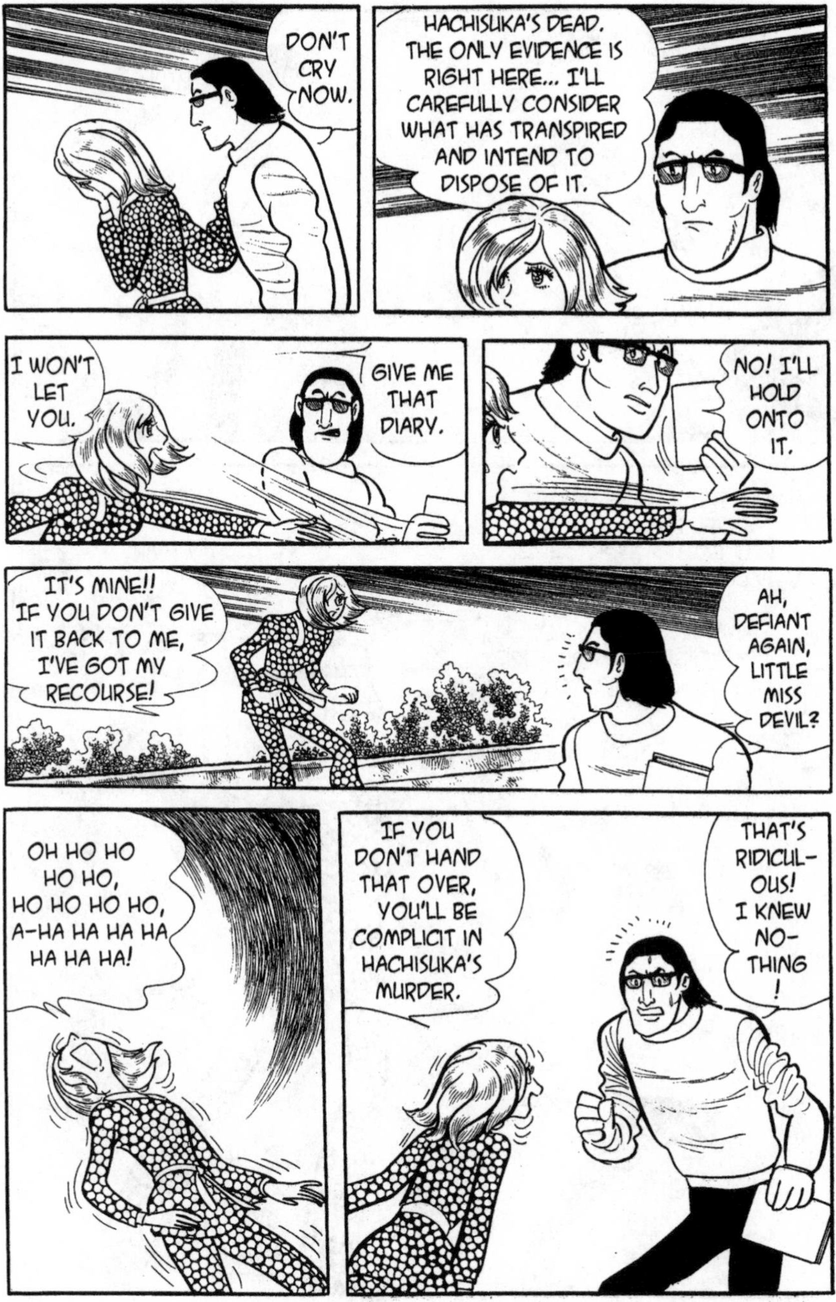
DON'T CRY NOW.
HACHISUKA'S DEAD. THE ONLY EVIDENCE IS RIGHT HERE... I'LL CAREFULLY CONSIDER WHAT HAS TRANSPIRED AND INTEND TO DISPOSE OF IT.
I WON'T LET YOU.
GIVE ME THAT DIARY.
NO! I'LL HOLD ONTO IT.
IT'S MINE!! IF YOU DON'T GIVE IT BACK TO ME, I'VE GOT MY RECOURSE!
AH, DEFIANT AGAIN, LITTLE MISS DEVIL?
OH HO HO HO HO, HO HO HO HO, A-HA HA HA HA HA HA HA!
IF YOU DON'T HAND THAT OVER, YOU'LL BE COMPLICIT IN HACHISUKA'S MURDER.
THAT'S RIDICUL-OUS! I KNEW NO-THING!

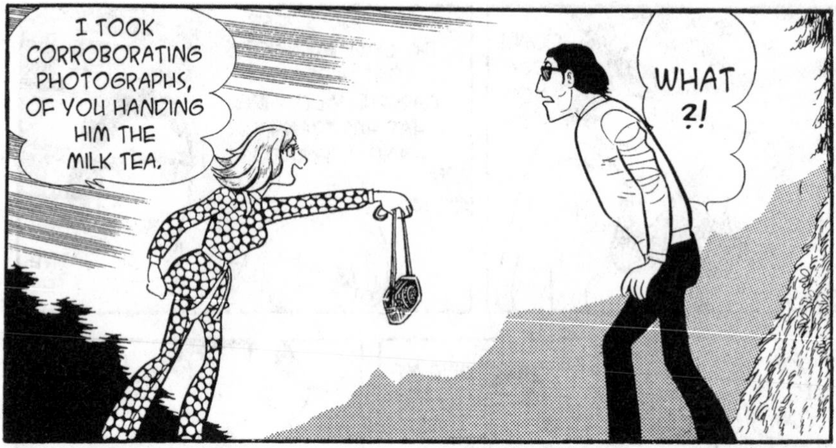
I TOOK CORROBORATING PHOTOGRAPHS, OF YOU HANDING HIM THE MILK TEA.
WHAT ?!

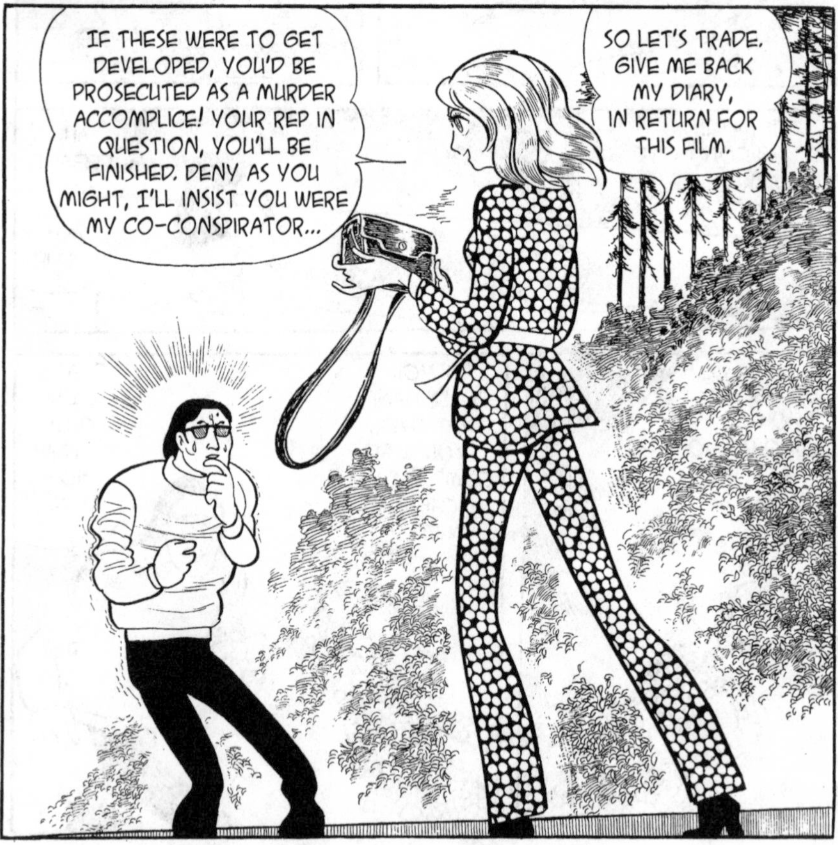
IF THESE WERE TO GET DEVELOPED, YOU'D BE PROSECUTED AS A MURDER ACCOMPLICE! YOUR REP IN QUESTION, YOU'LL BE FINISHED. DENY AS YOU MIGHT, I'LL INSIST YOU WERE MY CO-CONSPIRATOR...
SO LET'S TRADE. GIVE ME BACK MY DIARY, IN RETURN FOR THIS FILM.

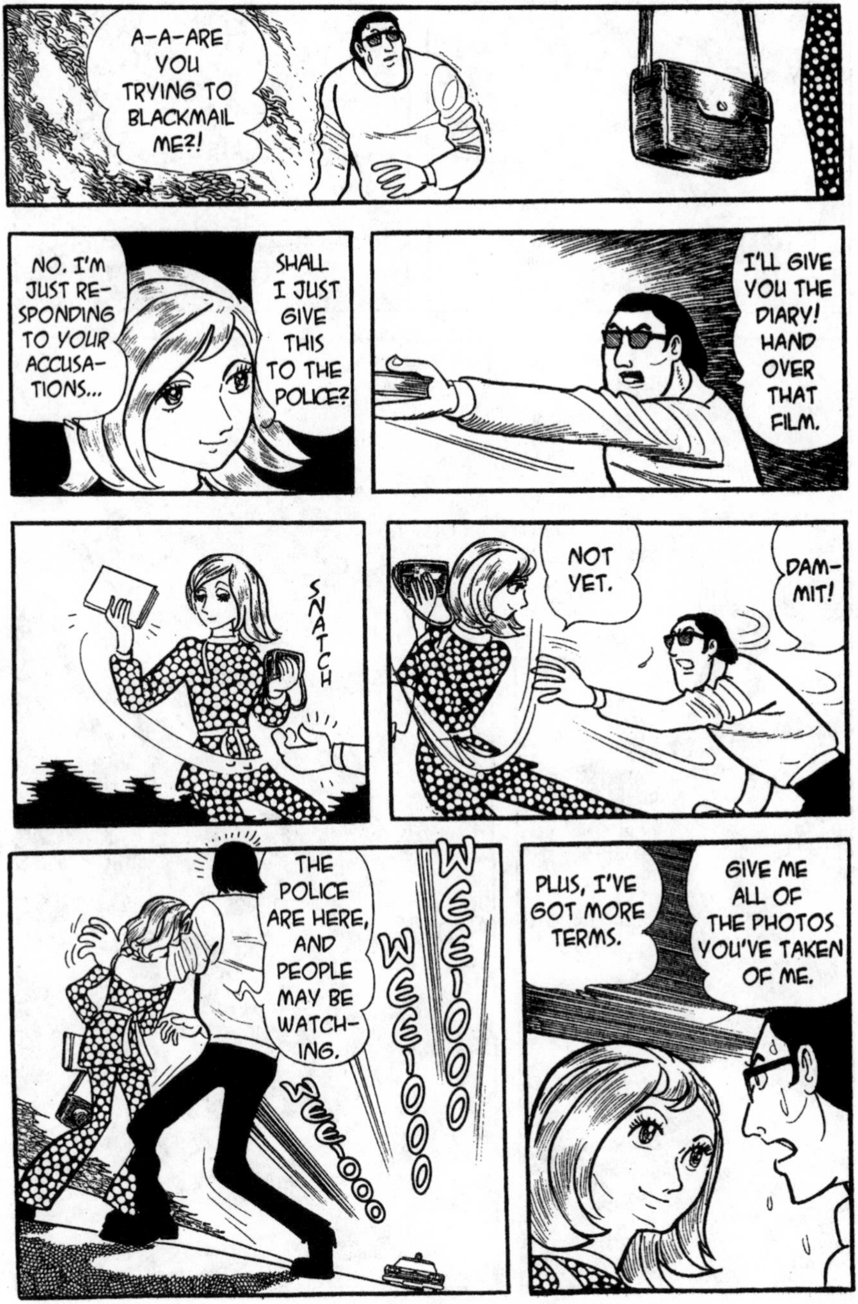
A-A-ARE YOU TRYING TO BLACKMAIL ME?!
NO. I'M JUST RE-SPONDING TO YOUR ACCUSA-TIONS...
SHALL I JUST GIVE THIS TO THE POLICE?
I'LL GIVE YOU THE DIARY! HAND OVER THAT FILM.
SNATCH
NOT YET.
DAM-MIT!
THE POLICE ARE HERE, AND PEOPLE MAY BE WATCH-ING.
WEE-OOOO
WEE-OOOO
WEE-OOOO
PLUS, I'VE GOT MORE TERMS.
GIVE ME ALL OF THE PHOTOS YOU'VE TAKEN OF ME.

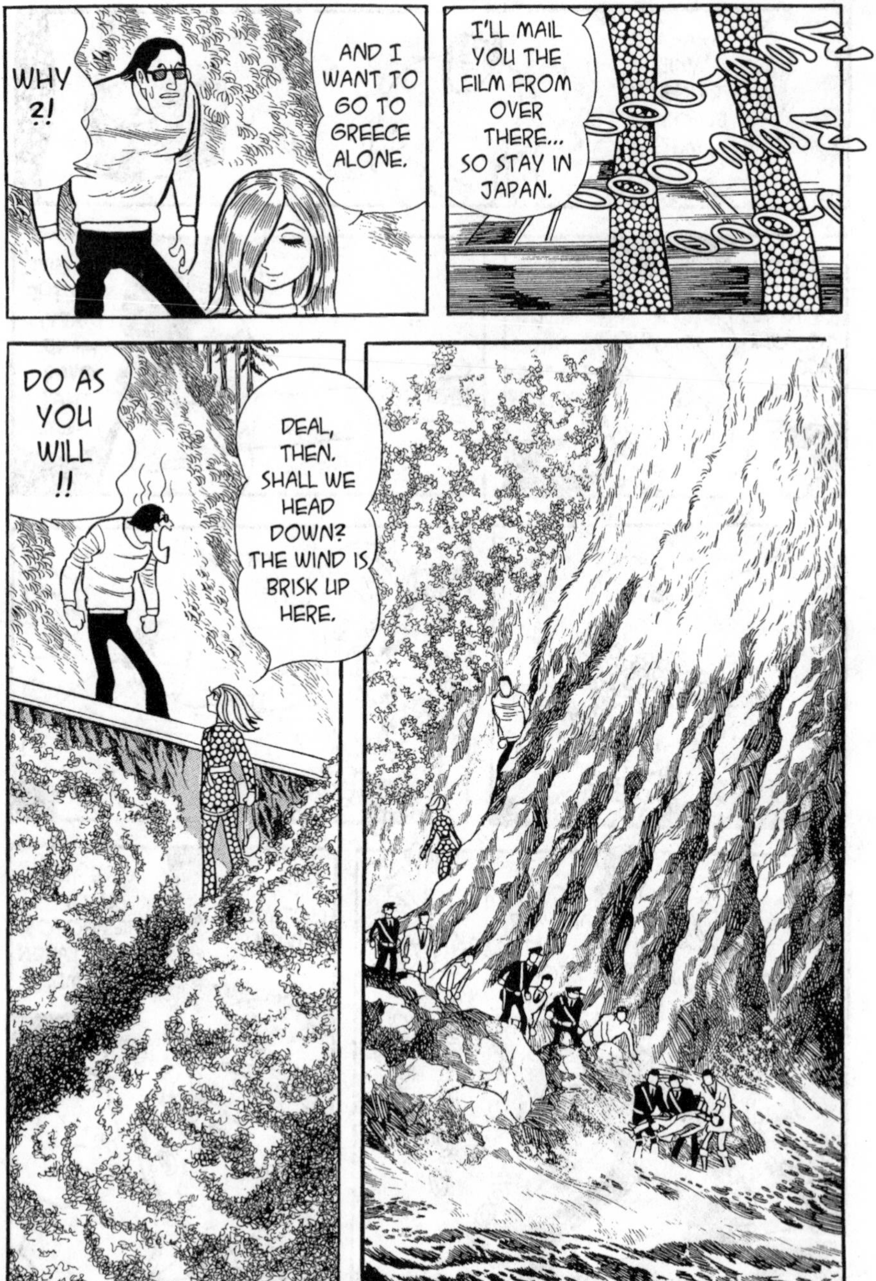
AND I WANT TO GO TO GREECE ALONE.
WHY ?!
I'LL MAIL YOU THE FILM FROM OVER THERE... SO STAY IN JAPAN.
DO AS YOU WILL !!
DEAL, THEN. SHALL WE HEAD DOWN? THE WIND IS BRISK UP HERE.

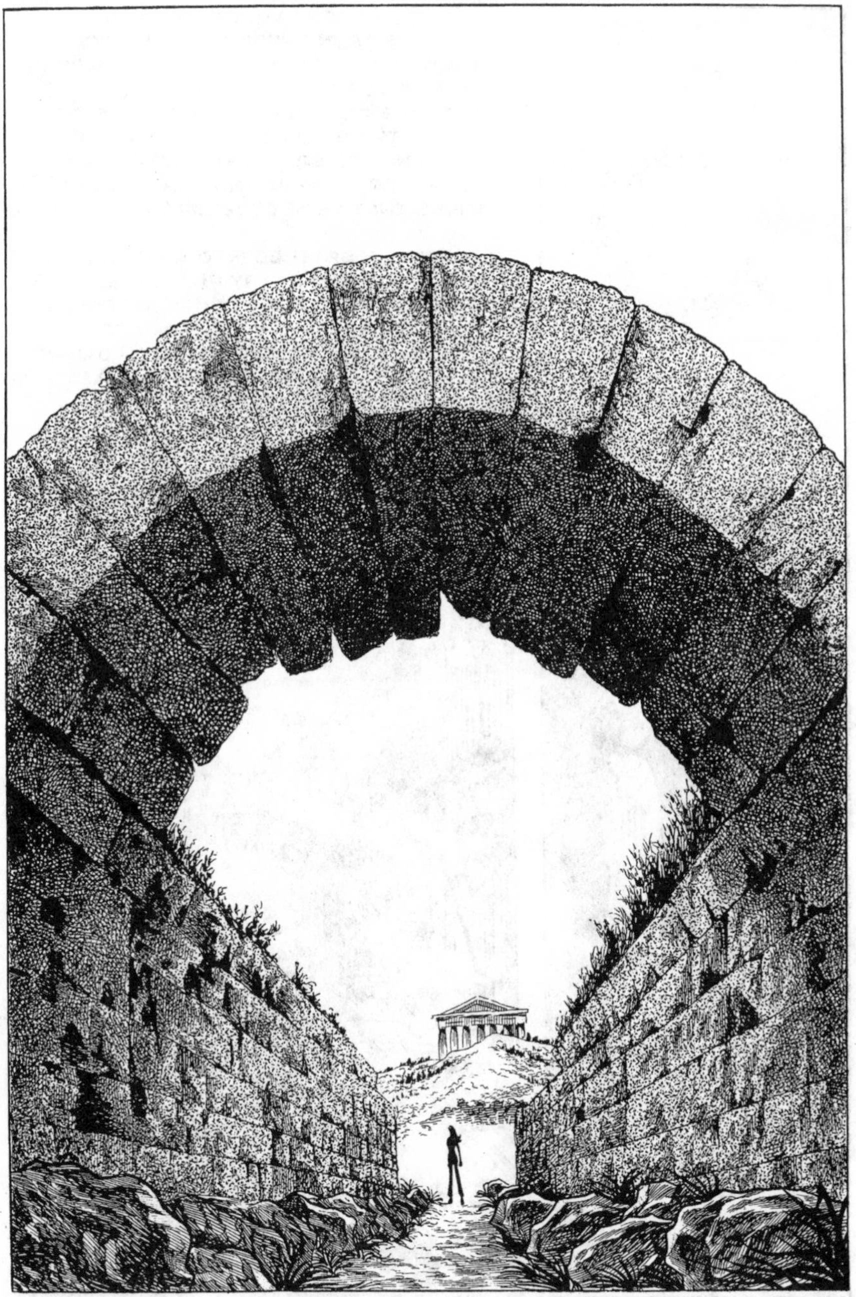

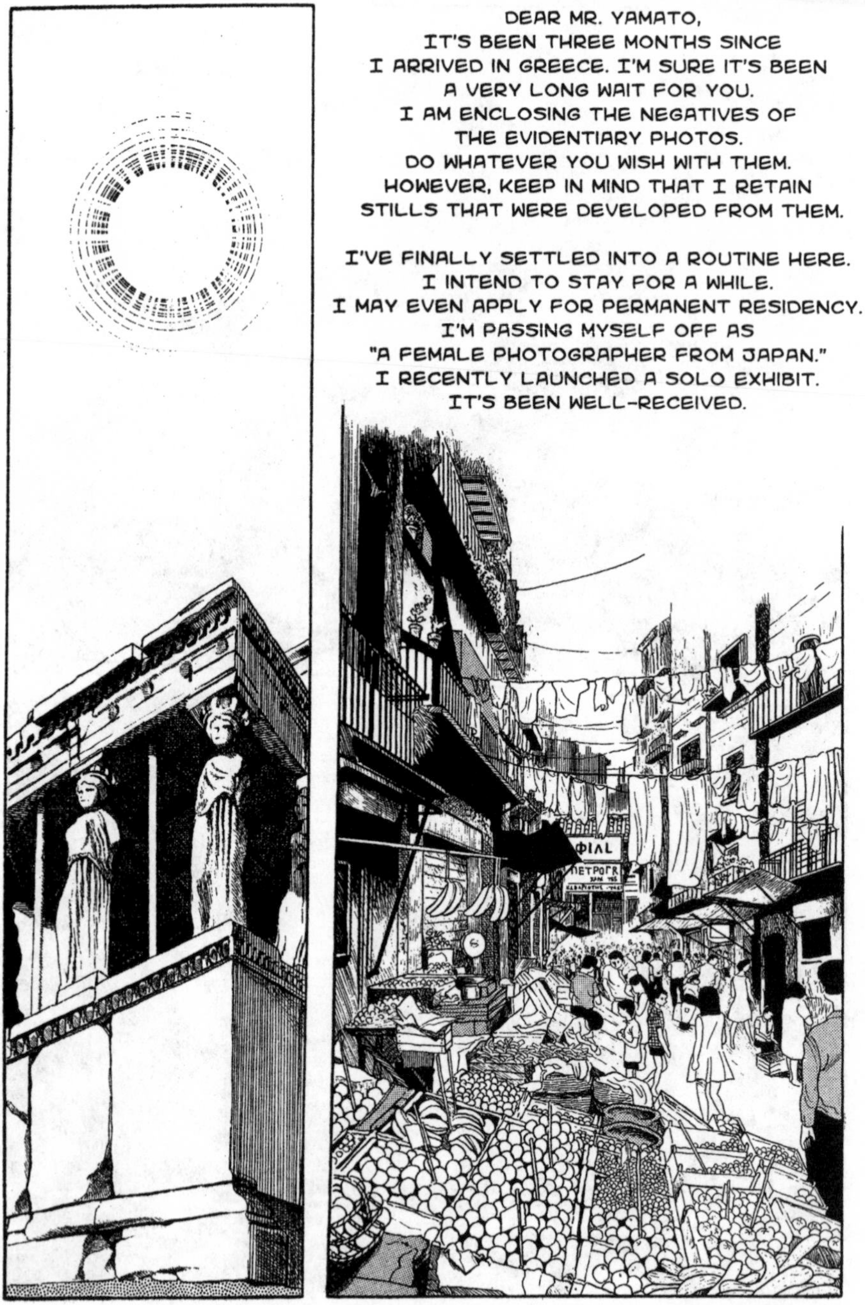
DEAR MR. YAMATO,
IT'S BEEN THREE MONTHS SINCE I ARRIVED IN GREECE. I'M SURE IT'S BEEN A VERY LONG WAIT FOR YOU. I AM ENCLOSING THE NEGATIVES OF THE EVIDENTIARY PHOTOS. DO WHATEVER YOU WISH WITH THEM. HOWEVER, KEEP IN MIND THAT I RETAIN STILLS THAT WERE DEVELOPED FROM THEM.
I'VE FINALLY SETTLED INTO A ROUTINE HERE. I INTEND TO STAY FOR A WHILE. I MAY EVEN APPLY FOR PERMANENT RESIDENCY. I'M PASSING MYSELF OFF AS "A FEMALE PHOTOGRAPHER FROM JAPAN." I RECENTLY LAUNCHED A SOLO EXHIBIT. IT'S BEEN WELL-RECEIVED.

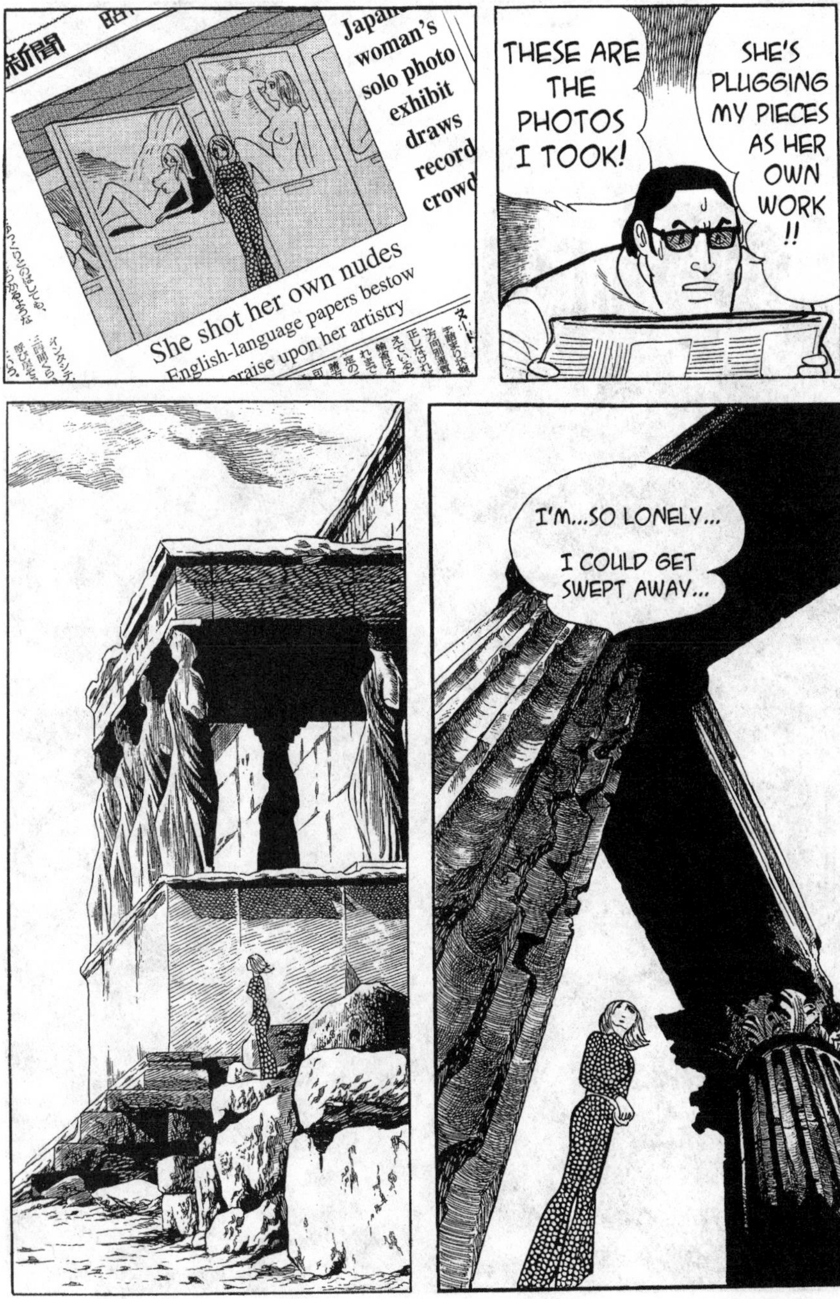
Japan
woman's
solo photo
exhibit
draws
record
crowd
She shot her own nudes
English-language papers bestow
praise upon her artistry
THESE ARE THE PHOTOS I TOOK!
SHE'S PLUGGING MY PIECES AS HER OWN WORK !!
I'M...SO LONELY...
I COULD GET SWEPT AWAY...

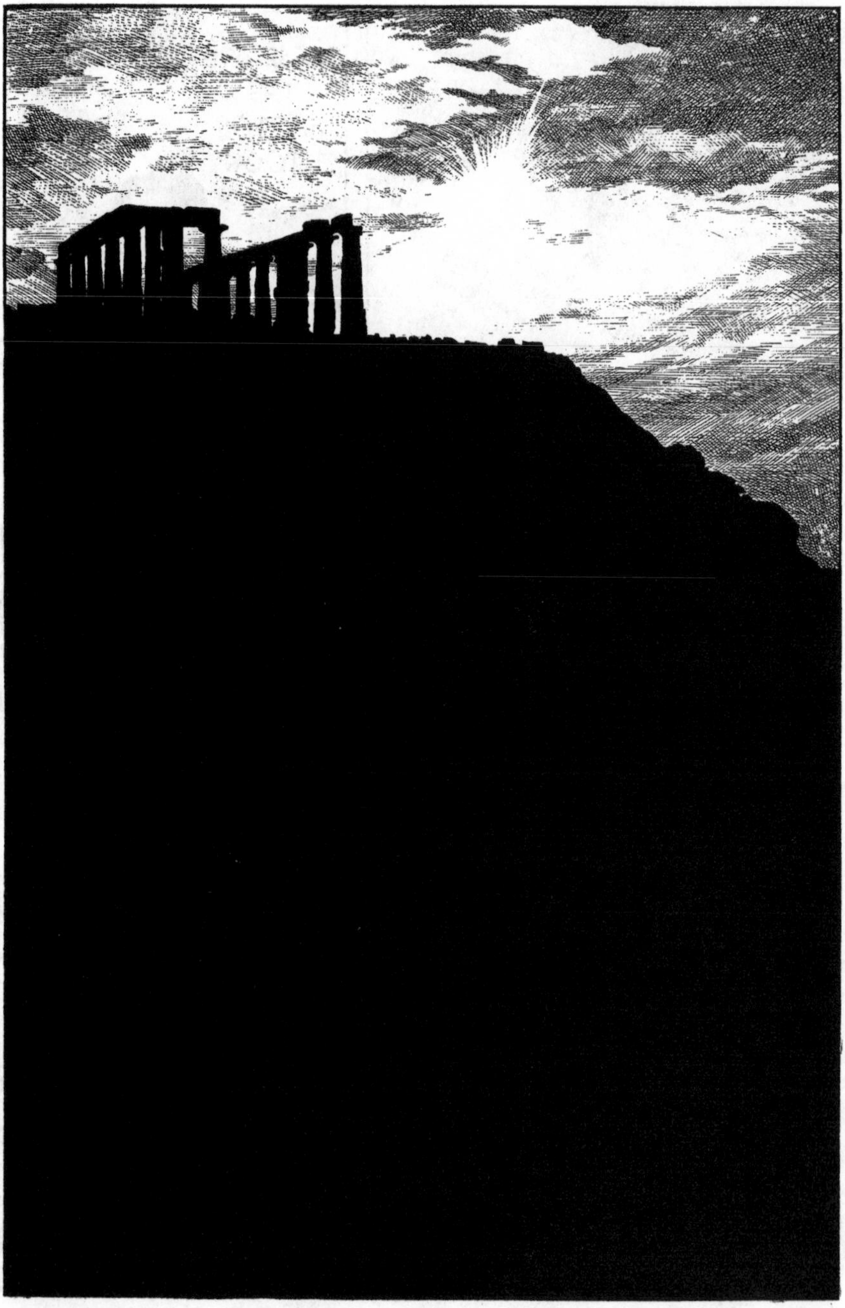

THE END

THE END

About the Author

Osamu Tezuka (1928-89) is the godfather of Japanese manga comics. He originally intended to become a doctor and earned his degree before turning to what was still then considered a frivolous medium. His many early masterpieces include the series known in the U.S. as *Astro Boy* and *Kimba the White Lion*. From the early seventies on, he increasingly targeted older readers as well, employing a grittier style and mature themes. With his sweeping vision, deftly intertwined plots, and indefatigable commitment to human dignity, Tezuka elevated manga to an art form. Since his passing, his international stature has only grown, his eight-volume epic *Buddha* winning multiple Eisner and Harvey Awards in the United States.